SOMEONE ELSE'S HOUSE

*America's
Unfinished Struggle
for Integration*

TAMAR JACOBY

THE FREE PRESS

New York   London   Toronto   Sydney   Singapore

THE FREE PRESS
A Division of Simon & Schuster Inc.
1230 Avenue of the Americas
New York, NY 10020

Designed by Carla Bolte

Manufactured in the United States of America

10   9   8   7   6   5   4   3   2   1

Library of Congress Cataloging-in-Publication Data

Jacoby, Tamar, 1954–
     Someone else's house : America's unfinished struggle for integration /
Tamar Jacoby.
        p.   cm.
     Includes bibliographical references and index.
     ISBN 0-684-80878-1
     1. Afro-Americans—Segregation—New York (State)—New York—
History—20th century.   2. Afro-Americans—Segregation—Georgia—
Atlanta—History—20th century.   3. Afro-Americans—Segregation—
Michigan—Detroit—History—20th century.   4. New York (N.Y.)—Race
relations.   5. Atlanta (Ga.)—Race relations.   6. Detroit (Mich.)—Race
relations.   I. Title.
F128.9.N4J34   1998
305.8'00973—dc21   98-11609
                                                                              CIP

For my parents, Irving and Alberta,
who cared so much about integration.

CONTENTS

PART THREE: ATLANTA

WHAT EVER HAPPENED
TO INTEGRATION?

I t was late one night at *Newsweek,* and I was filing my story at the last minute, rushed and a little bleary-eyed. *Newsweek* in the late 1980s was not a happy place to work. Much of the editorial staff was disgruntled— hemmed in by editors, frustrated by the corporate culture, resentful of a schedule that required us to work till midnight and beyond most Friday nights. Many writers vented their unhappiness in e-mail messages: this editor cut my lead paragraph to shreds, that new layout leaves no room for my story. Sometimes the collective malaise got so bad, one colleague claimed, you could use it to power the computer system.

That Friday night, as I was finishing up, I stopped by my researcher's empty desk to look something up in a reference book. In those days, *Newsweek* writers were assisted by researchers, and I was working with a young black woman: attractive, able, personable, making her way up through the ranks at the magazine. I sat down in her chair to use the heavy volume and found myself staring at her computer screen, where she had left her e-mail open. The words jumped out at me, and though I knew I shouldn't, I couldn't stop myself from reading on. There were about two dozen messages sent and received over the past few weeks: another *Newsweek* litany of discontentment. The difference was that, unlike my own stored mail, virtually all of hers made some mention of color: that white editor won't give me an assignment, that white scheduler put me on the late shift, that white librarian was rude to me, the white system will never be fair—to me or to us.

1

Like everyone in my generation, I had grown up hearing blacks talk about their anger at white society. As a student in the sixties and seventies, I'd met my share of black activists. More recently, as *Newsweek*'s law reporter, I had spent several weeks visiting juvenile detention centers and had been struck by the alienation I encountered among black inmates: kids who seemed to feel no sense of connection with the society whose laws they had broken. But my researcher was neither an activist nor an impoverished outsider. On the contrary, she seemed to be a privileged insider. The racial changes of the past few decades had opened doors for her at school and in the workplace. As far as I could tell from her lifestyle, there was little to distinguish her from other middle-class professionals her age, and already on a fast track at a national magazine, she faced a promising career in mainstream journalism. Besides, we all felt put upon by the system at *Newsweek*. Why had she come to see this common professional problem in racial terms, and why did she feel so irreparably cut off from her white peers?

The young woman's alienation stayed with me in the weeks to come, the kind of glimpse few of us ever get into how someone else sees the world, and the more I thought about it, the more I wondered: what exactly is the goal of race relations in America today—and is there any hope of achieving it if even this successful young journalist still does not feel she belongs?

Like most whites of my generation, I had always thought the goal was integration. I came of age politically in the years when the very word had a kind of magic to it—a vague but shining dream of social equality and fairness for all. In the years that followed, I watched as both blacks and whites fought for the ideal on a variety of fronts: first taking the signs off water fountains, then securing the right to vote, desegregating local school systems, bringing blacks into the corporate world, struggling to create a sense of political cohesion between cities and their suburbs. Inclusion turned out to be a delicate, time-consuming process; the front keeps moving, and the challenges grow more and more subtle. But blacks as a group have made enormous progress in three or four decades. The middle class has quadrupled, education levels have soared, blacks are increasingly well represented in electoral politics and other influential realms of national life.

Still, as I thought about my *Newsweek* researcher, I had to wonder if full integration was really possible. Like a growing number of blacks in America, she was leading an integrated life, but for her this hard-won achievement seemed all but meaningless. Accomplished as she was, she still felt deeply alienated, an uncomfortable and unwelcome visitor in someone else's house.

"I've seen plenty of physical integration," a black college student said to me a few weeks later. "That doesn't guarantee integration of the heart." Like my researcher, he seemed to feel irreparably cut off from what he saw as the white world, and the more I thought about them both, the larger the question loomed: how close have we come to integration, and can we ever hope to bridge the remaining gap?

If integration is still most Americans' idea of the goal, few of us talk about it any more. The word has a quaint ring today—like "gramophone" or "nylons," it is a relic of another era—and the ideal, under any name, has just about fallen out of most discussions about race. The focus now is on diversity, and few of us stop to ask if it is really compatible with the goals of the civil rights movement. We reflexively honor Martin Luther King, Jr., but not many still pursue the vision he called "the beloved community": a vision of a more or less race-neutral America in which both blacks and whites would feel they belong. Today, the word "community" means not one integrated nation but a minority enclave, as in "the black community." "Brother" evokes not the brotherhood of man but the solidarity of color. "*It's a black thing, you wouldn't understand,*" the T-shirts say—and few of us question the underlying assumption.

Only a tiny minority, black or white, have repudiated integration outright, but increasingly on both sides there is a new contrary mood. Some whites, tired of the issue and the emotion that comes with it, have grown indifferent to blacks' problems. Others, black and white, think of integration as a sentimental notion, more or less irrelevant to the real problems of race in America—black poverty, black joblessness, black advancement. Still others, particularly blacks embittered by a long history of exclusion, view the old color-blind dream as a pernicious concept, rightly superseded by identity politics. Left, right, poor and middle class all have their own reasons: everything from anger to callused neglect. But together, wittingly or not, we as a nation are dropping the flag, turning our backs on the great achievement of the civil rights era—the hopeful consensus that formed in the 1960s around King's vision of a single, shared community.

In fact, since Emancipation, most blacks with any realistic hope of inclusion have chosen to try to make their way into the political and economic mainstream. The first nationally known black spokesman, Frederick Douglass, was an ardent integrationist, and the popular thrust from the nineteenth century onward was for incorporation in the body politic. Of course, there was always another tendency, too: the proud and often angry separatism that flourished in the ghetto in periods, like the 1930s, when integration looked least likely. Yet even when the prospects were bleakest, most blacks nourished some long-term hope and pursued every chance they got to participate in the mainstream. Eventually, in the early 1960s, a critical mass of whites espoused the ideal, and the nation set out on the difficult course of trying to accelerate the long-delayed process. But paradoxically, even as America moved toward full inclusion, more and more younger blacks began to turn away, embracing a modern-day variant of separatism.

This new insularity has emerged starkly for everyone to see in the years since I stumbled on my researcher's e-mail. Unlike the street-corner chauvinism popularized by Marcus Garvey and others in the 1930s, today's separatism does not dream of a return to Africa. Unlike the Nation of Islam, it involves few rituals or regimens. Following in the path set by these predecessors, its first tenet is self-respect, although like both of them it also has a sharper edge. More an attitude than an ideology or even a political program, it is part pride, part disappointment with whites, part diffidence—an uneasiness about competing in the mainstream—part defensiveness and part resentful defiance. It shows up most plainly in Afrocentric curriculums and celebrations of black culture, but also in the NAACP's public ambivalence about school desegregation and the widespread feeling among black youth that to do well in class is somehow shameful—"acting white."

This new, "soft" form of the old separatist vision is capturing poor and better-off blacks alike. It caught on first on the left, among movement veterans, but then spread through the moderate middle and on to the new black right, where prominent conservatives like Clarence Thomas now doubt the value of mixed schooling and maintain that only blacks can help less privileged blacks out of poverty. Gangsta rap, Louis Farrakhan's Million Man March, Spike Lee's film *Malcolm X* and the reverential following it awakened all reflect and enshrine the credo—that the system is inherently prejudiced, that blacks are somehow fundamentally different from whites, that they will never be fully at home in America, that they are right to be angry and that only good can come of cultivating this bitterness.

Unlike old-fashioned black nationalism, the new separatism often coexists with functional integrationism. Young black professionals are making their way into the system and up the ladders of mainstream success, but a large number of them cling to their mistrust even as they enjoy the fruits of the "white world." Accomplished as they are, many seem to feel the system is rigged against them and that as long as racism exists, their abilities will carry them only so far. After decades of effort, some of their parents too have managed to create comfortable, middle-class lives, all but indistinguishable from those of white middle-class families. Yet even these prosperous citizens, wary of prejudice, often prefer to live in a realm apart: to buy homes and worship and spend their leisure time in the racial comfort zones of self-segregated suburbs.

Strangest of all, the white mainstream is encouraging this clannishness—in the name of integration. The government fosters color-coded hiring, voting and school admissions. Businesses like Time Warner lead the way in promoting gangsta rap; others have remade their corporate cultures to nourish a sense of diversity and color consciousness. Philanthropic institutions like the Ford Foundation fund the development of black curriculums. Magazines like *The New Yorker* publish profiles of black figures—intellectuals, celebrities, sports heroes and others—that make a shibboleth of "how black" they are. In the name of racial justice, of accommodation and respect, the mainstream culture has embraced the new black separatism. The idea is to make blacks feel more welcome, to honor their historical grievances and incorporate their culture into the mainstream. But in the long run, this well-meaning endorsement of separatism can only help prevent the realization of the civil rights vision.

Even under the best of circumstances, nationalism of the kind coursing through the black community would be difficult for Americans to accommodate—hard to square with our universalist values and our sense of a nation based not on blood but on political principle. But whatever the benefits of the new separatism in promoting pride and self-esteem, the overlay of anger and alienation that comes with it is poisoning our lives, both black and white.

Underclass youths ruin their own futures by declining to make an effort in "the white man's school." Others refuse to obey the "white" law. Even the most promising, middle-class black students are encouraged to feel put upon, different and forever apart. In the image of Malcolm X, they embrace anger as their identity—and then spend the rest of their lives trying to deal with its corrosive side effects. As for whites, the conventional wisdom that there are two separate and different communities has become an excuse for ignorance, indifference and worse. Increasingly resentful and put off by racial rhetoric, many feel little responsibility for even neighboring black poverty. Others—including those who believe themselves free of prejudice—still harbor half-conscious notions of black inferiority. Cut off from all but superficial contact and encouraged to think that black culture is different, their stereotypes only grow worse.

When did this happen? How and why? Have we Americans really agreed to give up on a common humanity? I don't think so. I believe most people still feel that what blacks and whites have in common is more important than their differences. Despite their anger and alienation, most blacks still want in—and most whites still want to do what they can to make this the land of opportunity they have been taught to believe it is. But if most Americans still believe in integration, they don't know how to reconcile it with diversity and identity politics—and meanwhile the nation is sliding haplessly toward a future that leaves less and less room for commonality.

What ever happened to integration? Do we as a nation recognize how dramatically we have changed course? What consequences will this unexamined turn hold for the future of black and white America? The answers to all these questions lie in the history of the past few decades and in choices made on the ground, at the local level, by individuals.

The failure of integration is a national failure, but as with politics, all race relations are local. The dynamics of our misunderstandings are invariably personal and shaped in some way by context—by a region's past, by its changing economy, by the quality of its civic leadership. Besides, wherever the mistakes begin, the tragedy usually plays out at the local level: in the streets; at City Hall; in a schoolyard or a downtown boardroom where blacks and whites encounter each other, both trying awkwardly to readjust their relationship, and end up talking past each other or worse. On the theory that the best way to see what went wrong is to look up close, this book traces race relations in three cities: New York, Detroit and Atlanta.

Why chart the history of a largely failed initiative? Integration's most convincing critics base their argument on history. We tried it, they say, and it didn't work. To a degree, the skeptics are right. Much of what we've tried in the past few decades hasn't worked. For all the progress made, the crusade has failed. But it failed, I am convinced, because we as a nation went about it wrong—and if we could learn from these years of mistakes, we could still, I believe, achieve real integration. That is why what follows is a work of history: an effort to disentangle the ideal from the flawed means used to pursue it. What dead ends did we turn down? What doubts led us to lose sight of the goal? What well-meaning efforts led in exactly the opposite direction, not toward a sense of community but toward ever more angry divisiveness?

In New York in the 1960s, as at the federal level in Washington, hopes ran high. Race relations, it was thought, were something white society could fix: with the right strategy and enough money, government could solve the problem. A handsome young mayor, John Lindsay, teamed up with the brilliant new president of one of the nation's most powerful foundations, Ford's McGeorge Bundy, and together they set out to make the city an experimental laboratory. "Little City Halls," neighborhood empowerment, community control of schools: all were tested in New York, as Lindsay, Bundy and their allies in the city's liberal elite moved to translate the integrationist ideal into a practical agenda. What can the government do to spur integration? How much can be ameliorated by caring and charisma like Lindsay's? The New York chapters are a lesson in the limits of white goodwill and sixties-style top-down engineering.

In Detroit, it was the election of a black mayor that made the city an important test case: just what difference can black leadership make? Already by the late 1960s, race relations were worse than almost anywhere else in the country. Blacks and whites reacted to the nation's most destructive riot by flatly giving up on integration. Whites moved to the suburbs; few blacks seemed sorry to see them go. A long court battle over busing between city and suburb only reinforced both sides' prejudices, and angry attitudes were still hardening when Coleman Young was elected in 1973. Could a longtime militant like Young come in from the cold and function successfully inside the system? Or would he see his mayoralty as a chance to create Black Power in one city, defying white suburbanites and alienating them further? Young's Detroit is a study in the consequences of choosing against integration.

If Detroit is a worst case—the failure of integration at its most stark—Atlanta is often celebrated as a model of racial harmony. The success story of the civil rights movement, now the jewel in the crown of the New South, it is a city where both blacks and whites prosper. Blacks have taken over local government but whites have stayed; a highly regarded affirmative action program has helped spawn a new middle class, and both blacks and whites feel they have a stake in a booming future. But even boosterish Atlantans have to admit that integration is eluding them. Whites live on one side of the city, blacks on the other, their tree-lined neighborhoods often indistinguishable but still color-coded—voluntarily so. Relations between black and white rarely go beyond workaday formality and, if anything, are said by many to be getting worse. "Race relations?" asked one man in the mid-1990s. "We don't have race relations in Atlanta any more." This half-success makes Atlanta a critical test: Is real integration possible in America today? Or is peaceful co-existence as good as it gets?

It's not a good record for three decades of effort. Yet most people still seem to believe in inclusion—still assume that's where we're headed in the long run. Corporations that insist on diversity training hope it will bring workers together. Middle-class blacks in segregated suburbs devote their lives to making it easier for their kids to join and prosper in the mainstream. Even whites who feel that race is no longer their problem, that there is nothing they or the government can do to help, assume that the field has been leveled and that most blacks are making it on their own. Ambivalent, inconsistent, hypocritical as we sometimes sound, the enduring moral power of integration still holds most of us in its sway, challenging us with the hope we once shared to return to the path we've lost.

What the past shows, more than anything, is that for thirty-five years we have been pursuing the vision with flawed means. Wholesale social engineering, color-coded double standards, forced interaction between people who are not social or economic equals; one after the other, the old stratagems have proved bankrupt or worse. But that does not mean the nation must give up its long-cherished ideal. Integration is in decline as a goal not so much because we don't believe in it but because we've failed to get there. The means haven't worked, or have made the problem worse, and when one road after another leads to a dead end, it's natural to start believing we can't get there from here. Devising new strategies will not be easy, but history can guide us, if we know how to listen.

Some readers will argue that I've made things too complicated. "'What ever happened to integration?'" they'll ask. "The answer is obvious. It was sandbagged by racism." They aren't wrong. The reason inclusion is a problem to begin with clearly traces back to bigotry: hundreds of years of shameful practice and attitudes with continuing consequences, painful and dehumanizing, for whites as well as blacks. Nor is racism dead. For all the whites who care about integration, there are plenty who don't—who never backed it, or who gave up long ago. Even whites who would like to think well of blacks and treat them fairly harbor all kinds of prejudices: irrepressible preconceptions and patronizing impulses. No honest white can pretend otherwise. Still, to say it was white racism that killed integration is not exactly right. Black alienation and black bigotry have played a part too, and though they may be rooted in white mistreatment, they have taken on lives of their own. No change in white attitudes alone, however dramatic, is going to solve the problem.

In fact, white attitudes have shifted significantly in recent years. As recently as 1940, more than two-thirds of whites believed blacks were less intelligent. Today, under 6 percent think so. Before World War II, no more than 40 percent, even in the North, endorsed desegregation of any kind. Today, it's hard to find a white person who will tell a pollster he does not believe blacks belong in the mainstream. Whites of all ages look back on the civil rights movement as one of the high points of American history, and more whites than blacks—in the 95 to 100 percent range—defend the idea of integration. Still, for all the progress, there is no denying that resentment persists. Large numbers of whites—40 to 60 percent—tell pollsters that blacks could do better if they tried harder. Whites from all regions bitterly condemn what they see as black demands for special treatment. And this anger often spills over into what sounds like old-fashioned prejudice—in corporate offices, on campus, in a resurgence of racial jokes.

Just what accounts for this new resentment is not easy to untangle, but it is not always the same as out-and-out bigotry. A white man who thinks a black woman on welfare should get a job may in fact be responding to her color, voicing an ugly and unthinking assumption about black attitudes toward work. Or he may be reacting to something he didn't like in the racial rhetoric of recent decades: the claim that white society is responsible for the problems blacks face. Thirty-five years of color-coded conflict have taken a huge toll on both sides, and fairly or not the showdown has left many whites embittered. Their feelings may be an obstacle to harmony, but they are not necessarily prejudice in the conventional sense.

Far more damaging today than the old bigotry is the condescension of well-meaning whites who think that they are advancing race relations by encouraging alienation and identity politics. After three hundred years of unfulfilled promises, it's not surprising that even the most successful blacks mistrust whites and that many hesitate to cast their lot with the system that held their people back for so long. But no one is served by a mainstream culture that spurs this estrangement, encouraging blacks to believe that the system is inherently racist and that all responsibility for change lies with whites. Well-intentioned as such deference is, it will not lead to inclusion. It will not empower blacks or make them feel more welcome. On the contrary, it can only delay the kind of push that is still needed to bridge the gap, particularly for the poorest blacks with the fewest chances and most meager skills.

As a white woman writing about race, I know my own color will be an issue for some readers. What do I know about how black people feel? How dare I presume to speak for them? How could I possibly describe what goes on between blacks and whites in a fair or objective way? I can only reply that this is what writers do. They tell stories about other people, usually different in some way from themselves, and they do their best to imagine those people's feelings, to recreate their thoughts and points of view. The racial perception gap may sometimes make this task a little harder. But as someone who believes that blacks and whites have more in common than what separates us, I don't think the difficulty is as great as some racial absolutists suggest, and I refuse to concede that racial inclusion is somehow a "black" subject. On the contrary, I believe it is a challenge for all Americans—the ultimate test we face as a nation. As for objectivity, readers will have to judge for themselves. This book contains heroes and villains on both sides of the color line. A small note tacked to the bulletin board above my desk reminds me daily: "If you can't call a black thug a thug, you're a racist." It is an idea I stand by.

Can the integrationist ideal be revived and reshaped to make sense in the racially jaded 1990s and beyond? I don't see any alternative.

Seductive as the other path may sometimes seem, it would soon lead into unlivable territory. How would the social contract hold in a nation where separate communities no longer felt bound or responsible to each other? Why should people pay taxes for social services to help others with whom they feel they have nothing in common? The rising indifference between city and suburb is already taking its toll, and it would only get worse if we were to give up all hope of a shared community. Then there's the law: the social order. The estrangement of my integrated, middle-class researcher is nothing compared to the alienation one hears from young people in prisons and reformatories. Poorer, less privileged black youth don't just feel like unwelcome guests in a white world; they believe they are trapped in an enemy camp. When they break the law—the rules of a game they feel they're excluded from—many express little or no remorse, and this in turn only erodes what white concern remains for blacks' problems.

In the end, we have no choice. The alternative to integration is not, as many hope, a rich feast of diversity. Far more likely, given America's history and the enduring problems many blacks face, a decision to give up on inclusion would leave us with a permanent, festering sore: a bitter juxtaposition of inside and outside that would consume all our energies and sap our morale.

Neither blacks nor whites would benefit, and no one could escape the moral corruption, which would eventually spread to all realms of national life. The political values we've inherited could not survive in a nation divided. If the civil rights era taught us anything, it was that—and slow as we were to grasp the lesson, it is not something we can forget now.

The corrosive effects of division—of living next door to someone with whom you feel no connection—are already all too evident in too many communities. Many of the people I spoke to in the suburbs of Atlanta and Detroit feel regretful about the way they've chosen to live: guilty, concerned—but, because of the gulf, often helpless to make a difference. Others live in denial, nostalgic for their cities but not sure exactly what it is they miss. Still others are simply hardened, and although they don't know it, they make the most powerful case for recovering a sense of shared community. By accepting the partition of city and suburb, giving up all sense of concern and responsibility, they have abandoned not just the poor blacks in their midst but also the ideals on which the nation is based. As for those blacks who choose separatism, it's hard to see how they benefit in the long run, cut off from the possibilities that the mainstream has to offer.

Just what would real integration mean? What would it look like? It's difficult to say from here. By definition, inclusion is an ideal—more a beacon than a concrete prescription. The closer we've come over the years, the more specifically and realistically we've envisioned the goal. We know now that it will take more than physical mingling; we know it starts but doesn't end with equal opportunity, and we know it won't look like the monotone conformity some people imagined in the 1950s. As my alienated *Newsweek* researcher makes all too clear, ultimately inclusion is about feeling you belong, but we still do not know much about how to foster that sense of a shared society. The government policies of the last three decades have met with mixed results, often unleashing more harm than good, though that does not mean, as some conservatives argue, that there is nothing the state can do.

Government, business, media, popular culture and activists on both sides of the color line: we have all contributed to the failure of integration, and we must all be part of a renewed effort. The best place to pick up the trail is where we lost it, bit by bit over the last few decades. Only by looking at the past can we see how much the turn away from integration has cost us. Only by understanding our failures can we hope to do better in the future—finding new, more workable ways to achieve the community most Americans long for.

Part One

NEW YORK

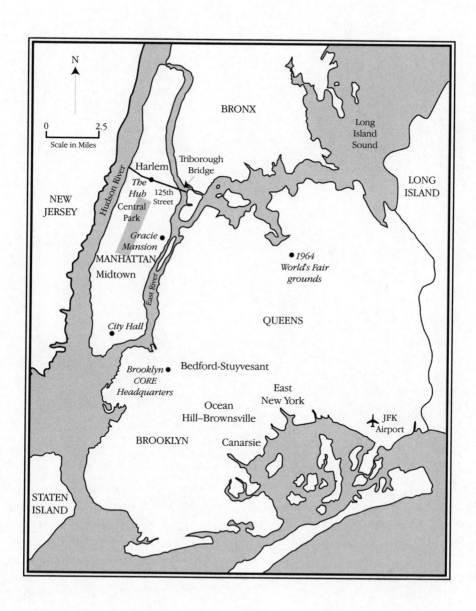

N

0   2.5
Scale in Miles

NEW
JERSEY

BRONX

Long
Island
Sound

LONG
ISLAND

Harlem

Triborough
Bridge

*The
Hub*

125th
Street

Central
Park

*Gracie
Mansion*

MANHATTAN

Midtown

*1964
World's Fair
grounds*

QUEENS

City Hall

*Brooklyn
CORE
Headquarters*

Bedford-Stuyvesant

East
New York

Ocean
Hill–Brownsville

BROOKLYN

Canarsie

JFK
Airport

STATEN
ISLAND

Hudson River

East River

Chapter 1

STALL-IN

To the impatient young activists of Brooklyn CORE, the 1964 World's Fair was a perfect target. In 1964, New York was a proud, glamorous city and it awaited the fair's opening day, April 22, with all the anticipation of a confident host. A quarter of a million people were expected. President Lyndon Johnson was scheduled to speak. The nation and much of the world would be watching on television. The Brooklyn chapter of the Congress of Racial Equality could hardly imagine a better audience for the protest it was calling a "stall-in."

The small, ragtag cell of black and white activists had been planning the demonstration for months. Up to two thousand five hundred cars would run out of gas on highways leading to the fair, clogging the streets and blocking access by visitors. Hundreds of other protesters would pull emergency brakes on subway trains and lie down on bridges between the city and the fairgrounds in Flushing, Queens. Still others would jam admission gates by insisting on paying all in pennies. Then, at the culminating moment of the festivities, when President Johnson got up to speak, CORE recruits would release live rats into the audience, causing unimaginable mayhem. Amid all the hoopla of the grand opening day, CORE would paralyze the city and close down the fair, lodging a huge symbolic protest against racial discrimination.

In 1964, CORE was working harder than any other civil rights group to bring the struggle north. But even as the ferment and protest activity spread up across the map, the new recruits were changing the face of the movement.

Unlike traditional CORE members, generally middle-class and among the most idealistic in the struggle, the new rank-and-file were overwhelmingly poor, black and uneducated. Most were emotional and impatient, without specific goals or a vision of the racial future. If anything, they were suspicious of the idea of racial understanding, and whatever CORE's long-time goal of integration meant to them, getting along with whites was not a priority. "I didn't know any white people," new recruit Sonny Carson said later, "and didn't particularly want to."

Every week that winter of 1963–64, a different local chapter tried out a different flashy, confrontational protest gambit. In San Francisco, demonstrators dumped shopping carts full of unpaid-for groceries on the floor in supermarkets they said were not hiring enough blacks. In several cities, protesters chained themselves to building cranes, stopping work at segregated construction sites. In Cleveland, one activist was killed when he lay down in front of a bulldozer preparing the ground for a new school. In city after city, even sympathetic liberal reporters began to write about the "anarchists" and "ultra-militants" making headlines with their sensational tactics. Whether or not they spoke for the black community was still unclear. But by the winter before the World's Fair, they were dominating the northern struggle, overwhelming other, more moderate black voices and triggering white alarm.

Founded in 1941, one of the oldest black protest groups in the country, CORE had always been at the radical edge of the civil rights movement. "The NAACP is the Justice Department," CORE leader James Farmer liked to say. "The Urban League is the State Department, and we are the nonviolent Marines." Leaving litigation and social services to other groups, CORE had pioneered the use of Gandhian direct action: protesting segregation on the spot—at restaurants, barbershops and swimming pools—with leafleting, sit-ins and old-fashioned picket lines. Already in 1947, almost a decade before the southern movement took off, CORE activists had put their lives on the line, daring to integrate interstate buses traveling through the heart of Dixie. And in those days, an era still dominated by Jim Crow, belief in integration was an essential part of what made the group radical. Indifferent to convention and censure, CORE fought unrelentingly not just for equal access, but also for an exalted moral vision of "understanding" and "reconciliation" between the races.

Commitment to the integrationist ideal permeated every aspect of the organization. Farmer and his colleagues insisted that all CORE cells be integrated; they opposed any effort, no matter how slight, to improve conditions in the ghetto—that might relieve pressure to get out. Their determined color blindness showed even in their jokes—like the one about the little boy who comes home from school excited about a new friend but can't answer when his mother asks, "Is he white or colored?" "I don't know," the punch line went. "I'll have to go back tomorrow and see." But more than anything, it was CORE's day-to-day tactics that revealed the full meaning of its integrationism: a determination in every instance to appeal to the decency of white people, shaming segregationists into moral recognition of blacks' dignity and worth. "When I look back," Farmer wrote later, "I am amazed at our patience and good faith. . . . In those days we were childishly literal-minded . . . [determined] to reach the heart of the restaurant owner with the truth. What we took to be his conversion was as important" as actually bringing blacks into the restaurant. Earnest behind-the-scenes negotiation preceded and followed every CORE protest. Activists sitting in at lunch counters remained calm even when served plates of eggshells and sandwiches made of lettuce retrieved from the garbage. They wanted to break down barriers—but only in a way that opened the door to dialogue. For them, communication was an end in itself: along with racial mingling, the only way for either black or white to find their full humanity.

The influx of new recruits in the early 1960s changed all of this, except for the emphasis on ever more radical tactics. More than anything, it was CORE's 1961 Freedom Rides that drew large numbers of northern youth into the organization by creating an image of courage and militancy with an all but irresistible appeal for restless young men in rust-belt ghettos. Freedom Riders daring for a second time to integrate interstate buses in the South were brutally beaten, then tear-gassed, but they persisted even in the face of hostile mobs: one of the most dramatic stands in the dramatic history of the movement. Much of white public opinion was troubled by the action and by what was seen as a deliberate provocation of violence. But blacks, particularly young blacks in the North, were thrilled by the Freedom Riders' boldness and their willingness to defy whites, physically if necessary, and thousands of northern youths were soon flocking into CORE offices asking how they could join in the struggle. In 1964, CORE's middle-aged national leadership still held to the principles that had driven it for over two decades. But the turbulence in the movement and the influx of new members in the North were driving grassroots chapters toward greater and greater militancy.

By the winter before the World's Fair, Brooklyn CORE had established itself as the toughest of the tough, a national model for other militant chapters and the most radical of New York's black protest groups. Though still a tiny cell, no more than a few score active members, poorly organized and without resources, it managed to cast to a larger-than-life shadow, thanks to the flamboyant daring of its tactics. Among the cell's stratagems were "dwelling in" disruptively at offices, lying down in front of delivery trucks and dumping bags of garbage on the steps of municipal buildings. In the summer of 1963, as Harlem erupted in a mini-riot—several nights of hand-to-hand combat between teenagers and police—Brooklyn CORE lived in for a tense week at the Board of Education. Then, with the city's temperature rising, the chapter helped orchestrate massive demonstrations at New York construction sites, and members were in the front ranks in ensuing tussles with police. Sometimes the group's goal was desegregation, sometimes better services in the ghetto. But as Farmer noticed, "often, for those recruits, what was important was not so much the outcome as the act of protesting."

Impetuous, quick on the draw, intoxicated by press attention, the youthful leaders of the Brooklyn chapter were not overly careful about the consequences of their actions. In one instance in 1963, they picketed the home of a supposedly discriminatory New York housing official only to learn afterward that they were persecuting the wrong man. That same year, they blamed a landlord for the death of a black baby, killed, they said, by the rats in a filthy tenement. An autopsy later showed that the child had died of pneumonia. Still, somehow, none of these mistakes proved damaging with ghetto followers, and the chapter's stature grew with every passing month. By late 1963, two of the city's two most prominent black pastors, veteran political organizers Milton Galamison and C. Gardner Taylor, were positioning themselves to catch some of the young Brooklynites' luster. Though not affiliated with Brooklyn CORE, both found themselves publicly supporting the chapter's actions and taking its side against moderate leaders like Farmer. "I think some of them would just as soon be dead as unfulfilled in this society," Reverend Taylor said of the young militants in tribute to their all-out tactics and daredevil intensity.

The reality out in Brooklyn was a little less glamorous. Headquarters was a ramshackle second-floor storefront above a barbershop on Nostrand Avenue. The walls were plastered with tattered maps and FREEDOM NOW posters. The one phone was in constant use—though as often as not for personal calls. Members talked proudly of their ties to the "grassroots" and made a point, to any visitor who would listen, of comparing the view from their storefront—the littered sidewalks of Bedford-Stuyvesant—with the midtown office towers outside James Farmer's window. Still, there was no way of knowing just who or how many the group spoke for in the neighborhood. The day *The New York Times* sent a reporter to Nostrand Avenue, several members with some time on their hands passed the afternoon outside on the sidewalk, arguing with an elderly black man who poked fun at their revolutionary pretensions.

Most members of the Brooklyn cell were ideologues and activists. Black and white, many of them from middle-class backgrounds, they ranged in age from high school students to middle-aged radicals—including several former Marxists involved in black politics in the 1930s and 1940s. For a leader, this motley group had settled on Isaiah Brunson, a gawky, rustic young man from South Carolina who had come to New York two years earlier in search of work. Largely uneducated and intensely shy, Brunson was soon devoting himself full time to Brooklyn CORE, working for free and sleeping on a cot at headquarters. The chapter's second-in-command was a young man named Arnold Goldwag. In his early twenties, the son of a Jewish garment worker, he had dropped out of college to make time for CORE. Frenetic and self-absorbed—one of his main preoccupations was a scrapbook of newspaper clippings about himself—he slept four hours a night, smoked eighty cigarettes a day and subsisted, he claimed, on cake and black coffee. But by the winter before the World's Fair, the chapter was also attracting ordinary black Brooklynites, mostly alienated young men roused out of hopelessness by what was happening in the South.

Sonny Carson was a fairly typical recruit: in his mid-twenties, out of work, brimming with unfocused anger at the world around him. One of several children from a poor working family, he always seemed to be in trouble. In elementary school, he was already stealing pennies from newsstands; by junior high, he had become an accomplished mugger. Before he finished high school, he was serving in a state reformatory, and even there he was known as one of the toughest youths. In the army, he chafed at the discipline and went AWOL several times before being wounded in Korea. Then for a time he tried family life, but ended up back in the streets, where he sold drugs and ran an illegal gambling joint. After a while, this too bored him, and he was drifting more or less aimlessly when he stumbled into racial politics. As for which branch of the movement spoke his language—the middle-class moderates or defiant nationalists—Carson never had a moment's doubt. "There was another brother," he wrote later, looking back on 1963, "named Martin Luther King. He was beginning to upset me because that philosophy he taught was spreading and it didn't seem to fit right with me. That 'turn the other cheek' business—shee-it. Malcolm, I think, was saying it right: that if someone hit you on one side of your cheek, then you lay him in the grave."

Different as they were in vision and temperament, James Farmer was thrilled that young men like Carson were joining the struggle. A strapping, good-natured man from a middle-class family, Farmer had come to the movement by way of divinity school and pacifist organizing. One of the original founders of CORE, he had been working as an activist for more than twenty years, struggling to spread the integrationist gospel to both blacks and whites. Educated, at ease in the white world—he was also married to a white woman—he deferred to no one in his color blindness, but by the early sixties he was urgently concerned to reach out and connect with youths like Carson. Pleased as he was by the way southern protests had galvanized the ghetto, Farmer knew CORE's northern chapters could not survive merely "on sympathy with the South." The traditional avenues that CORE had sought to open up—access to jobs and other opportunities in the white world—had little application for flailing street kids in Brooklyn. When Farmer went out in the wake of the Freedom Rides to rally would-be recruits in Harlem, he began as usual by talking about integration, but found all too often that he was met with boos. "Don't tell us about no nonviolence," he remembered one heckler shouting. "We don' wanna hear that shit." Already in the early sixties, Farmer grasped that he would have to find another way to speak to the anger and frustration in the northern ghetto.

Farmer's answer in 1962 was a sharp shift in methods and rhetoric. For the first time in the organization's history, CORE activists were told to put aside their color blindness. A new agenda was issued, urging chapters to get to work improving life "in segregated areas." Farmer modified what he said in Harlem, and when he got no response to talk about CORE's efforts on housing and unemployment, he changed the subject, rallying youthful crowds with angry complaints about racist white authority figures. The term "integration" did not disappear from his speeches or from CORE literature, but the old themes of reconciliation and understanding were no longer sounded much in public. Most significantly, Farmer encouraged lieutenants to start recruiting directly from the street, reaching out to the "gangs and crowds from which Malcolm recruited." Years later, Farmer maintained that he had known exactly what this would lead to. "I knew what we were chancing—changing the class content, bringing in all those people who were uncomfortable around whites and who had no interest in integration." A life-long integrationist, convinced that blacks' future lay in the mainstream, Farmer felt he had little choice. He made a point of listening to young recruits like Carson, and he could only swallow hard when he heard them talk about his cherished ideals. "Harmony is not the goal and never should have been," Carson said later. "The struggle is about power—power to control our own destinies. For black people, integration means relinquishing power. Why should we want to do that?"

By the winter of 1963–64, with the Brooklyn chapter emerging as a force to reckon with in the city, Farmer found himself being swept along willy-nilly in their direction. Though CORE was still an integrated group—as much as half the national membership was still white, and almost all of the funding came from white liberals—Farmer bowed to grassroots pressure to ease whites out of leadership positions. "It tore me up inside," he later said, but it was the only way to stave off "a nationalist takeover" from below. Instead of objecting to Brooklyn's confrontational tactics or trying to dissuade the group's impatient activists, he mostly bit his tongue and looked the other way. His relationship with the chapter was strained and uncomfortable, and he was nagged by growing fears that its tactics would lead to violence. Yet, at the time, it seemed possible to him that the organization could absorb and contain newcomers like Carson. They were still young, he insisted to himself and others, malleable and unclear about their goals; it should not be that hard, he maintained, to "channelize them constructively." For Farmer and others committed to CORE's old ideals, it still seemed possible that blacks and whites could forge the future together, particularly if white America was willing to meet the protesters halfway.

That winter, most white Americans were just waking up to the race problem. The Supreme Court's *Brown* v. *Board of Education* decision was almost a decade old, and polls suggested that by now about two-thirds of the public approved of it—though not even 10 percent of the schools in any region had been desegregated. But it was only with the demonstrations in Birmingham, Alabama, in the summer of 1963 that race had become a central issue in the nation's public life. Suddenly Americans of all kinds took note; the moral power of black demands hit home, and for a few months everyone talked excitedly about the pressing need for change. Still, it was far from clear how deep the goodwill went or what it would mean in practice. Though Farmer among others took heart from the change and committed himself to a working alliance with President Johnson, for the tough youths of Brooklyn

CORE the white awakening had little impact. "White folks are not honest and never have been," Carson explained his reaction years later. "It was all a trick. Emancipation was a trick. That talk in the sixties was just another trick. Who did they think they were fooling? The dishonesty is enmeshed in the foundations of the relationship."

Farmer continued his edgy dance with Brooklyn CORE through the winter of 1963–64. The two partners first quarreled publicly in January, when Brooklyn threatened a massive protest—one that "would bring New York to a complete standstill"—if the state would not release a chapter member arrested at a demonstration the summer before. Isaiah Brunson shot off a menacing telegram to Governor Nelson Rockefeller, followed a few days later by an angry press conference, both hinting broadly at giant sit-ins that would tie up traffic on the city's bridges and tunnels. The threat could not have come at a worse time for Farmer, who was just then flying back and forth to Washington to confer with Lyndon Johnson on the passage of the 1964 Civil Rights Act. Farmer didn't mind telling Johnson that his followers were angry and impatient. It even did him some good at the grassroots to show he could stand up to the president, proving his grit and militancy in the face of white authority. But Farmer also knew full well just how overwrought Brooklyn's threat would look from Washington. Caught between his own men and the president, he waffled evasively for a few days, then issued an awkward statement supporting massive civil disobedience in principle—but not to get one individual out of jail.

The two sides—leader and rank-and-file—managed to paper over their differences briefly for the historic 1964 New York school boycott. The action was conceived by the national CORE office and carried out by a broad coalition of activists, including some of the most venerated of the movement's old-guard leadership: the NAACP, the New York Urban League and Bayard Rustin, organizer of the 1963 March on Washington. The goal—desegregation of the city's schools—came straight out of the older generation's playbook. Some of the early preparations even had what reporters called "a Deep South flavor," with demonstrators gathering in local churches, swaying hand-in-hand and singing "We Shall Overcome."

The boycott came off dramatically on February 3, one of the first and most impressive protests organized by the movement in a northern city. Activists maintained the illusion of unity. All factions of the coalition paid lip service to the ideal of integration. Roughly 45 percent of the city's public school students stayed home, and 3,500 demonstrators rallied at the Board of Education. Despite some random black threats and much white fear of massive disruption, there was no violence anywhere in the city.

Then, within days, things began to fall apart. When the board of education declined to respond to the boycott, the coalition's leader, militant minister Milton Galamison, declared he would rather see the school system "destroyed"—"maybe it has run its course anyway," he said—than put up with continued segregation. He escalated his demands, asking now not for a timetable but for "immediate" integration—an impossible request. *The New York Times,* speaking for the city's liberal establishment, denounced him as "tragically misguided." "The battle for equality of opportunity is the common responsibility of all New Yorkers," an editorial argued. "It will not be won by tactics that tear the community apart." Galamison paid no attention to the reproach. He had made his demands and did not intend to take no for an answer. On the contrary, the more resistance he met, the more angry and insistent he became. He called on the board of education to produce and immediately implement a massive busing plan, even if this meant pitched battles with white parents. Then he announced a second boycott to take place within the month.

The next few weeks brought steadily growing tension across the city as groups like Brooklyn CORE ratcheted up their protest activity. Unlike old-time movement leaders who counted on liberals' sympathy and support, the new breed of activists was largely indifferent to white criticism. If anything, they seemed encouraged by white anger; it proved just how much consternation their protests had caused. In the wake of the boycott, their tactics grew still more theatrical, more symbolic and expressive and deliberately disruptive. One of the newest ideas was the use of rats. The first effort arose out of a rent strike, common enough in those years in Harlem and Bedford-Stuyvesant. In this instance, about one thousand Harlem residents had refused to make further payments until landlords repaired their crumbling apartments. The landlords procrastinated and attention flagged—until activists collected several bags of dead rats and dumped them in front of the judge arbitrating the dispute. The tactic did nothing to persuade the court or landlords, but as sheer troublemaking it was hard to beat. The effect in the black community was electrifying, and within months there was a rash of actions involving rats in Harlem, Brooklyn and dozens of other northern cities.

New York CORE members' next big flamboyant protest targeted the Triborough Bridge. Just a month after the school boycott, some two dozen members of a Harlem chapter gathered on the bridge and linked arms across the roadway, blocking traffic between Manhattan and Long Island. Demonstrators had come prepared with bags of garbage, which they dumped ceremoniously here and there on the span. Several were then arrested and carried off with due fanfare. Their announced goal, which had nothing to do with the bridge or garbage, was to draw attention to the need for better schools in Harlem. The board of education declined to react to the protest, but CORE activists were thrilled by the outrage they caused among press and public. Farmer hesitated to denounce his grassroots and struggled desperately to put the best face on the action. Fudging his lifelong belief that protests should be carefully targeted at specific offenders—and meant to inspire them toward good, not merely harass or threaten them—he reluctantly endorsed the traffic snarl-up. Meanwhile, more or less indifferent to his approval, local activists promised yet another round of disruptive protest. "More dramatic [demonstrations]" Bronx chapter chairman Herbert Callender warned, "will take place at locations where there are large crowds."

Other New Yorkers, black and white, were increasingly troubled by the escalating chaos. The *Times* called the Triborough action "a disservice to civil rights." A few brave black spokesmen, Bayard Rustin among them, expressed their disapproval of unfocused demonstrations, aimed not at biased individuals or groups, but, indiscriminately, at the general public. But it was among ordinary white New Yorkers that the new angry tactics took the greatest toll. The protests mushrooming around the metro area sometimes resembled those of the southern movement—actions that increasing numbers of whites found moving and sympathetic. Northern black activists too quoted Gandhi and chanted, "Jim Crow Must Go!"; some continued to invoke the ideal of integration. Still, it was evident even to distracted New Yorkers that there was something different about the big-city northern protesters: they were angrier, more impatient, less likely to believe that white people were basically decent and could change. Certainly, their new confrontational tactics seemed to have little to do with any practical political goals, whether integration or economic advancement for blacks. The rage and recklessness—the sheer destructiveness—that came with the demonstrations were incomprehensible to the larger public. And before long, even the most sympathetic whites were turning away, dismayed by what Brooklyn congressman Emanuel Celler—a key backer of the pending Civil Rights Act—called the growing "nihilism" of the northern movement.

The reasons for the difference between North and South were not hard to grasp and, given black impatience with the pace of change, perhaps inevitable. The methods of the southern movement—civil disobedience and the legal changes it was meant to bring about—could do little to improve life in the ghetto. Almost by definition, the old protest tactics could not deliver, and when they did not, frustrated activists only grew more impatient. Still, understandable as the new mood was, already in 1964 it was undermining the struggle. The less effective the movement, the more militant it became, and growing numbers of poor northern blacks latched onto the idea of protest for protest's sake: expressive, symbolic actions aimed at everyone and no one in particular. The idea, as one CORE man put it, was to do something that "drastically inconveniences people." The purpose of the inconvenience—for negotiating leverage or simply to annoy whites—was already cloudy and beside the point.

Galamison's second boycott, scheduled for Monday, March 16, fell clearly into the category of expressive politics. The weeks since the first boycott had brought intensified scrutiny of the city's schools—and growing skepticism, on all sides, about the possibility of desegregating them. White opinion was all but unanimously opposed to busing. Education experts, including the respected black psychologist Kenneth Clark, were warning that the proportion of black and Hispanic students (already about half) and their geographical distribution in the sprawling city made the dream of racially mixed classrooms unattainable. Reporters sampling ghetto opinion found parents if anything even more skeptical: fearful of the long bus trips, suspicious of white teachers, worried that their children would be met by gangs of hostile white kids. In early March, a group of forty-two Harlem ministers came out against Galamison's plan. "We are for integrated schools," the pastors said, "[only] where bringing this to pass will not disrupt the processes of quality education. . . . We do not believe that the continuation of school boycotts is in the best interest of our children." Still, Galamison pressed on, dealing a fatal blow to his rickety coalition that made up the New York integration movement.

The NAACP and Bayard Rustin quickly repudiated a second boycott. Farmer and Urban League chief Whitney Young hedged for a few days but eventually backed away from Galamison. The moderates were immediately replaced at his side by ten-term Harlem congressman Adam Clayton Powell, Jr., nine of fourteen local CORE chapters, and Malcolm X, who appeared at a rally in Harlem and urged the ghetto to arm itself for "self-defense." Asked if he would join Galamison's picket lines, Malcolm answered probably not—but not because he didn't support the protest. "If I got in line," he explained, "other believers of non-nonviolence would join it, and when we met up with

white non-nonviolence believers, there might be violence." A longtime opponent of racial mingling, in schools or anywhere else, Malcolm made no
mention of the boycott's ostensible goal. Apparently, for him, as for much of
Harlem, "integration" was already an all but meaningless word—the empty
pretext for a gesture of defiance.

By the day before the second boycott, many white New Yorkers were prepared for a full-scale riot. No one knew exactly who was going to show up on
the picket lines or what kind of chaos they might cause. Police commissioner
Michael Murphy warned that the force would not allow black radicals to
"turn New York City into a battleground"; even the liberal press sounded
frightened. The next morning, 270,000 children stayed away from school.
This was only about half the number that had stayed out in the first boycott,
but most black and Puerto Rican schools were 90 percent empty. Whatever
they felt about integration, most of the city's blacks had backed Galamison,
lining up behind his noisy show of anger, even though it was unlikely to
bring about any change. As luck would have it, the day came off peacefully,
but race relations in the city would never be quite the same again. Already in
1964, moderates like Young and Farmer could no longer carry the ghetto,
and militants like Galamison were setting the agenda for the movement.

The change was apparent all along the spectrum and on both sides of the
color line. Within weeks, even Farmer had stopped arguing for school desegregation. For many white parents, the boycott was just the excuse they
needed to justify their opposition to busing. Grassroots "parent and tax-
payer" groups sprang up overnight in the outer boroughs and began organizing counterprotests in their neighborhoods. Meanwhile, Manhattan's liberal
establishment hedged uncomfortably, trying to paper over its confusion;
both the *Times* and the board of education were firmly committed to school
integration, but without black partners, they were at a loss for what to do
next. The boycott's consequences were felt as far away as Washington, D.C.,
where Senators Hubert Humphrey and Thomas Kuchel, leading backers of
the pending Civil Rights Act, announced that unruly, illegal demonstrations
were endangering the bill. "Civil wrongs do not bring civil rights," they
scolded righteously, completely unaware how little weight their opinion carried in black New York.

In early, April, Brooklyn CORE stunned New York with its plans for the
stall-in at the World's Fair. By now, the chapter was no longer pretending
that there was a connection between its disruptive protests and the wholesale

changes it was demanding of what it called "the system." Activists conceded that the fair was in no way discriminatory, and the ultimatums they put to the city—including "immediate" integration and the elimination of slum housing—were so sweeping as to be unmeetable. As the cell's press statements made clear, the impetus behind the protest was largely emotional: "We do not see," a leading member, Oliver Leeds, explained, "why white people should enjoy themselves when Negroes are suffering." "I think it had something to do with jobs," Sonny Carson later said, "but it wasn't important what it was all about; what was more important was the effect it had. . . . It brought about [a] kind of pandemonium." Just to threaten to close down the fair gave him and his fellow activists a moment of delicious revenge. "We wanted to cause some pain and get some attention," he explained. "We wanted to put the city in the position that black people always find themselves in. Those people needed to suffer some indignities that we were in control of."

Panicked New Yorkers, anticipating the worst, made plans to try to contain the threatened disruption. Thousands of police leaves were canceled, elaborate security deployments were drawn up, extra towtrucks were arranged for and the city's mass transit schedules were revised. Dozens of black and white notables condemned the protest, including President Johnson, Robert Kennedy, New York's mayor, Robert Wagner and most moderate civil rights leaders.

As the alarm mounted, Farmer, too, decided he had to take a stand against the stall-in. He held several closed meetings with the young Brooklynites; one emotional session in his own apartment lasted until four in the morning. Even then, Farmer did not dare talk about the ideal—understanding between black and white—that had guided him through twenty years of civil rights activism. Instead, he made the case entirely in the young militants' own terms. Lacking clear targets, he tried stiffly to explain, the stall-in could not possibly produce a "relevant confrontation with those responsible for discrimination." Worse still, the action could be self-defeating, alienating white liberals and working-class blacks. The scruffy-looking young members of the Brooklyn group listened impassively to the older man's pleas. When they insisted they were going ahead anyway, Farmer suspended the entire chapter.

Farmer spent the next two weeks on the offensive. He explained his position over and over again to the press; he sent urgent memos to other CORE chapters pleading with them not to join in Brooklyn's "hare-brained" scheme. Finally, in desperation, he tried letters to the other major civil rights groups, asking their rank-and-file for a vote of confidence. But by the middle of April, Farmer could see that the campaign was futile. Nothing he could do was going to stop the Brooklyn militants from protesting. Martin Luther King and other moderate movement leaders pressed their membership, but not even the Southern Christian Leadership Conference (SCLC) would issue a statement denouncing the stall-in. Two weeks before the fair opened, the local media was giving Farmer and Isaiah Brunson equal time, playing up the head-to-head battle and what had become a major test of the older man's leadership.

White New York was baffled by the contest; it was a standoff they imagined Farmer would win hands down. He had a huge reputation; national CORE was a big, rich organization with a venerable history, and the awkward, rustic Brunson seemed no match for the veteran director. But the duel between Farmer and his grassroots had nothing to do with money or even leadership. Though Brooklyn CORE had no tangible backing and no particular talent, it had one towering advantage: it spoke for the anger stirring in the ghetto. To criticize Brooklyn CORE was to criticize that anger, or—even worse—to make light of it. Foolhardy as the militants were, brash and overreaching, to dismiss them was political suicide.

No one understood this better than Farmer. An unstinting integrationist, a man who had spent his life trying to communicate across the racial divide, he could not have been more troubled by the new protests, designed to anger and humiliate whites, that if anything widened the gulf between the races. He felt he had to stop the stall-in—to maintain some discipline and avert a citywide tie-up. But he also knew he could not afford to alienate the younger men's growing following. If he wanted to maintain his leadership in the ghetto, he would have to match Brooklyn's militancy with some defiant gesture of his own. He began with tough talk: continuing to denounce the stall-in, but also drawing attention to what he called its legitimate roots—black New York's "growing frustration, anger [and] militancy." Then, as the weeks went by and the stakes grew higher, he moved to make up for his censure of the Brooklyn cell by announcing his own showy, disruptive protest at the World's Fair.

With only a few days to go before the gala opening on April 22, Farmer scrambled to put together what he called a "counter-demonstration." He would, he announced, bring a thousand protesters into the fairgrounds. Some would climb the "Unisphere"—the great silver thirteen-story globe that dominated the exhibition. Others would demonstrate the use of south-ern-style cattle prods. Still others would block major doors and entryways with sit-ins and lie-ins. Together, the small annoyances would dominate opening day: a massive demonstration, like the stall-in, scheduled to coin-cide with President Johnson's speech.

Farmer tried painstakingly to explain to reporters exactly how his protest would be different from Brooklyn CORE's. All disruptive activity would take place inside the fairgrounds. Targets would be carefully chosen. The counterdemonstration would, he promised, be "positive," disciplined and "focused." Still, for all the differences, the two protests seemed to New Yorkers to have a lot in common. Much like the stall-in, the counter-demonstration was meant to serve a "gadfly" function, disturbing the peace and "courting" arrest. Farmer had understandable rationales for some of his targets: the pavilions of southern states, for example, and cor-porations with a history of discrimination. But others—like the Uni-sphere—made little sense. At best, his protest seemed designed to call attention to discrimination, but beyond that it was hard to see what con-structive goals it would serve: just whom exactly Farmer hoped to convince to make what changes, integrationist or otherwise. More and more, as the day approached, he seemed to want to have it both ways, denouncing the stall-in even as he imitated it.

President Johnson knew all about the struggle that had been going on in CORE that winter and spring, but he was still looking forward to his trip to New York. It was no accident that Johnson was known to Farmer and others as "the civil rights president." Assuming the helm in the wake of John F. Kennedy's assassination, he had taken up the cause with striking speed and confidence. His first priority in office was passage of the Civil Rights Act, a bill languishing obscurely at the time of Kennedy's death. Limited as it would seem even a year later, in 1964 the bill promised a huge step forward: the end of legal discrimination and the desegregation of all public places. At the time of the World's Fair, many white voters were still skeptical, and pres-idential hopefuls Barry Goldwater and George Wallace were already cam-paigning against the new law. But Johnson had not hesitated to stake his political future on passage. More far-seeing still, he was urging aides to de-vise a remedy for the economic and social gaps that separated most blacks from the mainstream—the strategy that would become the War on Poverty. Preparing his speech for the fair, the president could think of no initiative he was keener to tell the public about. With many of the movement's top leaders and fund-raisers based in New York, he also expected a warm welcome there. The disappointment in store for him could not have been greater.

Opening day of the fair dawned cold and rainy, more like November than late April. The Unisphere stood out starkly against the gray sky, emblem of the stylish exhibition and the universalist hope behind it. The police were out in force, manning the highways that converged on the fairgrounds. Tourists and others trying to make their way to Queens reported some civil disobedience on the subways. But the anticipated stall-in on the city's roadways fizzled. The cold, wet weather did not help. The expected twenty-five hundred cars did not appear, and those that did were vastly outnumbered by policemen and police towtrucks. Reverend Galamison was one of the few who tried, braving the chill rain only to discover that it was impossible to pull over on the side of the highway. Many of New York's main arteries stayed eerily empty through the day: wet ribbons of black asphalt lined by knots of yellow slicker–clad cops. Fewer than 93,000 visitors attended the fair—some 250,000 had been expected—but authorities insisted the fall-off was due largely to the weather. The next day, Isaiah Brunson went into seclusion, leaving the press with no explanation of the year's most spectacular flop.

Farmer's counterprotest was more successful. National CORE fielded over seven hundred demonstrators, including well-known social democrats Bayard Rustin and Michael Harrington. Bearded, scruffy, wet and covered with mud, the protesters both repelled and fascinated fairgoers. The opulent fountains and futuristic architecture of the grounds made a stunning backdrop for press photographers, and CORE members played their part for all it was worth. Demonstrators blocked gates and sat in doorways; when police tried to arrest them, they sank limply to the ground. Farmer himself was arrested and physically removed from the entrance to the New York City exhibition. "Farmer is our leader. We shall not be moved," young CORE members chanted as he was carried away in the rain past the Unisphere. For most of the morning, the leadership's discipline held and the protest unfolded peacefully. President Johnson, taking no chances, decided to deliver his speech behind closed doors, to an invitation-only audience. It was only when he emerged into an open area and tried to say a few words that the demonstration turned ugly.

The misunderstanding could not have been greater or more excruciating. As Johnson saw things, he had sided with the struggle, moving at enormous risk to do the right thing by blacks. Yet, in the eyes of even moderate CORE members, because he was white he was the enemy. "We do not try to mask our national problems," the president declared earnestly to a group of milling demonstrators on his way out of the fair. "No other nation in history has done so much to correct its flaws." The crowd responded with angry chants: "Freedom Now! Freedom Now!" "Jim Crow must go!" It was the litany of the southern movement, but in the circumstances bizarrely off-key. The president tried to continue—anything he could think of to reach the protesters—but the distance was unbridgeable. His last intent pleas were barely audible above the venomous shouting. His peroration about the future—"a world in which all men are equal"—drew derisive laughter from the noisy crowd.

The moment passed quickly, hardly noted in the press, but in its small, symbolic way it contained the seeds of much racial misunderstanding, and worse, to come. The white establishment was trying finally to deliver on the nation's promises, moving, albeit haltingly, to grant at least formal equality to black citizens. But the effort, earnest and repentant as it was, struck many blacks as meaningless, even contemptible: much too little, too late. The young blacks heckling the president were already beyond the reach of his integrationist agenda, and the alienation they spoke for would dog its implementation for decades to come. There was, to be sure, already enough blame to go around. But even in 1964 this was almost beside the point. The racial mismatch—in hopes and fears, grudges and energies—was already enough to spell the likely failure of the integrationist dream.

Despite the failure of the stall-in, Brooklyn CORE emerged unscathed and by most accounts more popular in the restless New York ghetto. The order suspending it from its parent organization was lifted, and several of the cell's most vociferous militants were promoted to national office. "We were on good terms after that," Farmer said later, "brought together by mutual respect." If anything, what happened at the World's Fair encouraged the Brooklyn activists, rewarding their threats and defiance with an intoxicating taste of power. Not only had white New York panicked, but the militants discovered just how easy it was to manipulate the movement's remaining moderates. Three hundred protesters had been arrested, thousands of fairgoers inconvenienced—not by a small group of radicals, but by one of the nation's largest and most respected civil rights groups. The brash young Brooklynites could hardly have asked for more. Already, less than nine months after the 1963 March on Washington, the militant tail was wagging the moderate dog, and black advocates of integration had been all but side-lined. White America was only just waking up to the need for change, moving to take down racial barriers and think through the difficulties of bringing blacks into the mainstream. But even as the nation took these first tentative steps, white liberals found that there was no one on the black side to talk to.

Chapter 2

OUT OF SYNC

In spring 1962, two years before the stall-in, Malcolm X and James Farmer met for an evening of debate entitled, without much ado, "Separation vs. Integration." The setting was Cornell University, before a packed and avid audience, mostly white. In 1962, the civil rights struggle had just begun to grab the public's attention. College students were fascinated and earnestly sympathetic to blacks' bid for justice. "Integration" was a word to conjure with among hopeful whites, and no one in liberal circles thought to question the concept. Most simply assumed it was the road to racial progress—that it captured the yearnings of most blacks and would catch on soon among a critical mass of whites. Yet even in the early sixties, the title of the Cornell event revealed, pockets of black America were skeptical. The integrationist Farmer felt he was arguing at a disadvantage and had agreed to participate only if Cornell would consent to conditions to offset what he saw as Malcolm's inherent edge. "Any black opponent was in an untenable position," Farmer later wrote, "trying to defend the white world against Malcolm's valid criticisms." Already in 1962, a black man defending integration knew he risked looking like a chump.

Standing up first in the campus auditorium, Farmer laid out a classic integrationist argument. He explained the problem with a string of anecdotes: catchy, down-to-earth examples of prejudice and the harm segregation did to both whites and blacks. From there, his logic was simple enough: if segregation was the disease, integration must be the cure. He didn't cite Martin

Luther King, Jr., but he might as well have: his assumptions were the same—that white Americans were basically decent people, that the movement should appeal to their consciences, that blacks and whites had to solve the problem together, that in the future color wouldn't matter much. "I tell you," he declared emotionally, "we are Americans. This is our country as much as it is white American."

Malcolm got off to a slow start—Farmer had stolen much of his fire with his indictment of white prejudice—but once the young Muslim minister got going, he made an electrifying case. Steely and intense in manner, as coolly humorless as Farmer was homey, he argued starkly that most blacks had no interest in integration. "The masses of black people don't think it's any solution for us to force ourselves into a white neighborhood," he said dismissively. "Integration," in his view, was just another word for white domination, a way to further rob blacks of their culture and identity. The only workable answer was "complete separation," if not in Africa, then in a black belt in the United States. Most of his presentation was calmly reasoned, but every now and again his smoldering anger burst through in bitter denunciations of white "hypocrisy" and "hand-picked high-class, middle-class Uncle Tom Negroes" who betrayed their race by trying to fit into the white world. The nastiest moment of the evening came when Malcolm turned personally on Farmer, asserting that he had no credibility among blacks because he was married to a white woman. It was a charge that would haunt black integrationists for decades to come—that, in effect, they weren't "black enough." But for the white students in the Cornell audience, this was overshadowed by a much more troubling message: that blacks didn't like or trust whites, that the ghetto wasn't interested in their help, that there was nothing they could do to make up for the past—no way, as King was suggesting, "to redeem the soul of America."

Few of those who heard him speak would ever forget Malcolm's acid tongue, but even after the debate it was hard to know what to think about his claim that the majority of blacks had no interest in inclusion. By the early sixties, most whites who followed racial questions—still a relatively small number—were aware of the Nation of Islam. A powerful CBS documentary, Mike Wallace's *The Hate That Hate Produced,* had aired in 1959, stirring a flurry of consternation. Then in 1962, James Baldwin visited Muslim leader Elijah Muhammad and included a telling portrait of him in a widely read *New Yorker* magazine piece, soon reissued in book form as *The Fire Next Time.* A vivid account of the Muslims' rising popularity, the piece described

growing black interest in "vengeance" and spreading "hatred for white men."
Cosmopolitan as he was, Baldwin himself seemed taken with the new mood:
"Do I really want to be integrated into a burning house?" he asked in what
became the article's most famous line. Leaders of the civil rights movement—and whites who sympathized with them—tried to play down this
troubling evidence of alienation. No movement chief but Farmer would debate Malcolm in public, and together the national spokesmen dismissed the
Muslims as a cranky fringe. Still, for the Cornell audience and others, Malcolm's repeated warnings were hard to ignore. "The people in the black community who didn't want integration were never given a voice," he charged.
"[They] were never given a platform. [They] were never given an opportunity to shout out the fact that integration would never solve the problem."

The word "integration" had gained national currency in the years just
before the Cornell debate, as King and other civil rights spokesmen put
it at the top of their list of demands. In 1957, the Southern Christian Leadership Conference appealed to President Eisenhower to appoint a cabinet-
level "Secretary of Integration." A year later, King told a mass demonstration
in Washington that "a hundred years from now, the historians will be calling
this not the 'beat' generation but the generation of integration." Even the
movement's opponents worked the term into their vocabulary: "Two–four–
six–eight! We don't want to integrate!" they chanted menacingly as they
milled around outside contested southern school buildings.

Still, even at this moment of maximum popularity, it was far from clear
what the word meant. As recently as the late fifties, it had denoted no more
than physical desegregation: access for blacks to southern schools and hotel
lobbies. But already in the early sixties, it wasn't hard to see that this would
not be enough to ease the black discontent spilling out across the South. To
the degree that the word "integration" stood in for the movement's goal, it
was an ever-expanding, grab-bag expression, as vague as it was promising.
What exactly was the ideal? How long would it take to get there? What could
the government do to help? And what kind of deeper change would be necessary—on the part of both whites and blacks? As late as 1962, few people
had thought about these questions.

The basic idea was hardly new, of course. Blacks had been yearning for inclusion for a hundred years, if not more, and, despite appalling obstacles, determined men and women had made their way into the mainstream even in
the nineteenth century. Yet for many blacks of that era, the goal had seemed

so distant and unlikely that its fulfillment had been hard to envision in a realistic way. Not even Abraham Lincoln could imagine that the Negroes he freed would be able to fit in. Through no fault of their own, blacks as a group were so far behind educationally and in other ways that well after the Civil War it was difficult for almost any whites or blacks to conceive of themselves as part of the same community.

No wonder that when Emancipation became a real prospect, many blacks' first impulse was not inclusion but emigration. Prejudice and white support for slavery only made the social gaps seem wider, and already in the 1850s, there was not a leading black in America—including integrationist Frederick Douglass—who did not at least toy with the idea of what was called "colonization." But what these men discovered was that as a large-scale solution, emigration was as difficult as integration—in the short run, virtually impossible. The late nineteenth century saw extensive fund-raising and planned pilot projects in Africa, the West Indies and southern enclaves, but none of these schemes came to much of anything. Questions about where to find the land, how to pay for it, how to develop an economy and then lure or transport enough poor freedmen and women: together, the obstacles were insurmountable.

What this meant was that from the start both of the freed slaves' options were essentially unrealizable. Both real inclusion and withdrawal were distant pipe dreams, as abstract and idealized as they were unlikely. Even during Reconstruction, most blacks remained a caste apart, with little hope of crossing the moat that divided them from the white world. In these conditions, separate yet largely dependent and uneducated, it made little sense to choose exclusively for either integration or separation. People understandably nurtured both yearnings—yet both remained remote, ill-defined ideals.

The result, persisting through the century that followed, was what W. E. B. Du Bois famously called "two-ness": the original and classic phrase for black ambivalence about integration. "One feels his two-ness," Du Bois wrote in 1903 in *The Souls of Black Folk,* "an American, a Negro, two souls, two thoughts, two unreconciled strivings, two warring ideals in one dark body." Still, the young scholar went on, the black man "wishes neither of these . . . selves to be lost. He would not Africanize America, for America has too much to teach the world and Africa. He would not bleach the Negro soul in a flood of white Americanism, for he knows that Negro blood has a message for the world. He simply wishes to make it possible for a man to be both a Negro and an American."

Optimistic and expansive as he still was at the turn of the century, Du Bois made his double self sound like a precious gift. For others, over the years, the feelings it evoked often weighed more heavily: rejection, confusion, anger, alienation. Yet through the decades, most blacks harbored a little of both contradictory impulses: some integrationist hope and some proud— or bitter or resigned—nationalism. "Deep in the heart of every black adult," James Farmer explained in the sixties, "lives some of Malcolm X and some of Martin Luther King, side by side."

In the years since Du Bois wrote, both inclinations had taken a variety of forms, some involving political initiatives, others more psychological. On the nationalist side, many blacks dreamed of physical withdrawal, whether abroad, in the South or, later, in a politically independent, self-governed ghetto. Others made do with color-coded insularity in the black church, black fraternal organizations, all-black schools or a self-conscious black worldview. For integrationists, too, the goal tended to vary with one's circumstances from mere physical desegregation to a full sense of belonging in the mainstream. At once more and less than conventional ideologies, both integrationism and nationalism were largely matters of personal temperament—fundamental attitudes toward the white world and one's place in it.

Amorphous, volatile, one the inevitable flip side of the other, the two moods alternated, not just within individuals but also in the community. When times were good, or as good as they could be for black people—during Reconstruction, say, or again in the 1950s—the optimistic, integrationist side of people came forward. When times were bad—when white society seemed unwelcoming or worse—frustrated, disappointed blacks turned fatalistically to separatism. Black intellectuals (and white historians) were sometimes tempted to say that one of the two strains was predominant: that one was figure and the other ground, or that one—integrationism—was merely an elite longing, while the masses of blacks were in fact deeply separatist. In truth, there was little evidence for either thesis and little basis on which to make claims about what the silent majority of blacks was aiming for, even when one or other tendency seemed in the ascendant.

The advent of Jim Crow seemed to many to end all hope, making integration, glimpsed fleetingly in the Reconstruction era, less and less of a plausible goal. Segregation was again legally acceptable; new draconian racial codes were transforming lives across the South. A sense of deepening gloom settled over the black community, and agitation for integration slowed to a minimum. "The goal seemed so hopeless," historian C. Vann Woodward would later explain. "Things can be so impossible as to discourage any effort." Still, even in the worst years of Jim Crow, integrationism survived. Working black families—what one sociologist called "exaggerated Americans"—struggled to live by the codes of middle-class white society. Devoting themselves to education and discipline, they prepared for the day when they or their children might slip into the mainstream. For this group, "two-ness" meant you never gave up on inclusion, though for other blacks, just as powerfully, it meant that one was always skeptical. Even when times were good and most people's prospects hopeful, the separatist tendency too was always present, and bitter, disappointed or defiant people were ready to rise up and follow nationalist leaders.

Uncertain black attitudes toward integration put a premium on leadership, on both sides of the black divide. Yet even integrationist leaders' definitions of the goal varied widely—once again, usually, what was plausible. For Frederick Douglass, born a slave, the focus was strictly legal: recognition as a citizen. In Douglass's day, that meant the right to vote, to own property and claim legal standing in court. When the post–Civil War amendments to the Constitution granted much of this and still integration did not ensue, later black spokesmen at the turn of the century had to rethink their concept of inclusion. It was the first of many such expansions of the definition: gradual political approximations of the still not quite articulable ideal of true equality and a full sense of belonging.

Conventional wisdom about black history usually paints W. E. B. Du Bois and Booker T. Washington as die-hard opponents: one integrationist, the other an unusually docile but still unmistakable separatist. In fact, while the two men were bitter personal rivals and their short-term strategies seemed diametrically opposed, they had more in common than is generally recognized: an early, stark example of just how differently different men could define integration.

By far the most popular black leader at the turn of the century, Washington was concerned above all with what he called the "development" of his people, and he devoted his life to a network of seemingly separatist black vocational schools and small-business leagues. Yet in its way, Washington's was a fundamentally integrationist vision. The goal, distant as it was in his era and hidden under countless layers of guile, was still eventual participation in the mainstream. Where Washington differed from his rival Du Bois was in his proposed means to that end. "The Negro must begin at the bottom," Washington insisted, "and lay a sure foundation, and not be lured by any temptation to rise on a false foundation"—by depending on paternalism, or forced, token integration.

Du Bois's alternative strategy, which would eventually carry the day, was more aggressive and political in focus. In 1905, the prickly northern scholar declared war on Washington's gradualist approach and organized a handful of black professionals and educators to form the vanguard Niagara Movement. Primary targets were legal disenfranchisement and the doctrine of separate but equal, and from the beginning the group's approach was based on protest. Washington's dream of inclusion had been implicit and low-key; he had, in effect, urged fellow blacks to grow into a place in the mainstream. The Niagara version of the idea had less to do with gradual development than with breaking down the door. The two programs were not mutually exclusive—certainly there was a need for progress on both fronts. But within a few years, the agitators had won the battle of ideas, ensuring that for decades to come integration would be defined as something that could be won in the political arena.

With the founding of the National Association for the Advancement of Colored People (NAACP) in 1909, the modern integrationist movement was born. From roughly that moment through 1955, the NAACP would dominate black political life. As later historians put it, the NAACP was the church and integration the religion of the community. A direct descendant of Du Bois's Niagara group, the new organization adopted its approach intact and unquestioned. Its primary battles took place in the courtroom, with lawyers hacking away at piece after piece of the Jim Crow system, while the group's pointedly noneconomic focus meant that self-help got little attention.

Whether or not the NAACP actually spoke for most blacks is a matter of some dispute. Card-carrying members—their number would eventually exceed half a million—were predominantly northern, urban and middle-class, while most of black America was still poor, rural and concentrated in the South. "Integration became the official agenda," James Farmer would note with some skepticism years later. "But most poor blacks were never very interested. Most of them didn't know any whites and felt only uncomfortable around them." Still other critics—nationalists like Malcolm X and the polemical black historian Harold Cruse—would claim that it was the whites in the NAACP who determined its objectives. Integration, Malcolm said, was an idea "invented by a Northern liberal." There is no question about white influence in the organization in early years; virtually all the original money and most start-up executives were white, as, well into the 1930s, were the volunteer attorneys. Still, from the beginning, members were overwhelmingly black, and they were the pillars of their communities—the doctors, barbers, undertakers, small entrepreneurs and church deacons who were the unelected leaders in the separate enclaves where most blacks lived. What exactly integration meant to these men and women is hard to say; it was still painfully remote to almost all. But by the early years of the century, they were willing to put their hope and faith and regular dues behind the idea.

Still, even as the integration movement took off, the old "two-ness" persisted, and its oscillations played themselves out in the ghetto street. The period following World War I was not a good time for blacks. Those who had fought overseas returned with heightened expectations of goodwill to find the same old prejudices, particularly in northern cities, where the two races were competing for scarce jobs. Poor black migrants flocking to the big factory towns were welcomed by rampaging white mobs, and in 1919 alone, more than seventy blacks were lynched. In this ugly climate, the nationalist temperament surfaced again: a generation of legendary street speakers, black book exchanges and storefront sects, interest in African history and left-wing politics—all evidence of the volcano lurking beneath the surface dominated by the integrationist NAACP. In 1919, one black journalist described the mood in his community as a recurring "feeling on the part of . . . Negroes that there was no future in the United States for them." Later that year, a Jamaican printer named Marcus Garvey purchased a hall on Harlem's 138th Street and began to preach his fiery nationalist message to anyone who would listen.

Garvey's meteoric rise and fall did not take long; within five years, he would be in prison on fraud charges. But in that time, he transformed black politics, giving form and substance to the separatist doubts coursing through the community—in effect, establishing an alternative church. A short, stocky man given to what one observer called "torrential eloquence," he was soon attracting up to six thousand listeners a night. His message was appealingly simple, particularly for poor, hopeless ghetto dwellers. "Up you mighty race!" he would thunder at his audiences. "I am the equal of any white man; I want you to feel the same way. No more fear, no more cringing, no more sycophantic begging and pleading." In addition to the galvanizing message, Garvey had a natural genius for political ritual. Followers were issued uniforms and organized for huge, showy rallies. They marched through Harlem, often led by Garvey himself, riding in a limousine in a lavishly plumed hat. Thousands of other blacks would line the streets to watch, clapping, waving flags and cheering themselves hoarse. Among the colorful banners: "We Want a Black Civilization," "Uncle Tom's Dead," "Africa Must be Free."

Garvey was not universally popular in the black community. Much of the middle class—people with a stake in integration and white standards of propriety—despised the populist, race-obsessed firebrand. The NAACP tried to undermine him. He was ridiculed mercilessly in the mainstream black press. Yet blacks of all backgrounds and viewpoints were welcome in his fold, and an astonishing variety came to pay court. Future congressman Adam Clayton Powell, Jr., then the privileged son of Harlem's most powerful minister, remembered riding down Seventh Avenue with Garvey in one of the big yearly parades. "It was one of the greatest thrills of my life," Powell said later. Integrationist Kenneth Clark, the psychologist whose data would clinch the *Brown* v. *Board of Education* case, watched the same processions from the sidewalk of 138th Street, awed by the uniforms and the audacity of the man who dared call himself "Provisional President of Africa." "What we now call his nationalism didn't seem to be anything other than part of the fight against racism," Clark recollected later. "At that time, the two approaches seemed complementary. Garvey was willing to stand up against racism."

At its peak in 1923, Garvey's organization claimed 6 million members and a sprawling network of small black businesses. All of this collapsed abruptly with his imprisonment and deportation a few years later. But the idea that one was part of a great, proud race, with no need of whites—and little hope of getting along with them—had made an indelible impression on black America. The writers and artists of the Harlem Renaissance gave voice to the new, defiant mood. "We younger Negro artists . . . now intend to express our individual dark-skinned selves without fear or shame," poet Langston Hughes wrote in 1926. "If white people are pleased, we are glad. If they are not, it doesn't matter." Even the aging Du Bois began to talk about "voluntary segregation" and what he called the "right to diversity." Realistic or not, nationalism packed an emotional power no integrationist program could match, and when it asserted itself, the fierce undertow could pull the firmest integrationist with it.

Ever the eloquent spokesman, Du Bois tried to explain why this was so. Increasingly disaffected as he was, the father of the integration movement still felt that inclusion was the black man's "natural" goal. Ahead of most contemporaries, he also grasped that racial mixing could be its own reward. "It gives wider contacts; it inspires greater self-confidence and suppresses the inferiority complex," he wrote. Why then did he renounce integration, opting instead for all-black schools? "We shall get . . . an infinitely more capable and rounded personality," he explained, "by putting children in schools where they are wanted, and where they are happy and inspired, than in thrusting them into hells where they are ridiculed and hated." Like countless blacks before him, Du Bois had come to nationalism by way of disappointment with the white world. The same line of reasoning would appear again and again in black biography: the separatist as rejected suitor. Often the disappointment would be compounded by anger or pride. But the primary source, potent for even the staunchest NAACP members, was a nagging sense of the hopelessness of integration. Du Bois's NAACP colleague, the great black man of letters James Weldon Johnson, made the point even more pungently. "What [else] is the Negro to do?" Johnson asked, explaining what he called his growing "isolationism." "Give himself over to wishful thinking? Stand shooting at the stars with a popgun?"

From the 1930s onward, the black movement found itself fighting a two-front war—against both white resistance and black uncertainty about integration. The primary battle, against segregation, began to shape up seriously in the interwar years. Boosted by an influx of money and a new generation of young black lawyers, the NAACP launched an intensified legal assault on the doctrine of separate but equal. The term "integration" came into use for the first time, in internal NAACP documents and then more broadly. Even more important from the point of view of the later struggle, activists discovered a powerful new tactic—direct action. The first practitioners were lonely individuals: Bayard Rustin and others, traveling around the South, simply refused to comply with Jim Crow rules. Then in 1941, labor organizer A. Philip Randolph threatened a massive march on Washington to protest discrimination in the defense industries. The march itself never took place, but the threat alone was enough to convince Franklin D. Roosevelt to desegregate munitions plants—a first major victory for the militant integrationist movement.

It was slower going on the other front—the internal one. Even into the 1940s, those who tried to assess black opinion found it surprisingly vague and changeable. The Swedish sociologist Gunnar Myrdal, researching his classic 1944 study of race, *An American Dilemma,* expected that the black experience of poverty and oppression would have produced a well-defined political agenda. Instead, he found "only a fluid and amorphous mass of all sorts of embryos of thought." Trying to predict the future, Myrdal thought the black masses might "rally around a violently anti-American, anti-Western, anti-White black chauvinism"—or, "just as likely, if only a slight change of stimulus is provided, join in an all-out effort to fight for . . . the United States."

What finally tipped the internal battle was a change of circumstance. As the prospects for black inclusion began to look more promising in the late 1940s, black opinion shifted markedly, rallying behind the integrationist agenda. The external changes were gradual, still generally two steps back for every one step forward. Growing migration from south to north meant better-paying jobs and an escape from the iron grip of Jim Crow. As black enclaves in the North grew to a critical mass, they began to elect black representatives who could bargain for them. Black soldiers came home from fighting in World War II with a new dignity, but also a fresh sense of indignation at the way they were treated. Having fought for the country and carried its colors, they saw no reason why they should be denied the right to take part in all aspects of American life. Even foreign affairs had a heartening effect on the integration movement as decolonization in Africa and Asia spurred both blacks and whites to think differently about the American race problem. Television news, just making its way into many homes, carried pictures of the new black heroes—both prime ministers and freedom fighters—and already by the forties Mahatma Gandhi had become a model for the emerging civil rights movement.

The result within a few years was not just more integrationism but also a shift in the tenor and quality of integrationist demands—another expansion of the vision. As black incomes, educations and aspirations rose, the humiliations of second-class citizenship—suffered for so long with virtually no hope of change—were suddenly unacceptable. Somehow, almost unnoticed, the old caste ceiling had been breached. In contrast to earlier NAACP officials, the activists who emerged in the postwar era—men like A. Philip Randolph, James Farmer and Thurgood Marshall—spoke in much stronger accents, no longer requesting but claiming their people's rights. As the emphasis shifted to activism and confrontation, poorer, less educated blacks began to get involved in the movement for the first time, taking risks in the name of integration. The old skepticism and sense of futility had not disappeared: many a hardworking, churchgoing black family still kept an old Garveyite uniform gathering dust in the hall closet. But in the forties, as the prospect of meaningful inclusion improved, the old bitter two-ness seemed at least to go underground.

Still, even as the movement took off, the definition of integration remained oddly unclear. Suddenly on everyone's lips, it remained a shadowy,
catch-all term: shorthand for racial progress—whatever that meant exactly.
To NAACP lawyer Robert Carter, "desegregated" was a synonym for "improved." "We [worked]," a more skeptical Carter later wrote, "on the theory
that equal education and integrated education were one and the same." Kenneth Clark, devoting his life to the ideal, understood it in even more elementary, abstract terms as simply "the antithesis of racism." Even into the
early fifties, few black activists looked beyond the struggle's immediate goals:
still very rudimentary kinds of physical mixing. If they did think into the future, most assumed that once they got the ball rolling—once they had broken through the color line—the rest would take care of itself. "I felt we were
of one mind," C. Vann Woodward later said about the NAACP strategists in
this era, "without a very careful definition of what we meant. We knew what
we were fighting. What was desirable to achieve was another matter."

The postwar era brought a shift in white attitudes, too—and with it, still
another new twist in the definition of integration. Mass black migration
into northern cities, the return of the black veterans, growing black electoral power and movement militancy: not all whites noticed these
changes—black and white Americans still lived very far apart—but in the
later forties, the political elite began to sense that the landscape was shifting.
The defeat of the Nazis and the advent of the Cold War spurred the change
in white awareness: what after all were Americans fighting for in Europe if
not racial tolerance and democratic values? Gunnar Myrdal's monumental
An American Dilemma became required reading in certain circles after the
war. McGeorge Bundy, among others, remembers devouring the book
when he came back from Europe in mid-decade. "My generation all read
it," he recalled later, "and we said to ourselves that we ought to just plain get
past these problems of prejudice and racial feeling."

As Myrdal's study and the reaction to it made clear, blacks and whites—
even well-meaning whites—already saw the racial imperative in starkly different ways. In contrast to blacks, historically driven by practical concerns—
what kinds of change were plausible, what burdensome restrictions could no
longer be borne—most whites who discovered the issue in the late forties
were driven by a sweeping, abstract idealism.

Not many people plowed through all 1,480 pages of Myrdal's survey,
filled with social science data on every aspect of the racial divide. But the
thesis, stated bluntly in the first chapter, so captured popular feeling that it

became conventional wisdom—for a certain class of privileged whites at least. Racial equality, Myrdal argued, was an implicit piece of the American social contract, part and parcel of what he called "the American Creed"—"the ideals of the essential dignity of the individual, of the basic equality of all men and of certain inalienable rights to freedom, justice and fair opportunity." The problem, as Myrdal saw it, was that whatever this contract promised in theory, it had not been extended to blacks. "In principle," he scolded, "the problem . . . was settled long ago, but the Negro in America has not yet been given [his] rights." The diagnosis hit Bundy's generation with the force of an obvious truth long denied. Suddenly, for them, race became a moral obligation—the need to deal with it, quickly and in an equitable way, inextricably tied to their sense of who they were as Americans.

Even so, for whites as for blacks, it was far from obvious just what it would mean to come to terms with race. Myrdalian goodwill, grand and far-reaching vision that it was, offered no better guide than the spontaneous promptings of short-term black needs. On the contrary, their very idealism and remoteness from the obstacles blacks faced made it all but impossible in the fifties for whites to chart a practical course toward one community, and so the white notion of integration, too, remained vague and ill-defined.

The common white assumption, so widely held that it was rarely discussed, posited that blacks, like other migrant groups, would simply assimilate into the mainstream. "The early definition of integration," James Farmer noted years later, "said forget you're black, forget that you're a Negro. Just think of yourself as an American. All you need is a little learning and you'll do fine." Once Jim Crow barriers had been removed, it was assumed, blacks would naturally and inevitably move into the system, climbing the familiar ladder—public education, on-the-job training, mom-and-pop entrepreneurship, ward politics—into the middle class and beyond. What blacks needed from whites was simply access to the ladder, and beyond that, they would require no further help. Indeed, what most whites imagined was more like an escalator than a ladder: once you got on, if you played by the rules, it would be hard *not* to succeed in due time. "Other groups had started at the bottom economically and politically and had risen," Nathan Glazer and Daniel Patrick Moynihan explained the assumption in their 1963 classic, *Beyond the Melting Pot*. "What was to keep the Negro from doing the same?"

Fueled by these changing attitudes on both sides, in midcentury, the push for integration finally took off. Still, even as the momentum gathered, it was a shaky start. In the aftermath of World War II, both Democratic and Republican parties took up the issue. President Harry Truman appointed a high-level commission; then moved to desegregate the armed forces and some facilities in the nation's capital. But the changes he initiated were extremely limited: a few integrated coffee shops and a lot of talk, with no movement toward enacting a civil rights bill or enforcing the Supreme Court's decision desegregating interstate transport. Many blacks were already deeply ambivalent, angry and skeptical of mainstream promises, and most whites still nursed intense, ingrained prejudices. More than two-thirds believed that blacks were less intelligent than whites, while the overwhelming majority—between 60 and 100 percent, depending on the region—endorsed some kind of segregation. Not even the forward-looking few who favored integration grasped what it really meant or how hard it would be to achieve it. Perhaps most troubling, though hardly discussed by anyone, were the developmental obstacles barring blacks from the mainstream.

What might be called Washingtonian integration—after Booker T.—had been proceeding apace for several decades. But through no fault of their own, most blacks were still way behind culturally. As recently as 1910, one-third were still illiterate, compared to under 5 percent of whites. Even at midcentury, the average black had no more than six years of schooling. Often just a generation removed from sharecropping, still excluded from most government jobs, businesses and labor unions, blacks earned on average a third as much as whites and knew nothing of the white-collar ethos taking over the culture. The push to break into the mainstream—with court cases, marches and desegregation orders—in no way blocked continued Washingtonian development. But the urgency and hope that drove desegregationists in the early fifties often blinded them to the social gaps still to be bridged.

The Magna Carta of integrationism, the *Brown* v. *Board of Education* decision enshrined racial mixing as a national aim—not just a policy objective but for many, both black and white, an article of faith. "Separate educational facilities are inherently unequal," the justices ruled, and from that moment on, Harold Cruse later wrote, "the uncommon word 'integration' would be added to the common lexicon of daily discourse as the media synonym for optimum race relations." The unanimous decision and the attention it received seemed to promise an end to the old white foot-dragging. Though the ruling referred only to southern schools, the NAACP was soon talking about extending it to all realms of American life. "By 1963," lawyer Thurgood Marshall claimed hopefully, "segregation in all its forms [will] have been eliminated from the nation." But just what real integration meant or how to get there was still far from clear.

In truth, the justices' definition was fairly narrow: negative rather than positive in thrust, more a repudiation of Jim Crow than a full-fledged vision of an interracial future. Both the justices and the NAACP hoped that eliminating legal barriers in public school systems would open the way to more profound changes in habits and attitudes—including, the decision's footnote to Kenneth Clark's work implied, radical improvement in black children's self-esteem. But neither the Court nor the lawyers behind the case had given much thought to how their vision of integration would be achieved. The opinion provided for no enforcement mechanism. As for the larger benefits—the promise of freedom, equality and self-confidence—like the NAACP and other liberals, the Court simply assumed most of this would take care of itself. Would physical mixing necessarily translate into a sense of equality? Would equal opportunity inevitably produce equal achievement? What would become of racial animosities? Would—or should—the future be color-blind, and was inclusion possible if it wasn't? Few people, white or black, anticipated any of these questions, even as integration was declared, officially, a national objective. The court set the ball rolling, mandating a minimum of physical mixing, and left it to the nation to give shape to the social forms that would grow up in the no-man's-land that divided blacks from whites.

The historic southern struggle—later widely referred to by Martin Luther King, Jr., and others as "the integration movement"—did not at the beginning posit racial mixing as a goal. Sparked in part by the *Brown* decision and its promise of inclusion, the movement grew out of hope but also out of long-simmering frustration brought to a boil by growing signs of white resistance to change. In the mid-fifties, blacks throughout the South hit on the idea of taking things into their own hands. The Montgomery, Alabama, bus boycott, in 1955–56, was only one of several local consumer campaigns, and like the others it brought out blacks from across the social spectrum—what King called "the Ph.D's and the no 'D's'." The outpourings were largely spontaneous, bottom-up and coordinated at first only by local clergy. To the degree the actions had goals, they were ad hoc and ill-defined. "People get tired of being trampled over . . . people get tired of being pushed. . . . We are here this evening because we are tired": King's rousing first speech in Montgomery said nothing about aims—and if anything, this helped propel him to the helm of a movement still unsure where it was going. Even when pressed by reporters, the young integrationist minister held back in deference to his followers. "We are not asking for an end to segregation," he maintained. "All we are asking for is justice and fair treatment in riding the buses."

Well into the sixties, it remained unclear just what the rank-and-file wanted. Even as the struggle gained focus, many protesters gave little thought to long-term objectives; what was important to them was the act of resistance. James Farmer spoke for many when he explained, "At three and a half, when I went downtown and couldn't go in any place to buy a Coca-Cola—I just felt that that was wrong. Was that integrationist? I'm not sure. I just wanted to get the Man off my neck." Already in the early days of the movement, long before it turned toward separatist militancy, the leadership worried that angry marchers would get out of hand, indulging the impulse to vent their anger at whites rather than appeal to guilt or good intentions. Among Andrew Young's most vivid memories of his years as King's lieutenant were of trying to contain what he called young "hotheads": undisciplined kids on a "freedom high" who would ruin peaceful demonstrations by throwing rocks or breaking windows. If Young had had his way, they would have been drummed out of the movement. But as King himself frequently reminded his aide, without the angry, confrontational kids, there would have been no struggle.

Just how and why integrationism emerged as the movement's goal is a disputed question. Was this a historical accident—a product of accommodationist, middle-class leadership papering over the angry protest welling up from the bottom? Were objectives determined by the courts—in effect, by white officialdom—and deliberately limited to what would be acceptable to white opinion? Or was the struggle's integrationism a true reflection of what most southern blacks wanted? Whatever the reason, by the time the movement coalesced, its perceived goal was unquestionably inclusion. "This is a revolution to get in," King told an interviewer.

More than anyone, it was King who was responsible for the blossoming of the word "integration"—by virtue of sheer usage, but also because of the way he transformed its meaning. In the beginning, from Reconstruction through the Niagara Movement, integration had been largely a political cause—a matter of votes and rights and the privileges of citizenship. Events of the twentieth century had introduced an economic dimension: to join the mainstream, it had become clear in the thirties and forties, required not just rights but also education and jobs. Some NAACP leaders talked vaguely of "social equality"—of what it might be like to know and get along with whites. But up through the forties, most Americans, black and white, saw desegregation as a physical thing: either a legal issue or, more basic still, a matter of mingling in public places. Gunnar Myrdal added a more abstract, moral component. Kenneth Clark introduced a layer of psychology. Still, even as the southern movement took off, "integration" remained an awkward, cloudy term—more a demand than an ideal, its full promise still unarticulated. What King did was stretch the concept in two different directions: making it at once more real—more concrete—and yet more exalted morally.

In 1955, King was still defining the goal as a matter of practical, legal change: an end to old Jim Crow repression. But within the year, he had begun pushing further, urging followers to look beyond a "negative" vision of integration to a larger, more "creative" aim. What, he asked, was the point of physical mixing? Why was it important, and what kind of changes would it work, on both sides of the color line? What he observed at Montgomery was that even a little desegregation had a way of exploding—conferring a proud, new boldness that encouraged blacks to demand more of white society and, at the same time, do more for themselves. This observation first sent him in a psychological direction, and he began to talk, Kenneth Clark–like, about how mixing on buses and lunch counters could convey "dignity" and "self-respect." But soon the psychological had taken on an added dimension, as King realized, in a way no one before him had seen, that integration was not just a means to achieve equality; in the right circumstances, it was an end in itself. Even before he had fully thought through the idea, he captured it in a phrase: "the beloved community." The theme appeared first in 1957, cropping up in sermons and in the Christian press. "Desegregation is not enough," King began to admonish his followers.

By 1962, he had spun the idea—integration for integration's sake—into a full-fledged argument: his sublime vision of what interracial mixing could produce. His thinking drew on theologians Reinhold Niebuhr and Paul Tillich, but also on the simpler spirituality of the black church, fellow ministers and the former leftists helping give shape to the civil rights struggle. Whether or not his writings truly represented that movement, King's eloquent synthesis was one of the first—and last—times a major thinker would outline the larger promise of integration, and it remains the classic definition of the term. Desegregation alone, he wrote, is "empty and hollow." "Physical proximity without social affinity," it produces a society "where elbows are together and hearts are apart." The true goal, he told whites as well as blacks, was to repair "the broken community"—to create "the good society" in which all men "treat other men as thou" and everyone has "the freedom to fulfill his total capacity." Real integration is a matter of "inner attitudes [and] genuine person-to-person relations." In contrast to desegregation, which is "an enforceable obligation," integration is an unenforceable goal—"like loving your children or being affectionate to your wife."

This was, King cautioned, a much bigger change than most people imagined, and it would not be easy for either blacks or whites. To blacks he explained soberly that real racial mixing would require more than beating down the door into the white world. "Integration is not some lavish dish that the federal government or the white liberal will pass out on a silver platter," he warned. The "primary responsibility" for making it work would fall to blacks. "The Negro will have to engage," he said, "in a sort of Operation Boot-Strap," finding the courage and discipline to compete in mainstream society. Not that this let whites off the hook. On the contrary, King argued passionately, whites needed integration as much as blacks did. "The Negro is God's instrument to save the soul of America," he wrote. As long as the country remained segregated, or even merely desegregated, whites would continue to deny the black man's humanity and compromise their own. For King, integration was nothing less than a religious imperative—the only hope that either blacks or whites would find the human dignity he referred to from then on as "freedom."

Rarefied as it was, King's vision struck a chord in early sixties America. The media, among others, needed a black spokesman to explain what was happening in the South, and already, at the start of the decade, the liberal elite was captivated by his resonant rhetoric. Still, it was plain to King, few whites had committed themselves to racial mixing, and even those who had failed to grasp the larger claims he was trying to stake. "The moral dimension of integration has not been sounded by the leaders of government," he said sadly in 1962. "They staunchly supported the principle . . . but their rationale fell short of being prophetic."

At best then, in 1962, despite King's eloquent efforts, "integration" was still an elusive doctrine, a media buzzword still defined differently by just about everyone who sought to pin down its meaning. As one skeptical black man, legal scholar Derrick Bell, wrote later about the southern struggle: "Racial integration [was that] era's idealistic equivalent of abolition. . . . Each represented . . . a polestar by which those seeking reform could guide their course. [But] while pointing the way, these beacons fail to provide us with a detailed blueprint of what to do on arrival." Nathan Glazer and Daniel

Patrick Moynihan, writing in the early sixties, made the same skeptical point. "No one has thought very seriously about what truly integrated communities would be like," they noted. "What would be the basis for common action, for social activities bringing together people of different groups?" What would real integration entail? How would Americans get there? What was the next step, and who should take it? In 1962, with the movement spreading rapidly north, the questions loomed more urgently than ever.

By 1962, the Great Migration had brought over a million blacks to New York City, and though they were beginning to fan out across the five boroughs, most still lived above 110th Street in Manhattan. The massive influx of poor, uneducated southerners had taken a toll on this black city-within-a-city, and the legendary Harlem of the 1920s had long since disappeared. Still, even as the migration tapered off around 1960, Harlem was a busy, awe-inspiring place, the shabby but proud de facto capital of black America.

Like all black communities, north and south, it was a self-sustaining, insular world, complete with its own businesses, theaters, newspapers, churches and exclusive social clubs. Even New York's most successful blacks still lived in the ghetto, side by side with the working poor and the still poorer, not yet settled migrants. Though unemployment, crime and the despair that came with them were on the rise, the *Amsterdam News* still carried stories about black debutante balls and a glittering black celebrity world. When it came to politics, Harlem had a proud reputation for militancy. It had been Garvey's home base and the site of the first black riots in 1935 and 1943. But in politics, too, Harlem's middle class provided ballast, maintaining a network of NAACP chapters and a strong Democratic Party organization: an old-fashioned machine, dispenser of jobs and patronage, with clout in City Hall and Albany. By 1960, Harlemites had elected a black congressman and several black city councilmen. Thanks to Tammany Hall, the Manhattan borough presidency was effectively a black seat, and the Harlem vote was a factor in all citywide races.

Still, for most Harlemites, segregation was the dominant fact of life. Local employers and unions were notoriously discriminatory. Even trained migrants found themselves barred from their chosen work, and many drifted into menial jobs. Unemployment rates were twice as high for blacks as for whites; average family income was roughly half the mainstream figure. Harlem's crumbling tenements were stifling in summer, then bitter cold through the winter months. Rats were a year-round problem; so was over-crowding. Most residents knew few white people, and those they knew, they often hated: beat policemen, the landlord, the local pawnbroker. Harlem's retail trade was controlled from downtown, and owners hired overwhelmingly in their own image—even the deliverymen working on 125th Street were generally white. Already in the early sixties, black New Yorkers were calling their city "the apple," but not because it was particularly delicious. "The Man," the saying went, "has taken the fruit and left the Negro the core."

The very early sixties were a deceptively quiet time in black New York. Among those who were following the southern movement and waiting for it to catch on elsewhere, it was still common to talk of the "apathy" of the northern black man. Harlem congressman Adam Clayton Powell, Jr., liked to point out that of some 19 million black Americans, only 900,000 belonged to the Big Six civil rights organizations. Among these, the NAACP was still the largest, but in New York it was losing members: the Manhattan chapter, for one, was down from twelve thousand to nine thousand in just five years. The *Amsterdam News* was officially committed to integration; staunchly pro-NAACP, it carried syndicated columns by Dr. King and NAACP head Roy Wilkins, along with occasional news stories about the demonstrations sweeping the South. But mostly, in deference to its comfortable middle-class readership, the tabloid avoided racial politics. Week in, week out, its pages were filled with news of local officials, wedding announcements, a "Prayer of the Week" and a regular feature on Harlem Boy Scout troops.

The reasons for this apathy were as varied as the people in Harlem. In the early sixties, many middle-class families still felt they had too big a stake in the system to support the protest movement. Others—poor, unskilled and uneducated—took little interest in politics. Journalists who ventured uptown in these years came back talking about "impassive faces" and pervasive hopelessness. One reporter tried to speak with a shirtless man sitting on a stoop. "Man, just lemme alone," the loiterer responded. "It's too hot to bother about all this noise about integration." Even working Harlemites were skeptical that the southern movement could do much to help them. "All this hollering over integration don't mean nothing to me," a woman told the same reporter. "I'm going to be working in a laundry all my life and there's no way out of it."

To the degree Harlemites were taking a new interest in politics, it generally had a militant edge to it. Even New Yorkers galvanized by the southern movement often had trouble with its integrationism. News from the front lines was not always good: there were as many brutal beatings as victories, and they did not inspire northern black goodwill for whites—any whites. One *New York Times* reporter visiting Harlem in 1961 stopped at the World History Outlet, a leftist bookstore on 125th Street, and discovered a stream of people looking for information about separatist speakers and rallies. "Damn the United States," one regular customer told him. "Crumbs from the tables of an abundant society have made millions of black men angry," said another. "That's why . . . the black nationalist movement is growing." Harlem's elected officials, most of them committed integrationists, strongly denied that these activists spoke for the community. But when the *Times* reporter set out into the neighborhood to ask ordinary Harlemites their opinion, virtually all the forty-odd people he stopped told him that nationalist sentiment was on the rise. "I don't belong to any of those militant groups, and I deplore their methods," *Amsterdam News* editor James Hicks noted tellingly. "But I sure go along with their spirit."

By then, there were ten to fifteen different separatist sects competing for the attention of black New Yorkers. Whether pressing emigration to the Nile Valley or a takeover of several southern states, most were dismissive of the civil rights movement and explicitly anti-integrationist. The groups ranged widely in size—from the Universal Association of Ethiopian Women Inc. to the local Muslim mosque, headed by Malcolm X. Most were small storefront or backroom operations, poorly organized and short-lived. In 1961, even the fearsome Muslims claimed no more than one thousand New York members. Still, sympathetic Harlemites countered, for every card-carrying member, there were many well-wishers who in the right circumstances would rally to the cause, and moderate black spokesmen were already beginning to feel some pressure. "We intend to press harder in the spirit of militance," Harlem lawyer Percy Sutton, then the president of the local NAACP, said in 1961. "Otherwise, we will not be accepted by the new Negro."

A year later, when Malcolm met Farmer at Cornell, that new spirit was carrying the day and Harlem's apathy was giving way to impatience. Demonstrations began to pick up in Harlem, mostly small and poorly organized. The nationalist speakers who regularly held forth at the corner of 125th Street and Seventh Avenue—a crossroads known as Harlem Square or "the Hub"—started attracting larger crowds. The long-simmering dispute over New York City school desegregation erupted in angry protests. Then, in early 1963, just as the southern movement was beginning to catch white people's attention, Congressman Adam Clayton Powell cast his vote for nationalism over integration.

After more than thirty years of activism, Powell was the undisputed voice of black New York: a ten-term congressman and pastor of Harlem's biggest, richest church, Abyssinian Baptist. From his first days in Congress in the 1940s, he had established himself as the prototype of a certain kind of ghetto leader: angrily defiant, yet willing to work within the system, a rogue who played by his own rules and was less concerned with solving problems than standing up to the white man. A canny horse-trading dealmaker, he rose eventually to be chairman of the House Education and Labor Committee. But to colleagues and constituents alike, he was known mainly as a gadfly. He called himself "the first bad nigger in Congress" and milked the part for all it was worth, deliberately playing the troublemaker to rally support from disaffected blacks. The more the white press criticized, the more black voters loved him. Campaigning for reelection in 1958, he rode around Harlem in an open car, reading critical *New York Times* editorials into a megaphone. Listeners cheered and threatened to march on the newspaper. To Harlemites, white criticism only confirmed that Powell was truly representing their interests.

By spring 1963, the southern struggle had begun to upstage black politicians like Powell who looked as if they were settling for the status quo. Sensing the changing tide, he first applauded the spreading protest and made a few halfhearted efforts to join in. But it wasn't long before he concluded, tellingly, that a more effective strategy—an approach more in tune with the mood of Harlem—would be to move out ahead of the integrationists by taking a more militant line. He turned up his attacks on white storeowners and white police in the ghetto. He began to throw around the nickname "Martin Loser King" and mocked the Big Six movement leaders as "old ladies [who] have not kept pace with the times." Then, in a brilliant stroke, he invited Malcolm X to join him for a major rally on 125th Street. Harlem's reigning patriarch, "the Prince of Abyssinia," would reach out over the head of Dr. King—who was not invited—to share a platform with the young Muslim. Already, it wasn't clear who would be helping whom more; by now a legend in his own right, Malcolm brought as much in fresh energy as Powell conferred in status. But what was plain was that militancy was now the name of the game: what black leaders had to prove to hold on to their constituents.

More than any black leader before or since, it was Malcolm who crystallized the modern alternative to integrationism. When he first joined the Nation of Islam in 1952, fresh from prison and before that a hustler's life, the sect had well under a thousand members, some say as few as four hundred. An indirect descendent of Garveyism, the Nation maintained all the trappings of the nationalist church—the emphasis on self-help and a largely symbolic ring of small black businesses—adding a bizarre racial mythology that predicted, among other things, Allah coming to earth to seek racial vengeance with a fleet of spaceships. But what appealed to young men like Malcolm—what made the talk of spaceships worth listening to—was the creed's emotional underpinning: an uncompromising hatred of whites. "The white man is the devil," the sect taught; "Separation, not integration." Malcolm and other young men like him, with little hope of making their way into the mainstream, were galvanized by the notion that they might simply thumb their nose at the white world.

The problem, as critics often pointed out, was that like most separatist visions before and since, the traditional Muslim credo had little to offer in place of integration. "Will [a black nation] have a General Motors," Farmer asked mockingly at Cornell, "a General Electric . . . a separate interstate bus line? . . . Will it be a rival economy? . . . Mr. X, what is your program?" Muslim leader Elijah Muhammad had no answer and seemed to feel no need of one: the antiwhite hatred he extolled was enough to sustain most followers. Angry as it was, Muhammad's Islam did not even counsel political action; indeed, it explicitly forbade voting and protests of any kind.

In his twelve years with the Muslims, Malcolm did not so much revise the creed as give it a new depth of meaning. It was partly by example and partly by the way he said things that he made a difference—with drama, flair, a sense of mission and charisma. Blacks who heard him speak or saw him in action dealing with the white man invariably commented on the same thing: his fearless, stand-up manner. "He didn't take no mess," was the way Louis Farrakhan, a onetime disciple, later put it. "I never heard any black man speak in the manner that I heard him speak, with the boldness." Malcolm looked whites in the eye; he said exactly what was on his mind. He refused, as he said, to "cringe" or "beg"—and by force of example, he taught followers they did not have to. Unlike his rivals in the movement, Malcolm had no faith that racial mixing would lift blacks' self-esteem. On the contrary, in his view, it could only mean degradation: an inevitably futile and humiliating struggle to fit in where you were not wanted. All of this was more attitude than ideology, but as Malcolm's stature grew, the attitude took on a life of its own: a new, psychological answer to the questions Farmer and others had posed.

As an alternative to integration, Malcolm started with the age-old nationalist nostrum: a deliberate effort to cultivate black pride. He used simple exhortations and a few recycled Garveyite ploys: the change from "Negro" to "black," a renewed glorification of all things African. But more and more, Malcolm discovered in himself and then began to teach others, the best way to find that sense of pride—to ease the humiliation history had tied to blackness—was through angry defiance of the white man and the painful differences his color brought to mind. Instead of counseling followers to move beyond their anger, Malcolm urged them to cultivate it as something healthy and positive. Exclusion and alienation were suddenly something to celebrate. "What to [some] is the American dream," he said, "to us is an American nightmare, and we don't think that it is possible for the American white man [to change]." Turning disappointment into defiance, he gloried in his own venom, cheering when a plane of white passengers crashed and when John F. Kennedy was assassinated. Not only did he say that white people stank and compare them to the lowest animals; he claimed that this was therapeutic—that blacks could not feel like men until they defied whites. There was no dignity except in revolt; to be polite or acquiescent was to degrade oneself before the enemy.

Finally, separatism had something to offer its followers—something other than showy parades and unlikely dreams of moving back to Africa. That American society is inherently racist; that skin color equals identity; that blacks form a community apart; that they are at least as African as American; that their rage is legitimate and that only good can come of expressing it— this was the credo that Malcolm taught, a faith built on anger and color consciousness and rejecting the white world before it rejected you. "Brother," Malcolm once asked a young black man during a debate, "why do you call yourself an American?" "Because I was born in this country," the young man answered, insisting several times, "I am an American." "Now brother," Malcolm said softly, smiling, "if a cat has kittens in the oven, does that make them biscuits?"

Already in the early sixties, moderate men like Farmer grasped that this was an all but unanswerable challenge to their integrationism. For most blacks, no matter what their politics, the appeal of Malcolm's militancy was immediate and intense—like a shot of good whiskey, one man wrote after hearing the young minister speak. "Malcolm says things you or I would not say," another, an NAACP official, confessed. "When he says those things, when he talks about the white man, even those of us who are repelled by his philosophy secretly cheer a little outside ourselves, because Malcolm X really does tell 'em and we know he frightens the white man. We clap." No wonder the fading Adam Clayton Powell was eager to tap into the electricity Malcolm generated among young men in the ghetto.

Powell's Harlem rally was exquisitely orchestrated. The Hub at 125th and Seventh was an old proving ground for Harlem nationalists—where everyone from Garvey on down had come to make their case to passersby. March 23, 1963, was a blustery day, and the brightly colored nationalist banners that draped the World History Outlet bookstore flapped noisily in the wind. An enthusiastic crowd assembled. Powell looked as sleek as ever in his stylish overcoat: open-faced, grinning, putting on the charm. Malcolm conveyed just the opposite impression; next to the big-boned, relaxed politician, he appeared even more taut than usual—lean, somber and characteristically intent. The congressman, playing magnanimous host, did most of the talking. Though careful to note that he did not endorse all Muslim lore, he declared that he counted Malcolm as a "friend" and shared his views about what methods would best advance the black revolt—methods that did not "depend on the white man." "We Negroes are not," Powell shouted, "going to get anything more in this life except that which we fight for and fight for with all our power." He paused for effect and looked significantly at Malcolm. "This may sound like black nationalism. If it is, then what is wrong with it?"

The next day, Harlem exploded in angry controversy. The old-guard leadership was dismayed. The *Amsterdam News* gave Jackie Robinson its front page for an open letter deploring Powell's speech. "You have grievously set back the cause of the Negro," he wrote. "The answer for [the black man] is to be found, not in separation or segregation, but in . . . moving into his rightful place—the same place as that of any other American—within our society." Roy Wilkins took up the gauntlet in *The New York Times:* "What is Adam Clayton Powell doing in Congress," Wilkins asked, "if he doesn't believe in integration? Logically, if he's given up on the system, or doesn't support what most Negroes want—integration—he ought to resign." Harlem's more militant young Turks, on the other hand, responded to the speech with a round of amens. *News* editor James Hicks called the NAACP "stupid" and in league with "the enemy," while his top political reporter agreed emphatically that Powell was onto something—that thousands of other blacks shared his feeling that "the Negro does not want charity or conscience contributions."

Integration or separatism—suddenly, the question was on everyone's lips. The March on Washington was five months away; President Kennedy still hesitated even to propose a significant civil rights bill. Yet already in Harlem, the old integrationist faith was faltering. Blacks "have already seceded" intellectually and emotionally from America, Malcolm told one interviewer. Downtown reporters who picked up on the dispute above 110th Street tried to make it sound like something reassuring—a more or less equal standoff between militants and moderates capable of holding them in check. "For the present," one article noted encouragingly, "the general Negro community continues to be swept along . . . on the wave of the integration movement." Be careful, though, the same story warned: that wave is rising "at an ever increasing tempo."

If anything, the debate swirling in Harlem was more alarming than it seemed. The arguments flashing back and forth may have been familiar— the old two-ness reasserting itself again. But by 1963, something new had crept into the equation. Even those blacks who opted for the mainstream were determined to move more quickly now. Even those who "wanted in" were growing impatient and volatile, possibly already beyond appeasement. More discerning white journalists understood this. "Black nationalism," one reporter wrote, "is a mood to be found in every segment of the Negro population," whether or not the people in question actually "renounce coexistence with whites." To the average Harlemite shaking off his apathy in 1963, the difference between the southern movement and the new militancy of men like Powell and Malcolm did not seem all that significant—a dispute, at most, about methods. The same rising anger and alienation underlay both views; the difference was one of degree and timing. No wonder most blacks saw no real need to decide the issue right away—and no wonder, before long, integrationism would look like the weak choice.

M ore than anything, it was the pictures that caught the nation's attention. It was on May 3, 1963—two months after the rally at the Hub—that Birmingham, Alabama, security chief Eugene "Bull" Connor first used dogs and high-pressure firehoses to disperse civil rights demonstrators, many of them children. Photographers and cameramen descended on the city just as black protest leaders had expected they would. That night the nation watched, riveted to its TV sets, as narrow jets of water sent black teenagers sprawling across sidewalks. One famous photo showed two black children taking refuge behind a treetrunk from the laserlike streams that, it was said, could strip the bark right off it. In another picture, a stony-faced policeman held a demonstrator by the sweater an arm's-length away as a snarling German shepherd lunged for the teenager's chest. Finally, at the end of two weeks, President Kennedy himself announced that the photos were making him "sick." For him, as for hundreds of thousands of blacks and whites, Birmingham was a decisive event. White policemen brutally manhandled passive young blacks—and it wasn't hard for most Americans to decide whose side they were on.

The surge of interest was intense and, for a while, all-engulfing. Virtually every magazine in the country—from the upscale *New Yorker* to the *Saturday Evening Post*—rushed into print with its effort to make sense of the black protest movement. One librarian estimated that each week of 1963 produced nine new books about race issues. Human relations councils were founded in cities across the country, and clergymen of every faith took up the matter in their sermons. The conventional wisdom emerged within weeks, stark and compelling: that, as one account put it, "racial prejudice was [an] unquestioned evil." Phrases like "Freedom Now!" and "The fire next time" burned themselves forever into the minds of ordinary whites, and civil rights surged to the top of the Gallup Poll's list of "the most important" problems facing the nation. By the end of the year, race had assumed its place—a place it would hold, on and off, for at least three decades—at the center of the nation's liberal agenda.

Still, for all their newfound interest, white Americans, the very liberal and less so, were astonishingly ignorant about blacks. The editor of *Newsweek* confessed his lack of knowledge that fall as the magazine published one of the first polls ever of black opinion: "What precisely [do] the Negroes want?" he asked. "How far were they willing to go to achieve their goals? What did they think of the white man? Not even Negro leaders could say for sure. . . . There was a deep and dangerous void between whites and Negroes in America, a no-man's land of ignorance."

This sweeping lack of knowledge was hardly surprising, given the distance between the races. No matter how liberal, in the early sixties, most whites still shunned social contact across the color line. North and south, neighborhoods were still strictly segregated. Outside of the military and selected professional sports, virtually no middle-class whites worked alongside blacks, and as recently as 1960, according to pundit Theodore White, race relations had still "seemed peripheral to national politics." Kennedy aide Arthur Schlesinger, Jr., recalled later that, like many of his class, the president "had an intellectual grasp of the black problem. But I don't think any of us sensed the anguish. Very few of us had seen how black people had to live." Whites had no way of knowing how blacks viewed the world—or how radically that view might differ from their own. The pollsters responsible for *Newsweek's* survey, Louis Harris and William Brink, found northern whites somewhat less prejudiced than southerners, but still clinging to a host of stereotypes. Between half and two-thirds of the whites polled believed that "Negroes laugh a lot," that they "tend to have less ambition," that they "have looser morals" and "smell different."

Nor in 1963 did the new white moral outrage usually translate into willingness to take action. Compassion for "the Negro" was still a new feeling, trendy and shallowly rooted. Most whites assumed that race was a regional problem—one that could be solved by a change of heart among a small number of southern whites. Polls showed overwhelming majorities—75 to 93 percent, north and south—in favor of fair housing, school desegregation, equal voting rights and fair job opportunities, but no more than 45 percent thought the government should move to implement any of these changes. Confronted with the possibility of blacks in their own neighborhoods, 78 percent of whites told Gallup they would move. It was an age-old gap that would endure for decades to come: abstract support for racial equality that ran well ahead of anything whites were prepared to do. "The colored got rights, just like us," the *Saturday Evening Post* quoted one northern man, "but I don't see why we got to mingle together."

Mindful of this reluctance, up until the time of the Birmingham campaign, President Kennedy had hung back cautiously, convinced that it would be futile to get out ahead of public opinion on race. The president waited more than two years to propose a civil rights act, and when he did, it was a weak, watered-down bill. Even then, Robert Kennedy recalled later, "there wasn't any interest in it. There was no public demand . . . no demand by the newspapers or radio or television. . . . Nobody paid any attention." Instead of championing the cause, JFK procrastinated, moving only hesitantly and behind the scenes—urging private employers to hire a few blacks, pressing foundations to contribute to the movement. Civil rights leaders were bitterly disappointed. "If tokenism were the goal, the administration moves us adroitly toward it," King wrote disparagingly.

With Birmingham, all this changed. Just weeks after the showdown, the president appeared on television to denounce prejudice and discrimination in exactly the prophetic terms King and others had been urging. Civil rights,

Kennedy told the nation in one of his most famous speeches, is "a moral issue . . . as old as the Scriptures and . . . as clear as the American Constitution." "I don't know why we didn't use the word," the president's speechwriter, Theodore Sorensen, recalled later, "but integration was certainly the implicit goal"—and the address can be read as a classic articulation of the ideal. As Kennedy made the case, integration was the inevitable culmination of the American dream: an explicitly "color-blind" vision of equal opportunity based on a moral appeal—"whether we are going to treat our fellow Americans as we want to be treated." A few days later, he introduced his version of what would eventually become the 1964 Civil Rights Act, then met with movement leaders to agree to the upcoming March on Washington. For a moment at least, however abstract and remote it seemed, the idea of integration seemed to have taken on the trappings of a national creed.

The president knew how big a risk he was taking. Reports of a new phenomenon called "back-lash" were already reaching the White House from Democratic districts in big northern cities like New York and Chicago. Appalled as they were by Birmingham, even the most liberal whites weren't sure the government should be putting its weight behind the unruly and unpredictable southern movement. Advisers warned Kennedy against sticking his neck out too far; according to one report, with the exception of his brother, not a single person he consulted in the White House supported his decision to propose a major civil rights bill. When he went ahead anyway with this and other initiatives that spring, they met with a decidedly lukewarm reaction. According to Gallup, 41 percent of the nation thought the president was pushing integration "too fast." Asked about the proposed bill, 49 percent of the public approved, but 42 percent found it too strong. By mid-fall 1963, Kennedy's advisers calculated that he had lost 4.5 million white votes by pressing the race question. "This issue could cost me the election," he told one civil rights leader.

Meanwhile, on the black side of the chasm, expectations were spinning out of control. For Adam Clayton Powell's audience at the Hub, the president's speech was just that—so much talk. Kennedy's civil rights bill struck blacks as timid and all but toothless: it did not even guarantee the desegregation of all public accommodations. As for his decision to sanction the proposed March on Washington, that too was only symbolism—and even so, the president was reluctant. Already in Birmingham, King and others had had trouble controlling recruits, and on at least one occasion, demonstrators' patience had given way, turning a nonviolent protest into something more like a small riot. Elsewhere, the courage of Birmingham's youth inspired both pride and anger at the status quo: in the next three months, there were eight hundred copy-cat boycotts and marches in two hundred southern cities, and within a year, more than fourteen thousand demonstrators had been arrested. But the stronger black emotions ran, the less focused the movement became. If anything, though conditions were often better outside the South, northern blacks inspired by the southern struggle were more bitter. Where white liberals and movement leaders saw events like Birmingham as moments of hope, young blacks in the northern ghetto saw an all-out race war, and they reacted to the hate in the faces of a few southern bigots with a hatred of their own that embraced all of white America.

For Kennedy, the 1963 initiative had been a huge step, principled and courageous. But in the larger scheme of things, given the climate and the urgency of the problem, it only revealed how far Americans were from coming to grips with race. Already, even before King's "I Have a Dream" speech, all the makings of future failure were present. Neither whites nor blacks were clear about the goal and no one, even the most concerned, had any real idea how to get there. More troubling still, the gap between black and white expectations already threatened to derail just about any move toward a solution. Kennedy had tried bravely to bridge this expectation gap, bolstering black moderates while goading a just-wakening white public, but the utter inadequacy of his effort was already painful.

The black community's changing mood was soon reflected in attitudes toward its leadership. King's renown among whites rose dramatically that summer, and *Newsweek*'s black poll showed him still the overwhelming favorite in the ghetto. Yet of all black spokesmen, it was Malcolm X who appeared most often on television that year. His scathing mockery of Birmingham was repeated as often as anything King said there. "Real men," Malcom noted, "don't put their children on the firing line." In July 1963, King visited Harlem and at one appearance was pelted with eggs by young hecklers chanting: "Martin Loser King." He tried to joke about the emerging divisions in the black world. "There go my people," he often quoted Gandhi. "I must catch them, for I am their leader." But he also knew he was asking a lot of his followers' patience, and he was increasingly concerned by what he saw developing in the ghetto. He began to talk worriedly about the fine line between "righteous indignation"—"the healthy discontent that will keep a revolution moving"—and what he admitted hesitantly could best be described as black "hate."

It was against this background, in spring 1963—still several months before the March on Washington—that Harlem exploded in a spasm of protest. A wave of sit-ins, sleep-ins, pray-ins, hunger strikes, boycotts and marches swept the metropolitan area, as thousands of New York blacks—including activists like those in Brooklyn CORE—went out to demonstrate in their own neighborhoods. Much of the protest was nominally integrationist and devoted to nonviolence. But on at least two occasions that summer, demonstrations turned into mini-riots. In June, picketing at Harlem Hospital gave way to a scuffle with police. Then, a few weeks later, as Kennedy met with Big Six leaders to discuss the March on Washington, cops battled angry kids for two nights running in Harlem.

The incident began when a group of youths meeting at the Hub's nationalist bookstore noticed policemen arresting a peddler on the street outside. The kids came out of the store and booed the cops, then pelted them with stones and bottles. The next night, two hundred youths massed on 125th Street, marching west in phalanx formation, knocking over garbage cans and smashing windows. The police made no attempt to spare their nightsticks. By morning, twenty-five kids had been arrested and several hospitalized. By midsummer, the spiraling unrest had led to over eight hundred arrests, and the city's black spokesmen were threatening more violence. "Blood may soon flow in the streets," Brooklyn pastor C. Gardner Taylor warned, "and if it does, the streets will be cleansed. If necessary, we will die like heroes." By the time of the March on Washington, *The New York Times,* James Farmer and even Kennedy himself were worried about the possibility of a full-scale riot in Harlem.

White ignorance and resistance, black violence and the backlash it was sure to produce: by 1963, the basic political obstacles to integration were already evident. But even before the March on Washington, those who knew the ghetto also saw a different kind of impediment emerging. With the white establishment starting to talk, however tentatively, about tearing down the walls that kept blacks out, journalists, social scientists and others began to ask how black America would respond, and already in the early 1960s, many saw reason for concern.

Some of the prophetic warnings had to do with poverty: a growing sense, among those familiar with places like Harlem, of the social and educational gaps that separated many blacks from the mainstream. Theodore White, chronicler of presidential campaigns, was one of the first to write candidly about this development chasm. There are "two Negro communities," he explained to readers—one middle-class and another, much poorer one—and the unacculturated black poor were not, he warned, going to dissolve easily in the melting pot. White looked hard at the northern ghetto and produced a graphic account of its pathologies. More than half the children in Harlem lived in homes with only one parent, and, White reported nearly a year before Daniel Patrick Moynihan, blacks were already bearing ten times as many illegitimate children as whites. Worse still, in one year in the early sixties, New York City subway crime had risen by 50 percent, and according to authorities, "non-white youths" were responsible for 80 percent of the rise. "This is a different kind of culture," White cautioned, one that would cause unexpected difficulties even if the mainstream were to open its doors unstintingly.

Other early warnings were more psychological in focus, none more eloquent or troubling than the distress signals from Kenneth Clark, the social scientist whose evidence had helped win the *Brown* case. Moderate, middle-class and at ease in the white world, in the sixties Clark emerged as a top consultant on race and poverty: what one magazine survey called "the principal intellectual leader of the Negro protest movement." A lifelong integrationist, by 1963 he sensed that the ideal was foundering. Concerned whites who sought him out to talk about the ghetto found him increasingly moody. Uncharacteristically angry at "the system" and preoccupied with John Brown's bloody slave revolt, he mused cryptically about what he described as the "cruel, horrible things [that often] have to be done to prepare the way for . . . change." Still other interviewers watched with fascination as Clark lit his cigarettes, then placed the flaming matches in an ashtray, leaving them to burn menacingly as he spoke. "In 1954, I thought the problem would be solved by 1960," he told one journalist. "That showed you how psychologically naive I was."

In interviews and in his classic 1965 book, *Dark Ghetto,* Clark tried to explain why he thought integration had not worked and would remain a problem into the future. Like all black spokesmen of his day, he laid much of the blame at whites' feet, but he was even more concerned about something that he sensed was holding blacks back—something in the psychological baggage many brought to their encounters with whites.

Clark's central metaphor for segregation was a prison or concentration camp, and as he saw things, the long, enforced isolation had wreaked so much psychological havoc that many blacks had lost the capacity to seek their way out. Though careful not to blame the victim, he spared nothing in his description of this "racial damage": a combination of defeatism and impotent anger that, he said, made blacks suspicious, predatory and continually resentful and left them ill-equipped to compete in the mainstream. Each individual was trapped by a "core of doubt"—a belief in his own inferiority and "the pervasive failure of his group." Many were so bitter that they would not even try to do well in the white world: to them, success seemed humiliating—a kind of betrayal of the race—because it meant seeking white approval and submitting to standards used in the past to keep blacks back. Even his own accomplishments, Clark admitted, felt like treachery. What he feared was that even when white resistance disappeared, the black man's "own inner anxieties" would hinder his move into the mainstream.

The alienation that would stop many blacks from pursuing integration was nowhere clearer than in a wrenching selection of quotations from Harlem residents in the prologue to *Dark Ghetto.* Struggling to sound optimistic, Clark tried to put the best face on the sampler, ending with a teenage boy who wanted to be "the first Negro president." But most of the comments, from people of all ages and all walks of life, were far from hopeful. "A lot of time when I'm working I become as despondent as hell and I feel like crying," said one thirty-year-old. "I'm not a man, none of us are men!" Another man expressed similar hopelessness: "No one with a mop can expect respect from a banker, or an attorney, or men who create jobs. . . . Whoever heard of integration between a mop and a banker." For still another man, the despair was curdling into anger: "The flag here in America is for the white man," he said. "The blue is for justice; the 50 white stars you see in the blue are for the 50 white states; and the white you see in it is the White House. It represents white folks. The red in it is the white man's blood—he doesn't even respect your blood. That's why he will lynch you, hang you, barbecue you and fry you." No wonder, already in 1963, integration seemed all but irrelevant to many Harlemites. "Segregation in itself is not the cause nor integration the answer to our problems," still another man, anonymous, wrote in a letter to the *Amsterdam News.* "We must first [find] dignity. Let us find ourselves."

Like Kennedy's 1963 speech, the March on Washington is now remembered as a high point of national idealism, a moment of moral clarity and universal concern about race. In fact, stirring as it was and celebrated by the media, the march was anything but a unanimous national commitment to integration.

The crowd that assembled on the Mall that sunny August day looked encouragingly mixed. Nearly 250,000 blacks and whites descended on the capital—just about double the expected turnout—singing, "Black and white together, We'll walk hand in hand . . . We shall overcome someday." Even more than their lyrics and King's famous speech, the marchers' good manners were touted as proof of their commitment to integration. "Instead of the emotional horde of angry militants that many had feared," *New York Times* reporter Russell Baker wrote, "what Washington saw was a vast army of quiet, middle-class Americans who had come in the spirit of a church outing. . . . Instead of tension [there was] sad music, strange silences and good feeling in the streets." As for the impact, organizer Bayard Rustin estimated hopefully that there were three hundred congressmen present; they came, he said, "and saw . . . [the] fantastic determination . . . [and] knew there was a consensus in the country for the civil rights bill."

In fact, at the time, most of white America was anything but enthusiastic about the march. One poll taken that week showed 63 percent opposing it—nearly two-thirds of the nation. Relatively few whites attended—only fifty thousand—and those who did were hardly representative middle Americans. Even sympathetic liberals ended the day less uplifted than relieved that there had been no violence or damage to the capital. President Kennedy's condescending reaction was typical: he "marveled, as the world marveled," one aide remembered, at the "self-discipline" of the marchers. As for the mandate Rustin and others had hoped to establish, in truth there had been about seventy-five congressmen on the Mall, and even when the day was over, few people in official Washington were sanguine about the pending civil rights bill. Kennedy warned black leaders who came to the White House that evening that they were letting expectations run far too high: he doubted that the demonstration had changed a single vote on the Hill. Not that the gathering had no effect. "People were moved," Arthur Schlesinger remembered, "Martin Luther King's performance lifted the debate to a higher plane and increased the moral balance for integration. . . . People had been shamed and pressured and they felt they ought to believe in [racial mixing]. But on the whole this was a rather abstract view."

On the black side, there could be no denying the enthusiasm—or the boost the day gave to integrationists everywhere. Even Harlem, still reeling from its first "long, hot summer," sent many busloads of demonstrators. The *Amsterdam News* called the march "the finest hour of Negro Americans . . . and in the history of America." The militant rhetoric that had been building through the summer in New York vanished without a trace as the newspaper gloried in "so many Negroes side by side with so many whites." For all their ambivalence, black Americans were not quite ready to give up on the white mainstream. Still, in the black world too, reactions to the march were far more mixed than most people remember—the old two-ness reasserting itself, even at this moment of integrationist triumph.

The dissent began at the top. Malcolm X, who mockingly called the demonstration the "Farce on Washington," famously refused to participate, watching standoffishly from a nearby hotel doorway. Adam Clayton Powell attended but was barred from speaking out of fear that he might say something radical or untoward. Those who did address the crowd were told to keep it vague and uplifting, and not even the most impressive of the speeches touched on ideas for concrete change. Student Nonviolent Coordinating Committee chairman John Lewis's suppressed speech—the day's more moderate organizers would not permit him to give it—conveyed a little of the ambivalence that could not be expressed on the podium. "We will march through the South," Lewis's prepared text read, "through the heart of Dixie, the way [Civil War general Tecumseh] Sherman did. We shall pursue our own 'scorched earth' policy and burn Jim Crow to the ground—nonviolently." But even Lewis's impassioned words were only a hint of what was being papered over. The anger and impatience, the racial perception gap, the daunting distances that still separated most blacks from the mainstream—all of this was too much for even the most skeptical dissenter to capture.

What the march meant to the black silent majority was hard to gauge. As James Farmer pointed out afterward, the crowd was far from representative. True, there had been some union groups—teachers, auto workers and government employees—but virtually no poor people. That, in Farmer's view, was why the day came off as it did—peaceful, hopeful and devoid of anger. Back in the ghetto, tuning in on TV or radio, poorer blacks "heard that they were 'free at last,'" Farmer said, "and they wondered what it meant." Certainly, in Harlem and places like it, nothing much had changed. "What the ghetto poor did not see or feel," Farmer said emphatically, "was integrationism. They saw black people standing up and fighting for themselves. Most of the blacks watching on TV had no idea what all those white people they saw were doing there."

Black spokesmen who spent time in the northern ghetto that fall saw little sign of new integrationist hope. In September, black writer Louis Lomax was booed in Harlem for advocating integration at an outdoor rally. Adam

Clayton Powell began to talk about the difference between "the masses" and "the classes." Make no mistake, he warned whites with a typical mix of mischief and militancy, poor northern blacks have very little in common with "the preacher, the teacher, the student [in the South] fighting for the golf course and the swimming pool and the restaurant." As for Malcolm, closest to the anger that was spiraling up among frustrated northern youth, whatever else he thought of integration by now, he doubted it was doable. "You can't integrate the Negroes and the whites without bloodshed," he predicted. "The only peaceful way is for the Negroes and whites to separate."

Louis Harris's important first poll of black opinion appeared that fall in *Newsweek,* reassuring white readers and confirming their belief that in racial matters things would eventually work out. More than one thousand blacks from all regions answered the pollsters' in-person questions. Asked about leaders, not only did they prefer King and the NAACP; they preferred them by huge margins. Between a third and a half had an unfavorable opinion of the Muslims. No more than 4 percent liked the idea of a separate state for blacks. Still, the picture was not all sweetness and moderation. More than two-thirds of those polled wanted to live and work with white people—but the rest weren't sure they wanted either thing. Only one-quarter thought white people wished blacks well, while roughly 40 percent believed whites actively wanted to "keep Negroes down." Perhaps most startling, among poor blacks in the North, only 50 percent thought their people's revolt would proceed in a nonviolent way: a full 25 percent thought the road ahead would surely lead to bloodshed.

Questions about integration turned up an even more marked ambivalence. On specific queries about schools, jobs and housing, blacks as a group were keenly interested in racial mixing, and a solid majority believed their children would do better academically if they attended school with whites. Most enthusiastic were educated, middle-income blacks, who felt integration was essential for equality. "As long as there is no mixing," said a student from Mississippi, "the Negro will be treated as inferior." At the same time, when asked about integration for its own sake, most blacks were pointedly uninterested.

"Do Negroes desire a lot of mixing of the races," one question asked, "or just being treated as human beings?" Respondents answered overwhelmingly (86 percent) that what they were seeking was "just being treated as human beings." Black leaders were badly out of step with their people: 25 percent of the spokesmen desired "a lot of mixing," while only 10 percent of their followers did. Asked to explain their answers, ordinary blacks were blunt. "I never wanted to visit with white people or go to parties with them," said one woman, "just to work where we could make the good wages." "I'm not thinking about mixing with anybody," echoed a tractor driver from Mississippi. "I just don't want to be treated like an animal." Many spoke not out of anger but sheer weary indifference. "I don't care if I never eat with one," said a housewife from New York.

By the time the 1964 Civil Rights Act passed, the gap between black and white attitudes had reached startling proportions—but it still went largely unnoticed by the media or anyone else. Sparked by the March on Washington, spurred by Kennedy's death and Johnson's leadership, white support for the historic rights bill built steadily through the winter and spring of 1964, and by the time of the Senate vote in July, polls showed nearly three-quarters of the public strongly behind the measure. The culmination of the great awakening that began with Birmingham, passage was regarded—at the time and since—as one of the nation's greatest triumphs. "There is an inexorable moral force that moves us forward," Republican senator Everett Dirksen of Illinois commented as he bowed to the weight of snowballing public opinion. "No matter the resistance of people who do not fully understand, it will not be denied." The new law was not without opponents: George Wallace confounded expectations with showings of 30 to 45 percent in northern Democratic primaries even as Barry Goldwater clinched the Republican nomination for president. But at the time of passage, the act's supporters dismissed the opposition as outmoded racists and cranks. When the vote came, all but seven nays came from predictably intransigent southerners, and few whites quarreled with the *New York Times'* assessment that the new law reflected a "flower of national consensus."

However far it reached on the white side, this consensus made a mockery of black opinion. With blacks of all kinds in all regions demanding immediate, tangible improvements in their lives—improvements, in most cases, no law could deliver—the bill was but a first, small step toward equality. What the new law did was remove the most obvious barriers that had been holding blacks back: blatant segregation and legally sanctioned discrimination. But beyond that, Congress and the white public would not go. The measure contained no positive racial remedies—not even the provision of equal voting rights. It removed the fences keeping blacks off the escalator into the mainstream—and in effect told them to get on with the climb. For blacks, virtually all blacks, this was far from enough. In Harlem, both Adam Clayton Powell and Malcolm X openly mocked the measure. A crowd of hopeful whites greeted passage with a vigil on the Capitol steps, but there was no elation on 125th Street. The day after the vote, the *Times* carried a small inside story: "Harlem greets passage of civil rights bill with a shrug of the shoulders." "It's still a piece of paper," one man said. "It's been long overdue," grumbled another. "What is there to celebrate about?"

In 1964, as the summer before at the March on Washington, whites still looked at blacks and saw what they wanted to see. *Newsweek's* editors chose to all but ignore the bitterness and disillusionment unearthed by their poll. "The Negro mood" was one of hope, the magazine concluded, "an abiding optimism about the future and an abiding faith in the human decency of whites." In 1964, most Americans were still confident about the future, sure that they could solve the nation's problems and live up to their highest ideals. The Kennedy assassination had shaken this sense of well-being and certainty, but not enough to dislodge it. "Vietnam" was still an unfamiliar word; GNP was growing by 7 percent a year. Race had emerged in the past year as a pressing national problem, but it was still—most whites assumed—a problem they could handle. Virtually no one had an inkling yet of what was going on in the ghetto—of the brewing anger of the developmental chasm. Not even the most concerned whites grasped just how much would eventually be required of them if the integrationist beacon were to become a reality. In 1964, "integration" was still a magical word, the heady liberal nostrum of the day, but already black and white America were tragically out of sync.

Chapter 3

LOOKING FOR
"THE SOLUTION"

It was exactly two weeks after the signing of the 1964 Civil Rights Act that Harlem exploded in the first major riot of the sixties. The trouble had begun a few days before on a quiet block on the Upper East Side. A building superintendent accidentally sprayed three black teens with a garden hose. They responded by throwing garbage and chasing him into a nearby doorway. An off-duty policeman who happened to be walking by showed the boys his badge and tried to stop the fight. But fifteen-year-old James Powell was beyond calming, and he lunged aggressively at the big, burly cop. Lieutenant Thomas Gilligan, who later said he saw the glint of a knife, took out his revolver and fired three shots, instantly killing the black youth.

The facts of the case would never be fully clear. Powell had a police record but nothing out of the ordinary: two "fare-beats" and one attempted robbery. The police department backed Gilligan in claiming that the youth had had a knife; fellow students insisted not. It was uncertain if he and his classmates had been provoked or provoking, whether Gilligan had acted hastily or not. Whatever the truth was, it didn't seem to matter much in Harlem, where anger and paranoia were already brimming over.

For two days and nights, rumors swirled in the ghetto. Residents, embittered by years of friction with white police, were sure Gilligan had acted deliberately. He had, the grapevine had it, emptied his gun into the boy's back, then planted a knife on the body—a cold-blooded racial murder. The next two days brought edgy demonstrations at Powell's school. Two hundred to three hundred kids showed up each day, picketing and shouting. Some still chanted the old slogans demanding "freedom" and the end of Jim Crow, but mainly now the cries were about the cops: "Police brutality must go!" "C'mon," one girl taunted an officer, "shoot another nigger!"

The first violence occurred on Saturday night outside the precinct house on 123rd Street. It grew out of a CORE rally at the Hub, a few blocks away. "It is time to let the Man know that if he does something to us, we are going to do something back," one activist shouted from the podium. "That's right, Brother," the crowd yelled in response, "blood for blood!" Another man then took the stage and urged listeners to march on the nearby stationhouse. Within an hour there were more than five hundred people milling outside the precinct. The first scuffles occurred as the police tried to set up barricades. Two activists were arrested, and the crowd started shouting. Police buckled on holsters and, braving a hail of bottles, forcibly herded demonstrators out to Seventh Avenue. There, on the broad boulevard, the crowd continued to grow. Finally, at about ten o'clock, the cops decided to break it up. Two squads of helmeted riot police leaped over the barricades shouting: "Charge." The first shots were fired shortly after—the first of thousands let off in the course of the night.

A series of pitched battles followed. All in all, several thousand demonstrators and more than four thousand policemen took part. The rioters' weapons of choice were bottles, bricks, rocks and garbage-can lids—all most effective when hurled from the roof of a five- or six-story tenement. Molotov cocktails were rarer, though highly prized. Police responded with nightsticks and by firing, mostly—though not always—in the air. Many streets were illuminated by blazing trash-can fires. Demonstrators would throw things, police would fire, the provocative youths would run off into the night. Other blacks watched from the sidelines, laughing and applauding. As the hours wore on, police grew more and more impatient, and by early morning they were freely clubbing anyone in sight. Officers roamed the streets with revolvers drawn; shuttles of squad cars removed youths holding their bloodied heads. During lulls in the fighting, the mob turned its rage on neighborhood shopkeepers, smashing windows, looting, ripping iron grates off stores. By two o'clock, the worst of the fighting was over, though sporadic incidents continued through the night.

The next morning, the streets glittered with broken glass, and the smell of smoke lingered in the air. The sidewalks were dotted with cartridges and stray booty—single shoes, plastic hangers, electrical appliances that had turned out to be too big to carry. Many grocery and liquor stores had been picked clean by looters; in at least two pawnshops, on West 135th Street, every single rifle was gone. The morning and afternoon hours passed in eerie quiet. Then, at dusk, the mayhem resumed again. This pattern continued for four days and nights in Harlem. On the third night, Brooklyn CORE held a midnight rally in Bedford-Stuyvesant, and it too turned to violence, which then raged for another three nights. Blacks in six other northern cities followed suit in ensuing weeks. All in all—in Rochester, New York, Paterson, New Jersey, Philadelphia, Harlem and three smaller towns—the rampages took five lives and did $6 million worth of damage.

The black reaction afterward was divided—the by now predictable split between old-guard leadership and grassroots. National civil rights spokesmen strongly deplored the disturbances and appealed for future restraint, declaring a moratorium on demonstrations to last until the November election. But virtually all black leaders with a base in Harlem found ways to justify and applaud the rioters. Malcolm X, who had been traveling in Africa at the time, told a reporter that if he had been in town, he probably would have died fighting the police. Congressman Adam Clayton Powell saw the disturbances as "a necessary phase" of his people's revolt. Powell, James Farmer and the New York chapter of the NAACP declared to the media that the police had been at fault, provoking the disturbance with their harsh suppression of black protests. As for ordinary Harlemites, it was hard to know what they felt. Only 1 percent of the population had participated, many of them underage. But journalists and others canvassing the ghetto found more approval than they expected. "White folks respect us more when they find out we mean business," one older man was quoted as saying. "When they only listen to our speeches or read our writing—if they ever do—they think we are just blowing off steam. But when rioters smash the plate glass windows of their stores, they know the steam has some force behind it. Then they say, 'Those Negroes are mad! What do they want?' And for a little while, they will try to give you a little of what you want."

One or two black commentators acknowledged that Harlem's problems might be bigger than the police. There was little question that during the riot some officers had gone too far. Police attitudes toward the ghetto were no secret in New York: city cops were rough and ready, if not racist and downright brutal. The overcrowded slums were thought to breed all manner of crime, and police did not expect to have to answer questions about what they did there—whatever it took to maintain public safety. Still, as even some angry black spokesmen conceded, the police also served as a kind of scapegoat, bearing the brunt of young blacks' unfocused rage at white authority. Harlem's unofficial poet laureate, Langston Hughes, tried to explain how this worked. "The prices for food in Harlem are higher," he wrote. "Rentals in Harlem are higher. . . . Graft [is worse]." All of this, and more, Hughes said, blacks blame on the white world—and "the cops, unfortunately being white, represent visually that world below Central Park that controls life in Harlem."

Nevertheless, when the dust had settled, all of Harlem stood together, moderates and militants united in their demand that the city do something about the police force. James Farmer found himself at the forefront of the campaign. Racist or not, the police had never been a priority for him, way down his list of concerns, after integration, jobs, education, improved living conditions. But as so often now, he was driven by the militants on his flank, and the police issue offered a sure way to establish his credibility. "It was a very live issue for the kids on the street," Farmer said later, "and for that reason alone we could not avoid it." Within weeks, the black demand had crystalized: a civilian review board to oversee police activity. By the end of the summer, the harder issues facing the ghetto—issues of poverty, pathology and ingrained race hatred—had taken a permanent backseat, as police brutality was dubbed the city's number one racial problem.

I t was almost a year later, in May 1965, that Congressman John Lindsay announced his candidacy for mayor of New York. It took exactly one week for the enthusiasm to kindle and catch in the city and the national political establishment. Within days, the candidate's clear blue eyes were gazing out at magazine buyers from the front of *Newsweek:* a stand-out, robin's-egg-blue cover that just matched the eyes and set them off to teen-idol perfection. The article inside the magazine was no less flattering. Lindsay, the story claimed, "is the hottest young Republican hope in the nation. . . . [This] is the most exciting and important political operation in America today. . . . [It] might even be the first chapter of the making of the president, 1972."

It wasn't hard to understand what made the fresh-faced congressman so appealing at just this point in the mid-sixties. Lindsay's resemblance to the Kennedys was lost on no one. His youth, his idealism, his can-do liberalism, the conviction that together Americans could make the nation great by taking care of its poorest citizens: Lindsay seemed to revive all the hope and promise that had been wounded at Dallas. That idealism was not exclusively about race, but race had a lot to do with it. To Democrats and Republicans alike, Lindsay offered a chance to implement the nation's new goodwill toward the black man: to take the dream outlined in the 1964 Civil Rights Act and make it real in the biggest, toughest city in the land. Just weeks after the march at Selma, Alabama, with the Voting Rights Act pending in Congress, he was promising to carry the fight to where it really mattered: the broken ghettos of the industrial North. Race, said Lindsay, is "the foremost issue of our time." "I deeply believe," he declared a few weeks later, "that the vast majority of the people of New York want an end to discrimination. [They] have themselves lived through prejudice of other kinds [and] they know that New York must solve this dilemma or die." Liberal Americans—still then the professed majority—could hardly imagine a bolder or more important mission.

As it happened—it would become clear years later—Lindsay declared for mayor at precisely the moment when American enthusiasm for racial change reached its historic high point. Much had changed since those first awful photos from Birmingham had prodded the nation's dozing conscience just two years before. Pollsters charting white feelings about the black movement had watched sympathy rise steadily until it peaked in spring 1965 after the dramatic confrontation in Selma between rampaging state troopers and nonviolent marchers led by Martin Luther King. President Johnson's speech backing the march, considered by many to be the most eloquent of his career, had met with impassioned applause on the Hill, then a flood of approval from both press and public. Congress wasted no time in hammering out the landmark Voting Rights Act, and as the year before with the civil rights bill, debate over the measure only piqued increased white interest and sympathy. Poll figures jagged upward: support not just for equal voting rights but also for integrated schools, enhanced job opportunities, even residential integration. The Harlem disturbance of 1964 drew little notice outside New York; the riot in Watts had yet to happen—and in most regions, white sympathy for the black man's cause was still growing faster than fear or disapproval of his tactics.

But even as the public's mood shifted, it became clear to concerned whites that the problem was much tougher than they had originally imagined. The challenge facing both Johnson and Lindsay was how, as the president said, "to fulfill these rights": how to make the integrationist ideal a reality. With the 1964 Civil Rights Act and the new voting rights measure, whites had met the southern movement's basic demands for removal of the legal barriers to black advance and equality. Yet, it had become immediately obvious, simple access—be it to schools or jobs or voting booths—was not going to be the answer for many black people, handicapped as they were by centuries of discrimination and backwardness.

The problem was nowhere clearer than in northern ghettos like Harlem, and it was already weighing heavily on movement activists. Bayard Rustin tried to explain it with a simple vignette of a kind that would soon become familiar. In the wake of the Harlem riot, he had found jobs for 120 teenagers. A few weeks later, only twelve of them were still employed. Some had met with subtle and not so subtle prejudice, but as often as not there were other reasons why things did not work out. One youth had found he could make more money selling marijuana; a second topped his salary by hustling at the local pool hall; still another turned down a scholarship because it would have taken him away from pimping. In the face of such evidence, James Farmer and other movement leaders had at first despaired and then begun to rethink their strategies. "[W]e can no longer evade the knowledge," Farmer admitted bluntly, "that most Negroes will not be helped by equal opportunity."

Johnson saw the problem as plainly as Farmer did, and he tried boldly, as one aide said, to "leap-frog the movement"—to get out in front of it and head off its demands. His historic speech at Howard University in June 1965 was a daring push forward, putting Johnson once again out ahead of most white voters, who, with the Civil Rights Act, had consented to no more than removing the legal obstacles to black advance. Johnson explained his leap with the famous metaphor of the "hobbled runner." "You do not," he said, "take a person who, for years, has been hobbled by chains and liberate him, bring him up to the starting line of the race and then say, 'you are free to compete with all the others,' and still justly believe that you have been completely fair." It was the argument that would eventually be used to justify affirmative action, but more immediately in 1965 it gave birth to the War on Poverty. The idea seemed obvious and compelling: the government would step in to bridge the moat that prevented most blacks from even trying to make their way in the white world. Johnson began with an array of social programs—compensatory schooling, job training and other experiments in acculturation. It was a hugely ambitious, unprecedented initiative and even so only a beginning of the effort that would be necessary to make integration a possibility for the poorest blacks.

John Lindsay responded to the challenge in an equally daring way. Seeing, as Johnson and Farmer did, that laws were not going to solve the problem, he decided to try to manage it personally—with charisma, caring and more effective government. Supporters were dazzled by his boldness: Johnson himself was said to joke admiringly that Lindsay had taken on the hardest job in country—harder still than the president's. But even those most impressed by the heady enthusiasm of Lindsay's bid could see that it would be a difficult mission.

L ike most of his class, Lindsay came to the problem of race through a learned sense of *noblesse oblige.* Born in New York in 1921, he had grown up in the world of the New York *Social Register.* His college career at Yale was conventional enough: the right clubs, the right friends, decent marks and a gentleman's sports record. A wartime stint in the navy, Yale Law School and a first job at the white-shoe Wall Street firm of Webster, Sheffield completed the perfect Park Avenue résumé. He encountered race for the first time in the mid-1950s, when he was lured to Washington by liberal Republican U.S. Attorney General Herbert Brownell. Lindsay's first job at the Justice Department, his initiation into politics, was helping to craft what became the 1957 civil rights bill. Two years later, he was back in Washington, this time as a congressman representing the tony East Side of Manhattan, and he made racial matters his first order of business. He still knew no blacks and had read little on the subject, but his "gut instinct" told him civil rights was an emerging issue.

Lindsay cut a dashing figure on Capitol Hill. A handsome young patrician with a cool, ironic smile, he was, rival William F. Buckley would later say, "first-class political horseflesh." Tall, slim, sandy-haired and classically featured, he was at once glamorous and earnest, privileged and used to power but also idealistic. Although a political maverick—an uncommonly liberal Republican—he was liked by colleagues and constituents. Some fellow representatives found him a little self-righteous, charming and witty in private but sometimes stiff and tending toward priggish. His crusading zeal waxed particularly hot when it came to race issues, and he could be fiercely intolerant of anyone he felt was obstructing the cause. The indignant young congressman was appalled by what he saw as President Kennedy's empty rhetoric on civil rights. Unlike JFK, Lindsay's proposals on a range of issues made clear, he believed government should use all the power at its disposal to force change in white behavior toward blacks. Also unlike the president, Lindsay was relatively unconcerned about consensus: he felt that leadership should be out ahead of the public. He rose to national prominence in 1963 by championing a far tougher civil rights law than Kennedy would consider, then helping broker the compromise that led eventually to passage.

It was a stance that played well in liberal New York, and Lindsay won his 1964 congressional contest by a wider margin than any other Republican representative in the nation. When he returned to the city a year later to run for mayor, friends found him still consumed by the race issue and as outspokenly righteous as ever. His crusading earnestness was evident in everything he said, and even in 1965, this utopian bent struck some people as anomalous—Pollyannish and unsuited to the gritty job of running a big city. "A lightweight Lochinvar," one journalist mockingly called him, "in New York's ethnic oriented political jungle." Yet in the wake of Selma and Johnson's inspiring address to Congress, many liberal voters felt the young representative was precisely what was needed, his gallant idealism just the answer to the city's race problems. What he intended to do to make integration a reality in New York was not so clear, but both he and his backers seemed to think that with the right kind of leadership, the details would take care of themselves.

Like most men of his class who came of age in the postwar era, Lindsay believed that Americans could solve any problem. As a young man in the 1940s and 1950s, he had watched as the nation rebuilt Europe with the Marshall Plan, jump-started the Japanese economy, turned the world into a global marketplace and made a sugary drink called Coca-Cola the symbol of prosperous modern life. Though inspired more by ideals than power, not even Lindsay was immune to the can-doism of this formative period. Not only was he convinced that it was America's job to save the world; with the right idea and the deft use of money and force, he saw no reason why that should not be possible. In Congress a decade later, he was applying this logic to race relations. Already in the 1950s, he claimed that the legislation he was backing was "the solution." In New York, in 1965, facing the developmental chasm that held poor blacks back, Lindsay was no less confident: he campaigned on a promise "to solve the crisis of the cities."

R ace questions were, from the start, at the center of the 1965 campaign. "There is no shortage of serious issues in New York," Lindsay claimed on the stump, "but no problem facing the people of this city cries out for greater understanding. . . . This issue may have more to do with the progress or decay of New York City in the next ten years than any of the other issues."

The specific planks of his program were not that different from the proposals of his Democratic opponent, drab-gray former accountant and party regular Abraham Beame. Liberal, optimistic, unsuspecting of the resentments emerging on both sides of the color line, Lindsay offered a vision of painless race relations: the city would restrain ghetto policemen even as it controlled spiraling crime and integrate education without destroying neighborhood schools. As for the development chasm, his answer followed the emerging liberal trend: acculturation programs on the model of the War on Poverty. But more than any specifics, what he campaigned on was his goodwill—his general, well-meaning determination to do the right thing by the black man.

He made a point in the first days after he announced his candidacy of going up to Harlem with reporters in tow. Speaking from scrawled four-by-five cards to a group of black ministers, he pleaded: "All I ask is that you . . . listen to me when I talk about justice." Journalists noted the "amens" in the back of the church. It was the first of many trips that summer, both to Harlem and Bedford-Stuyvesant. Charming as ever, Lindsay walked the streets, ringing doorbells and lingering at storefronts, shopping from sidewalk vendors and chatting with loiterers. Uptown and downtown, he played on the Kennedy resemblance for all it was worth, constantly invoking both brothers and holding up the pen Lyndon Johnson had given him at the signing of the 1964 Civil Rights Act. A number of the city's prominent blacks supported his campaign; not many elected officials (they were Democrats), but movement types like James Farmer and former King aide Reverend Wyatt T. Walker, as well as celebrities like Jackie Robinson, Ossie Davis and Dick Gregory. "It is time for a change," Lindsay boomed downtown, probing for his white listeners' idealism, "time for us to exchange respect rather than to exchange insults."

Lindsay's promise of racial harmony was part and parcel of his larger personal appeal—an appeal he made as much with style as with anything he said. He ran against both politics- and government-as-usual, promising to give the city back to its citizens, black and white. The hallmark of his campaign was its down-to-earth style, small-d democratic and appealingly irreverent. As a progressive Republican in a city where three out of four voters were Democrats, Lindsay made a virtue of his alienation from the GOP. (In an old New York tradition that had benefited progressives as far back as Fiorello La Guardia, he was also running on the Liberal Party line, sparing Democratic voters the need to pull the Republican lever.) Instead of party organization, he relied on youthful volunteers and storefront neighborhood offices. His own personal example reinforced everything he said: that people could make a difference, that New Yorkers could be proud of their city, that they could be proud of themselves because of their concern for the less fortunate among them.

Though race and its discontents were the spiritual heart of the campaign, the closest Lindsay got to specifics was the ghetto police issue. His first full-fledged speech broached the idea of a civilian police review board, still a key demand among the city's black spokesmen, and by the end of the summer this was one of the central planks of his platform. A review board would not, the candidate understood, be "the solution" he was seeking to the race problem; it was less promising certainly than the ten-point plan he had developed for cleaning up the ghetto. But somehow in the heat of the campaign, the ghetto proposal never caught on as the review board did. Besides, Lindsay and aides figured, police reform was what blacks were insisting on, and easing those tensions would be a start—proof positive of the white goodwill they so badly wanted to get across.

Even more than Lindsay, his Conservative Party opponent William F. Buckley put race at the top of the electoral agenda. Witty, flamboyant and irrepressibly combative, Buckley delighted in flouting the conventional wisdom on civil rights. Crime, illegitimacy and welfare dependency were staple issues of his campaign. The police review board was a favorite target, as were black politicians and militants: Adam Clayton Powell, he said, was "a scoundrel and an opportunist," doing a disservice to his people with his "special pleading" on their behalf. A master of innuendo, Buckley called black juvenile delinquents "junior savages." Among his most shocking ideas was a proposal to "relocate" welfare recipients outside city limits in enclaves his rivals likened to concentration camps. Buckley's popularity among Republicans and ethnic Democrats was an early sign of the trouble Lindsay would have as mayor when he tried to give blacks more say and standing in the city. But not everything Buckley said about blacks was wrong or racist; and if Lindsay or his followers had listened, it might have helped them refine their own still-unfocused policy ideas.

The serious idea behind Buckley's pandering campaign was that government could not solve all the problems blocking black entry into the mainstream—could not eradicate illegitimacy or make rebellious teenagers into scholars. He opposed not just busing but all "synthetic integration." Arguing that "racists are those who treat people primarily as members of a race," he denounced the color consciousness he saw coming into vogue among angry blacks and patronizing liberals as something that in the long run could only block more meaningful inclusion. The truths he wanted to air were not always pleasant: that the ghetto had spawned a vicious culture, that many blacks were not prepared to compete in the mainstream, that the black crime rate was soaring, hurting no one as much as other blacks. It was the kind of thing no liberal wanted to hear, but Buckley was right that Lindsay and his allies were setting themselves up for failure, ignoring the thorniest aspects of the challenge they had taken on. "Mention the fact," he said, "that Negro illegitimacy is a grave social problem, mention such a thing in front of say, Mr. Beame or Mr. Lindsay, and they will either simply vanish from the room in a cloud of integrated dust; or else they will turn and call *you* a racist."

In different circumstances, Buckley and Lindsay might have had an honest, useful debate about how to make integration a reality without alienating the city's ethnic whites. Instead, both men played divisively on the race issue, rallying supporters with code language and scare tactics. Rather than try to talk to liberals and convince them with reasonable arguments, Buckley pressed further with the mischievous race baiting that made him and his followers sound even more prejudiced than many were. Meanwhile, on the other side of town, Lindsay made hay with Buckley's welfare camps, evoking just the rise he wanted, particularly from Jewish audiences. Bewildered New Yorkers looking for a way to talk about color were put off by both candidates' rhetoric. Even when he made sense, Buckley's example suggested it was impossible to be honest without also—inevitably—sounding bigoted and insulting. Instead of digging deeper, instead of going beyond fear and sentimentality, both candidates made it harder to think seriously about race—and harder for Lindsay to develop a practical agenda.

For the Lindsay campaign, Buckley's candidacy was a godsend. It was as if Barry Goldwater or George Wallace himself had come to run in New York, the perfect foil for a righteous liberal crusading against intolerance. The city's liberals got the message and rallied behind Lindsay, coming out for him but also against the specter of Buckley. The conservative's campaign, with its cynicism and mean-spiritedness, set off Lindsay's idealism in exquisite relief. The intense young congressman pointed to the bigotry of the worst of Buckley's followers, and, as columnist Murray Kempton said, "scared the liberals to death."

By the time of the election, if anything Lindsay's appeal was more potent than when the campaign began. By then, four days of rioting in the Los Angeles ghetto of Watts had left thirty-four people dead and the civil rights vision badly wounded. The costs, in the $40-million range, were still being tallied, and the rioters' call—"Burn, baby, burn!"—was echoing from coast to coast. In the shadow of the disturbance, Lindsay's hopeful vision gleamed all the brighter. That summer of the Voting Rights Act and the War on Poverty, liberals' feelings about race still hung in the balance, torn between hopeful confidence and a new sense of foreboding, and Lindsay promised to appease the gathering anxiety that America might not measure up to its ideals. Progressive whites who embraced his candidacy liked the image of themselves he reflected. Like Kennedy, Lindsay made upscale New Yorkers feel he could help them forge the kind of city they wanted to be—not just physically integrated, but also enlightened and generous, civilized in the largest sense of the word. Goaded by both his scare tactics and his idealism, the city's powerful liberal establishment rallied around his candidacy: the Liberal Party, the Citizens' Union, Americans for Democratic Action, *The New York Times,* the *New York Post,* the *Herald Tribune* and a host of cultural luminaries—everyone from Ethel Merman and Sammy Davis, Jr., to Philip Johnson, Jane Jacobs and Norman Mailer. Most didn't see a need to look beyond the image and prod the candidate about what exactly he planned to do to bring about the racial change he promised.

The appeal to hope and conscience paid off in a November victory, albeit a narrow one. Lindsay took 45 percent of the vote, Beame 41 and Buckley 14, but the critical margin was fewer than 110,000 votes. Celebrating the next evening at the Roosevelt Hotel, both Lindsay and his aides knew what had made the difference for him. Despite Buckley's right-wing challenge, the new mayor had held on to three-quarters of the GOP vote. But it was the classic liberal coalition of blacks and Jews—he got about 45 percent of both groups' support—that had pushed Lindsay over the top. The first thing he did the next morning, on three hours sleep, was drive back up to Harlem, then Bed-Stuy and ghetto Queens, thanking black voters even before he held a press conference. The earnest lawyer's abstract commitment to civil rights had been planted in political earth, giving him a special bond with the black people of the city. Now finally, it was time to get down to the difficult business of delivering for them.

The city Lindsay inherited was not in good shape, already beginning the downward slide that would overwhelm it in the next few decades. The early sixties had brought increased prosperity to the nation but not, for a variety of reasons, to New York. The five boroughs cost more to run than any comparable northeastern city, yet municipal services were deteriorating, and New York was already tottering on the edge of bankruptcy. The problems were not exclusively racial, but race played a large part in many of them. Between 1950 and 1960, some 800,000 whites had left the city for the suburbs, while an almost identical number of relatively poorer blacks and Puerto Ricans had moved in. New York's great manufacturing base, once the largest in the nation, had been eroding for more than a decade, and 14 percent of the city's blacks were unemployed. By 1965, blacks accounted for one-seventh of the city's 8 million people, yet one-half of the budget was being spent on them—for welfare, schooling, public housing and the like.

New York's reputation as an unusually enlightened city—a place that managed race and poverty with more decency than most—was also already wearing thin around the edges. Miles of substandard housing, a decaying infrastructure and deteriorating school system: Harlem's physical troubles alone were beginning to discourage even the most ardent liberals. Add the other boroughs' black neighborhoods and their social problems and it wasn't hard to understand why skeptics were asking if the city was "governable." Crime had grown by 15 percent in the last year, by nearly a third in the last decade. The de facto segregation and prejudice that hemmed in the ghetto were not getting worse, but after a decade of protest they were exposed for all to see. In New York as nationwide, the black movement was in disarray, wondering what to press for now that legal barriers had been removed. Meanwhile, in the outer boroughs, as Buckley's popularity proved, white middle-class voters were growing edgy, worried that they were going to have to compete with blacks for civic spoils they were already being short-changed on.

Undaunted, the mayor-elect moved ahead with plans for what his campaign had called "Fun City." He assembled a team of bright, energetic young men compared headily to the one JFK had attracted: a staff determined to put New York on the cutting edge of the nation's great new experiment with social engineering. They hailed from Harvard Law School and from Washington's most respected congressional staffs; several of the hottest prospects came by way of the Ford Foundation—the largest and most influential philanthropic institution in the country, already a pioneer of experimental social policy. Then, just weeks before he took office, it was announced that White House insider McGeorge Bundy, one of the architects of the deepening Vietnam War, was resigning to take the helm at Ford. A man of Lindsay's class and upbringing, close in age, Bundy had come to a conviction like the mayor's own that the cities and their problems were as important as any facing the nation. His decision to manage Ford's multi-million-dollar experiment in social engineering only reinforced New York liberals' hopeful sense that, bad as things were, the ghetto's problems were solvable.

Lindsay's ghetto walking tours began in early 1966 in the first few months of his mayoralty, and from the start they were a symbol of his government. He went typically in an unmarked car, often in shirtsleeves, with an aide or two and a plainclothes policeman, usually black. Soon the press caught wind of the outings and a reporter was allowed to come, often with a TV camera. The walks were generally scripted—or as scripted as they could be—but they also struck observers as spontaneous and natural. Lindsay would get out of the car at a predetermined spot and stroll, thumbs in pants pockets, seemingly wherever his interest took him, like any other man out for a walk. What everyone noticed right away was the mayor's easy rapport with ghetto people: he wasn't condescending, he didn't grin like a movie star, he didn't peer curiously around the neighborhood or try, like a candidate, to attract people's attention. He waited for passersby to recognize him and when they approached engaged them cordially. He listened as much as he talked and never seemed afraid.

With time, as the walks became more regular, he developed a routine. Some days he went to trouble spots, other times to stable, working-class neighborhoods. He stopped for food and sometimes drink; he signed autographs on every conceivable surface. Things didn't always go well—from the beginning there were hecklers—but kids in particular seemed taken by the powerful visitor, and Lindsay's easy manner relaxed everyone around him. One hot night in Brooklyn, the entourage stopped in a bar, and the mayor found himself elbow-to-elbow with a regular who launched into a long, slow tale of woe. Aides fidgeted nervously, but Lindsay listened intently and after a few minutes put his arm around the man. "You think you got problems?" he said with a smile. "Just listen to mine for a while, will you?" The black man laughed, then others in the bar joined in. Whether in Harlem or Bed-Stuy, Lindsay was eager to engage and when possible responded to complaints—arranging for a special garbage pickup or a new basketball hoop, finding someone downtown to donate books for a community center.

Lindsay never claimed that the walks were a substitute for a ghetto policy, but in an important way they embodied the essence of his approach and his ideas about integration. Blacks had to be made to feel included, shown that they mattered to the city, and that the city could make a difference for them. Downtown in the white world, Lindsay liked to project an aggressive image. He was, he often said, "tough" on unions, "tough" on bureaucrats, "tough" in the assertion of his principles. When it came to blacks, though, both the mayor and his brash young aides were forever telling reporters how much they "cared." "Discontent and alienation [in the ghetto] were at breaking point," Lindsay said. "These visits . . . offer[ed] some sign that the city cared." "I think it's important," he told another reporter, "for the people of the ghettos to see their mayor. They've got to feel somebody is interested in them."

The problem for Lindsay, uptown and downtown, was how to move beyond street theater and make good on his promises. He saw for himself on his walks through Harlem just how difficult the ghetto's problems were. Idle men hanging around on street corners; youths killing time throwing stones at school buildings; the dirty, dilapidated housing and what he called "the ugly silences": Lindsay felt, he said, "how deep poverty was"—how different, and just how discouraging. What had happened that summer in Watts only confirmed his growing sense of urgency. Blacks, he now saw, were far angrier than he had imagined, and what he called their "social problems" were much worse than he had thought. Young and old, he tried to tell whites, they were tired of "the same old trite phrases . . . [of] vague generalities about equal rights and equal opportunity." Even the can-do problem solver in Lindsay saw that it would not be easy to deal with the ghetto's pathologies or the frustration they produced—and daunting as these problems were, there was something encouraging about his realism.

His first impulse was to attack the pathologies head-on: to step in with government aid and eradicate them. His proposed program reflected the newest liberal thinking, in the same mold as Lyndon Johnson's Howard University speech. The idea was to move beyond rights to ghetto conditions, giving blacks a leg-up so they could compete more effectively. The eventual goal was still inclusion, but plainly, for many blacks, this was going to require extensive preparation—remedial education, job training and acculturation programs in the ghetto. So, in the name of integration, the government took on that job.

Most of Lindsay's initial ideas seemed modest enough; certainly they were needed. Like the federal government and much of the movement's leadership, he saw that change had to start with the ghetto's physical problems—renovating schools, repairing housing stock and building new hospitals. From Farmer, among others, he had learned that jobs were key—for economic reasons but also as an antidote to marginalization—and he now devised a package of initiatives to get blacks working. Like Kennedy before him, he put a premium on hiring visible black officials. At the same time, in keeping with the newer ideas of the War on Poverty, he saw that many in the ghetto would probably need more than role models, and he made plans to bring them into the workforce through unskilled public works jobs. Both businesses and unions would be cajoled to help with job creation and training. The city would expand Head Start and other "education enrichment" programs. In most of these ideas, Lindsay was neither behind nor ahead of other liberals, including Lyndon Johnson and Robert Kennedy. The difference was that he had a giant laboratory at his disposal: a city on the brink, where he could test the best new ideas about how to bring blacks up to the starting line and get them in the race.

If Lindsay grasped how he was raising the stakes, he did not let on. This was the moment, the historic turning point, when pursuit of equal rights gave way to a promise of equal outcomes. It was a turn that would be criticized for decades to come, but at the time, it seemed a humane and apt response to the gaps revealed once racial barriers had been lowered. The rationale put forward by Johnson and others sounded compelling. The country was prosperous and powerful, and people felt they could afford to be liberal. Lindsay and others like him saw acculturation programs as the logical next step, the only answer to the painful centuries in which segregation and subordination had prevented many blacks from learning how to participate in the mainstream. Neither he nor the architects of the Great Society grasped how intractable the ghetto's "social problems" would turn out to be. They didn't anticipate a shrinking economy, or a reluctant white electorate that would resent special privileges based on color. Besides, neither Lindsay nor his counterparts in the White House saw any danger in aiming a little high. If anything, the challenge the mayor faced in the ghetto only spurred him to think bigger. He had no idea what kind of extravagant hope he was spurring or what anger would be unleashed when he proved unable to deliver.

The difficulty, as Lindsay saw it, was where to find the kind of funding he needed for his ambitious acculturation effort. He began the search at home in New York with a pitch based on the idea of the social contract: that the better-off were responsible for helping the poorest in the community. In the mid-sixties in New York, this appeal still worked among wealthy liberals: foundations, old-money friends and civic-minded businessmen came through for Lindsay, providing funds here and there for special neighborhood projects. Still, the mayor knew, these private donations were hardly enough to underwrite the city budget or the large-scale social transformation he was dreaming of, and he soon found himself looking further afield: devising new taxes on the city's middle class. The package he proposed in spring 1966 included a broad range of new levies—higher business taxes, a stock transfer tax, the first personal income tax in city history—each more controversial than the one before.

None shocked New Yorkers more than the commuter income tax. It was a classic Lindsay idea: to try to force a sense of a shared future by making suburbanites who worked in the city pay for the services that kept it clean and safe. The proposal was met immediately with a firestorm of protest. Wall Street brokers, union bosses and incensed suburbanites joined together in an unprecedented coalition to block the tax. Lindsay mounted a major lobbying effort in Albany; he went directly to the people with a high-profile TV ad campaign, appealing to the city and suburbs to pull together as one. Finally, after months of bitter back and forth, the state legislature approved the package; but even after the tax went into effect, New York found itself woefully short of funds. Having lobbied for a $520-million package, Lindsay came away with $283 million: just enough to cover the city's current budget, with nothing left over to upgrade services or infrastructure in Harlem or put aside for acculturation programs. Far from feeling more sympathetic to the city, as Lindsay had hoped, suburban whites were grudging and furious. He had achieved temporary financial integration in New York, but there was no integrated community to sustain it.

Having failed at home, Lindsay turned increasingly to the federal government. Even as a congressman, he had foreseen what growing social problems would do to municipal budgets, and as early as 1960 he had recommended the creation of a cabinet-level department of urban affairs. Now with New York's annual expenses rising three times as fast as revenues, he saw that only the feds could possibly provide the kind of money needed to transform the ghetto, and he devoted himself to opening up a permanent pipeline. He met with other big-city mayors and in their name made himself a leading advocate for more urban spending. New York established a lobbying office in Washington. Lindsay wrote articles for national magazines and made himself a fixture at conferences and on television, tirelessly reminding people of "the crisis of the cities."

The problem already in 1966 was that federal money was increasingly earmarked for other things. With Johnson escalating in Vietnam and Congress already losing patience with the War on Poverty, Lindsay's trips to Washington grew more and more frustrating. In August 1966, he testified in the Senate that New York would need $50 billion over the next ten years. At the time, Washington was not providing even $1 billion annually and, despite rising demands, was cutting back—slashing funds for housing, urban development and antipoverty programs. Lindsay stopped cajoling and attacked the Johnson administration head-on, insisting that the nation would have to choose between Vietnam and ghettos like New York's Brownsville. He cut a dramatic figure and scored points with the liberal press but went home empty-handed to face the people of Harlem.

Without more money, Lindsay had few options, and he fell back on an early campaign promise: the idea known in the social science jargon of the day as "ghetto empowerment." It was a fashionable new concept—along with its handmaiden, acculturation, the essence of the War on Poverty—and it was at the heart of Lindsay's vision for accelerating black entry into the mainstream. The idea was simple enough, and compared to acculturation programs promisingly easy to implement: blacks and other poor people would be given a chance to have more say in the administration of local government. Running their own services would teach people dignity and work habits. Even as the government stepped in to refashion the culture of the ghetto, participation in the process would free residents from dependency. Like other aspects of the War on Poverty, empowerment was meant to make up for the past—in this case years of disenfranchisement. But even more than that, bringing blacks into the process of government would, it was hoped, be an antidote to ghetto alienation. "I propose," Lindsay told Harlemites, "to make the people . . . the partners of their city government, not its adversaries."

By 1966, the War on Poverty had given over nine hundred grants to experiments with this kind of empowerment. Blacks and whites below the poverty line were receiving money to man their own neighborhood cleanups, preschool education, dropout programs and other services. Already in 1966, it was clear that many of the experiments were running into difficulty. Alongside those seeking dignity and self-reliance, other, more militant participants were trying to use the programs to wrest power and money for themselves. Politicians and civil servants in cities across the country sensed the threat to their authority and tried to obstruct projects. One of the War on Poverty's earliest experiments, at a social service agency in New York called the Mobilization for Youth, was beset by scandal a year before Lindsay ran for office. Financial mismanagement was only part of the problem, as organizers were accused of stirring up trouble in the ghetto, radicalizing residents by teaching them complaints about "the system" they had not previously known they had. Reports filtered back of angry, name-calling meetings: gatherings devoted more to denouncing the government than devising ways to take responsibility for its chores.

Still, Lindsay was not to be deterred. Spreading riots and angry rhetoric from the black community only reinforced his sense that empowerment was the answer. If the youth of Watts and Harlem had not felt so powerless, he reasoned, they would have felt no need to rampage through their cities. The mayor pooh-poohed the risk that community action would put New York in the business of hiring militants and ghetto toughs. "Of course," he wrote later, "there were . . . mistakes and there was conflict. Had we wanted a trouble-free program we would have had no program." Headstrong as ever, Lindsay felt that the potential gain was worth the risk. Community action was not, in his eyes, just a bureaucratic reform or a more effective way of delivering city services; despite the separatist rhetoric of many of the militant leaders involved, it was the best way he could think of to translate the integrationist dream into reality.

Lindsay's empowerment proposals went even further than the community action programs of the War on Poverty—not just allowing blacks to run new social services in the ghetto, but actually breaking up the existing municipal bureaucracy. City Hall would ease centralized control of a wide range of city functions, including schools, hospitals and public housing. Neighborhood health clinics, "satellite" welfare centers and storefront job-training programs, all locally run, would replace the old unfriendly white-staffed offices. Thirty-five "Little City Halls" dispersed in New York's poorest neighborhoods would provide a gamut of municipal services, sparing ghetto residents the need to come downtown and spend a day on line at a big agency every time they had a gripe or needed to renew their driver's license. "I want to humanize the government," the mayor insisted to skeptics. "[This] is a very modest expenditure to bring some sense of participation to the people."

Lindsay put enormous store by this experiment and spent untold political capital touting it. A tiny number of pilot offices were opened, generally with foundation help or privately raised money. Just how much difference they made to citizens was hard to say—there was no groundswell of gratitude from the ghetto. Meanwhile, the city's political establishment went all-out to stymie the idea. Harlem's Democratic regulars were anything but enthusiastic. Borough presidents complained of confusion, expense, duplicated services and bureaucracy. They also accused Lindsay of scheming to use the new neighborhood offices for political purposes, reinventing ward politics in the expectation of running for president. Within a year, the initiative was all but dead. Still, even as it ran aground, it gave important support to the idea that City Hall held the answers for what was wrong in the ghetto: that with social services, administrative reform or simply more money, government could somehow magically step in and eradicate whatever was keeping blacks from making it in the mainstream. For better or worse, the idea grew—in the establishment and in Harlem—that the problem was less poverty or social pathology than the way power was distributed between black and white.

Race was not the only realm where Lindsay floundered during his first year in office, proving the limits of charisma and crusading willfulness in government. Blaming New York's troubles on bureaucracy and tired officialdom, the mayor and his whiz-kid staff made it their business to undermine what he called the city's "feudal hierarchies." Every young aide had a different horror story and a different set of procedures he wanted to revise: union work rules for Gracie Mansion janitors, hospital procurement guidelines, the telephone system in the mayor's office and the very structure of the city administration, divided as it was into nearly fifty overlapping departments. No reorganization was too large or too small, no rules or conventional boundaries sacrosanct. Lindsay's promise could be summed up in one word, "change"—and as he saw things, you could not make changes unless you were willing to poke people in the eye. Both he and his young aides set to it with some gusto, but soon found that their reformist end runs were no match for the entrenched power of the city bureaucracy. "Sometimes I feel I'm pushing my shoulder against a mountain," he told a reporter near the end of the first year. "My feet are churning away and the mountain won't budge."

When change proved slow or yielded meager results, the mayor resorted to style and symbolism. Fit-looking, energetic, brash, he rode the subways, walked the streets, showed up at theater openings, fires and other emergencies, single-handedly keeping a pack of news photographers busy. Enchanting as it seemed at first, it was an approach that quickly wore thin. Voters had plenty to gripe about: the transit strike that shut down the city during Lindsay's first two weeks in office, then a bus and subway fare hike, the new income tax and a threat that the New York Stock Exchange might move to

New Jersey. Not all of this was the mayor's fault; everyone knew he had inherited a city in financial difficulty. But New Yorkers caught on quickly enough: ever self-righteous, Lindsay had trouble compromising—and his petulant stubbornness was hurting the city. His campaign to restructure the bureaucracy pitted him against his own civil servants. Union chiefs complained he didn't have time for them. ("Labor hates his guts," one man put it bluntly.) *The Wall Street Journal* noticed a "puzzling tendency to go it alone," treating "every other politician as his natural enemy." One small group—Manhattan liberals—continued to be encouraged by his optimism and engagement. In their view, style was substance and Lindsay was doing just what was needed to transform the city. But before the first year was out, even the press found him a little quixotic, a judgment reflected in his many nicknames: Mr. Clean, Captain Marvel, Prince Valiant, Sir Galahad, among others. Most disgruntled were middle-class whites in the outer boroughs, the kind of people who had lost two weeks' pay when they couldn't get to work during the transit strike. The mayor's predecessor, Robert Wagner, summed up the verdict that first year. Lindsay was "the greatest mayor the city ever had," Wagner said, "before he took office."

Meanwhile, the problems Lindsay had discovered in Harlem proved no more tractable than the city bureaucracy. In his first year, the mayor delivered virtually nothing for the ghetto: nothing but symbolic gestures and inflated promises—of short-cut acculturation, money and power he was unable to produce. If anything, his extravagant pledges—part of the shift from equal rights to equal outcomes—only exacerbated race relations in the city. Lindsay and other liberals had jumped from a goal they could meet—a field without barriers—to a vow no outsider could possibly guarantee: that blacks would find it in themselves to make good on opportunities. Even as they meant to free the ghetto, to enable people to stand on their own feet, the reformers encouraged blacks to believe that white society was responsible for all their frustrations. Decades later, blacks and whites alike would still be mired in the confusion this created, blaming white neglect and bigotry for age-old problems with far deeper origins. Lindsay and other reformers weren't wrong to try to create the conditions in which change would be possible. What they didn't foresee was how, because of their rhetoric, they and those who came after would be blamed when their decent gestures fell short. They had no clue what unforgiving expectations they were raising: what profound dependence and inevitable rage when government could not produce the kind of change that only individuals can create for themselves.

Outside New York, in the movement and on college campuses, 1966 was a year of deepening turmoil. The escalation in Vietnam proceeded relentlessly, and the first campus teach-ins of the year before, "Flower Power," miniskirts and macrobiotic food were giving way to a harder-edged kind of rebellion: massive antiwar protests, psychedelic music and LSD. In the wake of the Voting Rights Act, the movement was at a loss for what to do next. After much deliberation, Martin Luther King made an effort to bring his operation north, establishing a toehold in the black neighborhoods of Chicago. But like Farmer before him, King found his Gandhian tactics of little use in overcoming the subtler barriers blacks faced outside the South. Malcolm X's assassination in February 1965 had left a leadership vacuum in the northern ghetto, but neither King nor his integrationist lieutenants seemed to have much appeal among the restless youth galvanized by the former Muslim minister.

The summer of Lindsay's first year in office proved a critical turning point, as a younger generation inspired by Malcolm took over the leadership of the struggle. A mid-May coup at SNCC catapulted Stokely Carmichael to power. James Farmer had already resigned from CORE, and his successor, Floyd McKissick, joined Carmichael in making bitter fun of the old goals and tactics. Flamboyant, menacing, powerful orators and brilliant manipulators of the press, the two men dominated the airwaves that spring, and it wasn't long before the meaning of their takeover became clear: finally, after decades of vacillation, the dethroning of integration as the movement's goal. With Malcolm's posthumous autobiography passing from hand to hand in the ghetto and winning him an influence even greater than he had known in life, Carmichael and McKissick wrapped themselves in his memory and expounded his views to a much larger, more frustrated audience.

More than anything, it was Carmichael's "Black Power" speech, in June 1966, that marked the end of the integrationist era. He had gone to Mississippi early in the month when activist James Meredith, walking across the state to protest discrimination, was wounded by a sniper. All the major movement leaders raced to the scene to continue Meredith's trek, but immediately disagreed over its purpose. Moderates wanted something nonviolent, interracial, inspirational—a way to rally support for the latest rights bill pending in Congress. Carmichael and McKissick, repudiating the bill, discouraged whites from marching and asked a group of armed black men to serve as "bodyguards." For nearly three weeks, King and Carmichael led a straggling pack of protesters through the state. Hoping desperately to maintain unity, King tried marching arm-in-arm with his young rival. But at every stop, their speeches veered further apart. Dozens of reporters were on hand to gauge which was more popular, and the fiery Carmichael won hands down. "White blood will flow!" "Seize power!" "We Shall Overrun!": the new slogans literally drowned out King and his followers. Carmichael's speech, in a schoolyard in Greenwood, Mississippi, merely gave the rising anger a new name. Forget "freedom," he instructed the crowd; "what we gonna start saying now is Black Power." As soon as he was finished, fellow SNCC member Willie Ricks jumped on the platform. "What do you want?" the little man shouted, raising his fist and punching into the air. "BLACK POWER!" the crowd roared back. "BLACK POWER! BLACK POWER! BLACK POWER!"

There was little original about Carmichael, nothing new about the alienation he voiced, but somehow—with his timing and brilliant attention-getting—he closed the door forever on an age of possibility in race relations. Integration, he wrote the following year in his widely read book, *Black Power*, is not only unrealistic, it is "despicable." "Based on the assumption that there is nothing of value in the black community and that little of value could be created among black people, [it] reinforces the idea that 'white' is automatically superior and 'black' is by definition inferior." No Americans, he argued, had ever been remotely color-blind—and even if they were, it would not be a good thing for blacks. "Race," he concluded, "is an overwhelming fact of life"; integration, by definition, "a subterfuge for the maintenance of white supremacy." Distilling Malcolm's teachings, packaging them as a coherent doctrine, like Malcolm before him, Carmichael struck a chord with virtually every black who heard him, even those who disliked him and were intent on getting by in the white world. "I was thrilled by the speech," New York activist Sonny Carson remembered. "What he said was exactly what I felt. What we needed was power—to control our own destinies. It was time to stop worrying about white people and what they thought of us."

In fact, by the summer of 1966, white concern about blacks was visibly flagging. Distracted by Vietnam and the social unraveling it had triggered, put off by the hardening of the movement, much of the larger public had simply lost interest. Even the liberal establishment was distracted and confused. The grandiose promises of the War on Poverty were hardly a year old, but already many of the men behind it had turned elsewhere. The fading attention and disappointment were painfully apparent that summer at the White House's conference on civil rights.

The title and goal of the meeting came from Lyndon Johnson's Howard University speech: whites and blacks coming together to devise a strategy "To Fulfill These Rights"—to move further down the road opened by the War on Poverty. When the conference was planned in 1965, this had seemed difficult but doable; by the time the meeting convened in June 1966, it was clear that little would come of it. LBJ was furious at the movement, stung by what he saw as its ingratitude and by leaders' opposition to the war in Vietnam. Meanwhile, the nationalist mood sweeping over the struggle made it all but impossible to talk about the goal of most poverty programs: an assault on ghetto culture. Daniel Patrick Moynihan's report on the black family had been bitterly condemned in the months leading up to the conference, effectively ending the possibility of the only step that could make integration an option for poorer blacks: that the government and the movement would come together and forge a realistic, long-term plan for encouraging individual acculturation.

The conference turned out to be a meaningless charade. Most of the young men who now spoke for the movement did not attend. Even the relatively moderate leaders who showed up could not keep the separatist rhetoric out of their speeches—mainly empty threats and flailing accusations. Instead of honest discussion or new ideas, participants heard a series of stale, predictable speeches, with Johnson at one point angrily swearing at King over his position on Vietnam. At the end of the meeting, the two thousand four hundred delegates dispersed with what one observer called "a feeling of emptiness."

Back in New York, Lindsay and aides had little time to worry about long-term strategy as they girded for the immediate threat of summer in the city. On July 4, CORE's annual national convention embraced the idea of Black Power. Adam Clayton Powell hailed it, too—and tried to take credit for inventing it. Within weeks, it was clear that Black Power was going to mean something different to everyone who invoked it. But this was little comfort in northern cities, where blacks hardly seemed to need a slogan to spur them into the streets. The first big disturbance of the season was in Chicago, followed by upheavals in Omaha, Des Moines, Philadelphia, Cleveland, Atlanta, Dayton, Providence, Oakland, Minneapolis, Milwaukee, St. Louis and three Michigan towns. Hardly a day went by without fresh news of black violence, and the Justice Department announced that forty of the nation's biggest cities were at risk of exploding. Lindsay, his staff, Robert

Kennedy and the Ford Foundation looked out at New York and saw what Kennedy described as a "riot . . . waiting to happen."

The Lindsay administration went into overdrive. The theme, as before, was reaching out to the ghetto, and as ever, Lindsay relied heavily on gestures. He stepped up his walking-tour schedule. Word went out that City Hall was open twenty-four hours a day and that no complaint from the ghetto was too small to get a hearing. Several young aides were dispersed into the city to make contact with youths who would be likely to take part in a riot. Once these toughs were identified, the theory went, the mayor's team would provide a more constructive way for them to spend the summer—working in the parks, perhaps, or putting their "leadership" to use in a city youth program. Lindsay scrambled to find things for them and others to do and came up, mostly, with neighborhood sports. The city borrowed private money to buy fire-hydrant sprinkler caps; "play streets" were cordoned off and athletic equipment trucked in. There were bus trips to the beach, occasional street theater and a specially rigged truck that projected movies on the walls of tenements. Most of the initiatives were cheap and hastily organized; everyone in the mayor's office knew they were just distractions. Still, Lindsay figured, they would at least buy some time—time to make the kind of changes that were really needed.

Well into the summer, the program seemed to be working—if not healing the ghetto, at least averting violence. By the time Carmichael made his "Black Power" speech, the mayor was spending all his spare time in Harlem. One night he went into the projects to listen to pianist Billy Taylor playing live from the city's newly inaugurated jazzmobile. "You going to treat us right, man?" one listener yelled. "You bet, baby," Lindsay shot back. A few days later, he was uptown again, installing sprinkler caps, and got into a squirting match with a throng of half-naked kids. Later in the week, still another walk made the front page of the *Times*. This time he was picking up litter—"Is this cat serious?" one youth asked—and trying his hand at a local man's bongo drums.

Not every venture was so carnival-like. In mid-August, Lindsay headed out to a remote enclave near Canarsie to break ground for an industrial park. A handful of suited executives were waiting for him, sitting quietly on folding chairs. Not far away about a thousand black demonstrators had gathered; their signs said the land should be used for schools instead of factories. Reporters noticed the crowd getting pushy and watched apprehensively as the mayor's limo pulled up. Lindsay got out nonchalantly and walked alone into the knot of demonstrators. It took a few seconds for people to recognize him. There was a moment of confused quieting. Then the protesters' angry shouts turned into cheers, and a group of burly black youths hoisted the mayor on their shoulders. "I'm all right," he yelled to his police escort, and after a few minutes the groundbreaking went ahead. It was, one journalist said later, "the year's most spectacular moment," proof positive that the mayor's "caring" worked.

Lindsay had exactly two days to savor his triumph before an incident elsewhere in Brooklyn sparked a weekend of rioting. East New York was the kind of neighborhood that some people mistakenly called "integrated"—actually in transition, from poor white to poor black. Tensions between the two groups were running high, and the most disgruntled whites had coalesced in a group known as SPONGE, the Society for the Prevention of Niggers from Getting Everything. One afternoon, Lindsay's grapevine picked up rumors of trouble in the area, and the mayor and aides sped out to East New York in unmarked cars. Nothing much seemed to be happening, and they walked around for a while in the white part of the neighborhood. Some Italian kids shouted, "We don't want you here, you nigger lover." Lindsay crossed the street and confronted the gang. Together, they trooped to a nearby pizza parlor and sat down to talk things through.

It was a classic Lindsay tableau: the mayor and aides, in jackets and ties, surrounded by a dozen kids in T-shirts, some sitting with them in a booth, others hovering in the aisle. The kids complained about blacks ruining the neighborhood. They took the cigarette packs out from folds in their shirtsleeves and smoked one after another as they talked. Older whites from the neighborhood gathered outside and gawked, peering in through the storefront window at the unusual powwow. Lindsay listened respectfully for an hour or so, then promised to do what he could to help. By the time he politely excused himself, the kids seemed relaxed, almost friendly. It was another victory for Lindsay-style government by charisma. Then, in the car on the way back to Manhattan, the mayor heard over the shortwave radio that a black eleven-year-old had been shot in the neighborhood he had just left. It was hardly Lindsay's fault; it may not even have been white kids. But it could not have been a grimmer lesson in the limits of what the mayor could do.

The disturbance followed the by now familiar pattern. By the time Lindsay got back to the neighborhood, there were a few hundred people in the streets, and a number of windows had been smashed. SPONGE pickets appeared, and before anyone could stop them, they were fighting the gathered blacks and Puerto Ricans. Lindsay and aides stayed in the neighborhood till after midnight, wandering aimlessly and unable to make much difference. The next night, Friday, things were considerably worse. Whites, blacks and Puerto Ricans showed up in organized gangs. Two Hispanics were shot. There were Molotov cocktails and a lot of sniping. The fifteen hundred cops on the scene, under orders of maximum restraint, stood their ground silently under a hail of angry abuse. By the end of the evening, there had been twenty-two arrests.

The next morning, Lindsay again tried diplomacy, this time at City Hall. Some fifty "representatives" from East New York gathered mistrustfully in an ornate reception room: shopkeepers, homeowners, several ministers and about two dozen gang members, black and white. Lindsay got up to open the meeting; an angry youth interrupted him—and this set the tone for the next three hours. Kids talked about "our turf" and "their turf"; they shouted and jabbed their fingers at each other. At one point, some older men had to step between two teenagers who were getting ready to use their fists. "I do not think," Lindsay wrote later, "City Hall has ever witnessed that kind of meeting—the language and the exchanges were brutal." When it was all over, photographers were admitted to the room and the mayor abruptly pulled two youths forward, slapping their hands together, black on white, just before the cameras snapped. The picture appeared the next day on the front page of *The New York Times:* an image of integration rising up out of the ashes of the East New York disturbance. This wasn't exactly the way it was supposed to be— not quite King's vision of "the beloved community." But by the week of the "Black Power" speech, in the shadow of national rioting, even this much black-white dialogue seemed like something to celebrate.

Within a month, the first "Little City Hall" opened, in East New York. Lindsay had raised the money privately, assuring the city this would help cool tensions. When the public was skeptical, the mayor responded indignantly: couldn't people tell blacks and whites in the neighborhood were now "communicating"? Later in the summer, he cut short his vacation and returned to the city to take a walk in East New York. All was quiet in the streets, but for the first time on a walk, aides and reporters noticed that people seemed indifferent, even hostile. "It will take more than walks," one man said, "to solve the basic problems of these neighborhoods." Lindsay's own press secretary, Woody Klein, concluded that the mayor's "visible caring" had reached the point of diminishing returns. The mayor let on nothing, but later even he admitted this had been a demoralizing moment. What happened in East New York, he said, was "a combination of work and sweat and luck. But we could not let that kind of ad hoc operation continue as a strategy, because it was no strategy."

Tired, out of ideas, desperate to do something to make good on his promise of improved race relations, at the end of the summer Lindsay turned his attention to the police issue still simmering in Harlem. Practiced by now in going over the heads of his own bureaucracy, he launched the initiative with an executive order, announced in his most charismatic, inspirational style at a televised news conference. Reminding viewers of his campaign promise the year before, now by fiat the mayor created a civilian police review board.

The order had been carefully prepared and packaged to appeal even to those who were skeptical of police oversight. There were slots on the board for cops and civilians, blacks, Irishmen, Manhattanites and spokesmen for the outer boroughs. But neither the police department nor borough whites were appeased by the promise that they would be represented on the panel, and before the month was out they made clear their intention to challenge it. Denouncing the mayor's order as "the property of bleeding hearts and cop-haters," a coalition of opponents circulated petitions to put the issue to a vote. By the time of the disturbance in East New York, they had collected enough signatures to get a question about the board on the ballot in November, and the campaign over police review took off in earnest: the city's first explicit, pitched battle over race.

Neither the mayor nor most of his aides—young men focused on the big ideas of the day—had initially put much store by police oversight. Compared to cleaning up the ghetto, job-training programs or school reform, it was a minor matter—at best one small, first step in a broader campaign to rein in the bureaucracy. Still, by the time the city started unraveling that summer, Lindsay could see he needed some kind of high-profile civil rights initiative. His acculturation programs were stuck on the runway. Whatever faith black New Yorkers had once had in integration was rapidly giving way to alienation. Two years after the Harlem riot, black demands for police review had taken on a hard, angry edge, blocking any hope for other progress in race relations. The creation of a review board promised some immediate payoff: easing tensions between the police and the black community might help New York avoid a major riot that summer. But as much an anything, the initiative was a diversionary goodwill gesture. "It was a symbolic issue," aide Jay Kriegel said later, "but an important symbol. We had to show people we understood what was bothering them."

In fact, the mayor's board fell somewhat short of what most blacks were demanding. Instead of an all-civilian panel, his seven-member board included nearly as many policemen as civilians, and its powers were sharply limited. Members were to concern themselves only with minor rule infractions—not brutality or other illegal conduct by officers. The panel had no enforcement power and could make no changes—in the internal command structure, training, discipline and accountability—of the kind most experts agreed were necessary to make a dent in police abuse. At best, Lindsay's board might improve cops' manners and make the streets a little more civil—might, as one campaign flyer put it, "raise the morale of the slum dweller." Still, the mayor announced his initiative with all the righteous fanfare he could orchestrate, putting the full weight of his office behind the idea. Political consultant David Garth was brought in to promote it, and together he and the mayor set out to make the case that this was something the enlightened city had to do for the ghetto.

All of progressive New York immediately rallied behind the initiative. Both the *Times* and the *Post* heralded the executive order. So did the American Civil Liberties Union (ACLU), the Liberal Party, the Urban League, the Citizens' Union, the City Bar Association, the Anti-Defamation League and the Council of Protestant Churches. When it emerged that the city's police officers and their allies were going to spare nothing to stop the board, Garth organized a coalition called FAIR—Federation of Associations for an Impartial Review Board—and anyone who was anyone in liberal New York rushed to join: black and white, Republican and Democrat, white-shoe elite and ghetto grassroots. Like Lindsay, the Manhattan establishment was hugely relieved to find something it could do for the ghetto. Unlike acculturation or empowerment, police oversight was something the city could deliver. It seemed to require little political or financial capital, looked virtually risk-free and promised a big payoff in race relations. Right or wrong, the activists advocating police oversight had assumed the mantle of the movement—with all the moral power that implied—and liberal whites, keen to prove their racial virtue, could not imagine saying no to them. If activists worried more about police misconduct than about criminals or the roots of poverty—well, FAIR and others reasoned, that was their prerogative, and concerned whites should follow their lead. As for the resistance from the boroughs, liberals figured it would pass—or didn't matter much.

The *Daily News,* then the voice of the city's ethnics, kicked off the opposition effort. Patrolmen's Benevolent Association (PBA) activist John Cassese lost no time in declaring the mayor's executive order "improper, illegal and undesirable." Right-wing groups rallied to the policemen's side: the Conservative Party, the John Birch Society, even the American Nazi Party. But the campaign to collect signatures for a referendum also galvanized part of the city that hadn't known it was conservative on race: middle-class or working people, mostly from the boroughs, union members, shopkeepers and homeowners worried about crime. William Buckley was the opposition's best-known partisan, though its real leaders were Patrolman Cassese and PBA public relations man Norman Frank. By July, the PBA and the Conservative Party together had collected over 91,000 signatures to get a measure on the ballot, more than three times as many as they needed by law.

The conservative opposition drew on a potent mix of feeling. As the opponents' chief spokesman, Buckley made a broad-gauged, principled case that spoke to the larger issue of police-ghetto relations. Poor blacks, Buckley said, were bearing the brunt of the city's rising crime, and they welcomed a tough police presence. It was demagogues who made a cause out of alleged police brutality—a phony charge, Buckley maintained, useful for whipping up racial resentment, but certain to make life even less safe in the ghetto. With militant blacks like James Baldwin claiming that black crime was a form of social protest, something to be understood if not justified, Buckley bluntly told followers not to be cowed by this racial rhetoric. Do not think, he insisted, "that Negro crime is any less criminal." Black complaints about police, he argued provocatively, had less to do with justified grievance than a misguided defense of lawlessness and racial hostility—and whites who cared about poor blacks were making a big mistake to encourage this.

Other opponents, in the police force and elsewhere, made a more pragmatic case. For many officers, the issue came down to a stark question—as one put it, "Who's going to run the police in New York?" Cops felt that Lindsay was playing political football with their department, using it carelessly to make a gesture to angry blacks. Others worried that the extra scrutiny would tie their hands in dangerous situations, endangering them and the people they were trying to help. This argument didn't necessarily have a racial edge: one poll conducted in the months before the election suggested that blacks were more concerned than whites about good police protection. Still, "crime" and "law and order" were crystal-clear code words, and the obviously biased cast of many of the board's opponents only hardened black support for the board.

Once again, as in the mayoral campaign, Lindsay and his backers seized on the bigoted-sounding arguments of the opposition to rally liberal New York behind their cause. Lindsay was thrilled when the John Birch Society came out against the panel. He didn't bother to refute the Birchers' arguments, simply denounced them as "terrible, infamous, hostile to everything I think decent." As the opposition gathered steam—and signatures—the ACLU accused Patrolman Cassese of "injecting a thinly veiled racism" into the debate. Lindsay complained that "highly organized, militant, right-wing groups [were creating] an inflammatory situation" in the city. The mayor was not wrong: the opposition did include some virulent racists. But already in 1966, the charge of bigotry had a McCarthyite edge to it: once you found someone "racist," you no longer had to argue with him. The more serious arguments against the board put forward by Buckley and the police force went unanswered. Instead of thinking through the problem or judging the mayor's proposal on its merits, liberal New York mobilized against racism—and the real question of how to improve ghetto-police relations got lost in the shuffle.

Meanwhile, Lindsay's dismissal of the PBA's claims rankled many ordinary citizens who weren't sure where they stood on the issue and wanted to hear some more substantive debate. Manhattan businessman and writer Roger Starr became a spokesman for this group, confused at first but growing ever more resentful. "The suggestion that anyone who opposed the board was per se a bigot," Starr wrote, "affronted those New Yorkers who considered themselves free of bigotry and who were nevertheless afraid in the streets." Many who might have been open to argument were annoyed by the mayor's contemptuous attitude, and their initial opposition only grew more entrenched.

As the summer wore on, the board's backers saw they had miscalculated, but instead of shifting strategy they became more combative. The idealism drained out of their campaign speeches; arguments grew more and more defensive. Finally, when they could think of nothing else, the liberals tried scare tactics. One morning in July, John Cassese and Norman Frank came to Gracie Mansion for breakfast with the mayor. "I told them," Lindsay reported later, "that if anything happened in New York—if there was a blow-up—they would be responsible." By now, both sides were talking past each other. Instead of addressing the issues, both played shamelessly on white racial fears, whether of crime or riots hardly mattered. And no one from the mayor's office went out to the boroughs to make a case that people there could hear: to listen to their concerns or win their confidence or inspire them to empathy with people on the other side of the color line.

By the end of the summer, the campaign conceived as a way to encourage trust was mostly stirring up paranoia and prejudice. "Why do you always kowtow to the coloreds?" one woman in Flatbush yelled at Lindsay. Even traditionally liberal members of an Upper West Side synagogue wanted to know why the mayor was always "doing so much" for blacks. The mayor's aides began to sense how poorly Lindsay's manner was playing among white ethnics, and they stopped bothering to campaign in the boroughs, concentrating instead on registering votes in the ghetto. More and more, both they and their black allies made the case in starkly racial terms. "The arguments against the board are shorn of their sophistry in Harlem," said black state senator Basil Paterson. "We in the ghettos have heard it before. . . . 'If you're black, get back.'" By now, thanks to the polarizing campaign, few people on either side were voting on the issue—simply for "us" against "them."

The odds grew longer and longer as election day approached. The press sensed the way the city was leaning and called the coming rout as plainly as they saw it. Journalists began to ask why Lindsay had risked so much for what was after all a largely symbolic issue—a telling gesture perhaps, but one unlikely to bring much change in the ghetto or accelerate integration. Lindsay, zealous as ever, soldiered on. The mayoral walking tours became high-profile, orchestrated events. He took at least one a day, sometimes several. In early fall, he started out at about 5:00 P.M. In mid-October, he shifted the schedule and left the office at three o'clock, often staying out until midnight and giving as many as five or six speeches in different neighborhoods. Aides noticed that now, as before, he seemed happiest on these walking tours, but they also worried that he seemed obsessed and was neglecting other, pressing city business. Even in the ghetto, aide Woody Klein felt, the mayor seemed to put more store by the board than the citizens who stopped to hear him. For his part, Lindsay was convinced the walks were working. "I can tell they are responding," he said, "I can see it in their eyes."

The only surprising thing about the vote was the margin: 63 to 36 percent in favor of abolishing the board—a crushing defeat. Of the city's five boroughs, only Manhattan voted for it; all the others went overwhelmingly against. Roman Catholic voters, many but hardly all related to policemen, came out 5 to 1 in opposition to the panel. Jewish New Yorkers joined them by a margin of 55 to 40 percent. (The Jewish vote was divided along class lines, with educated professionals going one way and poorer, working Jews another—squarely with the PBA.) Black and Puerto Rican neighborhoods were for the board, as expected, but the turnout there, unlike in the boroughs, was dismally low. "They just hadn't registered," said Garth, still disappointed many years later.

Conventional wisdom quickly tagged the vote as a defeat for civil rights: the first time in the sixties voters anywhere in the nation had explicitly rejected a black demand. The mayor, righteous as ever, scornfully dismissed those who had voted against the board. Asked if the vote had hurt his credibility, he replied that he didn't know and didn't care. "I would regard that as irrelevant in any case. The important thing is that we did what we thought was right. It was worth fighting for, even though we lost." By the time the postmortems were written, the stereotypes of the campaign had hardened into received truth: that the whites of the outer boroughs were hopelessly racist—and that any improvement in the city's racial climate would mean overriding them.

It was not until some years later that anyone looked more carefully at what the vote had signified. A team of social scientists, working at Harvard University in 1969, tried to correlate the outcome with a survey of attitudes in a middle-class white neighborhood in Brooklyn. Edward Rogowsky, Louis Gold and David Abbott found, as they expected, that "on balance, race was the most significant factor" in the way people voted. But unlike those partisans who felt that anyone against the panel was an outright bigot, these pollsters found that Brooklynites—even those who rejected the board—held strikingly ambivalent views on many race issues. Three-quarters of the Brooklyn respondents said they would not mind a black family in their neighborhood; 85 percent believed that "Negroes learn as well as whites." Given the way the boroughs had been pilloried, these were startling numbers, even allowing for people's reluctance to reveal their prejudice to strangers. The rejection of the review board had not, the Harvard team found, been evidence that most white New Yorkers were inherently "racist."

What the vote did signal was a complex set of misunderstandings, which with some leadership the city might have bridged. In 1966, most whites had no idea what blacks suffered at the hands of policemen. Then, as for decades later, even as they argued about the issue, neither black nor white understood what the other side was talking about: whites simply could not comprehend blacks' fear and resentment of blue uniforms, and blacks could not understand why whites did not get it or seem to care. Beyond that, by 1966, many whites were truly frightened by the city's growing crime rate—and, for all the code words, they did not have to be racists to vote against a measure that seemed likely to put them at greater risk.

To the degree the Brooklyn voters were driven by race, the Harvard pollsters found, it had less to do with color per se than with racial politics. More than anything, the whites surveyed were scared by the anger that was surfacing in the black movement: by the riots in Harlem and East New York, by the protests for protest's sake and the talk of separatism and violence. More than two-thirds of the Brooklyn sample felt the movement was "pushing too fast" and turning in a "generally violent" direction. Whether or not they liked blacks, and many probably did not, what they feared and resented most was the angry pressure. Rightly or wrongly, black complaints about the police department were seen as the property of a few extremists. And already, by 1966, it was easy for whites to blame the protest movement, citing its excesses as a rationale for resisting change—especially if they wanted to resist in any case. To those who were racist and many who were not, acrimonious color-coded demands had given whites an excuse to act their worst—to hunker down and block reform and vote as selfishly as they liked.

Rather than bridging this gap between black and white, the city's liberal leadership only made it worse. Both sides were to blame for the campaign's shrill fearmongering rhetoric, but Lindsay and his backers should have known better—and their cause suffered most. In order to win, in order to convince the city to try change, proponents of the board needed to go more slowly. Rather than blaming people in the boroughs, they needed to talk to them, reassuring frightened whites and appealing to their decency. Instead, to the people of Brooklyn and other boroughs, the mayor seemed to side reflexively with the ghetto, whether or not its demands made good policy. He made it look as if City Hall were going to choose between Brooklyn and Harlem—that blacks would get favors while white neighborhoods were short-changed. Because of his poor leadership, most whites never saw the board as a step toward justice or inclusion; they merely felt, according to the Harvard team, that they were being asked "to create special procedural guarantees for blacks and Puerto Ricans."

In the months after the election, Lindsay managed to establish another board, instituted without challenge from voters. Though staffed entirely by police employees, it had a powerful investigative arm and handled as many complaints each month as the civilian panel had. Still, to the city's blacks, it represented a stinging defeat. From Harlem's point of view, white New York had sent an unmistakable message. By more than two to one, the backlash vote had triumphed over the liberals, and the widespread bias that blacks suspected had been revealed for all to see. It wasn't important that many blacks had seemed indifferent to the review board, that most had not even bothered to come out to vote. What mattered was that the city had said, as Basil Paterson put it, "If you're black, get back." And like whites who used Black Power as an excuse to act their worst, many blacks felt their bitterness vindicated by the hostile message they heard.

The city would never be the same again. Well short of bigotry, the 1966 campaign showed, it was easier for black and white to misread than hear each other, easier to overreact than to listen and respond. Turn for turn, each side fed on the other's mistrust and resentment, and each bad experience paved the way for worse. From now on, all New York elections would be tinged with racial politics. People were no longer embarrassed to make color an issue, or to vote whatever racial prejudices they had. As for the rest of Lindsay's civil rights agenda—his ambitious plans for the school system, housing, job creation and the like—whatever chances it had once had were all but dashed now. The deeper problems of the ghetto had been buried by the symbolic police issue; the wisdom of the War on Poverty—that integration meant acculturation—was lost in the acrimony between black and white. Instead of fostering better race relations, the liberal establishment had fanned both black anger and white resentment, and New York was no closer than before to "solving" the problem of race.

Chapter 4

THE FIRE NEXT TIME

By spring 1967, by Lindsay aide Barry Gottehrer's own account, his special city "task force" had every street-corner speaker in Harlem on its payroll. Still trying to reach out to ghetto leaders, hoping to enlist their help in preventing another riot, Gottehrer did not bother with New York's black elected officials or old-guard civil rights pillars; he went directly to rising younger men—local nationalists, Black Power activists, wheeler-dealers, angry kids. He saw that his open invitation for "complaints" was attracting all manner of troublemakers. He also knew there would be criticism that the city was paying off militants and criminals. Still, with another hot summer looming, the Lindsay team did not feel it could afford to be choosy, and it was willing to remunerate activists for what it billed as intelligence and "liaison" work.

Just thirty years old, Gottehrer was a former city reporter with a passion for the nitty-gritty of the ghetto. Ivy League–educated, settled with a wife in suburban Scarsdale, before he came to work as the mayor's all-purpose troubleshooter he had had only one black friend. His immersion in ghetto life began gradually, handling the occasional crisis in Harlem or Brooklyn. But by June 1967, he was spending most of his time uptown, desperately trying to make contact with people he felt were likely to take part in a riot. Eschewing suit and tie, all but abandoning his marriage, he spent the summer crisscrossing the city in a battered car: from Brooklyn high school to Harlem bar, out to Rikers Island to visit a jailed informant, then up to the South

Bronx to meet someone on a street corner. He laughed at the idea of a work-day; he was on call around the clock. His marriage crumbled; other friend-ships slid; his ghetto contacts became all-consuming; and before long, he was talking about moving permanently to Harlem.

His task force coordinated a wide range of activities: everything from play streets and jazzmobile concerts to emergency negotiations with militants. The busiest part of the operation was the hot line into City Hall. Some days Gottehrer felt he got wind of every rumor in Harlem. According to Lindsay, over the course of the summer, there were more than one thousand official complaints, as well as countless unofficial late-night calls and other casual tips. Some were old-fashioned gripes about city services, others false alarms about teenage brawls and family quarrels. Occasionally, callers provided the kind of intelligence Gottehrer was looking for—word about a protest action or other incident that might turn into a riot. Meanwhile, the mayor's aide was also cultivating restless youth in Harlem and Brooklyn, paying them as much as $75 a week to run street sports programs and clean up abandoned lots. But the most important part of the outreach effort, the part Gottehrer put most store by, was his search for "potential leaders"—the men likely to start or in some way control a street rebellion.

The police department provided lists of men reputed to have followers, and Gottehrer went out, usually alone, to track them down. He made cold calls, followed faint leads and met with whoever would see him—no matter where, no matter when. He found what would become one of his best con-tacts in a place called the Glamour Inn, a seedy one-room lounge on 127th Street, frequented mostly by gamblers and pimps. The air conditioning didn't work; the upholstery in the booths was cracked and fraying. Some reg-ulars sported old-style hustler outfits—platform shoes and lamé shirts; the more up-to-date preferred dashikis and then still eye-stopping Afro haircuts. Gottehrer immediately fell in love with the place—with the air of shabbiness and danger—and he was soon spending as many as four nights of his week there, trying earnestly to convince regulars that rioting "would hurt the poor far more than the rich."

Before long, he had more contacts than he could handle and the prob-lem became weeding through them: deciding whom he could trust and whom he couldn't, who could really do something in the ghetto. Some of the hustlers were more obvious than others. During one particularly hot spell, an anonymous telephoner requested $500,000 from the city for seed-ing the clouds above Harlem with rain. (Nothing did more than a rainstorm to defuse a riot, dousing the swirling rumors and restlessness of a hot city night.) Still another caller wanted several million dollars to install air conditioning in the city's tenements. Gottehrer laughed and told himself he was getting to know the community. He was more disappointed by the ghetto's big-name spokesmen, whom he took to calling "power brokers" and "poverty pimps." His growing skepticism about their leadership was confirmed at a meeting in early June. He had arranged for CORE chief Floyd McKissick, Manhattan borough president Percy Sutton and a handful of others to come to Gracie Mansion and brief the mayor on the mood uptown. After an hour or so of speeches and appeals for money, Lindsay tried to slip quietly out of the room. He stopped in his tracks when several men got up and threatened citywide riots if he left before they had a chance to talk. More and more, as he explored the ghetto, Gottehrer felt that the big-time leaders were out of touch or, worse, playing their own self-serving game, pressing for riots as an "expression of racial unity" from the safety of a well-guarded downtown office.

Still, as the summer wore on, the mayor's young aide felt he was making progress. His biggest find at the Glamour Inn was a much-feared local militant known as Allah. A small-time hustler, then a Muslim, by now head of his own nationalist group called the Five Percenters, he was, Lindsay would later say, "the Al Sharpton of his day." According to the police, Allah's group had no more than a few hundred members. They weren't particularly sophisticated politically: their creed combined a bit of Islam with a ganglike esprit de corps. But they had reportedly played an important role in the 1964 Harlem riot, leading some of the worst pitched battles with police. Another of Gottehrer's mainstays went by the name of Kenyatta. His group, the Harlem Mau Mau, was even smaller—perhaps ten members—but Kenyatta had acquired a media following when he appeared on the evening news and threatened to lead a mob down Park Avenue. His friendship with Gottehrer also drew a good deal of press attention, perhaps because of the way he dressed—in military buff and pith helmet, carrying a long machete.

Even in 1967, radicalized as black America was becoming, it was hard to imagine that these men represented Harlem—the churchgoing ladies, the middle class or the silent majority of hardworking people. Still, Gottehrer's instincts told him, they were the people he had to get to know. The mayor's aide grasped that many of the young people likely to take part in a riot were motivated less by ideology than alienation—sheer despair and personal hopelessness. Restless, frustrated, at loose ends, they were as interested in getting a little attention as in making a political statement. "There were lots of kids with nothing to do," Gottehrer said later. "They were not organized. But anyone who wanted to lead a parade could run in front of them with a sign." Many of these self-styled spokesmen were demagogues: big talkers, with little or no following, their reputations made by a sensationalist press. But Gottehrer had seen for himself how much trouble they could cause. "They would stand on a soap box or go on TV," he explained, "and say black babies were being murdered," emboldening youths to loot and burn and needlessly provoke police.

Like many concerned whites, Gottehrer and his boss were still confused by what they had seen of ghetto riots. What were they about exactly? How much was targeted protest, how much sheer frustration and unappeasable rage? The Lindsay team didn't know, but when pressed, they fell back on their own conventional political assumptions: deciding that riots were a kind of focused rebellion, that they were meant to express specific gripes about ghetto conditions—and that they could be prevented if the city addressed those legitimate demands. Gottehrer's outreach effort was based on the theory that if people groused, they would not riot, and that government could deliver the kinds of change that would ease black alienation. It did not occur to either him or Lindsay that the anger went deeper than any problems they could address—that much of the leadership in the ghetto might be beyond reasoning, beyond negotiation or even pragmatic goals.

In spring 1967, less than a year after Stokely Carmichael's "Black Power" speech, the protest movement of the early sixties seemed a distant memory. Activists' clothes, their talk, their image, their very body language had changed completely. The word "Negro" was virtually dead, so was the phrase "civil rights" and the idea of a multiracial crusade. King's last push for integration—his Chicago campaign for open housing—had been interrupted by rioting and ended in a disastrous melee: white bigots throwing bricks and bottles at columns of black and white marchers. Fanned by this and other resistance, the idea of Black Power swept through the cities. Young militants shouted down their elders; age-old ideals were trampled underfoot. "A black man today," one activist told a reporter, "is either a radical or an Uncle Tom." Both CORE and SNCC went through a rapid turnover that year: the rise of a new generation inspired by Malcolm X. In addition to Black Power, talk now centered on "community control" and the idea of a black "identity." "What the Negro wants is total equality," Floyd McKissick declared.

"And that does not mean integration all the time. He wants his self-identity, he wants his culture."

The old movement, with its rational leaders and targeted demands, was desperately on the defensive. This was nowhere clearer than at the NAACP, still the largest and richest of the Big Six groups. Presiding over the organization's yearly meeting in July 1966, Roy Wilkins and Hubert H. Humphrey had pleaded passionately with middle-class delegates to keep their eyes fixed on integration. Black Power, Humphrey said, was just another word for black racism—"the father," Wilkins added, "of hatred and the mother of violence." Eloquent as he was, Wilkins looked old and tired, and many in his organization were no longer listening. "What we need is a few more riots," the head of the Philadelphia NAACP chapter told the press. "I'm in full accord with Black Power. You name me a Negro who isn't anti-white. This damn moderation will make the bigots bolder." Even whites who had never heard of the NAACP two years before could sense that it was now the struggling rearguard of the movement.

CORE's annual convention, held the same week, bristled with the same kind of unappeasable bitterness. Martin Luther King had originally been scheduled as the main speaker, but he canceled at the last minute, and Stokely Carmichael was invited in his stead. The SNCC chief was fresh from Mississippi, the talk of black America, and his charismatic presence electrified the meeting. On the podium, he picked up right where he had left off in Greenwood: "We don't need white liberals," he thundered. "We have to make integration irrelevant." Floyd McKissick brandished the same nationalist banner. "I don't want to be a white man," he shouted. Speaker after speaker attacked middle-class black "sell-outs." Carmichael talked reverentially of the martyred Malcolm X, and the still-orthodox Muslim minister Lonnie X—surrounded by a phalanx of uniformed Fruit of Islam guards—addressed an overflow audience.

Even as the slogan swept through the ghetto, an overnight household phrase, no one was exactly sure just what "Black Power" meant. At SNCC, the youngest and most militant of the national movement groups, it began with the exclusion of whites from the movement and already pointed in the direction of guerrilla warfare. CORE was still a more diverse body, and even as members tried out the new phrase, they quarreled about its meaning. Some said they would be satisfied with "self-determination": black control of schools, cops, courts and businesses in northern ghettos. Still others, a small, now besieged faction of moderates, said Black Power should mean black political power and the building up of a black business class. James Farmer pleaded with delegates to imagine how frightening the new demand would sound to many whites. "We are not anti-white," he insisted, "this is not a racist organization." Still, even he could not resist the new mood. "If I am against Black Power," he said, "I would be against myself."

To the degree the new shibboleth had an agreed-upon definition, it was largely negative—the end of integrationism. "What Black Power is all about," rising New York CORE activist Roy Innis explained, "is that we have to demand that we be accepted for what we are, and insist that we don't conform or blend with the rest of society." For him, the new creed was an answer to movement old-timers who "wanted to break down the barriers one by one, and then finally people would intermarry and that would solve the racial problems. . . . They had found the solution all right, the 'ultimate solution'— just like Hitler. Hell, they were talking about my genetic destruction." The CORE convention adjourned without settling on a definition, but members formally adopted the Black Power slogan and rescinded their commitment to nonviolence. That "dying philosophy," McKissick said, could no longer "be sold to the black people. . . . You can't have white people who practice violence and expect black people to remain passive."

Without a clearer goal or coherent philosophy, many movement activists found themselves at a loss for what to do. Unlike the SCLC ministers who had organized the rural South in the early sixties, spurring people into the streets to demand desegregation and voting rights, the SNCC workers who now traveled the same areas had little to propose—little but racial bitterness and revulsion for the system. SNCC organizers focused increasingly on the cities, but there too they seemed to have few concrete aims and devoted themselves mainly to getting media attention and spreading the Black Power slogan. In part, this lack of focus was inevitable—a product of history and welcome change. In many cities, the government had taken over traditional movement concerns: voter registration, monitoring employment practices, improving ghetto education, even community organizing. Legal parity had been achieved, and there was no obvious way for even the most constructive activists to attack the social and economic problems many blacks faced. "There are no longer available major issues," one CORE member explained, "around which communities can be organized." Yet the rise of Black Power only aggravated the aimlessness. "I agree with you about the importance of pride in being black," Bayard Rustin chastised some younger men, "but being black is not a program."

The feelings of the black silent majority were as hard as ever to gauge. Back in mid-1966, forty-eight leading black clergymen had issued a statement against Black Power; some weeks later, another hundred ministers met in Chicago and signed a similar document. A *Newsweek* poll suggested that the black rank-and-file was less taken with Black Power than their leaders were: about a third of the spokesmen approved of Carmichael and McKissick, for example, compared to merely 20 percent of the community at large—both figures dwarfed by King's resounding 85 percent approval rating. Still, as the months wore on, it became harder and harder to ignore the news from the street. "Burn, baby, burn!" and "Kill Whitey!": the slogans spoke louder than any reassuring pollsters' figures. Then, in the early fall, new survey data showed that a third of the black community felt the riots of the summer before had helped more than they hurt—and many fearful whites wondered if even this figure wasn't low. Even remote white newspaper readers could see that the movement's aging, middle-class spokesmen were no match for the dashing and dangerous Carmichael. More ominously still, every time a new leader emerged from the ghetto—and the turnover was getting faster all the time—he was angrier and more outspoken than those who had come before.

By fall 1966, most whites grasped that the movement had been captured by radicals, and many, across the spectrum, turned away in disappointment. Already, several weeks before the November elections, the press predicted a severe backlash. President Johnson held a news conference pleading with people not to vote their racial fears, but it seemed to have little effect. Across the country, thirty to thirty-five identifiably liberal congressmen lost their seats to more conservative candidates. Republicans gained eight statehouses and three Senate seats. The strongest antiblack vote was still in the South: Lester Maddox took over as governor of Georgia, and George Wallace's wife Lurleen won handily in Alabama, positioning her husband to make another run for the presidency. But the frightened white reaction was not confined to the old Confederacy. In California, badly shaken by the riots in Watts and at Berkeley, Ronald Reagan was elected governor by a margin of more than a million votes. On the same ballot, in another color-coded referendum, Los Angeles declined to build a badly needed hospital in the ashes of the neighborhood that had once been Watts. Then, in early 1967, an overwhelming majority of newly elected congressmen went on record against passage of another civil rights bill.

Repelled by the bitterness sweeping over the movement, even the staunchest liberals seemed to lose interest. Several of CORE's prominent white donors quit in anguished protest after the 1966 convention. SNCC, King's SCLC and the NAACP reported that giving was down by as much as 50 percent, and all three organizations were forced to slash their staffs. In mid-autumn 1966, a survey of campus political activity found a dramatic drop in student interest in civil rights: what had been *the* cause the year before was no longer attracting followers, and many who had participated were now turning away. "Students don't see what role they can play in the South and in civil rights," said one young man who had spent the summer before in Mississippi, "since Snick made it clear they don't want white students working in the black community." By the end of 1966, there were four hundred thousand American ground troops in Asia, and liberals disappointed by the movement were turning en masse to a new cause, opposition to the war. Not yet four years old, the era of racial goodwill was all but over.

B y the start of 1967, the growing discontent was getting scary. Harlem in 1964, Watts in 1965, twenty-one different cities in 1966: the riot season had grown more damaging with every passing year. In early 1967, Martin Luther King said what everyone feared: that the new year would bring worse. As the days would surely get longer, as the heat and humidity would mount, so too, inexorably, the hot nights would bring violence. The question was not if, but rather where and when exactly: how many, how bad, how much warning and—the bottom line—could the conflagration be contained?

In Washington, New York and other cities, politicians wondered what to do. The debate had an anguished yet weary edge: people were desperate to contain the explosion, but also dogged by a sense of impotence and, as spring wore on, increasingly irritable. Martin Luther King, Robert Kennedy, LBJ, Congress—all talked almost matter-of-factly through April and May of the disturbances to come. Recriminations flew back and forth between Democrats and Republicans, administration and Congress, within the movement and between black and white. The president requested $75 million from Congress for job-training and recreation programs: diversionary field trips, playgrounds and sports leagues. The appropriation passed easily enough, but no one imagined it solved anything. Movement leaders scored the government for doing too little too late. King and Wilkins complained bitterly about "the long, cold winter" past when few measures were taken to meet the fundamental needs of the ghetto. Liberals, in Congress and out, compared Johnson's $75 million to the $2 billion a month the nation was now spending in Vietnam.

The unstated argument implicit in all these reproaches was that the rioting could be stopped—if only the nation would move to heal the ghetto. The nation's mayors talked wistfully about wholesale solutions when they gathered in Honolulu in June for their annual conference. "[We thought] integration was going to bring a lot of trouble," said Mayor Glenn Hearn of Huntsville, Alabama. "But our experience has been that when you're integrated, there is no trouble." Johnson's critics, including Lindsay and Bayard Rustin, came up with a blueprint for the fundamental change they claimed was necessary to avert violence—not just desegregation but long-term acculturation. Still, even as they made the request, no one imagined that much funding would be forthcoming. The price tag was startling—$100 to $185 billion. Even sympathetic liberals found the proposed programs troublingly vague, and by now, two years into the War on Poverty, many wondered if the government knew how to jump-start blacks' entry into the mainstream. It was a watershed debate, but mostly the two sides talked past each other, and neither seemed to have come to terms with how long it would take—probably a generation, if not more—for acculturation to bear fruit in a way that might ease the discontent in the ghetto.

With large-scale change ruled out, instead, as spring wore on, both black and white turned to stopgap measures. At once angry and worried, King spoke of organizing the dissatisfaction in the ghetto, channeling it into peaceful demonstrations instead of arson and looting. Even coming from King, the idea sounded far-fetched. If it hadn't worked in Harlem three years ago, why should it work now, in a nation ten times angrier and twenty times more polarized? The far right drew up police contingency plans and took advantage of the occasion to score the left. (FBI chief J. Edgar Hoover, already working to discredit King with COINTELPRO surveillance, accused him of fomenting trouble in the cities—issuing, Hoover said, an "open invitation" to ghetto youth.) LBJ, reduced to symbolic gestures, appointed Thurgood Marshall to the Supreme Court. Other white politicians ducked for cover, positioning themselves to avoid too much blame, even as they watched the fuse burn down. What everyone recognized, but no one could admit, was that although they saw the outbursts coming, they had no idea what to do.

Outside of Washington, the temperature rose and the rhetoric grew wilder. By now, Stokely Carmichael and others were talking without restraint about violence. "It is time to let whites know," Carmichael said in early summer, "we are going to take over. If they don't like it, we will stamp them out." In May, he was replaced at the helm of SNCC by the still more embittered and sullen H. Rap Brown. That same month, a seven-month-old self-defense organization called the Black Panthers carried loaded weapons onto the floor of the California state legislature. Still more obscure and even more bewildering were smaller groups like Ron Karenga's US, based in Watts: members wore African tribal regalia and organized their children in paramilitary drills. Perhaps the most threatening, with fear of riots spiraling, was the Revolutionary Action Movement (RAM), which was said to have laid out detailed plans for armed insurrections in several cities.

In New York, the Lindsay team dug in for another summer. By now, after eighteen months in office, the mayor had established his bona fides in the ghetto but still had accomplished relatively little in the way of concrete change. His walking tours remained popular. He had gone to some length to recruit black city officials. He was making a particular effort to attract more minority cops, and outreach efforts had brought him in touch with a new generation of black leaders: not just the ministers and NAACP officials who had worked with previous mayors, but tough race men and grassroots activists. In the bitter climate of the mid-sixties, even this—the simple contact—seemed an achievement. But the more fundamental changes Lindsay had promised were still just that, promises. There were plans for thousands of new housing units, plans for a sweeping reorganization of the school system, plans for more jobs programs—all awaiting money and the ever more elusive support of middle-class white New Yorkers.

Conservatives and other critics were more skeptical than ever. Men like William F. Buckley and businessman Roger Starr persisted in warning New Yorkers about the limits of what government could do. Critical columnists noted how the mayor was alienating the white middle class—yet still not delivering much of substance to the ghetto. Even Lindsay's own team was careful not to overstate the case. "Sure," aide Jay Kriegel told a reporter, "opening up a few more play streets and getting the sanitation department into a ghetto neighborhood is not in the same league as new housing and schools and jobs. He knows that."

Both the mayor and his aides still maintained they were on the path toward a "solution" for the ghetto. Unlike many officials in Washington and other cities, Lindsay refused to give in to fatalism about race. Asked if New York was proving ungovernable, he insisted, "No, I don't believe so. I think that human ingenuity today, plus the resources of this great, powerful country can be brought to bear to solve any problem that we have in any city." Still, as he rushed around putting out fires, it was hard not to feel that his goals had shrunk—from a large, idealistic vision of inclusion to sheer damage control. Whatever promises he held out, already by 1967, the most liberal city in the nation had no real racial agenda except to contain the anger in the ghetto. And now, as another menacing summer approached, the Lindsay team too began to panic.

The ever necessary appeal for money took on a new edge, based less on the social contract than the looming threat of riot damage. "Last summer," Lindsay told one group, "New York was one of the few large cities to pass the summer without significant racial disturbances. This summer we may not be as fortunate. . . . We do know that the teenagers of the slums are angrier than their elders, and they have much less to lose in the midst of a mob." He ended the speech with a plea to the private sector to develop nine thousand summer jobs, to pay for play streets, portable swimming pools, sports equipment and theatrical props—more stopgap measures. It was not a pitch that went down well in the boroughs; as people there saw things, the mayor was participating in a shakedown—raising payoff money for militants and criminals. But the Manhattan establishment came through again: $100,000 here, five play streets there, jobs for one hundred youth. Robert Kennedy did even better in raising funds for his Bedford-Stuyvesant Restoration Corporation, a community development project in poor, black Brooklyn. Add that and federal riot prevention aid, and by the end of the summer, New York had spent $49 million in its black enclaves. Some of it, like Kennedy's investment in minority businesses, promised to have a relatively enduring effect. How much difference the rest would make was anybody's guess.

The mayor, ever upbeat, stepped up his ghetto walking schedule, often with philanthropists and other businessmen in tow. The diversionary recreation programs were ready right on schedule on the Fourth of July: more hydrant sprinklers, more block parties, basketball tourneys, a jazzmobile and movies. The police department was enlisted to help: one plainclothesman in each of the city's seventy-nine precincts. Like the mayor on his walking tours, these cops hung out with local kids, played cards and checkers with them and listened to their gripes. Lindsay defended all of these programs in appealingly integrationist terms. The important thing, he told aides, was "to get to" ghetto kids, not so much to convince them of anything but simply to reach out to them—to give them a sense that they too had a stake in the city. In the long run—the very long run—his outreach strategy might have helped, particularly if the city had combined it with more substantive efforts to spur integration. The problem in 1967 was that there was no time for long-run strategies—and even integrationists like Roy Wilkins mocked Lindsay's efforts as "lollipop programs."

Trouble started in earnest in early June: major outbreaks in the Roxbury section of Boston, in Tampa, Cincinnati, and Buffalo. In just about every city, the pattern was the same; an incident involving a white cop, a rapid swirl of rumors and within hours the black part of the city would be in flames. If indeed there were local leaders, they were rarely visible during a disturbance. As for proximate causes—ghetto problems white authorities could have addressed—they usually involved the police, but not even cities with the most enlightened departments seemed able to prevent those frictions. The difference now, compared to even a year or so before, was that the drill was much, much faster: muscles were tensed and readier for the spasm—and often the triggering touch seemed to come from outside. Even as the first violence erupted in June, boxer Muhammad Ali went to trial on charges of draft evasion. He had, as every admiring black child knew, refused to serve for reasons of conscience, noting, with a racial edge, "I ain't got no quarrel with the Vietcong." The draft board's case against him was perceived as pure persecution, and it added fresh fuel to the already smoldering rage in the ghetto. Outrage spread from city to city, and within days, there was a new round of rioting: Dayton, Des Moines, Kansas City, Philadelphia, Atlanta and Lansing.

In New York, with small disturbances flaring here and there in virtually every black neighborhood, the Lindsay team stepped up its efforts to reach out to local race men. Barry Gottehrer wooed the Five Percenters with a picnic and a bus trip to the beach. Lindsay took a group of kids for a joy ride in an airplane provided for the occasion by Eastern Airlines. The outing was seen as a great coup, more proof that the mayor's "caring" outreach worked. *The New York Times's* front-page story featured a photo taken inside the cabin: beaming Lindsay, in shirtsleeves, surrounded by smiling teenagers and cradling a queasy baby in his lap. "[These kids] now believe," Gottehrer boasted to the press, "that everyone—whites and blacks—should learn to live together in harmony, and that is precisely why we are working with them in every way to [help them] help themselves." Still, even as Lindsay reached out, he sensed that the problem was bigger than he knew. He watched apprehensively as other cities burned. He talked in private, to aides and others, about the danger posed by demagogues like H. Rap Brown. Ever upbeat and righteous, he never admitted publicly to any doubt. But it was becoming plain even to him that he was fiddling at the edges.

With violence spreading from coast to coast, the walking tours became much tenser. One evening in Brownsville, a leering youth taunted the mayor with a dead rat, swinging it by the tail menacingly close to Lindsay's face. The mayor nodded grimly and moved on his way. A few nights later on 135th Street, about five hundred kids were waiting at the YMCA, and by the time Lindsay arrived, militant strike leader Jesse Gray had whipped them into a nasty mood. The crowd blocked the entrance to the building, chanting, "We want jobs! We want jobs!" As the mayor made his way past, they began shoving and punching. Inside, Gray made clear that this was no idle request. Lindsay, he said, was "on notice to find 1000 jobs . . . by Monday." When the mayor left the building, he was followed by chanting youths. A few blocks down the street, with the mob growing behind him, he had no choice but to radio for his car. He climbed into the limo, grinning stiffly, as the youths surrounded the vehicle, pounding angrily on the roof and windows.

As the summer wore on and disorders multiplied, experts began to categorize them. A "minor" riot, according to the official taxonomy, meant only a few fires, lasted no more than one day and could be controlled by local cops. A "serious" disturbance was a little bigger but not as bad as a "major" riot. Those continued for more than two days—often as long as a week; they involved many fires, intensive looting, the use of guns and sizable crowds. By definition, they required federal troops or National Guardsmen to restore order. Already, in June 1967, the Harlem riot of three years before hardly counted as a significant disturbance. But even as white authorities measured and categorized, their local statistics seemed somehow beside the point. More and more, it was plain to all, the local outbursts were part of a swelling river—one large, national conflagration, feeding on itself, each outbreak spurring others as the violence spread from city to city.

In most places, there was no political organization behind the rampaging: no planning at all, not to mention cadres or conspirators. Riots were as spontaneous as basketball pickup games. They were rooted in deep popular feeling—an inchoate frustration that no one could have staged—and the larger public looking for conventional leadership was almost always disappointed. At the same time, local activists and—even more important—the national climate of opinion played a critical role in fanning the uprisings: making violence fashionable, fueling and occasionally dampening it. Though bottom-up and impromptu, the riots were focused and legitimized by a spreading culture of protest and the power of example—as seen on TV news. Whether or not rioters meant to send a message when they went out into the streets, their actions were viewed as part of the snowballing movement for Black Power. Flailing anger was perceived as a political gesture that provoked more of the same in the next city the next week.

Nationally, the momentum built steadily as the summer grew warmer and violent examples multiplied. In June, there were three upheavals that qualified as "major," three "serious" and ten "minor." July brought five major riots, twenty-two serious disorders and seventy-six minor ones—rhetoric spurring riot spurring more angry talk and then more violence in another city halfway across the country. The drama came to a climax in the last two weeks of the month—first Newark, then Detroit.

The uprising in Newark, New Jersey, began on Wednesday, July 12, with the reported beating of a cab driver by a policeman. Rumors spread, people gathered, several black leaders tried to disperse the crowd, to no avail. Eventually, state police and National Guard were called in and by most accounts battled the rioters with little restraint. For three days, off and on, uncontrollable youths swept through the streets, looting and setting fires over an area of ten square miles. Then for two more days, nearly five thousand law enforcement officers waged a deadly battle with elusive "snipers." In the end, the disturbance was smaller than Watts, but much more destructive. Twenty-three people were killed: one white cop, one white fireman and twenty-one blacks, including six women and two children. Police reported 250 fire alarms, 1,300 arrests and $10 million worth of property stolen or destroyed. Meanwhile, trouble—if not full-scale riots—spread out across black New Jersey: to New Brunswick, Englewood, Paterson, Elizabeth, Passaic and Plainfield.

On July 20, with violence still sputtering in the state, a thousand militants converged on Newark for the first National Conference on Black Power. Beseeched to convene elsewhere where their presence would be less of an incitement, Floyd McKissick defiantly asked what better place to consider how to "unify and empower black men than in Newark, the most recent symbol of the oppression of the black man?" Delegates covered the spectrum of black politics from James Farmer and SCLC minister Jesse Jackson to Ron Karenga and the Harlem Mau Mau. Farmer later remembered that a majority were packing guns. The only whites allowed were reporters, and they were publicly insulted, even manhandled; one journalist was actually thrown out of a window. Among the final resolutions: demands for a national guaranteed income and a "dialogue on the desirability of partitioning the United

States into two separate nations, one white and one black"—all delivered with explicit threats of bloodshed. "I love violence," H. Rap Brown cooed, urging followers to "wage guerrilla warfare on the honkie." "Everyone knows Whitey's a devil," Ron Karenga remarked. "The question is what to do about it." Even as the conference adjourned, a thousand miles away, black Detroit offered its desperate answer.

No one, white or black, who saw the television footage would ever forget it. The usual incident, an early morning police raid on a speakeasy, brought thousands of people into the street, some still in pajamas. That first day, it seemed almost jolly: looting was a kind of a kick, there was no one to stop you, it was all very liberating and carnival-like. The wind was brisk, fanning fires sparked by Molotov cocktails. Soon hundreds of houses were burning and several looters had been shot. At the end of the day, Governor George Romney flew over the area, still billowing with smoke, and reported that it looked as if it had been bombed. Night brought the curfew, and police roamed the empty streets, searching for invisible snipers. Monday morning brought another carefree looting spree.

It was only on the second night that the mood grew ugly. By then there were nearly 10,000 uniformed troops in town: 4,700 army paratroopers, 5,000 National Guardsmen and the police. Poorly trained, frightened, confused, they responded to the violence in the streets with even greater violence of their own. The city was eerily dark by night—many streetlights had been shot out—and soldiers roamed the sinister streets, gun barrels protruding from jeep windows. Heavy firing, from rifles and machine guns, broke out at the slightest pretext. Unverified reports of trouble could bring a marching row of troopers to surround a building and open fire on it. Just how many blacks were still fighting back at this point has never been established.

During the day, tanks patrolled the streets; choppers flew overhead. Squads of young white men in helmets strode around the ghetto, bayonets at the ready. Police searching for snipers broke into homes and tore them apart; of the four thousand people arrested, scores were brutally treated. Day and night, war-zone confusion reigned, and many innocent people were caught in the crossfire. In the end, all national riot records had been broken. After eight days, forty-three people were dead, twenty-eight of them reportedly at the hands of uniformed officers. The public, watching on TV and imagining the worst, was told that $500 million worth of damage had been done. It wasn't until months later that the true figures appeared—somewhere in the vicinity of $45 million.

Even as the fires spread through Motown, H. Rap Brown addressed a rally halfway across the country in the sleepy town of Cambridge, Maryland. The tall, sour-looking activist stood on the hood of a car and harangued three hundred excited youths. He began by glorifying the burning of Detroit and of Harlem and Newark before that. He extolled the killing of a white cop in New Jersey: "The brothers . . . stomped [him] to death. Good!" Then, when he felt his audience was ready, Brown turned his attention to Cambridge. "Get your guns," he shouted, "You gotta take over these stores." He pointed to a row of shabby buildings not far away. "Don't you see what your brothers in Detroit are doing? Now it's time for Cambridge to explode!" A few hours later, the black section of Cambridge looked exactly like smoldering Detroit. The fire leveled a school, a church, a motel, a tavern and the few stores where black townspeople had worked and shopped.

New York's first spasm of violence occurred on July 23, even as Detroit went up in flames. Concentrated for the most part in the Puerto Rican section of Harlem, it raged intermittently for several days. The police were under orders of maximum restraint: rather than battle the looters, they looked the other way as windows were smashed and merchandise removed. Though later much criticized by local shopkeepers, for better or worse, the strategy seemed to work. By midweek, some two dozen Third Avenue stores had been destroyed, but calm had been restored to the volatile neighborhood. From City Hall, Lindsay played down the incident. It was merely "a disturbance," he told reporters, "a demonstration, not a riot."

The next night, far more alarming to white New Yorkers, a band of 150 youths rampaged through midtown. It was one of the only incidents of its kind that summer: one of the few times that violence spilled out of the ghetto. The trouble started, ironically, at a city-sponsored concert in Central Park meant to distract and entertain ghetto kids. Smokey Robinson and the Miracles lured a large crowd down from Harlem. Several youths were annoyed that they were not allowed on stage with the musicians. They rallied others; an angry pack left the park and headed downtown just as Broadway was letting out, jostling theatergoers and pilfering several purses. The kids' destination was the Blye Shop, a small haberdashery store on Fifth Avenue; what they were after, it turned out, were Blye's $56 alpaca sweaters. By the end of the evening, seventeen youths had been arrested. The next day Lindsay toured the neighborhood, reassuring merchants but also scolding white New Yorkers, who he felt had overreacted. "People who woke up this morning were left with the impression that midtown Manhattan was ravaged," he complained. Once again, in his view, it seemed preferable to swallow a little trouble than to respond angrily and risk an all-out fight.

Meanwhile, Lindsay and Gottehrer persisted in their search for local leaders. Even more than Harlem, where by now Gottehrer had several contacts, black Brooklyn stretched, mysterious and confusing, an expanse of trouble waiting to happen. The Lindsay administration included several blacks from Brooklyn—most prominently, former activist Major Owens, commissioner of the city's community development agency. But with the summer growing ever hotter, the mayor felt he needed a different kind of connection, and he urged Gottehrer to reach out over the heads of his own men—to find some grassroots leaders he could work with.

By now, Sonny Carson was head of Brooklyn CORE. The chapter had dwindled over the years to only a shadow of its former self, but Carson traded on the name, still fearsome to many New Yorkers. He had no practical program for Brooklyn; if he had a grassroots following, it was unorganized. But his big Afro and bright dashikis had caught the attention of both blacks and whites, and the police unit that tracked militants put him "close to the top" of its short list of supposedly dangerous leaders. His background in the gangs of Bed-Stuy, in reform school and the adult underworld: all enhanced his reputation as a militant and a man who owed nothing to the white world. Committed to black secession and armed self-defense, he seemed to personify the fearless bravado of the Black Power movement, and he plainly thrilled to the violence sweeping through the nation's cities. "We didn't own nothing of our own in those communities," he said later. "We should have burned them all down. That was a good way to get the kind of attention we needed." By midsummer 1967, this alone was enough to make Carson popular in the ghetto—and compelling to whites trying to understand it.

Flamboyant and quotable, he began by attracting the attention of reporters, who turned to him for comment when things got hot in Brooklyn. This gave Carson a podium and an aura of leadership, soon noticed by liberals trying to communicate with poor, angry blacks. Robert Kennedy chose him to sit on the board of the Bedford-Stuyvesant Restoration Corporation, and this in turn attracted the Ford Foundation's interest. Asked why he was flirting with toughs like Carson, Kennedy replied impatiently, "These are the people we have to reach. Some people may not like it, but they are in the street and that is where the ball game is being played."

All of this made Carson exactly the kind of local leader Gottehrer was looking for. The mayor's aide had some initial doubts—about Carson's following and his character. The young man's intuition told him Carson was different from the other militants he had been cultivating that summer: harder, cannier, more scornful of the white world. Nor was Gottehrer sure he could trust the Brooklyn activist; he was convinced that Carson was "committed to change" in the ghetto, but he also found him manipulative, ever looking for a chance to make the mayor's men squirm a little. Brooklyn CORE was not a large organization; as far as Gottehrer knew, Carson commanded no more than eight or ten followers. The mayor's aide believed that Carson spoke for many more in ghetto Brooklyn, though just how many he had no idea.

Still, both Gottehrer and his boss felt obliged to take Carson seriously. If anything, his extreme positions had a kind of appeal for the mayor's team. By 1967, white liberals knew all about "Uncle Toms"—and the last thing they wanted was to make common cause with someone who spoke for no one. The Lindsay team could see that Carson "represented something in the community," and the very unrelenting and unappeasable quality of his resentment gave him an allure that eluded more reasonable spokesmen. He knew how to give a name to the formless anger of the kids hanging out on the corner. He made young toughs feel like racial heroes, justifying their violence as something strong and proud. Whether or not the press had helped create him, people seemed to listen when he talked. No one stood up to gainsay him, and the street kids obeyed his orders. Gottehrer wasn't sure what to make of this power; he didn't want to give it too much legitimacy. But even without understanding, he knew that Carson was "somebody we had to deal with."

The Lindsay team took pains to nurture its connection with the Brooklyn militant. The mayor paid a first, formal visit to the CORE office in Bed-Stuy. Several of Carson's followers received stipends to work in the play-street program, and Gottehrer had soon established a regular telephone relationship of a kind he had with several ghetto spokesmen that summer. "These guys would call on Friday," he remembered later, "and tell you that all hell was about to break loose. 'I'll be on the streets,' they'd say, 'doing all I can to stop it.' Then on Monday, they would call in again and say, 'God, it was close.' Sonny did it too. It was part of the game." Gottehrer was onto this hustle, but he didn't feel he had much choice. "If there were an incident," the mayor's aide explained, "Carson could make it worse. He could go on TV or on the radio and say that nine black kids had been mercilessly beaten by the police—and before you knew it, you'd have hundreds of people in the street." City Hall wasn't counting on Carson to stop a disturbance from turning into a riot. "I doubt he ever stopped anything," Gottehrer said. "But he didn't always inflame it."

The first close call in Bedford-Stuyvesant came toward the end of July, just as the National Guard was leaving Detroit. A handful of kids—nobody knew who or why exactly—had gone on a rampage just before dawn on the main shopping thoroughfare, Nostrand Avenue. One hurled a metal trash can through a plate-glass window; others liked the effect and began to imitate it up and down the street. There wasn't much looting, but by dawn nearly thirty big windows had been broken. Lindsay hurried out to the neighborhood and went straight to CORE's shabby second-floor office. About seventy-five people had gathered in anticipation of his visit. No one pretended these were the same people who had been out on the street the night before. Lindsay did not ask how or why they had taken it on themselves to speak for the community. Like the rioters in the street below, these "representatives" needed no mandate. It was understood by all that as long as they were standing up to the white man, few other blacks would question them or the importance of their being heard.

Carson opened the meeting. Though relatively short and physically unprepossessing, he had a presence that dominated the room. He hovered over the seated mayor, waving his finger menacingly in Lindsay's face. "The main reason for the small insurrection this morning," he said, "is because certain things have not been done." When he finished speaking, others in the room had their turn: a torrent of demands, some answerable, some simply bitter. Where were the checks for the antipoverty program? Where were the swimming pools Lindsay had promised? Why were there white policemen stationed in the neighborhood?

Lindsay waited for the barrage to subside. "We have a long way to go," he said earnestly. "A lot hasn't been done. I'm as worried as you are." He started to explain in some detail about the city's job-training program. He'd gotten out a sentence or two before Carson cut him off. "We're tired of waiting," the militant barked. "You should have started all this months ago." "Yeah! Yeah!" the room erupted, and before the mayor could go on, someone brought the conversation back to the morning's disturbance. "This was only a skirmish, and only that, because some brothers and sisters wanted to keep the community from burning." At that point Carson stepped forward again, wordlessly hushing the men around him. Neighborhood merchants have failed to provide jobs, he said, and now, "if [their stores] are burned, it won't be CORE's fault. . . . These kids are sore, they're angry and your training programs are obsolete. . . . We don't want [the neighborhood] burned down, but CORE won't stand in the way."

Ever upbeat, the mayor left the meeting convinced it had been useful: a confirmation of his view that the city had to do more in the ghetto—or face still more, bigger, less containable riots. He reiterated this message downtown in the next few days, and later that week again in Washington. No matter how many militants he met or how much anarchic looting and arson he witnessed, Lindsay persisted in his belief that the riots were a rational response to particular ghetto conditions—an awkward but still straightforward, answerable demand for better city services. If he heard Carson's truculence, he said nothing about it. Nor did he seem to notice that he and the militant were on different wavelengths: that no matter what he offered to fix or change, Carson interrupted him to say it was too little too late. Earnest, well-intentioned, worried about the city, Lindsay may simply have had too much at stake to see through the Brooklyn militant. But it did not seem to dawn on him that Carson might thrive on trouble—that if things were fixed and ghetto grievances eased, Carson might find himself with nothing to do. For his part, Carson could not have been more pleased by their encounter. "That was power," he said later. "That was the kind of power black people need." Plainly enough, the more menacingly he threatened Lindsay and Gottehrer, the more eager they were to mollify and appease him.

For the next few weeks, the last of the summer, Lindsay's visit to Brooklyn CORE seemed to be having the desired effect. His "discussions" with Carson appeared to have eased the anger in Bed-Stuy, dampening the street violence if not extinguishing it. Gottehrer, still spending all his time in the ghetto, was counting the days until September, when, he hoped, the autumn cool would bring an end to the riot season. Then, just before Labor Day, he received a call from Carson. "A white cop shot a black kid for no reason," the militant declared angrily. "This place is gonna burn."

Lindsay raced out to Brooklyn, where a knot of angry blacks had already gathered outside the Bed-Stuy precinct house. The cops and the militants glared threateningly at each other. "I have never seen a crowd in an uglier mood," Lindsay commented later. Gottehrer immediately regretted advising his boss to come out and confront Carson directly. "[The mayor's] presence tended to escalate the demands and to magnify the importance of all the issues," Gottehrer recalled. "We had tossed our ace out on the table before all the cards were dealt." But by now Lindsay and his aides had little choice or room to maneuver. They had spent over a year scouring the ghetto for someone like Carson, then they and the media had done everything they could think of to enhance his stature. Now they could hardly ignore the complaints they had solicited, no matter how reminiscent of a shakedown.

Lindsay and Carson met inside, in the backroom of the stationhouse. The mayor sat quietly for half an hour, listening to Carson and several followers vent what Lindsay later called "pure fury." They blamed him for the shooting; they complained about racist police. (In fact, it turned out later, the offending cop had been black, not white, and the youth he shot—inadvertently, he claimed—had been mugging someone.) Carson's lieutenants cursed and taunted the mayor with racial epithets, hinting menacingly about the crowd milling in the dusk outside. Lindsay, as usual, listened attentively. Then, when the men were done, he tried to call Carson's bluff. "Look," he said sternly, "you've got two choices. You can burn down the community or you can change it. Now, do you want to burn it down? Is that what you want to do?" Carson didn't answer—Lindsay hardly expected him to. But by the end of the meeting the activist had agreed to leave the precinct house with the mayor and help him urge the gathering crowds to "cool it."

Lindsay was thrilled by Carson's promise, convinced that at last he had gotten through. He had made a deal that might save the neighborhood; he had proved he could communicate across the racial divide. "[Those black men in Brooklyn] recognized that I was listening," he later wrote, "that I was not reading from a script or telling them what I thought they wanted to hear." Gottehrer was even more gratified: this was the scenario he had been preparing for all summer. Now the tough leader he had been cultivating so patiently would emerge from the shadows and help the city take control of the streets.

In fact, nothing came of the conversation in the Bed-Stuy precinct house. Carson and Lindsay came out of the building and announced their intention to walk the streets together, calming the crowd. But then Carson turned on his heel and strolled off into the night alone. No one in Bed-Stuy that evening recalled hearing him tell anyone to cool it. His own account of what happened—and of Lindsay's walks in general—could not have contrasted more sharply with the mayor's. The neighborhood, Carson wrote acidly, was "honored by the exciting presence of tall, blond John, sporting his blue television shirt and red tie, walking tall and majestically down the most protected main street, patting the woolly heads of the citizenry and remarking, 'We can work it out, we can work it out.' . . . Anybody with a little common sense knew that walking around The Community couldn't repair anything."

As it was, mayhem raged in the neighborhood, on and off, for four hot nights. There were Molotov cocktails, what Gottehrer called "a lot of gunfire," eleven injuries and five arrests. A year or two earlier, the incident would have been called a riot. Now, because of the way things had escalated, it was relegated to the back pages of the newspaper. Still, in Lindsay and Gottehrer's view, the evening at the stationhouse had been a success. Carson's tip that something was happening in the neighborhood had given their team a three-hour start in cordoning off the area and deploying police, and if they noticed the militant's duplicity, they did not seem particularly troubled by it. The important thing was the immediate outcome: there had been no major disturbance to ruin Lindsay's clean record, and neither he nor his aide seemed to have any regrets about what they had done to bolster Carson and the anger he stood for.

Nationally, the riots continued unabated through the summer until the heat and the fury that came with it were spent. By the time the worst was over, almost every town with a large black population had experienced some kind of disturbance; by one journalist's count, thirty-one cities had been ravaged. The human toll dwarfed that of summers past: 86 dead, 2,000 serious casualties, more than 11,000 arrested. Property damage ranged from under $100,000 in smaller cities to $10 million in Newark and $45 million in Detroit. The damage to the national psyche—and the idea of integration—was beyond measuring.

Most whites had no idea what to make of the uprisings, and the media coverage hardly helped. As Lindsay and other liberals liked to point out, TV news had exaggerated and sensationalized events. Viewers saw only the fiery violence, not the years of slum life behind it. Swashbuckling militants made good copy, and the press—print and broadcast—tended to dwell on them. It was often possible, on television, to mistake a minor incident for a big riot, and as a result many viewers imagined the mayhem to be worse than it actually was. Perhaps most misleading, watching white troops battle black youths, TV audiences were led to believe that the violence had been directed by blacks against whites, rather than, as was almost always the case, at their own miserable neighborhoods. To a degree, the media critics were right. Certainly, the picture drawn by the press had looked senseless: frenzied, random aggression, directed at no one in particular and, in virtually every case, hurting no one as much as the perpetrators themselves. What no one dared say as the smoke cleared in 1967 was that perhaps this picture was a largely accurate one—that the riots had made no sense at all and served no useful purpose.

The one thing that was clear as the violence subsided was that it had brought blacks and whites no closer together. By late summer 1967, much of white America was a backlash waiting to happen, and no one was surprised to see the hostile reaction forming even as the fires sputtered out. All but the most liberal politicians hastened to denounce the disturbances. Former president Dwight Eisenhower wrote the classic conservative attack: a bitter screed in *Reader's Digest.* California governor Ronald Reagan made front-page news calling the rioters "mad dogs against the people." For the already bigoted and those frightened by change, the disturbances became an occasion to vent pent-up hatreds—another excuse for their ugliest stereotypes. Georgia governor Lester Maddox described ghetto participants as "a bunch of savages, rapists and murderers." Student leader Tom Hayden, wandering in the streets of Newark, watched a crowd of whites urge National Guardsmen to "go kill them niggers!" The week between Newark and Detroit, Congress met to consider a bill that would grant money to the cities to help them eliminate slum rats. Making open mockery of a southern-born black man's slurred speech, members made punning reference to "anti-riot"—pronounced "anti-rat"—legislation and the "civil rats bill." One representative suggested that "the rat smart thing" would be "to vote down this rat bill rat now."

This and other calls for increased spending in the ghetto were spurned as rewards for violence, and the men behind the already languishing War on Poverty braced for a drastic cut in funds. "Congressmen who are elected by white middle-class voters are in real trouble with our programs," one insider said. "Their people are as mad as hell." Even the most open-minded, well-intentioned whites were at a loss to understand the blowups. The pictures on their television screens seemed utterly alien and terrifying. Mindless violence or targeted rebellion—it hardly mattered to most viewers. Few middle-class people could empathize with the fury. Fewer still could understand the rioters' wild sense of nothing-to-lose. "It's like laughing at a funeral," New Jersey governor Richard Hughes said after a predawn tour of the rubble that had been Newark. Who would burn down their own blocks and churches and schools? What possible good could come of the rampaging? Could black and white people really be so deeply different? Daniel Patrick Moynihan, not yet an elected official, caught the essence—and significance—of the common white reaction. "At a time," he commented, "when there is more evidence than ever about the need for integration, rioters are undermining the grounds for integration and letting all the whites say, 'Those monkeys, those savages, all Negroes are rioters. To hell with them.'"

In New York, there was no major riot that summer. By September, the city had weathered five minor disturbances—any one of which would have been called a riot in years past—but not 1967's culminating explosion, which many people had expected to come in Harlem. For Lindsay and his team, this was seen as a stunning coup, vindication of their liberalism, their vigilance, their ideas about race and police work. New Yorkers heaved a sigh of relief; other cities watched with awe and made plans to imitate Lindsay's strategy in the coming year. In the heat of the moment, no one wanted to probe too deeply—to talk about what wasn't being accomplished or ask about possible costs.

What had caused the violence, what role leadership had played, what the city could have done to avert it with structural changes or stopgap measures: none of this was any clearer now than it had been in early spring. It would be months before anyone, in New York or elsewhere, would begin to come to grips with the violence or what lay behind it. What was plain already as the leaves began to turn was the disastrous effect even in New York, where there had been little rioting. Lindsay's dreams of making integration a reality for the city's poorest blacks were not forgotten, but they might as well have been. There had been no progress in that direction, and if anything, the insights of the War on Poverty seemed to have gone disastrously askew. Instead of understanding that inclusion was a long, difficult process, one the government could perhaps spur but not guarantee, most of those who cared, both black and white, had clung to the mistaken idea it was something that could be produced on demand. When change did not materialize, when it emerged just how long it might take, impatient blacks had lashed out furiously—but by doing so, they only set back the cause.

What little money had been available for the ghetto that summer had been spent not on better schools or jobs or training, but on play streets—and police equipment. From now on, there would be much less money and less white goodwill. Worst of all, the idea of acculturation would be all but dropped from the nation's racial agenda. It was easy to blame activists like

Carson or H. Rap Brown—men who had no interest in integration in any case. But Lindsay, so earnestly committed to black inclusion, had played at least as big a part in slowing the process. He and his well-meaning aides had not just appeased the city's nihilistic militants; they had encouraged and legitimized and amplified these men, giving them a reach and power they could never have hoped to achieve on their own. Instead of bolstering a black leadership that could get things done, the mayor's team had fostered a class of professional grousers—people who derived their power and prestige from their readiness to badger white authority. Thanks to Carson and others like him, many blacks were only angrier than when the riots started—at the cops, "the Man" in general, the system Lindsay and others wanted to include them in. Meanwhile, most whites were only further put off by the black struggle, less sympathetic to blacks' problems and less inclined to help. Worse still, now that Lindsay and others like him opened the door, there would be more and more black spokesmen who would use it as Carson had—in an unending ritual of protest that would do nothing to close the gap between black and white.

Gottehrer had two more run-ins with Sonny Carson in 1967: more of the same, only worse. The first came just a few days after the August disturbance in Bed-Stuy. Even as the fires cooled and shopkeepers boarded up their windows, Carson invited the mayor's aide to what he promised would be a grassroots meeting—a chance, he said, to hear how neighborhood people saw the shooting that had prompted the violence and how they felt about the city's response. Gottehrer drove out to CORE headquarters on Nostrand Avenue, accompanied by three black policemen. As soon as he walked into the second-floor office, he knew he had fallen into a trap.

As usual, there were no neighborhood people present, only Carson and his men. But this time, they had gathered a roomful of reporters to witness their confrontation with white authority. Carson launched into his usual monologue, berating Gottehrer, Lindsay, the cops. The mayor's aide, ever mindful of the journalists, felt obliged to agree with Carson's indictment of the system and promise to try to make some of the changes he was demanding. Unwilling to argue publicly with a black spokesman or even state the facts of what had happened, Gottehrer watched passively as Carson tongue-lashed the three black cops and accused them of betraying their race. The militant leader and his men made no secret of their delight at the visitors' discomfort, and when Carson had finished, one of his tougher-looking lieutenants decided to make the newspapermen squirm a little, too. The activist got up abruptly, walked over to a photographer, picked up his camera from the chair next to him and smashed it violently to the floor. The journalist, terrified of a confrontation, looked away as if nothing had happened—and neither Gottehrer nor the humiliated cops moved to lift a finger. "The meeting simply went on," Gottehrer recalled later, still mortified by the position he had let Carson put him in.

It was exactly the effect Carson had been aiming for. "That's power," he said years later, "when *you* are in control of the situation. White people need to know what it feels like—what it's always felt like to be black." Never mind that the Lindsay team had come out to Brooklyn begging to be told what they could do to help, and that nothing had come of their meetings—nothing substantial for the people of Bed-Stuy. What mattered to Carson was the power of defiance, not the power to deliver or effect change. It did not occur to him even to follow up on his scattershot demands or to use his riot-hedged leverage to make sure that something constructive got done.

A few months later Carson called Gottehrer again, this time in the middle of the night, and demanded that the staffer come out "immediately" to meet with him in Brooklyn. Once again, the mayor's aide got in the car and made his way across the river, this time to the transient hotel where Carson had recently moved his headquarters. When Gottehrer arrived, he was kept waiting for nearly an hour, then admitted to a small, makeshift office. The urgent matter turned out to concern a group of Sunni Muslims who held services in a nearby brownstone. Some weeks before, the FBI had chased someone into the building and, not knowing it was a mosque, had neglected to take off their shoes. There was nothing Gottehrer could do now in the middle of the night, and probably not even in the morning. The "crisis" had been a pretext, he explained later. "Sonny was mainly interested in proving that he could pull Barry Gottehrer out of bed." The mayor's aide came away seething, but again absolutely powerless. For over a year, he had been bolstering the influence of men like Carson, and now he and his boss were prisoners of the game they had created. Gottehrer went home to Manhattan, but he knew this would not be the last call for a "meeting." Worse than that, he knew, invariably he would go—and in the name of all New Yorkers would submit to yet another round of racial threats.

Chapter 5

THE LAST GASP
OF LIBERALISM

From the beginning, Lindsay set the tone—both the style and the direction—for the Kerner Commission. It was in July 1967—the climax of the riot season—that Lyndon Johnson asked the mayor and ten other prominent men and women to form the blue-ribbon panel known officially as the National Advisory Commission on Civil Disorders. Together, they were the political mainstream personified: black and white, Republicans and Democrats, labor, business, a southern police chief and NAACP head Roy Wilkins. The president asked them to answer three questions about the riots: what happened, why, and what could be done to prevent it from happening again? As much as anything that had occurred in the nation's cities over the past few years, the Kerner Commission's findings would shape the legacy of the long, hot summers of the 1960s. Though chaired by staid and centrist Illinois governor Otto Kerner—President Johnson did not want any surprises—the panel's work would be anything but bland, thanks in large part to the galvanizing presence of the crusading mayor of New York.

Lindsay's leadership began, as ever, with his personal style. He would be the first in the room to take off his jacket and open his shirt—and within five minutes most of the others would have followed. The New Yorker was not only the body's official vice chair; his personal dynamism and high-profile expertise on urban issues made it all but inevitable that he would take charge. Much of the group's working method was his idea: the field trips, the outreach to black activists, the intense personal involvement of members at every stage of the process. Lindsay aides—Jay Kriegel, Barry Gottehrer and others—dominated the commission staff. Even the press releases were pure Lindsay: all righteous zeal and combative edge. The first, issued several months into the commission's research, warned the public and the president almost gleefully that the medicine would be bitter—the group's conclusions, as Lindsay put it, "abrasive."

Lindsay was among the panel's more liberal members, but few of the others were so far to his right that they could not be tugged in his direction. Centrist or liberal-leaning—in 1967, the political establishment didn't yet include full-blown conservatives—all were impressed by his evident self-assurance. Certainly, he seemed to be doing something right in New York, managing against all odds to stave off a major explosion. More important yet, at a time of great national confusion, he was holding fast to ideals that most others on the commission still found deeply attractive: that the problem *was* solvable, that the races could be brought together, that America could still live up to its promise of equality for all. "He was engrossed. He was passionate. He was the only one there trying to run a city," Kriegel remembered. "People listened and deferred to him."

The commission convened in Washington, D.C., even as the embers cooled in Detroit, and members got down to business with all the can-do confidence and problem-solving method that NASA brought in those years to putting a man on the moon. Determined to be thorough, the panel left no question unasked: not just what had caused the violence and what could be done to avert more, but also a host of subsidiary queries about black history, city government, the role played by the media, the police and organized crime. An impressive staff was assembled: nearly one hundred professionals from a variety of disciplines. Originally given a year to prepare its findings, the panel decided in advance to finish ahead of schedule—in time, members hoped, to have an impact on the summer of 1968.

The intense involvement of members began right away, at the research stage. Lindsay and Kriegel spent a day or two each week in Washington, and unlike many executive commissions, no principal missed a session without a good excuse. All eleven read extensively. "I began feeling as though I had checked out half the Library of Congress," Oklahoma senator Fred Harris later joked. Researchers pored over police blotters and census data, FBI records and newspaper reports. Data from each city was compiled on huge wall charts; riots were reenacted with the help of detailed maps.

Panelists visited eight cities; staff studied the disorders in twenty-three more. Together they questioned city brass, policemen, activists, shopkeepers, teachers and local kids—over twelve hundred people in all—and by the time they sat down to prepare their findings, staffers would claim they had consulted every relevant "expert" in the nation, including Stokely Carmichael and Ron Karenga. The larger white public might be reeling, bewildered by the violence and what it seemed to say about blacks. But the establishment commission, undaunted, was convinced that it could get to the bottom of things.

By the standards of 1967, the panel was anything but radical; in fact, it came under stinging attack by black activists and their peace movement allies, who wanted to know why it was manned by stodgy old-timers like Roy Wilkins and Otto Kerner instead of Stokely Carmichael, James Baldwin or student leader Tom Hayden. Still, centrist and mainstream as they were, all eleven shared Lindsay's sense of civic responsibility. As they saw things, their job was not just to explain the riots. Their mandate was to restore the community shattered by three summers of violence: to translate the cry from the ghetto, to prod the nation to respond, to mediate between black and white and pull America back together again. Frightened by the riots, but determined to absorb whatever lesson they taught, the panel saw itself as the conscience of the nation: the liberal establishment stepping forth to come to terms with the crisis and persuade the public to do the right thing by blacks.

It was an earnest and concerned response, a last gasp of sixties liberalism—and it embodied the assumptions of the generation that had made the civil rights revolution a reality. Johnson, Vice President Hubert Humphrey, Lindsay, Kerner Commission members Roy Wilkins and Congressman William McCulloch—all had been playing leading roles already in 1963 when the civil rights era began, with the watershed battle to pass the 1964 act. Now, as then, they did not agree completely on strategy, but together, they were still driven by the same shared vision. The ideal was still inclusion, the engine of change still the federal government. Perhaps most important, they were all still convinced that the black man's problems were the white man's problems too—that America was a single community and a single body politic. If one part of the body was not well, then the other part was of necessity concerned. Black discontent put all Americans at risk, physically, but also for deeper reasons—because it diminished whites' humanity and tarnished the nation's ideals. "The situation facing the Negro," Lindsay wrote that winter, "is not solely a matter of Negro concern. . . . [It] is the responsibility of each of us." In this, its sense of shared community, the panel represented the best of liberal integrationism—now in the aftermath of the riots, facing its hardest challenge yet.

Most members of the commission hardly realized what they were taking on: how far most Americans, black and white, had moved away from a sense of one community. Even at its peak, in the mid-sixties, integration had been a fragile, tentative ideal, and blacks' and whites' differing reactions to the riots had all but decimated the vision. The black mood had been furious before the disorders began, and it had only grown angrier as the violence raged. Meanwhile, try or not—and most did not—whites just could not understand the black grievances that lay behind the looting and arson. Where most blacks and some liberals saw a justified rebellion, most whites saw inexcusable lawlessness. This wasn't just a matter of different racial lenses; it was as if the two groups were looking at different events—and the gap made it all but impossible even to talk about things afterward.

In the wake of the violence, all but a few partisans were at a loss for what to do next to ameliorate blacks' problems and speed their entry into the mainstream. It was unclear that even the best-intentioned whites knew how to foster integration. Even if they did, no one had any idea where to find the kind of money that would be needed to make a difference. As the riots showed, black expectations were already running way ahead of anything whites could deliver, and the larger white public was less and less certain that it made sense to get involved. Even those who saw the need in the ghetto and felt the government should be helping were put off by the rioters' rage and nihilism, and many took refuge in the theory, being put forward by police chiefs and other conservatives, that the violence had been caused not by ordinary, representative blacks but by rabble-rousing militants and "outside agitators"—people, by definition, with little claim on the mainstream.

Still, even in this climate, the Kerner Commission was determined to mobilize the public to help. The panel's first big fight, early on, was over the scope of its recommendations: should it limit itself to one or two politically practical measures, or go all out and argue for a complete overhaul of the ghetto? Members were divided, with Lindsay heading the all-out faction; but it took only a few late-night sessions that fall for the New Yorker to win over his colleagues. More than ever, in the wake of the riots, the liberal establishment was convinced that whites could solve blacks' problems for them—not just get the ball rolling, or create conditions for blacks to help themselves, but step in with money and a few ideas and somehow right what was wrong in the ghetto. It was a noble, generous impulse, all the more impressive now with the civil rights consensus unraveling. But already, even as it made its first decisions, there were signs that the Kerner panel's integrationist impulses were driving it toward unrealistic promises and misleading paternalism.

A s the commission formed, the nation's black spokesmen came forward to explain the rioting, and together they agreed as one that far from being the work of hoodlums or aimless rampagers, it was a form of targeted political protest. The movement's young militants made the sharpest, most insistent claims. H. Rap Brown called the looting and arson "dress rehearsals for revolution." Floyd McKissick chided the press and public for even using the word "riot." "The explosions of this summer," he said, "[should] be recognized for what they are—rebellions against oppression and exploitation." Both men were seconded by the ever more outspoken Adam Clayton Powell, now evading a lawsuit on the island of Bimini: the blowups, Powell said, were "a necessary phase of the black revolution—necessary!"

Nor was sympathy for the rioters limited to the Black Power wing of the movement. The NAACP issued a declaration disapproving of the means but full of understanding for the rampagers' need to lodge some kind of protest. "We condemn such violence," the unanimous resolution read. "However, much of the blame . . . must be placed on the [local authorities that failed] to meet any of the grave social ills of the Negro community." Martin Luther King, Roy Wilkins, Bayard Rustin and Whitney Young—the pillars of the old movement—released a similarly equivocal statement. At once stern and saddened, they declared that "killing, arson, looting are criminal acts" and that nothing could justify such violence. Yet even this clear-eyed judgment came with a litany of complaints about the ghetto, implying as the NAACP had, that ultimately the riots were society's fault.

The sheer rage behind the looting, burning and rampages could not be ignored: what else but rage could bring people to destroy their own homes and ruin the few businesses that survived in their neighborhoods? No one suggested that conditions in the ghetto were anything but appalling. But even sympathetic liberals could see that there was something irrational about the anger surging in the streets: that it was aimless and self-destructive and had if anything grown stronger in the past few years, at a time when most blacks' prospects were improving. The usually liberal *New York Times* editorial page took a hard look at the rioters and described them with some skepticism as "young men without . . . constructive outlets for their energy. To many of them, a riot is a welcome escape from the boredom and hopelessness of daily life, a chance to prove their manhood and an opportunity to steal a television set. . . . They feel they have nothing to lose and they speculate that performance in a riot may gain them prestige among their peers." A handful of commentators, mostly white, warned against glorifying this flailing or reading too much into it. Still, black spokesmen of every political variety came forward to endorse the rage brimming over in the ghetto.

The first to weigh in were moderate, old-guard leaders. Whitney Young's thoughtful face gazed out at readers from the cover of *Time;* Bayard Rustin's carefully reasoned explanations filled *The New York Times Magazine.* Neither man could have seemed less like the angry mobs on television; all they appeared to share with the street kids was the color of their skin. But commonsensical and pragmatic as they were, both men embraced the rioters' anger as their own. Both told their white audience to put aside its judgments, to listen to the raging youth in the ghetto. A coolly precise writer, Rustin was careful not to overstate the case: the disturbances, he conceded, "were less than politically coherent rebellions." Still, he explained, within the black community, "they became more than riots pure and simple." They "set off a chain reaction" involving "people who ordinarily would not be found looting," and snipers and arsonists were regarded as heroes in the ghetto. Make no mistake, both he and Whitney Young warned the white public, the rioters represent black America.

Following on the heels of the organization men, black psychiatrists and psychologists took over, striving to explain to whites why rage was an understandable response to the way blacks had to live in America. Suddenly, the new clinical vocabulary was everywhere—in the press, on TV, wherever people talked about the violence. Professionals cited "the difficulty of the young Negro in developing a feeling of self-esteem"; they talked about poor youths' "unbalanced tendencies," their "self-destructive" and "suicidal" feelings. Each practitioner had a slightly different theory—a different model of anger and catharsis—but their larger message was the same. The rioters had indeed been representative of the black community; the anger vented in the streets was not confined to looting youths. Every black person, old and young, was said to deal with this anger differently: some expressed it, some suppressed it, some channeled it into crime or competitive sports. But underneath even the "coolest," most obsequious or "happy-go-lucky" black, there seethed, these experts asserted, emotion as strong as any rioter's. Not only that, noted many, including the dean of the doctors, Kenneth Clark, but the street kids' anger was entirely appropriate. "I find myself," Clark commented, "becoming more and more extremist. . . . I am becoming less moderate and less balanced."

Few black spokesmen made the case more strikingly than Mississippi psychiatrist Alvin Poussaint, later a friend and adviser to Bill Cosby. Poussaint's article about the reservoir of anger behind the riots appeared in *The New York Times Magazine* in mid-August, just as the Kerner Commission was holding its initial meetings. "This rage was at fever pitch," he wrote, "months before it crystallized in the 'Black Power' slogan," and no blacks, young or old, were immune. The article was filled with examples, among them an apparently happy and successful young man, one of Poussaint's patients, who had been known for his sweet temperament. A promising graduate student, liked by friends and colleagues, he discovered on the therapist's couch that he was consumed with racial anger. He grew more and more bitter as the treatment proceeded; he began to see subtle bigotry where he had never noticed it before. Some days, he felt so furious that he was overcome with nausea. Finally, beside himself, he abruptly left job and fiancée and moved to a different city to join the militant underground. "The implications for American society are clear," Poussaint concluded, indulging in a little angry flourish of his own. "Stop oppressing the black man, or be prepared to meet his expressed rage."

So evolved what became the black and liberal consensus on the riots. Born of adolescent anger, spontaneous and seemingly nihilistic, they had in fact, this interpretation held, been a legitimate and appropriate political act. Impetuous and unreliable as the messengers seemed, the content of their message had been true—and it was a critically important message. The rampaging youths were right to blame white society for what was wrong with their lives; they were right to think of protest as the best path toward change—perhaps the only one. Far from being tragic or misguided or futile, it had been nobly heroic for them to vent their anger as they did. What had looked like destructive carnivals were in fact glorious, proud rebellions—endorsed by most of black America.

In reality, it was hard to gauge just what the black silent majority made of the violence. Surveys revealed considerable support for the rioters, though not quite the resounding approval most movement spokesmen claimed. According to pollsters, no more than 15 percent of ordinary blacks said they would join another upheaval if the occasion arose. The fact that one-third felt the disorders had been justified was frightening to the white public, but not exactly an overwhelming endorsement. The strongest support was among educated, middle-class blacks: up to 40 percent of them were convinced the violence would advance racial justice. But even that was short of a majority, and the feeling was not shared among poorer people who had borne the brunt of the rioting; they told pollsters they felt strongly that it had done more harm than good. There was no question in anyone's mind in 1967: most blacks were disappointed by the outcome of the civil rights revolution. For large numbers, perhaps a majority, virtually nothing had changed yet, and many reacted with rage at the white world. Perhaps, as the psychologists said, everyone felt some anger. But there were other responses too—everything from confusion and despair to quiet determination to make the best of the new opportunities—and a raging youth with a Molotov cocktail did not represent them.

If any of the moderate spokesmen tapped by the media to respond to the violence were tempted to speak for these people instead of the rioters, they did not give in to the temptation. Ever fearful of looking like Uncle Toms—in 1967, the phrase was "the white man's errand boys"—even the most centrist spurned any position that would make them look "moderate" or "gradualist." The movement as they had known it was running out of steam; the moral leverage that had served so well in the early sixties was visibly weakening. For better or worse, the violence in the streets seemed to give black spokesmen just the tool they needed to prod the white world. Caught on the horns of their own "two-ness," not even the most ambivalent wanted to disown youthful protesters willing to put their lives on the line in the name of the race, and before long even the strongest misgivings were buried in a tide of racial solidarity.

By the time the Kerner Report came out, on the last day of February 1968, America was already experiencing the first wrenching sensations of the turbulence that would be the hallmark of that unforgettable year. There were 525,000 soldiers in Vietnam, more than the total number that had gone to fight in Korea, and nearly 16,000 American servicemen had been killed. The antiwar movement had passed from the counterculture into the establishment—leaders now included Dr. Benjamin Spock, Robert Lowell and Norman Mailer—and that fall it had brought over 700,000 people into the streets of New York for a demonstration.

The news from black America was hardly more encouraging. In the wake of the riots, H. Rap Brown announced provocatively that "violence is necessary. It is as American as cherry pie. If you give me a gun and tell me to shoot my enemy, I might just shoot Lady Bird." Stokely Carmichael traveled to Havana, where he held a press conference with Fidel Castro, urging American blacks to take up arms and "liberate" themselves. Back at home, second-tier CORE leaders, chafing under what they saw as the moderation of Floyd McKissick, declared that armed conflict between black and white could no longer be averted. Sonny Carson announced plans for a nation within a nation: an exclusively black agricultural settlement somewhere in the Deep South. In the aftermath of the Six Day War, anti-Semitism swirled openly in the movement. By winter, the larger public was so unnerved that even Martin Luther King began to look threatening: his plan, announced in December 1967, to lead an army of poor people to Washington struck many whites as an invitation to violence. Then in early 1968, just days before the Kerner Report was released, what was left of SNCC merged with the Black Panther Party, and in case anyone misunderstood its objectives, designated Carmichael as "prime minister."

Kerner Commission members readied for the release of their report with if anything more care than they had taken in writing it. There were plans for an elaborate publicity campaign: advance press briefings, in-depth interviews and talk-show appearances to prepare the press and public for the thick, data-filled tome. As Lindsay remembered, "We knew it would be controversial—and we knew our presentation would be critically important if we were to win over a skeptical public." All this careful preparation went up in smoke when the text was leaked, three days early, to *The Washington Post*. A few days later, *The New York Times* managed to get the entire executive summary into print. Bantam Books rushed to press with an instant paperback, and within a month nearly a million copies had been sold, making it what the *Times* called "one of the best-sellers in history." (The Warren Report on President Kennedy's assassination had sold only 200,000 copies in its first month.) Lindsay and other panel members spent much of those first weeks on television, explaining what the data meant and why it mattered. Hearing that the commission had condoned the riots, Lyndon Johnson canceled plans to receive its findings at a White House ceremony. But other national public figures scrambled to comment one way or another. "It is hard to overstate the importance that was placed on the . . . report," one reporter remembered years later, reliving "the sense of excitement and anticipation" that swelled in many circles that spring. Even in the wake of the riots, conscience, the Constitution and a sense of the nation America ought to be still prompted many whites to want at least to understand the ghetto's frustration. Whether they would accept the Kerner explanation—and, more important, move to act on it—was another question.

The report itself, if not exactly "abrasive," was unvarnished and hard-hitting. It had not been easy for panelists to come to a consensus. Through February 1968, members had spent untold hours closeted together, arguing late into the night, usually in an empty room, formerly a snack bar, in the Senate office building. Debate was cordial but intense, mostly over the reach of government programs to be recommended. Lindsay and Democratic senator Fred Harris led the ultra faction; Republican congressman William McCulloch and the panel's businessman, Litton Industries' chair Charles Thornton, argued for a more moderate approach. Sometimes the gap between left and center loomed so wide that there was talk of two reports. But in the end the liberals won, and all eleven signed on to a document that pulled no punches. When it was finished, Lindsay aides Kriegel and Peter Goldmark sat down to craft an introduction. "We wanted something with a cutting edge," Kriegel said later, "something tough and fiery." The two young men read through the text, taking notes for an essay, and found to their surprise that the existing language was so strong that an executive summary would be as catchy and urgent as anything they could write. "Our ultimate coup," Kriegel said, "was to get the commission to support the summary—and it was a stunner."

What the public read that spring—the cheap paperbacks seemed to be everywhere—was part investigative journalism, part history, part sociology. Each of the season's major riots was described in painstaking detail. There was a long section tracing the background of the black protest movement, an account of conditions in the ghetto, an analysis of what members felt had caused the violence—definitely not, they concluded, any conspiracy by outside agitators—and an unflinching discussion of police practices in black neighborhoods. But all of this was really prologue. The culmination and heart of the report was the admission of guilt and the call to atone for it by moving once and for all to heal the ghetto.

To many who read the text and millions more who did not, all 500-plus fact-packed pages boiled down to the blunt, two-sentence *mea culpa*. "What white Americans have never fully understood—but what the Negro can never forget—is that white society is deeply implicated in the ghetto. White institutions created it, white institutions maintain it, and white society condones it." Controversial as they would turn out to be, these two sentences had provoked virtually no dissent among panel members: only a minor quibble over wording—whether it should be "white society" or "white morality" that was deemed responsible. (Elsewhere, the report would talk more sharply still about "white racism.") For better or worse, Lindsay's zealous idealism had overcome all objections. The commission decided, Fred Harris said, straining for contemporary resonance, "to tell it like it is." Liberal and moderate members alike saw it as their mission to startle and goad. "It was a report about choices," Kriegel said later, "and about opportunities. It was an appeal to people's best instincts. We hoped that it would galvanize the country."

For panel members, what was important was what was supposed to follow from the admission of guilt: what white America would do to make up for its racial past. The report's recommendations were numerous and wide-ranging—some 160 in all—and they touched on virtually every aspect of race relations, from police practices to the hiring of black reporters. Many of these demands had originated in the ghetto and been passed on to Kerner during field-trip interviews. Not all were expensive; many called less for funding than for changes in habits and attitudes. Won over by Lindsay's view that the riots would not have happened if local government had seemed more accountable, commission members embraced proposals for symbolic "Little City Halls," civilian-staffed police review boards and improvements in ghetto services. But at the center of the blueprint—in the panel's view, the key to change—were a handful of big-ticket items: 2 million new jobs, 6 million new housing units, higher welfare payments and, eventually, a guaranteed annual income for all poor people. Commission members declined to put a price tag on their vision, but it surprised no one to hear them estimate that it would cost at least as much, over an extended period, as the $2 billion being spent every month in Vietnam. The report stated bluntly: "These programs will require unprecedented levels of funding."

Perhaps it was the long-term costs; perhaps there were other reasons, but in 1968, most of the public, black and white, paid little attention to the call to action. What stunned the nation, those who were sympathetic and those who weren't, was the report's admission of responsibility. "We're on our way to the moment of truth," CORE's normally dyspeptic leader, Floyd McKissick, declared excitedly. "It's the first time whites have said, 'We're racists.'"

McKissick's endorsement would be echoed in ensuing weeks by amens from every corner of black America: recognition, even before the full impact was clear, of the historic importance of the panel's admission. To most of the liberal establishment, the report's statement about white responsibility seemed unobjectionable enough—if anything, obvious and long overdue. Concerned, well-meaning integrationist commission members had empathized with black frustration and tried to explain it to white America. Nor was their *mea culpa* out of line with the other assumptions of their generation that lay behind the Kerner Report: that white society was responsible for the poverty in its midst, that change would come from the top down, in the form of massive federal philanthropy. But the panel's statements about white racism took this reasoning a giant step further, all but ignoring what had become apparent in recent years about the cultural roots of what was wrong in the ghetto and what it would take to fix it.

Kerner members had no idea what kind of message they were sending. The commission's report was perhaps the last time that the word "integration" was used in the mainstream debate about race, and members assumed implicitly that their admission of guilt would bring blacks and whites together. They were a little nervous about their use of this old-fashioned term. They saw the difficulties involved in trying to engineer social change of such magnitude, and even in the long term, panelists recognized, many blacks "would voluntarily cluster together in largely Negro neighborhoods." Still, search as they did, in their hearts and in the ghetto, members could envision no other long-term answer. Driven by this hope and faith, the report was filled with ideas for accelerating integration: not just "empowerment" and participation in the political process, but also school desegregation, an open-housing law, public housing built outside the ghetto and increased access to jobs in the mainstream economy. "Integration," the report concluded, "is the only course which explicitly seeks to achieve a single nation"—the only logical remedy for "two societies . . . separate and unequal."

Yet if anything, by encouraging race consciousness and endorsing the anger in the ghetto, the Kerner panel helped to widen the gap between black and white. Over half the white public disagreed with the commission's claim that white society was responsible for black poverty, and even many who accepted the burden of the charge worried that the finger-pointing would be counterproductive, spurring black paranoia and white defensiveness. Public figures as diverse as Richard Nixon and Hubert Humphrey concurred that, in Nixon's words, this sort of accusation could only "divide people. . . . [It] doesn't help in breaking down [their] prejudice." Humphrey spoke for other old-style liberals when he said the nation should focus on "reconciliation," not "group guilt." Still others, well-meaning whites and black moderates like

Bayard Rustin, complained that the *mea culpa* would reopen old wounds, even as it drew attention away from the ghetto's real, pressing problems. Commission members said they meant their admission of guilt as a goad, the first step on the road to change. But critics felt it could only spur anger, setting black against white and vice versa.

The black reaction to the *mea culpa* more than confirmed these fears. Moderates and militants alike exulted at the white admission of guilt. Kenneth Clark among others wondered wearily how long—how many decades or longer still—it would take white society to make up for what it had done to the black man. This was hardly an unusual comment in 1968; what was surprising was to hear it from Clark—the man who had originally diagnosed the indigenous ills that, along with white racism, were barring poor blacks from the mainstream. His insightful analysis of the self-defeating attitudes of black children no longer seemed relevant or even mentionable. The breakdown of the black family, the inadequate educational backgrounds, the alienation that was making it so hard for many to find a way into the mainstream economy: all of this was forgotten now—or jettisoned. Three years after the publication of Daniel Patrick Moynihan's 1965 report on the black family, censure by blacks and white liberals had made it unacceptable to appear to "blame the victims" in the inner city, and Clark too now seemed to believe that white society was entirely responsible for blacks' problems.

Intentionally or not, the Kerner panel's findings dovetailed perfectly with the spin that most black spokesmen had put on the riots. Rather than clearing the air, the *mea culpa* only inflamed black anger, boosting the sense of grievance and separatism already poisoning the atmosphere in black America. By implying that the disorders were not only understandable but an appropriate reaction to ghetto life, both the black and white establishments signaled to young blacks that they were right to blame their frustrations on white society—and that there was no meaningful distinction between generalized racial rage and focused, constructive political demands. Ghetto kids and others were not encouraged to see that they faced two different kinds of problems, some that whites could solve and some that they would have to tackle themselves. On the contrary, they were encouraged to lay every setback, no matter how personal, at the door of the white world. Instead of talking candidly about what was necessary to heal the ghetto—some combination of white help and black acculturation efforts—the president's establishment panel had encouraged blacks to blame whites, and to wait angrily for whites to make things better.

Many of the consequences, particularly the subtler, psychological ones, would not be exposed for years to come. It would be more than two decades before black intellectuals began asking why so many of their people had trouble seizing opportunity—why they seemed so mired in a politics of rage and grievance. It would take still another five years before the focus of the debate began to shift from blame to self-help: to acculturation and community building. And even then, the rage would still be self-defeating, the blame and pessimism still choking hope—driving young blacks to thumb their noses at the law and disparage the effort it takes to do well in school.

In the wake of the riots, much as in the launching of the Great Society, the liberal elite was trying to do the right thing by blacks. Yet, instead of helping, the Kerner Commission had echoed and endorsed the most misleading of black assumptions, sending a message about rage and responsibility that would haunt the nation for decades to come. For better or worse, already in 1968, the report had effectively fixed the terms of future debate about race. From now on, with the consent of even the most moderate black spokesmen, black anger and black threats—as much as guilt and moral leverage—would be the engine that would drive relations between blacks and whites. More damaging still, by signaling that there was little blacks could do to help themselves, the commission only helped delay the very healing it had hoped to spur.

For Lindsay, the months after the release of the Kerner Report were an intense and hectic time. The panel's diagnoses were all but unanimously endorsed by the liberal establishment, and Lindsay was fêted seemingly wherever he went. New York's congressional delegation threw a breakfast in his honor, welcoming him into the room with a standing ovation. That same week, at a Republican dinner in Boston, the governor of Massachusetts called him the "greatest mayor in our country." Lindsay's effort to sell the report took him back and forth across the nation, and by the end of the year, he had given more than three hundred full-length speeches, most of them outside New York. Combative and crusading as ever, he defended the report word for word: "'white racism,'" he told audiences, was "exactly the right phrase." His impromptu additions to his written remarks invariably turned up the passionate rhetoric, and he openly relished the idea that Kerner was "making all America uncomfortable."

Interest in the panel and its findings continued to run high for many months. A second million paperback copies were sold before the year was out. Debate raged in the press and Congress. "White racism" was a key issue in many of the year's electoral contests, and it came to be widely accepted, in liberal circles at least, as the root cause of the ghetto's problems. Still, as Lindsay and other panel members suspected, the larger public was not buying into their vision. Critics complained about the report's tone. They questioned its specific recommendations. Even after it appeared, a Harris survey showed, close to a quarter of whites polled were convinced that rioters had been driven by an idle desire for violence and looting, and nearly two-thirds still believed that the blowups had been organized—the work of a criminal conspiracy. Right-leaning politicians drove home the point, with Nixon, among others, talking about ghetto "perpetrators," and Chicago mayor Richard Daley accusing the Kerner panel of confusing petty crime with political protest. Congress heard the message from the public and voted to make incitement to riot a federal offense. The Kerner Commission, critics said, was offering "excuses" for the rioters. All 250,000 words, one wag remarked, could have been conveyed in three: "Spend more money."

A year later, very little had been spent—and almost nothing changed in the nation's approach to race relations. Liberals and conservatives alike found a wholesale assault on black poverty hard to imagine in 1968. The report's critics, who doubted that the government knew what to do to heal the ghetto, charged that even $100 billion would not cover the bill, that a 50 to 100 percent income-tax surcharge would be needed. Even supporters wondered where the money would come from, what with the war and the space program and the cities' shrinking tax base. "We have the problems," said San Francisco mayor Joseph Alioto, "and everybody else has the money." Well-intentioned mayors and congressmen tried to push ahead with the panel's cheaper recommendations. Some cities tinkered with their police practices; a liberal-sounding open-housing law circulated on Capitol Hill. But there was no massive spending at any level of government on the panel's big-ticket recommendations. Where the report asked for 550,000 jobs (the first installment toward 2 million), the administration moved to create only 100,000. There was no push for increased welfare payments, limited money for educational change, and cities like New York found their federal aid shrinking rather than growing. Lindsay became more and more agitated. The country "is not getting the message," he told a group of students. Congress was responding "with vacuous debate." "This is not the time [for] slogans," he insisted. "For heaven's sake, this is the time—once and for all—for performance."

Commentators trying to explain white America's sluggish response diagnosed it first as old-fashioned selfishness and passivity. A Harris survey conducted in April 1968 found that "although whites approved the principle of giving cities enough money to rehabilitate their slums . . . [they] also rejected the suggestion that they pay higher taxes to accomplish the task." Call it Myrdalian schizophrenia: the old gap between ideals and action diagnosed by the Swedish sociologist over forty years before. Like Birmingham and Selma and the debate over the landmark civil rights laws, the Kerner Report pushed whites' Myrdalian buttons, evoking an outpouring of idealism and concern. Much of the larger public wanted to do the right thing by blacks—as long as it did not cost too much, or inconvenience them. Yet when asked to reach for their wallets, only 45 percent were willing to pay for healing the ghetto.

But by 1968, in addition to this perennial ambivalence, it was clear to Kerner panelists that something new had crept into white attitudes toward race: an unembarrassed combativeness provoked by the riots and the Black Power rhetoric that came with them. Daniel Patrick Moynihan and Nathan Glazer were among the first to remark on the shift: "in the course of the 1960s," they noted, "the etiquette of race relations changed." Nationally, as in New York in the wake of the civilian review board fight, people no longer hesitated to voice and vote what they saw as their racial interests. Black and white alike grew far less squeamish about their prejudice, and the old Myrdalian schizophrenia became noticeably worse. As the initial reaction to the Kerner Report showed, the public had not lost its sense of concern and obligation toward the ghetto. Spurred by their most deeply ingrained ideals, many white people still dreamed of an open, equitable society. But as the Kerner panel's ultimately unsuccessful campaign revealed, when the idealism kicked in, it was much less of a goad to action than it had once been, even a few years before—in 1963, say, or 1965. Shame and moral exhortation no longer had the same effect. In the wake of the riots, even the most eloquent appeal fell flat, and the public sat on its hands.

In New York, by spring 1968, the erosion of racial etiquette was palpable, integration close to a dead letter. The mood in the outer boroughs, increasingly truculent and assertive, showed its face plainly at a series of open hearings on Lindsay's plan for "scatter-site" public housing. The idea behind the program was simple, physical desegregation: people displaced by urban renewal in Harlem, Brooklyn and the South Bronx would be moved to highrise projects in white middle-class neighborhoods. Borough whites had opposed the idea from the start, but even the most outspoken rarely mentioned race, talking instead about the number of people to move in, the inadequate parking and transit facilities. Then, early in the year, the dam broke. The occasion was a tumultuous nine-hour public hearing in Queens. More than one hundred speakers rose to object to the city's plan. The audience was in a restless, jeering mood, and speakers were candid about the racial basis for their resistance. "We homeowners have a right to live where we are," one man said, "and we want to maintain it the way it is." Lindsay and his aides were appalled by the homeowners' lack of embarrassment. "The primary reason for the opposition is bigotry," one staffer told the press, "outspoken, vulgar bigotry." The scene repeated itself again and again in the months to come wherever the administration tried to muster support for desegregated housing.

In the wake of the riots, blacks too seemed to retreat into cynicism, and not even the most moderate of ghetto spokesmen now deigned to use the "I-word." "We do not seek integration," said old-time civil rights pillar Whitney Young. "We seek an open society. Discussions about separatism and integration are irrelevant." Floyd McKissick avoided the term completely and, when prodded, dismissed it curtly: "It didn't come about," he said. By 1968, even integration's historic champion, Kenneth Clark, was flirting with separatist ideas like community control of schools and other institutions in the ghetto. Not all of these spokesmen rejected the old ideal outright; many held out some hope that it could still be achieved, some day in the future—when the black identity was more firmly established, when white prejudice ebbed, when blacks were strong and confident enough to join the mainstream as equals. But in the short term, even men like Clark conceded, integration just did not seem feasible. Let's try Black Power first, the conventional wisdom held. Let's build black institutions and develop black pride. Then, when we are ready, sometime down the road, blacks will come back around to the idea of integration.

By spring, left-leaning white intellectuals were following this lead and openly disparaging the ideal of a shared community. "Racial integration in the United States is impossible," said writer W. H. Ferry in one public forum. "[Let us settle for] peaceful coexistence between blacktown and whitetown." "The assimilationist argument" is based on false assumptions about black culture, wrote Christopher Lasch in *The New York Review of Books*. *Partisan Review* ran a symposium of opinion pieces questioning the old dream. *The New York Times* published a story on the trend. The intellectual magazines began to talk about building up "Negro institutions," about the beauty of Black Power and the virtues of the ghetto, both as political base and cultural proving ground. "Separatism has become the fashionable thing in some liberal circles," said Thomas Pettigrew of Harvard. In the spring of 1968, it was still a minority view, but, as the *Times* noticed, it was "gathering momentum steadily." And much like the Kerner Commission's endorsement, the intellectuals' approving justifications only encouraged black isolation and standoffishness.

As ever, the black silent majority was all but forgotten. One of the few major polls of blacks conducted in this period found an astonishing number firmly committed to a mixed society. Roughly 80 percent wanted to work, live and send their kids to school among whites. Asked if the record of recent years had led them to give up hope of working for change within the system, 72 percent rejected the idea. As for what kind of change they wanted, given a choice between "integration" and the newest Black Power vision, "community control," a full 78 percent chose racial mixing. Though blacks had long been on the record demanding equal access to jobs and schools, never before had such a proportion opted, in the abstract, for integration. Yet in the furor of 1968, these ordinary people were never heard from. Neither black spokesmen nor their white allies seemed to give them a second thought—a majority more hidden than ever now as the black political agenda shifted leftward.

That agenda was on full display in Harlem in late February 1968 at a meeting to commemorate the third anniversary of Malcolm X's death. City authorities were leery of the memorial even in its planning stages, but they could not prevent the sponsoring activists—a coalition in favor of community control—from staging the protest in a public school auditorium, at the new Intermediate School 201 on 127th Street. Anticipating an inflammatory gathering, the school board forbade teachers from encouraging or requiring students to go with them. Still, when the day came, some 600 people gathered at I.S. 201: teachers, activists, neighborhood folks and several dozen twelve- to fourteen-year-old students.

The gathering opened on what seemed like a celebratory note. Newly acquired Afros and dashikis were on proud display. The program included music by black composers and other segments promoting the idea of black culture. James Baldwin was among the featured speakers; the centerpiece of the evening was a skit by poet and playwright LeRoi Jones. As was increasingly common at ghetto meetings, reporters—black and white—were barred from the room. They huddled instead in the principal's office, listening to the proceedings on the school public address system. But even there, as the night wore on, it was easy to feel the temperatures mounting in the auditorium. The strains of rhetoric coming in through the loudspeaker grew sharper and sharper. One speaker raged at "the white man and his bitch"; another denounced "America, the Fourth Reich." Several segments of the program traded openly in Jew-baiting stereotypes, and a character in the Jones play predicted that "All white people will be killed." (*The New York Times* was at a loss even to report on much of the language, filling its front-page story with partial quotes and strange-looking blanks. "White people," a leading paragraph read, "your——will be set on fire.")

The climax of the evening was a speech by militant Herman Ferguson, till then a relatively little-known figure outside of Harlem activist circles. A former city school principal and a member of the Revolutionary Action Movement, he had been arrested the year before in connection with an RAM plot to murder Roy Wilkins and Whitney Young. Though still awaiting trial, he had been released on bail and was working as a paid consultant to the group demanding community control of Harlem schools. It was nearly midnight when he came to the podium at I.S. 201 and launched into a short harangue urging his listeners to take up arms. Go out and buy yourselves guns, he instructed the audience of impressionable teenagers. Begin to practice using them. The government is stockpiling weapons, and blacks must prepare for "hunting season."

The next day, white New York exploded with outrage. Angry parents and taxpayers wanted to know why the meeting had been held in a school auditorium and why students had been permitted to attend. The board of education retook control of the school building, then disciplined several teachers who had defied the order not to participate in the memorial. Flouting the conventional wisdom that said only whites could be bigots, the president of the board accused the activists behind the program of "racism." Even New York's usually liberal press seemed to share the board's appalled reaction. It looked for once as if Manhattan and the boroughs agreed, with even liberals recognizing finally that black protest could go too far, that it wasn't always constructive or morally justified. Then City Hall weighed in, followed by its ally, the Ford Foundation.

A Ford grant, it came out, was funding the group demanding community control; the foundation had been paying Ferguson's salary, and even now hesitated to denounce him. Called for comment after the meeting, a foundation official hedged: the fact "that such pilot efforts may produce controversy, and even conflict, should not overshadow the difficult effort to solve educational problems in the cities." Lindsay, caught off guard on a skiing vacation in Oregon, reacted in the same vein, defensively. "People like Ferguson," he said, "are bound to come to the forefront during a transition." Once again, as with Sonny Carson and on the Kerner Commission, Lindsay and his allies instinctively sided with aggrieved black activists, even if that meant endorsing separatism and violence.

Assailed from all corners of the boroughs and the schools bureaucracy, by the time he got back to the city, Lindsay knew he had to temper his response. He called a press conference and began as sternly as he could. "I'm sure I can speak for lots of other people in condemning that kind of talk," he said of Ferguson's comments. Still, the mayor went on, he could see lots of reasons for black unhappiness with the public schools. He still endorsed Black Power, still felt the community should run its own institutions—even if its "meetings are sometimes very difficult to control." Besides, he saw no point in getting into a "showdown" with someone like Ferguson. When the mayor was finished, an aide took over, deflecting questions about the memorial with angry criticism of what he saw as white New York's overreaction—a response, he said, that only "fanned the flames of racial hatred." Lindsay, standing by, said nothing, implicitly endorsing the idea that, as ever between black and white, it was racist whites who were causing the problem.

Whatever else went wrong in New York, whatever happened to the racial etiquette, no one could say that the liberal establishment did not try through the sixties to do the right thing by race. For all the angry blacks who argued then and later that white society did not care, that it never tried to help, what Lindsay proved in New York was that, if anything, sometimes well-meaning whites tried too hard, humoring blacks just because they were black and giving credence to irresponsible leaders. In the name of integration, the mayor felt, white America had to be a little tolerant. He didn't see, and perhaps couldn't, that tolerance was not always benevolent, and that what his tolerance encouraged might not be the best thing, for blacks or anyone else.

L indsay was at the theater when the news broke on April 4. A detective brought a note to his seat in the middle of the second act: Martin Luther King, Jr., had been assassinated in Memphis. The mayor dashed to a pay phone and called police headquarters, then headed to Harlem. At Second Avenue and 125th Street, he and adviser David Garth got out of their car and continued on foot. Garth, who years later would still be in awe of Lindsay's physical courage, thought to himself, "my life is over." The night was hot for spring. There were crowds of people milling in the streets. Sirens and burglar alarms sounded in the distance. Some people were openly weeping, others looking for a fight. Several of the record stores on Harlem's main thoroughfare, which usually blared music from outdoor speakers mounted above their doorways, had gotten hold of King's speeches and were playing them over and over. The incantatory phrases echoed along the busy boulevard, adding to the confusion and the eerie, volatile atmosphere.

Lindsay could feel the anger as he made his way westward into an ever-thickening sea of people. The black detective who had accompanied him from the theater told him it wasn't safe to be in Harlem. The mayor ignored him and walked on, shaking hands where he could, or merely pressing his palm on a passing back or shoulder. He didn't say much, just a quick "I'm sorry" or a nod. He was aware of currents within the crowd—groups of young men running quickly by, some compacted jostling and, occasionally, fighting. The sound of breaking glass mixed with the smell of acrid smoke, and at one point Lindsay had the impression that he was surrounded by several large men. Reporters would later say he had been caught between two hostile militant factions. Lindsay believed the men were trying to protect him. Somewhere along the way, he attempted to speak to the milling throng. "Brothers—" he began, shouting through a bullhorn. "You've got some nerve using that word," came the answer amid a hail of obscenities. Still, as far as Lindsay could tell, the neighborhood "was holding": scattered window-breaking and looting had not turned into anything worse. An hour or so later, across town from where he started, the mayor ran into black borough president Percy Sutton, also walking the streets and trying to calm the crowd. Persuaded by Sutton that he had done whatever he could, Lindsay headed back to Gracie Mansion to hear if the rest of the city was holding.

The nation's other cities were not faring well. Almost immediately after the bullet struck home in Memphis, rioting broke out in black enclaves across the country: from Washington, D.C., to Oakland, and everywhere in between. The National Guard was called out in Chicago, Detroit, Pittsburgh and Boston. Washington, Chicago, Detroit and Toledo imposed dawn-to-dusk curfews. Some of the time, in some cities, the atmosphere was carnival-like. In Washington, a *Newsweek* reporter came across a matronly woman emerging through the shattered plate glass of a ghetto storefront: "Cohen's is open," she declared nonchalantly, even as a second looter lobbed a liquor bottle in the journalist's direction. But in most cities, even newsmen who had witnessed other riots were stunned by the bleak mood in the streets—furious, desperate, no-holds-barred. In Minneapolis, a black man with a gun pumped half a dozen bullets into a white bystander. "My King is dead, my King is dead," he sobbed without restraint. In other cities, the usual street battles, arson and looting were accompanied by interracial brawls in public high schools.

The political message of the violence was as tangled and hard to read as ever. Many rioters seemed to see only color: a black leader had been shot by a white gunman. Still others, as in earlier upheavals, seemed thrilled mainly by a chance to break the rules—to walk in and out of store windows, to thumb their noses at cops, to defy the white system and all it stood for more or less with impunity. Some—it was impossible to know how many— seemed to be mourning the death of both a man and his program. But whatever drove the mayhem, few people watching from a distance could see how the destruction of more black homes and shops would advance King's dream. Even the style of the rioters—the nihilism and the self-destructive flailing—seemed to mock his life of hope and careful, strategic thinking.

The dead man's ideological rival, Stokely Carmichael, was in Washington that week, encouraging violence wherever it waxed hottest. "Go home and get your guns," he counseled one group of young people. "When the white man comes, he is coming to kill you. . . . I don't want any black blood in the street. . . . Go home and get you a gun." The next day, Carmichael sounded if anything even more incendiary. "When white America killed Dr. King," he warned a reporter, "she declared war on us. . . . We have to retaliate for the deaths of our leaders. The executions [are] going to be in the streets." Extreme as it was, in most cities, Carmichael's vision had replaced King's. In Chicago, with sniper fire crackling and whole city blocks enveloped in flames, one journalist stopped to talk with a band of roving youths. "This is the only answer," one said jubilantly. "It feels good," interrupted another: "I never felt so good before." "When they killed King," the leader said solemnly, "I came to life. We gonna die fighting. We all gonna die fighting."

Lindsay went back to Harlem that night and walked the streets again till close to dawn. The next evening he returned three times, and then again on Saturday. Sometimes he watched the crowds from a second-floor police command overlooking 125th Street. Gottehrer's hangout, the Glamour Inn, served as another, impromptu headquarters: a place for the mayor's team to coordinate with militants they persuaded to work the streets, urging angry youth to "cool it." Lindsay was everywhere on the airwaves that weekend— the city-owned stations but also Harlem's WLIB—taking calls, answering questions, trying to tell people he understood. In between times, he walked the streets, often, at his insistence, without reporters. He wanted to go directly to the people, he said. This was no stunt, and—he told the press frankly—he was scared for the city.

By now, whatever else it had learned about race relations, the Lindsay team was good at emergency damage control. In addition to militants, clergymen walked the streets urging calm. Ghetto churches kept their doors open around the clock. Encouraged by authorities, parents found ways to keep their kids at home. Both the police and the fire department deployed special riot techniques: New York's now patented policy of maximum restraint. Everywhere Lindsay went in Harlem, he criticized the city government and its "older established persons." He knew, he said, that the city hadn't come through for blacks. He promised to do better. "I think I understand," he empathized. "I understand the temptation to strike back. I hope the young men of the city will help me to cool it. I need strong arms to keep the peace."

As ever, the walks met with mixed reactions. On at least one occasion Lindsay was jostled, and frequently heckled. Once, on 125th Street, he met two teenagers with their arms full of new dresses, still on plastic store hangers. The mayor strode up to the kids and stuck out his hand. "Hello, I'm John Lindsay," he said, "and I'd like to thank you for all you've done these last few days." "Mr. Mayor," one youth replied, without missing a beat, "how would you like to buy this woman's dress for five bucks?" More often, though, the reaction was solemn, the mood tense but largely calm. Even as other cities went up in smoke—Lindsay and his aides stayed up late at night watching the hair-raising footage on TV—the violence in New York was on the scale of the 1964 Harlem blowup: hardly, in 1968, even worth talking about. There was only one night of what could really be called rioting and, according to the police, only one death. Whatever the reason—police restraint or Lindsay's personal chemistry—something worked in New York, and the city held. In the short term at least, both Lindsay's touch and his vision of race relations seemed vindicated.

Still, both the mayor and his aides sensed, this time around keeping the lid on would not be enough. In the wake of King's death, with Black Power raging in the ghetto and middle-class whites turning angrily away from blacks and their problems, the idea of integration seemed imperiled as never before—and Lindsay felt desperately that he had to do something to keep the ideal alive. At rally after rally, on TV and in the streets, he insisted that

King's dream had not died with him. Whites were urged to join peaceful marches mourning the tragedy: to help create the impression of a shared sense of loss. Working overtime on spin control, aides even argued that the anger swirling in the streets uptown was a "tribute" to King's vision: what one staffer would later call "a riot of remembrance." "You have kept the faith of Martin Luther King," Lindsay told a large, mixed crowd in Central Park. "The [skeptics] were wrong. . . . The dream lives." An impressive group of speakers, black and white, was on hand to prove the point: theologian Abraham Joshua Heschel, Governor Nelson Rockefeller, Terence Cardinal Cooke, several black pastors including King's former aide, Wyatt Tee Walker—all trying to convince themselves and their audience that the integrationist movement was still a force to reckon with. The crowd held hands and sang "We Shall Overcome." "It may be that in this tragedy we shall find promise," Lindsay said hopefully that night on national TV. "I think Americans are preparing themselves anew for [the] journey" to the mountaintop.

In the days and weeks that followed, Lindsay kept up the drumbeat, trying with every means he could think of to get the city back on the path toward integration. Partly, as ever, this was a matter of outreach. Of all the eloquent and urgent remarks he made the week after the shooting, none were more dramatic than his late-night radio broadcasts. "Good evening," Lindsay began the first with wartime solemnity. "As I speak shortly before midnight, New York is relatively peaceful. . . . I want especially to talk to the young men of our city. . . . I hope you will listen to my message." It was a clever statement, well-pitched and well-written, but the mayor's most effective word, sounded again and again, was the simple "you"—creating somehow, across the divide, an instant sense of relationship with the city's black youth. Lindsay told them he thought he knew what they were going through: "You feel the wind has been knocked out of you, that your legs have been knocked from under you." He reassured them that he and other whites shared their feelings, that whatever had happened, whites and blacks must face the future together. "You, the young men of our city," he pleaded, "[we] will not abandon you. . . . As one who has worked in the streets with you . . . I ask your help . . . this evening, and tomorrow, and the tomorrow after that." Even in the wake of Black Power, with the city on the edge of violence, Lindsay was still trying—to his credit—to reach out across the color line and find a sense of shared community with the youth of Harlem.

But King's death also seemed to remind the mayor that outreach alone was not enough, and he turned back with a new sense of urgency to his original mission: making inclusion a reality for poor blacks in New York and elsewhere. Within days of the assassination, Lindsay began to push for reconvening the Kerner panel. Walking the streets of New York, traveling to King's funeral in Atlanta, holding press conference after press conference aimed at whites as well as blacks, the still earnest New Yorker pleaded desperately with the nation to turn crisis into opportunity. "It is too late to answer the martyred Dr. King," he said. "It is too late to grant reprieves to the cities in which riots have broken out since his assassination. . . . It is not too late, however, for the nation to move against this crisis with the urgency and enterprise that the commission sought to generate." He talked about specifics, about jobs and congressional funding, but mostly he hammered home his vision of the big, elusive dream. To those who shared his idealism, it was one of Lindsay's finest moments: leadership at its most eloquent and ennobling. His appeal was still to white people's conscience, to their sense of fairness and decency. Even now, his vision was still inclusion, and it was still color-blind. We must find the "resolve," he urged both black and white, "to create a single society and a single American identity." For a moment, listening to the inspiring rhetoric, it was easy to lose sight of just how tragically— unintentionally and with only blacks' best interest at heart—Lindsay himself and his approach to ghetto grievances had helped in the last few years to set this vision back.

In the gloom of spring 1968, Lindsay's New York stood out as an emblem of racial success. There were calls from mayors in over forty cities asking Lindsay how he had kept the lid on. Gottehrer's "urban task force" became an idea to conjure with, and City Halls around the nation began to talk of reaching out to militants. Requests came in from further and further afield to accompany Lindsay on his walking tours: not just from reporters and politicians but also movie stars and other celebrities. Lindsay and Gottehrer's buddy Allah appeared together on the cover of *New York* magazine: a jokey photomontage that showed them putting out a fire on the Empire State Building. The piece inside, by Gloria Steinem, was upbeat and celebratory. Columnist Jimmy Breslin entertained tabloid readers with a description of the scene at the Glamour Inn. Kenyatta, still in a pith helmet and carrying his machete, went on TV to praise Lindsay and testify to his rapport in the ghetto. As usual, those New Yorkers who saw through the success—in the boroughs and the ghetto—were not heard from or, because of their bigotry, were discredited. The image of community would hold for a while, but appealing as it was, most people knew, it was ultimately hollow.

That spring of 1968 brought no discernible progress toward more meaningful integration, locally or in the nation at large. Together, what became known as the "King riots" were the worst America had seen yet. It was nearly two weeks before calm was restored and the damage could be reckoned. By then, there had been disorders in more than 125 cities, 46 people had been killed and 50,000 troops mobilized, more than had ever been required in America to quell a civil emergency. Lindsay's effort to revive the Kerner Commission went nowhere. King's death spurred passage of a pending Civil Rights Act with a largely toothless open-housing provision. But more than that, Congress made clear, it would not do. If anything, members seemed intent now on dismantling the Office of Economic Opportunity, the agency that had been responsible for the acculturation programs of the War on Poverty. Even with another hot summer looming, federal aid to cities was slashed dramatically: New York's allotment shrank from $9 million to under $5 million. As for the larger public, it was soon distracted by other events: disruptive campus strikes, Robert Kennedy's assassination, the Democratic National Convention in Chicago. The erosion of white concern and goodwill toward blacks was obvious to all. By now, instead of disappointment or even outrage, the rioting evoked mostly belligerent shrugs, and, in most of America, the phrase of the summer was "law and order."

In New York, it wasn't long before Lindsay's aides began to feel they were back more or less where they started. "We're slapping Band-Aids on," Gottehrer told a reporter, "but Band-Aids won't cure a cancer." Sonny Carson saw the truth as plainly as anyone, and he made bitter fun of Lindsay and his staff. "This is nothing but a riot-stopping committee," Carson jeered. "It's just a lot of screaming and hollering and promises." It was some time that spring that the Black Panthers opened an office in New York: yet another generation of aggrieved black militants more angry and ruthless than those who had come before them. Still, it did not occur to Lindsay or his team that in their way they had helped to encourage this. The mayor and his inner circle took a deep breath; 1968, they could see, had only just begun.

Chapter 6

"IT'S NOT AN EITHER/OR"

McGeorge Bundy had been at the Ford Foundation for all of nine months when the memo about community control and integration crossed his desk. In 1967, "community control" was little more than a slogan and no one, white or black, was sure what it would look like in practice. But already, whatever it meant, it was a phrase to conjure with among militants in New York, who saw it as the first step on the road to their larger dream, Black Power. The razor-sharp, patrician Bundy had come to Ford fresh from the White House, where as national security adviser he had been all but running the Vietnam War; and already, in his first few months as president of the foundation, he had made the race issue his number one priority. Like Lindsay and the rest of the liberal establishment, Bundy assumed that the long-term answer for blacks—the only answer that made any sense—was inclusion in the mainstream. Now, with Ford's considerable clout and resources at stake, he was being asked to decide if Black Power was consistent with that older goal.

The phrase "community control" had come into currency just the summer before, in 1966. Malcolm X was the original father of the idea. Unlike earlier nationalists who dreamed of a nation apart, whether in Africa or the Deep South, Malcolm had reminded blacks that they already lived in a separate world: each ghetto, as he saw it, a kind of independent city-state. Encouraging followers to embrace and revel in their alienation, he gloried in the segregation of black neighborhoods and urged residents to take charge in their separate enclaves. In the years since Malcolm's death, Stokely Carmichael had taken up the idea, and community control figured prominently in his widely read book, *Black Power.* "Control of ghetto schools," Carmichael maintained, "must be taken out of the hands of 'professionals,' most of whom have long since demonstrated their insensitivity to the needs and problems of the black child. . . . Black parents should seek as their goal the actual control of the public schools in their community: hiring and firing of teachers, selection of teaching materials, determination of standards, etc." The idea spread quickly in the roiling ghetto, and by 1967 militants in northern cities were clamoring to take over from all manner of local bureaucrats. Schools, hospitals, police precincts, welfare services and more: these, the movement reasoned, were the institutions that made the difference in black lives—and they were institutions, now run by white people, that the black community should control for itself.

By the time Bundy arrived in New York, everyone in town seemed to be buzzing with the new concept. Not just militants and ghetto parents, but also downtown liberals, teachers, schools experts, even the board of education: though different factions used different terms—whites generally preferred "decentralization" or "empowerment"—all seemed to agree that this was an idea whose time had come. Even those with only a passing knowledge of the ghetto could sense that residents felt ill-served by local government. Schools in particular seemed desperately in need of some change. More than ten years of on-again off-again efforts to integrate the system had made virtually no difference, and even desegregation's most ardent advocates were conceding that it might be impossible in New York. "We had to do something," Lindsay said years later. "Something had to happen. And it seemed to make sense to listen to the community—to get them involved and try whatever it was they wanted."

There were hints already even as Lindsay and Bundy took up the issue that blacks and well-meaning whites might be imagining the ideal differently. For ghetto activists, community control held out a promise of black teachers and a "black curriculum." For Lindsay—whose term of choice was "empowerment"—it had more to do with Jeffersonian democracy and an antidote to big bureaucracy. While Carmichael and his followers talked angrily about separating from the white world, Lindsay anticipated that black cooperation in running schools and cops and hospitals would eventually spawn a sense of belonging: a kind of political shortcut into the mainstream. Still, whatever their differences, the mayor embraced New York advocates of community control, endorsing their demands and their Black Power slogans, and Bundy, studying the question from his new office at the Ford Foundation, saw no reason to doubt his friend Lindsay's analysis.

In late fall 1966, Lindsay reached out to Bundy for help in making community control a reality in New York. As the largest, richest foundation in the nation, on the cutting edge of social policy, Ford had been experimenting with ghetto empowerment for a number of years already. Its innovative Gray Areas program, tried first in New Haven, Connecticut, and other cities, had pioneered the idea of helping ghetto people help themselves, and former Ford staffers committed to the concept had helped make it a central tenet of the War on Poverty. By 1966, one of Bundy's top lieutenants, education expert Mario Fantini, was spending a lot of time in Harlem meeting with advocates of community control, and by late fall Fantini's passionate memos were winning over his boss.

Knowing of Bundy's interest, Lindsay suggested that he form a blue-ribbon task force to plan how the city might implement the idea. Ostensibly, the panel's job was to reconcile the different visions of empowerment being floated around the city: visions that ranged from the board of education's proposal for slightly enhanced parental involvement to ghetto activists' radical demands for completely autonomous school districts. In fact, Lindsay made little secret of his hope that the bold and forceful Bundy would take charge of the panel and push through a sweeping empowerment plan. Together, the two men would define decentralization their way, and backed up by the power of the Ford Foundation, would effectively pressure the board of education to cede control of the city's schools.

If there was a sticking point for Bundy, it was the issue of integration, and Fantini had been trying for months now to convince him that it could be pursued in tandem with community control. As Fantini knew well, when it came to race, his boss was a classic liberal. "My idea of the solution was fairly natural," Bundy said years later, "to get past all those racial feelings—to get back to the country that our great-great uncles fought for in the Civil War." As late as 1967, his vision of the future was still explicitly color-blind. He could no more imagine a nation divided up into separate ethnic enclaves than he could conceive of a city divided into male and female camps, and he saw America as a single community structured by a single set of ideals. The problem for Fantini was to reconcile this long-term ideal with a plan for dividing the city school system into districts—districts that in many cases would be defined by color and controlled by activists whose declared purpose was racial separatism.

It wasn't an easy circle to square, though Fantini's memo made a clever start. His argument began with the familiar point that school desegregation no longer seemed possible in New York. Besides, the staffer was blunt, integration had fallen out of favor among ghetto activists. "It implies," Fantini wrote, "that Negroes have to be with whites to receive a good education." With old solutions passing out of fashion, the community was looking for new answers. "Now the cry is that Negroes can do it alone," Fantini explained, "if they have their own control." This control would not be so much about separatism, he wrote hopefully, as about parent participation, innovative teaching, creative curriculums and extracurricular programs geared to the needs of children from minority communities.

More than that, Fantini emphasized at several points, community control need not mean abandoning integration. Part of the memo made this reconciliation sound slightly cynical: an on-paper consistency useful mainly for tactical purposes. Whatever their true feelings, the blacks Fantini was talking to in Harlem understood that community control could not "be presented" as an alternative to integration. They grasped how much the old ideal still appealed to white liberals—and knew that in order to win support for decentralization, they must say that their long-term goal was racial mixing. But Fantini's pitch was not only tactical. In the long term, he argued, community control would improve the education in ghetto schools and, as a result, would serve as an incentive to desegregation. Black Power and integration, he concluded, need not be antithetical. Paradoxical as it sounded, separate development could be a route to racial mixing. Let blacks run their own schools, let them teach race consciousness and race-based self-esteem—and after a few years, Fantini speculated with a hopeful leap of faith, the schools would be so good that white students would be clamoring to get into them.

Could the circle indeed be squared? Bundy pondered the question through the winter of 1966–67. It was, he knew even without Fantini's guidance, the most important issue he would face that year and perhaps well beyond. Could the Ford Foundation ease integration by promoting separate education? Could New York nourish both separate enclaves *and* a sense of overarching community? Could "black culture" and "black education"— what would later be called "Afrocentrism"—be separated from the anger that seemed to drive so many of its proponents? As the call for Black Power ricocheted from city to city, much of liberal America was asking itself the same question. It was one of the hardest choices liberals would make in the sixties, and it would shape race relations for decades to come.

Like his friend Lindsay, Bundy had no doubt that the nation's race problem was solvable. In his case, as in Lindsay's, this was the confidence of his class and background. Born into the heart of New England privilege, the product of Beacon Hill, Groton and Yale, Bundy had grown up among men who naturally assumed they would lead the nation—and lead it to reshape the world. A dazzling young Harvard professor, then dean of the college, he was a natural choice for the Kennedy White House, itself the most vigorously activist administration in decades. Slenderly built, with sandy hair and pink cheeks, Bundy was a shining star even in the Kennedy firmament, where his rare intelligence and cool, decisive manner came to epitomize Camelot style. His certainty that America could impose its will on any problem was part of what lured the nation to disaster in Vietnam, but even then Bundy did not lose faith, and he was confident as ever in the spring of 1966 when he sidestepped from government to the Ford Foundation. "The idea," he said in his first months in New York, "is to do things society is going to want after it has them." Legendarily able and devoted to public service, he still believed it was up to men like him to shape a better world—and now he had the resources of the nation's most powerful foundation at his disposal.

Both Bundy and the Ford board of directors that chose him understood before he started that, more than anything, this would mean tackling the race question. "It was the obvious issue of the moment," he said later, "and Ford was already involved. All that was needed was a public declaration—that we were going to make this our top priority." Bundy made the announcement that summer at a meeting of the National Urban League. By then, he understood as well as anyone that formal equality and basic rights were not going to be enough. "The road from right to reality goes through thick and tangled country," he told the Urban League audience, and he saw it as Ford's job to help the black man make this all-important leap, moving beyond legal parity to "improvements in skills and schools, in real opportunity and in the quality of life itself." Nimbler than any government agency and free to try even the most experimental approaches, Ford seemed ideally situated to accomplish the kind of social engineering that was eluding men like John Lindsay and Lyndon Johnson.

Bundy attacked the issue with the same vigor and confidence that he brought to everything he did. He began, typically, with a thorough course of study. He read everything he could get his hands on and spared no effort to get to know "Negro leaders." He reached out to individuals and heads of organizations, meeting them individually and in small groups. There were Sunday lunches at his home and dinner meetings at the elite, all-male Century Club. These Century roundtables were the most agreeable kind of homework: a dozen or more black and white men, from government, social work and academia, would gather on the club's musty top floor and take turns around the table, each speaking his piece, then removing their jackets and arguing late into the night. Meanwhile, wasting no time, Ford stepped up its grants to black activists: the NAACP, the Urban League, Martin Luther King and several middle-class black colleges, but also, further to the left, CORE and other grassroots groups committed to Black Power. Asked at the time if he was nervous about funding militants, Bundy grimaced slightly and recited the then current cliché: "Picketing is better than rioting." Before long, the foundation's race-related grants had doubled—to nearly $40 million a year by 1968.

A s Bundy learned soon enough in his first weeks at Ford, the background to the New York school situation was a course of study in itself. School desegregation had emerged as an issue in Harlem as early as 1954, and it had been a source of continual controversy ever since. Bundy immersed himself in the details provided by Fantini, painstakingly reconstructing the history and the outlines of the debate. It was a bitter, complicated story, full of missed opportunities for change. New York was reputed to have one of the most progressive and inclusive school systems in the nation, but after more than a decade of effort the board of education had been unable to implement any significant desegregation. Scores of pilot projects and piecemeal innovations had done little but exhaust school authorities and irritate parents. By the time Bundy arrived in town, the failure was so widely acknowledged that it had a name: "the New York City syndrome." Just who had been at fault was hard to say, even after extensive study. All that was clear to Bundy was that New Yorkers had been talking about integration for twelve years, and now in 1966 the schools were more segregated than ever.

The story began just weeks after the Supreme Court's *Brown* decision, when Kenneth Clark got up at a New York symposium and denounced city authorities for maintaining what he charged was an entirely separate, inferior set of schools for black children. New York's liberal establishment responded quickly and sympathetically, agreeing that northern de facto segregation— caused by habits and residential patterns rather than by law—was as bad as the legally mandated southern kind. Virtually no one among the city's elite questioned the need for racially mixed schools. The issue was not whether but how to implement desegregation as quickly as possible.

The board of education swung into action as only big bureaucracies can swing—with a combination of great fanfare and slow-moving cumbrousness. Members organized a commission to look into the problem; they issued a policy statement, held a series of hearings, considered a range of options and talked among themselves about drawing up a master plan. With this, New York seemed to confirm its reputation as the most enlightened school system in the country. Still, two years later, nothing concrete had been accomplished. The problem already in the late fifties was that increasing residential segregation made it all but impossible to integrate the schools without extensive long-distance busing. Over eight hundred thousand blacks and Puerto Ricans had poured into the city in the previous decade, clustering together in run-down enclaves. Schools in these areas were soon overcrowded and overtaxed by migrant children with scant educational preparation: students and schools sure to put off the middle-class white parents who would have to be involved in any busing scheme.

Desperately hoping to avoid busing, the schools bureaucracy tried everything else it could think of: creative zoning, encouraging the system's best teachers to transfer to ghetto schools, building new schools in "integrated" fringe areas between neighborhoods, replacing junior highs (grades seven through nine) with intermediate schools (grades five through eight) that would pull kids out of their color-coded neighborhoods at an earlier age. None of these efforts produced much in the way of results, and with each halfhearted try, the board looked more foolish, its high-flown rhetoric more at odds with its inaction. Black advocates of integration grew more and more frustrated and began to make additional, angry demands—for at least a voluntary busing program. Coming as it did from impatient activists, the proposal took on the air of an extremist ultimatum. Advocates upped their pressure, organizing demonstrations and boycotts: pressure that paradoxically only made it harder to implement the idea. The board held off as long as it could but finally agreed to transfer four hundred kids—only to find white parents mounting feverish protests of their own. In the end, the tiny pilot program did almost nothing to alleviate the city's growing segregation. Yet blacks and whites were already at a standoff, and the board, trying to appease both sets of parents, grew ever more hesitant to do anything at all.

Finally, in 1960–61, under pressure from activists, the board agreed to expand the experiment with voluntary busing, inviting anyone in the city to apply. Authorities anticipated a flood of black applicants, but much to their surprise, only a small number of ghetto parents showed interest. The long distances between neighborhoods, the surging racial hostility, the vacillating and apparently untrustworthy school board: together, it was all too much for even those black families seeking a way into the mainstream. Already in the early sixties, school desegregation had lost its appeal for most New Yorkers. Still, ignoring the signals from their constituency, movement activists once again escalated their demands—now for nonvoluntary busing and "guaranteed integration" for all children.

The long-brewing conflict came to a head in the winter of 1963–64 with the historic, citywide school boycotts. Longtime Harlem activist Milton Galamison reached out to Bayard Rustin, who had organized the 1963 March on Washington, and asked him to do something like it in New York: a mass protest action, this time on behalf of school integration. Moderates and militants, black activists and white liberals all came together behind the cause—and school desegregation looked again, for a few weeks at least, like something that might bring blacks and whites together instead of dividing them. When the day of the first boycott came, in early February 1964, some 450,000 children stayed away from school—nearly 45 percent of the student body. National news media were mesmerized; activists claimed a resounding success for the integration movement—though all the boycott really showed was that black New Yorkers were dissatisfied with the city's failing schools. Just what they wanted—or what could realistically be done to fix the system—was another matter.

When the first walkout failed to produce immediate action from the city, Milton Galamison escalated his demands, insisting on the imposition of a nonvoluntary, busing scheme that would "immediately" desegregate every school in the system. "Anyone who talks about integration and is against busing is not serious about the matter," he said provocatively, adding that he would rather see the system "destroyed" than watch it go on as it was, perpetuating segregation. School officials told him they could not produce the "instant" racial balance he was insisting on. Even stalwart integrationist Kenneth Clark declared the demand "unrealistic." Still, Galamison pushed ahead with his second boycott, this one deliberately punitive: calculated to deprive the city of state education funding.

The event itself only exacerbated racial tensions in the city. Just six weeks after the first walkout, the boycott movement was unrecognizable. Kenneth Clark, Bayard Rustin and most national civil rights leaders had distanced themselves, leaving only Galamison, Malcolm X and a ragtag band of local grassroots militants. The southern-style church rallies and hopeful odes to racial harmony that had accompanied the first boycott were replaced by ultimatums and threats of violence. White liberals, strongly supportive of the first walkout, now wondered if Galamison were trying to provoke a riot. The city's black parents backed the action, the vast majority keeping their children out of school. But the downtown liberal establishment was bewildered by the vindictive nihilism that seemed to be driving the protest. In early 1964, these well-meaning whites were still intent and hopeful about integration—both school desegregation and black inclusion in the mainstream—and they could not see what Galamison was doing to advance either cause.

In the boroughs, the two boycotts spurred still more fear and more resistance to desegregation. Only a year before, the antibusing movement had been made up largely of activists: self-styled education experts and conservative camp followers, few in number and evoking little sympathy even in their own neighborhoods. Now, abruptly, the character of the struggle changed. Housewives who had never before thought about political action suddenly grasped that they too could organize to make themselves heard. Lower-middle-class, hardworking, often second-generation Americans, they met in the rumpus rooms of their apartment buildings and agreed among themselves that something had to be done.

It was the board of education that finally drove them into action. Prodded by the boycotts, in early spring, the board began to talk seriously about an involuntary busing plan. Anxiety spread through the boroughs. Frightened parents egged each other on at neighborhood rallies. Then in March, some twenty thousand middle-class activists came together for a major counterdemonstration, descending on Manhattan via the Brooklyn Bridge. Picket signs read: "Have child—won't travel" and "Can a bus bring a sick child home?" Virtually none of the slogans were explicitly racist, though it was not hard to see the glint in many eyes—a glint of panicked fear and anger that would show itself again and again as the decade wore on. Some months later, white parents organized their own school boycott and the board of education backed away from the idea of busing. Though still not as strong as the integration movement, the white resistance had shown itself as a force to be reckoned with. By 1964, the two were poised for a long standoff, and every passing day made compromise seem more remote.

The battle over school desegregation would continue for two more years, though by now virtually no one had much hope of a happy outcome. The board of education persisted with its piecemeal experiments. There were more commissions, more reports, more poorly implemented changes.

Whatever the board's intentions, these efforts looked by now like so many gimmicks, designed mainly to forestall criticism. By mid-decade, it was increasingly clear that integration was a lost cause in New York. The problem was part demographics (by then there were just too few whites in the system), part geography (with bottleneck bridges and tunnels separating Harlem from the outer boroughs, most kids' daily bus rides would have been interminable), and over ten years of racial conflict had made the difficult all but impossible. Segregation, as measured by statistics, had more than doubled since 1960. Hope had given way to stalemate and recriminations, and forty thousand white students were leaving the system every year.

Meanwhile, the schools deteriorated further. Overcrowding and double sessions were the norm, delinquency and gangs more and more common. New York was still spending more money per pupil than any other big city and most suburbs in the country. But reading scores were falling steadily, and black students, on average, were two years further behind than whites. The dropout rate, shooting upwards, had reached 50 percent among blacks. Most troubling of all, blacks in higher grades did even more poorly than young ones—suggesting that their schooling was of no help, or worse.

Bundy and Lindsay had read all about this history and the many, tangled reasons for the failure of desegregation in New York. Still, as the two men saw things, ultimately white New Yorkers were to blame: previous administrations, self-serving educators, hesitant liberals and plain, old-fashioned white prejudice. "It was the principal obstacle," Bundy said later, "here as in the South. It took some time to understand that, but those resistances were obdurate and built-in." In 1966, there was no one in New York to tell Bundy that this might not be the whole truth—that black activists and their angry, unrealistic demands were part of the problem, too. For better or worse, he had read the history his way, and his reading was the one that would shape the future.

By the time Lindsay and Bundy got ready to tackle education issues, the city's black activists had lost all faith in the school system. The focus now was on white staffers and the harm they allegedly did black students—by ignoring or scorning them or simply not expecting as much from them. White teachers and the white-run bureaucracy, it was said, were committing educational "genocide"—why otherwise did blacks fall further behind as they advanced through school? On this as on other matters, the liberal establishment followed the vogue in the movement, and both Lindsay and Bundy were inclined to believe the charges being leveled by activists, no matter how sweeping or unsubstantiated. Integration—still the school board's stated goal—was rarely mentioned by the new mayor. Both he and Bundy became convinced that traditional education was somehow damaging for black children, and they and their staffs reflexively sided with angry critics of the system. "New York City schoolteachers were one of the most obnoxious groups I've ever encountered," one Lindsay aide said years later. "They were hateful of blacks, condescending, horrible. That wasn't just militant rhetoric. I know. I met some."

The conflict between black activists and white teachers emerged in the open during Lindsay's first months as mayor in a bitter dispute over Intermediate School 201. The school had been a source of controversy for over five years even before the cornerstone was laid in 1964. The board of education had had the highest hopes for the new building: a major step, officials felt, toward desegregation in Harlem. Not only was it among the first of the experimental intermediate schools, but it was strategically located near the Triborough Bridge—just a short bus ride away from large white neighborhoods in the Bronx and Queens. The city spared nothing in its plans for the five-million-dollar facility, and this, plus the school's superior academic programs, was meant to attract voluntary transfers from the boroughs. Still, no matter what the board promised, Harlem activists were suspicious and accusatory. They didn't like the school's location. They found the design an affront to the community. They wanted to be consulted on even the smallest construction decisions. They took offense at the proposal that it be called the Arthur Schomburg School. (Schomburg was a black bank clerk who had given the city his library of books about black history, but militants who had never heard of him assumed that he was Jewish.)

By the time the building neared completion, in the spring of 1966, these dissatisfied activists had come together in what was known, somewhat misleadingly, as the Ad Hoc Parent Council. The New York school integration movement had never been a grassroots effort, and even after ten years, ghetto parents remained largely apathetic. Most members of the Ad Hoc Council were activists schooled in the ideology of "participation"—the idea that the official bureaucracy was the enemy—and they came openly eager for a power struggle with the board of education. Just how much support they enjoyed in Harlem was always murky, though when they stood up angrily in the name of "the community," no one came forward to question their role as representative spokesmen.

Early in 1966, they issued a list of demands: the power to hire a principal of their choosing, to mediate between the board and teaching staff, to launch after-school and weekend programs—fish fries, rent parties, weddings, even funerals—that would bring the community into the school building. School desegregation still appeared on the agenda, but the activists' emphasis ran strongly counter to the principle of genuine integration. What defined "the community" for them, their early documents made clear, was precisely its alienation from the mainstream. They made a shibboleth of skin color and claimed, as blacks, to have different educational priorities, different "interests . . . values and life styles." When it came to hiring, they demanded not just a principal who would be "accountable" to them instead of to the school board, but also—and this, they said, was non-negotiable—a principal who was black. Inspired by the teachings of Malcolm X, the activists' program embraced not just color coding, but also—and apparently inseparable—a large dose of color-coded anger. The Ad Hoc group was explicit: members looked forward with pleasure to "the controversy and conflict" their ultimatums would produce.

Desegregation emerged early on as a major source of contention. Nothing the board could propose was good enough for the council. Mixed black and Puerto Rican would not do; nor would the board's proposal for a magnet school that would attract voluntary transfers from the boroughs. What activists wanted, they told school authorities, was nothing less than mandatory busing of large numbers of white kids into Harlem—though after twelve years of back-and-forth, all of New York knew this to be impossible, and their own documents made clear that the I.S. 201 activists themselves had scant interest in racial mixing. Still, the council held adamantly to its demand—clearly less a goal than a bargaining chip. The ultimatum was simple: either immediate, guaranteed racial balance, exactly half white, half black, to be imposed by the board on white families—or, if that could not be delivered, then activists must be allowed to run the school their own way. "Integration or community control!" they demanded. Either forced busing—or the city should hand the school building and its budget over to them.

The city establishment responded with earnest good faith, looking for ways to meet the activists' demands. School superintendent Bernard Donovan entered into around-the-clock negotiations with the Harlem group. *The New York Times* endorsed these talks and encouraged the board to make concessions. Even the teachers' union seemed willing to suspend judgment. "We feel that the involvement of the parents . . . if done in a constructive way, could result in great educational improvement," union chief Albert Shanker noted. Manipulative and angry as some activists plainly were, they still drew on the moral capital of the civil rights struggle, and no one in liberal New York dared suggest that they might not be in good faith—that they seemed more interested in power than justice and relatively unconcerned with black children.

The issue came to a head in late summer, just as the idea of Black Power swept over the ghetto. Eager as they were to accommodate the uptown activists, school authorities were unprepared to give up all control of I.S. 201, and they insisted on choosing the new school's principal. The man they picked, Stanley Lisser, had a good reputation and extensive experience in Harlem. He happened to be white—in 1966, there were few blacks on the civil service list of qualified principals—but when he in turn chose a teaching staff, he made sure that it was half black. Still, activists rejected the instructors sight unseen. The board offered a compromise: The community could screen candidates and advise on hiring. The Ad Hoc group would have none of it and threatened to boycott the school on opening day.

Emboldened by the board's concessions, the militants grew still more intransigent, and by the time school started in September 1966, the two sides had come to a standoff. The council talked less and less about education, more and more simply about color—theirs and the white teachers'. Rumors swirled through the city that activists from SNCC and the Black Panthers were advising the Harlem committee. The militants began to threaten violence, noting that they could not be "responsible for any action the community might take" against the board's chosen principal or teachers. The first day of school arrived without an agreement, and some sixty black pickets showed up at I.S. 201, shouting, among other things, "We got too many teachers and principals named Ginzburg and Rosenberg in Harlem. This is a black community. We want black men in our schools."

Still, neither the board nor City Hall was prepared to turn the activists down. No one questioned the council's plainly false claim that it was made up of concerned parents. No one asked whether the militants' preoccupation with color would be good for education or race relations in New York. Lindsay met with members of the Ad Hoc group at the barricades outside the school building and encouraged them in their bid for increased control. Superintendent Donovan, ever eager to compromise, offered them a right to veto staff choices. With the city establishment apparently backing out from under him, Lisser offered to resign as principal. After a week-long boycott, the community seemed on the verge of winning. Only then did the tide turn—thanks to a few dozen of the teachers, some black, some white, who had been chosen to staff the new school.

Terrified by the precedent, fearful that the board would sell them out too, this handful of employees stood up and did what the city was afraid to do: say no to the brazenly bigoted militants determined to take over I.S. 201. Acting entirely on their own, without the backing of their union or school authorities, the teachers declared that they would not enter the school until Lisser was reinstated. Goaded by this show of courage, the rest of Harlem's principals came out in support of the teachers' position, as, belatedly, did some of the mainstream press. Lisser took back his resignation and showed up at school, surrounded by a heavy escort of policemen. Classes resumed and eventually calmed down. The board of education heaved a sigh of relief. Whites would not be barred from teaching at I.S. 201. The militants had lost this battle; yet even as they folded up their banners and trudged home, the idea of color-coded community control was taking root across the city.

The phrase caught on overnight in Harlem and Brooklyn. Stokely Carmichael suggested blacks secede from the public school system. With talk of "educational genocide" now commonplace in militant circles, ordinary parents too began clamoring for "accountability," and there was a rash of boycotts at other ghetto schools. Even Kenneth Clark, who until now had been strongly critical of the I.S. 201 activists, made common cause with their effort to wrest the district away from the school board, putting it into the hands of a coalition of parents and education experts.

Downtown, in white New York, it was the mayor who led the push for change. In the wake of the I.S. 201 crisis, Lindsay invited members of the Ad Hoc Council to meet with him at City Hall. He listened quietly to their complaints and when they were finished picked up where they had left off, lashing out angrily at the board of education and its resistance to community control. Aide Woody Klein asked his boss if he was sure he wanted to take sides so clearly. "Look," Lindsay insisted, irritated and impatient, "we either have to do what's right in shaping up this government, or the hell with it." The signal could not have been clearer—to the visiting Harlem activists or the education establishment. The mayor was declaring war on the city school bureaucracy.

He moved ahead that winter of 1966–67 with quiet determination. New York tradition did not give City Hall much role in school matters. The board of education was an independent body, and no mayor since La Guardia had dared to meddle in its business. But none of this deterred

Lindsay, never one to put much store by established ways of doing things. His first step was to recruit Bundy and plant the idea of a blue-ribbon task force. Then he lined up an array of important allies, including Kenneth Clark, and stepped up his complaints about the school board—about its record on race and the "poor return" it got on its budget. By the start of 1967, the trend was clear: some form of community control was in the cards for New York. The only questions concerned degree and timing: just how much control would the central school board be asked to cede—and to whom exactly? As the idea gathered momentum, all the interested parties—from the board of education to the teachers' union, grassroots black Brooklyn and the Ford Foundation—began to piece together their own visions of just how the devolution should work.

In white New York as in Harlem, there were many different arguments in favor of change. The mayor saw the schools as a place to advance his larger mission: to cut back bureaucracy and empower poor, black New Yorkers. Education experts were willing to try any remedy that promised to save the sinking school system. Even borough-based parents were interested; by now they grasped that decentralization could mean some power for them too. The board of education was the most reluctant backer, but it too joined in the chorus of support—a calculated effort to preempt more sweeping reform from outside. Educators and foundation heads, politicians and patrician do-gooders fell over each other through the winter and spring figuring out how to hand the schools over to "the community." Yet none of them, liberals or moderates, seemed to take account of the lessons of I.S. 201. Determined to do right by the city's blacks, liberal white New York picked up the militants' banner, assuming they could have reform but shed the bitterness that came with it.

Lindsay maneuvered behind the scenes all winter, and in late spring 1967 his work bore fruit: an invitation from the state legislature in Albany—the body that ultimately controlled the board of education—to submit a proposal for decentralization. It was at this point that the Bundy task force finally took shape: an advisory citizens' panel charged with formulating a blueprint for the legislature. The idea, plainly enough, was to make an end run around the schools bureaucracy, and the mayor did not hesitate to stack the panel in favor of just the kind of far-reaching decentralization he wanted. It did not seem to occur to him that such an end run might be dangerous—that even if New York's racial past was as shameful as he believed, it might not make sense to give carte blanche to angry activists.

There were plenty of warnings from the ghetto that winter and spring about just who was behind community control and what they would do with it. Less than six months after the I.S. 201 episode, Milton Galamison and activists from the Ad Hoc Council disrupted a meeting at board of education headquarters. The meeting was forced to adjourn—and as soon as members left the room, militants took over their seats. Calling themselves the "People's Board of Education," they occupied the hall for the next three days, rallying like-minded activists and demanding community control. Within weeks, Sonny Carson, CORE activist Roy Innis and several other, lesser-known militants in other parts of the city had come out with threats to take over their local schools, imposing segregation and color-coded curriculums even more "radical" than those suggested at I.S. 201.

As usual when Sonny Carson joined the battle, he took it several steps further than any of the city's other militants. With no particular authority but that of Brooklyn CORE and the ever amorphous "community," he announced in May 1967 that he was going to "evaluate" thirty-two teachers in the Bedford-Stuyvesant public schools. He and a band of followers entered several school buildings, stalked menacingly from classroom to classroom, and demanded that the instructors under suspicion show them detailed lesson plans. Then, a few weeks later, Carson declared that all but five of the thirty-two were "fired," in most cases on the grounds that they were white and could not help black students. "If [the schools superintendent] thinks we are kidding," Carson threatened, "he had better wait until September and see what happens when those teachers . . . try to come back to our community."

When neither the board of education nor the teachers' union responded, Carson took the battle directly to them. First, he and a group of followers took over union headquarters, spending a night on office couches and making free use of the telephones. Some weeks later, he tried the same tactic at the board's central office. This time, the cops were there ahead of him and—by Carson's own admission—he and his group provoked a nasty brawl that landed one policeman in the hospital. (The officer was struck on the head with a three-foot metal ashtray, then taunted with shouts of "I hope you die.") Also that summer, Carson invited teacher union head Albert Shanker to a "community" meeting in a Brooklyn school. Shanker was heckled and then prevented from leaving. When he appealed to Carson to call off the thugs blocking the door, Carson merely laughed at what he later described as "this great big honky union chief standing there, blotchy with apparent fright." By September, Carson's gang was regularly entering school buildings and accosting teachers in the halls, telling them among other things, "The Germans did not do a good enough job with you Jews."

Brazen and bigoted as Carson was, the basic elements of his approach—color coding and confrontation tactics—were by now commonplace in the community control movement. With both the War on Poverty and the Ford Foundation strongly encouraging ghetto empowerment, the emphasis of many antipoverty agencies had shifted dramatically, and the new focus had less to do with running substantive programs—education, health care or job training—than teaching people to organize so they could challenge the government. Liberal theorists argued that the very act of challenging would be healthy for ghetto residents mired in powerlessness and resignation. Grassroots politics would teach them to assert themselves, taking responsibility for their own lives even as they secured better public services. Already, like Carson, many of the empowered participants were sounding shrilly resentful, more interested in telling "whitey" off than in making changes in their rundown neighborhoods. Still, the shift toward activism was welcomed by white liberals. By the summer of 1967, in the name of empowerment, Ford was funding separatists and street gangs, including a Cleveland CORE chapter that championed armed revolution and "race hatred." "Empowerment was a means," Bundy said years later. "At the time it seemed an effective means of getting black people involved in solving their own problems. Yes, there were difficulties. But if you didn't expect some difficulties, why did you bother to get into it in the first place? You can't expect effort-free social revolution."

In New York, Bundy's blue-ribbon panel worked through the spring and summer of 1967, hashing out the fine points of its decentralization plan. Even before he started, Bundy knew what he wanted the blueprint to look like, and he laid out his vision in a series of internal memos. The proposal looked great on paper: a model of grassroots democracy. Small districts, each with real operational autonomy, should be free to innovate in the classroom and control their own budgets, contracting with people in the neighborhood to provide the services that kept the schools running. The only thing that was missing was a sense of the context in New York: the real conditions in the ghetto where community control would be implemented. On the all-important question of hiring and firing—the central issue at I.S. 201 and already in Bed-Stuy—the memo said nothing. Color coding was not mentioned, and although Bundy imagined that each district would elect a local committee to take over from the central school board, he showed little concern about militants stepping in to make decisions for the community.

Ever impatient, Bundy was eager to try his plan out in practice, and his panel had just gotten started, filling in the details, when he moved out ahead of it—an end run on his and Lindsay's own end run around the board of education. Without waiting for the state legislature, without permission from the board, Bundy went into action, putting Ford's money behind his enthusiasm: a groundbreaking grant for decentralization in "demonstration school districts" in three of the poorest neighborhoods of the city. Ford would supplement their budgets, liberating them from the board of education and allowing them to experiment with community control. In each case, the grants were funneled to well-known militants—among them the activists who had led the I.S. 201 fight and those who, along with Galamison, had been arrested for taking over the school board building that winter. There was no evidence that these people knew anything about education or that they were representative spokesmen for their neighborhoods. Still, more important to Ford, they were the ones who had ideas about community control. Years later, asked if he had made a bad choice, Bundy would not comment directly. "You can't just start something," he answered. "You can't run it yourself. You have to back who's out there. You've got to find someone in the community."

The New York establishment was thrilled by Bundy's bold move. The liberal press applauded his take-charge innovation. The teachers' union talked eagerly about participating in the experiment. The board of education was the least enthusiastic, but by now even it had little choice: it could hardly block a Ford grant for improvement of ghetto schools. Intoxicated by the hope and promise of decentralization, no one in New York seemed to hear the warning signals from the ghetto, and no one looked too carefully at just who or what was going to be empowered. Proud of their extreme rhetoric, flamboyantly disruptive, committed to hiring and firing on the basis of color: there can be little doubt that if the recipients had been white, they would never have been considered for a Ford grant. Still, in their passion for racial progress, few white New Yorkers noticed the patronizing double standard at work. Confident, righteous, keen to get on with his experiment, Bundy did not hesitate, and no one in liberal New York counseled caution.

It would have been hard in 1967 for the Ford Foundation or anyone else to find a more benighted enclave than Ocean Hill–Brownsville in which to launch a high-profile experiment. It was not a neighborhood in the conventional sense, merely a border area between two ghetto pulse points, Brownsville and Bedford-Stuyvesant. Ninety-five percent of the residents were black

or Puerto Rican. Well over half had recently moved into the area, and virtually all were poor by any standards. The enclave's garbage-strewn streets were
lined with run-down tenements and rooming houses, many of them abandoned. Rusty automobile hulks were as common as trees. Three out of four
families were on welfare, the others mostly unskilled and often only casually
employed. Residents wrestled daily with every imaginable social problem,
and most of them had no experience of politics—nothing to guide them in
the experiment in self-government they were about to undertake.

The eight public schools in the neighborhood were predictably besieged.
One building was ninety-two years old; classrooms in all eight were chronically short on supplies. The student absentee rate was the highest in the city,
and more than 40 percent of the teachers came and went every year. Hardly
a preferred assignment, the district employed more than its share of tired,
mediocre teachers: people who had long ago given up hope for ghetto students. "There was plenty reason for blacks to be offended by the white teachers in that district," one journalist later remembered. "They were punching
their time cards and blaming black kids instead of teaching them." Still, even
in these conditions, a few educators were struggling to make a difference,
and they had recently worked impressive changes, winning citywide attention and several prizes for improved reading scores. Just which faction—the
tired holdovers or the young idealists—was in the majority was hard to say,
but there were few people in the city more enthusiastic about Ford's experiment than the younger teachers in Ocean Hill.

Energetic, reform-minded, willing to put their lives on the line behind
their ideals, many of these people had gone into teaching precisely because
of their concern for civil rights. Naturally left-leaning, they gravitated to the
ghetto and the United Federation of Teachers (UFT), a union known for its
commitment to racial justice. Science teacher Frederick Nauman, chairman
of the UFT chapter at Ocean Hill's Junior High School 271, was a Jewish
refugee from Germany who felt he had a special stake in fighting prejudice.
In addition to his teaching and union work, he was an active member of the
NAACP. "I had been a strong supporter of the civil rights struggle," he said
later, "a strong supporter of Martin Luther King. I didn't back the Black
Panthers or the militant black movement, but every time there was a confrontation between black and white, I tended to side with the black." The
union representative in the district, Sandra Feldman, was a longtime
CORE activist who had been arrested on the Freedom Rides and helped to
organize the 1963 March on Washington. Overseeing the UFT, former

teacher Albert Shanker was a veteran of ghetto schools—he began his teaching career in Harlem in the early fifties—and a charter member of CORE who had marched at Selma.

When Feldman first went out to Ocean Hill, just as the Ford experiment was getting underway, she found a number of the teachers "defensive" and worried about the disruption that would come with community control. Still, she reported later, there was also genuine hope stirring in the district, with many staffers "excited and enthusiastic about the possibility of really working in a creative way to change the schools. . . . There was a feeling that if we could really have the possibility of the parent support and the community support and get the resources that we needed to help the kids, then this could be a very exciting thing." Instructors were proud of the recent improvement in the Ocean Hill schools; most were committed to their calling as teachers. But more than that, like the Manhattan establishment, Feldman and Nauman and others were driven by concern about the city's poor blacks. They believed in activism as a path to progress. They saw the push for empowerment and participation as a continuation of the inspirational southern struggle. They wanted desperately to like the black community's representatives, to agree with them and see them succeed in the district. If this made them, like Ford and City Hall, a little credulous or uncritical, that didn't seem such a bad thing. Like the Manhattan establishment, they were swept along by their goodwill and hopeful commitment to racial change.

Ford's initial grant of $44,000 sparked a flurry of activity when it was delivered to Ocean Hill in July 1967. The official recipient of the money, now responsible for the district's schools, was a small, ad hoc group, much like the group behind the I.S. 201 controversy, that called itself the People's Board of Education for Ocean Hill. Founded by self-styled "worker priest" John Powis, pastor of a local church and leader of that winter's takeover of the city school board building, the People's Board consisted mostly of activists— poverty program organizers and Brooklyn CORE members—with a smattering of local parents. When the Ford grant came through, the People's Board put together a "planning council," and it held a series of start-up meetings with outside education experts. Teachers were invited to take part and several did, expressing their strong support for the idea of parental involvement in the schools. They were surprised to find parents playing little or no role in the meetings, which were dominated by Powis and other militants, including his close friend, Herman Ferguson, recently indicted for conspiring to kill Roy Wilkins and Whitney Young.

The People's Board got down to business in earnest that summer, laying its plans for the community's takeover of the Ocean Hill schools. Ferguson made no secret of his hostility for white teachers, and they began to feel uncomfortable at planning sessions. Science instructor Fred Nauman, initially among the most enthusiastic, recalled later how white staffers were shut out of decision making: "Any suggestions that were made by the teachers were either disregarded or, actually, they were insulted about making them." The more the teachers tried to help, the angrier the community people seemed to grow, denouncing them as bigoted, incompetent, obstructionist. As the summer wore on, activists stopped informing the educators about meetings; the teachers stopped attending, and none were present when the planning council selected Rhody McCoy to run the experiment in Ocean Hill.

Mild-mannered and pipe-smoking, McCoy had worked in the New York school system for eighteen years, rising to the rank of acting principal. A guarded and inscrutable man, he lived in suburban Long Island in a middle-class neighborhood and seemed as comfortable at the Ford Foundation as on the streets of Brownsville. He had a different manner—a different demeanor and vocabulary—for each setting, and from the beginning, he was everything to everybody. Activists in Ocean Hill saw a fellow militant, a friend and devotee of Malcolm X, while sympathetic liberals saw a sober, dedicated educator, a man who could help the community find power and autonomy without sacrificing school standards.

Together, McCoy and Powis's People's Board forged ahead through the summer, working out the mechanics of community control. Under pressure from Ford and others to involve parents and Ocean Hill residents, Powis's group came up with a plan to replace itself with a "governing board" that would include teachers, elected parent representatives, "community representatives" and an academic expert. The plan looked democratic enough, but it was accompanied by strangely belligerent rhetoric: "The ending of oppression and the beginning of a new day has often become a reality," the preamble stated, "only after people have resorted to violent means." And the elections, held in August, proved highly irregular. Several would-be "parent representatives" neither lived in the district nor had children in the schools, but they played a prominent part in organizing the election, registering voters and carrying ballot boxes door to door, and not surprisingly, they won seats on the board. As it turned out, no more than a quarter of district parents had voted, and when it came time for the newly elected "parent representatives" to chose "community representatives," they picked the very people who had hired them to conduct and run in the elections: Powis and his militant allies, including local minister Reverend C. Herbert Oliver, who was designated chairman of the new board. The Manhattan establishment, apparently not watching too closely, was encouraged by what it took to be the empowerment of the district.

The governing board's first official task was to choose five new principals for Ocean Hill's schools, and members insisted up front that all five must be black. The UFT, which had fought for years to introduce merit ranking into the school system, was troubled that none of the proposed names were on the civil service list. Teachers like Nauman were even more unsettled to discover the confrontational Ferguson being put forward for the top job at I.S. 55. Asked why he was chosen, one governing board member answered candidly: "He's the person to keep teachers in line." But anxious as they were, teachers were reluctant to act against the experiment, and none could bring themselves to vote against Ferguson. Still cautiously hopeful about community control, they hesitated—in Nauman's phrase—to take sides against a black man, particularly one who wrapped himself in the mantle of racial justice.

Then, in September, after an awkward, edgy summer, relations between the Ocean Hill teachers and the community board finally broke down. The issue that provoked open hostilities—a citywide teachers' strike over the union contract—had nothing to do with the district or community control. Still, Ocean Hill activists took offense at the walkout, arguing that the teachers were trying to sabotage their experiment by closing down the schools just as it was getting started. Unlike in the rest of the city, schools in the district remained open through the two-week strike. Local activists were brought in to take over classes. Sonny Carson appeared in the neighborhood, as ever accompanied by a band of "bodyguards." Union pickets were regularly jostled and bombarded with obscenities. One teacher was stopped in the street on his way home from a morning at the barricades. A car pulled up in front of his, blocking his way, and four men got out and gathered menacingly around him. "Don't come back here or else," they threatened, before letting him go on his way. On another occasion, a pro-union principal discovered that his car was not where he had parked it. Several days later, someone noticed that it had appeared mysteriously on a different street not far away.

Meanwhile, inside the Ocean Hill schools, community control got underway. The five new principals chosen by the governing board took over. Together, they and the board moved ahead to replace the teaching staff: encouraging union teachers to transfer out and hiring new ones, mostly from outside the school system. Curriculum changes began to take hold, with all subjects soon being cast in the light of race and politics. White teachers felt increasingly unwelcome in the schools; many complained that discipline was flagging and academic skills getting short shrift. Indifferent if not hostile, the governing board brushed aside their complaints. "It was not skills we were interested in," McCoy said later. "[That] wasn't going to do anything for the [kids'] lives."

The governing board made little effort to disguise its militant purposes, which turned out to reach well beyond classroom issues. In addition to transforming the schools, members were intent on what they called the "education" of Ocean Hill residents. Parents were invited to meetings to discuss their children's progress, only to find when they got there that Ferguson had prepared a lecture on the evils of white America. Teams of volunteers circulated through the neighborhood, filling "data books" with residents' complaints: gripes about their kids' education, but also about neighborhood housing, shoddy city services and "the white system" in general. Like other community organizers of the late sixties, the board was determined to "rub raw the sores of discontent"—to make people "conscious" of complaints they were not aware they had, to concentrate their fury and help them act it out. "[We were] taking on not just the school system," McCoy said later. "[We were] taking on white America."

As ever, it was difficult to judge just what the community made of the activists speaking in its name. It was clear even at the start that students, particularly older ones, were intrigued by the change in the air. Parents' reactions were less visible, and though often evoked, the neighborhood was rarely consulted. White teachers like Fred Nauman were skeptical. "We didn't feel that Carson or the governing board or even McCoy were representative of the real community," the instructor said, "not what we saw as the community—people living in the area with children in the schools." A poll taken in early 1968, after nearly a year of militant efforts to mobilize the neighborhood, seemed to confirm this view. The survey showed that only 29 percent of Ocean Hill parents supported the governing board. A third said they feared they would get into trouble if they denounced it, and nearly half told pollsters they were not sure where their sympathies lay. Even journalists who looked favorably on the experiment were dubious about local people's sympathies. "The hope was that once they saw they could have an impact, they would appear and engage in the process," *New York Times* reporter

David Shipler said years later. "But it didn't happen. They didn't come forward. The community didn't exist."

Already that autumn, it was hard to say who was calling the shots in Ocean Hill. Though nominally in charge of everything that happened in the schools, the governing board frequently claimed that "the community" was driving its actions, and as often as not Sonny Carson then came forward to speak on behalf of what he claimed was an angry neighborhood. Carson and his men—usually eight or ten followers—seemed to be everywhere by now, in and outside school buildings, guarding the doors, leading student rallies, menacing white teachers. Nauman and other teachers wondered if these toughs were being paid by the governing board, if Powis and Ferguson were using them, or the other way around. Decades later, Carson would still maintain he had been "advising the board" in the name of Ocean Hill residents. In fact, it was never clear whether he was taking orders, giving them or simply acting on his own initiative with the board's acquiescence.

Rhody McCoy's role—and his relationship with the militants on the governing board—was equally murky. Talking to white people, at the board of education or the Ford Foundation, he liked to give the impression that he was caught in the middle, keen to do the reasonable thing, yet somehow unable to because of pressure from the community or the governing board. True or not, this was a useful bargaining tactic: it allowed McCoy to look cooperative and trustworthy even while presenting the district's most outlandish demands. On other occasions, when pressed on how he got along with the board, McCoy talked warmly about a "family-like" relationship. "I'm locked in with them," he told a reporter. "When their hearts beat, mine beats."

As the year wore on, even initially sympathetic white teachers began to sense that the so-called moderates and militants in Ocean Hill were closer than they thought. With confrontations between the district and the board of education growing more and more frequent, the supposedly reasonable McCoy always seemed to be at the forefront of these standoffs. Staffers began to see the smoldering anger beneath his affable surface—an eagerness, as he later put it, "to destroy the system." In 1967, McCoy still made some effort to conceal this bitterness—enough at least not to frighten liberals supporting the Ocean Hill experiment. "At the time," Nauman later recalled, "I didn't think McCoy was an ideologue. At the worst, I thought maybe he was being pushed by the militants. Later, looking over the things he said, I realized I was probably wrong. He may even have been out ahead of people like Powis and Ferguson."

Meanwhile, relations between the teachers and the governing board grew more and more tense. In the wake of the September strike and the harassment that came with it, large numbers of white staffers requested to transfer out of the district. The UFT joined in a lawsuit challenging the governing board's selection of principals on the grounds that it was racially motivated. The more the board made itself felt in the schools—with new hires, menacing pronouncements, through proxies like Carson and others—the more open the racial friction in the hallways, at staff meetings and even in class. Still, teachers like Nauman did what they could to accommodate the board, hoping against hope that some kind of parent participation would materialize and the Ocean Hill experiment would take off.

Back in Manhattan that fall, Lindsay and Bundy continued their push to make decentralization official—to convince the state legislature to institute local control, not just in three demonstration districts but throughout the city. If anything, despite growing tensions in Ocean Hill, the momentum behind the idea grew stronger. Details about Ferguson and Carson and their intimidation of teachers did not get much attention in the Manhattan press. The teachers' union and the board of education remained guardedly in favor of decentralization, and the rest of the well-meaning Manhattan elite, apparently oblivious to what was going on in Brooklyn, saw no reason to back away from the idea.

No one was more enthusiastic than the Ford Foundation. Mario Fantini pressed ahead with research to substantiate the blueprint that the Bundy panel would submit to the legislature. He and his staff spent considerable time in the three demonstration districts, and they could hardly have missed the mood of the activists in charge of the schools. Still intent as they were on change, these foundation staffers believed that community control could be made to work. Their heavily theoretical report hardly mentioned Ocean Hill–Brownsville, and they had a well-reasoned rebuttal for every likely objection to the breakup of the school system. Addressing concerns that Black Power activists might take over in local districts, the report confidently affirmed that this would not be allowed to happen. "[We] put our trust," the document said, "in the collective good sense of the . . . parents. . . . [They] can be trusted to care more than anyone else for the quality of the education their children get."

It was also in these months that Bundy himself finally decided that the circle could be squared. Even as the Ocean Hill experiment took off and the idea of Black Power swept the ghetto, he remained firmly committed to the ideal of integration. Like most traditional liberals, he had little tolerance for what he called "racial feelings" and was determined to stand firm against the threat of balkanization. "There is only one bar and bench," he wrote eloquently that fall, "only one system of government, only one national marketplace, and only one community of scholars. Our great national institutions . . . will have to be open to all"—and, the implication went, would have to do for everyone. Still, after extensive study, Bundy was convinced that integration could be compatible with Black Power. Community control, nationalist pride, separate black institutions: paradoxically, in his view, they could provide a path to racial harmony. "It's not an either/or," Bundy would say, still absolutely confident, years later. "There are two tracks."

In part, this was a practical accommodation. Over the years at Ford, Bundy would fund a wide array of black opinion—including people as mainstream as Bayard Rustin—and even in the foundation's most radical years, Ford grants to militant groups accounted for no more than 10 percent of its giving. Still, by 1967, Bundy saw how the tide had turned in the movement, and he felt it made little sense to fund likable, reasonable-sounding integrationists if they had no following in the ghetto. Like all good foundation executives, he knew that change had to come from the bottom up: that to be effective, he had to reach black people where they lived, speaking their language and addressing their concerns. Still more important, Bundy believed that most blacks would eventually see the limits of separatism. "It seems to me the plainest of facts," he wrote, "that the destiny of the Negro in America is to be both Negro and American. . . . He will take pride in his particular group at the same time that he insists on full membership in society as a whole." Bundy saw the paradox at work here, but he felt that blacks would resolve it as other American groups had: that a period of separate development would prepare, embolden and fortify, then lead eventually to participation in the mainstream.

His mistake, in Ocean Hill–Brownsville and elsewhere, was underestimating the ferocity of black anger. He saw the bitterness plainly enough— you could hardly miss it in 1967—and he had little sympathy for what he called "the preachers of hate." Still, Bundy believed that their alienation was transitional: "spume on the wave of the past," he called it. Convinced, like so many liberals, that the main problem was white racism, he felt that black anger was "legitimate" and justified—and that, if white bigotry could be eliminated, the rest would eventually take care of itself. If only the nation could put its house in order, if whites could do the right thing by blacks, then, Bundy was sure, the race-based hatred swirling in the ghetto would disappear. He apparently did not worry that by funding radicals he might encourage them—might seem to reward them for their militancy and crowd out other, more moderate black spokesmen.

The Bundy panel's report, released in November, recommended more radical decentralization than anyone in the city had suggested before. Typical Bundy, the argument was crisp and to the point: the schools bureaucracy was the problem, the key obstacle to learning and integration. Remove that bureaucracy and the schools would surely flourish. Teachers would feel freer, energies would be released for innovation. Ghetto scores would rise to suburban levels, and white students would flood back. "Integration must be deferred, though not abandoned," the text insisted. "[It] is most likely to come only after a drastic improvement in the general effectiveness of the schools. . . . This will be the strongest possible magnet to draw *all* kinds of parents back to the city." It was an appealing vision—community control for the sake of integration—and in the panel's view, it justified radical dismemberment of the New York school system. The proposal submitted to the legislature, with Lindsay's emphatic backing, called for the system to be broken up into sixty small districts, each governed by a local board with significant power over budget, personnel and curriculum.

A handful of die-hard integrationists objected to the Bundy plan. The report "shows an incredible lack of understanding of New York today," Puerto Rican Bronx borough president Herman Badillo declared. Far from encouraging inclusion, he predicted, neighborhood boards would exacerbate racial tension. "Candidates would be running along ethnic lines. . . . Extremists would be running for office. . . . I can't think of anything that would be more conducive to civil strife." Union head Albert Shanker saw the same danger—as he put it, "Negro teachers [being] hired in Negro areas and white teachers in white areas." A board of rabbis called the Ford plan "a potential breeder of apartheid." Even the usually liberal *New York Times* was skeptical, in favor of some form of decentralization, but worried about "interference by political or racist-extremist pressure groups." The strongest opposition came from the board of education and the teachers' union, but like most of the report's critics they were dismissed in liberal circles—written off as interested parties.

Two incidents in the demonstration districts that winter argued somewhat alarmingly in favor of the skeptics' view. The first, in early February

1968, took place in Ocean Hill–Brownsville. A black junior high school student got up in the middle of class and left the room without permission. The teacher in charge followed him and led him back into the classroom. The youth picked up a chair, threw it at the older man and bolted. The next day, instead of rallying around the instructor, the local board accused him of assaulting the student and fired him without further ado. Albert Shanker went immediately to the press, warning anyone who would listen about the "terror" taking over in the schools. "Threats and intimidation are the order of the day," he charged in a full-page ad in *The New York Times.* "Teachers are beaten in their classrooms. . . . School after school has been enveloped by a climate of fear and chaos. . . . [The city is] kowtowing to irresponsible extremists whose terrorist tactics are in proportion to the lack of community support." The second incident, even more widely publicized, was the infamous Malcolm X memorial at I.S. 201 at which Herman Ferguson urged students to arm themselves in preparation for a coming race war. Still, even the board of education and the UFT remained cautiously in favor of decentralization.

Debate over the best way to break up the school system raged through the winter and spring. In addition to the Bundy plan, two other proposals circulated in Albany, one, slightly more conservative, the other even more radical than the Ford Foundation's. Discussion centered on a variety of theoretical issues: how would decentralization affect the civil service merit system, what would it mean for the schools budget, how many districts should there be and how exactly should they be overseen? The skeptics—mainly the teachers' and principals' unions and the central board—continued to push for a range of safeguards for school staffers. Still, virtually no one took heed of the warnings from Ocean Hill–Brownsville, and few reporters even bothered to visit the district.

That spring, as before, the question was not if, but how exactly to implement decentralization. The liberal press remained staunchly committed to the concept, and by April 1968 all of the Manhattan establishment had lined up behind one or another of the proposals circulating in Albany. Republicans and Democrats, state and federal education authorities, Governor Rockefeller, *The New York Times* and *The New York Review of Books:* the consensus was overwhelming and unequivocal, even among those whose own experience argued against it. The hope inspired by the civil rights struggle— and all the romance and idealism that came with it—was now riding on the idea of ghetto empowerment. The angriest activists in the movement had set the terms of the debate, and the white establishment, moderate as well as liberal, had uncritically adopted their ideas. Almost no one seemed to notice the difference between Ford's aim—to involve minority parents in their kids' schools—and the outcome of its experiment—creating a platform for disruptive militants. The liberal establishment congratulated itself on its efforts to promote racial inclusion and willfully ignored the separatist hatred it was unleashing in Brooklyn.

By spring 1968, the atmosphere in the Ocean Hill schools had undergone a marked transformation. White teachers were transferring out in droves; others were calling in sick on a regular basis. McCoy was hiring outsiders to replace the old staff, and the newcomers were transforming what went on in the district's classrooms. Parents, community people, activists, many of these new, nonunion "aides" had no teaching experience, and they gravitated toward unconventional, alternative curriculums: instruction in black culture, bilingual education, non-graded classrooms and the like. This was exactly what Bundy and others behind the experiment had hoped for, and in other circumstances it might have been cause for celebration. But in Ocean Hill, the district's original teachers knew if no one else did, the innovation came with a heavy price: poisonous levels of black anger and vituperation.

For the governing board and most of the new replacement teachers, the schools' number one priority was racial consciousness raising—to the district's white teachers, it seemed more like schooling in race hatred. McCoy's first order of business was to develop a black curriculum: lessons, laced with hostility for "the power structure," that only black teachers could teach and that left little room for what some were already calling "white learning." White teachers felt that district activists were inciting restless kids to make trouble, defying authority and rampaging in the halls. By spring, student discipline was nonexistent. Relations between black and white staffers were openly antagonistic. Community people increasingly blamed union teachers for sabotaging the experiment, and many white instructors were afraid to come to school.

District activists showed scant interest in the policy debate swirling in white circles. "We have authorized no one to speak for us," one grassroots activist wrote to the legislature. "We would oppose *any* legislation on decentralization." Legally and bureaucratically, the district needed an official go-ahead from state authorities, but the last thing many seemed to want was white people's permission—they could hardly claim to be launching a revolution if they had to ask city or state officials. The more sympathy well-meaning whites showed, the more it seemed to grate on the district's militants, and the further they went to provoke their would-be allies.

When the central board revised its procedures to accommodate the district, activists responded with a volley of petty complaints. Salary checks were coming late, they said; requests for supplies were being lost at central headquarters. It was hard for anyone in Manhattan to know what to make of these accusations, but even the most sympathetic were stunned by the local board's claim that white teachers were setting fires in the schools. In fact, several fires did break out in Ocean Hill that spring. School furniture was thrown from classroom windows, and vandalism skyrocketed. But there was never any evidence that teachers were responsible—if anything, they tended to be victims of the vandalism.

Try as it might, the education establishment was unable to come to any agreement with the district. The Ocean Hill board wanted to control its own budgets, to operate its own bank accounts, to hire and fire at will and to contract out locally for all support services. When the board of education balked at this, district activists claimed it was not serious, that the empowerment being offered them was nothing but a charade. The central board offered to work around the law and delegate fiscal powers to the district. Albert Shanker suggested that teachers and parents combine forces behind a bill to abolish the board of education. But every time the school authorities made a concession, McCoy and Powis and the others escalated their demands—and at one point stated explicitly that they would accept no compromises. When the central board and the union refused to capitulate, they were accused of racial genocide.

Even the Ford Foundation came in for a drubbing. By June 1968, according to one estimate, the foundation had spent $1 million on decentralization, some of it in grants to the Ocean Hill board, some of it paid indirectly to consultants. Still, McCoy and the board maintained that they were being shortchanged—and that they needed another $5 million immediately to cover the hiring of supplementary teachers. Sonny Carson, as ever one step ahead of the board, called a meeting to discuss Ford's relationship with the district. Reporters were summoned to his headquarters, where they found the militant and his followers waiting in a conference room surrounded by over $60,000 worth of office machinery—all of it, together with the rent, it turned out, paid for by a Ford grant. Without a trace of irony, Carson repudiated the foundation, raging at the strings that came attached to its money, and made bitter fun of Uncle Tom blacks who supported themselves by "begging for funding." "By 1970," he concluded, apparently on behalf of black America, "we'll either be independent or we'll be dead."

The board of education and the governing board were still negotiating—and still getting nowhere—when Martin Luther King was assassinated on April 4. By the time J.H.S. 271 opened the next morning, some of the students had been out all night on the streets of Brooklyn, and the atmosphere in the school, volatile now on even the calmest of days, was on the verge of exploding. The school's popular "Black Power bulletin board" was plastered with new material. "Wake up black people!" one run-off leaflet urged. "Martin Luther King . . . has been shot down by a vicious *white* man. Wake up! . . . As a black individual *prepare!!!*" Classes were effectively suspended; students milled angrily in the halls. At eleven o'clock, the principal called an assembly. Several members of the governing board got up and spoke, then the principal announced that white teachers were free to leave if they wished. For Fred Nauman, who had turned a blind eye on so much for so long, this was the most painful moment yet. "That principal was saying to the students," he recalled, still incredulous years later, "that because we were white we could not share in their remembrance of Dr. King."

Even then, those who stayed were unprepared for what happened next. The assembly culminated in a long, incendiary speech by popular black teacher Leslie Campbell. "[S]top fighting among yourselves," he told the students. "[G]et your minds together. You know who to steal from. If you steal, steal from those who have it." The agitated students listened raptly to their charismatic teacher. "If whitey taps you on the shoulder," he counseled, "send him to the graveyard." When Campbell finished, the remaining white teachers scrambled to leave the hall, and many were followed by bands of students. "We were frightened," Nauman recalled later, "really frightened. We had no idea what was going to happen next." Students roamed the corridors in search of white teachers. One was punched and pelted with beer cans; another, a young woman, was surrounded in the hall, her dress ripped and clumps of her hair pulled out. By the time the rampage subsided, a third staffer had been knocked unconscious and taken to a hospital. "It was totally out of control," Nauman remembered. "People were harassed and beaten. From then on, we knew the threats were real, and a lot of people began to see things differently."

Yet even this incident had little impact in Manhattan, where liberal support for community control was running as strong as ever. Bundy and Lindsay continued to press Albany to pass a law implementing citywide decentralization. Most of the Manhattan newspapers stood behind them. Even the board of education continued to try to come to terms with the district, offering ever more in the way of formal authority and autonomy. Still, with the Brooklyn activists explicitly ruling out all compromise, no agreement was reached. Nothing the city, the Ford Foundation or the central board could do seemed to appease the anger in Ocean Hill—and no amount of vituperation or even violence seemed likely to stop the Manhattan establishment from granting ever more power to the district's militants.

The rhetoric coming out of Ocean Hill grew more and more belligerent, and by late spring 1968 the board was openly spoiling for a fight—what Powis called "a confrontation with a sick society." "Maybe hunting season will start early," one militant threatened. Decentralization is but "a mechanism to contain guerrilla warfare," another declared. "We must destroy the mechanism. We must encourage incidents." That the city was already moving full speed ahead to empower the district seemed to mean little to these activists. That their experiment was already transforming the schools and the neighborhood of Ocean Hill did nothing to ease their impatience. What the board wanted, it made clear in its statements, was the emotional punch of revolution. The only question was the pretext—over which of its many disagreements with the educational establishment the district would launch a confrontation. The punch came in early May with the arbitrary firing of nineteen union staffers.

Chapter 7

"CONFRONTATION WORKS"

I t took the activists in Ocean Hill–Brownsville several weeks to prepare
the shot that began their revolution. It wasn't easy to pick a fight with
the city's education establishment on any issue, particularly not on matters of hiring and firing. Movement activists had made no secret of their antagonism toward conventional teaching, and sympathetic Manhattanites
had grasped from the start that community control would mean personnel
changes. Firing tenured faculty was out of the question, all agreed. But the
Ford Foundation, the board of education and even the teachers' union had
agreed to look the other way if the district wanted to replace a few staffers.
Still, intent on confrontation, the Ocean Hill board ignored these offers to
bend the rules.

The local board's militant flank set the conflict in motion in early spring
1968. Father John Powis and Reverend C. Herbert Oliver formed a personnel committee and declared belligerently that it would write its "own
rules"—ignoring tenure, seniority and merit ranking. Then, in mid-April,
the committee called for the removal of nineteen staffers: thirteen teachers,
five assistant principals and one of the district's few remaining white principals. When the full governing board met to consider the recommendation,
Sonny Carson and his thuggish followers burst into the room halfway
through the meeting and arranged themselves menacingly against the wall.
They had come, they claimed, on behalf of the neighborhood, and they
wanted the ousters to go ahead. Liberal whites told themselves that "the

community" was forcing Rhody McCoy's hand, though in the weeks ahead, the district's activists acted as one—and with scant input from parents—in engineering the confrontation.

The unlucky teachers were notified by registered letters, delivered to their classrooms, telling them they were no longer wanted in Ocean Hill. Fred Nauman, who like the others had had no previous warning, remembered later that the communication left him "totally numb." "At no time," he recalled, "had anybody mentioned that there was a problem with my service or, for that matter, with any of the people who were named." Neither the central board nor the union were informed of the dismissals. No due process was observed, no formal charges lodged. In a particularly Kafkaesque twist, the letters left unclear whether staffers were being fired or merely transferred. The curt notes directed them to report to the board of education for "reassignment," but the district's public statements threatened worse. "Not one of these teachers," McCoy told the press, "will be allowed to teach anywhere in the city. The black community will see to that."

The local board's explanations for the ousters were blustery and vague and charged with racial resentment. Asked what was wrong with the nineteen staffers, all but one of whom were Jewish, activists talked mainly about their "disloyalty." The ousted teachers didn't support the experiment; they didn't want to help black students. They weren't teaching—only "baby-sitting." There was some talk, then and later, of the fired staffers' incompetence. But their main crime, McCoy said candidly, was that they represented the system—the system of "white domination that would never relinquish its . . . mind control." When urged to file more specific complaints, McCoy and the governing board objected—on principle. "Decentralization means *we* decide," a board handout declared. "No Shanker, No Lindsay, no 500 cops—WE DECIDE!!!!"

The confrontation grew uglier still when the ousted teachers showed up for work the next week and found that "the community" had turned out in force to stop them. Sonny Carson and a small detail of militants were waiting on the steps of Junior High School 271. Arrayed in quasi-military gear and helmets, several of them carrying large sticks, they screened people at the door and denied entry to five of the fired teachers. Confused and frightened, the five stood awkwardly on the sidewalk from early morning until midday. Just after noon, several police vans pulled up. But before the cops could escort the teachers into the building, a throng of students gathered around Carson in front of the door. "The kids don't want [the teachers] to come in," one of Carson's toughs declared. "If [the five] persist, everything may explode, and it will be their fault." Students began setting off cherry bombs; the sound of shattering glass filled the air. The cops did nothing— they were awaiting orders—and the atmosphere grew more and more ominous. Finally someone announced that the board of education had decided to shut the school for the day. The police drove off, the spurned teachers went home, and Carson's improvised militia lingered to savor its victory, shouting Black Power slogans and pounding on the cars parked in front of the school building.

The confrontations at J.H.S. 271 continued through the month of May. Carson seemed to be everywhere, straggly followers in tow. When they weren't wearing helmets—those were reserved for formal skirmishes—many sported Black Panther berets and strings of 50-caliber machine-gun bullets draped over their dashikis. The first standoff set the pattern: the toughs waited intimidatingly on the school steps every morning, making it necessary for police to accompany the ousted teachers into work. Then, in mid-May, the activists organized a boycott, shutting district schools entirely for several days rather than let the nineteen come to class. By the end of the month, low-level violence—pushing, shoving, racial epithets, shouting matches with police—had become common currency at all eight of the Ocean Hill schools.

Audacious as it was, the board's revolutionary punch did not at first create much of a stir in Manhattan. Mayor Lindsay publicly deplored the ousters but declined to blame the district, coming down instead on the board of education. The school authority had failed to define the local board's duties, he charged. The "transfers," though abrupt, had been perfectly understandable: the district's effort to establish just where exactly its power stopped. (In fact, the central board pointed out, it had defined the district's powers precisely. Local board members had refused to accept the definition—and brazenly defied it with the dismissals.) Determined to support the experiment, to make it work no matter what, both the mayor and McGeorge Bundy attempted to smooth over the crisis—trying behind the scenes to convince the nineteen to go quietly, urging the local board to file formal charges and make the transfers legal.

After more than a decade of disillusionment with the board of education, Lindsay's reasoning made sense to many well-meaning New Yorkers, and they too ignored the cherry bombs exploding in Ocean Hill, the daily threats and the harassment of white teachers. The Urban Coalition, the New York

Urban League, Kenneth Clark, the Board of Regents, the liberal press, other leading civil rights groups and social service agencies: most of progressive Manhattan affirmed its support for the district during the month of May. Surely, they said among themselves, this small dispute can be papered over. The local board did not mean ill; these teachers can be mollified. Decentralization must go ahead.

It was a familiar reaction and by now, after a year of back and forth, a familiar pattern of threat and accommodation. The activists running Ocean Hill were intent on an extreme course, determined to provoke a confrontation no matter what it took. At the same time, still intoxicated with the idea of community power, the city's liberal establishment was determined to encourage the experiment, bending as many rules as possible to give the district what it wanted. Can-do, confident, paternalistic as ever, Lindsay, Bundy and others in Manhattan liberal circles were not going to let a few details derail their important experiment—and once again, as so many times before, they averted their eyes. The difference this time was that finally someone else stood up to the local board, resisting its rebellion as destructive for both the schools and the city. As a result, Albert Shanker would eventually be blamed for starting the conflict, though it had been set in motion long before he intervened.

Son of Eastern European Jews, raised in poverty on Manhattan's Lower East Side, Shanker was a born fighter, though always for an idealistic cause. His first love had been socialism, then union politics tinged with civil rights. He formed the United Federation of Teachers in 1960, an amalgamation of smaller pressure groups, and within a decade made it a force to reckon with in New York. When he started, there were twenty-four hundred members; by 1968, more than fifty thousand, and they had engineered a revolution in personnel practices in the public schools. Union work brought out Shanker's tough side. "One strike is worth a thousand settlements," he once said. Though not a temperamental man, he was stubborn and often self-righteous. He never lost a chance a make a point or get in a dig at an enemy, and on several occasions went to jail for the UFT. On the matter of decentralization, he was still guardedly for it in April 1968, though he worried more and more about balkanization. "The [smaller] the district," he said, "the [less] integrated it will be, and the [more] likely that it will be controlled by a small band of extremists using threats of violence."

In the days after the ousters, Shanker came out with guns blazing, determined to do whatever it took to stop the Ocean Hill board. As soon as the firings became known, he declared that the nineteen would report to work as

usual. When staffers were met on the school steps by Carson and his hench-
men, Shanker insisted that Lindsay himself accompany the teachers to work.
When he got no response from the mayor or others in Manhattan, he went
further still, insisting—an unthinkable demand in the spring of 1968—that
the Ocean Hill board be removed. Finally, when McCoy and his board
closed the district schools with a boycott, Shanker responded in kind: with a
strike. When the boycott ended and the Ocean Hill schools reopened their
doors, all 350 union teachers in the district stayed out, refusing to return to
work until the nineteen got their jobs back. Shanker was adamant: unless the
nineteen were reinstated or, at the very least, given a hearing, he would, he
threatened, shut down all of the city's public schools.

Shanker was not the only person in the city or state who was troubled by
the firings and what followed in the district. Teachers throughout the system
were taken aback. The dismissals had a slight chilling effect in Albany, convincing the state legislature to vote against the Bundy plan and for a more
limited decentralization bill. But even this was only a delaying tactic—it put
off the breakup of the system for a year—a weak, indirect signal that in no
way met or checked the district's aggressive punch. With the legislature tem-
porizing and most of Manhattan ignoring the crisis, only Shanker stood up
decisively to say that the intimidation must be stopped.

Unfazed by race or by the romance surrounding the Ocean Hill project,
Shanker stated bluntly what no one else dared say: that the emperor had no
clothes—that the activists on the governing board did not represent the district or the civil rights movement, that their vituperative anger would do no
good for anyone in the city. "We in the UFT," he declared, "strongly favor
more community participation. [But] we do not favor . . . extremist groups
[being allowed to] take over the schools." The question, now after two years
of encouragement, was whether the militants and their message could be
contained. Shanker had made a good start: a clear, unequivocal statement
that race hatred had no place in city politics. But there were signs from the
beginning that he was up against something stronger than he was: that whatever he did to fight the fury in the district might only make it worse, and that
he and his union risked being engulfed by the very passions they were trying
to staunch.

In June, with the first shock and countershock subsiding, the conflict entered a new phase. By now, eight of the nineteen dismissed staffers had
lost heart and agreed to accept their transfers. One—the only black one—

had been reinstated by the governing board. But ten aggrieved teachers—
and 350 striking supporters—were still demanding reinstatement, or at least
due process. Lindsay and Bundy, still determined to paper over the crisis,
continued to press the district to make a legal case: the ousters could be made
to seem acceptable, they insisted, the local board could have its way, if only it
would go through the motions of bringing formal charges. Finally, after
nearly a month of exhortation, McCoy agreed to file a complaint, and one of
the city's few black judges, the elderly Francis E. Rivers, was brought out of
retirement to hear it.

It was a rare moment of truth for the experiment. Now, finally, the community and its spokesmen had a chance to make their case. If Kenneth Clark
and others, including the activists in the district, were right—if it really was
white teachers who were holding blacks back—this was their opportunity to
demonstrate the wrongdoing. Unsavory as Sonny Carson was, troubling as
the abrupt ousters had been, if the community could prove its allegations, it
might make sense for the experiment to go ahead. Even the district's bristling
defiance could be understood if there were some substance to its claims.

The local board and its backers struggled for several weeks to formulate
their charges. McCoy continued to talk about white staffers' incompetence
and their efforts to "sabotage" the experiment. They had, it was said, started
fires in the schools; they had let students run wild in the hallways. They
wouldn't visit black homes or stay after school on their own time. One man,
it was even alleged, had installed a mistress in an apartment across the street
from the school where he worked. By the time the case came to court, some
of the wilder smears had been dropped. But the district's bill of particulars was
still an odd mix of the serious and the trivial: everything from unwillingness
to maintain order and "inappropriate remarks to a girl student" to "failing to
decorate the classroom properly and excessive use of the blackboard."

The charges were presented in June. Judge Rivers deliberated through the
summer. His findings, presented to the city in late August, were thorough
and carefully reasoned. If, as the local board later claimed, the verdict was
skewed by race or politics, this was nowhere apparent in Rivers's workmanlike report. In all ten cases, the black judge ruled, the ousted teachers should
be reinstated.

Charge by charge, he found the district's complaints false or unsubstantiated—what his report called "hearsay on top of hearsay." None of the five
said to be incompetent could be proved to be so. On the contrary, several
had recently received good ratings or recommendations from supervisors.

No accusations of corporal punishment, profane language or lewd remarks could be made to stick. Three of those said to "oppose the experiment" were completely exonerated. In a fourth case, the only evidence the board could bring was a report of a conversation at a Christmas party in which the accused complained to a friend about what was going on at work. Judge Rivers considered the episode in detail but decided the comments were "constructive criticism." As for the teacher accused of failing to maintain order, letting his students get so wild that they threw chairs around their classroom, it turned out, according to the school custodian, that the furniture in the room in question was screwed to floor.

Striking as it was, Judge Rivers's verdict had virtually no effect, either in the district or on the city's sympathy for the project. The local board shrugged off the report. "[We] never formally discussed the Rivers findings," chairman Oliver said later, "to say nothing of voting on them." Instead of dismissing the board or moving to restrict its power, the city suggested arbitration—as if both the district and the UFT had elements of right on their side and what was needed was to find a balance between them. The Ford Foundation continued to pour money into the district. Lindsay, Bundy, Kenneth Clark and others in the liberal establishment continued to justify what they called the "transfers." The Ocean Hill board may have meant the firings as an angry revolutionary punch; to well-wishers in Manhattan they were an awkward but welcome step toward independence and political maturity. Besides, proof or no proof, the district's basic charge—that white teachers were racists—was beyond the reach of any facts.

If anything, in the wake of the Rivers report, well-intentioned whites rallied around the district with new enthusiasm. Both the city and state education establishments moved that summer to give still more autonomy to the militants in Ocean Hill. Even as it voted to delay citywide decentralization, the state legislature also moved in the opposite direction, giving Lindsay a chance to stack the board of education with new members favorable to community control, then authorizing this revamped board to grant local districts whatever powers it saw fit. Among Lindsay's five new appointments was schools boycott organizer Milton Galamison, longtime advocate of community control and mentor to several members of the Ocean Hill board. Sonny Carson delivered the district's reaction to his selection: "We think Mr. Galamison is a great guy." A month after the central board was expanded, it produced an interim decentralization plan, granting more independence to the city's local school districts than any blueprint yet.

Nothing the district asked for seemed too much to grant; no step it took, no matter how unsavory, elicited criticism in Manhattan. Siding unequivocally with the district and against the teachers' union, in August 1968 the new board of education authorized McCoy to appoint 350 new, nonunion teachers to replace the 350 UFT staffers who had gone out on strike in support of the ousted nineteen. None of the district's liberal well-wishers seemed to care that the replacements would be scab laborers, hired without pretense to break a union strike. When the UFT demanded due process, some of Manhattan's leading lawyers dismissed the claim. Then, when McCoy had trouble finding qualified candidates, the central board stretched itself to the limit to help with unconventional recruitment and emergency qualifying exams. Even so, four-fifths of the new hires squeezed in just under the wire, making the grade as substitutes but not as regular teachers. Ocean Hill activists could not have cared less. They put no store by merit-based hiring and felt that what black kids needed was black role models—and as long as black spokesmen said so, liberals reasoned, it must be true.

By the time the schools were ready to open in September, a showdown was all but inevitable. Activists in the district still defended their right to dismiss whoever they liked—and they made clear they planned to defy Judge Rivers's order that they take back even ten of the nineteen. As for the 350 union teachers who had struck the district in May, by the end of the summer, their number had dwindled dramatically; more than 200 of them who had seen all they needed to see of Sonny Carson and his methods had requested and received transfers out of the district. This erosion left a total of seventy-nine disputed union teachers. Not only did the district not want them, but now it had no need of them. Now that McCoy had hired 350 replacement teachers, he had all the ammunition he needed to go into battle with the UFT.

With school opening day approaching, all seventy-nine disputed teachers announced their intention to return to work in Ocean Hill. McCoy made plain they were not welcome and declared he was under no obligation to take them back. As the year before, only Shanker said no. "[McCoy] takes the position," the union chief charged, "that he has the right to overrule all duly constituted authority, claiming, 'I don't care what rights exist. I am a dictator. . . . I am the law.'" Shanker, for one, had no intention of submitting, and he threatened to strike citywide if the seventy-nine union teachers were not allowed to return to work in Ocean Hill.

Hoping against hope, up until the last moment, many teachers in Brooklyn and elsewhere thought the educational establishment might intervene, chastising the district or at least brokering a compromise. Instead, the board of education, now controlled by Galamison and his allies, moved to grant local boards in Ocean Hill and elsewhere yet more leeway on hiring and firing. Shanker denounced the new rules in no uncertain terms: they would, he charged, "open up a field day for bigots and racists." Decades later, Sandra Feldman, by then the head of the teachers' union, was still smarting with disappointment. "The fact was that the Board of Ed in the city of New York seemed to have washed their hands of the thing," she said despairingly. "They just weren't helpful at all. They weren't exercising any authority."

For the city's teachers, in the district and elsewhere, this episode said all that needed to be said: they were wasting their time waiting for someone from Manhattan to stop the angry, color-coded harassment they were suffering under community control. Instead of providing leadership—playing referee and brokering a consensus for change—Lindsay, Bundy and the board of education were going to support the governing board no matter what. Liberal staffers like Sandra Feldman and Frederick Nauman were still deeply troubled by the prospect of taking sides against a black experiment. But by the time school was ready to open, even they felt that someone had to put a stop to what was happening in the district, restoring some sense of limits and a common code of conduct. "The union really had no choice," Feldman said later. With opening day approaching, UFT teachers voted to stay home from work, striking not just Ocean Hill but the entire school system.

Ninety-five percent of the city's teachers stayed away on September 9, 1968—more than fifty-four thousand in all. Pickets circled every school in the city. Most principals, siding with the union, locked their doors and sent students home. In all three demonstration districts, community people helped keep classrooms open. Attendance was light, but in Ocean Hill the schools buzzed with activity—mostly assemblies and political discussions.

The board of education and the UFT sat down to negotiate and had little trouble reaching a compromise: a "memorandum of understanding" that preserved the idea of decentralization but granted teachers many of the safeguards missing from the board's recent empowerment plan. Among other things, the agreement extended the union's contract to local districts and promised to protect school staffers from arbitrary dismissals. On the question of the ousted ten, the memo committed Ocean Hill to taking them back. But the settlement did not in any other way diminish the local board's powers, and it made clear that Shanker would be punished for the illegal strike. The union, the school authority, Lindsay and the Ford Foundation accepted the agreement. After only two days of missed classes, the city's teachers prepared to return to work. The only party that was not satisfied was the Ocean Hill board, still unwilling to brook any compromise. The district responded with a sullen statement acknowledging the settlement but refusing to cooperate. Among other points, the board declared that it would "no longer act as a buffer between this community and the establishment"— would no longer even pretend to restrain Sonny Carson and his men.

The full force of the militants' violence was unleashed the following day, September 10, when the seventy-nine disputed teachers attempted to return to work in the district. Staffers arriving at J.H.S. 271 girded for trouble as they approached the front steps, manned once again by Carson and a gang of his "bodyguards." A large brigade of cops was on hand, and the atmosphere was ugly. After some harassment, the union teachers were allowed to enter the building. Sandra Feldman went directly to McCoy's office, hoping to persuade him to welcome the staffers back. He was busy with a journalist and had no time to talk. But it took Feldman only a minute to grasp that there was trouble brewing. Every few moments the phone rang, and McCoy answered as if at military headquarters. Yes, he told caller after caller, the plan should be put into effect. At all eight district schools, union teachers reported to their principals' offices, only to discover that they had been relieved of classroom duty. They would learn about their new jobs, they were told, at an "orientation session" starting soon in the auditorium of I.S. 55.

When the teachers arrived in the large, windowless hall, they found that Carson and his men had gotten there first. Some fifty toughs were lined up along the walls of the auditorium, now arrayed in helmets, carrying sticks and draped with bandoliers of bullets. The teachers were showered with curses as they filed in. Frightened and confused, they huddled together in the middle of the room. McCoy appeared and tried to speak but was drowned out by the jeers of Carson's men. McCoy shrugged as if helpless and left the room. "Wait till we get the lights out," one of the thugs shouted. "We'll throw lye in your faces. You'll be very visible."

All in all, it would be nearly two hours before the teachers were allowed to leave. The lights in the hall were repeatedly flicked off and on. There were scuffles in the darkness. Staffers were called "faggots" and vermin; the hoodlums threw bullets, hitting one man squarely on the head. The threats were explicitly racial and often personal, directed at the teachers' families as well as themselves. At one point, paper and pens were circulated and teachers were made to write down their addresses. Later, with the chaos mounting, they were pushed and shoved and told that they would leave only in "pine boxes." Sandra Feldman bore some of the worst of the abuse. "You think this little lady can protect you?" one activist asked. "Let her come near us and we'll show you how she will protect you. You'll see what we'll do to her." One teacher, pregnant, was reportedly punched in the stomach. Just when they thought they could stand it no longer, staffers were released from the auditorium.

Most headed back to their own school buildings, only to find more of the same treatment waiting for them there. The schools had been emptied of students; there were no teaching assignments, not even time cards to punch. At J.H.S. 271, a mob blocked the steps and more of the usual harassment occurred. One group of teachers that made it inside was accosted by the principal, who proceeded to lock them in a medical examining room, ostensibly for their own protection. "He told us to stay where we'd be out of trouble," Nauman recalled. "Then Sonny Carson and a number of his people appeared. It was the first time I'd seen him roaming on his own inside a school building. We were outraged—and terrified." Closeted together in the small doctor's room, the activists called the teachers "pigs" and taunted them menacingly at close range. "Why don't you go teach in your own community?" one man said. "You can see you are not wanted here." Finally, some time after two o'clock, a police unit arrived and escorted the union teachers to safety, outside the building.

Back in Manhattan, it was as if the incident in the auditorium had never happened. The strike settlement made the front page of *The New York Times,* but Sonny Carson and his thugs were not mentioned. Indignation was minimal, and the establishment continued to side with the district. If anything, now that a fight was brewing, editorialists, columnists, liberal lawyers and armchair do-gooders began to take a more avid interest. Most perceived the dispute as a classic racial standoff: struggling, courageous, put-upon blacks versus selfish, bigoted white teachers. *Village Voice* columnist Nat Hentoff, *New York Post* editorial page editor James Wechsler, intellectuals Dwight Macdonald and Jason Epstein, well-connected minister Donald Harrington, the New York Civil Liberties Union and black moderate Whitney Young: the rush to take sides with the district was deafening and, in the intellectual world, all but unanimous.

Even as word filtered back about what had happened at I.S. 55, these well-wishers brushed it off as if it were a nasty rumor. As ever, Lindsay took the lead, making light of what had happened when union teachers tried to go back to work in Ocean Hill. The abuse of the returning teachers was "99 percent verbal," he declared dismissively. Besides, he reasoned, whatever was said or done was surely understandable: striking staffers could hardly expect the district to feel "affectionate" toward them. As for the larger dispute between the district and the union, the mayor left no doubt about whose side he was on, announcing—apparently oblivious of the facts—that he thought the Ocean Hill board had "more or less" lived up to its agreement to take back union teachers.

It took several months for *The New York Times* to report on what had happened that day in the district, and when it did, the account was not in the news pages but an opinion-laden magazine piece: an article by a replacement teacher—one of McCoy's 350 new hires. Young, idealistic, a declared partisan, Charles Isaacs was on the job at J.H.S. 271 the day the union returned to work. If he knew about what happened around the corner at I.S. 55, he did not mention it, commenting only in a general way on the hostility that passed between teachers and activists. Given the built-up resentments, he reasoned, "there had to be harassment on both sides." But "all of the abuse was verbal . . . the harassment was petty and, to the best of my knowledge, it never escalated to threats on people's lives." The article backed up this claim with a quote from governing board chairman C. Herbert Oliver: "I wish people wouldn't interpret an exclamation of 'drop dead!' as a threat on their lives."

In place of the assembly incident, Isaacs's article related an entirely different episode that occurred on the same morning, in his math class. Isaacs was busy conducting a lesson when suddenly, according to his account, a UFT teacher barged into the room. Without a word to teacher or students, the intruder began picking papers up off the floor and rummaging in the wastebasket. Isaacs told him he was disrupting the class and tried to show him the door. "The students (13 to 15 years old) looked at him," Isaacs wrote, "their eyes filled, some with amazement, some with hatred, some with confusion." Finally, "for no apparent reason," the interloper "turned to the class, belched loudly and walked out." It wasn't a major incident, but the innuendo was clear: that union teachers were bigots trying to kill community control.

The magazine articles piled up through the autumn. The *Times, The Village Voice, The New York Review of Books, Commonweal,* even *Time* and

Newsweek ran pieces glorifying community control and blaming the UFT for trying to scuttle it. The same reasoning ran through all the stories: that anyone who opposed the black experiment in Brooklyn was by definition a racist. That the teachers were obviously bigoted was proven by their failure to educate black children. Worse yet, they had the gall to put their own interests first, worrying more about job security—and safety—than about racial redress. Didn't they understand, liberal journalists asked righteously, the importance of the race issue? Didn't they see that justice had to come first, trumping other, more petty concerns? Viewed from this larger, historical perspective, little things like what happened at I.S. 55 were insignificant. Given their race and their righteous cause, the militants running the Ocean Hill district could do no wrong, and ordinary standards—no matter how basic—did not apply to them.

All in all, there would be three strikes, one after the other as the fall wore on. In the wake of the I.S. 55 episode, Shanker felt the city lacked the will to enforce an agreement, and he ordered union teachers to walk out again. The second strike lasted more than two weeks. It too was followed by a settlement reached without the participation of the Ocean Hill board—activists from the district still refused to negotiate. Once again, union teachers returned to the district; once again, they were met with vigilante violence. After a week of harassment, they and their colleagues walked out a third time and stayed out for over a month. By Thanksgiving, New York's 1 million public school students had missed nearly forty days of class, disrupting life across the city as parents scrambled to make other arrangements for their kids.

On a typical strike day, roughly 85 percent of the city's schools were closed. In Ocean Hill, McCoy's 350 replacement teachers kept classes and community activities going strong; local activists and volunteers did the same in other black enclaves. UFT teachers turned out en masse to picket these open schools and others, and in black areas they clashed on a daily basis with activists and students. Most ghetto schools were ringed, as if permanently, by blue police barricades. White teachers carrying picket signs lined up on one side of the wooden horses; embittered blacks clustered on the other. The police, often dressed in riot gear, did their best to keep the two groups apart—not always successfully. "There were a lot of volatile moments," Sandra Feldman remembered of her experience at J.H.S. 271, "when crowds were being kept away from the school by the police, and teachers had to walk through a gauntlet of shouting, jeering people . . . to get to where the picketing took place. . . . It was very painful and very frightening. . . . These were teachers who had spent years and years coming to the school. And suddenly they found themselves so pilloried, so much anger out there at them."

The bitterness was catching among both teachers and neighborhood people, and it was not confined to adults. School-age kids in black districts often spent the day hanging out on the streets near their school buildings. Stunned, they watched their parents and teachers, filled with rage, glare and scream at each other without reserve, and not surprisingly it wasn't long before the poisonous "us" versus "them" engulfed the children, too. "No one was immune," one Brooklyn student, then thirteen, recalled. "You go to watch the picket line, and when you watch the picket line you choose sides, and before long you end up joining the picket line." For that kid, the young Al Sharpton, it was a defining experience, and though as an adult activist he later took the lesson further than many others, he was not alone. "You couldn't avoid it," he explained. "There was nothing else for us to do. And a lot of kids who would otherwise never have gotten involved got involved in the struggle then. Our going to school for two months or however long it was, our daily lesson was joining a picket line."

For many black students throughout the city, this political education continued inside the schools. In Ocean Hill, the governing board was determined to keep classes running, and all eight of the district's schools remained open through the fall. In other ghetto areas, learning moved into churches, storefronts and brownstone basements as well as "liberated" school buildings. Overall, several hundred thousand minority students attended alternative classes at one time or another that autumn.

Classes in the district were manned by the 350 irregular teachers McCoy had recruited over the summer. The replacements were a mixed lot: neighborhood people, movement veterans and hangers-on, former gang members, recent teaching graduates of southern black colleges and—the largest group—middle-class white kids looking for a way to make a difference. Most of them had been too young to march in Selma or work for SNCC, and for them teaching in Ocean Hill was the next best thing: a chance, as the phrase went, "to be part of the solution." The press could not help but be captivated by them and by the spirit of change in Ocean Hill. Newspaper and magazine articles celebrated the influx of "teachers who give a damn." The district schools were featured almost every night on the TV news: the dashikis and bright billboards, the buzz of political organizing in the hall-ways. For many New Yorkers, the experiment captured all the charged promise and hope of the era: the same romance of spontaneity and freedom and redemptive social action that were swirling around the Prague Spring and Robert Kennedy's campaign for president. Central to this romantic image was the district's educational vision: the idea, still new and untested then, of a specifically black curriculum that would instill pride in black children and inspire them to learn.

Every aspect of what went on in the district schools was informed in some way by race consciousness. Texts circulating at J.H.S. 271 included works by W. E. B. Du Bois, Malcolm X, Marcus Garvey, H. Rap Brown and Mao's *Little Red Book*. Courses taught that civilization began not in Greece or Rome but in Africa. There were lectures by big-name militants and informal chats with Black Panthers. Students assumed African names. They were taught that everything they studied was "political"—or that, if it couldn't be made political, it probably didn't matter. Rhody McCoy and other district spokesmen made no effort to conceal their vision of education as indoctrination. "I don't want you reading the book to these kids," McCoy lectured a group of teachers. "I don't want these kids reading the books. I want you to take them down to the courts, to the [state] assembly, take them where they can see, then you come back, you dissect it and talk about it." In place of old-fashioned academic instruction, there were "liber-ation classes," "community workshops," lessons in self-defense and "how to stage a demonstration." "You can't just have biology class," one junior high student explained, "with all the political science going on. So, basically, [we had] political science."

Friends of the district took it on faith that black educators knew what was good for black children. Then, as in years to come, theories about identity and self-esteem seemed plausible and appealing to white liberals. Certainly, many black children were having trouble with conventional "white" teach-ing methods, so why not try piquing their interest with race-conscious cur-riculums and role models? Patrons who visited the district came away impressed by what one called the "atmosphere of warmth and dignity." "The holy flame of learning," Alfred Kazin reported in *The New York Times,* "[burns] hotter than ever" in community-controlled Ocean Hill. Other New Yorkers, particularly educators, were less sure. "I can see," Albert Shanker told the press, "why kids would want to know more about their heritage." Still, he worried—on the basis of some knowledge of community control—

that this might not be all that was going on in Black Studies class. "The real problem," he warned, "is to make sure that white and black racists do not teach hatred at the expense of the child."

Intrigued by the innovation and the "relevant" black curriculum, some students seemed to show new interest in school, and many plainly liked their dashing, new black teachers better. But the reasons they gave for this preference did not always sound like good ones—that the new staff let them play soul music at lunch or skip chemistry class—and already it often seemed that what was being encouraged was old-fashioned bias. The black teachers "were human beings," one student declared, not—like whites—"some abstract something." Teachers made no secret of their alienation from mainstream America; many saw it as their mission to pass this anger on to students. And nine times out of ten, the "political" cast of class sessions was explicitly racial: that black was always right and white by nature alien and oppressive. Then, as for decades to come, few whites dared suggest that this sounded like racism.

In addition to what went on in class, the district's activists helped indoctrinate neighborhood kids, mesmerizing them with their style and swagger and the shadow they cast over the city. Al Sharpton, who lived in the nearby neighborhood of East Flatbush, was not exposed to any classroom learning in Ocean Hill. Still, he later said, he was forever transformed by what he glimpsed of the men running the experiment. "I saw them as exciting," he remembered. "I saw them as role models. It was the first time I met black men who were constantly in the media—who had gotten white people's attention." Carson, Ferguson, McCoy, C. Herbert Oliver, Leslie Campbell and Albert Vann: the different militants involved in the experiment played a variety of different parts—teacher, administrator, strategist, enforcer. But separately and together, they conveyed the same message: that what was happening in the district and the city was a war between black and white, and that the struggle justified just about any means.

No one articulated the vision more clearly than Leslie Campbell. Tall, striking, charismatic, a natural organizer, Campbell had come to the district from I.S. 201, where he had been one of the organizers of the infamous Malcolm X memorial. From the beginning, he helped set the tone in Ocean Hill, and by fall 1968 his dashikis and his "Black History bulletin board" had become the hallmarks of the experiment. Students were fascinated and Campbell had attracted a large following. But it was increasingly clear that his passionate race consciousness could not be separated from color-coded anger at the white world. His most famous lesson, documented in a teachers' newsletter in 1967, began with a comparison between Martin Luther King and Malcolm X. "Whitey doesn't listen," Campbell said, disparaging King's peaceful tactics. "Whitey doesn't want to give us anything," one eighth grader dutifully echoed. "The only thing [the Man] understands," Campbell pressed his point home, "is when we get up and start throwing bricks and Molotov cocktails." The district's white well-wishers tended to gloss over this kind of incitement; it was overshadowed, they said, by the racial dignity Campbell inspired. But for Campbell, as for Malcolm, the different parts of the lesson were of a piece: the dashikis, the bulletin board—and the open incitements to violence. What he taught, in class and by example, was that racial pride was the same as racial anger. A moment's flare of resentment—at a cop or a teacher or a hard test—could and should be nurtured into a generalized hatred of whites.

Sonny Carson took a different tack, less about ideology than action, but if anything he was more influential than ideas men like Campbell. Both students and teachers found Carson inscrutable: "I'm not sure what if anything he believed," Nauman said later. Still, like him or not, there was no ignoring the impact of his tactics. Playing guard on the school steps, intimidating teachers, defying police: as much as any of the ostensibly more powerful men on the governing board, it was Carson who frightened and provoked the UFT, prolonging the strikes that shut down the school system. Many white liberals, in 1968 and later, were tempted to dismiss him as a rabble-rouser, a hired thug far more extreme than other activists in the district. In fact, he was not only powerful but widely popular among the neighborhood's alienated youth. "I transformed thousands of black kids into little Sonny Carsons," he boasted later.

There was little mystery about his appeal. Confused, impulsive, uncertain about themselves, defiant but, as everyone recognized, low on self-esteem, the youths of the district thrilled to an angry black man who dared to thumb his nose at white people. Carson's troublemaking demagoguery appeared to them as manly strength, and they thronged around him whenever he took over the steps of the school or roamed the hallways intimidating teachers. Unlike their fathers or their neighbors or black teachers eager to ingratiate themselves in the mainstream, he was big enough to stand up to the white man and tell him, without blinking, just where to get off. To these kids, Carson's Manichean picture of black and white was all the more appealing for its starkness. More important still, he was not just talking; he was hitting white

New York where it hurt. Brazen and unrestrained, Carson made violent confrontation seem not just acceptable but glorious, and he convinced an entire generation of New York kids that white people were the enemy.

As ever, it was hard to gauge just what the adults in Ocean Hill made of this militancy. Few of the district's parents seemed curious about the experiment being run in their name, and only a tiny percentage participated, either at the barricades or in the classroom. McCoy and the governing board were invariably disappointed by the showings at rallies: after making preparations for hundreds, they often found themselves waiting hours to address a few dozen neighborhood people. Even the most successful gatherings only proved the thinness of the community's support. More than half of those who showed up at the larger rallies were white, and all but a few were what the *Times* called "frequent demonstrators": dashiki-clad, in blue jeans, brandishing their fists, activists and intellectuals committed to left-wing causes. Journalists looking for engaged community people could rarely find anyone to talk to, and as a last resort often settled for an interview with one always available, eccentric neighborhood woman. Dressed in leopardskin and carrying a chieftain's staff, she appeared several times that fall on the nightly news. "White people," she muttered, "you'd better be out of this district. Get out by sundown and don't you never come back."

Still, virtually no one in the city's black community—in Brooklyn, Harlem or anywhere else—came forward to naysay the district's militant leadership. No journalists visiting the district reported parents restraining their children from joining Carson at the barricades. Youths like Sharpton who came under the influence of Ocean Hill "role models" remembered no countervailing influence from ministers or other political leaders. Movement old-timer Bayard Rustin, who had organized the March on Washington and the first New York school boycott, was conspicuous in his solitary opposition to the local board: the only prominent black in the city to side with the UFT, he was widely repudiated as a cranky old sellout. Not only had Malcolm X's separatist notion of community control won the day even among Harlem's old-guard integrationists like Kenneth Clark and Whitney Young; more striking still, no mainstream blacks dared to stand up and denounce the violent intimidation of white teachers. "I don't recall that there was any repudiation of Carson," Fred Nauman said later, "not by Kenneth Clark or anyone else." As ever, the centrists knew it would not pay to chastise militants: that to ordinary blacks, apathetic or ambivalent as they were, this would seem like the worst kind of racial betrayal.

As the second strike wore on, racial polarization spilled across the city, spreading beyond the district and the school system. No one with children could ignore the disruption, and eventually even the childless felt compelled to take sides. There were street protests and mass meetings in all five boroughs. The conflict dominated the newspapers: ordinary news stories and a war of full-page advertisements in *The New York Times*. Color-coded fears and resentments, never very far from the surface, surged into the open, ugly and unashamed, spreading poisonously among adults and children who had never thought of themselves as bigoted before. Professionals, liberals, most of better-off Manhattan and the opinion-shaping elite sided with the district—as, in their own largely passive way, did the swelling minority population in all boroughs. A tiny handful of intellectuals—in addition to Bayard Rustin, the most important was social democrat Michael Harrington—supported the UFT. But apart from them, the union's support came almost entirely from borough-based whites: other civil servants, ethnics, cops, frightened parents, less prosperous Jews.

In late September, with New Yorkers already divided into hostile camps, Shanker stunned the city with an anti-Semitic leaflet he said he had discovered circulating in Ocean Hill. The pamphlet was semiliterate, crudely typed and mimeographed, and according to Shanker, it had been used to threaten Jewish teachers, who found it one morning stuffed in their school mailboxes. The subject was educational genocide—in this case by so-called "Middle-East murderers." "If African American history and culture is important to our children," the leaflet read, all capital letters, "the only persons [who] can do the job are African-American brothers and sisters, and not the so called liberal Jewish friend. We know from his tricky deceitful maneuvers that he is really our enemy and *he* is responsible for the serious educational retardation of our black children." Shanker reprinted five hundred thousand copies of this text and distributed them widely to the press. Surely, he reasoned, this would make clear to skeptical liberals just why it was that he and his union felt they had to go out on strike. Instead, far from shedding new light on the conflict, the pamphlets dramatically escalated it.

It was hardly the first anti-Semitism to surface among black activists, in Ocean Hill or elsewhere. Harold Cruse's much-publicized 1967 book, *The Crisis of the Negro Intellectual*, had provided the intellectual framework for others to fashion old resentments into a case: to argue that Jewish merchants robbed the ghetto, that Israel was an oppressive power, that patronizing Jew-

ish advisers had misled the movement—and that, in the name of racial grievance, blacks had a right to say whatever they wanted about Jews. The climate
had grown more vicious still with the outbreak of the Six Day War: SNCC
had sided against Israel, while the Black Panthers seized the chance to vent a
blanket hatred of all things Jewish. "We're gonna piss upon the Wailing
Wall," the Panther magazine declared. "That will be ecstasy, killing every Jew
we see." In New York, Sonny Carson had been among the first to air his prejudice openly, singling out Jewish teachers for special treatment in Bedford-
Stuyvesant. "The Weinsteins [and] the Goldbergs are wasting our kids'
time," he charged, "on other people's cultures." In Ocean Hill, Leslie Campbell gave the same sentiments a more respectable veneer in his newsletter,
The African-American Teachers' Forum. "The Jew," one issue noted, "our
great liberal friend of yesterday . . . is now our exploiter. He keeps [black]
women and men from becoming teachers and principals . . . he keeps our
children ignorant." Still, until September 1968, no one in the Manhattan establishment had called Ocean Hill activists on their anti-Semitism.

Shanker, it would turn out later, got a number of his facts wrong. The
pamphlet he distributed most widely was probably a composite of two
leaflets, and both were as venomously antiwhite as they were anti-Jewish: the
combined text gave as much space to "whitey" and "whitey textbooks" as to
"Middle-East murderers." The number of copies originally handed out
could never be determined, but it was well below the hundreds of thousands
Shanker spread around the city. Nor, as Shanker implied, was the Ocean Hill
board responsible for the literature. More likely, the texts were the work of
one Ralph Poynter, a freelance hatemonger and enforcer who operated, on a
smaller scale, in the same autonomous way that Carson and his thugs did.
Still, exaggerated or not, there was no disputing that Shanker was onto
something, and that it was being spread in the district with the acquiescence
of the governing board.

Shanker's revelations brought a raft of denials and countercharges. Members of the governing board insisted they were not anti-Semitic. McCoy
claimed he had never seen the handouts, that it was white teachers who had
produced or distributed them. Still, open-minded as he claimed to be,
McCoy refused to go on television to denounce the leaflets; he felt, he said
candidly, that this would impair his credibility. "You have to understand," he
told reporters, "I have to work with both worlds." Predictably enough by
now, none of the district's white well-wishers pressed McCoy to make a statement. On the contrary, instead of looking into the matter or chastising the

board, most of the Manhattan establishment attacked Shanker for drawing attention to the pamphlets. Journalists, foundation executives, Christian clergymen and city officials all lashed out indignantly at the union leader. Columnist Jimmy Breslin compared him to demagogue George Wallace. "The UFT is trying to pin responsibility for the . . . leaflets on the Ocean Hill [experiment]," declared the New York Civil Liberties Union. "This is a smear tactic reminiscent of the days of Senator Joseph McCarthy."

If anything, in the short term, the episode enhanced the district's standing with a certain kind of New Yorker. Liberal friends of the experiment seized on Shanker's exaggerations and mounted a public relations field day. All the teachers' talk about death threats, about black thugs and black racism: that too, many Manhattanites now felt certain, had been an exaggeration at best. In fact, it would turn out, Shanker was anything but wrong about the anti-Semitism in the Ocean Hill district. Before the year was out, an impartial panel convened by the mayor would more than vindicate the union chief's charges. "The countless incidents, leaflets, epithets, and the like in this school controversy," the group's investigative report stated, "reveal a bigotry from black extremists that is open, undisguised, nearly physical in its intensity—and far more obvious and identifiable than that emanating from whites." But in New York in 1968, not even hard evidence like Ralph Poynter's pamphlets could disabuse sympathetic whites of their illusions about the black protest movement.

In the wake of the leaflet incident, the level of venom in the city—already near intolerable—spiked upward. From now on, Shanker's name alone would be enough to start quarrels among New Yorkers. Long suspect in Manhattan circles, he was now viewed as a confirmed racist: liberal contempt grew so strong that Woody Allen could play off it, joking in a coming film, *Sleeper*, that his worst nightmare was Shanker with a nuclear weapon. But for most of the city's middle- and working-class Jews, the union chief only looked more heroic: someone willing to stand up to surging bigotry that no one else in a position of power would even acknowledge. For better or worse, in the boroughs and in black neighborhoods, the Ocean Hill controversy was redefined overnight. What had seemed to be a struggle between teachers and community—a conflict between two interest groups that could find a compromise—was suddenly a set-to between two tribes. And with the stakes raised to involve racial honor, no black or Jew could avoid taking sides.

Even formerly uncertain Jews, many of whom liked to think of themselves as liberal, were unable to evade the call of "us" and "them." The UFT pickets circling the Ocean Hill schools made less and less of an effort to disguise their resentment. The shouting matches at the barricades grew uglier and uglier, and many of the striking teachers began to look as hate-filled as the militants on the other side, fed up and spoiling for a fight. Shanker and Nauman were treated like movie stars as they traveled around town, approached by white working people eager to commiserate and congratulate them. "At this point," Nauman recalled, "we had become sort of heroes to the city—to some of the right people and some of the wrong people. . . . [Among] the things that you heard was, 'You got the guts. You put the blacks in their place.' It was disturbing." By the end of the year, Jews were even forming their own vigilante groups: the best known, in Brooklyn, led by Rabbi Meier Kahane. A newspaper survey of the rising polarization quoted borough Jews at their brazen worst. "Lindsay leans over backward to help the Negroes," one woman complained. "He's a blankety-blank nigger-lover," an older man echoed.

There were those, on both sides of the conflict, who felt that the issue of anti-Semitism was a red herring. "When [the militants] say 'Jew,'" James Baldwin insisted, "they mean 'white.' . . . The hostility is toward the whites." Twenty years later, Sonny Carson seemed to confirm this view, announcing provocatively that he was not anti-Semitic but "anti-white." "Don't just limit me to one little group of people," he said of his own antagonism. Even the Jewish refugee Fred Nauman saw the Ocean Hill controversy in broader terms: "The fact," he said, "that many of the teachers who were fired were Jewish, I think, was incidental." True or not, in the aftermath of the leaflets, with all of the city taking sides in the ethnic standoff, anti-Semitism spread through the ghetto—suddenly not just acceptable but a matter of honor. Menorahs, swastikas and Hitler talk became common currency among the mobs harassing UFT pickets. Anti-Semitic rhetoric became standard patois among New York ghetto kids. Jewish teachers in particular were convenient victims, hapless and unprotected, easily accessible to men like Carson and his followers. The fact that they were especially sensitive to bigotry and rarely fought back only made it easier to pick on them. With the Manhattan establishment explicitly blaming the teachers and refusing to hold the district responsible for its anti-Semitism, both Carson and the kids who admired him believed they could now taunt Jewish staffers with impunity.

By the end of September, New York students had missed only thirteen days of school, but the city was embittered beyond the point of no return. The transformation of the conflict—from political dispute to tribal war—

was a disastrous turning point for both blacks and Jews. But the ill effects did not stop there—because once the conflict was recast in communal terms, there was no settling or containing it. Bigotry surged on both sides. Clan and color consciousness trumped all other judgments and loyalties, and as the poison welled up, no one in the city could avoid being engulfed. What had once been considered unspeakable was now hardly even startling, and brazen racial hatred became the order of the day. "Jew pig!" "Nigger lover!" "Middle East murderer!": the epithets shouted over the barricades were soon commonplace around New York, and now that the union too was caught up in the swirling hatred, there was no one to stop it from spreading.

The settlement that ended the second strike differed little from the first agreement of two weeks before. At Shanker's insistence, the new deal provided a measure of protection for UFT staffers returning to the district, but once again they were met with harassment and violence. Angry crowds gathered around the schools and taunted the teachers on their way into work. Not one union teacher at any of the eight schools received a classroom assignment. Students were hostile and defiant, and as usual the worst trouble occurred at J.H.S. 271—another scuffle on the steps that ended with nine arrests and ten injured policemen.

The days that followed brought more of the same at J.H.S. 271 and throughout the district. There were no teaching assignments. Union staffers were continually harassed. Finally, at one building, the threats and tension got so bad that the principal closed the school for the day. By the time the week was out, not even the Manhattan establishment could ignore the chaos. Divided and somewhat reluctant, but under pressure to take action, the board of education suspended the local board and relieved McCoy of his duties. It was a sweeping, dramatic step: the action the teachers had been waiting for since summer. The problem was that by now, even this was too little too late. After months of vacillation and open encouragement for the local board, the city authorities had little power over the experiment. If anything, the pressure spurred the district to new defiance. McCoy simply ignored the ruling and went to work as usual in Ocean Hill, shrugging off the central board's order that he rein in the activists wreaking havoc in the schools.

The rampage that occurred at J.H.S. 271 on Wednesday, October 9, was one of the worst yet. Two hundred demonstrators battled cops in front of the building. Inside, neighborhood activists roamed the halls at will, assaulting union teachers and uniformed police. Students were encouraged to act out in corridors and classrooms. Notation on one blackboard—a scrawled list of white teachers' names—suggested that the kids had been told whom to target. In late morning, classes were herded to the auditorium for a rally. "We will die for Rhody McCoy," the junior high schoolers shouted joyously. The next Monday, October 14, the teachers' union struck the system for the third time, claiming that the city still had not made it safe for them to work in Ocean Hill.

The third strike was the longest of all—a full five weeks—and the most bitterly divisive for the city. By now, both teachers and parents were at the end of their tethers: teachers angry, confused and missing pay, parents at a loss for what to do with their children. Determined not to send his people back to work until every one of them could return safely, Shanker went all out, dramatically escalating his demands. Neither legal guarantees nor observers nor a massive police escort would satisfy him: nothing short of the abolition of the Ocean Hill experiment. City authorities were furious but helpless, and they scrambled to woo Shanker with compromise proposals. The union chief refused every one. He simply no longer trusted the mayor or the central board to guarantee teachers' safety.

By the time October turned to November, there was hardly anyone in the city who had not taken sides. After three strikes and two months of missed classes, parents were desperate to send their kids back to school, but no one imagined that this would put the genie of race hatred back in the bottle. From one end of town to the other, blacks and whites alike were ready to rally behind extremists. Virtually all had lost sight of what one school official called the "specifics" of the dispute, and even reasonable people stopped making a distinction between angry activists and ordinary people of the other race. Sometime in early November, it became clear that the denouement was coming, but this did nothing to appease the bitterness dividing the city.

Lindsay experienced the spreading fury firsthand when he drove out to Flatbush with his wife to address a group at the Midwood Jewish Center. The mayor had chosen his audience carefully. Middle-class Jewish Flatbush would naturally be sympathetic to the teachers' union, but also, Lindsay hoped, generally liberal on race issues. He prepared a speech supporting decentralization but denouncing anti-Semitism; his point was that compromise was still possible—if only people could see beyond the few "extremists" in the spotlight. A year or so before, this argument might have worked in a Flatbush synagogue. By mid-fall 1968, that was out of the question.

Two thousand people were waiting in the street when Lindsay arrived, chanting, "We want Shanker!" and brandishing picket signs. The mayor had trouble making his way through the crowd. Inside, the boos and jeering started with the first word of his speech, spiking upward whenever he mentioned the activists in Ocean Hill. About ten minutes into his remarks, he was shouted down, and the synagogue's rabbi took over the podium, hoping to quiet the audience by reminding it of its own rationality and tolerance. "Is this the exemplification of the Jewish faith?" he asked plaintively—and, to his astonishment, the crowd roared, "Yes!"

Finally, his face twitching with rage, Lindsay decided he had had enough. Surveying the room quickly, he moved to leave by a side door. His wife Mary followed dutifully onto what turned out to be a fire escape. Cameras flashed as they stopped short on the cramped balcony. There were now five thousand people massing on the street below, angrily shouting, "Lindsay Must Go!" The couple backtracked awkwardly up the fire escape, then emerged from the temple's front door, protected by a shoulder-to-shoulder line of cops as they made their way to a waiting limousine. The mob pounded the car as it pulled away, kicking at the doors and flinging trash. Lindsay had gotten this kind of treatment in Harlem, but never before in a middle-class Jewish neighborhood. Not only had anger bred counter-anger, but there seemed no way of containing the spreading poison. A few loud bigots on one side of the color line had embittered an entire community on the other. No one of any color or creed was immune, and all were beyond the appeal of reason.

The settlement, when it finally came, was a product of exhaustion. After nearly ten weeks without pay, the union was on the verge of splintering. The city could no longer resist mounting pressure from angry parents, and finally in mid-November the two sides reached a weary compromise: an anticlimactic, ambiguous deal that did nothing to break the spiral of hatred.

The conventional wisdom at the time was that Shanker had won hands down. The Ocean Hill project survived, but just barely. The governing board was temporarily suspended; top staffers were reassigned elsewhere in the city. Rhody McCoy remained, but without much power, subject to being overridden at any time by the state-appointed trustee who now ran the district. A permanent panel was established to protect teachers' rights, and the disputed UFT teachers were reinstated in Ocean Hill.

Still, in the long run, Shanker's victory proved of dubious value. Ocean Hill remained a dismal, polarized place, inhospitable to Jewish teachers.

Chastened as it was, the experiment was not abolished, and it continued to spawn angry activists intent on defying "the white system"; they managed to make life so unbearable for the state trustee that three different men came and went in that post in the first month after the settlement. As for Shanker and his union, they had won the strike but lost what many members would call their soul: not just their liberal image, but their faith in universalism and the possibility of racial harmony.

On the larger racial issues at stake in the controversy—community control and Black Power—little if anything had been learned. After more than a year of threats and violence and indoctrination in race hatred, Manhattan liberals still did not see the truth about the activists who had taken over in Ocean Hill. City Hall was still convinced that ghetto empowerment was the key to better race relations. Lindsay and aides still blamed the conflict on the union. Recalling years later what had happened in New York that fall, staffer Barry Gottehrer wrung his hands and mused bitterly about "what Shanker had done to the city."

McGeorge Bundy's reaction was even more astonishing: in his view, the "disruption" caused by the Ocean Hill experiment "was not all that distressing." By his account, neither he nor Lindsay had any regrets at the end of the school strike. The controversy that tore the city apart that autumn merely proved "how difficult the problem" was—and how many small-minded New Yorkers had balked at a fair solution. Community control of schools and other neighborhood institutions remained a central focus of Ford funding. Not even militant Black Power was discredited in Bundy's eyes. To him, it still looked like a necessary and helpful phase on the way to eventual racial harmony. "I still believe in that track," he said years later, "and I'm not going to judge those who choose it—then or now. You can't blame blacks for their alienation."

Even in the wake of the strike, New York State continued to press ahead with school decentralization. Advocates and opponents moved camp from Ocean Hill to Albany and prepared for an entrenched legislative battle. Frightened, angry, misunderstood, by now the teachers' union would not take no for an answer—would not accept any compromise on the issue of job protection and other safeguards. But the UFT was more than matched by the bill's liberal supporters, more righteous than ever now and convinced that anyone who opposed decentralization was a racist. Both sides pressed their case through the winter and spring: a bitter standoff of epic proportions. When the battle reached an impasse, Governor Nelson Rockefeller brokered a compromise: yet another fuzzy and ambiguous deal between the school authority and the teachers' union. Finally, in April 1969, decentralization passed into law: a weak and uncertain measure, not particularly satisfying for supporters or opponents.

The city was divided into thirty-two school districts, each overseen by an elected community board. Although meant to please alienated minorities, in the end the division did little to empower them. Part of the problem was the plan itself, with its awkward restructuring of the board of education and unusually powerful schools chancellor. But even more critical in the long run, ghetto people failed to vote in community board elections—in Ocean Hill, no more than 2 percent of residents would participate in any school board vote in the next twenty years—leaving neighborhood say over the schools in the hands of a few busybodies and activists. In some districts, it was ideologues who moved in to take over the local board; in other cases, self-promoters eager to get their hands on a school budget. Ironically, in many districts where there was no one else to fill the vacuum, the UFT determined the composition of the board. Almost nowhere did ordinary parents get more involved. And in the end, the structural change triggered by the 1968 strikes did little if anything to improve the city's public schools.

Both in the ghetto and the boroughs, local boards proved a disappointment and worse. Chronically short of money, often corrupt and driven by ethnic chauvinism, mostly they supplemented the central bureaucracy with an equally pernicious local one. Members stole school supplies; they let contracts to friends; they hired by color and neglected to oversee appointments. Many seemed indifferent to the quality of education in their districts, and this soon showed in school performance. After two decades of local control, only 26 percent of the students in Ocean Hill were reading at grade level—close to the worst scores in any district in New York City.

As for decentralization's original political goals—integration in the classroom and mainstream entree for ghetto parents—these had been lost in the shuffle well before the idea became law. Not only had Bundy failed in his attempt to involve the black community in the schools; his wager—that Black Power could prepare the way for inclusion—had backfired disastrously. Liberal integrationists, trying to do good, had backed and bankrolled a band of angry separatists, then watched, not understanding, as the militants killed all hope of racial harmony. After nearly a year of racial conflict, city authorities finally moved to rein in the activists they had encouraged in Ocean Hill. But by then it was too late to block the consequences of the angry, race-obsessed experiment. From now on, for better or worse, tribalism and identity politics would be the order of the day in the school system and the city at large.

Though widely remembered as a critical turn in black-Jewish relations, the Ocean Hill experiment's greatest impact was on a generation of young blacks radicalized beyond the point of no return by the racial conflict that engulfed the city in 1968. This legacy showed itself almost immediately in a new round of unrest in Ocean Hill. Though officially barred from neighborhood schools, militant members of the governing board and their freelance enforcers continued to show up on a daily basis, disrupting classes and intimidating union teachers. But even when there were no adult militants present, chaos reigned in the district schools. Students rampaged through the hallways on their own. Staffers found it impossible to maintain order. In late November 1968, Fred Nauman was assaulted by a band of junior high students, who shoved and punched him and threw two chairs in his direction.

Nor was the disorder limited to Ocean Hill. Infuriated by the union's victory, too restless to settle down to work, ghetto students from all over the city skipped out of school to mount protest rallies in the street. In the weeks after the settlement, there were large, unruly demonstrations in Brooklyn and Harlem and even downtown Manhattan. Both Sonny Carson and Leslie Campbell were heavily involved in these events. But by now, after nearly a year of training and example, the city's black teenagers needed little help or goading.

The downtown demonstrations usually began in an orderly way. Young people gave the first speeches, calling for "student power" and solidarity with Ocean Hill. They were followed by older militants: someone from the district or, on occasion, a big-name movement figure. As the rally proceeded, the rhetoric would escalate. "We're going to have Operation Liberation today," eighteen-year-old Ellen Sheppard shouted at one crowd, urging kids to return to their schools and wrest the buildings back from the UFT—by force if necessary. On another occasion, H. Rap Brown took the podium to call for self-defense classes in ghetto schools. "You better get your gun, brother," he told the crowd of teenagers. "You better stop smoking your reefers and use the money to buy bullets."

What happened next was predictable enough—more or less the same after every rally. Over a thousand young people left a Washington Square event in November and headed for the subway to Ocean Hill. Small groups swarmed through the trains, chanting militant slogans, breaking windows and intimidating passengers. The several hundred who made it to Brooklyn provoked a melee with police: more of the same rock- and bottle-throwing they had been practicing all autumn. Rousing speeches at a Union Square rally several weeks later also sent hundreds of teens into the subways, arming themselves as they ran with rocks and bottles and wooden sticks. They scattered in every direction intent on disruption and harassment. Incidents ensued that afternoon at half a dozen public schools, on subway trains, at a parochial school and in the busy commercial neighborhood around Penn Station. In one week during this period, more than 125 youths were arrested and a large number of others injured in set-tos with police. Sonny Carson was jubilant. This was exactly what he had hoped to produce—a generation of "little Sonny Carsons" irrevocably alienated from the white mainstream.

The months that followed the school strike brought a steady stream of protest activity in ghetto schools. Al Sharpton, then a student at Tilden High in Brooklyn, remembered the "excitement" continuing for roughly a year. Students organized their own Black Panther chapter; others joined ethnic gangs like the Latino Young Lords. "It wasn't just a few of us," Sharpton said. "Everyone was involved in something." The most disruptive of the protests at Tilden occurred not long after the strike settlement when a group of students formed an African-American Club and invited Leslie Campbell to give a talk. The principal declared he would not permit Campbell into the building, provoking several dozen black youths to march to the cafeteria and begin smashing dishes. "It was like a rampage," Sharpton recalled. "It started with only a few kids, but then the police came and everybody got into it. We had a riot in the school."

Radicalized students were also at the center of the renewed controversy that flared between blacks and Jews after the strike. Sia Berhan and Karima Jordan were two of Leslie Campbell's most devoted protégées at J.H.S. 271. Both had immersed themselves in Black Studies, changing their names, joining the African-American Students Association, hanging around Campbell and doing his bidding. Berhan's notorious poem, "Anti-Semitism," was written in his office and inspired by his teaching. Campbell decided to read it, along with several other student efforts, when he appeared on a radio call-in show in late December. The show's host, Julius Lester, was a writer and militant nationalist; his regular Thursday night program, aired on WBAI, was known as a forum for activists, and Campbell was eager to participate. The two men agreed that the important thing now, in the wake of the settlement, was to prove that the spirit of community control had caught on among youth in the ghetto.

On the night of the broadcast, Campbell brought a packet of poems, and it was Lester who chose Berhan's: short, punchy and dedicated to Albert Shanker. "Hey, Jew boy," the infamous opening declared, "with that yarmulke on your head,/You pale-faced Jew boy—I wish you were dead." When Campbell was finished, Lester opened the telephone lines, and the two men took calls for several hours. "People should listen to what a young black woman is expressing," Lester said. "[W]hat she said was valid for a lot of black people, and I think it's time that people stop being afraid of it and stop being hysterical about it."

The broadcast triggered a roar of outrage from Jewish New Yorkers, but if anything this only seemed to encourage district activists and their young followers. Shortly after the initial broadcast, Campbell and Lester appeared together on TV, declaring that the poem was "beautiful" and "true." Lester aired the verse again and then again, every week for three weeks. Former Ocean Hill teacher Al Vann held a press conference to defend Berhan and her work. The poem had "no anti-Semitic overtones," he insisted, it was merely "critical of Jews. . . . Are Jews beyond criticism? We don't think so." A few days later, a lesser-known militant teacher, Tyrone Woods, appeared on Lester's show. "As far as I'm concerned," he declared, "more power to Hitler. He didn't make enough lampshades out of them. He didn't make enough belts out of them."

The Jewish community exploded with angry indignation. The major organizations ran full-page ads in all the newspapers. Jewish supporters of WBAI canceled $15,000 worth of subscriptions. By mid-January 1969, the protest had become so loud that even Lindsay had to react. "I'm particularly disturbed," he wrote to the school board, "by the public statements of the teacher involved, which strongly suggest that not only was the poem's content consistent with the teacher's view but also that children in his classes were being encouraged to express themselves in this manner."

Then, at the end of January, just as the controversy seemed to be subsiding, the Metropolitan Museum released the catalogue for its new photography exhibit, *Harlem on My Mind*—a lavish, handsome volume with an introduction by another radicalized black teenager. Sixteen-year-old Candice Van Ellison was not a student in the Ocean Hill schools, but as her essay—originally a term paper—made clear, the bias that been incubating in the district all year had now spread throughout the city. "Behind every hurdle that the Afro-American has yet to jump," she wrote, "stands the Jew who has already cleared it." Coldly resentful and matter-of-fact, she saw nothing wrong with black anti-Semitism. "Blacks may find that anti-Jewish sentiments place them for once with a majority," she noted. "Our contempt for the Jew makes us feel more completely American in sharing a national prejudice."

Once again, the Jewish community protested. Once again, the Manhattan establishment moved to deplore the show of bigotry. Still, as so often in the previous year, the repudiations seemed tepid and halfhearted. The exhibition catalogue remained on sale, unchanged, and the curator responsible for it defended Ellison's essay. "I assumed that everyone knew that black anti-Semitism existed," he wrote later. Within a few weeks, the flurry of mainstream indignation had passed—and if anything the response had fueled the tension flaring between blacks and Jews.

As spring wore on, the promises to crack down on black bigotry in the school system were forgotten. Lindsay vowed to press the matter with the board of education, but later went back on his word. The board did nothing to chastise Rhody McCoy for defending Campbell's freedom of speech to say whatever he wanted about Jews. Though eventually indicted for intimidating white teachers in Ocean Hill, Campbell was not fired or even disciplined by the city. For young blacks like Berhan and Ellison and Sharpton, the signal was as clear as it could be. Not only could blacks get away with anti-Semitism. Not only could they call on their sense of grievance to justify even the angriest race hatred. But they could win almost anything they wanted from "the system" with defiant, disruptive protest of the kind they had seen in Ocean Hill. "What I learned from Ocean Hill–Brownsville," Sharpton said years later, "was that confrontation works. The black community won. They got community control. They transformed the school system in the largest city in the country—and they did it with confrontation politics. I saw it with my own eyes at the impressionable age of thirteen or fourteen, and it changed the way I looked at the world."

The last installment of the Ocean Hill–Brownsville saga did not come until the year after the settlement: New York's bitterly contested 1969 mayoral election. As four years before, the race was regarded as a national bellwether—not this time an emblem of hope, but a test of creeping backlash. By now, every newspaper and magazine in the country had done its special feature on the new mood. Call it "the silent majority," "Middle

America," "the average man" or "the forgotten American," just the year before this group had been responsible for a conservative landslide, electing
Richard Nixon and a host of local law-and-order politicians. New York City
was not exactly Nixon country, but after more than a decade of school wars
and the battle over civilian police review, the outer boroughs were as ready as
anyone for a change. A poll commissioned in March 1969 by Rowland
Evans and Robert Novak found widespread dissatisfaction among New
Yorkers: by nearly three to one, they felt Lindsay had bungled the school crisis, and only 25 percent backed his core belief that government should be
doing more to heal the ghetto. "The days," Evans and Novak wrote, "when
liberal politicians could take a strongly pro-Negro position and carry along a
substantial white civil rights following (mostly Jewish) are ended." Less than
four years after he was elected on a wave of liberal exuberance, Lindsay now
faced a very real possibility of defeat.

The primaries, in June, were not encouraging. The large, star-studded
field included an array of appealing liberals, both Democrat and Republican: former mayor Robert Wagner; promising young Puerto Rican, Herman Badillo; novelist Norman Mailer; and Lindsay himself. Bruised as he
was, Lindsay was still one of the best-known mayors in the nation: glamorous, idealistic, can-do, now also experienced. Even after his tough first
term in New York, he was still on many people's short list for president. By
comparison, the field's two conservative candidates—there was one running in each primary—were decidedly second-tier. Both Republican John
Marchi and Democrat Mario Procaccino were obscure, lackluster political
operatives, and both campaigned almost exclusively in the boroughs, focus-
ing narrowly on law-and-order issues. Republicans and Democrats alike
were stunned when these two men won their respective primaries. Lindsay,
ever righteous and a touch apocalyptic, said what much of Manhattan felt
the next morning: "The forces of reaction and fear have captured both
major parties in our city. The question is whether New Yorkers will surrender to fear and backlash."

Lindsay's defeat in the GOP primary left him to run on the Liberal Party
line in a three-way race against the two law-and-order men. By the time the
campaign kicked off in earnest, John Marchi was already way behind, leaving the field to Procaccino and the mayor. Together, they made one of the
oddest couples ever thrown together by electoral politics. At least a head
shorter than Lindsay and three or four times his size around, Procaccino was
an easy mark for the city's caricaturists. His pencil mustache and popping

eyes gave him the look of a silent movie villain. A trademark cigar and bungled syntax stamped him as a leftover from an earlier era, before men like Lindsay and the Kennedys transformed the art of politics. Lindsay's whiz kids dismissed him with a laugh line: "What's a Mario Procaccino?" Woody Allen made fun of him: in his undershirt, drinking beer and watching *The Lawrence Welk Show*. But the best Procaccino jokes were things he came up with himself. When Lindsay said he had a melodramatic manner, Procaccino replied that this was true of history's greatest men—"Moses, Jesus, Joe DiMaggio and Joe Namath." On another occasion, at a ghetto rally, struggling to endear himself to a cool crowd, Procaccino bellowed out, ingenuous as could be, "My heart is as black as yours." In any other circumstance, Lindsay would have crushed him. It was a measure of the climate—of the growing revolt against everything Lindsay stood for—that Procaccino gave the glamorous mayor a run for his money. In fact, he did more than that; he almost beat him.

Both sides knew from the start that the race would hinge on the very people most embittered by Lindsay's mayoralty: disaffected ethnics in the outer boroughs. Now as ever, Lindsay's natural constituency was in Manhattan: better-off, better-educated, liberal professionals. Yet powerful as this group was, it alone could not reelect him; all of Manhattan together accounted for only 1.6 out of 8 million New Yorkers. Nor, even with his record, could Lindsay count on ghetto voters: blacks and Hispanics did not, it was well known, come out to vote in very large numbers. In 1965, he had squeaked by on a high ghetto turnout and a patchwork of borough-based support: Jews, blue-collar Italians and Irish, a smattering of loyal Republicans. But by 1969, all of these groups were up for grabs. The high-minded, patrician Lindsay had never understood or particularly liked these people, and he made little effort to disguise his distaste; to him, their lives seemed stultifying, their concerns selfish and small-minded. But now, like it or not, he needed them. The question was how many were still in his column—how many could still be wooed with liberal hope and ideals.

As all three candidates' surveys showed, the borough-based voter bore a strong resemblance to the "forgotten American" recently discovered by the media. Construction workers, cabbies, cops, teachers, low-level tradesmen, factory and office workers: though not entirely working-class, the boroughs had a blue-collar sensibility. Their children went to public or parochial school. Many worked in the city bureaucracy. They had no cushion in their lives, and most said they felt threatened by the way things were changing in the city. Procaccino knew his customers and could describe "the average man" as well as any journalist. "He's the guy who works hard all day," Procaccino said, "and maybe comes home too tired to move, but he has to moonlight anyway to pay his bills. He wants to educate his kids. He wants his neighborhood to be peaceful and clean. He doesn't have a doorman. . . . He rides the subways and the buses. He never burned his draft card or the flag, and he never will. He tries to play the game by the rules, and for that he's getting pushed into a corner."

Though not an explicit topic in the campaign, race was the subtext of virtually every speech and every TV ad. Procaccino, betting on backlash, pushed every button he could think of. He complained about "relief chiselers." He excoriated black militants. He denounced "limousine liberals" for encouraging activists, whom he portrayed as simple criminals. If he were elected, he promised, there would be "one standard for everybody." Most important, every chance he got, he talked about rising crime, and though he did not mention race, everyone knew what he was getting at. He had had enough of "coddling criminals," he fumed, and if a burglar broke into his house, he wouldn't call the cops, he'd "blow [the guy's] brains out."

In fact, whatever the conventional wisdom said about their bigotry, race was only one of many issues troubling borough voters, and in many cases their negative feelings were rooted in real complaints. Rising crime, color-coded double standards, the growing tax bill for ghetto services: for middle-class New Yorkers, these were issues, not excuses. New York's welfare rolls had swollen by 200 percent under Lindsay: with over 1 million recipients, the program now accounted for nearly a quarter of the city budget. What the police called "offenses against persons" had more than doubled since 1960—and black spokesmen from James Baldwin to Eldridge Cleaver were now openly saying that, just as many whites suspected, black crime was driven by anger at the white world. "[For me] rape was an insurrectionary act," Cleaver wrote in 1968, a way of defiling white women and "trampling upon the white man's law." Middle-class whites were appalled by this lawless defiance, and whatever they felt about color was compounded by fear and distaste for what they saw as the new black attitude. Of course, there were real bigots in the outer boroughs—more than journalists or pollsters could keep track of. But well short of racism, there were plenty who felt that they had suffered from the way racial politics were transforming the city.

More than anything, borough voters feared that what Procaccino called "the rules of the game" were changing—and that the black man was benefiting while they got left behind. Cops and teachers were convinced that their careers were in jeopardy. Parents feared their children were being sacrificed. Second-generation immigrants felt they were paying the bill for a failure that occurred long before their families arrived in America. And while all of these groups sometimes blamed blacks, they were even angrier at the Manhattan establishment—no longer, in their view, doing its job refereeing the city's ethnic rivalries. "The backers of the Negro are making them think that *we* owe them," one New York cop complained to a pollster. Grudging as this view might sound, it was not the same as prejudice, though by 1969 many borough-based ethnics were so mad—and so determined to make themselves heard—that they no longer cared what kind of impression they made. "All right," one New Yorker shouted, speaking for many, in front of a TV camera, "I'm a bigot if that's what you want."

Lindsay and his aides were appalled by this sort of talk, but they also realized shrewdly that it played right into their hands. Like Buckley in 1965, Procaccino was a perfect foil for the mayor. All Lindsay had to do was point to him and his prejudiced followers, and huge numbers of other voters would go running in the opposite direction. Vote your hopes, not your fears, the mayor said over and over again. "If you want a mayor who speaks the language of fear and repression," he told other crowds, "I'm not the man you want." By 1969, after nearly ten years of upheaval, the nation was tired and retreating. In New York, after four years of Lindsay and McGeorge Bundy, middle-class voters were more than wary; many had already given up. Still, even now, chastened as they were and generally gloomy about race relations, the voters Lindsay was targeting did not want to look as if they were racist. More than anything, the mayor understood, they wanted to think of themselves as decent people—if not exactly crusading liberals, certainly not, as one put it, "anti-black."

The biggest question in New York in 1969 was whether or not Jewish voters were still susceptible to this kind of appeal. As September turned to October, it became clear to both sides how most other blocks were going to go. Manhattan and the ghetto would stay with Lindsay; working Italian and Irish would vote conservative. Most people in the boroughs were fed up with the mayor—everyone except, maybe, the Jews. How frightened were they by Ocean Hill–Brownsville? Had they abandoned their old liberal instincts? Were Meier Kahane's vigilante followers typical—or the earnest, conscience-stricken Fred Nauman? And would even Nauman and others like him now vote liberal or conservative? Both Lindsay and Procaccino understood, as one put it, that "the Jewish vote is the ball game"—and with election day approaching, neither candidate spent much time in any other kind of neighborhood.

Lindsay traveled from borough to borough, yarmulke glued to his head, braving dubious crowds in synagogues and community centers. He denounced anti-Semitism at every turn; he apologized abjectly. "I made a mistake," he admitted in one of media adviser David Garth's most famous spots; with the school strike and in other ways, "I made a mistake." But more than anything, the mayor appealed to Jewish voters' idealism—their need to think of themselves as decent people, on the side of justice and fairness for all. It was, Lindsay knew, a huge gamble. In the wake of Ocean Hill–Brownsville, no one was more aware than Jews of the dangers of black militancy: the rage, the violence and the spiral of counter-hatred it spawned among frightened whites. At the same time, no one was more sensitive to the risks of bigotry. Few groups were keener to preserve an open society—or to avoid the taint of prejudice themselves. "The Jewish voter," one Lindsay staffer explained, "has always been the most liberal voter in America. On election day, they just won't be able to pull the Procaccino lever. Talking about voting for a law-and-order candidate is one thing. Doing it is another."

On election day, this combination of hope and guilt triumphed, but just barely, saving Lindsay by a hair from an overwhelming defeat. The final count made the point: the mayor won just 42 percent of the vote, giving his law-and-order opponents a combined total of 58 percent. In a two-way race, even a mediocre conservative candidate would have prevailed. As it was, only one in four working people cast their ballots for Lindsay. He had spent more than $3 million—and humbled himself more than most New Yorkers thought possible—to split the Jewish vote down the middle with the amateurish Procaccino. The next day, Lindsay proclaimed the outcome as "a victory for the liberal faith." In fact, what the vote revealed was a swelling backlash, disguised by a thin overlay of liberal reticence and good intentions.

New York Jews were not the only white Americans still driven in 1969 by a need to feel and look fair on race issues. The liberal establishment, particularly the media, and much of the middle class shared their reluctance to say anything that might offend blacks or raise an obstacle to racial harmony. This wasn't necessarily a bad impulse; on the contrary. But in New York and elsewhere, the concern not to look prejudiced could have disastrous consequences for race relations. By making it impossible—unseemly and apparently bigoted—to talk about ghetto crime or thuggish militants, the climate of opinion only made it harder to deal with the problems in the black community. Liberal reluctance to face the truth about things like the hatred in Ocean Hill–Brownsville skewed and distorted the debate, forcing whites caught in the middle to side with bigots: to join the brawl at the barricades or vote for Procaccino. The result was polarization, and between liberals and blacks an awkward, artificial relationship: double standards, patronizing dishonesty and, inevitably, resentment on both sides. Manhattan liberals set the pattern, but the problem would get worse—far more widespread—as the years wore on. Because they did not want to look "anti-black," more and more whites would simply look away—or paper over race-related problems.

Lindsay's friends in Manhattan celebrated his inauguration much as they had celebrated the first one four years before. Their crusading mayor was back in Gracie Mansion; McGeorge Bundy was still at the helm of the Ford Foundation. Liberal social engineering, if not integration, was still the name of the game, and the media was still calling New York "the Athens of American liberalism." But whether or not they could admit it, the New York establishment knew things were different now. Lindsay had failed to bring racial harmony or integration to the city, and there was little hope that he would do better in his second term. His good intentions and ghetto walks, his empathy and his effort to shift resources: much as they had done to project an image of racial peace, underneath, things were as bad or worse than they had been before he took office.

Lindsay could not be blamed for New York's tribal politics. He had tried the best he could to overcome both black rage and white bigotry, but in the end he didn't know how. He pushed when he should have waited; he criticized when he should have empathized; he looked the other way indulgently when he should have held out standards; and he set one group against another when he should have split the difference between them. Even in 1969, besieged on all sides, he remained an eloquent liberal, speaking out every chance he got in favor of hope and integration. It was a noble ideal, still the only plausible goal for a decent white man. But even now Lindsay had no idea how to get there—and no sense of how much he had done to set the dream back.

Part Two

DETROIT

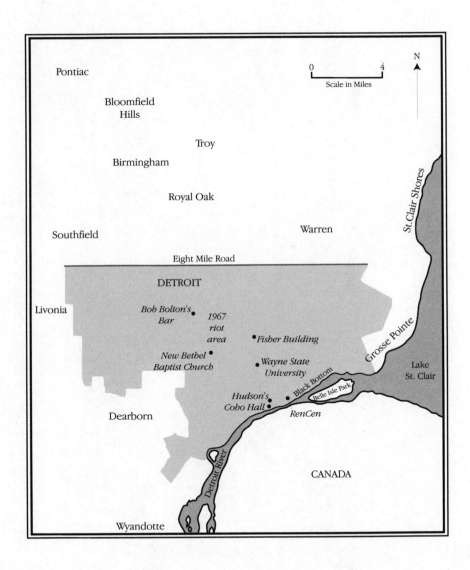

Pontiac

Bloomfield
Hills

Troy

Birmingham

Royal Oak

Southfield

Warren

St. Clair Shores

N

0   4
Scale in Miles

Eight Mile Road

DETROIT

Livonia

*Bob Bolton's
Bar*

*1967
riot
area*

Fisher Building

*New Bethel
Baptist Church*

*Wayne State
University*

Grosse Pointe

Lake
St. Clair

Black Bottom

Hudson's
Cobo Hall

Belle Isle Park

RenCen

Dearborn

Detroit River

CANADA

Wyandotte

Chapter 8

BENDING THE RULES

The fires of the July 1967 riot were still burning in the streets of Detroit when the city's biggest businessmen got on the phone and asked each other what they were going to do. Oil magnate and Republican fundraiser Max Fisher was among the first to reach out. Though he lived fifteen miles out of town in a sprawling home on the golf course in Franklin, Fisher still considered himself a Detroiter, and when the violence started, he knew he had to look in on his city. He drove into town and stood at the window in his office on the top floor of downtown's most imposing skyscraper. It was not yet midday, but the sky was black with smoke, and fire pockmarked the city twenty-eight floors below, spreading here and there into large, angry patches. More than anything, Fisher felt helpless. "It was quite a shock," he recalled years later, "people burning their own homes, people happily burning down their city." He watched silently for a minute or two, then picked up the telephone and called his close friend, Republican governor George Romney.

A wealthy, aging Jewish businessman, Fisher could hardly have been more remote from Detroit's increasingly poor, black residents. A self-made man, the son of an immigrant peddler, he had made millions in the oil business, then, like many of the city's biggest entrepreneurs, amassed a second fortune from the growth of the suburbs—fueling the cars that made them possible. Now, in his newest career as a real estate investor, he was multiplying his money yet again in the new towers and subdivisions springing up on the empty land beyond the city line. Still, like his friends, Henry Ford II and

Alfred Taubman—Ford built the cars and Taubman developed the shopping malls that pulled Detroiters to the suburbs—Fisher continued to feel loyal to the city that had given him his wealth.

Even as the city emptied of business, Fisher had maintained his base of operations in town. As late as 1962, with downtown real estate values already plummeting, he had bought a majestic skyscraper in the heart of central Detroit. An ornate Gothic leftover from the Motor City's glory days, it happened to be called the Fisher Building—named after the family, unrelated to Max, that produced auto bodies for General Motors. There, on the top floor, Fisher kept his office, long after friends and subordinates had abandoned the crumbling center of town. Dogged for years by anti-Semitism, he was now a charter member of Detroit's small, WASPish elite. In a city known for its philanthropy, he was one of the biggest givers: a legendary fund-raiser for, among other causes, the United Way, the state of Israel and the Republican Party. Well before the riots, he and other local businessmen had taken the initiative on civil rights, pressing for reforms and meeting quietly with black leaders. "I'd lived here for sixty-three years," he explained later, "I'd started a business here. I identified with the city and felt a commitment to it. I felt a responsibility to try to do something"—particularly when things started to go wrong, as they did that Sunday morning, July 23, 1967.

By Tuesday, his idea had caught on. With the city still burning and federal troops patrolling the streets, Governor Romney was acting on his and Fisher's shared assumption that Detroit's business elite should be mobilized to help. The calls ricocheted around town, and when the executives weren't reachable, there were telegrams. Joseph L. Hudson, youthful president of the region's largest department-store chain, remembers hearing in one afternoon from Romney, Mayor Jerome Cavanagh and Cyrus Vance, President Lyndon Johnson's emissary to the city. The appeals to get involved knew no boundaries: Democrats and Republicans, business and labor, still based in town and long ago displaced to the suburbs. It was, in some sense, a call to serve, but most business leaders needed little prodding; this was the kind of role they had always played and there was no question that they would come forward now. Henry Ford, Fisher, Hudson, UAW president Walter Reuther, GM president James M. Roche, Chrysler president Lynn Townsend and American Motors president Roy Chapin, Jr.: all agreed to come to an exploratory meeting with spokesmen for the black community.

The five hundred black and white Detroiters who gathered two days later at the City-County Building had no one to turn to but each other, and powerful as some of them were, they were deeply uncertain about what to do next. Smoke still hung over the city as they met. Thousands of police, National Guardsmen and federal troops were still struggling to maintain order in the streets. Both the media and the grapevine were spreading wildly exaggerated reports of riot damage. Most businesses were still closed; a 5:30 P.M. curfew was in force. Gasoline, liquor and guns sales had been prohibited inside the city line, but all three were doing brisk business in outlying areas—and police and fire departments in the suburbs were standing ready in case trouble spread in their direction. One of the nation's most enlightened cities had had the era's worst riot—and all its hopeful conventional wisdom about race relations had been shattered overnight.

The gathering itself had an oddly upbeat air: the adrenaline rush of rallying to cope with an emergency. Every segment of the community was represented: business, labor, public officials, black churchmen, newly emerged militant leaders and block association types. The City-County Building where the assembly took place was the seat of city government, but it was as plain as the chaos outside that the government had essentially collapsed. The handsome and charismatic Mayor Cavanagh, once seen by Washington and the national media as a man who might solve the urban problem, looked puffy and depressed, more an observer than a player. "The world of Jerome P. Cavanagh has come down like an old pair of socks," a local journalist would write shortly. "He's just like Job. The only thing he hasn't got are those sores."

In the government's place was the economic power structure—the businessmen plus the UAW's Walter Reuther. Their first priority was emergency relief. Reuther undertook the physical cleanup of the riot area. GM's James Roche pledged "the facilities, skills, resources and people" of the largest corporation in the world. But the executives' earnest, emotional speeches also promised more: a new civic compact between business and the deteriorating city. It was just what many blacks in Detroit and elsewhere had been waiting for: spurred by the uprising, corporate America had finally woken up, and now it was going to reach into its bottomless pockets and solve the problems that had given rise to the riots. "They thought we could pour money in," Joseph Hudson recalled, "and that would take care of everything."

Near the end of the meeting, the city's businessmen agreed to form an interracial organization called the New Detroit Committee. Hudson, Fisher and the others behind it would later admit that they had little idea how exactly business could help, beyond perhaps providing advice and a semblance of order as the government got back on its feet. At the most pragmatic level, their goal was to prevent further rioting. "We got involved partly for selfish reasons," Hudson admitted later. "We were concerned about down-town." Most of the executives still had financial interests in town; and even those who had shifted their money to the suburbs sensed that their invest-ments would be at risk if the city were destroyed. But Fisher, Hudson, Reuther and the others also agreed idealistically that they had to do more than what Fisher called "putting out fires"; they had to try to "change atti-tudes" and "bridge differences." Prodded by the riot, the businessmen were hoping against hope that they could do something about the sea change coming over their region: the ever-quickening slide toward an all-black city surrounded by white suburbs. "We thought we could halt or reverse that," Fisher remembered. "We thought we could avoid a situation where all the whites would move out. We were hoping for a fifty-fifty relationship."

None of the blacks or whites involved in New Detroit were exactly text-book integrationists. Black members were angry and skeptical of the old dreams of color-blind unity. Whites like Hudson and Fisher were more inclined to use the term. "It was a new thing," Fisher said later, "something we felt we should try." But even white members with black acquaintances knew little or nothing about the ghetto, and even when they tried to be forthcoming—Fisher remembers making an effort in this period "to invite blacks to parties"—they grasped that meaningful inclusion was at best a good way off. Still, in their ways, all five hundred Detroiters who gathered at the City-County Building were clinging wistfully to an image of one com-munity. Whites, even whites who lived fifteen miles away, wanted to help and felt they could contribute. Even the angriest blacks seemed to welcome the concern and to hope still for some kind of alliance. No one imagined any more that the task would be easy. All had driven through the same deserted streets; all had passed the same smashed storefronts and the FOR SALE signs that had mushroomed in white neighborhoods since the riot. But at the moment of crisis, at least, it seemed that they were all in it together. "No matter where we live in this metropolitan complex," an early committee document declared hopefully, "no matter who we are or what we do, it isn't 'we' and 'they.' It's just 'we.'"

The evolution of the two Detroits—black city and white suburb—had been a long, slow process. In its glory days, when the auto industry was growing, the city had been one of the nation's most impressive. At the center, perched on the broad Detroit River, was a small but imposing downtown. Built largely in the 1920s—the decade the automobile caught on in earnest, and money flowed into Detroit as if nothing could stop it—the hub was dominated by eye-catching Gothic and Art Deco skyscrapers. Stretching out from them in a rough semicircle were block after block of proud family houses. Some were grand, some modest, but each had its own yard and each street had trees, and together the orderly ranks of homes marched for miles across the flat landscape, giving Detroit a distinct style befitting its sober, working-class residents. Even in the first decades of the century, the city's orderly map was divided into ethnic enclaves known, without ceremony, as Poletown, Germantown, Jewtown, Hunkytown, Corktown, Greektown and Black Bottom. In Detroit, as in all immigrant cities, some of this clustering was voluntary, but from the 1920s on there was nothing optional about the segregation of black from white.

Always a rough-and-tumble factory town, Detroit had a long history of racial conflict. The population was heavy with physical laborers, many of them newcomers lured to town by the auto industry's famously high wages. Henry Ford first laid the bait in 1914 with the then incredible offer of five dollars a day, and the hungry workers had been coming ever since: mostly rural people from the American South and Eastern Europe. Black and white, Catholic and Protestant, often with little English, what they had in common were their strong backs and rudimentary educations. The southerners, black as well as white, brought their racial attitudes with them, and most were what the first black mayor, Coleman Young, would later call people who "dealt in harsh realities"—unfamiliar with "the niceties of life" and easily given to violence. They streamed into the city in the early decades of the century, quadrupling its population in just twenty years. The black community grew proportionately at first, but then in later decades—particularly after the start of World War II—blacks made up more and more of the influx. In 1925, they accounted for only 4 percent of the population; by 1950, 16 percent. By 1960, the figure was 29 percent: nearly double in a decade and already close to one-third of the city.

Black Bottom, also known as Paradise Valley, was a typical northern ghetto. Hemmed in by segregation, it was always much too small for its population. When Joe Louis grew up there before World War I, it was a jumble of workers' wood-frame houses, most of them without electricity or indoor plumbing. In the thirties, the hardest hit center of a hard-hit town, the enclave was transformed into a hotbed of unionism and radical politics.

Largely poor and chronically crime-ridden, Paradise Valley was also rich in color and culture, home to a small black middle class as well as factory workers. Black funeral parlors, barbershops, blue-collar bars and lawyers' offices, rib joints, fraternity houses and all manner of churches: together, they crowded into a few dozen square blocks on the east side of the city near the river.

As the North's third largest concentration of blacks—the first two were New York and Chicago—Detroit saw its share of history, including the beginnings of the Nation of Islam and, in the fifties, the birth of Motown. But what made the city's black community distinct was the same force that shaped its white culture: the many-tentacled and all-powerful automobile industry. Generous auto wages created a solid black working class: persevering, disciplined, churchgoing people with a strong stake in the system. An unusual percentage of black Detroiters owned their own homes. Even at its peak in the thirties and later in the sixties, black nationalism failed to catch on big among them. And even into the later sixties, what militancy there was translated mostly into politics—strengthening the already important black political machine. Still, in the brusque and brawny cauldron of Detroit, not even staid, working-class blacks could avoid trouble with their white neighbors.

As the city's population expanded, the ghetto inevitably grew with it, and from the beginning, that growth met sharp resistance from white homeowners. The first incident to attract national attention occurred in 1925, when a black doctor named Ossian Sweet tried to move into an all-white enclave and was met by a mob of angry neighbors. A shot fired from Sweet's house killed a white man in the mob and occasioned a celebrated trial involving Clarence Darrow. Sweet was eventually acquitted, but his experience would long discourage other blacks from thinking about moving into white neighborhoods. Tensions grew still worse in the following decades as more and more black migrants poured into the city. The lines between black and white enclaves were set down in restrictive covenants, and as often as not the boundaries were enforced by cruder means: cross-burning, rock-throwing, arson and homemade explosives. Before long, Detroit had earned a national reputation as a place of unusually bitter racial hatred.

The economic hardship of the 1930s only inflamed passions and further tarnished the city's image: easterners who knew nothing else about Detroit knew it as the home of the automobile but also of demagogic radio preacher Father Charles Coughlin, white supremacist minister Gerald L. K. Smith, the pro-Nazi National Workers League and one of the largest northern factions of the Ku Klux Klan. In 1924, the Klan, then said to number more than thirty thousand in Detroit, almost succeeded in electing the mayor of the city, and well into the thirties Klansmen were an important force in the police department. A 1943 race riot—a two-day free-for-all between ten thousand whites and their black victims, fighting hand-to-hand in the streets of downtown—sealed Detroit's image for a generation, and things grew even worse with the beginning of World War II, when the black influx picked up in earnest.

By the late 1940s, the expansion of the city had pushed most working whites to the outer edges of town, with the biggest clusters in the northeast and northwest corners. Largely isolated from the ghetto but increasingly frightened of it, the residents of these enclaves came together in homeowner associations often explicitly devoted to keeping blacks out of their neighborhoods. Panicked whites looked on with horror at a deepening ghetto culture: poverty, crime, alcohol abuse, single-parent families, rootless children, seeming indifference to education and other bourgeois norms. The homeowners' rhetoric grew uglier and uglier; their newsletters spoke of resisting the "Negro invasion." The mayoral elections of 1945 and 1949 turned explicitly on race and real estate, making Detroit already one of the most polarized cities in the nation.

At the same time, the city's reputation could be misleading, and in the late fifties and early sixties, a very different, liberal-minded Detroit emerged. This Motown too had roots in the auto industry. Henry Ford, an active anti-Semite, was anything but a liberal, but he was one of the first northern industrialists to hire blacks in significant numbers. The jobs were generally second-rate—if not strike-breaking, then dirty, menial work—but they were jobs, and they were available to blacks. Ford also made his presence felt in the ghetto, supporting churches and social services as a way of maintaining a hold over his black workforce. His approach was the essence of paternalistic benevolence, at once appreciated and resented by black Detroiters, but it opened the door to a long tradition of business civic-mindedness. The small and tightly knit structure of the city's economy—centered as it was on one industry—made for a small, tightly knit business elite. Largely WASP, Detroit money was a loyal, insular world, and through most of the century it organized itself to shore up the city by means of philanthropy, boosterism, urban renewal and, in the sixties, civil rights reforms.

The other pillar of Detroit's liberalism was organized labor. During World War II, when blacks began to compete in earnest for the better jobs in the auto plants, racial antagonism ran so high that there were fistfights and sit-down strikes on the shop floor. But even then, for the most part, the unions did what they could to restrain racial tensions, actively recruiting and promoting blacks, working to transmute racial passions into labor solidarity. United Auto Workers' union president Walter Reuther was a stalwart of the early civil rights movement, marching in Selma with Martin Luther King, prodding the city to integrate and provide better services for its black community. Factional politics plagued the labor struggle from its earliest days, and Reuther was not always popular among the UAW's radical blacks. But no Detroiter, black or white, could ignore the union's hold on the city's voters—an influence it used to keep them largely liberal and Democratic.

In the early sixties, the business elite and union leaders joined forces with blacks to elect a whiz-kid liberal mayor—Jerome Cavanagh. Like John Lindsay in New York, Cavanagh was a dashing young man and a dedicated reformer, a politician who made liberalism seem glamorous and all but invincible. Known as "Jerry the Giant Killer," he was committed to healing the ghetto, involving the federal government in the cities and bringing blacks into the middle class the same way his Irish brethren had come in—by way of city politics. Racial integration was an article of faith—he welcomed Martin Luther King to Detroit in 1963—and in his view there was no problem he and his can-do government could not solve. Much like Lindsay a few years later, Cavanagh was a name to conjure with in the early 1960s: one of John F. Kennedy's favorite mayors, then a top recipient of Great Society dollars. Under his leadership, Detroit finally shed its bad reputation, becoming known nationwide as a beacon of liberal hope: a place where school integration, police reform and black political participation were proceeding apace—a city where blacks had a real stake and blue-collar whites were learning to make room for them. Even when the long, hot summers started, no one expected a major riot in the Motor City.

At the beginning, the move toward the suburbs had nothing to do with race. Detroit's first factories were at the center of town, near the harbor and the railroad terminal. But as early as the 1920s, when the car and truck freed manufacturing from these moorings, the auto industry began moving away from the heart of the city. The land was flat and featureless, seemingly unlimited in supply, and in a make-money, migrant town like Detroit there seemed no reason—sentimental or economic—to retool an old plant in an old neighborhood. When factories became obsolete, they were simply abandoned, and new ones were built a little further out along the city's spokelike avenues. Workers and the merchants who serviced them then moved out along the spokes, leaving the poor and powerless—both black and white—behind. The result was a vast, sprawling city: always vital and developing at the edges, but increasingly impoverished and physically rotten at the core.

In the booming forties, this development finally spilled over the city line. Defense plants were the first to go: the giant Willow Run aircraft assembly, employing more than 42,000 workers, was built in virgin territory, 25 miles from downtown Detroit. In the decade after the war, the Big Three followed with twenty new factories beyond the city limits. Complementary industries, parts suppliers and services were not far behind, bringing more jobs and, before long, real estate speculators to the open land north of the border at Eight Mile Road.

As they developed, sometimes overnight, the suburbs provided much easier living than the city: land was cheap, the houses larger, both driving and parking far less troublesome. Zoning made many outlying areas more attractive still, guaranteeing bigger yards and homogeneously middle-class neighborhoods. The federal government did its part, first with subsidized mortgages and homeowner tax credits, then in the mid-fifties with the interstate highway system. But the coup de grâce was the shopping malls, the first of which—the legendary Northland—opened in the suburban township of Southfield in 1951. Unlike earlier commercial strips, which developed along with the neighborhoods they served, the great malls of the fifties were designed to attract and anchor residential growth. Like magnets, they drew other stores and shoppers, and made it easy for them to build and decorate homes. Together, the jobs, the shops, the roads and the tax breaks were an irresistible combination, and by 1960, one in four Detroit whites had moved from city to suburb.

For many suburbanites, these economic reasons combined with racial ones. Neighborhood panics of the kind that began in the forties continued into the fifties and contributed to the growth of the suburbs. As Coleman Young would later say about the transformation of Detroit: "White people cannot abide a situation they don't control—and when such a situation arises, they move." But already in the fifties and sixties, as suburbanites looked back over their shoulders, they did not have to be racists to feel that they had found a better quality of life. "The people who moved to the suburbs," one outlying newspaperman maintained, "wanted what everyone in America wants—to lead a safe and comfortable life, to get a good education for their kids, to live in a comfortable house and cut the lawn on weekends. It isn't complicated—it's the American Dream." In Detroit, as in most cities, the truth lay somewhere between these two interpretations: not necessarily innocent, but usually more complicated than simple bigotry. The move out of town was an economic slippery slope, sometimes greased by racism, sometimes not. Still, whatever the reasons, already even before the 1967 riot, no one in the region was color-blind, and it was plain to everyone just what the growth of the suburbs was doing to the city.

What happened in 1967 set race relations back by years, if not decades. The bloodiest and most destructive riot of a bloody, bitter year, it ignited with casual spontaneity. Then, even when things began to get out of hand, with the arson, the occupying tanks, the pitched gun battles and punitive curfews, no one grasped just how much damage was being done—either by the spreading fires or the fear and anger taking root on both sides of the color line. For both whites and blacks, 1967 was the moment that forever sealed the fate of Motor City: for whites, the end of an era, for blacks, the beginning of history.

For the vast majority of whites, racist or not, it signaled that Detroit was beyond the point of no return. Thousands of families that had been vaguely aware of the suburbs and thought they might move "some day" realized that they too were going to have to leave, probably sooner rather than later. Some put FOR SALE signs on their houses even as the fire spread through the ghetto. Others, with friends or relatives across the city line, made arrangements for their children to move in with them immediately. Still others decided they would bide their time—but only until the schools in their neighborhood tipped black. Suburban developers went into high gear, as did real estate agents in the city, triggering a round of blockbusting from which property values would never recover.

Black Detroiters' interpretation of 1967 could not have been more different. Some of the poorer blacks who lived close to the riot area were angered by the violence that destroyed their homes and neighborhoods. But others, particularly the black middle class, saw the disturbances as a welcome political watershed—not a riot, but a "revolt" or "insurrection." Coleman Young's interpretation was one widely shared by black Detroiters: "What you had in 1967," he said, "was a major one-sided confrontation between certain elements in the black community, mostly young people, and a lily-white police department, lily-white state troopers . . . and a largely lily-white National

Guard." In the black mythology of Detroit, 1967 became the point that blacks finally stood up for themselves—what *Ebony* magazine called "the birth pangs" of a new city. Former head of the Detroit NAACP Arthur Johnson used the same metaphor. "What we had in 1967 was a surprise pregnancy," he said. "The baby had to be delivered. . . . We had to go through some kind of trauma."

It would be a few years before Detroit would technically become a black city—before the population tipped and political control fell into black hands. But plainly, for most residents, the riot was the turning point that mattered. People began to talk proudly about the emerging "Black Metropolis." A popular Motown song captured the new reality with a homey image: a "chocolate city" ringed by "vanilla suburbs." The question from 1967 on was what kind of accommodation the two parts of the region would make with each other, and whether there was still any hope of maintaining a sense of one community.

In the two weeks between the disturbance and the New Detroit Committee's first meeting, the mood in the city grew even more tense. It was as if the very act of rioting had unleashed a flood of rage. A new generation of black spokesmen emerged overnight. Services memorializing those who died in the "rebellion" attracted large crowds of black youths and adults. "Negroes in Detroit are walking taller," one man told a reporter. "There is no such thing as moderate any more," another declared, "only militant and more militant." A mushroom crop of new organizations formed. Invoking Malcolm X, Chairman Mao and the image of a "New Africa," most were committed to the use of guns. Even the most sober, working black Detroiters now seemed unable to resist the call of racial anger. The churches themselves began to shift ground—and membership in Reverend Albert Cleage's Central United Church of Christ shot upward when he renamed it the Shrine of the Black Madonna and dedicated it to black nationalism.

In white neighborhoods, fear was turning to outrage. About a third of the whites polled in this period were convinced that "criminals" had been behind the riots; 70 percent felt that blacks were demanding too much, too fast, and that they now had only themselves to blame for their circumstances. The white side of town spawned its own fanatics, the worst of whom joined a vigilante group called Breakthrough. Organized by city employee Donald Lobsinger and popular among blue-collar ethnics, it met in American Legion posts and drew followers from police and firefighter associations.

Openly hatemongering, with roots in the John Birch Society, Breakthrough maintained that the riot was a provocateurs' effort to spread separatism among the black masses. Members demanded that Cavanagh be indicted for failing to crack down on what they too called the "insurrection." In anticipation of "civil war," they stockpiled a frightening variety of weapons and mapped out a block-to-block home defense system.

Every fearful or angry move in a white neighborhood provoked the same on the black side of town, and vice versa. Truckloads of illegal guns poured from out of state into the ghetto. In response, outlying police departments ordered the latest high-tech weaponry, including, in some cases, armored vehicles. Within a few months of the riot, regional handgun sales would double, trade in rifles and shotguns nearly triple. A sensationalist media only fanned the flames. One famous evening newscast that particularly upset the black community featured a group of suburban housewives at the target range, trying out their new revolvers. The nationalist call to arms most often cited by frightened whites was a SNCC manifesto reprinted in the conservative *Detroit News:* "It is our duty to revolt against the system," the document declared, "and create our own system." The *News* also spurred white fears—and outraged blacks—with a daily crime blotter that identified the race of perpetrators. In the suburbs, Philip Power, publisher of the weekly *Observer* chain, urged readers to recognize that Detroit was still "our city" and the riots "as much our problem" as anyone's. But many suburban families vowed once and for all in the weeks after the disturbance never again to cross Eight Mile Road into the city.

Even so, the members of the New Detroit Committee were determined to step in and stop the polarization. They came out of business, not politics, and most would have laughed at the idea of large-scale social engineering. But they were convinced that, with their guidance, the city could come together—could, as Fisher put it, "bring blacks into the process." No area of urban life would be off limits: who knew what business could do to improve housing, education, employment or even community services? Even before the committee met for the first time, a full-time staff of high-ranking personnel was "loaned" by the corporate sector, and a general working objective began to crystallize. The goal was not to raise funds or to replace the city government. It was rather to serve as a kind of interim board of directors, providing a strategy at this critical point to hold black and white Detroit together.

Hudson set out to find a group of blacks who would be included in the committee. He called around in black circles, starting with middle-class moderates and others in the political establishment; but he also pressed them to suggest younger, more "representative" figures. "We knew," he explained later, "that a big proportion of the city's blacks were educated and middle class, but we had to reach out beyond them to the community that was causing trouble." Of the nine blacks originally chosen to serve on the thirty-nine-member panel, three were avowed nationalists. When the powerful Reverend Albert Cleage called them "Uncle Toms" and announced to the press that "the Hudson committee will take orders from us," Hudson immediately met with Cleage and agreed to "recognize, welcome and cooperate" with the still more radical street leaders he recommended. With this, Hudson and his behind-the-scenes adviser Max Fisher made the same choice that McGeorge Bundy had made in New York: they felt they had to listen to the depth of black alienation, even if that meant seeming to encourage the community's anger.

No one, black or white, knew quite what to expect when the committee met for the first time in early August. The room was in carefully chosen neutral territory on the Wayne State University campus. "It was a pretty wild situation," Hudson recalled. "Street kids and CEOs coming together to talk." He opened the meeting with an earnest speech, laying out the committee's raison d'être. Several other corporate heads rose to state their aims and their estimates of what might be accomplished. There was talk of hiring ten thousand hard-core unemployed, securing passage of an open-housing law and prying $5 million in school aid from the Michigan state legislature. It was a solid, practical agenda, based on a sophisticated understanding of integration. Members understood they would have to go beyond legal changes. The challenge as they saw it was to give blacks a boost up the socioeconomic escalator: jump-starting what Fisher called "the natural Americanization machine"—public schooling and the job ladder—that had traditionally helped immigrants and their children become "part of American society and capable of taking care of themselves." The unquestioned aim was inclusion, and Detroit's businessmen were confident that they could play a role in helping blacks achieve it. Hudson stated breezily that he thought the committee could do its job "within a fairly short space of time." Then the meeting turned to its other agenda: what Hudson introduced as "listening."

Fisher would later call it "ventilation," Hudson more plainly "haranguing," but even years afterward the group's corporate leaders saw what happened next as an important part of the process they had initiated. "It was a place for airing," Fisher recalled. "The minority community needed a place to express its grievances." The committee's three separatists were the loudest voices, here in committee, as out in the streets, drowning out more reasonable black spokesmen. Lena Bivens was a tough, squat community activist with roots in the poverty program bureaucracy. Teenager Norvell Harrington's main qualification was his youth and his closeness to the mood in the street. Frank Ditto was the professional: a rough-and-ready career activist who had come to Detroit just as the riot was starting expressly to act as a "catalyst." Most of their complaints were sweeping indictments of "the system"; almost none touched on matters the committee could do anything about. Fisher remembers a lot of talk about institutional racism and corporations making money on the backs of black people. "We crusty CEOs bit our lips," Hudson remembered, "and asked ourselves why we had to listen to this stuff. We would ask, 'Do we have to do it this way?' They'd say, 'Forget civility. This is the real world.' We'd ask, 'What are the issues?' And they would come back with more four-letter words." At the end of the first meeting, the committee agreed to a schedule of monthly sessions, and the Big Three heads themselves promised to return for more "ventilation."

Out in the streets, the gulf between black and white was growing steadily wider. Crime and the perception of crime rose dramatically: there would be nearly twice as many murders the year after the riot as the year before. Downtown offices hired guards and installed bulletproof windows. Students in the riot area were at first said to be "dazed"—what one administrator called a sea of "stone faces." But it soon became clear that, as in New York after Ocean Hill–Brownsville, the disturbances were radicalizing a generation of black teens. The winter after the riot brought daily skirmishes in school corridors, boycotts, vandalism, classroom fires and a much-publicized stabbing of a teacher. At one junior high school, students went on a violent rampage, demanding that their white principal be replaced by a black one. Screaming teenagers disrupted board of education meetings, shouting that they would not listen to "honkie" officials. By the middle of the term, school officials were locking classroom doors, and white families were evacuating as if from a plague. Twice as many whites fled the city in 1967 as had left the year before. In 1968, the figure would double again, to more than eighty thousand.

The ten-month newspaper strike that began in late autumn 1967 only poisoned the atmosphere further. Rumors swirled back and forth over the city line, unchecked by reality and fueling paranoia. Whites talked of black plans to set fire to the expressways by rolling lit gasoline drums onto the roads. Others imagined schemes to mine the highways, to cut off the suburbs' phones and water supply. Killer squads would be dispatched over the city line; maids would poison the families they worked for. One suburb prepared to meet the threat by buying $12,000 in riot equipment, and the towns of Dearborn and Warren passed stop-and-frisk laws that permitted police to search anyone suspicious. Meanwhile, in the city, blacks imagined parallel nightmare scenarios. Whites were planning an invasion. The police force was said to be training white civilians. Agents would provoke racial incidents and use them as pretexts to march on black neighborhoods. The goal, if not genocide, would be the establishment of concentration camps. Reverend Cleage urged followers to stockpile food; militant rallies turned into how-to lectures on building bunkers and surviving a white siege. By May 1968, a third of the region's residents would say that they expected another riot soon, and most were preparing for it.

Inside New Detroit's Wayne State meeting room, the panel's militants took full advantage of the mood raging outside. Sessions grew stormier and stormier as fear spread in the city and the activists grasped just what kind of specter they were conjuring with. Norvell Harrington began to come to meetings accompanied by an "honor guard": four other teenagers in fatigues and berets. Career organizer Frank Ditto and his "youth patrol" took up a position outside Hudson's downtown department store. The chain's money-making branches were by now all in the suburbs, hubs of Northland, Eastland and the other great malls, but the company still maintained its elegant old flagship in the heart of downtown. "White customers were upset at us for listening to the strident voices," the young president recalled. "We had [Breakthrough head] Lobsinger protesting at one door and Frank Ditto at another. Thank goodness we had a big building."

From the beginning, New Detroit had stressed that it was not a fund-raising organization. Though it would "set priorities" and "identify sources" of aid, corporate members had no intention of funneling their own money into the ghetto. The militants in the group had a different idea, and it became clearer and clearer as the city's mood worsened. "If you fat cats don't give us what we want," Harrington told the executives, "it won't be our places that will be burning next summer. It will be yours." There better be "some crumbs on the table," Ditto echoed, or the angry youths in the street "might burn down some shit." More and more, as the committee fell into stride, it grew clear that its minimal goal was going to take priority: if nothing else, the businessmen had to prevent further rioting—and the best way to do that was with money.

The grants were small but strategically placed. Ditto netted about $250,000 for his paramilitary groups and other activities. Cleage's nationalist consortium came away with over $100,000. Ditto used his to pay the street kids he recruited to attend "classes" and for a newsletter that advocated "bloody" revolution. Other small grants boosted black arts projects, black theater, black business and summer recreation programs. Not all the money went to activists or street kids: there was also a grant to draw up plans for low-cost housing and a large lump sum for the Detroit public schools. But even money earmarked for black businessmen and housing development went in significant part to militants, and before long many of Detroit's black moderates were criticizing the committee. "Financing the man who says 'Burn whitey' isn't common sense," noted prominent trade unionist Horace Sheffield.

Over the next two years, the committee would raise and give away $10 million in thinly disguised riot insurance. Whatever hopes they had had at the beginning, as time went on the businessmen shed their illusions, and few imagined that their grants would solve any long-term problems. This was a long way from the integration they dreamed of, a long way from a harmonious "fifty-fifty" relationship." "There was a great, great need," Hudson said later, "and there was no way for us to snap our fingers." Still, the city's big businessmen reasoned, they could make a show of racial goodwill and sympathy—and if that turned out to mean paying off militants, so be it. "The committee did what it could," Reuther's top aide Irving Bluestone noted years later with a sigh of resignation. "It was a place to talk. It eased the antagonism and put a quietus on the situation."

New Detroit had been meeting regularly for over a year and a half when word came through to Fisher, who had replaced Hudson as chairman, that the city was on the brink again. As usual, the trigger was an incident involving blacks and white cops. Angry rumors were spreading fast, and it looked as if the black community was gearing up for a major confrontation.

The trouble started in March 1969 in the heart of the 1967 riot area, at the New Bethel Baptist Church, where one of the more radical groups formed in the wake of the disturbances was celebrating its first anniversary. The self-proclaimed "provisional government" of black America, the Republic of New Africa (RNA) was a small but by now national organization with a military arm. Committed to establishing a separate black nation in the Deep South, members rallied around Malcolm X's ideas that whites were inherently racist and integration a form of genocide. Their armed wing, the

Black Legion, was modeled on the Fruit of Islam. Dressed in black uniforms with leopardskin epaulets, black berets and combat boots, legionnaires were trained in "self-defense" tactics and ready for confrontation with their sworn enemy, the police. Shortly before midnight on March 29, 1969, a dozen of these militants, some of them armed, were standing outside the New Bethel Church when two white officers from the Detroit force cruised by and stopped to question them.

The last the precinct heard over the radio from rookie officer Michael Czapski was that he was getting out of the car to investigate some "guys with rifles." No evidence suggested that he or his partner Richard Worobec approached the Black Legion cadres in a threatening manner; no later investigation unearthed any wrongdoing by either officer. The next thing that came over the radio was the unmistakable sound of gun shots. By the time reinforcements arrived from the precinct, Czapski was lying dead on the sidewalk, his revolver still in its holster, and his partner, seriously wounded, had dragged himself back to the patrol car.

What happened next remains unclear, a matter still in dispute between black and white Detroiters. The police reinforcements would later testify that they saw the armed legionnaires flee back into the church. A knock on the door, according to the cops, was met with gunfire, and militants inside the church continued shooting as the police streamed into the sanctuary. The church janitor and representatives of local community groups told a different story: that police were never fired on from inside the church and that it was they who entered shooting, creating hysteria among women and children lingering after the RNA meeting. The two sides agreed that after several minutes of gunfire the police arrested all 142 people present—in fact, they were mostly adults, men and women, and many were in uniform—confiscating a dozen guns and a cache of ammunition. The RNA later charged that the police fondled female members as they searched them and taunted the prisoners with racial epithets.

It was just the kind of spark to start a riot, Fisher knew, the kind that by now had triggered trouble in just about every ghetto in America. As in 1967, the police herded their black prisoners into vans and ferried them across town to headquarters. As on that warm Saturday night nearly two years before, there were a lot of people in the streets, and word spread like wildfire through the neighborhoods. In Detroit as in most heavily black cities, relations between blacks and white police could not have been much worse, and an incident like this was sure to set people off.

Detroit cops were known as the toughest and meanest of a tough, mean, white working class. Some had been recruited in the South specifically for their experience handling blacks; others were hardened by the job and the brutality it required, particularly in the city's increasingly poor, black, crime-prone neighborhoods. In the 1930s, police officers had formed the backbone of the Detroit KKK. Cops had played a notorious part in the 1943 riot: many stood idly by as white mobs had their way with innocent blacks. For decades, the department screened out most black applicants, and well into the fifties those who were admitted were shunned by fellow officers. In the early sixties, when other whites' racial attitudes began to soften, many cops' experience of soaring crime rates bred still more mistrust, and by then, the antipathy was mutual. Two-thirds of all offenses in Detroit were committed by blacks, and as in all cities, the black community needed the cops as much or more than anyone. But policemen didn't need to be racist for ghetto kids to fear and resent them. Whether or not the cops wielded a brutal hand, blacks bristled at the idea of a white man in authority giving them orders.

In the sixties, cop-community relations became a political issue, further exacerbating tensions between the two groups. The 1961 mayoral campaign turned on police matters, and the liberal Jerome Cavanagh was elected by a huge black turnout. Cavanagh made it a top priority to reform the force, hiring blacks in large numbers and endeavoring to change the climate in the department. The police reacted with defensive stonewalling. Then the 1967 riot further inflamed feelings on both sides. Seventeen of the twenty-five blacks who died in the disturbances were killed by policemen, and the infamous Algiers Motel incident that week, in which cops were accused of shooting three subdued black men at close range, quickly became a cause célèbre in the community. As for the police, the riots only confirmed their notion that many blacks were indeed committed to lawlessness and disruption.

Black and white, city leaders struggled to find ways to defuse the mounting tension. The New Detroit Committee appropriated $300,000 for a study of how to overhaul the department. Cavanagh appointed an interracial task force and beefed up human relations training for officers. But like earlier reform efforts, these initiatives only seemed to make things worse. Resentment seethed through the rank-and-file, with officers complaining that the white establishment was ready to "sacrifice them to appease the Negro community." With both sides growing more bitter and entrenched every day, there seemed to be nothing anyone could do to ease the hostility.

Within hours of the New Bethel shooting and raid, word went out in the black community. The church's pastor, C. L. Franklin—the singer Aretha's father and a much-respected figure among black Detroiters—alerted Judge George W. Crockett, Jr., early the next morning, and Crockett rushed to the stationhouse where the RNA prisoners had been taken. The distinguished, aging judge was a pillar of black Detroit. His progressive credentials dated from the New Deal and culminated in the civil rights movement's Freedom Summer—he provided critical legal backup—with a long stint in between working for the radical wing of the UAW. His proudly leftist past—he also defended blacks at HUAC hearings and went to jail for contempt of court at the 1948 Smith Act trials—enhanced his reputation in the community, and he was committed to advancing black interests whenever the chance presented itself.

Like much of black Detroit, Judge Crockett made no secret of his mistrust of policemen and did not hesitate to act on that suspicion in his courtroom, relentlessly challenging police evidence and testimony and leaning whenever possible in favor of black defendants. He made it a policy to sentence black first offenders as leniently as the law allowed, and once ruled that a thief was not responsible for his actions because he was high on drugs when he committed his crime. Detroit police contended that Crockett was not just distrustful of cops but hostile to law enforcement. Colleagues on the bench grumbled behind his back and complained to reporters. "He has developed such a prejudice against the police," one said, "that he doesn't belong on the court." "Crockett has instilled in the mind of the thug and the con man and the pimp on the street corner a sort of security," charged another. "He's given them carte blanche."

When Crockett arrived at precinct headquarters at 5:30 Sunday morning, police were still trying to process their large intake of RNA prisoners. Ignoring the hubbub, the judge set up an impromptu court and began releasing the militant legionnaires, in many cases before they had been questioned. Police officials objected strenuously. Many of the activists had long criminal records. Nitrate tests showed that several of them had recently fired weapons, making them prime suspects in the death of Officer Czapski. Still another prisoner, none other than Herman Ferguson of Brooklyn, had been convicted not long before of conspiring to murder three national civil rights leaders and had jumped bail while awaiting an appeal.

Crockett could not have cared less. He brusquely ignored the officers' objections and went on methodically with his paperwork, releasing prisoner

after prisoner on the grounds that their constitutional rights had been violated in the raid on the church. Helpless officers looked on angrily. Waiting
RNA suspects cheered and taunted the cops, punching the air in the Black
Power salute. When white prosecutor William Cahalan arrived and protested Crockett's actions, the judge threatened to charge him with contempt of court. It took Crockett all day to process the RNA cases, but by
nightfall, he had released all 142 prisoners, including the three later tried
for Czapski's murder.

By the time most Detroiters heard of the incident, some time Sunday,
there were two versions of the story—one black, one white. For Crockett,
what happened in the church had been a police riot and a gross infringement
of his people's rights. For the department, it was cold-blooded murder: the
politically motivated slaying of a fellow cop. Both sides could make the facts
fit their interpretation, and neither wanted to hear any other view.

The initial reaction in the larger white community was anger and all but
unanimous censure of Crockett. Three out of four whites told pollsters they
believed he had acted illegally; 84 percent defended the police decision to
enter the church. No one was surprised when the conservative *News* came
out with an editorial questioning the black magistrate's judgment. But people began to take notice when Mayor Cavanagh, a stalwart liberal, declared
that the police had acted "in the only appropriate way." The state's new governor, William Milliken, also a liberal, went one step further, calling for a
judicial oversight committee to investigate Crockett's behavior. Before the
week was out, the state Senate passed two resolutions calling for punitive
action against the judge.

Then the black community began to make its defense: a political case for
Crockett's creative law enforcement. The support was virtually unanimous,
from Reverend Franklin to Reverend Cleage, from black elected officials to
the neighborhood youth groups organized by militants Frank Ditto and
Norvell Harrington. A majority of the city's blacks told pollsters they
thought Crockett had acted legally. The black lawyers' association, the black
policemen's league, black union groups and the black bourgeois version of
the Junior League all sided with the RNA, demanding police apologies and
damage payments. A long-scheduled testimonial breakfast for Crockett
turned into a show of defiance of the white community's censure—universally dismissed by Crockett and others as so much racist aggression. Among
those who got up to speak was former city councilman William Patrick, the
leading black member of New Detroit, who saluted the judge as "an authen-

tic hero of these trying times." Street kids demonstrating outside his court-room expressed their support even more vehemently: "If Crockett goes," they chanted menacingly, "Detroit goes!"

Buoyed by this acclaim, Crockett escalated his attacks on the system, assailing not just the New Bethel raid but the very foundations of the legal code. "The law," he told a group of fellow black lawyers, "is [a] camouflage . . . for racism." He boasted of his long-standing practice of stretching the rules for black defendants. "The people who elected me," he explained to a reporter, "expect me to take care of the shortcomings of the law as applied to them. A black judge has to be a nonconformist. He can't just do business the same old way." Implacable and righteous, Crockett shrugged off white Detroiters' criticism. "If the white judge's law in Alabama must be obeyed," he declared, "then a Negro judge's law in Detroit must also be obeyed." He announced that from now on he was going to take the law into his own hands on a regular basis, offering black defendants a chance to prove that police had mistreated them—and releasing any suspects who could make a case, guilty or not. In his view, he made clear, the fight against racism justi-fied almost any tactics. "I think black judges have an obligation," he said, "to pore through the law books to find new remedies for the ailments of their people."

By the time the New Detroit Committee met, four days after the raid at the New Bethel Church, the city was split down the middle. Crockett had framed the issue as starkly as it would ever be framed, asserting his and oth-ers' right to bend the rules in the name of racial justice, and the black com-munity had rallied behind him, adding that if "justice" were denied, there might be violence. The ball was now in the white establishment's court: just how far would the system go to accommodate blacks' demands that the law be stretched and if necessary suspended for them?

By the time the committee gathered, Fisher was convinced that the city was about to erupt, and any doubts he had were dispelled by Norvell Har-rington. Several corporate members got up as the meeting opened to express their concern about police attitudes. Someone suggested that a special sub-committee be formed to investigate the New Bethel incident. Then, abruptly, Harrington jumped to his feet and insisted he couldn't wait for a subcommittee's report; he wanted to meet immediately with the police com-missioner. "If you don't get me an appointment," Fisher recalls him threat-ening, "I'll burn the city down." Fisher watched anxiously as Harrington stalked out, praying that no other blacks would follow. None did, but outside the hall Harrington upped the ante, repeating his ultimatum to reporters. "You don't know what kind of hell I can raise," he threatened. Asked if that meant a riot, he answered, "It could."

Fisher came out moments later to speak to the press on behalf of the committee. "Let us examine what is happening in a calm atmosphere," he pleaded, "on the basis of facts, not rumors. . . . We as a community are at a crucial time. . . . Let us not go back to 1967." This was all the oilman had intended to say, but even as he spoke, he felt something more was needed. His mind raced back over the last few days, then over the meetings of the past eighteen months. He thought of the hours of talk, the "ventilation," of what he had learned and what he had promised. With black and white poised yet again on the brink, he asked himself what he could do to stave off disaster, and he made a snap decision. Surveying the gathered reporters, he said he would like to make a personal comment. "In my honest judgment," he declared solemnly, "Judge Crockett is an honest man who is trying to do what is right."

Fisher remembers the moment as one of the most important in his life. "It was a hard call, but I was right," he said later. "When you are a leader, every once in a while you have to take a position." As he understood the situation, he had done what it took to prevent a riot—and if that meant agreeing with a black man's claim that the law was racist and could be ignored, so be it. The city's most powerful businessman had lent his prestige and authority to the idea that the law could be applied selectively on the basis of race.

The rest of the city establishment immediately followed suit, rallying in support of Crockett's idea that racial sensitivity could trump justice. Fisher launched a campaign to convince the press of his view and made several public statements on local television and radio. Within days, his praise of the black judge had been seconded by the ACLU and a range of political figures. New Detroit released a strongly worded statement in defense of Crockett: there was, it declared, "more than merely a justifiable basis for his conduct and exercise of judicial discretion." Criminal law instructors at two Michigan law schools endorsed the judge's action, and several other prominent civic groups issued statements of support. Most stunning of all, within a few weeks, the *Detroit Free Press* published an editorial stating that its coverage of the New Bethel incident had been inaccurate and expressing its "regret" to the black community. Suburbanites and other whites who objected to the establishment's change of heart were written off as racists, and by the end of the month, all talk of censuring Crockett had been dropped.

Just what effect the New Bethel controversy had on the rule of law in Detroit could not be easily measured. Crime had been rising rapidly through the 1960s. Both homicide and robbery rates were already twice as high as elsewhere in the nation—violence fueled by demographic patterns, the business cycle and inner-city joblessness, among other trends. Yet for whatever reason, or combination of reasons, things grew significantly worse in the late 1960s and early 1970s.

The law seemed to hold less and less sway in the years after the incident. By 1970, there were half a million guns in Detroit, four-fifths of them unregistered. Fender-benders on the expressway regularly turned into shootings, and in the course of that year, several municipal employees were raped during the day in the halls of the City-County Building. Over the next five years, homicide and robbery rates rose between 25 and 30 percent. An aide to Jerome Cavanagh's successor, Roman Gribbs, recalled that the mayor himself was afraid to walk the streets and that he put off a visit by Richard Nixon because he felt he could not guarantee the president's security. "Cops began to see enforcement as a losing battle," the aide remembered. "Imagine a cop who sees a robbery in progress. He says to himself, 'I'm going to get out of here as fast as I can. Either he'll shoot me or I'll shoot him—and then there'll be a complaint and an investigation and I'll lose work for months and maybe even lose my job and my pension.'"

By the early seventies, Crockett's creative law enforcement and Fisher's endorsement of it were distant memories, but the breakdown of legal authority was making life in black Detroit more and more difficult. Blacks bore the lion's share of the city's rising crime: half of the robberies and 80 percent of the rapes and murders. Yet, by their own accounts, blacks were considerably less concerned about lawlessness than whites—only one in four thought it was Detroit's most pressing problem—and many were as wary of police as of the criminals they were battling. By 1971, a full half of the city's blacks told pollsters they mistrusted the police and had complaints about them—double the number who had felt that way just four years before. Two 1971 jury trials demonstrated how far the mood had swung. Many people predicted the first acquittal—of fifteen Black Panthers involved in a fatal shoot-out with police. But even jaded Detroiters were startled when a largely black jury decided that a black veteran who had gone on a rampage in a Chrysler plant and killed three white coworkers with his M-1 carbine should be excused because of the racist treatment he had received as a young man.

The effect on race relations was stark and irreversible, as more and more whites came to see crime as a racial issue. By the early seventies, a majority felt that violence was the city's leading problem, and *Time* magazine reported that "almost every white [in Detroit] claimed to know someone who had been mugged or robbed by black thugs." Karate and gun clubs flourished in the suburbs. Outlying whites dubbed the city "Indian country," and the few commuters who had to venture in made sure to be back across Eight Mile Road by nightfall. At holiday shopping time, cops with megaphones patrolled downtown. "Walk in twos after dark," they advised suburban shoppers. "Keep your hands on your purses. Stay away from alleys and have a merry Christmas." Whites leaving the city for the suburbs no longer needed to explain what was driving them out. As violence rose, the exodus swelled—it was even greater in the early seventies than in the late sixties— and with it went the businesses that might have given poor blacks an alternative to criminal activity.

As the years went by, the New Detroit Committee found it harder and harder to make a difference. There were some successes, most of them the fruit of members' personal influence: under pressure from the big auto companies, the state legislature passed an open-housing law, and local banks made more mortgages available in the inner city. Henry Ford II convinced Lyndon Johnson to try some of the group's ideas at the national level, and Max Fisher later goaded Richard Nixon in the same direction. Still, the committee did next to nothing to overcome the region's ever-deepening polarization or jump-start what Fisher had called "the natural Americanization machine." Try as he would, Fisher found that even the middle-class blacks on the panel did not come when he invited them to his house: "they didn't seem that interested in integration," he remembered. Poverty and its pathologies raced on unchallenged. White suburbanites were not only frightened of the city; they grew ever more indifferent to its problems, more and more put off by its festering anger. Eventually even members of New Detroit began to throw up their hands. Fisher complained of "volunteer fatigue"; committee meetings dissolved in bickering. Periodic progress reports admitted that the group's goals remained "largely unfulfilled," and instead of new initiatives, members fell back on recommending that the federal government spend more money.

Whether the obstacle was hate, indifference, economic conditions or simply geography, just about everything New Detroit attempted proved how hard it was to bring blacks into the system. Nothing made the point more starkly than the committee's hiring program, widely considered to be one of its most successful. Ford Company employee Levi Jackson, a black man and former Yale football star, came up with the concept, and his boss, Henry Ford II, put it into practice, announcing in late 1967 that he was going to hire five thousand "hard-core unemployed." By then, after several years of Great Society efforts, reformers had grasped that ghetto joblessness was a many-sided problem, caused in part by limited job availability but also by the mismatch between workers and slots. The hard-core unemployed were mostly high school dropouts, many with criminal records, no work history, fewer skills and mixed feelings about "fitting in" to the system. The idea in hiring them was to get them off the street and out of trouble but also, more ambitiously, to trigger the "Americanization machine": to bring them into the mainstream by placing them on the job ladder, and hope that the rest would take care of itself.

It was no small thing for the Big Three automakers to revamp their hiring standards and procedures. In a few short weeks in 1967, fifty years of habit flew out the window. Application forms were redesigned, written entry-level tests eliminated, rules about dress and deportment abruptly scrapped, questions about work experience and police records simply no longer asked. Long-proven procedures were deemed not just "unrealistic" but "irrelevant"—and a major reason for the dissatisfaction that had led to ghetto rioting. In the past, one guilt-ridden New Detroit document stated, "employers unwittingly supported the myth that job seekers were a poor risk if they didn't hold a high-school diploma, or if they had been convicted of a crime, or if they had a bad employment record. By systematically excluding such job seekers from employment, employers themselves may have been as much to blame for 'hard-core unemployment' as any lack of ability on the part of job seekers." Once again, as in the New Bethel incident, Detroit's elite decided that racial justice—and racial peace—demanded a radical bending of mainstream standards. "For over 75 years," one employer noted, "business tried to screen people out. Now we are trying to find reasons to screen them in."

The hiring program produced immediate and numerically impressive results. For the first time in company history, Ford set up recruitment centers in the ghetto. More than fifteen hundred people lined up overnight to apply for work, and within weeks, the company had met its quota of five thousand hires. General Motors followed suit with a similar number, and Chrysler outdid them both with eight to nine thousand. In some cases, new screening procedures replaced old ones: one recruitment initiative looked exclusively for prison parolees, another accepted only youths at risk of dropping out of high school. Michigan Bell, Detroit Edison, Hudson's and others soon had programs of their own, and by spring 1968 some twenty-eight thousand people had been hired, many of them street kids, gang members and others who had never held a job before.

The journey from street corner to shop floor was not always a smooth one, but the automakers bent over backwards to ease the transition. Orientation programs stressed a basic work ethic. Several companies handed out alarm clocks to all new recruits; others provided bus fare and lunch money along with advice about how to budget a weekly salary. Buddy systems were encouraged; a foreman who complained about the new hires' work was told that it was up to him to help them fit in—and that his own job might depend on it. When Chrysler discovered that a large number of its new workers could not read, it hired fifty high school teachers for a tutoring program. Both Michigan Bell and Detroit Edison set up summer training sessions to help with grooming, deportment and telephone skills. In March 1968, the federal government was so impressed with Detroit's efforts that President Johnson called Henry Ford to Washington and asked him to launch a similar campaign on a national scale: the National Alliance of Businessmen's JOBS program would find work, heavily subsidized by the federal government, for one hundred thousand hard-core unemployed.

The campaign's longer-term success was harder to measure. Undoubtedly, for a number of hires, particularly the younger ones, New Detroit's efforts opened a critical door into the mainstream economy. What the committee called "retention rates" varied widely: at some companies no more than a third of the new hires worked out, but in other places it was 75 percent—as high or higher than the rate for ordinary employees. By the end of the decade, the black presence at the Big Three had grown markedly; many plants in the city were now majority black, and unlike in the past, black workers could compete for any job.

The problems began to emerge in the winter of 1969–70, when a slump in the auto industry caused severe layoffs and many of the hard core were the first to go. Then, with programs closing and the pressure off, word began to leak out about other disappointments. It was rumored that the young clerks hired by Hudson's had pilfered a staggering amount of merchandise. Union officials complained of an upsurge in racial strife on the shop floor, and the press reported a sharp rise in drug use at the auto plants, where a weekly assembly-line wage could more than support a robust heroin habit. Most troublingly, economists studying the recruitment effort began to notice that, for all the goodwill and the subsidies, virtually no company had created any new jobs; they had merely put new hires in old slots, now being eliminated by larger forces.

In the end, New Detroit's hiring was simply no match for the economic realities besieging Detroit. By the time the program was initiated in the late sixties, jobs were leaving the region at a torrential rate. The exodus had nothing to do with race and everything to do with global economic changes: foreign competition for the auto industry and the lure of lower production costs outside the city, whether in the suburbs, the South or overseas in a Third World country. Foreign-car imports skyrocketed in this period, up by more than 2 million a year. Pinched American automakers had little choice but to move their production where taxes and wages were lower. Mayor Cavanagh made Herculean efforts to make the city hospitable to business, but for every company that stayed, two others left town. Even as Henry Ford recruited 5,000 unemployed ghetto kids in Detroit, his company's domestic workforce shrank by 8,000—and its overseas employment grew by 50,000. By the early seventies, just about half of all Ford jobs were overseas; fewer than 35,000 remained in Detroit, and more than 150,000 were spread elsewhere in the United States. If ever there was a "shrinking pie," it was Detroit in the late sixties, and there was little the city's corporate leaders could do to make it go further for either blacks or whites.

Ford and Fisher knew as well as anyone where the jobs were in the late sixties. Troy, just north of the city in Oakland County, was the new suburban enclave of choice, picked by Chrysler among other companies when it built a new 1,700-acre complex. Troy was only seventeen miles from the center of black Detroit, but it was an entirely different economy. Most of the jobs were in offices in the new glass towers along the expressway—in corporate headquarters, small electronic companies, consulting firms and other professional services—and they required a different kind of education than the old jobs in Detroit. No relaxation of standards and no amount of extra bus fare could equip the city's street kids for this work, and not one of New Detroit hard-core recruits benefited from the thousands of jobs opening up in the new town. Try as they might, Fisher and his fellow businessmen could do nothing to fight the economic restructuring of the region, and by the time the recession lifted, their hiring program had been quietly dropped.

If anything, members of the New Detroit Committee were contributing to the problem, quietly moving their own wealth from the city to the suburbs. Well-intentioned as they were, in their business decisions, they were driven by business—and by the late sixties, everyone knew, the best opportunities were out of town. Even at the peak of Max Fisher's involvement in New Detroit, most of his new real estate business was on the outskirts of the city. Joseph Hudson was concentrating more and more on his chain's suburban outlets, gradually cutting advertising and inventory at the old downtown store, and Henry Ford's investment focus had shifted to the Fair Lane mall, part of a $750-million cluster of homes and office blocks he was putting up in suburban Dearborn. Like many New Detroit members, Ford rarely even came downtown except to committee meetings: morning and night, he sped across town on the expressway—from his home in a northern suburb to his office in Dearborn, south of the city line.

By the early 1970s, the two Detroits had settled into uneasy coexistence, with most residents on both sides of the line determined to pretend the other world did not exist. Few city blacks had ever set foot in the suburbs; suburbanites saw the trip downtown as a perilous journey. City and suburb, though rarely more than twenty miles apart, might as well have been on different planets.

Pollsters gauging the mood of the black community found it radically transformed in the years since the riot. The upsurge of political activity had produced a proud new self-reliance. "Black Power" was the phrase of the moment. The word "Negro" had fallen abruptly out of use. In 1968, it had still been the term of choice for 71 percent of black Detroiters; by 1971, a large majority preferred "black" or "Afro-American." Black history, black culture, black clothing and black solidarity were rapidly replacing the deference of the city's old southern-born, churchgoing black working class. The myth of the riot as rebellion helped cement this sense of solidarity; so did a new mood of aggressive skepticism about race relations in the region. Emerging middle-class blacks told questioners that group identity was what mattered most to them—more important even, they said, than their own personal success. "We became aware of ourselves," one assembly-line worker later told a reporter. "'Black is beautiful, black is power.' We had a unity there. You passed somebody on the street and you were 'sister,' you were 'brother.'"

Against this background, the paternalism of the New Detroit Committee seemed less and less relevant. Committee members, long tired of ventilation, itched to move on to other things. "We realized," Hudson later said, "that New Detroit had become a debating society, and we all felt that we had to go beyond this." Henry Ford was the most impatient, bored by committee meetings and irritated by the insults. "We have to get down to programs," he insisted. "We have to get out and do things. I'd rather get something done than sit around and talk about it." The problem in Detroit as elsewhere in America was that no one knew what to do. It was partly their own fault and partly due to circumstances beyond their control, but try as they might, Detroit's civic leaders had failed to jump-start poor blacks' "natural" rise into the mainstream, and after three years they still had no idea how to ease black poverty or assuage the ghetto's anger.

Yet neither Fisher nor Ford liked to give up, and finally in 1970 they fell back on what they knew best: perhaps simple investment could solve the problem. New Detroit was not disbanded, but a new entity was formed alongside it—Detroit Renaissance Inc.—and it became the focus of the businessmen's activity. The players were the same: Fisher, Ford, Hudson, the other top auto executives and their biggest suppliers. But the style could not have been more different. Gone were the militants, the social programs, the monthly complaint sessions. Detroit Renaissance was a high-level investors' club and its modus operandi was strictly corporate. Fisher, once again the behind-the-scenes ideas man, commissioned an expensive study of the prospects for downtown development. Ford Company staffers told their boss that the project Fisher envisioned was unrealistic; no matter how cheap the land or what kind of breaks the city would give them, there was simply no market for a complex of tony shops and apartments in the heart of devastated downtown Detroit. Fisher brushed off the doubters and brought in his own gung-ho consultants. He invited Ford to his home and cajoled him over drinks at poolside. "We'll force the market," Fisher and his advisers insisted. "[We can] stimulate economic growth in Detroit."

The idea was a huge downtown development project that would change the face—and image—of the city. A string of parks, stores, office towers, high- and low-rise apartment buildings would replace the abandoned lots and warehouses that now lined the riverfront, and would provide a glamorous catalyst for other new downtown development. Ever confident, Ford and Fisher convinced each other that they could halt the decline of the city—could single-handedly reverse the disinvestment that had been disfiguring the region since the 1940s. Their new riverfront project would be big enough to counter the lure of the suburbs, pulling white money, white shoppers and eventually white residents back into the city. Hard as it had proved to bring poor blacks into the mainstream, why, with enough money and clout, could they not bring the mainstream back into the black city? Only men as powerful as Fisher and Ford could even have contemplated the possibility, and even for them, it was a breathtaking endeavor.

The two men tackled the project with characteristic energy and commitment. Ford took on the fund-raising himself with a flurry of letters, lunches and dinners, twisting the arm of every executive in the region who had ever done business with the Ford Motor Company. A number of CEOs were skeptical: "You won't get the multiplier effect you're looking for," Hudson warned him. But Ford and Fisher left even the skeptics no choice: "Detroit has been good to you and your companies," Fisher harangued a room of executives. "[Now] you have an obligation to give something back."

Within a few months, Ford and Fisher had put together the largest private investment group ever assembled for an urban redevelopment project. As they imagined the future, the automobile industry would step in where the poverty program had failed, and with the sheer force of real estate dollars, do what it took to heal the ghetto. The original investment was not huge—about $120 million, one-third of it from the Ford Motor Company—but the executives behind the venture were persuaded it would pay off big, if not for themselves, then for their city. In the early seventies, there was no one to tell them differently—and little else on the horizon that promised change. The polarization of the region now had a momentum of its own, and left to itself, in a matter of years, it could only produce two irreconcilable communities. Fisher and Ford were brimming with enthusiasm, but behind their bravado lurked a growing desperation. Their riverfront project was a bold, brash bid, but if it failed, there would be nothing to hold the region together—nothing to bind the two Detroits, neither of which could hope to survive alone.

Chapter 9

BLOCKING THE BUSES

I rene McCabe was a reporter's dream: the larger-than-life local character who perfectly captured the national mood of the moment. Local media could not get enough of her when she emerged in autumn 1971, leading antibusing demonstrations in the town of Pontiac. Eighteen miles north of Detroit, Pontiac was a grimy industrial center in its own right, one of the largest and oldest nodes in Motown's diverse suburban ring. Roughly one-third black, the rest tough blue-collar ethnic, the town had not reacted well to a busing order handed down the year before by a federal judge in Detroit. Pontiac's white mothers were gathering at playgrounds and in the supermarket; fathers were grumbling among themselves on their way to work in the town's sprawling GM factories. There had been meetings after school and then more over the summer, devising tactics to stop the buses on school opening day. Reporters looking for a way to cover this grassroots flurry fell immediately on Irene McCabe. Blond, thirty-something, shapely and engaging, she was not only photogenic and appealing to TV viewers, but in her die-hard beliefs she seemed to represent the soul of the "silent majority" that had been preoccupying the media and the public since Nixon named it in November 1969.

McCabe could have come straight from Central Casting or off the set of *All in the Family,* which first appeared on national television just as she made the evening news in Detroit. Middle-income, high school–educated, wife of a postal worker and mother of three, she sounded almost boastful when she told reporters she was "blue-collar working-class." True to type, she was fiercely patriotic, committed to law and order and family values, and inexperienced as she was, she gave the perfect interview. Though largely unconcerned with anything ethnic—of Greek extraction, she had married into a clan of Irish immigrants—she knew enough to talk about her roots to reporters looking for an angry hyphenated American. "I never used to even stop to think I was Greek," she explained ever so coyly, "I always thought I was just an American. Now people are going around calling themselves Afro-Americans. So I now tell everyone I'm a Greek-American." It was almost as if she knew she were playing the nation's newest stock character.

McCabe liked attention and knew how to get it, whether with a combative stance or a little old-fashioned coquettishness. (Though a staunch defender of family morality, she noticed that reporters could not help mentioning her slogans if she wore them blazoned on a tightish-fitting T-shirt.) She hadn't planned to get involved in the antibusing crusade: she just happened to stand up and speak one night at a mothers' meeting where TV cameras were rolling. She hadn't been recruited by anyone; she had been taught no set of coordinated beliefs. She was a housewife, irritated by a few local issues, and in another era she would have been content merely to gripe about them. What made her and her moment different was television.

She found her politics on the evening news, in its portraits—and caricatures—of other blue-collar conservatives. She learned her tactics from her enemies: the student antiwar protesters and black activists featured on the airwaves. Louise Day Hicks (another former housewife who made a name for herself by opposing busing in Boston), Martin Luther King, even the Black Power movement all helped to form McCabe's political imagination and inspired her stratagems. Her goal, in just about all she did, was media coverage for her cause. "That's what we've got to have," she told anyone who would listen. "Publicity, attention—every day." American original that she was, Irene McCabe was nobody's stereotype. Yet with the media's help, she emerged in no time flat as a full-blown representative of "the forgotten American," voicing the same set of concerns, in just about the same language, as other activists like her all over the country, whether in Mario Procaccino's Queens or Mrs. Hicks's South Boston.

McCabe's first splash on the evening news was in September 1971, when she led a school boycott in Pontiac. A handful of housewives appeared on camera carrying flags and blocking the path of a yellow bus. "You can't run over the American flag," one woman taunted the driver. She was quickly removed by a policeman, but her cry was taken up by a group of other women, who chanted it rhythmically several times, then switched to "God Bless America." It was the second day of school, the second day the buses rolled in Pontiac, and thanks to the housewives' efforts, about half of the system's white students were absent. Irene McCabe spoke for the protesters at an impromptu news conference. Wearing a wine-colored minidress, carefully made up, her hair swept back in a loose bun that framed her face in golden ringlets, she could have been advertising shampoo or cold cream—if she hadn't seemed so fiercely earnest. In 1971, Pontiac was one of the first northern cities under a court order to introduce busing for racial reasons, and the housewives' protest attracted national attention. Open conflict over integration, commentators noted ominously, was now moving to the industrial heartland.

Before the week was out, McCabe and her fellow housewives had organized a second protest, shutting down two of the big GM plants that employed much of Pontiac's workforce and, as it happened, built most of the nation's yellow school buses. This action was much larger than the first, involving hundreds of pickets, mostly women and children, who came out at five o'clock in the morning to march in front of the Fisher auto-body plant. More than half the factory's employees declined to cross the picket line. GM was forced to close the big facility and a car-assembly plant not far away. All in all, some seven thousand workers lost a day's work and pay. "We've shown what the people of Pontiac think about busing," McCabe told reporters.

Spread out over six counties, the sixty-five-plus suburban enclaves that ringed Detroit in 1971 were almost as varied as the city had once been in wealth, class and ethnic origin. Warren and Pontiac were older manufacturing cities, both by now outmoded and declining. Grosse Pointe was a wealthy bedroom community. Birmingham and Bloomfield Hills were newer, but also conventional residential enclaves. Troy, Southfield and Dearborn were different: along with subdivisions, they were sprouting high-rise towers. Close to the auto industry but clean and modern, they would soon have as much office space as downtown. Also new but different in their own way were the vast malls at Northland, Eastland and Fair Lane, all of them ringed by seemingly endless retail strips. In 1970, the city population was down to 1.5 million; together, the suburbs totaled nearly double that—2.9 million. In contrast to the city, now equally divided along racial lines, the suburbs were under 5 percent black.

On race as in all things, the suburbs were anything but uniform. Some rich, some poor, some liberal, some conservative, some largely Jewish and some Polish, they differed greatly in the degree to which they did or didn't seem to welcome blacks. Some, like old-money Grosse Pointe, were notoriously exclusive, hostile not just to blacks but also to Jews, Catholics and people of Mediterranean descent—anybody but WASPs. Other enclaves, like working-class Warren and Dearborn, home to the Ford Motor Company and eighty thousand of its employees, were simply and unashamedly antiblack. Still others, like the upscale Southfield and Oak Park, were known to be more tolerant: they even began in the late sixties to try to counter the trends that were keeping black families out. But whatever the reasons, almost no blacks followed whites to the Detroit suburbs in the fifties and sixties— and no suburbs were beset by the social problems increasingly common in the city.

Many working-class whites in places like Warren and Dearborn came directly from embattled Detroit, and they tended to bring both the fears and the tactics that had made their old neighborhoods so ugly. Residents talked of "undesirable elements" and unwelcome "hordes," and they elected aggressive, brazenly bigoted officials to protect them from a black influx. No one symbolized the crusade better than Dearborn's segregationist mayor, Orville Hubbard, who was elected in 1941 and ruled the city for more than three decades. "If whites don't want to live with niggers," he declared, "they sure as hell don't have to. Damn it, this is a free country. This is America." Warren officials were a little less flamboyant but no more tolerant. Thirty percent of the workers in Warren's factories were black; but at the end of the day, virtually every one of them drove back across the Detroit line. In 1970, Warren went so far as to turn down a $30-million HUD grant rather than build a low-cost housing project, establishing itself, in the eyes of *Time* magazine, as "the nation's most racist city." The homes in both Dearborn and Warren sold in the middle range of regional real estate prices—by 1970, affordable to many black working-class families—but between them, the two outlaying cities counted no more than 133 blacks in a combined population of 300,000.

People in better-off and better-educated enclaves like Southfield and Bloomfield Hills talked a nicer game than people in Dearborn: more than three-quarters told pollsters they would not mind a black in their neighborhood. But in their way, they too were resisting blacks—albeit with subtle barriers and hidden discrimination. As in the past, in upscale towns like these, much of the dirty work fell to real estate brokers, who knew where blacks were welcome and where not, and how to steer unwanted inquiries away from white neighborhoods.

Black realtor John Humphrey worked for many years in an area near the Detroit line where the covert discrimination was practiced and unrelenting. Often, white realtors lied to Humphrey and his clients about prices and rental fees, quoting ridiculously high figures and insisting on unreasonable down payments. On other occasions, the agents told black customers that all available units had been sold or rented. In still other cases, suburban realtors tried to discourage blacks by denigrating the property that interested them. "I don't know why you'd want to buy this house," one white salesman told Humphrey, "because it floods every time it rains. [Even] a good heavy dew [is enough]—and things are flooded all over." Federal officials investigating the Detroit area confirmed Humphrey's experience; according to one study, black families faced a 60 percent probability of receiving some sort of unfavorable treatment from suburban realtors.

Still, for all the covert discrimination, civil right activists trying to pry open the suburbs wondered if there wasn't also something else keeping blacks out, particularly in upscale, professional enclaves more and more likely to be liberal in the sixties and seventies. Although discrimination was abating, both whites and blacks seemed to have what sociologists called "a mental map" of the city. Both groups professed support, in theory, for the idea of residential integration, and yet both continued to live in almost entirely segregated neighborhoods. As early as 1963, a liberal organization devoted to fair housing gathered sixty listings of available homes in affordable white enclaves—Palmer Woods, St. Clair Shores, Livonia and Oak Park, among others—but could find only two black families who were interested in looking at any of them. "Both blacks and whites," one researcher explained, "are very knowledgeable about where they and the other race 'belong.'"

Social scientists working from testimony and anecdotal evidence explained these "mental maps" in a variety of ways. Both whites and blacks in the Detroit area were haunted by memories of racial conflict. Whites recalled how former neighborhoods had tipped overnight, transforming schools and driving families from the city. Blacks remembered the friend or relative who had bought a house in an all-white enclave and was forced, by violence or ostracism, to sell again within the year. As late as the mid-seventies, 40 percent of Detroit whites believed property values would sink if a black family moved onto their block, and about the same proportion of blacks expected to be made uncomfortable in a white neighborhood. True or not, these expectations often loomed larger than more reasoned calculus, and for many people, they were reinforced by natural clannishness. When white Detroiters left the city, they often went en masse, whole neighborhoods together: WASPs moving out along one spoke, to the northeast, Jews along another, heading northwest. Germans, Poles, and Irish moved to neighborhoods where they knew other people and expected to feel comfortable—and with or without bigotry, this tended to produce segregated enclaves. Still, powerful as they were, even these inclinations did not seem enough to explain the persistent segregation of the Detroit area.

The man who finally cracked the riddle of Detroiters' mental maps was Reynolds Farley, a sociologist at the University of Michigan, and his work in suburban Detroit remains the reigning explanation of residential segregation. Frustrated for years by the evasive answers people gave to pollsters on race issues, Farley developed an ingenious technique to explore what they really felt about their neighborhoods. The device was a series of flashcards depicting a variety of segregated and mixed neighborhoods. At one end of the series, all fifteen houses on the card were white; the next card had one black house among fifteen, the next card two, and so forth, until at the other end of the series, all fifteen houses were black. Farley showed the complete set of cards to blacks and whites in the Detroit area, asking each which diagram represented their ideal neighborhood. Already in the mid-seventies, both groups endorsed the idea of desegregation. Still, Farley found, there was a fundamental mismatch between black and white preferences. While even the most recalcitrant Detroit whites would accept a small number of blacks in their neighborhoods, blacks were most interested in living in enclaves that were at least half black.

The difference seemed small, but it was critically important. For most whites, Farley found, one or two black families on a block—a proportion that reflected the population—did not seem to threaten the quality of the neighborhood. But more than that, people worried, would make the area identifiably black, probably bringing crime and lowered property values. Call it prejudice or realistic fear, whites expected that a black neighborhood would be a poor one, with different social norms than they were used to. At the same time, blacks did not want to live as a minority among what they feared would be hostile neighbors, and they did not feel at ease in an area until at least half the families looked like them. Translated into real neighborhoods in a changing region like the Detroit area, this fundamental mismatch made residential integration all but impossible—no matter how much the law changed or discrimination abated.

Whatever the reasons, by the early 1970s, Detroit was well on its way to de facto apartheid. Not only did the city line divide black from white; it also divided wealth from poverty, and economic growth from looming decline. The older, inefficient plants in town were far less pleasant places to work and far more vulnerable to the business cycle. Even in boom times, unemployment in the inner city rarely dropped below 30 percent, and more than 70 percent of the housing in town required major repairs. The schools had long ago tipped from majority white to majority black, and by now two-thirds of the youths looking for jobs were dropouts. It would be some years before the trends of the postwar era became fully apparent, but by the early eighties, the city's share of regional manufacturing had dropped from 60 to 25 percent, its share of retail from 73 to 15 percent. Already in the early seventies, things were so bad in the city that many neighborhood shopping streets looked like ghost towns, and an increasing number of black Detroiters regularly traveled to the suburbs to buy not just their clothes and household goods but even their groceries.

Eight Mile Road, Alter Road, Telegraph Road and Tireman Avenue: though originally arbitrary—lines on a map—the boundary between Detroit and its suburbs had become a chasm between two social classes. In some places, usually where the road was wide, it divided slum from new, upscale housing development. At other spots, once similar houses on either side of the street now looked like pictures before and after a natural disaster. Heavily industrial, largely ethnic, already plainly on the decline, working-class Pontiac was more like the city than almost any other enclave in the region, and it already had enough black families to make school segregation a problem. But what frightened Irene McCabe and the other mothers who picketed with her was not only the few blacks who had made it out to Pontiac. By the early seventies the race relations that mattered in metro Detroit were not between blacks and whites in the suburbs, or even between blacks and whites in town, but between the increasingly black city and its all but lily-white suburbs.

L ike most of the grassroots activists who would emerge out of nowhere in the next few years to oppose busing in the Detroit area, Irene McCabe had to educate herself as she went—about politics, the law and the tangled school integration issue. When she began, she said later, "I was so naive I didn't even know how to make a picket sign. I wrote on a brown paper shopping bag and stuck it over a broom." McCabe and the local lawyer she found to help her remember struggling to grasp the difference between de jure and de facto segregation. "We're dumb and we're blue-collar," McCabe told a reporter. "But that will change. We're learning." Meanwhile, suburban opposition to busing was picking up steam, and with it McCabe's organization, NAG—originally the Northside Action Group, soon redubbed the National Action Group.

The group's early activities had a wholesome, small-town feel, something like the PTA or a local church affiliate. There were raffles and garage sales to make money. Headquarters were in McCabe's small frame house, meetings in a basement rec room. Would-be supporters were invited to drop by at McCabe's "office" to pick up T-shirts, buttons and bumper stickers or simply to chat. Others learned about the group's activities from its crudely mimeographed newsletter. The movement's rhetoric made little mention of race, and McCabe never tired of insisting how much she abhorred bigotry. "Years ago," she liked to tell reporters, "one of my closest girlfriends was a wonderful black girl. We worked together as X-ray technicians at Pontiac General Hospital. One day we went to Detroit and tried to join the Waves. We were eighteen and too young to get in. Later I worked as a bookkeeper for a fine black man. I have nothing against individual blacks. I went to school with them. I wouldn't mind my children going to school with them. It isn't that."

The housewives' tactics gradually grew more sophisticated. The demonstrations in September 1971 failed to block the buses in Pontiac, but McCabe continued to organize local mothers, both in her own town and further afield. Soon the women were tracking legislation, organizing speaking tours, testifying at hearings and backing local candidates. The cheerful PTA friendliness gave way to something harder-edged, and there was talk of shifting children permanently to neighborhood academies. As time went on, even the most restrained mothers seemed to show a certain relish for confronting opponents. NAG regularly demonstrated at schools and school board meetings, organized parades and car caravan protests. One group of mothers even traveled downtown to picket Detroit businesses that contributed to the NAACP.

Yet reporters looking for the face of hatred were usually disappointed by Pontiac's housewives. The dynamiting of ten school buses late one night in a Pontiac parking lot sent shock waves through the region and attracted national media attention, but no one was ever able to prove that NAG had encouraged the action. McCabe immediately denounced it, insisting on her group's commitment to peaceful protest. Future rallies were called off at any hint of violence, and McCabe made certain that speeches were positive—not so much against busing or even intrusive judges as in favor of the security provided by the neighborhood school. "A mother is a mother," a typical NAG leaflet read, "no matter what her color, creed or ethnic background. Her first concern is her child, who she wants to be near." Intensely conscious of their image and of the way they were portrayed in the media, Detroit mothers remained for the most part earnestly patriotic and upbeat, convinced, despite all negative coverage, of the justice of their cause.

It was hard to tell what they really felt about race matters. Mostly, when they talked about busing, what they seemed to object to was the government intrusion. They complained about being "guinea pigs," about "losing control" of their lives and the lives of their children; they resented being forced to take part in a "giant social experiment" they did not believe in. On the rare occasions that McCabe mentioned race, it was usually to complain about the rise of militancy. Whether or not she liked blacks, she didn't hesitate to voice her dislike for the turn black politics were taking. "In 1969," she declared, "I read in the paper a statement by a leader of the National Association for the Advancement of Colored People here saying he was going to advise his people to get more militant. That's when all the trouble started in Pontiac. There were school riots. Children were injured. I think the black parents instilled hatred of whites in their children."

The issue of ghetto violence was an even bigger concern. One of McCabe's comrades in arms, Shirley Wohlfield, traveled around the region giving speeches about what she called the "crime-blackboard jungle" in the Detroit public schools. There is "no discipline, no learning," she said. "Students are physically and verbally abusive and seldom expelled for it." In Pontiac, McCabe feared sending her daughter to the elementary school she had been assigned to under the busing plan. "It's in an area of town the fire department won't even go to," McCabe complained, "unless accompanied by armed guards." In the minds of many suburban mothers, black meant poor meant less carefully brought up meant probably violent. "There was an incident," McCabe told a reporter, "where a black child didn't want to wait for his turn on the slide and he threw a white child from the top of the slide. Who knows what kind of a home that child came from. Maybe there's no father, maybe the mother was out all night. I don't know, but I don't want my child to suffer."

In fact, it would have been hard for the region's parents, white or black, to exaggerate the turmoil taking over in city public schools. Even before the 1967 riot, the Detroit system had been in a tailspin. An influx of black children from poor, uneducated migrant families had overwhelmed the schools, and conditions were so bad that about half the city teaching staff turned over every year. Visitors noticed that students were fighting in the halls and urinating behind radiators. It was not unusual for kids to reach eighth grade without being able to write the alphabet. At Martin Luther King High School, only one in seven hundred sophomores could read at grade level and many graduates could not decipher their diplomas. First in the inner city and then in a series of concentric circles, schools turned from mostly white to mostly black in under five years. Fairly or not, white parents blamed blacks for the poor quality of their kids' educations, and thousands moved to the suburbs to escape the decline.

In the wake of 1967, already bad conditions worsened dramatically. Several largely black high schools exploded. There were boycotts, demonstrations and angry campaigns to fire white teachers. Student grievances varied widely, from calls for "quality education" to complaints about locker assignments, but in the months after the riot even the smallest demand was backed up by protest—and, increasingly, it became difficult to distinguish political acts from sheer vandalism. Armed intruders roamed the halls in ghetto schools. Carrying knives and guns, they came to sell drugs, to shake down smaller kids or snatch teachers' purses. Windows were broken and school equipment stolen faster than anyone could replace it. There were skirmishes between black and white students, then an epidemic of small fires in school buildings. One local adult activist—a professor at Wayne State University— spoke for striking students in 1968. "In some schools," he warned the city, "we're going to have teachers who are going to be injured." In 1968, fifteen white principals quit, and the city began to find it difficult to replace teachers. For suburban mothers like Irene McCabe, the idea of busing inner-city blacks into their kids' schools seemed tantamount to inviting the 1967 riot into their living rooms.

For McCabe and others like her, the hated yellow buses symbolized precisely what they feared and wished to avoid in the dangerous inner city, be it Detroit or downtown Pontiac. Race plainly fed their fears, and many were driven by bigotry. But others were protesting an arguable social policy: an insistence by the government that they could not protect themselves from a class and culture they found dangerous. "If you think about it," liberal suburban newspaper publisher Philip Power noted years later, "there is a great deal of emotional power and reasonability to the cry of a mother asking, 'What gives some judge the right to send my child to a violent, deteriorating school in the inner city?'"

The irony, in Detroit as elsewhere, was that it did not matter whether the white parents who opposed busing were driven by prejudice or not. Whatever feelings the mothers harbored, however reasonable or unreasonable their objections, in the eyes of the region's blacks, the suburbs' rejection of integration looked like bigotry—with all the inevitable, poisonous consequences for race relations. Angry ghetto youths rebelling against what they saw as "the racist system" now had all the evidence they needed. Rejectionist militants spreading counter-hatred said, "I told you so" and made converts without an argument, even in Detroit's deferential, churchgoing black community. Black support for school desegregation dropped sharply—according to one measure, from 88 percent in 1967 to 68 percent in 1971—and even those who supported the idea were less and less willing to take steps to achieve it.

In Detroit as in other cities, the push for school desegregation was undergoing an abrupt change when Irene McCabe appeared on the scene in the early 1970s. Detroit's school authorities, like those in New York, came out of a paternalistic, liberal tradition committed to reform and to the latest theories of education. The civil rights revolution had only intensified these good intentions, and the push for change that began in the early sixties put Detroit in a class by itself, out ahead of even the most liberal northern cities. By then, middle-class whites were abandoning the city in droves and the schools, already overburdened, were plainly heading for trouble. But well-meaning, liberal educators were still convinced they could make a difference. In Detroit, as elsewhere, schooling was the front line of integration—the area where, it was thought, it made most sense to give blacks a leg-up into the system.

Still, as in New York and other big cities, desegregation proved all but impossible. No amount of new building or voluntary transfers made a dent in the demographic pattern. In Detroit, as elsewhere, the cry went up: "There aren't enough whites to go around" in a desegregated system. What whites there were huddled together on the north side of the city, leaving three-fourths of Detroit's black pupils in schools that were more than 90 percent black. An ambitious magnet school program led to few interracial assignments. Even in the few schools—mostly high schools—attended by both blacks and whites, students remained strictly self-segregated, avoiding each other in the lunchroom, if not openly clashing in the halls.

White integrationists on the school board and in parent councils began to notice that blacks were abandoning the cause, complaining that in the face of white flight it seemed foolish to hold out for desegregation. Pollsters showed black support for all forms of integration slipping sharply in the five years after the riots, and even those who continued to use the term seemed to see it more as a synonym for equal opportunity than a vision of living among white people. A small, experimental busing program launched by the school board in 1970 led to protests by black mothers who traveled to the state capital in Lansing to complain. "They did not want their children bused, period," reported a state education official. Even the NAACP, still battling in court for desegregation, seemed to be revising the goal beyond recognition. "None of us," a Michigan NAACP lawyer noted, using a stock phrase of the era, "was convinced that a black child could only learn while sitting next to a white child." The old ideal was being replaced by a new beacon, "quality education"—and as one black Detroiter commented in 1971, "most people [in the community] no longer see integration as being the way to achieve that objective."

In place of integration, black activists and their white allies turned, as in New York, to community control. The idea cropped up first in militant circles in the years after the 1967 riot. Then, at the end of the decade, inspired by visiting lecturers from Ocean Hill–Brownsville, moderate blacks and liberal whites endorsed the idea, followed by suburban conservatives, who recognized that the breakup of the system could be a windfall for them, too. As in New York, at least some Detroit backers believed community control could be consistent with integration, and in 1969 the state legislature passed a far-reaching decentralization bill. Only as the plan began to be implemented did integrationists see the writing on the wall. Even as the school board met to divide the city into local districts, black activists and parents petitioned against making them integrated. Then, in August 1970, four integrationist board members were voted out of office—by an unusually heavy, negative turnout in white enclaves and a relatively light vote in black precincts. The verdict was unmistakable, an increasingly familiar pattern. Working-class whites and ghetto spokesmen were joining together to reject integration, while ordinary blacks remained largely apathetic—and a few dwindling do-gooders struggled vainly to advance the old dream. It was at this point that the NAACP stepped into the Detroit controversy.

The venerable civil rights organization was not in the best of form at the turn of the decade. With integration waning as a goal, chapters were hemorrhaging members as well as funding. Still largely focused on legal action, the association had also lost much of its raison d'être. In the decade and a half since *Brown* v. *Board of Education,* the courts had played a relatively minor role in race relations. What cases there were had served mainly to clarify the 1954 landmark, and virtually all had been focused on southern desegregation. Now that the civil rights revolution had begun to take root, it looked as if voters and elected officials—if not simply private citizens in their daily lives—would step in to advance race relations in a more consensual way, without the need for divisive suits or coercive court decrees. And the NAACP, with a diminished role, was slowly dying a natural death. But then, in 1968, the Supreme Court issued its first racial landmark since the *Brown* case, requiring school systems not just to try but actually to succeed in desegregating. Civil rights lawyers went back to the drawing board to develop new theories to present in court and began once again to drum up plaintiffs in cities where they hoped to press suits.

In Detroit, the NAACP suit started small. Backed by the national organization, the local chapter assembled a team of black and white lawyers. Together, they recruited seven families, black and white, with children in the Detroit schools, who claimed they had suffered from the segregation of the system. With the plaintiffs listed alphabetically, six-year-old Ronald Bradley lent his name to the suit, and his mother, Virda, helped stiffen the backbone of the other parents. "If you don't know anything about asking or demanding," she would later say, "you don't get anything." The NAACP's immediate goal was to press the school board to implement a limited desegregation plan.

Yet from the start, the *Milliken* v. *Bradley* case was about something much bigger than the situation in the Detroit schools. Integration was fading as an ideal in Detroit. There were no longer enough white children to sustain a desegregation plan, and even the black plaintiffs recruited by the NAACP were ambivalent, more interested in improved facilities than in mixing black and white children. Virda Bradley was seeking less crowded classrooms; thirteen-year-old Jeanne Goings's mother, Blanche, wanted cleaner facilities and toilet paper in the lavatories—as they had in "white schools." Yet the NAACP chose to turn the Detroit suit into a heroic make-or-break case, and the Motor City emerged as the front line of the national struggle for busing. "The issue had been drawn," one of the plaintiffs' lawyers, Paul Dimond, noted years later. "For better or worse, Detroit was the place where the NAACP would test the constitutionality of Northern segregation."

By the time the case got to court, in April 1971, it was on its way to becoming a national landmark. The national NAACP and the NAACP Legal Defense Fund had joined together despite growing differences to make the suit a major test case. Not only were they suing Michigan governor William Milliken and the state school establishment, the Detroit Board of Education included; they were also seeking greatly to expand the role of the courts in enforcing civil rights—to press the battle against injustice not just in new locations but in new realms where it had never been fought before. How far should the Supreme Court's reach extend, and what kinds of behavior should it regulate? How active should judges be in forcing change? And what exactly should they be striving for? All of these momentous issues had presented themselves in the Detroit case in a deceptively technical guise: a legal controversy over the distinction between de jure and de facto segregation.

The problem of de jure segregation had been settled long ago, in the *Brown* case. There, the Supreme Court had ruled plainly that deliberate southern-style barriers to racial mixing were illegal, and that the state was obligated to remove them, ending all racial separation in public facilities. But in the seventeen years since *Brown,* the Court still had not addressed the issue of northern-style de facto racial clustering. Was racial concentration (as found in the North) the same as racial exclusion (as produced by southern Jim Crow laws)? Was the difference between the northern city and its suburbs a crime—or a kind of natural accident? Even harder to say, was the separation of blacks and whites in places like Detroit and its outlying white ring a result of something the state did and thus something the state should be responsible for fixing?

For the lawyers of the NAACP, the answer to all three questions was yes, and the goal of several late sixties suits was to convince the nation. "We were groping for ways," the organization's top lawyer stated, "to prove that what most judges and the public perceived as de facto or adventitious segregation was what we knew to be . . . de jure or official segregation and intentional discrimination, public and private." The distinction sounded arcane and abstract, but it could not have been more significant. After all, if racial clustering were more or less voluntary, if it had arisen by accident and without ill will, it would hardly seem fair to most Americans for the government to step in and "fix" it, particularly if this imposed undue burdens on some large, unwilling part of the population. Truly de facto segregation was not illegal and never would be, any more than de facto separation of rich and poor into separate neighborhoods was illegal.

But if what seemed like de facto segregation turned out to be de jure—if the NAACP could prove that even northern clustering involved deliberate, state-sanctioned exclusion—then it would be only fair and just for the state to take steps to break up the clusters, no matter how painful that intervention proved for either blacks or whites. If the NAACP prevailed, the Detroit case would have consequences far beyond Michigan: not just in other school systems, but wherever disproportionate statistics suggested racial concentration and, in the NAACP view, covert racial exclusion—be it in the workplace, in medical school admissions, on a jury or in a legislature. Racial justice would be forever defined not as the absence of barriers but as even mixing—voluntary or not. The goal of color-blindness would be all but lost in the pursuit of a color-conscious balance and remedies. And the courts, until now pressing integration only in the school systems of the South, would have license to intervene in a dramatically wider sphere wherever the numbers of blacks and whites seemed somehow out of equilibrium.

De facto school segregation cases like Detroit's were thus the all-important thin edge of the wedge: the first chance for civil rights lawyers to prove that differential outcomes were inherently suspect. No wonder the NAACP lawyers were excited. As they saw it, they were tearing a veil off a hideous injustice, until now unrecognized by the public and working untold harm on generations of blacks. Liberation seemed just a step away—all they had to do was prove that Detroit's blatant segregation was no accident.

The first obstacle in the NAACP's path was the district court judge assigned to the case. Nearly forty years of local politics and courtroom experience had brought Stephen Roth's stern character to the surface in a hard-bitten, unsmiling face. Born in Central Europe, Roth had come to America as a child and settled in upstate Michigan. Blue-collar, Roman Catholic, instinctively conservative, he worked several years in a Buick factory before making his way to college and law school. As a fledgling lawyer in politics, he was principled to the point of stubbornness and jeopardized his career by defying the state Democratic establishment. Better suited to the bench, he was a deeply private man who refused interviews, and what little he said to reporters only confirmed his obstinate, flinty image. Though sympathetic to integrated schooling—he ruled in favor of an early magnet plan—he stood firmly against mandated, involuntary desegregation: what he called "integration by the numbers," "forced feeding" and "integration for integration's sake." To the NAACP lawyers, it seemed at first that they could not have drawn a worse judge, one more likely to side with Detroit's resentful ethnics.

The trial began in early April 1971. The courtroom was largely empty except for the judge and several teams of experts—from the NAACP, the school board, the state education bureaucracy—and the atmosphere was reminiscent of a tutorial: a government-sponsored seminar with a large team of teachers and one star pupil. Roth was initially frosty, unconvinced as he put it that the school board was guilty of anything but "a conscious, deliberate, progressive and continuous attempt to promote and advance the integration of both pupils and faculty." Still, cantankerous as he was, he was also willing to listen.

The first phase of the trial dealt exclusively with residential segregation. A historian described the white mobs that once prevented blacks from moving into Detroit's white enclaves; black realtor John Humphrey told poignantly of his long career trying to break down the residential color bar. For days, the witnesses came and went, and many grew intensely personal as they testified, hoping to sway the judge with graphic anecdotes about the discrimination they had experienced in the Detroit area. Gruff and seemingly implacable, Judge Roth peppered them with skeptical questions. Other immigrant groups, he noted, had settled in "pockets . . . and they did it for their own protection because they didn't know the language . . . nor the customs nor ways. . . . Wasn't it natural for them to collect in a group so they might better conduct their business and social intercourse?" The lawyers dutifully answered his queries and continued to pile on the evidence. None of their data bore on the school board's guilt, but as they and their witnesses made the case, Detroit's racial geography seemed every bit as bad and in need of remedy as the Jim Crow–style exclusion of the Deep South. And as the days wore on, the NAACP team could see that Judge Roth was troubled by the picture they painted. "The quandary of a man testing his own lifelong beliefs was apparent," commented one lawyer.

In the middle of the second week, the NAACP team moved on from the real estate case to present evidence about the Detroit school system. Educators testified about construction patterns, district boundaries, faculty assignments and parents' choices—facts, figures and anecdotes stretching out over several days. At the very least, the NAACP charged, school authorities had passively acquiesced in the city's segregation, building schools at the center of neighborhoods, almost always, if they were stable, one color or another.

Worse still, knowingly or not, the board might have subtly encouraged color-coded enclaves; after all, didn't many families move precisely to get within reach of a "safe," all-white school? If nothing else, the lawyers argued, there was guilt by omission: the board's integration efforts had not gone far enough—had not been strong enough to counteract demographic patterns.

It wasn't exactly a ringing indictment. But according to the NAACP's logic, it didn't have to be. At the heart of the lawyers' case was an implied theory of guilt: that it could not be divided. The NAACP maintained that it had taken layer upon layer of discrimination—by homeowners, realtors, government housing authorities, legislators, cops and school officials—to create the Detroit color line. And the lawyers didn't feel they had to prove that the school board was responsible for what was wrong—merely that it had been unable to halt the socioeconomic trends of a century. As long as the school authority had played some role, however tiny, the court was justified in taking over and carving up the entire school system.

The trial went on for forty-one days, through the spring and early summer of 1971, and by the close of proceedings, NAACP lawyers were confident the judge was leaning their way. He talked indignantly about the "forces of evil" responsible for housing discrimination. He let slip that he thought the legal necessity to distinguish between racial clustering and racial exclusion was "unfortunate." But even the civil rights team was unprepared for the stunning victory Judge Roth gave them when he issued his written opinion on September 27. The ruling was sweeping and stark enough to make the front page of *The New York Times:* an unequivocal declaration from a mainstream federal judge that what was once thought to be de facto was indeed de jure—and that the state was justified in stepping in to enforce northern desegregation. The NAACP team was overjoyed, jubilant at what it called the "conversion" of the stern Michigan jurist. A legal revolution had taken place—and would now make waves in courtrooms across the nation.

Judge Roth did not view the facts of the case exactly as the NAACP did. He went out of his way to commend the Detroit school authority's enlightened racial outlook and its tireless efforts to integrate the city's system. If anything, he devoted more space to praising the education establishment than to listing its shortcomings. Still, on the central legal point, the judge stood with the NAACP, endorsing its basic premise that the cause of segregation was ultimately beside the point.

City, suburbs, school authorities, realtors and state officials, ordinary citizens' choices as well as government action—all had played a part, Judge

Roth believed, in creating the problem. "There is enough blame for everyone to share," he wrote, "including of course, the black components. . . . Blacks, like ethnic groups in the past, have tended to separate from the larger group and associate together." Racial clustering, in the judge's view, was as bad as exclusion. Any and all kinds of separation violated the Constitution, whether the people who were separated desired it or not. What mattered to him now was not the cause of segregation but the fact that he might step in aggressively to fix it—not just removing barriers but mandating racial mixing.

Judge Roth's ruling caught the city and suburbs of Detroit by surprise. The trial had not been well attended. It was hardly covered in the press. There was no Detroit constituency for integration, and few people were waiting for the verdict. The judge's far-reaching decision and the national coverage it received were all the more astonishing, emerging as if from out of nowhere. Even before Roth announced his remedy, alarm spread through the region like floodwaters pouring out over the flat land. If he was really serious about racial mixing, everyone knew, he would have to include children from the white suburbs that ringed the city.

Housewives jammed the telephones; workers stood in worried knots around the auto plants. For both city families and suburbanites, the uncertainty was excruciating. Would there be a metropolitan remedy, linking the city and suburbs? And if there were, how far would it reach? Rumor had the plan extending even into the suburban ring's three worst racial flashpoints, Dearborn, Warren and Grosse Pointe. A rash of newspaper articles on city school violence brought the region's anxiety to the boiling point. With the grapevine working overtime, parents, realtors, teachers and local politicians speculated wildly about just when the judge would rule and how much busing he would insist on.

Irene McCabe's experience and know-how were suddenly in great demand. Judge Roth's ruling came just three weeks after NAG's first splash of publicity, and the Pontiac mothers were now looked upon as veteran activists. Parents from all over the region began to telephone frantically. Would McCabe come to speak next week to a meeting in a Warren basement? Could she tell another caller where to get bumper stickers printed? McCabe didn't always have the answers to these questions, but she was more than happy to help out as the suburbs erupted in protest in the days after Roth's ruling. Small-town newspapers across southern Michigan denounced the meddlesome judge. Rallies, large and small, were organized overnight, and within a few days tens of thousands had signed antibusing petitions. Even before Judge Roth announced what the next stage of his process would be, sixty suburban school superintendents had met and agreed to hire a lawyer. Before the week was out, McCabe had issued a call for a statewide school boycott.

At the end of the week, Judge Roth held an unprecedented news conference in his courtroom. The sleepy chamber was transformed under the glare of klieg lights. Where once a single reporter had sat—the *Detroit Free Press* had been the only paper to cover the trial—national and local media now elbowed each other for space. Black and white Detroiters, suburban lawyers, a sprinkling of the city's liberal establishment crowded in to see the dour immigrant judge's moment in history. "The court has made its determination of things as they are," he proclaimed dramatically. "Our concern now—to take a thought from Aristotle—is of things as they might be, or ought to be. . . . It appears to us that perhaps only a plan which embraces all or some of the greater Detroit metropolitan area can hope to succeed in giving our children the kind of education they are entitled to." Suburban Detroiters heard only one word—"metropolitan"—and most gasped audibly at the idea.

The judge had plainly made up his mind, but he was determined to go through the motions of deliberating on a remedy. He set up an elaborate process that would last though the winter. A variety of interested parties would submit desegregation blueprints. A team of experts would help him write a mandate, and school authorities would be charged with drawing up the actual plan. To suburban Detroiters, it all seemed like so much sinister machinery—an elaborate ruse to help the arbitrary judge impose his idée fixe upon them.

On paper, for a man like Roth, the idea of metropolitan busing had a stark and obvious appeal—the only way to include enough whites to make desegregation worthwhile. With the school-age population in the city already close to two-thirds black, a Detroit-only plan would make little difference for most ghetto schools: at best they might go from, say, 95 percent black to 75 percent. By including the suburbs, on the other hand, Judge Roth could create a 75 percent *white* district, and his plan could result in schools where the racial mix looked almost like the national population.

Beyond the proportion issue, metro desegregation was one of the few ways to mix rich and poor. City-only plans tended to pull in mainly working-class kids, but including the suburbs meant tapping the middle class—

and exposing poor kids, black and white, to middle-class enthusiasm for schooling. In a semicircular city like Detroit, a metro plan could also mean shorter bus rides and a cheaper transportation bill. It held out the possibility of significantly more money for inner-city schools, since the tax base in the suburbs was already far flusher than the city's. Finally, and critically important in a shrinking city like Detroit, a metro busing plan might halt the white flight that was disfiguring the region. After all, wishful liberals reasoned, if white families had nowhere to run, they might stay in town—or even move back—and try to make the city work again. No wonder, by 1971, integration enthusiasts throughout the nation were buzzing with the idea of metropolitan school districts. If mixed classrooms were the goal, this seemed the only truly workable way to get them—the obvious and imperative answer to ghetto isolation.

The hearings Judge Roth held through the winter of 1971–72 were an exercise in utopian planning. A dozen different blueprints were considered: everything from a voluntary magnet scheme to the mandatory consolidation of eighty-six townships, some of them not even suburbs but quasi-rural areas. Racial percentages, gasoline costs, daily commute times and real estate markets: like an engineer or an inventor, the scrupulous judge wanted to leave nothing to chance. Judge Roth made no secret of his goal: to determine and maintain the ideal numerical balance between black and white children.

Where the Roth of just six months before had argued that only voluntary mixing could bring harmony, the newly converted judge was now convinced that he could calculate and implement the perfect racial blend. The district had to include enough blacks to ensure meaningful exposure between the races. It had to include enough whites to ease blacks' sense of isolation, but not so many that it would mean smothering ghetto kids with middle-class culture. And it had to be big enough to discourage white families from moving out of reach, but still small enough to avoid unreasonably long bus rides. By the time the judge's plan was done, it would be a masterpiece of abstract design—and a recipe for enduring color consciousness. What's more, if even a few whites moved, the racial balance could tip abruptly—and the court would have to start all over again.

Neither black nor white parents' concerns were aired in the courtroom as Roth deliberated on his remedy. News accounts from Detroit and elsewhere underlined blacks' growing uncertainty about busing. One local poll found black parents ranking integration twelfth in a list of seventeen factors that might contribute to "quality education." Still, through the winter, Judge Roth soldiered on, convinced that he was doing right by the black city. He would allow no discussion of the educational effects of desegregation. (In fact, at just about this time, many experts for and against busing were coming to the conclusion that it probably had little bearing on black achievement.) Nor would he admit testimony about white fears of ghetto violence. "Rumor and mythology," the court noted, "about incidents and difficulties in the schools is exaggerated and exacerbated by all kinds of fears which are irrational and which come from stereotypes."

Was involuntary mixing in this climate the best way to introduce black and white families? Was it likely to ease prejudice or exacerbate it, as kids with widely disparate school ability were thrown together under pressure? Forced, uncomfortable and often frightening, might it not erode support for more gradual, natural mixing? These questions did not come up at the hearings. In Judge Roth's eyes, they were beyond his scope. Now that he had found, for better or worse, that Detroit segregation violated the Constitution, he was duty-bound to remedy it, whether or not the solution was sound social policy.

By spring 1972, anxiety in the suburbs was at a fever pitch. Liberal and conservative, middle-class and blue-collar ethnic, the more they thought about busing, the less they liked it—and the more willing they grew to express their feelings, whether or not it made them look like racists. "Busing is the most deeply felt issue to hit the area since the Depression," wrote Philip Power, "and the overwhelming majority of people living in the suburbs detest the idea." Irene McCabe found herself a national celebrity—and a seemingly respectable one at that. There were appearances on *The David Frost Show, Firing Line,* even Walter Cronkite's CBS Evening News. NAG's focus shifted to Congress and the possibility that it might pass a constitutional amendment against busing. The organization's folksy mimeographed newsletter was replaced by a professional-looking printed pamphlet, and Washington politicians began to reply when McCabe wrote to request a vote or a signature.

Try as it might to look civil and rational, the grassroots antibusing movement could not always control members' angry instincts. Bumper stickers appeared in the thousands from the southwestern suburb of Wyandotte to the northeastern enclave of St. Clair Shores. "Roth is a four-letter word," they proclaimed, "Pith on Roth" and "Roth is a child molester." Federal marshals were assigned to protect the judge when he came to court in

Detroit, and local police guarded his home in the upstate city of Flint. In 1972, when he was hospitalized after a massive heart attack, opponents deluged the hospital with calls, cards and telegrams: "I hope the bastard dies," read a typical message. But the region's more genteel middle class too was concerned about metro busing, and as the months went by and anxiety grew, liberals too began to voice their doubts. Philip Power editorialized regularly on the subject, stating his own ambivalence and noting that even his progressive friends were "ducking the issue" rather than take a pro-busing stance. "Parents who may be the farthest thing from being bigoted," Power wrote, "resent the idea of their child being bused for an hour every morning and afternoon in service of a principle that seems to have little application to their own community."

Prosperous middle-class and blue-collar ethnic alike, what Detroit suburbanites resented as much as anything was their vulnerability to the court's pending edict. "We were losing control of our lives," Irene McCabe complained. Parents from Dearborn and Livonia could hardly believe that the solitary, moody Judge Roth, appointed years before in far-off Washington, was going to determine their children's fate without any evident checks or balances. To suburbanites scanning the paper anxiously for news of a court decree, the judge's very timetable—or lack of one—seemed to underscore the arbitrariness of his process. Would their children be bused in September or January; would they ride a few miles or way across town? The most intimate personal routines seemed to be hanging on one man's whimsy. Worse still, there was virtually nothing anyone could do to sway or stop him. Wielding the ultimate trump card—the Constitution—he was all but immune to dissent. "The ordinary guy," Power wrote, "who hates the idea of seeing his kid bused . . . stands around wondering what in blazes he can do."

This did not stop suburbanites from making their views known, and while they had no effect on the court, they transformed Michigan politics. Antibusing meetings drew huge crowds merely for venting steam about the judicial process. Town after town held "advisory votes" of no-confidence addressed to no one in particular. Local candidates with no influence in the state legislature or in Congress—where the only effective countermeasure, a constitutional amendment, would have to be initiated—made busing their number one issue. The August 1971 Democratic and Republican primaries were decided almost entirely on busing, with the rawest and most vocal candidates, local and national, making a clean sweep on the issue.

By 1964, the civil rights struggle was spreading north, but protest actions like the "stall-in" at the New York World's Fair (above) were confounding many whites who supported the movement. President Lyndon B. Johnson's opening-day speech endorsing racial change was drowned out by hecklers at the fairgrounds (left). *(AP/Wide World Photos)*

Under pressure from impatient recruits in northern cities, movement groups such as CORE, once committed to integration and nonviolent methods (above), mounted confrontational demonstrations like the tie-up on New York's Triborough Bridge (below). *(AP/Wide World Photos)*

Martin Luther King, Jr.'s dream of integration was beginning to catch on among the larger public, but many blacks were giving up hope. Malcolm X (top) drew large crowds in Harlem, which was torn, in 1964, by the first major riot of the postwar era (center), while psychologist Kenneth Clark (left) warned that, without internal change, some blacks would have a hard time fitting into the mainstream. *(AP/Wide World Photos)*

Well-intentioned liberals like New York's mayor John Lindsay tried, with ghetto walks (above) and other gestures, to show blacks that whites cared. Lindsay managed to head off demonstrations in Brooklyn (center left) and elsewhere. But spurred by angry black leaders like Stokely Carmichael (bottom left) and Sonny Carson (center right), devastating riots spread through black America, culminating in the July 1967 disturbance in Detroit (top right). By the time residents of East New York, Brooklyn, started throwing Molotov cocktails, even Lindsay and his aides (bottom right) were wondering how much their caring and charisma could help. *(Carson photo: NY Daily News. All others: AP/Wide World Photos)*

Though committed to integration, Lindsay and Ford Foundation president McGeorge Bundy (above right) found themselves backing activists like Rhody McCoy (above left) who were intent on Black Power. Granted "community control" of the schools in Ocean Hill–Brownsville, these militants fired several Jewish teachers, including Frederick Nauman (below right), provoking the teachers' union to go out on strike.

Nonunion instructors like Leslie Campbell and Al Vann (right) took over the schools, radicalizing students with lessons in separatism and racial anger. With most of the city's liberal establishment still supporting the Ocean Hill experiment, union head Albert Shanker (above) strove to expose the terror taking place in the district — here he holds up a bullet that had been thrown at a white teacher — while the racial tensions that erupted at the barricades (top) polarized the city. *(Campbell and Vann photo: NY Daily News. All others: AP/Wide World Photos)*

In the wake of the Detroit riots (above), civic leaders like Max Fisher (below) struggled to f
ways to help blacks and whites come together. But the fatal shooting of a white police off
and the response by Judge George Crockett, Jr. (center right) sparked angry demonstrations (
right and bottom right) that divided the city still further. *(Bottom right: The Detroit News.
others: AP/Wide World Photos)*

With Detroit and its suburbs growing ever more estranged, antibusing activist Irene McCabe (above) led a wave of suburban protests against busing (below). *(AP/Wide World Photos)*

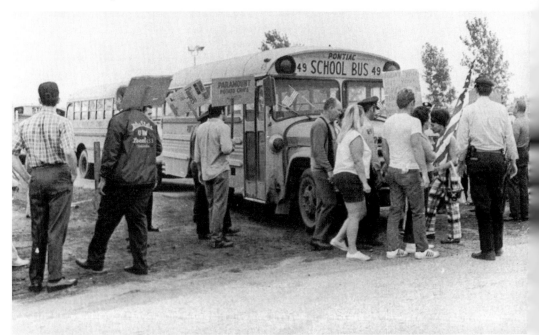

In 1974, former militant Coleman Young (above, left) was sworn in as mayor of the nation's largest majority-black city. Among his first steps was a campaign to integrate the police force (below). *(AP/Wide World Photos)*

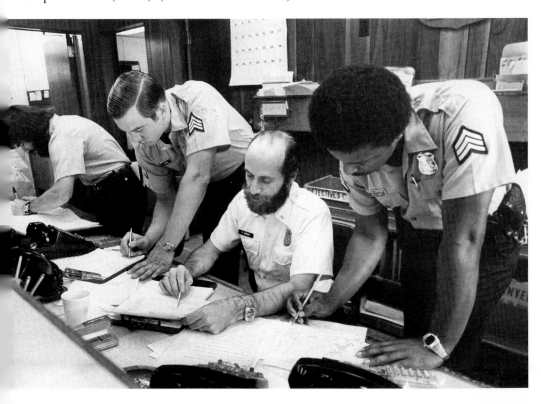

Young's efforts did little to improve police–community relations or control crime, and black officers were unable to dispel the discontent that erupted in 1975 when Andrew Chinarian shot a youth outside a neighborhood bar (above). The opening of the Renaissance Center (below left) failed to revive downtown, and by the early 1980s even the legendary Hudson's department store (below right) stood empty and abandoned. *(AP/Wide World Photos)*

Race relations were better in Atlanta, where blacks and whites came together in 1980-81 to search for the bodies of missing black children (above left). But Mayor Maynard Jackson (above right) had to twist arms behind closed doors to launch the city's affirmative action program. That effort enabled more black contractors to participate in the renovation of the airport (below left), though critics claimed that the middle-class blacks building homes in suburban Atlanta (below right) would have flourished with or without racial preferences. *(AP/Wide World Photos)*

The next mayor of Atlanta, Andrew Youn; (above), charmed whites and blacks (left) alike. He expanded the city's affirmative action program, helping successful businessmen like Herman Russell (top right, second from left) fare even better, but doing little to help poorer black Atlantan: Still, Young's relaxed approach to race proved more popular with whites (center right) than blacks, and in 1984 he had a bitter run-in with Jesse Jackson (bottom right). *(Top left:UPI Corbis-Bettmann. To right: Carol Muldawer. Bottom right and bottom left: AP/Wide World Photos)*

Young was still trying to reach out t
whites in 1990 when he campaigne
at Carey's Bar (left) but by then few
Atlantans had much hope for the k
of integration Young and Dr. King
had once envisioned. Race relation
Atlanta (below) were as good as the
got in America, but many wondere
if this was good enough. *(Both pho
Carol Muldawer)*

In June 1972, Judge Roth finally announced his remedy, and it was even more sweeping than most people had anticipated. The plan involved not just the city but 53 suburbs including Pontiac—a total of 780,000 children. More than 310,000 of them, from kindergarten through high school, would be bused for up to an hour and a half each day—from the ghetto to tree-lined suburbs, and also the other way. By far the most extensive and ambitious integration plan yet proposed in a courtroom, it reflected a vision of judicial power undreamed of even by the NAACP. "It makes all previous busing programs look like class excursions," said one editorial comment. A coalition of lawyers from the suburbs and the Detroit education establishment immediately appealed, and the case began to make its way up through the federal court system. It would be another two years before the Supreme Court would rule on the suit. But the damage had been done to race relations in the Detroit area, and it would not quickly be undone.

In the summer of 1972, George Wallace swept the Michigan Democratic primary by a historic margin of 51 percent, while large numbers of other suburban whites—no one knew how many—quietly turned their backs on the goals of the civil rights movement. Whatever idealistic stirrings they had felt in 1964 or since, they were now convinced that the liberal push to help blacks had taken a wrong turn—and for them, from now on, it would be forever suspect. "Busing legitimated a white backlash," Philip Power explained later. "It made people feel reasonable and justified in their inclination to wash their hands of the black city."

Judge Roth's rulings hit the national political scene with even more impact than they had in Michigan. When the 1971 decision spurred a rash of eye-catching protests in the Detroit area, reporters checked across the country for other cases and discovered what looked like a pattern. Magistrates were testing the boundaries of desegregation law in half a dozen cities, including Los Angeles, San Francisco, Pasadena, Indianapolis and Richmond, Virginia—and all were hatching experiments that pushed well beyond anything Congress or the Supreme Court had sanctioned. The worried public grasped immediately: busing had crossed the Mason-Dixon line, and it was heading north and west faster than defendants could hire lawyers.

Overnight, the images filled the airwaves and the pages of national news-magazines: the distinctive yellow buses, the police barricades at protest sites, the heart-rending photos of eager black children, scrubbed and combed and dressed up for the first day of school. "The Agony of Busing Moves

North," blared *Time* magazine's headline, and parents from Boston to San Francisco asked what it would mean for their kids. Within weeks, formerly liberal congressmen from half a dozen northern states were openly strategizing with southerners they once had shunned in public. One hundred representatives announced their support for a constitutional amendment banning busing. Others scrambled to add restrictive language to education funding bills. In Washington as in the suburbs, it was often women who led the battle. "I've never bought a home without looking first to find out about the schools my boys would attend," declared Oregon congresswoman Edith Green in one high-pitched exchange on the floor. "If the federal government is going to reach its long arm into my house and say, 'We are sorry but your children are going to have to be bused 30 miles,' I say the government has gone too far."

Busing was not a new issue on the national scene, but until now it had not been a particularly emotional one, mainly because in the past it had affected only a small number of families. Even when the Supreme Court began to enforce desegregation in the late sixties, it hesitated to mandate too much involuntary change. The Court did not explicitly endorse busing until 1971, and that decision, a North Carolina case called *Swann* v. *Charlotte-Mecklenburg County,* covered only southern school districts. Seventeen years after *Brown,* school integration was still largely an abstract goal, virtually unimplemented in any region of the country.

By then, it was widely recognized by left and right alike that the civil rights revolution was taking—that the mainstream public, in principle at least, was increasingly committed to racial justice. Seventy-five percent of Americans supported the idea of mixed schooling, nearly 90 percent the idea of equal job opportunity. Even after the riots, the spread of white goodwill toward integration was, in the words of one pulse-taker, "merely slowed, not reversed." And the debate about busing, when it first began, was very much a debate about means: a respectful, more or less gentlemanly argument about the best route to a common end. Even as President Nixon excoriated busing, he pledged $1.5 billion in emergency aid to school systems desegregating by other methods, while most liberals, committed as they were to racial mixing, were ambivalent about forcing kids to travel long distances to school. "Two valid aspirations are in conflict," the usually liberal *New York Times* noted in an editorial in early fall 1971. "Most parents want to obey the law and help this country end the shame of racial segregation. [But] each family [also] wants the best possible education for its children."

Then, in late fall, when busing began to move north, the debate was abruptly transformed. Both supporters and opponents escalated their rhetoric, liberals excoriating the "racism" of northern ethnics, conservatives denouncing the "Marie Antoinette liberalism" of judges who made grand moral gestures that had to be paid for by working-class families. Newspapers and magazines were filled with stories about the violence erupting in cities where court orders were in the offing: the Chicago kids being rolled for lunch money, the Annapolis students afraid to use the cafeteria, the heroin being sold openly just a block from a Detroit school. Antiblack graffiti, self-segregation on buses, handguns circulating in ghetto playgrounds—there was something to frighten everyone, and within a few weeks everyone was frightened. By mid-November, Congress was obsessed with busing, and a Gallup Poll showed 76 percent of voters against it.

Threats of massive civil disobedience spread through the cities where busing plans loomed. In Augusta, Georgia, six thousand parents crowded into a stadium in the pouring rain to express support for a pending school boycott. In Denver, protesters staged a mock funeral—complete with hearse and pall bearers—for a small wooden model of a neighborhood schoolhouse. In Memphis, a crowd of white parents buried a life-sized bus in a gigantic ditch. North and south, city and suburb, the grassroots organizations were strikingly similar: ordinary housewives like Irene McCabe banding together to defy the courts and lobby Congress. In early 1972, McCabe brought two hundred local activists together for a "national conference" in Pontiac. Canny as ever, she made sure to give ample speaking time to the black delegates. "Busing is destroying what it set out to do!" declared a black woman from Delaware. "I feel like I'm inferior now, and I never felt that way before."

A traveler returning to the country after just weeks abroad would hardly have recognized the policy debate of the early fall. Liberals accused antibusing activists of apartheid and genocide. "This busing is callous and asinine," retorted George Wallace. Gone were the thoughtful equivocal newspaper editorials; gone the respectful understanding for the other side's arguments; gone, most tragically, the shared sense that a reasonable solution could and would be found. Liberal and conservative, both sides were now in high dudgeon, consumed by fear, anger and righteous fury that what they felt were their legitimate gripes had been brushed aside. At issue now was not a means to an end but rather which of two opposing sides could be shown to be the greater evil: the arrogant elite depriving ordinary people's kids of education, or the racist blue-collar workers trampling the nation's most glorious ideal. Conspicuously absent from the uproar were any strong black voices in favor of busing or integration. The nation was tearing itself apart—opening wounds that would not be closed for decades—over a policy that no one in particular wanted and even supposed beneficiaries mistrusted.

By early 1972, Congress was in a kind of frenzy. Like suburban Detroiters with no recourse, congressmen could do very little about busing. An amendment to the Constitution could stop the Supreme Court, and by February, there were a dozen different proposed amendments floating around the Hill. Popular pressure was intense; one Michigan senator received sixty thousand letters and telegrams endorsing his version of a constitutional measure. But even its most avid supporters knew that an amendment was unlikely to pass. So Congress, like parents in suburban Michigan, turned instead to expressive politics: showy votes of displeasure and defiance designed more to mollify voters than change policy. There were votes every couple of weeks that winter, each more implausible than the one before—votes to cut money to pay for gas for school buses, to restrict the length of rides that could be ordered, even to preempt lower court judges from acting on Supreme Court precedent.

Michigan representatives were at the forefront of these efforts. Democratic congressman James O'Hara was a lifelong friend of labor and an advocate of racial equality. Yet within weeks of the Roth ruling, he announced that he was ready "to do whatever is necessary . . . to prevent implementation of the [metro busing] decision." Senator Robert Griffin, a moderate Republican with a long civil rights record, looked sure to lose his 1972 reelection bid—until he proposed an antibusing amendment and immediately soared in the polls. Representative William Broomfield, another lifelong liberal, was responsible for the season's most effective nuisance measure: an ordinance preventing court-ordered busing from going into effect until all legal appeals had been exhausted. When the bill came to the floor that winter, fifteen out of sixteen Michigan congressmen voted for it, delaying Judge Roth's order, among others, for more than two years. As court orders spread across the North and West, delegations for other states caved just as Michigan's had, and liberal congressmen from Massachusetts, Delaware, Colorado, Ohio, Illinois and Indiana were soon voting dutifully for the House's symbolic measures. Even Congress' most progressive members, those who could not bring themselves to vote against civil rights in any circumstances, often left the chamber when busing came up rather than defy their constituencies and vote the wrong way.

No wonder, in this climate, civil rights advocates concluded that the nation had given up on the cause. More than anything else in the sixties or seventies, the antibusing movement fueled blacks' claims that America was inherently and unredeemably racist; not just misguided in its racial policies, but by nature evil and inhumane. "It's not the distance, it's the niggers," NAACP lawyers angrily paraphrased what they thought white parents were thinking. "The North," charged Kenneth Clark, "is trying to get away with what the South tried. If the North succeeds . . . it will make a mockery of our courts and laws." Clark and other infuriated blacks blamed the white working class, they blamed Congress, they blamed the conservative president and they blamed "the system." It never occurred to anyone to blame the civil rights establishment for asking middle-class parents to support something that most could not possibly stomach: risking their children's education for a policy that seemed neither fair nor practical.

In fact, for all the anger swirling in the streets and Congress, opinion polls that winter and spring found a strange contradiction in public attitudes. Even as feelings toward busing hardened, large majorities of whites continued to affirm their faith in integrated schooling. A major *Newsweek* poll conducted in March 1972 showed 66 percent nationwide for integration, 69 percent antibusing. Other surveys were even more striking, showing as much as 80 percent of the country ready to accept mixed education. Nor did this support seem to be merely lip service. By September 1973, a Gallup Poll reported only 5 percent of the nation for busing but found between a fourth and a third willing to endorse other integrationist methods, including building low-income housing in middle-class neighborhoods. Even the most ardent champions of busing had to recognize the paradox. "Taken together," social scientist Gary Orfield noted, "these surveys show that a great many people wish to do something. . . . For most Americans, the busing issue remains separate from the question of integration."

Yet this ambivalence did not stop people from going out in the streets or voting for strident antibusing candidates. North and south, political observers were astonished by the numbers willing to pull the lever for George Wallace. The Alabama governor made busing the central issue in his presidential campaign and ran particularly strong—winning up to half the Democratic primary votes—in states like Michigan, Wisconsin and Florida, where it threatened most imminently. Exit polls showed that many who voted for him did so in spite of their better instincts: they opposed busing so much, they would even vote Wallace to say so. "At a certain point," Irene

McCabe explained, "you rebel—and you don't think too much about the consequences." Conflicted as they were, busing was bringing out the worst in many whites, interfering with their growing goodwill toward blacks and poisoning their view of race relations.

The storm came to a peak in spring 1972 as the nation headed into the presidential election. By March, just about every major candidate except George McGovern had come out against busing. Wallace's stunning victory in the Florida primary sent his rivals into high gear, all scrambling desperately to present themselves as more respectable versions of the outspoken governor. At the end of March, Nixon gave a major speech on national television in which he proposed a broad package of antibusing laws and even seemed to be considering a constitutional amendment. Hubert Humphrey, among other liberals, supported him. So did an even stranger group of bedfellows—the national convention of black leaders, meeting that week in Gary, Indiana. Nationalist and integrationist, dressed in tailored pinstripes and dashikis, delegates were united on few things, but busing was one of them. "We condemn racial integration of schools," their closing statement said. Busing is a "bankrupt and suicidal method . . . based on the false notion that black children are unable to learn unless they are in the same setting as white children."

It was at just this peak of excitement that Irene McCabe and several of her followers decided to walk from Pontiac to Washington to galvanize congressional action on a busing amendment. The idea was borrowed from the black protest movement. Imitating the Meredith-Mississippi March of 1966 on which Stokely Carmichael launched the Black Power slogan, McCabe mapped out a 620-mile walk through Michigan, Ohio, West Virginia, Pennsylvania, Maryland and Virginia. The distance was no accident. House Resolution 620 was the "discharge petition" required to pry the pending constitutional amendment loose from committee and bring it to a vote on the floor of the Senate, and like everything McCabe did, the mileage was a perfect attention-getting gambit.

McCabe and five other women left Pontiac early one morning in midMarch 1972. They were accompanied by two borrowed Winnebago campers and a gaggle of reporters. None of the women had ever done much physical exercise, but together they covered fifteen miles each day—rain, shine or blisters. The roadside reception was uniformly warm. "People are always inviting us for lunch or dinner," McCabe told a reporter. She would stop to talk to any gathered crowd, no matter how small, and she made great copy all across the continent, noting at one point that she had failed to watch the television coverage of the Wisconsin primary—a big Wallace coup— because she had been up till three in the morning helping one of "the other girls" bleach her hair.

McCabe's march was hardly the largest or most dramatic antibusing protest of the year, but somehow it captured the essence of the grassroots movement: the women's inexperience, their fervor, the almost entirely expressive nature of their politics. Even hostile reporters had to concede that some of the friendliest people who gathered by the roadside were black, and by now there could be little doubt that a national consensus backed McCabe's opposition to busing. Still, as often as not, press coverage pilloried the housewives as racists, dangerous cranky extremists allied with the likes of George Wallace. Popular and influential as McCabe's position was, the press and other liberals held housewives like them responsible for the busing controversy. Their resistance and alleged bigotry had become the focus of the national debate, and any reasoned discussion of the issue went by the wayside.

Meanwhile, for all the attention and controversy, in the end McCabe's march fell strangely flat. The women arrived in Washington exactly on schedule, tanned, tired, and limping slightly after six weeks on the road. A hundred supporters joined them at the Lincoln Memorial, and still a hundred others were waiting on the steps of the Capitol. Representative Gerald Ford showed up to greet them and announce to the world that five more Michigan congressmen had signed the discharge petition while McCabe was en route. It wasn't a terrible showing, but not exactly a revolution, either. Even the two thousand people who came out the next day for an antibusing rally registered as a disappointment—far short of the quarter million McCabe had originally said she hoped for.

As spring turned to summer and then fall, a strange quiet fell over the busing battle. The warmer months brought surprisingly few protests, and many, like McCabe's, seemed to fizzle. Despite Wallace's victories and several stunning state referendums, once an assassination attempt forced him to quit the presidential race, the campaign veered in other directions. Even where local candidates pressed the issue, pollsters noted a dramatic drop-off in interest. Large majorities of whites and blacks, neoconservative intellectuals and black militants, Congress, the president and the mainstream of both parties were lined up against the idea—with only the courts and a handful of lawyers supporting the spread of busing. To many opposed parents, it now seemed unnecessary to agitate—and they were spared the embarrassment of having to take sides against what looked like justice. It was one thing to stand by the roadside when Irene McCabe came marching by, quite another to travel to Washington for a protest rally; one thing to talk angrily to a pollster about busing, another to vote on it in November. If busing did not threaten in their own city, most people seemed willing, even relieved, to let go of the issue.

The one place the subject did not die was the nation's courtrooms. By the time Judge Roth issued his sweeping remedy in June 1972, there were metropolitan busing plans pending in Boston, Buffalo, Hartford, Atlanta and Indianapolis, among other cities. In December 1972, a three-judge panel of the Sixth Circuit Court of Appeals affirmed the Michigan decision and the regional remedy that came with it. In June 1973, the full Sixth Circuit Court followed suit, this time with all nine judges voting. That summer, the case headed for the Supreme Court, where it was heard in February 1974.

B y the time the Supreme Court decided Detroit's *Milliken* v. *Bradley* case, in July 1974, the problems of black America had all but disappeared from public consciousness. The big news of 1973 had been the end of the Vietnam War, *Roe* v. *Wade* and, increasingly, overshadowing all else, the Watergate scandal. The racial turmoil of the late sixties seemed like a memory from the distant past. Few people imagined that the problem had been solved, but most of white America seemed content to ignore it—to give the matter what Daniel Patrick Moynihan called a period of "benign neglect." Those few liberals who cared about integration had focused their attention on busing—mainly on reviling busing's opponents—and virtually no one was giving much thought to other, more workable strategies for bringing black and white together or helping blacks into the mainstream. As for the dour Judge Roth, one of his state's last integrationists, he had had three heart attacks and died just two weeks before the Supreme Court's decision.

It was the most important ruling of the justices' term, though at the time almost buried by Watergate. When Solicitor General Robert Bork argued the case before the Supreme Court in February, even his flamboyant, ideological performance received little press attention: far less, certainly, than his recent firing of Special Prosecutor Archibald Cox. On July 4, the Court's term officially ended, with no word about the historic busing suit still pending. On July 8, the justices heard arguments about the White House tapes. Two weeks later, they sealed President Nixon's fate by ordering him to turn over the recordings. Then finally, on July 25, almost as an afterthought to the Court's term, came a decision in the Detroit case. After three years of bitter national controversy over busing, it could not have seemed more anticlimactic.

The decision was anything but ringing. The Court was split 5–4 along political lines—Republican appointees versus Democratic ones. A welter of dissents diluted the majority's impact. The ruling was specific to Detroit and on the face of it fairly narrow. Yet, as the dust settled and the distracted public took note, it became clear that the decision was indeed momentous—that in the long run, it was going to spell the end of busing.

Of all the issues raised by the case, the Court had chosen to focus exclusively on Roth's metropolitan remedy, and it had ruled that there could be no transport between black city and white suburb. In Detroit and other places, the justices would allow lower court judges to spread around the few white students still living inside the city line. Blue-collar workers who could not afford the suburbs, upscale city liberals who preferred public to private school, blacks and whites in the few small towns that managed to remain stably biracial: a tiny number of parents might still see their children ride off to a different-color neighborhood. But by ruling out exchanges between city and suburb, the justices had effectively sidelined the busing issue. The majority of the nation's blacks, now living in large, deteriorating northern cities, were not going to be part of any court-ordered mingling.

The ruling was met by intense indignation among liberals and civil rights advocates. For more than two decades now, the Supreme Court had been perceived as the black man's patron, his only reliable friend in government, and the NAACP and its allies had been hoping that *Milliken* would be another *Brown* decision: a unanimous and unequivocal statement that would serve as a beacon for the future. Instead, Justice Thurgood Marshall complained in his dissent, they got "a giant step backward." For the first time since the fifties, the justices were seen to be cutting back on civil rights enforcement. The Court's new conservative majority—four out of five of them appointed by Nixon—was accused of working a crass political rollback under the cover of jurisprudence. "*Milliken* ended a dream," one critic wrote. Still others charged that it ended an era, just twenty years after *Brown*, ushering in a "second post-reconstruction." Even liberals willing to admit that they had doubts about busing charged that the Court was cutting off hope for black progress.

In fact, the Court's decision was far from hostile to racial justice. The majority opinion, by Chief Justice Warren Burger, upheld Judge Roth's verdict about the Detroit school board, finding it guilty on a number of counts of failing to integrate the city system. Even the more conservative justices embraced the principle of integrated learning. Discrimination, the decision said, must be eliminated "root and branch" from the nation's schools. More important still, the ruling affirmed Judge Roth's idea that what looked like de facto segregation could be de jure. Racial disproportion, whether in the schools or other institutions, was potentially a sign of intent to discriminate. If the numbers looked bad, school authorities and others could be brought to court and asked to prove they were not guilty, and even in the absence of tangible racial barriers, judges could step in to order a remedy. Though the Court pulled back slightly from the role the NAACP would have it play, it hardly closed the door on future efforts to engineer integration—even in cases where the racial clustering looked innocuous.

Where the Court drew the line—where it differed from Judge Roth and the NAACP—was in deciding just who was guilty of the constitutional violation in this case. "Disparate treatment of white and Negro students occurred within the Detroit school system, and not elsewhere," the opinion said, "and the remedy must be limited to [the Detroit] system." The segregation of Detroit's schools, the Court agreed with the NAACP, was not an accident or a natural occurrence. But neither was it a crime to be blamed broadly on society, a wrong that could be attributed to "the system" at large, and one that everyone and anyone was responsible for fixing. With this, the decision struck a fine balance: what looked like de facto segregation might, the Court conceded, actually result from wrongdoing, but in those cases especially, trial judges had to be unusually careful about assigning blame. Specifically—the ruling at the heart of this case—the Court found that the Detroit suburbs were not guilty. They had played no role in the segregation of the Detroit schools and thus could not be asked to bear the burden of the remedy.

The justices remanded the case back to a Detroit district court, ordering it to proceed with a city-only desegregation plan. The Detroit school system was required to undo the harm it had done to the city's black children. But the suburbs, not involved before, did not need to be involved now or in the future. It did not matter to the Court that there were virtually no whites left in Detroit; it was not the Court's business, the majority insisted—a gentle scold for the dead Judge Roth—to produce an ideally integrated outcome in the Detroit area. That, the Court said, "is a task which few if any judges are qualified to perform," a task that must be left to "the people . . . and their elected representatives."

In fact, in the wake of the ruling, neither the people nor their elected representatives came forward to pick up where the Court left off with new ideas or compromise measures. Instead, like the long busing controversy and the ruling itself, the back-and-forth commentary that followed focused almost entirely on the question of guilt. To critics, the Detroit decision was a criminal "act of absolution"—a declaration that white America was no longer responsible for the black man's plight. Liberal columnists like Tom Wicker and James Wechsler made long lists of guilty actions the Court seemed to have forgotten: the zoning regulations, the unequal school funding, the mortgage practices and school construction policies. On the other side of the argument, suburbanites across the nation heaved a nervous sigh of relief. "We never felt we were guilty of any wrongdoing," one Michigan school official said defensively. Once again, as at every step along the way in the Detroit case, dialogue was overshadowed by finger-pointing—and virtually no one gave any thought to how blacks or whites might move beyond the divisive issue of busing.

Whatever the justices had hoped, by summer 1974, a more constructive approach to school desegregation was out of the question. The long, bitter fight over busing had spoiled much of what goodwill there was for any kind of racial mingling. The legislatures that might have picked up where the courts' mandate stopped—looking for consensual rather than prosecutorial answers—had been riven by years of angry, polarizing debate. Even liberals, in Congress and elsewhere, who might in other circumstances have pointed the way to a better solution, were too caught up in recriminations to give much thought to the next step forward. It hardly mattered that 80 percent of the public now endorsed the idea of mixed schooling; any shared concern or sense of responsibility was lost amid the shouts of a sterile blame game. Whatever trust blacks had felt for whites, whatever enthusiasm Middle America had mustered for civil rights enforcement: probably neither had been as strong as they once seemed, but both were heavily damaged now, perhaps beyond repair. "Busing is going to destroy integration in the name of saving it," one op-ed piece predicted after the Detroit decision. "A whole generation and maybe another will be embittered. . . . Forced busing will set back the advances of civil rights made during the past generation by 20 years."

S till, it turned out, busing was an issue that would not die—not in the schools, the streets or Congress. The fall of 1974 brought the first battle royal in Boston. All of the nation watched, transfixed, as mothers chanting

"Hail Marys" pushed through police lines and white teens spat at black students trooping off buses. The TV footage stunned viewers, much as the coverage of Selma and Birmingham had done a decade before. "I'll never forget the faces filled with hatred," black moderate Kenneth Clark commented years later. "Until then, I hadn't understood how deep the racism went, how much it is and always will be part of this country." Whites and blacks alike stared at their television screens and gave up hope that America would ever find racial harmony. In the shock of the moment, no one stopped to ask if this was a fair test of integration—if this was the best or only way, if the opposition was to the means or the end.

The controversy dragged on grimly for two years after the Detroit decision. The Supreme Court had restricted busing between city and suburb, but this did not stop local courts from ordering city-only plans in many northern towns. In some cities like Detroit, where the city plan kept busing to a minimum, the protests were relatively limited. (Judge Roth's successor, Judge Robert DeMascio, used busing only as a last resort in a scaled-back decree that emphasized "quality education" for the now 75 percent black schools in the city of Detroit.) In other cities, where the busing was more extensive, parents' fury seemed bottomless. Boston whites boycotted city schools for a full year, reducing attendance rates to an average 48 percent. By autumn 1975, parents' protests had become a yearly ritual, not only in Boston but also in Louisville and several other cities.

The longer the controversy simmered, the worse the damage to race relations, yet national leaders, both right and left, found reasons to keep the issue alive, even after the judiciary began to back off. Sometimes it was conservatives who raised busing on the stump, hoping that it would rally a sluggish constituency. In other cases, it was liberals who picked at the scab, using charges of bigotry and threats of a national swing rightward to boost support for the Democratic Party. George McGovern, Gerald Ford, Ronald Reagan and Teddy Kennedy all made busing their cause célèbre at one time or another, each for his own reasons delighting in the polarization his rhetoric produced. Ordinary blacks continued to show little interest, and if anything, their leadership grew increasingly opposed. "I see no point," said Coretta Scott King in 1975, "in the futile shuffling of students from one school to another with scant prospect of a meaningful educational experience in either." Still, white liberals continued to grandstand in favor of busing, and conservatives made hay by denouncing it.

It wasn't until the late seventies that the controversy faded from the nation's streets. Busing for integration remained in effect in a number of smaller towns—roughly a million kids nationwide rode a bus to a mixed-race school—but in big cities like Detroit, segregation grew steadily worse, often exacerbated by what busing there was. By the end of the decade, nearly half the white students in Boston's public schools had left, most of them fleeing to the suburbs. In Detroit by then, the school population was more than 80 percent black, and a third of the city's schools had no white children at all. Detroiter Claud Young, national vice president of the SCLC, reported that even in the city's nominally desegregated schools, "there is a total black and white segregation. . . . Blacks and whites stay on opposite ends of the cafeterias and playgrounds. There's no fellowship."

He could have said the same thing about the Detroit region. In the end, Irene McCabe had gotten her way: she had kept the riots and all they symbolized out of her neighborhood. For better or worse, she and her neighbors had made their choice; they would spend the rest of their lives cut off from the city they once called home. Of course, they might have stayed away in any case, frightened by rumors and crime statistics, along with their own stereotypes. But by the time the busing wars were done, neither black nor white had any inclination to cross the city line. Whatever McCabe was avoiding, blacks in town were now happy to avoid her too and her still mostly white neighborhood. The integrated metropolitan region that Judge Roth had dreamed of was rarely mentioned, or only as a subject for sarcasm. "That was the end of it," Philip Power remembered, "the end of all hope and all common involvement." For all practical purposes, both blacks and whites knew, Detroit was now permanently divided into two cities.

Chapter 10

"THE PEOPLE'S MAYOR"

I t would come to be known as "the coronation," and for good reason. The official feasting and fêting began early Wednesday morning and ended in the wee hours of Saturday. Events included a prayer breakfast, a swearing in, a business-labor luncheon, a senior citizens' reception, a concert and an inaugural ball—each in its way an extravaganza worthy of a king's ascension. All in all, over twenty-five thousand people attended the official events, with many times that number celebrating at home through the weekend. When Coleman Young took over as the first black mayor of Detroit in January 1974, no one knew he would remain in office for twenty years and become synonymous with the Motor City. But most people, black and white, recognized that a torch was being passed and that Detroit was now officially a black town.

The hopeful tone of the inauguration was set at the start at an early morning prayer breakfast at the convention center, Cobo Hall. The temperature was just above zero and the streets were filled with fresh snow. But at seven-thirty on New Year's morning, more than three thousand Detroiters lined up for tickets. Mostly black and working-class, dressed respectfully in Sunday finery, they paid five dollars for scrambled eggs and sausage and a glimpse of their charismatic new mayor. The theme of the morning was reconciliation. A huge banner hanging behind the podium proclaimed: "Let There Be Peace in Detroit, and Let It Begin with Me." At the center of each table stood a small paper cutout: a black hand and a white one, clasped in prayer for a better future. The assembled preachers and gospel singers put on a fine show, but the mayor-elect owned the morning. Grinning broadly, witty, charming, nattily dressed in a trademark three-piece suit, he knew he was on home turf and he spoke magnanimously, picking up and expanding on the theme of racial unity. "As of this moment," he declared, "Detroit is coming together. As of this moment, we are going to turn the city around."

The next three days brought more of the same—more hope and more celebration, by white and black alike, of a happy racial milestone. The three-day party had many moods and many different kinds of music as it moved from place to place in the big, sprawling city. The Wednesday night concert, which drew an audience of three thousand, featured both the Detroit Symphony Orchestra and Motown singer Diana Ross. The inaugural ball, on Friday night, boasted two full orchestras, a rock band and free champagne for eight thousand people. The celebrants could not have been any more diverse: black, white, rich, poor, workers and auto executives, Motown starlets, union organizers, street kids and suburban society matrons. The dress code was as varied as the crowds and much commented upon by the newspapers: everything, one noted, "from Superfly to super straight," including broad-brimmed hustler hats, sweatshirts and dashikis, as well as the ordinary ball gowns and tuxedos. The business-labor lunch, for thirty-five hundred, drew by far the whitest group, but it was as enthusiastic as any about the new mayor. Henry Ford II, UAW president Leonard Woodcock and Governor William Milliken, among others, came to the podium to promise support. As for the mayor, he seemed as much at ease here as anywhere, plainly relishing every moment.

The mayor's political signals, like the music, included a little something for everyone: both black solidarity and hope for a new era of racial unity. The black triumph and the pride that came with it were palpable at just about every event. The mayor's old friend, black federal judge Damon Keith, introduced the theme early, on Wednesday morning. "Let it be said," he noted, "that this is one of Detroit's finest hours." Then he turned to Young and challenged him to prove "that a black man can run this city in an outstanding manner and bring it new honors."

Young was hardly the nation's first big-city black mayor; Gary, Indiana, Cleveland and Newark had been run by blacks for several years now. Nor was he the only black man elected in a large city in 1973; Tom Bradley of Los Angeles and Maynard Jackson of Atlanta had been voted into office at about the same time. But unlike Bradley and Jackson, who were elected by the white majorities of their cities, Young was brought to City Hall at the hands of blacks. Though he had campaigned in white neighborhoods and wooed most of his funding from the white business sector, in the end he polled only 8 percent of the white vote. It didn't matter; Young needed no more than a sprinkling of white support because—and this was the real significance of his triumph—black Detroiters now outnumbered their white neighbors. In the three years since the 1970 census, more than one hundred thousand whites had moved out of town, tipping the racial balance and paving the way for a black mayor's election. For most blacks who participated or watched on TV, the inauguration celebrated far more than an electoral victory; it marked Detroit's emergence as the largest black-majority city in the country.

Everything about the inaugural ceremonies reflected this triumphant sense of having arrived. Speech after speech, by Young and others, referred to "the people's city" and "the people's mayor." Diana Ross interrupted her singing to reminisce nostalgically about the nearby projects where she had grown up. The mayor recalled his roots and rallied his followers by slipping every so often into street dialect—white reporters called it "soul talk"—smiling broadly at his audience before switching back to mainstream diction. None of the mayor's inaugural addresses had a separatist message, but most were unabashedly race-conscious and often directed at the blacks in the audience. "We must first believe in ourselves," he said at one gathering. "We must first do for ourselves. The job begins here and now—with us."

At the same time, the mayor made it known that racial healing also had a place on his agenda. Young did not use the word "integration"—it would have sounded quaint in 1974—but there was no mistaking the signals sent again and again during the three-day revel. The black-and-white centerpieces at the prayer breakfast were the most explicit, singer Diana Ross's Wednesday night finale the most rousing. "Reach out and touch somebody's hand," she crooned. "Make this world a better place if you can." TV cameras panned the room as the mixed black and white crowd rose together, blue-collar black and white businessmen clasping hands and swaying in unison. There was no reason, both she and Young seemed to be saying, that being proudly black was necessarily incompatible with racial harmony. On the contrary, perhaps a majority-black city, where blacks no longer felt like second-class citizens, could achieve a kind of equality impossible when whites were in the driver's seat.

Not everyone in white Detroit was convinced, but many seemed willing to give Young the benefit of the doubt. The business community came out in

force behind the mayor it had helped to elect. Even the *Detroit News,* generally the more conservative of the city's two papers, ran a hopeful editorial
during the inaugural celebration, suggesting that perhaps Young was the
man to bring the divided city together. As far away as Washington, the Joint
Center for Political Studies, a Ford Foundation–funded institute devoted to
advising black elected officials, noted the integrationist promise of Detroit's
new executive: "The biggest chore facing any new black mayor is to convince
his citizens that he will be mayor of all the people. In that respect, Coleman
Young has the best chance of any black yet elected."

It seemed an extraordinary moment, rare in Detroit and in American history—a moment of hope for true racial harmony predicated on equality.
Here was a man and a city on the brink of achieving real Black Power, and
amazingly enough, instead of shouting and posturing and insisting on separatism, the new mayor seemed to be reaching out to white people. Liberal
whites across America held their breath and hoped as they watched the celebration in the Motor City. Old-style desegregation had not come to much.
Its proponents, now widely written off as Uncle Toms, had accepted their
failure and fallen silent. But here was a blacks' black, a proud and defiant race
man, proposing a new kind of integration—of equals.

Only once in three days was there a lapse—an oddly jarring false note
amid the harmony. Both at the time and in retrospect, it was hard to tell
exactly what it meant or how significantly it was intended. But for many
Detroiters, particularly whites, it was the one moment that counted: the
moment that defined the inaugural and would still define it twenty years
later—for many, the moment that defined the Young mayoralty.

It came during the formal swearing-in on Wednesday. The event was
attended by seventeen hundred people: the by now familiar, orchestrated
blend—black, white, rich, poor, in- and outsider. When it came his turn to
speak, Young stepped to the podium without notes. Charming, breezy, the
master of the moment, he talked for several minutes, eloquently and often
inspiringly. "We can no longer afford," he preached, "the luxury of hatred
and racial division. What is good for the black people of this city is good for
the white people. . . . What is good for those who live in the suburbs is good
for those of us who live in the central city." Both blacks and whites
applauded heartily, and if they didn't hear exactly the same speech, all heard
what they wanted or needed to hear: for blacks a promise of equality with
whites, for whites a guarantee that a black takeover would not relegate them
to second-class citizenship.

But then Young shifted into street vernacular and his tone changed abruptly. "I issue a formal warning now," he said, "to all the pushers, to all rip-off artists, to all muggers. It is time to leave Detroit for Eight Mile Road." Suburbanites in the audience stiffened uneasily at the mention of the street that divided the city from its outer ring. "I don't give a damn," the mayor went on, "if they are black or white, or if they wear Superfly suits or blue uniforms with silver badges: Hit the road!" Young would later claim that the remark was "innocent enough." It was a line, he said, borrowed unthinkingly from the sheriff in a John Wayne movie. True or not, by 1974, there could be no innocent, offhand exchange between Detroit and its white suburbs. Even the slightest ambiguity was sure to be misunderstood, and whatever Young meant by his inaugural comments, after years of rising crime and riot threats, for white suburbanites, it could mean only one thing: the new black mayor was urging the city's black criminals to head for the suburbs, encouraging them to prey on outlying whites in some kind of vengeful racial vendetta.

The tangle of misunderstandings that surrounded Young's speech was hardly surprising in Detroit in the mid-seventies, and it was only one sign of how hard it would be to achieve the racial harmony promised at his inauguration. By now, more than ten years after the March on Washington, the civil rights era was the faintest of memories, and most of the interracial hope it had sparked had all but evaporated. Blacks and whites who looked back over the decade came to very different conclusions. For most blacks, the sixties and early seventies had been a story of disappointment and broken promises—too little, too late, too slow, too grudging, and all of it untrustworthy. Many whites, in contrast, felt that a sea change had taken place and could not understand why blacks were still so angry.

The rhetoric on both sides of the color line was if anything more bitter than in years before. George Wallace's flamboyant campaigns, the Black Panthers' raised fists, Richard Nixon's "Southern strategy": there were ample provocations on both sides, and together they fed an air of confrontational crisis. Worse still, unlike in previous years, the anger now masked widespread weariness and disappointment, and many Americans—black and white—were giving up on each other. Spiro Agnew's infamous campaign quip captured the fatigue setting in around the country. Asked by a reporter why he had visited only one ghetto during the 1968 campaign, Agnew replied, "If you've seen one city slum, you've seen them all." Just as cynical, on the black side of the divide, more and more activists were writing America off as irredeemably racist.

In whites' eyes, blacks had made enormous progress. Southern schools and other public accommodations had been desegregated; blacks had registered to vote in record numbers and were being elected all over the country. The black middle class was growing, educational levels rising at a rapid clip. Many whites were convinced that the playing field had been leveled and they felt it was now up to blacks to take advantage of their new opportunities. Blacks, on the other hand, looked around and saw only that they were still hopelessly behind in most realms of life: in educational achievement, earning power, wealth and political clout, among others. Black journalist Roger Wilkins voiced a widely felt sense of despair in an article in *The New York Times Magazine:* "The question is whether the momentum generated by the activities of the last 20 years . . . will almost automatically lead to racial justice in this country, as some whites seem to think, or whether, as most blacks hold, the largest and hardest job is yet to be done, and whites have quit the game before the first quarter has even ended."

By the early 1970s, attitudes on both sides were hardening. Polls showed that white prejudice was abating, and white acceptance of racial equality had risen markedly. But whites were also weary of the racial struggle and irritated by black demands. In 1971, only one American in ten saw much hope for what one pollster called "settlement" of the nation's racial problems. By 1974, the ills of black America were ranked thirtieth on a list of thirty issues. Similarly, on the black side of the divide, the mood was increasingly detached, uncomprehending and angry at what blacks saw as white resistance. Frustrated expectations were turning into permanent alienation, and the black community seemed less and less interested in finding ways to take part in the mainstream.

In contrast to early civil rights activists, by now, the movement was hardly talking to white people at all. Some of its leaders had turned to politics, often politics in black jurisdictions, and staked their future on racial block voting. Others, particularly at the grassroots, were pursuing community development. Still others like Huey Newton, Angela Davis and the Soledad brothers had even less faith in the system and had devoted themselves to armed struggle. One hero of the black movement after another was involved in a shootout with legal authorities, and by 1971, more than two dozen were reported to have died in these engagements—making them, in black eyes, instant martyrs. Though never more than two thousand strong, the Black Panthers entranced the liberal media and, in the absence of other leaders, became the de facto stars of the black struggle. Prison revolts, murder trials, guns and underground cells become the trappings of a movement once devoted to peaceful sit-ins and church oratory. "Offing the pigs" was enshrined as a political ideal, armed defiance sanctioned and glamorized. In poor cities, many grassroots leaders were too alienated even for protest. Liberal Democrat George McGovern described their troubling silence: "Our cities and ghettos seem to be quieter today than they were a few years ago. But it is a stillness born more of resignation and despair than from any confidence in progress or the future."

In 1974, the 1967 riot and all it stood for still hung heavily over Detroit. The riot zone remained an ugly scar on the landscape. Most of the decimated buildings on Twelfth Street had been torn down, and the lots had been cleared of rubble. But nothing had been done to start the lavish rebuilding promised by city authorities and the New Detroit Committee. In that neighborhood and elsewhere in the city, a new style of architecture had emerged. Caustically dubbed "Riot Renaissance," it featured bars and bricked-in windows, concrete slabs, barbed wire and heavy metal sheeting.

Black Detroiters were inheriting the aging and dilapidated remains of what had once been a glorious, wealthy metropolis. Business flight to the suburbs was emptying the great buildings downtown; blocks from the center, what should have been prime commercial real estate had been simply deserted and left to rot. The next ring of neighborhoods, those with the city's oldest houses, had fallen into the hands of slumlords and poor tenants unable to provide for upkeep, and many enclaves were beginning to look like ghost towns. Decrepit houses alternated with abandoned lots, once-thriving shopping strips were boarded up and empty. Even out toward the city line, many of the old orderly rows of houses now looked like a witch's gap-tooth smile: you could tell exactly where each home should be, but often, instead of a house, there was a ragged meadow—grass tangled with weeds and littered with broken bottles. On some blocks, the only usable buildings left were the churches: ornate stone reminders of now dispersed immigrant neighborhoods. Even the great monuments of the auto era were falling to ruin. Frederick Law Olmsted's elegant Belle Isle Park, in the middle of the Detroit River, was among the most haunting—it looked as if, sometime before World War II, the picnickers had gotten up and left in mid-meal.

Demographic statistics told the same story in a different way. In the decade before Young came into office, Detroit had lost 10 percent of its population and one out of every three jobs. Since 1950, the peak of Motown's power and influence, a full one-third of the city's residents had abandoned it—bringing the census down from nearly 2 million to something more like 1.4 million. In the same twenty-five-year period, 40 percent of all commerce, retail and wholesale, had moved beyond city limits. Between 1956 and 1974, twelve Fortune 500 companies—two-thirds of the total—had fled, and virtually no enterprises of any size had grown up in the city to replace them. The departure of business and commerce was painfully evident in the city's streets: largely denuded of shop signs, billboards and the other trappings of capitalism, much of downtown had taken on the gray, forlorn look of an Eastern European capital. More troubling still were the human consequences: by the time Young was elected, one in five city residents was living below the poverty line.

In Detroit as elsewhere in the nation, indifference had set in like thick fog, as both blacks and whites disengaged from an issue that seemed too charged to deal with. Both sides were turning inward, to solidarity and Black Power, and in the white case, retreating to the suburbs. Hardly anyone on either side of the divide had much good to say about the other race. A frightening 57 percent of Detroit blacks reported that "many" or "almost all" blacks disliked whites; 47 percent of the city's whites admitted as much about "other whites'" feelings about blacks. By the time Young was elected, expectations ranged from guarded to outright cynical. At best, ordinary people seemed to hope for a kind of cold peace—live and let live, but without much contact with the other race.

Economic circumstances didn't promise to make healing any easier. Just as Young carried the city, the oil shock hit, sending Detroit into a major tailspin. By the time he was inaugurated, auto production had sunk to its lowest level since 1950. The deepening national energy crisis was causing thousands of layoffs at the Big Three and among the many smaller businesses that supplied them with parts and services. Rough-and-tumble Detroit had always been known for its high crime rates, but hard times combined with the stress of the riot years had triggered an unprecedented spasm. In many neighborhoods, black and white, small shops were being driven out of business. Burglarized as often as twice a week, merchants tired of replacing their hundred-dollar windows and many simply decided to close their doors forever. Virtually every issue of the black bourgeois weekly, the *Michigan*

Chronicle, was blazoned with a banner headline about a recent death, and inside pages were dominated by ads for window bars and security alarms. Known as "Murder Capital, U.S.A.," Motown averaged two slayings a day, and would reach a record total of 801 in 1974—about twice as many deaths per capita as in any other large American city.

As elsewhere, much of this carnage pitted black against black, and it was ruining life for Detroit's black working-class backbone. But whites were hardly immune to the violence, and it only fed their desire to separate themselves from the poor, crime-ridden black city. Some whites were still hoping against hope that a black mayor could improve things. Perhaps, they speculated, he would be able to crack down on lawlessness in a way no white mayor could. Or perhaps his coming would ease the alienation that was giving rise to crime and rioting: maybe his presence would give ghetto youth a sense that this was their city too, and that they should think twice before they destroyed it. Young catered to all these hopes in his campaign, striving to reassure whites as well as frightened blacks, and when he was elected, many white Detroiters heaved what one called a "sigh of relief." What wasn't clear in 1974 was whether these whites still felt they had a stake in their city—whether their audible sigh was a sign of hope or a sigh of letting go.

Coleman Young was a man who did what he wanted, when he wanted and according to his own rules. He saw himself and the world primarily in racial terms and always began his life story—a story that came to have legendary proportions in black Detroit—with an account of his racial awakening. Both his parents, who migrated from Alabama when he was five, were educated, hard-working people, by Depression-era black standards decidedly middle-class: his mother a former schoolteacher, his father a night watchman who moonlighted as a tailor. Mrs. Young ran a disciplined, orderly home, and Coleman was sent out of the neighborhood to a Catholic school, where he and his four siblings were among the only blacks. Coleman was a good student, dazzlingly smart and eager to please, and he was caught completely offguard in the eighth grade when his class went on an outing to the Boblo amusement park, located on an island in the Detroit River. The children were boarding a boat to cross the river when a member of the crew lifted Young's cap and scrutinized his hair, then gruffly informed him that no blacks were allowed on Boblo. Young recalls feeling numb and later infuriated. "I was never quite the same person again," he would say bitterly. The next fall, he tried to enroll in a Catholic high school and was again denied on account of his race. "I got screwed," he would later tell interviewers, "and resented it very much. Almost subconsciously, I [was] beginning to take on an adversary role toward society."

The "adversary role" came easily to a black youth growing up in Detroit in the 1930s. With blacks being turned out of jobs, harassed by white cops and hemmed uncomfortably into the ghetto, Young came of age in what he would later depict as a world of frustration and defiance. His father stood out even in this climate as an angry man. A self-described militant, "proud," "ornery" and a heavy drinker, according to Coleman, "he hated white people." The elder Young introduced his son to black history and black letters—W. E. B. Du Bois was an early favorite—but also to the idea of what Coleman would call "tweaking the system" with "scams" and "hustles." Meanwhile, the years after high school brought still more discrimination: first, the loss of a college scholarship; then, after a Ford Company apprenticeship, being passed over for a skilled job. Young's growing resentment drew him to union work, and this in turn led to a shop-floor fight with a Ford union buster that got Young fired from the company. "Certainly," he would later say, "I have been eternally mad, consistently angry and . . . resentful. It causes you to have an extra antenna, [a] sensibility in which you can detect racism where other people can't, a form of a sixth sense."

Already at nineteen turned off regular work and alienated from the system, Young looked around at his prospects and decided to devote himself to political organizing. He took a job at the Post Office in order to organize a union there and then, when he was fired, spent a few years as a freelance activist. He learned his politics from fellow organizers in the radical wing of the UAW, but also in the ghetto, at a barbershop hangout run by Communist Party recruiter Howard Maben. Young was among the sharpest of Maben's protégés, and though there is no record that he ever joined the party, he was a member of the Communist-backed National Negro Congress, founded in the thirties to eclipse the NAACP. "If Coleman wasn't a Communist, he cheated them out of dues," said Douglas Fraser, a member of the anti-Communist wing of the UAW and later a close friend of the mayor's. Young's attraction to the Communist orbit was by no means unusual for a young black in the thirties: the party was among the only national organizations interested in the ghetto or its problems. But in Young's case as in many others, the experience would leave a permanent mark. "It was a climate," he later recalled, "very conducive to the nurturing of young radicals," and by the time he was drafted, in 1942, he was by his own account a confirmed subversive—someone who saw himself permanently outside the mainstream, hostile to it by training as well as instinct.

Young's years in the armed forces completed his racial education. As in the past, things began well enough, with Young's abilities landing him a good slot at the air force officer training school at Tuskegee. Yet, reluctant to serve and resentful from the start—"in our neighborhood," he would later boast, "only fools went off to war"—he did not take long to run afoul of the service. He found the authority oppressive, the expected obedience so much "Uncle Tomming," and when he washed out as a fighter pilot, he blamed it on FBI intervention. For the next three years, he served, he liked to say, "on the Southern front": organizing antisegregation protests on one stateside army base after another. Almost court-martialed for one action, he emerged from the war more alienated than ever from "the system" and more convinced of the righteousness of his fight. By then, his habit of defiance was so entrenched, he remembered, that he "deliberately screwed up the paperwork" on his formal resignation from the Air Corps.

Back in Detroit, Young returned to political work, in the far left union movement and on the fringes of electoral politics. A professional agitator, he flitted in and out of Communist circles and learned, as he put it, to "hate liberals." UAW president Walter Reuther was his most despised enemy, and some of Young's most vicious battles were against mainstream union men. With tactics ranging from vote-getting to old-fashioned fisticuffs, he cultivated a reputation as a ruthless fighter. "I reveled," he wrote later, "in the trouble I now had the license to cause for those who had it coming."

Young's run-in with the House Un-American Activities Committee was the pinnacle of these years, his moment of greatest glory as a radical. He was called to testify in February 1952 when the committee held hearings in Detroit, investigating Communist involvement in the union movement. Young was a natural target, as was the organization he was running: a confederation of Communist-friendly unions called the National Negro Labor Council (NNLC) that used boycotts and other protest tactics to win black workers jobs at department stores. He came to the hearings determined to make trouble and proceeded to use the witness chair as his own political platform. Asked about the NNLC, he interrupted, "That word is 'Negro,' not 'Niggra.'" "Speak more clearly," he admonished his questioner, a southern senator. "As a Negro," Young explained frostily, "I resent the slurring of the name of my race." Turning the tables on committee members, he told them that *their* politics were "un-American" and brazenly defied their queries: "You have me mixed up with a stool pigeon, sir."

Young emerged from the hearing a local celebrity, his reputation forever made among black Detroiters. A smuggled tape of his testimony was pressed into a phonograph record that circulated in the community like so much contraband. Walking through the city's black East Side, Young would later say, "I felt like Joe Louis home from a title fight. People called out my name . . . small crowds gathered when I stopped. Guys patted my back in the barbershop. . . . I felt like a fucking hero. . . . I had said words that the people of Black Bottom had dreamed all their lives of saying to a Southern white man. . . . I had spoken for all of them, and they were standing a little taller." It was an experience Young would not forget—and one that would guide him for the rest of his life.

The later fifties were a time of transition for both Young and Detroit's black population. The triumph of UAW moderates made it impossible for him to work in the union or, he maintained, in any factory where Reuther had influence. Instead, he flitted in and out of the labor force, putting in a few months now and then behind the wheel of a cab, hauling beef or spotting clothes at a friend's dry-cleaning business. He was divorced once in 1954 and again in 1960. He was, he claimed, dogged constantly by the FBI. Meanwhile, black Detroit was slowly coming into its own. More than half a dozen blacks won seats in the state legislature in these years; then in 1954— a huge event—Black Bottom's Charles Diggs, Jr., was elected to Congress, the third black representative in the nation. As in all northern ghettos, there were occasional flurries of militancy through the fifties and early sixties. But for most of black Detroit, the new "activism" of the civil rights era meant registering to vote or helping with a campaign, going to the polls and electing someone who could make a difference—whether another black first or, in 1961, a liberal white mayor.

Young was never one to miss an opportunity, and by the late fifties he was thinking about running for office. There were plenty of practical hurdles— rebuilding bridges to the union and its ally the Democratic Party, not to mention raising money and organizing at the precinct level. But the more important question was a personal one: could Young find it in himself to "come in out of the cold" and build a career within the system? Could a man who had lived his whole life as an angry outsider suddenly become an insider? Could he shed his contempt for whites—and for blacks who tried to "fit in"? It was a question that would haunt many blacks his age and younger when the opportunity finally arose to integrate, and it would be the hardest test that a generation of black politicians—from Marion Barry to Jesse Jackson and Kweisi Mfume—would face. Could a man like Coleman Young operate inside the system and make it work to blacks' advantage, or would he find it impossible, even inside, to move beyond protest politics?

Young's answer in the early sixties was a cautious yes. His old East Side reputation served him in good stead, electing him narrowly as a delegate to Michigan's 1961 constitutional convention. In 1964, on his second try, he won a seat in the state Senate, and by 1973, he was ready to run for the mayoralty. An insider now whether he liked it or not, he still had not resolved his outsider's doubts or shed his lifelong street fighter's reflexes. Venturing in the mid-sixties into a neighborhood barbershop, he was greeted in the customary manner. "Hey, motherfucker!" someone called out. "From now on," Young answered, charismatic as ever but straining to have it both ways, "it's *Senator* Motherfucker."

He entered the 1973 mayoral race late and way behind, but together his ghetto following and natural political talent quickly put him in the running. Young hoped to appeal to both black and white voters, and from the beginning, he ran what amounted to two separate campaigns. Charming, well-spoken, well-informed, he stumped extensively in white enclaves, working hard to assuage white fears about his past and his intentions. No one mistook him for the old-fashioned, deferential black candidate, Richard Austin, who had run unsuccessfully for mayor in 1969 on a promise of racial healing. But in his way, Young too seemed to promise that he could be mayor of all the people, and for a while, on the stump in 1973, his reassurances seemed to work. Liberal, civic-minded Detroit was enthusiastic about his candidacy, generous with its money and its all-important imprimatur. No one expected many working-class white Detroiters to vote for Young, but at the start it looked as if he could reassure even them— could avoid scaring them to the point that they turned out in large numbers for a white opponent.

Still, even as he campaigned in white neighborhoods, Young found it hard to mask his angry color consciousness. Try as he might, he couldn't always contain his resentment—couldn't mute his barbs or disguise his redistributionist politics. Though cordial enough with New Detroit businessmen, he never quite brought them into his confidence. In black neighborhoods, he campaigned explicitly on his skin color. "Now is the time," he said on the stump. "We need to have a black mayor." Where

Richard Austin had pleaded hopefully for integration, Young talked combatively about community control, ethnic curriculums and the unfairness of "the system."

Longtime outsider that he was, Young was not exactly a separatist. He had attended the 1972 black political convention in Gary, Indiana, but walked out in the middle. "The black agenda" espoused by most of the three thousand delegates was "completely off-target and unacceptable," he later said. "It consisted of bullshit like taking over five states for black people . . . and I, for one, wasn't buying it. I refused to surrender the belief that any black solution will derive from unity between the races and maintained, then as now, that separatism is asinine and suicidal." Still, there could be no mistake: Young was not really an integrationist, either. "I do not believe that integration is an end in itself," he declared. "I do not shrink from it. But I do not believe that integration in itself will come to a damn thing." As his prickly campaign made abundantly clear, he had no intention of compromising his blackness, and even inside the system, he would go on rebelling against it.

On the stump in 1973, it looked like a brilliant balancing act. Neither a deferential white man's black like Richard Austin nor a committed militant like his friend and backer Reverend Albert Cleage, Young seemed to have found a way to tap black anger and ride it into the system—to be at once an inside player and a classic race man. The question, already in 1973, was whether he could maintain the balance, and as the campaign wore on, the answer was increasingly unclear.

His plain-spoken, street-smart appeal was a huge success in inner-city neighborhoods. Six years after the riot and still in the throes of the busing wars, black voters thrilled to Young's defiant style and unabashed race consciousness. The black political establishment rallied around his campaign, and buoyed by their enthusiasm, Young found himself growing ever more combative. "The black man has the feeling he is about to take power in the city," commented white businessman Joseph Hudson, and few people were surprised when Young came in an easy second in the nonpartisan "primary" that constitutes the first round of Detroit elections. His impressive showing was widely interpreted as a racial victory, and blacks and whites alike girded for the general election to come. Young himself could hardly have invented a better foil than the man who beat him in the primary and who he would now face in the runoff: Police Commissioner John Nichols, a crew-cut, career law-and-order man with a large following in working-class neighborhoods.

Like most of black Detroit, Young made little secret of his hostility for the police; he was convinced, as he put it in 1973, that the "criminals on the streets were seriously rivaled by the ones in squad cars." As a young ghetto hustler and left-wing organizer, he had learned early in life to hate white men in uniform. In the legislature, police matters were his number one issue and primary vote-getter. Young had sponsored bills to add blacks to the state police and to local departments in towns with mixed populations. He had prodded Mayor Cavanagh to hire more black officers. He and other promi-nent blacks had formed a statewide committee protesting "police harass-ment" of the Black Panthers. He had even brought Bill Cosby to Detroit to help the police recruit in the inner city. For more than ten years, he would later say, "I carried on a crusade against the police department," and by the early seventies he was convinced that there would be no change in Detroit policing until there was a black mayor.

Though the city's murder rate had nearly doubled in four years, antipathy toward the police seemed if anything more raw than ever in black Detroit. Complaints centered on an undercover unit known by the acronym STRESS. The squad focused its efforts in the inner city, mainly at small mom-and-pop groceries, where it used decoy officers disguised as drunks or hustlers. Highly effective in curbing robberies, the unit promised to make a big difference for declining neighborhoods, but it was also responsible, in just two years, for nineteen fatal shootings, many of them of black youths. Most of those who were shot had been caught in the act, robbing a store that served the ghetto. Still, in the eyes of Detroit blacks, STRESS was a racist "execution squad"—what Young called "an official vehicle for killing black people in the alleged line of duty." As one of the main architects and defend-ers of the unit, Commissioner Nichols hardly dared campaign in the ghetto.

Caught up in the police issue, encouraged by the response among blacks, Young paid less and less attention as the campaign wore on to his interracial balancing act. Stumping in Black Bottom and other enclaves, he not only mentioned STRESS at every stop but also warned apocalyptically that "a vic-tory by Nichols would deliver a . . . message to the rest of the country and goose it along toward a coast-to-coast police state." "The pattern was devel-oping," Young later explained, "with police chiefs being elected mayors of cities. . . . I felt deeply that unless blacks were given fair representation within the department, the police would [soon be running] our cities." Whether or not he believed this, Young knew exactly how it would strike black Detroi-ters—and how much it would help bring them out on election day. What he didn't calculate was how his charged campaign would sound to white Detroiters or what it would cost in the long run in alienation between black and white.

In the end, the 1973 campaign was one of the most racially polarized contests in Detroit's polarized electoral history. Both candidates made a show of campaigning all over the city. But as Young conceded later, underneath it all, the election was "a classic confrontation"—as everyone in town understood, "the black community against the white." The code language was obvious: not just cops and crime, but Nichols's crew cut, his supporters' suburban hobbies, Young's salty street talk and his constant hints about demographics. As the voting approached, few Detroiters mistook the real issue: a pitched racial battle to gain control of the tipping city. On election day, Young won by the slimmest of margins, taking virtually all the black vote and a small percentage in white districts.

Once the campaign was over, victorious and faced with the challenge of governing, Young again made some effort to reach out to white Detroiters. The mayor-elect took pains to reassure white audiences about the city's future. He pledged repeatedly that his administration would be staffed equally with blacks and whites, strictly fifty-fifty, in every department, including his own security detail. "I'm a mayor," he said, his meaning plain, "who happens to be black." Even his infamous "warning" speech at the inauguration had a little something for everyone—digs at criminals as well as cops, and a promise to crack down on lawlessness in the city—and that was exactly the way Mayor Young wanted it.

Not everyone was convinced, certainly not in the city's northern pockets. But most liberal white Detroiters, eager to give Young the benefit of the doubt, were happy to put the bitter campaign behind them. The business elite, union leaders, the press—both liberal and conservative—told themselves as they milled around the inaugural that if anyone could bring the city together, it was Coleman Young. In polarized Detroit, his interracial appeal seemed a crucial asset. Who else in the region could talk to both blacks and whites? Who else could give frustrated blacks a voice and help to ease their long-stored anger? "Many of us had great hopes," Philip Power remembered. "Many of us saw it as a new beginning." Together, the businessmen and the mayor-elect talked about reconciliation, harmony, rebuilding. It was hard to tell exactly what Young meant by "reconciliation" or, given the circumstances, to imagine a "harmony" that went beyond peaceful coexistence—a wary truce between two largely hostile communities. Still, Detroit's white elite were encouraged by Young's promises, and they reassured themselves that he could heal not just the city but also race relations between city and suburb.

Defiant and color-conscious as he was, Young knew he could ill afford to alienate the white suburban ring. By the time he was elected, there were already twice as many people in the suburbs as in town, far fewer of them unemployed and most earning considerably more than city residents, black or white. Increasingly self-sufficient, many outlying whites worked and shopped beyond the city line. Still, in the mid-seventies, not all had cut their emotional ties to Detroit. Many still came into town to the theater, the symphony and the Detroit Institute of the Arts. Others came for baseball games or hockey and stayed afterward to eat dinner. With the lion's share of downtown stores and restaurants already closed or closing, Young knew just how desperately the city needed this business. At the very least, to remain alive, Detroit had to seem hospitable to suburban visitors. But the city's need did not stop there, and never a man to settle for the minimum, Young had ambitious plans for revitalizing Detroit with white help.

His first priority was a $500-million downtown redevelopment scheme— a plan that could be financed only with suburban money. Henry Ford II's half-finished complex, the Renaissance Center, would provide the anchor for a string of grand, large-scale construction projects on the riverfront: office buildings, hotels, shopping plazas and convention space. This development would in turn create a favorable climate for smaller businesses: light industry, white-collar services, stores and restaurants. Many of the new enterprises would, Young hoped, be owned and run by blacks, but even then the city would require goodwill from the suburbs. By the mid-seventies, Detroit was heavily dependent on outside aid: everything from block grants to the food stamps that sustained one-third of its residents. And with more than half the state's voters living in the white ring outside of town, Young depended on them to support the crumbling city not just with their business, but also with their taxes and by electing a generous state government.

Michigan suburbanites weren't the only people in a position to help, but they were the most likely—if only they could be reminded of their stake in the city. What they needed to understand was that Detroit was *their* city too, that its problems were their problems and its success their success. Call it "regionalism" or "integration," what Detroit needed was a renewed sense of community and of the commonality of interest between black and white. Shrewd operator that he was, Young understood this as well as anyone.

"There is no way in hell or in heaven," he told one audience not long after he was elected, that city and suburb could survive without each other. "If the heart stops, the body dies. If the roots wither, the tree will fall. . . . My future is your future, and yours is mine. The more we recognize that, the better we'll move forward together." Yet, in case after case, he proved unable to act on his understanding—and instead, through the seventies, regional antagonisms grew steadily worse.

Young's first year in office was hellish by any standards. The 1973 oil shock had plunged the city into its worst recession in three decades. Auto production fell; unemployment soared, particularly among young black men in the inner city. Layoffs and hard times cut deeply into city tax revenues. In Young's first week alone, there were sixteen violent deaths: just above par for that year—roughly two a day—in "Murder City." Add the continuing drift toward the suburbs, festering school budget problems and a failed HUD mortgage program that left the city with twelve thousand abandoned houses, and it wasn't hard to imagine why the new mayor felt beleaguered. Much of what was wrong in Detroit was, as he argued, beyond his control: the fault of the Arab oil boycott, of fuel-efficient Japanese cars, of shifting demography and regional economic change. No one was surprised when he appealed for increased state and federal aid, or called on the area's big businessmen—Ford, Fisher and other New Detroit members—to pump additional money into the city. Mayors across the country, black and white, were doing the same thing. Still, from the start, there was something different about Young's demands. Even when he tried to be diplomatic, there was no mistaking the racial edge to his accusations.

Reporters could not write enough that first year about Young's "style" and unorthodox methods. His salty language—described as the mayor's "street talk"—made it into every story. The self-proclaimed "people's mayor" let it be known that he liked to spend time with old buddies, playing poker or just hanging out on an empty lot, drinking out of a brown paper bag with guys named Dirty Red and Skate Key. He answered the phone with a gruff "What's happening?" He bragged to reporters that he carried a gun. He drew attention to himself at official gatherings by abruptly turning on the street style and exchanging a flamboyant high five with an old acquaintance. Journalists didn't like to say so, but most Detroiters, black and white, understood: the manner Young was cultivating was a stylized black manner—a not-so-subtle message that the city administration was black now and it was going to do things differently.

From the start, this public personality had two sides, one triumphant and carefree, the other slightly menacing. Young's trademarks were his catbird grin and the devil-may-care shrug with which he responded to even the gravest questions. Asked about the crime that was destroying the city, he put on his best dialect: "I'm a victim of it, baby." Both this irreverence and the other, darker side of the persona harked back to one of Young's favorite historical figures, Adam Clayton Powell, Jr. "He was an arrogant son of a bitch," the mayor would say. "That's one of the reasons I loved him. . . . he didn't back off of anybody." Young imitated the never-back-off style in all things large and small. From his first weeks in office, he was pointedly casual about appointments. He liked to make a show of telling off federal officials, in unprintable street language if possible. And he soon made clear that the press—like everyone else—was going to have to deal with him on his terms. He was just three months in office when the memo went out, forbidding city employees from talking to reporters without his explicit permission.

Like most of the white establishment, the media was initially sympathetic to the mayor, and most journalists were baffled by his evident mistrust. By temperament and training—as a former radical—Young was naturally suspicious and somewhat secretive, and he gravitated toward a solo, behind-the-scenes style of governing. He confided in few advisers, avoided standard procedures and saw no reason why outsiders had to know how he got things done. Affronted by this standoffishness and bewildered by the secrecy, the press was at a loss to cover his administration, and many reporters were irritated by the obstacles he threw in their path. But even the city's most prickly, combative journalists were stunned by the way the mayor seemed determined to pick a fight with them.

The growing animosity broke out in an open, angry quarrel when someone leaked the mayor an internal memo from an editor at the *Detroit News* praising a recent article about a black man who had raped a white woman. "It was an example," the memo said approvingly, "of just the horrors that are discussed at suburban cocktail parties." From Young's point of view, he had caught the newspaper red-handed, and he went public with the memo, accusing the press of sensationalizing Detroit crime and sowing ill will between city and suburb. The *News* immediately apologized for its editor's callousness, running a large disclaimer on the front page of the paper. But there was no appeasing the mayor—and no undoing the black public's suspicion that the paper was racist—and from that day on, whenever Young disliked the *News*'s coverage, he dismissed it as so much bigotry. "He got most people in the city to believe," *News* columnist George Cantor recalled, "that any criticism was part of a white conspiracy." When journalists claimed this meant the mayor was unaccountable, Young insisted he had every right to tell employees not to talk to the press. "If they work for me," he declared defiantly, "well then, I control what they say and do."

From then on, throughout Young's twenty years as mayor, his administration went largely uncovered in the Detroit newspapers. The mayor rarely came to the offices of either the *News* or the *Free Press* to meet with editors or editorial writers. Reporters looking for routine city documents had to go to court to get them or file a time-consuming Freedom of Information Act request. The mayor granted occasional interviews to selected journalists, but these highly controlled sessions yielded little of use. If Young didn't like a question, he would stare at the TV always on in his office or tinker with the solitaire game lying on his desk, and usually, when he chose to answer, his responses fell into one of two predictable categories: suburb-bashing or Detroit boosterism. The few serious or critical stories that did get into the papers brought angry delegations of Young supporters to the offending newsroom, charging the staff with racism and threatening a reader boycott. In any other city, voters would have sided with the press—their ally, after all, in holding the government accountable. In Detroit, where the mayor was black and the press largely white, Young used the running feud as a way to rally supporters. "He was a fairly obvious politician," said one editor, "pandering to his support group."

The quarrel with the press set the tone for the besieged Young mayoralty, and journalists were only one on a long list of enemies. The federal government made another favorite, easy target. For years, according to Young, it had been actively encouraging whites to "abandon" the city, and now—now that Detroit was black—Washington was cutting back on social spending. Within the government, the Department of Housing and Urban Development and its mortgage program were a particular scourge. Enemy number four was the police department, accused of harassing innocent teens and running the city's drug trade. All four villains figured so regularly in Young's public remarks that soon he hardly had to lay out the case against them, and even when he didn't mention race, it wasn't hard for black Detroiters to catch his drift. HUD, the cops, the feds, the establishment press: from Detroit's point of view, this was the face of white authority. As the city's first black mayor, Young might have taken it on himself to ease black relations with the white world. Instead, in case after case, there seemed no escaping old racial antagonisms, and Young soon emerged as commander in chief of what appeared to be unending racial warfare. "He just didn't have the confidence to build the bridges," Joseph Hudson noted years later. "Some deep combative influence would come out. His suspicion that people were trying to get something away from him always got in the way."

More and more, in speeches and interviews and out among the people, Young spread a stark and unrelenting picture of a world divided by skin color. The image struck a chord among Detroit blacks and it was soon accepted as conventional wisdom—the official mythology of the black city. Confident and at ease in any crowd, Young had plenty of white friends, and he kept his promise, all through his years in office, of a staff that was half black and half white. Still, whether for political reasons or out of deep-seated personal antagonism, he couldn't seem to help fueling the city's racial hostility.

By the early seventies, regional cooperation had become a kind of hobby-horse for suburban newspaper editor and publisher Philip Power. The ambitious, idealistic son of a well-connected Michigan family, Power had dabbled in Democratic politics before buying a string of folksy, small-town newspapers in 1965. Just as he predicted, his chain grew with the suburbs, until in the mid-seventies it rivaled Detroit's two older, in-town papers in both readership and advertising revenue. By then, there were eleven different local newspapers in the group, each called its town's *Observer & Eccentric*. With white Detroit emerging as a city in its own right, these weeklies became the voice of the suburbs, and by the time Coleman Young took over the city, Power was a leading player in the region's liberal civic-minded elite.

Power had written his first column on metropolitan cooperation even before the 1967 riot was over, and he continued, week after week, for the better part of a decade. "Suburban isolation is not inevitable," he insisted in one piece. "We're all in this together," he went on in another. "We'd better start doing something about it." Spurred by Power and other well-meaning liberals, a fledgling movement took root in the better-off suburbs. There were conferences to discuss the metropolitan concept, inspirational speeches by Governor Romney and his successor, William Milliken. Teams of high school students from Livonia spent weekends rehabilitating houses in the ghetto. Churches in Southfield and Bloomfield Hills sent volunteers. One group of suburban residents from Farmington went so far as to urge their town council to send money to the city.

Even idealists like Power knew that a single metro government was a pipe dream in the Detroit region. By the early 1970s, the city was in a virtual free fall, with poverty and crime rates rising faster than suburbanites could keep track of. Even the declining industrial suburbs were downright wealthy by city standards, and the newest outlying towns—self-sufficient, high-tech "edge cities"—were among the most prosperous, fastest-growing enclaves in the nation. Detroit's social service bill was skyrocketing. The in-town tax rate was two to five times the rates in the suburbs, and the still-sputtering busing battle made amply clear how hard it would be for the two sides to get along. Metro cooperation was sure to be awkward and expensive—the last thing most people in the suburbs felt they needed. Still, dryly technical as most of the proposals sounded, by now everyone understood: in Detroit, regional cooperation was a euphemism for racial cooperation—if not full-fledged integration, then at least a form of interracial partnership. And the worse things got between black and white, the more passionately Power and his allies felt that it was necessary. "We need the city," he would argue later, "and it needs us. The angrier people got, the more polarized, the more urgent it seemed to try to do something."

Metropolitan alliances were catching on in other midwestern cities—Cleveland and St. Louis were among the most progressive—and Power and his friends urged metro residents to consider a variety of communal projects. City and suburbs could join to build the mass transit system desperately needed to take suburban shoppers downtown and connect urban workers with outlying factories. Better-off suburban townships could take financial responsibility for regional assets like the city zoo and museum. As nearby Minnesota proved, even metropolitan tax sharing was a possibility: pooling regional business tax revenues in a common pot and then distributing it according to need. Air and water pollution, industrial development, the increasingly fierce competition to lure business away from other states: all were common problems, Power argued, and none could be solved except with regional answers.

Power estimated that "a sizable minority" of suburbanites shared his hopes for racial and regional cooperation. "We didn't have enough support to elect a candidate," he recalled later, "but we were something like a forty-five percent view." In 1974, as Coleman Young took office, a survey of elected officials, city and suburban, found them split down the middle on the metro question, with just about half expressing support for strong regional governance and some pooling of resources. The new mayor himself seemed to be of two minds. Partnership—what he called "unity"—was an old favorite theme of his, going back to his days in the labor movement. Suburban investment in Detroit development remained the centerpiece of his financial plan for the city, and whatever quarrels he picked with white people in Detroit or elsewhere, he still seemed to recognize the need for tactical cooperation. "My modus operandi," he would later say, "has been to build coalitions that bring together the parties, the classes and the races in a common self-interest." It sounded like a recipe for a pragmatic metro alliance, and even after the inaugural speech, suburban liberals were hopeful. Yet, once again, Young proved somehow unable to act on his better impulses. "He wasn't acting rationally," one out-of-town black friend commented years later. "He would get pissed off and shoot from the hip. He knew he needed the white businessmen and the suburbanites, but then he'd get mad and tell them to get the hell out of town."

A regional bill pending in the state legislature provided the first flashpoint. The aim of the measure was to create a loose metro confederation by transforming an existing body, the Southeast Michigan Council of Governments, known as SEMCOG. Underfunded, entirely voluntary and devoted mainly to information gathering, SEMCOG was a well-meaning but toothless group, more a liberal think tank than a government-in-waiting. The legislature's proposal to overhaul it—by requiring all local governments to take part, collecting "dues" and letting residents elect some members—would have been a major step toward regional integration, and it was the subject of a fierce, statewide debate. With all eyes on newly elected Mayor Young, he made his opposition clear in several interviews. "Those people who fled to the suburbs to escape Detroit's problems in the first place," he griped, "aren't going to help support Detroit now." No suburbs had spoken, no votes been taken, but for Young, the outcome was already clear. Anticipating white rejection, the black city said no first and aggressively laid the blame on the suburbs.

Baffled by this reluctance and apparent hostility, the region's liberal whites tried repeating their offer. A few months later, with the SEMCOG bill still pending, leading supporters of the measure convened a meeting with Young and other prominent Detroit blacks. The two sides agreed on the issues they needed to discuss: the regional water supply, the city bus system, the zoo, the library and the art museum. To white liberals, each was an opportunity—a realm in which city and suburbs could cooperate, with the suburbs assuming more of the cost and the two sides sharing in management decisions. Yet once again, city blacks responded negatively with an immediate, angry rejection. "Detroit's fiscal problems," Young declared, "stem from the fact that we furnish services to people who don't pay for them because of an unequal tax structure. We must achieve some equity before we'd be willing to go further or exchange any power. I'll tell you up front, I'm not willing to deal with people who have refused to deal fairly with me. . . . I have to look askance at this whole proposal."

Rebuffed and confused, Power and others pored over the mayor's statements and reexamined their proposals. Finally, Power recalled, it began to dawn on them: Young and his staff saw metropolitan cooperation as a threat—an act of racial aggression by the suburbs. "In Young's eyes," the editor said later, "it was a battle for control. He saw the situation as an either/or, win/lose struggle, and he believed that partnership would mean a reduction of his control." Mistrustful of whites, bruised by past encounters, Young could see only ill will in the liberals' outstretched hand. "I might feel differently," he asserted, "if there were some way [Detroit] could get in on the suburban tax base." Indeed, he made clear, there was only one kind of cooperation that interested him: cash payments from the suburbs, the fewer strings the better.

The Detroit Water Board was just the kind of arrangement he liked: an ostensibly cooperative body that gave him the upper hand. In fact, when it came to water, city and suburbs had been cooperating for decades. Rather than maintain their own wells and purification plants, the outlying townships had always bought water from the city at a price fairly negotiated between buyer and seller. The 1973 election created a new body to coordinate the rate. Composed of four Detroit members and three suburbanites, it answered directly to the mayor. Through spring 1975, both Young and the commission assured customers that rates were stable. But then in April, the board's Detroit members held an impromptu meeting and, without consulting their colleagues from the suburbs, unilaterally raised prices by 35 percent. The suburbs were furious, particularly when it turned out that Young had approved the stealth maneuver—and that, far from needing the money, the Water Authority was operating at a surplus. Even liberals like Power were appalled. The board, he charged in an angry column, was "ripping off the suburbs without warning or representation." One suburban commission member—the mayor of Livonia—protested, and Young fired him on the spot. In Young's view, the suburbs were trying to "take over a city utility." In the eyes of the suburbs, Young was simply fleecing them.

On this as on most things, black Detroiters rallied around the mayor. His election and the transfer of power that followed had had a profound effect on the mood of the city. Detroit was now a proud black town, the largest black-majority city in the country—and the one where blacks wielded the most political power. The mayor's office, the school board, the city council and the courts were increasingly African-American. Outside of government too, black professionals were gaining ground. Though most finance and industry were still in the hands of whites, a small black elite was emerging: sleek, well-dressed developers and money people, many of them newcomers, doing a thriving business with the city government. As exciting for many Detroiters, the public face of the city was changing. The images on billboards, the mannequins in department stores, the television personalities and radio announcers all seemed to have changed color overnight. Black music filled the airwaves; soul food restaurants opened around the city, and even traditional restaurants downtown were suddenly filled with black people. For many city residents, it added up to a cultural revolution. "Blacks," one resident noted jubilantly, "are saying 'Detroit's ours now.'" The change was palpable and apparent to any visitor in people's bearing, their clothes, the proud way many kept their houses and lawns. Even the culturally remote *New York Times* understood. Detroit was becoming the black capital of the nation, it wrote, "certainly, the black working-man's capital."

Just like white suburbanites a few miles away, heady black Detroiters saw less and less reason to reach out across the city line. Regional governance would have meant the dilution if not the end of their newfound black power. Not only would it have required compromise with the suburbs; it would have meant a return to subordinate, minority status. An earlier generation of blacks might have seen the appeal of cooperation. But for the hungry young professionals coming up in Detroit—men and women looking forward, at last, to shaping their own destiny—metropolitan integration was unthinkable. What they liked about Coleman Young was what black Detroit had always liked about him. "He'll tell white people off in a minute," said his authorized biographer, black political scientist Wilbur Rich. "He's tough, combative, confrontational. That's reassuring to a lot of black people." Detroit blacks believed their mayor when he told them they could extract cash from the suburbs—and from the state and the federal government—without any strings attached. They rallied behind him when he blamed whites for what was wrong in the ghetto. They identified with his alienation;

they drank satisfaction from his anger. And when Young talked about the suburbs' "need for control," his constituents counted on him to repel it— even if that meant financial loss for the city.

The fracas over the water board put an end to all hope for metro cooperation in the Detroit region. Whatever restraint Young had shown in the past went abruptly out the window, and he began lambasting suburbanites in speeches and interviews. "Get the hell out of the way," he bellowed at one group; stop "blocking" Detroit's efforts to build a rapid transit system. He accused suburban developers of sending "raiding parties" to snatch tenants from downtown buildings, of "stealing" money from the city and "sabotaging" his development plans. (In fact, through the seventies, the suburban ring would provide virtually all the money that went into Young's ambitious downtown redevelopment schemes.) Even as he berated outlying whites, he maintained his willingness to cooperate: "If some of the people in the suburbs who are throwing all those rocks would come to Detroit as often as I go to the suburbs, we probably would be able to achieve a degree of unity." But by now not even the most liberal suburbanites could take his occasional peace offerings seriously.

By the later seventies, attitudes were hardening on both sides of the line. "When Young talks about suburban cooperation," complained the mayor of Westland, "he wants everything on his own terms." "I think he uses racism as an alibi," said another local politician. "I wish he'd just lay out the problems and the solutions." Even liberals like Philip Power conceded sadly that the city and suburbs were effectively "at war." The SEMCOG bill went nowhere; tax revenue sharing dropped off the agenda. And when the federal government gave the region $900 million to build a subway—a huge, unprecedented grant—disagreements between city and suburb stalled and eventually killed the project. Liberal Republican governor William Milliken continued to press for state aid to the city and succeeded in appropriating a package for the zoo, library and museum—money effectively culled from suburban taxes. But this and other occasional dollops of aid were nothing compared to the potential investment and business revenues that Detroit sacrificed by alienating whites from the suburbs.

Meanwhile, inside the city line, the suburbs eclipsed even the press and the feds as black Detroiters' racial enemy number one. Outlying whites— "our assailants"—had not simply moved from the city; they had, Young charged, "abandoned" it, for no other reason than because it was black.

Residing beyond Eight Mile Road—and paying taxes there—was not a way of life but a deliberate act of aggression: what Young called "economically pillaging the city." "The suburbs," he claimed, "have disassociated themselves from the problems of Detroit even as they have maneuvered to control our assets." "Whites," he explained on another occasion, "can't stand for black folks to run a damn thing . . . and if we do, they're going to destroy it." According to Young, both at the time and later, as mayor he devoted himself tirelessly to easing these tensions, making friendly overtures and proposing regional cooperation. "I'm honestly not dumb enough," he wrote in his autobiography, "to tell the suburbs to fuck off." Still, Young somehow just couldn't bring himself to do what it took to get along with the region's whites. "When somebody steps on my toe," he defended himself combatively, "I'm going to say 'ouch.'"

Given the differences that divided the Detroit region, even the most conciliatory, diplomatic mayor would have had difficulty convincing whites that they were part of the city. But Young, with his overheated rhetoric and paranoid siege mentality, discouraged even the most well-intentioned, forthcoming suburbanites. More and more, outlying whites stopped coming into town. Many stopped calling themselves Detroiters and, when asked about the city's woes, shrugged indifferently. Meanwhile, inside the city line, any whites who could afford to move began to look elsewhere. "Coleman Young as much as told people to leave," Irene McCabe said years later. "He wanted everything black and treated whites as second-class citizens." Many felt he was deliberately cutting corners in their neighborhoods. "He was trying to drive whites out," charged *News* columnist Pete Waldmeir, a crusty spokesman for blue-collar Detroiters, "and he cut their services." True or not, between 1970 and 1975, another 12 percent of the city's whites made the move across Eight Mile Road. "I'm not going to say I staunched the flow," Young conceded years later, with a laugh. As the first black mayor of black Detroit—he made no secret of it—his priorities were elsewhere.

With his anger, his defiance, his blaming and his "us" versus "them" views, Young encouraged both blacks and whites to cling to their suspicions and do the easy thing—resist—no matter what the long-term costs. He wasn't responsible for white racism or selfishness. There wasn't much he or anyone else could do about the decline of the auto industry or the global economic restructuring that was splitting the region into two worlds, one rich, one poor, one modernizing and one sliding off the economic map. But by fueling the color-coded antagonism on both sides of the city line, Young all but ensured that the region's division would be permanent. He not only spurred both black and white to act on their worst impulses; he also encouraged the black city to cut itself off from its own best hope for prosperity. "We need a metropolitan partnership," he would say at the end of his mayoralty. "We need the suburbs' dollars, their jobs . . . their cooperation." Yet even after twenty years, he didn't see what he had done to discourage this.

Chapter 11

A MANDATE FOR ANARCHY

reddie Williams remembers the first years of the Young mayoralty as a sudden burst of light in a bleak landscape. One of eight hundred-plus black cops on the Detroit force, Williams had been waiting for change for more than two decades. When he joined the department, in the mid-fifties, he was one of a few dozen blacks, most of whom had signed up because it was the only steady work they could find. After twenty years, unlike white officers who thought of the force as their extended family, Williams looked backed over his career and could remember little but the discrimination: the added recruitment hurdles, the virtual impossibility of promotion, the segregated assignments and continual humiliation.

"Blacks were confined to three precincts," Williams recalled of the 1950s, "black precincts." There was no chance to join the department's specialized units, no hope of working at headquarters. Only one or two black men in the city had made sergeant, and black cops were barred from patrol cars. "You walked the beat," Williams remembered, "and when you got back to the squad room, white guys wouldn't play Ping-Pong with you. If you picked up a paddle, they put theirs down." Other black officers remembered even worse: pictures of gorillas taped to their lockers, a sign in the men's room, pointing to a urinal, that read, "NAACP Blood Bank." By the late sixties, attitudes were changing. "The guys weren't all bad," Williams remembered, "they probably weren't much worse than your average white guy out there." But in his eyes and the eyes of most black cops, the world turned over when Coleman Young became mayor.

By the time Young was elected, the Detroit establishment had come to a consensus about the police department. Most Democratic and Republican leaders, businessmen and union officials understood that an overwhelmingly white force probably could not police a black city. White liberals had begun to grasp the ghetto's historic fear and hatred of policemen. They had followed the increasingly bitter grudge match between the police and the city's black leadership, and even if they understood that there was right and wrong on both sides, most believed that the only answer was to change the culture of the department. After all, they reasoned, the population shift was inevitable, and the city needed a police force that could handle the change.

The city's blue-collar whites were more skeptical, and many of them worried that liberal-minded reforms would weaken the department. If you weren't for the police, people like Irene McCabe reasoned, you were against them—and if you were against them, you were for the criminals. But even Irene McCabe's lawyer Brooks Patterson, elected in 1972 as the law-and-order prosecutor of Oakland County, believed that adding blacks to the city force might help it fight crime more effectively. As far back as 1961, a majority of Detroit voters—white and black together—had been electing mayors who promised to integrate the police and stiffen civilian review procedures. Whiz-kid Mayor Jerome Cavanagh had made a start on both fronts in the early sixties. His successor, Roman Gribbs—a former sheriff and favorite son of the city's blue-collar ethnics—had done better still, pressing both integration and oversight with greater zeal than Cavanagh. By 1973, the number of blacks on the force had tripled to 16 percent and recruitment in the ghetto was a top priority.

Still, Williams and others understood that Young's commitment to change was of a different order. "There were reformist efforts before Young," said one of the mayor's police commissioners, UAW leader Douglas Fraser, "but for him it was a raison d'être, the centerpiece of his mayoralty." Young had made law enforcement issues his first concern for a decade in the state Senate, then put police accountability at the top of his mayoral platform. "It wasn't the main issue," he would later say, "it was the only issue." He viewed his election as a mandate for radical reorganization of the department, and he could hardly wait to get started.

He had been in office only a few weeks when he made his first move: a package of vigorous reforms welcomed by the city establishment and its black cops. A mayoral executive order began where Young's campaign left off, abolishing the undercover antitheft unit, STRESS, seen by many in the black community as a racist execution squad. In an effort to bring the department closer to the people, the order also announced plans for fifty police "mini-stations": storefront outposts, to be manned mostly by black cops and, in each case, a team of civilians who would take neighborhood complaints about police brutality. Most dramatic and important for the long term was the provision on affirmative action; one way or another, through recruitment, attrition or other means, the Young administration promised to deliver a 50 percent black police force.

Well-meaning whites and blacks throughout the country applauded the mayoral order. Young's commitment to a fifty-fifty balance was seen as ambitious but doable. The mini-stations seemed a brilliant innovation—the germ of the idea that would become known as "community policing." The press covered the first storefront openings in two of the city's most notorious projects with cheerful hoopla and earnest hope that this simple gesture would be enough to restore the community's faith in the department. The media's first progress reports, a few weeks later, were even more glowing. Project dwellers had welcomed their new protectors enthusiastically with food and potted plants for the mini-stations. One preschool child brought in his puppy and an obliging cop allowed the dog to sit on his desk. In another project, the first month of neighborhood friendly policing actually brought a reduction in crime—from ten robberies to two.

The next round of changes involved more radical surgery on the structure and color of the department. The first step was to revise recruitment procedures. Scouts were sent into ghetto areas to sign up potential applicants. The police entrance exam, revised once just before Young's election in an effort to make it easier for black applicants, was changed yet again, to make it even easier. The test for promotion to sergeant and lieutenant was also changed, and when the group that passed still did not meet the mayor's racial targets, his administration hit on a way to get around the exam. Instead of promoting those officers with the best results, Young simply divided the rank-ordered list of scores into two lists—one black, one white—and promoted one black candidate for every white one. When critics on the force and elsewhere complained that this was reverse discrimination, he replied, "You're damn right—the only way to arrest discrimination is to reverse it." Finally, hoping to clear the way for more black officers, Young ordered the department to start enforcing its residency requirement, firing cops—and they were all white—whose primary home was beyond the city line.

Young's police recruitment and promotion initiatives put Detroit on the frontline of the nation's new experiment with affirmative action. Proudly race-conscious, audacious, aggressive, the overhaul was widely viewed as a long-overdue effort to right past wrongs. Black cops like Freddie Williams were thrilled. "The mayor gave black officers the idea that they could go for things," declared Gil Hill, a young black policeman who went on to become one of the department's most successful detectives. "He instilled the idea that you could qualify, and if you qualified, you too would rise." Even ghetto youth responded with interest. Between 1974 and 1975, there was a 25 percent jump in the number of black applicants looking to join the force, and within a few years the police academy was half black.

As Young's reforms got underway, virtually no one in Detroit, black or white, thought to question them. The press supported the initiative; the liberal civic establishment was pleased; even some of the region's conservative law-and-order types remained hopeful. "It had to be done," white union leader Douglas Fraser recalled. "The department had to change, and change fast. It was the only way to win the trust of the community." No one asked if color coding was likely to ease black animosity toward law enforcement, or if other, deeper changes might be needed. No blacks came forward with other ideas; no establishment whites, few of whom lived in town, thought too hard about possible consequences. If a black man like Young said this was the answer, liberals like Fraser—and Max Fisher and Henry Ford II—saw no reason not to support and encourage him.

Young threw himself into the reform effort with an intensity that surprised even his inner circle. City council members recalled later that he focused on virtually nothing else his first year in office, and some began to detect what struck them as an excess of zeal. Labeling the patrolmen's union "a bunch of out-and-out racists," Young seemed to get a thrill from opposing it and thwarting department brass. He relished even minor disagreements over wages and sick leave; his strict enforcement of the residency requirement had an unmistakably vindictive air. Several of his initiatives seemed to go beyond what was necessary to end discrimination or open up opportunity for black officers, and no charge against the force, no matter how speculative, seemed to strike him as outlandish. One day, talking off the cuff, the mayor claimed that the department's senior-ranking white officers were involved "at the top" of the city's drug trade. Later, lacking evidence, he dropped the accusation—but made no effort to repair the damage he had done to police authority. Intent and inventive, Young was full of new ideas for reforming the department. But he also seemed to harbor an animus for the force that set him apart from his white backers—an animus most liberals were only dimly aware of.

What Young's white supporters did not grasp was the racial dimension of his crusade. Raised since childhood on the politics of "us" versus "them," a former radical and union tough, Young came into office not just seeking reform but girding for war with the department—race war. In his eyes, as in the eyes of many blacks, ten years of liberal tinkering had changed little or nothing. "The same problem exists throughout most police departments," he said in 1974. "They are predominantly white and racist." In an era of pitched gun battles between police and Black Panthers, he saw the force less as an arm of the law than an army of repression—the paramilitary wing of a white society determined to crush black pride and autonomy. "As everyone knows," he told a group of black professionals, "law and order is a code word for 'Keep the niggers in their place.'" Everything else was secondary, even the crime rate in Detroit. "Crime is a problem," he declared, "but not *the* problem. The police are the major threat . . . to the minority community." For Young, police issues had less to do with public safety than with a larger and, to him, far more important power struggle between black and white. "I have to decide," he said early in his mayoralty, "who is going to run the city—the police or the people."

Morale on the force, already beaten down by the late sixties and the New Bethel controversy, sank further still as Young's initiative took root. White cops began to count the days until they could retire with a vested pension. Others who had gone to court in the past to fight the city residency requirement wondered why they had bothered: "I'd planned on building a house in the suburbs," one told a reporter, "but now I'm just going to look for a job out there." Still others admitted to journalists that they regularly turned their backs on criminal activity: what was the point of risking your life to make an arrest if it was going to lead to a citizen complaint that could eventually block prosecution of the suspect? Fearful officers braced for massive firings and the wholesale reorganization of the department. The mayor's new police chief, though white, was deeply distrusted by the rank-and-file, and the several black deputies installed below him were even less popular.

As for Young's promise that affirmative action would make the cops more effective, officers on the beat saw little evidence. "With a shooting in a bar," one told a reporter, "you'll have 30 people tell you they were in the john at the time—the same time." Mistrustful of the criminal justice system, loathe to appear in court or side with white authority against a neighbor, many potential witnesses still refused to cooperate with the police. Others would offer to help but then give the cops what turned out to be a false name or nonexistent address. Many black cops reported that they were getting to know the neighborhoods they patrolled, that they hung out there on their days off and were cultivating informants. But others, even successful ones like Gil Hill, admitted that they were seen as "traitors" by fellow blacks who scorned their cooperation with the white system. "You join up and say to yourself, 'I'm going to try to help,'" said twenty-four-year-old Officer Larry Walker. "But all of a sudden the black group you grew up with shuts you right out. You no longer relate. You'd be surprised how you're not black any more."

If anything, Young's all-out war on the department only seemed to fuel the community's mistrust and hostility. Though the mayor talked earnestly, particularly with his white supporters, about the need "to bring the force closer to the people," his actions and attitude conveyed a very different message. Unlike the Black Power movement, he didn't exactly glorify criminal violence, but he made no secret of his view that it was more important to understand criminals than to blame them. Everything he said and did encouraged the ghetto notion that the law was white and alien and fighting racism more important than maintaining order. He milked his conflict with the department for all it was worth in the eyes of black constituents, and as in his other feuds, they rallied around him. "The typical [black] resident of the city," Young said years later, "is naturally concerned about the safety issue but not preoccupied with it. . . . [Black Detroiters] considered the local police to be every bit as dangerous and threatening to their welfare as crime."

Despite the encouraging news from the first few mini-stations, crime rates rose inexorably through Young's first years in office. Violent crime was growing everywhere in this period—for demographic reasons as well as social and economic ones. But Detroit figures were in a class by themselves, well above the national average—for some crimes, double the rates in other cities. No one really knew why things were so bad in Detroit. Some traced it back to the city's rough-and-tumble, factory-town origins. Others looked to the 1974 recession and the frustration that came with it; still others to the unusually large number of guns that had been circulating since the 1967 riots. With the police force demoralized, the hard drug trade just taking off and teenage gangs mushrooming across the ghetto, it made little sense to try to isolate one reason; and to the degree Young's crusade contributed, it was impossible to measure its effect. But whatever the explanation, the fact was plain: a different kind of culture was taking root in Detroit's inner-city neighborhoods.

In Young's first year, there were 801 murders, up from 508 just three years before, and the old label "Murder City" gave way, in the press and the streets, to the grimmer still "Kill City." Even as the numbers rose, the crimes themselves grew nastier: old-fashioned one-on-one sexual assaults became gang rapes, stabbings were replaced by shootings, and unruly fights by execution-style slayings. Hardly a week went by without a major horror story on the front pages of the papers. Police investigators were shocked, as one put it, by "the way the public accepts the homicide rate." Indignation, the cop told a reporter, had been replaced by "ho-hum, another murder." The department was baffled by a rash of inquiries from citizens about the number of slayings in a given week—until it came out that the curious callers were organizing office betting pools. By 1975, the idea of killing had become so banal that the department reported a spate of what it called "insurance murders"—for the cash benefits. Crime, one wag remarked, had become the city's leading growth industry. Private guards, locksmiths, manufacturers of anticrime devices and perpetrators: these, the joke went, were the only people making money in Detroit in the mid-seventies. "It's wild, just wild," one cop told an out-of-town reporter. "You see it on TV. Here in Detroit, we practice it."

The summer of 1975 brought a major escalation in the mayor's war on the department. With the national recession dragging on and the auto industry at a virtual standstill, unemployment rose into the 25 percent range, and among young black males, roughly double that. Facing a budget deficit of nearly $50 million, Young announced massive cuts in public service spending, and despite the soaring crime rates, he let it be known that more than half would be borne by the police. Defensive, suspicious, resentful of the mayor, union officials rejected Young's proposal that patrolmen agree to an across-the-board pay freeze. Then, before the cops' rebuff hit the papers, Young fired back with an even less appealing order: a sweeping cut in personnel that would eliminate more than eight hundred officers, or about 15 percent of the force. This was a losing proposition all around: for the crime-ridden city, the beleaguered department and the mayor himself—his low-seniority affirmative action hires would be the first to go in any large-scale firing. The only way it made any sense was from the point of view of the mayor's spiteful crusade. Even when it undermined his own policies, he couldn't seem to help lashing out at the force.

By the time the dispute was reported in the newspapers, Young had cast it as a conflict over affirmative action. Grasping that his draconian cuts would hurt black officers more than white ones, he blamed the police union for making the firings necessary, deliberately sabotaging his effort to integrate the department. The city's black police associations rallied behind the mayor, and the administration took the matter to court, asking a judge to override union seniority protections so that Young could avoid firing black cops even as he eliminated eight hundred white officers. The police rank-and-file responded with a rally, to be held in front of the courthouse where the case was being heard. Sympathetic fellow cops made plans to travel from as far away as New York and California. Concerned not to seem bigoted or anti–affirmative action, the police union appealed to Detroiters' labor solidarity: full-page ads in the newspapers denounced the mayor for trampling the shibboleth of seniority. Still, at the rally, simmering racial resentment spilled over, and a fight erupted among the gathered cops: one black officer against a clique of hostile, rowdy white men.

It was only a momentary flare-up, but it would loom large for years to come among both black and white Detroiters. By the time the rally started on May 9, 1975, the day had grown hot and sultry. Many of the thousand picketing cops were drinking beer. One threw an empty can in the direction of the courthouse, and when a black officer, also in civilian clothes, reprimanded him, he shot back abruptly, "Get fucked." A scuffle ensued, and before it was finished, ten other whites were involved against the black man. Just when he drew his gun was never clear, but he was quickly outmanned by white officers who whipped out their revolvers. Surrounded and outnumbered, the black cop gave up his gun and was led away to the hospital to be treated for a broken nose.

As it happened, both *The New York Times* and *The Washington Post* had photographers on the scene and both played the story in a big way, using it as an occasion to look at length at racial tension in the declining city of Detroit. The photographs were unforgettable: the sun-dappled all-American downtown street, the bewildered, innocent black victim, the circle of hostile working-class whites in sunglasses, pointing their guns at the lonely black man. The implied analogy was as clear as the pictures: in a city where the pie was shrinking, small-minded whites opposed racial justice—in the form of affirmative action—just as others like them had once opposed the end of Jim Crow. The national papers ran several follow-up stories, all of them with the same well-meaning, righteous slant. Like Detroit's civic-minded elite, no one asked any hard questions, either about the mayor's quota system or what it might really take to ease tensions between blacks and the police department. In the liberal press as in Detroit, it was assumed that the mayor's initiative was only fair, the cops' opposition unreasonable and racist.

The usually reticent Young all but gloated to the press. "Violence and racial problems in the police department don't really surprise me," he noted. "The officers who took part in last Friday's display of public drunkenness and beer-can throwing . . . aren't doing a bit of good and they are a danger to the city." Right or wrong, the mayor had won the publicity battle and dealt another body blow to the police force and all it stood for. Whatever Detroit blacks had thought of the department before, now they were convinced of the very worst.

The first serious test of Young's police force came ten weeks later, in midsummer 1975. By then, the dispute over layoffs had been settled to save the four hundred or so new blacks on the force, and Young felt confident that he was winning his war to transform the department. Otherwise, the first year and a half of his mayoralty had not gone well. Banking on outside money to revive the city, Young had devoted most of his time to importuning the federal government and waiting for Henry Ford's big waterfront project, the Renaissance Center, to be completed. Meanwhile, the city's long-running recession had bottomed out in depression, and thousands of unemployed youths sat idle through the long summer days. No city in the country had had a major riot since 1968, but the combination of the heat and record joblessness sent tremors of fear through the Detroit establishment.

The *Detroit Free Press* reported widespread discontent in the city. Half of the population, including 43 percent of black residents, said they would move out of town if they could, and when asked why, a large majority cited the climate of fear. "I'd leave in a minute," said one man, a black auto worker. "There's no law in the city, no substantial law—and you're just a sitting duck." Cutbacks in city services had begun to take effect, removing both cops and firemen from active duty. Crime rates continued their grisly course upward, and radical black union groups sprouting in the auto factories spread talk of armed revolution. Still, white executives reassured themselves over lunch, if anyone could keep the racial peace, Young could. "I'd say we're fortunate to have Young there now," said GM vice president George Morris. "Even though I didn't vote for him—maybe he can keep the lid on."

When it happened just after dark on July 28, the trouble followed the classic pattern. White bar owner Andrew Chinarian came out of his workingman's hangout in the racially mixed Livernois neighborhood and noticed some black kids breaking into a car in the dimly lit parking lot. When he approached the car, rifle in hand, one of the youths turned toward him, and Chinarian thought he saw something glinting in the kid's right hand. The shots the bar owner fired hit eighteen-year-old Obie Wynn in the back of the head in what would turn out to be a fatal wound.

Within a few hours, three hundred people had gathered in the street outside Chinarian's bar. Egged on by troublemakers, they stormed the place, driving out the few remaining customers, then divvied up the liquor and trashed the small wooden building. By midnight, the three hundred had grown to seven hundred and split into small bands that roamed the city streets, breaking windows, looting shops, overturning cars and torching them. One unfortunate white man who happened to make a wrong turn was dragged from his car and beaten close to death. The mob's main targets were police and firemen, and though Young told the force to deploy only black cops—and ordered them to use the utmost restraint—the roving youths showed little mercy. The kids used mostly stones and bottles, the cops nightsticks and tear gas. Black or white, restrained or brutal, in the eyes of Detroit's blacks, it hardly mattered; the police represented authority—hated authority—and the way to prove yourself was by defying them. Young and other black leaders wandered the streets through the night, trying to calm the mob, to little effect. Finally, after ducking a rain of bottles and stones, the mayor gave up and went home.

The next day, Young struggled to put the best face on what had happened, appealing, as usual, to black solidarity. "We had a great number of black commanders to help control the crowd," he boasted, "and not a single shot was fired." Also in the name of race, he took a jab at legal authority—not at the cops this time, but at the judicial system. Passing quickly over the behavior of those responsible for the disturbance, he lambasted the judge who had handled Chinarian's arrest, letting the bar owner out on merely $500 bail. "I'm just as disappointed as the crowd," the mayor proclaimed, "that this man is released on a murder charge when people who get caught stealing a dress get stuck in jail." Though Young plainly hoped that his comments would calm the rage in the street, if anything, they seemed to have the opposite effect, and the looting, arson and pitched battles continued unabated through a second night.

Finally, on the third day, in a brilliant bit of spin control, the Young administration claimed victory. The city had had a minor riot that had spent itself. The black police had proved no more popular or trusted than their white counterparts. And Young, as ever, had chosen to play the race card rather than stand up for the law and order his city desperately needed for residents, black and white, to feel safe in their homes and for new, job-creating businesses to take root. Still, in Young's hands, the episode became a political triumph. The mayor took credit for keeping the peace, earning support for his police reforms among regional businessmen, even as he sowed still more resentment of legal authority in black Detroit, further undermining the rule of law. "To me," Young said later, "this was the turning point," the vindication of his campaign to transform the department. As for city whites who weren't so sure—who worried that the civic order was collapsing around them—no one with any power in Detroit was particularly interested in their opinions.

Young's war with police brass and unions simmered on through that fall and winter. Disputes over affirmative action and the residency requirement worked their way up through the court system. Resentment seethed among the rank-and-file. Superior officers reported that cops were leaving the force in droves and that they were having trouble finding new recruits. Meanwhile, the newest cohort of officers—the affirmative action cohort— was having problems fitting into the department.

Young's all-out effort to hire from the community had included a radical "streamlining" of procedures. Applicants were no longer interviewed at home, family records were not checked, prior employers often went unconsulted, and only cursory inquiries were made about prior arrest records. This aggressive recruitment and the quotas that came with it had come close to achieving Young's racial targets: in just two years, the number of blacks on the force had risen from 16 to 22 percent. Then, in early 1976, the scandals began to break. One rookie was arrested for selling marijuana to high school students; several others were charged with dealing heroin. Still others, who confessed that they had been using or dealing drugs when recruited, resigned before charges could be pressed, and one trainee was suspended when she shot and killed her husband, ostensibly while learning how to load her service revolver. Determined to press ahead with its quota system, the administration ignored the flap. "The recruitment process is subject to the mores of the society from which we recruit," said a police official fending off inquiries.

"The officers we are getting have the same mores as the other people in the community." Some white officers who worked alongside the new recruits could not resist a gleeful "I told you so," but most despaired at what was happening to their department.

Young's final and worst assault on the police came in the spring of 1976: another round of cutbacks, this one non-negotiable, that threatened to devastate the already hemorrhaging force. Another year of high oil prices, flat auto production and spiraling inflation had brought the city to the brink of fiscal disaster. Crime figures for the first quarter of 1976 once again put Detroit near the top of the list of the most dangerous American cities, and many in the regional establishment urged the mayor to find some place else to cut—anywhere except the police force. But Young insisted that there was no alternative—that other monies could not be tapped for the department—and that the crime problem was much exaggerated anyway by hostile reporters and white suburbanites. People complaining that downtown Detroit was unsafe had, he complained, "a racist perception of the city."

Even police brass expecting the worst were stunned by the magnitude of the layoffs: close to one thousand officers, or a full one-fifth of the department. The rank-and-file responded with an angry case of "blue flu." But Young was undeterred; if anything, he seemed encouraged by his adversary's resistance. Appealing to the community for "volunteers"—to replace cops to be fired and those out on strike—he began the layoffs by dismantling the department's specialized units, including the one responsible for patrolling the city's expressways.

It was the last straw for the rule of law in Detroit, and what little order there was broke down completely. Within days of the cutback in highway patrols, teenage bands from the neighborhoods descended on the roadways. Rocks, bricks and masonry rained down on passing cars from pedestrian bridges above the expressways. Youths roamed the highway system in old jalopies, "accidentally" bumping better-looking cars, and when the drivers pulled over to exchange insurance information, the kids surprised them with a gun in their ribs. One man who stopped to change a tire was beaten senseless by a pack of roving teens. A woman whose car broke down was abducted to an abandoned house and raped repeatedly over several days. Elsewhere in the city, cutbacks in transit police led to a rash of crime on city buses: mostly robberies at gun- or knifepoint. By midsummer, the department reported that it was taking up to four hours to respond to 911 calls, and reductions in courtroom police had led to several violent incidents, including one in which a lawyer pulled a gun and fired wildly at judge and jury. In August, half a dozen terrified judges announced that they could no longer take the risk of appearing in court to hear cases.

Just what lay behind the violence that erupted that summer was probably beyond explaining: some combination of rage, frustration and boredom in broken-down neighborhoods where unemployment reached the halfway mark. Cutting back the police, Young had merely taken the lid off, and what emerged from underneath had a momentum of its own. Still, there could be no denying the role he had played—not just in trimming the force but by undermining respect for what it stood for. Together with New Bethel judge George Crockett and the Black Panther movement, Young openly encouraged the city's youth to see the law as an alien enemy: the inherently racist arm of a white system determined to crush and control them. The mayor set the example himself: defying the cops was good sport and an important way to stand up for one's people. No wonder the city's teens saw the police—and the law—as something worthy of their contempt.

The summer of 1976 was shocking even by Detroit standards. Looting of downtown stores became an everyday sport—not something reserved for special occasions. In one struggling neighborhood in the northwest of town, shopowners reported replacing plate-glass windows as often as twice a week. Black and white, shopmen and customers, in big department stores and mom-and-pop groceries: among the few businesses remaining inside the city line, no one was spared. Against this background of daily robberies and muggings, a handful of particularly grisly individual crimes stood out. A popular community priest was robbed and brutally murdered in his rectory. A legal aid lawyer's leg was broken when an auto thief ran over him in his own car. But most terrifying—and relatively new to most whites—were the teenage gangs that flourished that summer. Groups called the Bishops and the BKs (short for Black Killers) waged open warfare in the neighborhoods. They also ventured occasionally into the central business district to prey on suburban shoppers and one evening rampaged through the expensive Pontchartrain Hotel. Coming by chance on a private party, twenty youths tore through the opulent dining room, overturning tables, stealing purses and screaming, "Black Killers! Black Killers! It's all about the Black Killers!"

The crime wave climaxed in mid-August with an incident at the Cobo Hall convention center. About eight thousand people, black and white, had gathered on Sunday night for a rock concert. About halfway through, as if on signal, 150 black youths leaped up from their seats and put what seemed to be a planned attack in motion. Members of the Black Killers and the Errol Flynns set upon concertgoers with canes and umbrellas. Dozens of people were robbed, one woman raped—by fifteen to twenty youths, in a public space. Many more, both black and white, were harassed and molested. "I don't care who you are," one gang-banger said to a black man. "Give us what you've got."

The mayhem continued for a full hour before police entered the hall—city authorities would later explain that there were so few police on duty in the area that they feared to confront the gangs before reinforcements arrived. By then, the youths had gathered dozens of wallets and purses and were pursuing concertgoers out into the summer night. Spilling into downtown, the bands roamed the streets for several hours, breaking windows, looting and causing thousands of dollars in damage. Cops investigating the episode in the weeks that followed could find no apparent cause or precipitating incident. This was not part of a gang war, not a racially motivated attack, just simple, wanton violence. The late-arriving police managed to arrest a handful of suspects, but failed to collect any weapons or connect with victims who would testify against their attackers. In a city where the rule of law meant as little as it meant in Detroit, no one was interested in stepping forth to help prosecute the Black Killers or the Errol Flynns, and all the youths arrested by the police were eventually released without charges.

The incident caused an uproar through the region and beyond. The national press descended on the city; there were articles about its decline in all the major papers and newsmagazines. Governor Milliken ordered the state police to take over patrolling the city's expressways, and the state department of transportation found funds to rehire cops to ride shotgun on buses. Regional businessmen with millions of dollars at stake in the Renaissance Center complex going up just blocks from Cobo Hall demanded that Young take the situation in hand. "It's time to clamp down, and clamp down hard," Henry Ford II declared, "on anyone who threatens the peace and safety of the people of Detroit." Still other prominent figures, black and white, called for reconstituting the STRESS undercover unit Young had dismantled just two years before.

Under intense pressure from the region's businessmen, Young went into action to restore the city's image. Nearly half of the laid-off cops were immediately recalled. Federal funds were found to begin rehiring others. A complicated system of curfews was imposed for youths as young as eleven years old, and a new police unit was created to try to break the gangs coming up in the neighborhoods. The mayor went on TV to address the city. "I want the pimps, prostitutes, gangs and youth rovers off the streets," Young proclaimed. "We're going to rid the city of them—beginning tonight." Still, many Detroit residents, white and black, were skeptical that a show of force could now deter the lawless youths. On several occasions, bands stopped by police after curfew responded with open defiance of the officers. "How come you're hassling us," one youth caught red-handed challenged a squad of cops, while others in the gangs and in local community groups denounced the mass arrests as draconian and racist.

In truth, whatever happened now, the damage had been done—to Detroit's image, its hope for economic revival, its chances of sharing in the prosperity of an integrated region. White perceptions of the city, already soured by 1967, would never recover from the summer of 1976. As local people would say for decades to come, it seemed as if the riots had never stopped—and weren't going to. Henry Ford's lieutenant, Wayne Doran, in charge of developing and renting the Renaissance Center, told reporters after the Cobo Hall incident that he wasn't sure he could fill the office towers. With only one-third of the space spoken for, other prospective tenants were calling worriedly to ask about security and police protection. Within three months, 20 percent of the city's downtown office space was vacant, and a number of conventions had been canceled. Many months after the August melee, city sports teams reported that attendance was still down. Midtown restaurateurs had their worst winter ever. Cultural institutions like the symphony and art museum suffered so badly that some people wondered if they might not move elsewhere.

Out in the suburbs, newspaper publisher Philip Power went on record: "I've been writing this column regularly for nearly ten years now, and never have I seen relations between the suburbs and Detroit grimmer." Left and right, blue-collar and better-off, from liberal businessman Joseph Hudson to Oakland County's law-and-order prosecutor Brooks Patterson, whites throughout the region would later recall this as the time when they or their friends and acquaintances finally cut their ties to the city. "By attacking the police," antibusing housewife Irene McCabe explained, "Coleman Young undermined the people, the only people, who could get a grip on what was killing the city—the crime. It was as if he said to the criminals, 'The city's yours now.' That's why whites left. And many—most of them—never looked back." Power remembers friends closing businesses and finding new jobs, taking losses on investments and canceling memberships in downtown clubs. The liberal newspaperman listened sadly as his neighbors talked about the city and its blacks: bigoted or not, their fear of gangs and roving hoodlums was turning into a more general fear—a poisonous racial paranoia. "Coleman Young had a chance," Brooks Patterson recalled. "He had a chance to stabilize the city. But he did what he did—and instead of teetering, it tottered. Then it was just a matter of time before the crime drove the businesses and the people out."

Even men like Hudson and Power, who had wholeheartedly backed the idea of police reform, could not help feeling that Young had squandered the mandate. Whatever he had done to change the color of the force, he had done it largely at the expense of department standards. However much he had achieved in winning the community's trust, he had also, in Hudson's words, undermined "respect for any kind of police enforcement." Wittingly or not, he had nurtured the blossoming of what scholars would later call the city's "oppositional culture"—and by encouraging that alienation, that anger and contempt for what was seen as the white man's law, he had all but guaranteed a permanent standoff between city and suburb. "The only issue I can think of," Power wrote glumly, "that in any way could bring the interests of Detroit and the suburbs together is that of crime. Until that is done, until the authorities in the city can get their crime problems under control, Eight Mile will really be a wall."

By the time the Renaissance Center opened, in the fall of 1977, the writing was on the wall for the future of Detroit. The center—widely nicknamed "the RenCen"—was a showpiece of modern urban architecture. Designed by the national firm of John Portman & Associates, it stood on a glorious piece of real estate where the radiating spokes of the city's main boulevards met the majestic Detroit River. Wrapped almost entirely in glass, on a sunny day the glittering cluster of cylindrical towers was a sight to behold. Some called it "an Emerald City of Oz." To others, standing in the heart of the Motor City, it looked more like an architect's ode to the internal combustion engine. By the time the center opened, Henry Ford II and his partners had invested $350 million, hoping that the new complex—the largest privately financed real estate development in the world—would spark the economic revitalization of Detroit.

The only thing grander and more portentous than the buildings was the rhetoric used to describe what they would do for the city. At the center of the cluster was the seventy-story Detroit Plaza Hotel, meant to welcome the thousands of business people and conventiongoers who would flock to what Ford and Young imagined was the emerging economic hub of the Great Lakes region. The four forty-story office towers that shot up around the hotel were to serve as the brain cell of the city's new professional economy. In the atrium below—the base from which the towers rose—boosters envisioned one of the country's most luxurious shopping malls: Courrèges, Cartier, Lanvin and the like, cheek-by-jowl with the region's best eateries. At the top of the hotel tower—the crown of the complex—was the world's largest and most opulent revolving restaurant, also meant to attract visitors from across the state and beyond.

Expectations for the complex had reached mythic proportions by 1977. The idea began with the project's godfathers, Ford and Fisher, seconded by Young and the national press corps. Their hope was that RenCen would keep Detroit alive—no more, no less—by restoring its ties to the surrounding region. Determined to refurbish the city's tarnished image, to counter the growing crime and racial alienation, Ford and Fisher calculated that the center would lure white business and consumers back inside Eight Mile Road and spark new development elsewhere in the midtown area. No one used the word "integration" in connection with the project—that would have seemed ridiculous in 1977—and no one imagined that it alone would heal the tension in the region. But for the white entrepreneurs behind it, RenCen had as much to do with social policy as with hardheaded real estate development. The culmination of the New Detroit Committee's efforts, the answer to Mayor Young's charges about racism and indifference, RenCen was a bullish last-ditch effort to bridge the widening gulf between black city and white suburb.

The lavish dedication ceremony harked back to the Young inauguration: another celebration of the new black Detroit, but also—with its hope and show of harmony—a promise of a new kind of racial partnership. The East Coast media showed up en masse to make the gala opening a national event. Reporters rode up and down in the glass-enclosed elevators, looking out over the exquisite view: Lake Erie, the river, Chrysler, General Motors and the legendary Ford River Rouge Plant. There was free champagne for all eight hundred guests and endless photo ops of black and white together: jaunty, triumphant Coleman Young and his "coalition" partners, Henry Ford and company. The adjectives flowed as freely as the champagne, and even the press corps seemed giddy with hope. Maybe the city would have a future, after all. Maybe money could actually solve the problem. Still, even the most enthusiastic journalists could tell, underneath the hype, something was amiss.

At the time the center opened, its office towers were about half rented—and the realtors in charge of filling the space had had a hard time doing even that well. Henry Ford had muscled everyone he could think of, and when that didn't generate tenants, he had moved several divisions of his own company downtown, filling nearly a quarter of the RenCen space himself. In a city with no rapid transit, the seventeen hundred employees he brought from suburban Dearborn complained bitterly about the long commute and about their fears of being mugged or murdered downtown. As was the case with most people in the region, the focus of their lives was moving in exactly the opposite direction—away from the city.

In the last 25 years, reporters covering the RenCen opening noted, 550,000 people had moved from Detroit to the suburbs. In the decade since the 1967 riot, the once-thriving downtown had turned into a disaster area. Retail had gone into a free fall; on many downtown streets, there were more vacant stores than open ones. Three major hotels had closed in the last few years, and like many of the city's once proud downtown buildings, they stood empty and abandoned—worthless even to real estate developers. The last of the city's theaters had gone dark a month before; another had just been turned into a parking lot. The football team had left for the suburbs, and the basketball team was scheduled to follow next year. Even stores and office buildings still in use had a lost, forgotten air—often half-empty, ground-floor windows boarded up, badly in need of painting and routine repairs. At Hudson's great flagship store on Woodward Avenue, the display windows were permanently covered and a uniformed guard manned every entrance.

Ford, Fisher and Young maintained that the RenCen would serve as a "catalyst" for development, bringing new life to this decaying city. Yet even as it opened, urban planners speculated that it might actually do damage to the downtown business climate, not adding to the dwindling number of firms and services but merely concentrating them in one place. With unemployment rates hovering between 20 and 40 percent, Detroit was desperately in need of new jobs. But it seemed unlikely that the RenCen's white-collar offices would have much to offer city residents. The word "underclass" made its appearance in the American vocabulary at about the time the complex opened, and already sociologists estimated that one in four black Detroiters were part of it: poor, uneducated, angry, alienated and even more isolated from whites than working-class blacks. With still-record crime rates, among the worst schools in Michigan and the most extensive heroin addiction of any city in the country, Detroit was banking on monumental bricks-and-mortar development to bring it back into the mainstream economy. The RenCen was a dazzling and impressive effort, a tribute to the business elite and its social conscience. But the odds against it could hardly have been steeper. "Would it spark a meaningful revival of downtown?" *Newsweek* wondered. "Or will it turn out to be another overwhelmingly white suburb that just happens to be downtown?"

Young and Ford shrugged off the naysayers, and the corporations with the largest investment in the complex ponied up another $200,000 for a national PR campaign. There were printed T-shirts: "Detroit—A Phoenix Rising." Max Fisher reassured would-be investors and Republicans in Washington with a glowing article about Detroit's economic future on the *New York Times* op-ed page. Both Ford and Young went so far as to tell reporters—with no evidence whatsoever—that the RenCen was already reversing the flight of business to the suburbs. Then, scraping together money from suburban investors and the federal government, they kicked off a second round of downtown projects, most of them cosmetic: turning one shopping street into a trafficless mall, restoring an antique trolley to a downtown boulevard, building a $2-million computerized fountain on the waterfront near the RenCen.

For a year or so following the RenCen opening, the hype campaign seemed to be working. The national media ran stories about the boom in downtown Detroit. Photos of the skyline emphasized the cranes and bulldozers at work. The ebbing of the mid-seventies recession brought a modest comeback in the auto industry, and foot traffic in the central shopping district seemed to pick up a bit. Even investors seemed heartened, and plans were made for several more substantial development projects, including another major shopping mall and renovating one of the city's old posh hotels. In Detroit in 1977 and 1978, the watchword was "comeback," and optimism spread among the city's black elite. "Detroit is a young woman with acne," said NAACP official Arthur Johnson. "It is troublesome, but it is by no means fatal." "For a city that was declared dead two years ago," Young seconded the notion, "we are very much alive."

Then, in 1979, the business cycle turned down again, and the true state of the Detroit economy was exposed in all its bleakness. Among the more substantial construction projects planned the year before, few had gotten beyond the blueprint-and-budget phase. Frightened by the downtown crime rate, several big developers had backed away, and neither the new shopping mall nor the hotel restoration had gotten off the ground. By then, city authorities were moving ahead with their own riverfront development: a sports arena and an addition to Cobo Hall. But City Hall proved unable to rally private investors and instead had to use federal funds originally intended for more essential needs. Even so, like Third World countries trying to spark development with lavish government projects, Young's effort inspired few imitators. Despite generous tax rebates, private developers remained skittish, and 85 percent of what was built in the region in the late seventies went up across the city line in the suburbs.

Whatever was happening in the central business district, virtually none of it was trickling down to ordinary Detroiters. Out in the city's decaying neighborhoods, "improvement" meant not building but mostly demolition. With thousands of residents and landlords choosing to abandon buildings rather than repair them, it fell to the Young administration to destroy the empty structures: knocking down ramshackle family homes and cleaning up the charred remains of those that had fallen prey to arsonists. Together, these efforts consumed nearly $30 million a year—three out of every five dollars that the feds gave the city in community development block grants—leaving precious little for the construction of new housing or for social programs of any kind. City council members, white and black, vehemently opposed Young's redevelopment strategy, arguing that far too much was being spent downtown and far too little on the neighborhoods. But the mayor held tenaciously to his theory that a thriving downtown was the key to economic renewal. Meanwhile, in the course of a decade, Detroit lost 10 percent of its population and a third of its jobs—commercial jobs, industrial jobs, retail work and even government positions.

Nothing the mayor or the private sector tried worked to lure suburbanites back to the crumbling city. As predicted, rather than sparking growth, the RenCen sucked firms and services out of other downtown office buildings: by the time it had been open a year, the occupancy of older buildings like the landmark Cadillac Tower was down by 40 percent. After five years, city retail jobs had shrunk by nearly a third. For a few months at the beginning, the RenCen itself did a decent business, but soon it too was failing to attract suburban customers. Many came for a meal or two, some even stayed overnight at the hotel, but once their curiosity was satisfied, most hesitated to make the trip into the city again. In the first five years after its opening, the complex lost $130 million in operating costs, and investors defaulted on two mortgages before taking a huge loss on their capital. "We were never in it for the money," Fisher commented gamely—though, if anything, his attempt at social engineering had been even less successful.

Lavishly landscaped, fantastically designed, the atrium of the RenCen was as remote from the Detroit streets as the suburbs beyond Eight Mile Road. Pedestrians had to cross a ten-lane highway just to get near an entrance, and according to white Detroiters, if anything, the compound's extensive security only spurred their fears that the trip into town was unsafe. "If that's what's needed," journalist George Cantor explained, "they figured things must really be bad." Black Detroiters called the cluster of towers "a Noah's ark for the middle class" and "a fortress for whites to work in while the rest of the city goes to hell around them." Critics would complain for years to come that things could have been done differently. If only the architecture had been less security-minded and more welcoming. If only the site were five or ten blocks further north, less isolated from the existing business district. If only the complex's thirteen thousand jobs had required less skill or paid a little better—then, perhaps, the RenCen would have worked, luring whites downtown and spreading their wealth through the black city. It was an appealing fantasy, then and later. But in truth, by the time the center opened, Detroit needed more than a little trickle-down business to recreate a functioning community.

To survive, the city needed a real partnership between white suburbs and black city—not just Henry Ford II and his million-dollar investment, but also Irene McCabe and her shopping dollars. It needed tax revenues. It needed professional know-how. It needed small business and light industry and entrepreneurs willing to open shops in the neighborhoods. It needed middle-class people committed to repairing their homes and maintaining the civic order that would discourage criminals. It needed not just capital but cooperation—sustained, wholehearted cooperation between those who were part of the system and those stranded outside it. Not all the things needed were by definition white, but as it happened in Detroit in the seventies, without help from the white suburbs, the city didn't stand a chance. Instead of coming together as one community, the region divided along the color line. In place of cooperation, there was race baiting. Instead of working to create a climate that might encourage suburbanites to remain involved in a declining downtown—not an easy task under any circumstances—the city pursued an angry, color-coded agenda that eroded the quality of life for everyone. What destroyed Detroit was part economic, part geographic and part technological. But a functioning, cohesive region might have withstood even the challenge of global economic restructuring. In the end, what really killed the city was its failure to hold and pull together as one community. If ever integration mattered, it mattered in Detroit—and when it failed, the city went under.

With suburbanites coming less and less into town, black Detroit fell back on itself, retreating into a segregated cocoon. Race and race consciousness dominated awareness in the neighborhoods and among the city's new professional elite. Young bragged to reporters about the blacks in his administration and the black entrepreneurs landing city contracts. Residents talked proudly about "doing for themselves," about "self-determination" and local leadership. Magazines like *Ebony* celebrated Detroit as the nation's black capital, the place where, as Mayor Young put it, "blacks exercised more power than blacks anywhere in the United States." A dozen years after Stokely Carmichael coined the term, Black Power was a fact—at least in one big city.

Most of the time, the mood was one of pride and enthusiasm, though every now and then it edged toward something more defiant. Only "sentimentalists," *Ebony* noted bullishly, missed the old integrated, mainstream Detroit. The city might be smaller now, it might be poorer, but at least, blacks maintained, "It's ours." "I've never been concerned," Young boasted, "about upsetting white people. I'd rather not, but I'm not going to back away from something I know is right just to please whites." "We refuse in Detroit," he told another reporter, "to kiss their behinds."

Divisive as it was, Young's proud black rhetoric served him well, boosting his popularity and influence. Glowing media reports sang the praises of the wily, no-nonsense mayor. "He's fighting back," said *The Washington Post*, "'kicking ass,' as he puts it. A troublemaker, proud, belligerent, 'bad'—an unlikely [but impressive] leader of a resurrection." Tough and angry enough to fill the shoes of the fading Black Power elite—Carmichael, Rap Brown, the Panthers—but pragmatic enough to run a big city, Young was hailed from coast to coast as the new answer to the black leadership vacuum. Politicians sought his endorsement, business and policymakers called for advice. In 1976, he provided critical black support for candidate Jimmy Carter, backing him early in the presidential race and then publicly pardoning his campaign remark about the "ethnic purity" of segregated neighborhoods. Isolated racial and ethnic enclaves were "as American as apple pie," Young said, and before long it was almost fashionable for white liberals to say they believed in separatism.

Carter's election boosted Young's stock higher still. Several of the mayor's top aides went to Washington to join the government. His blueprint for federal aid to cities became the cornerstone of Carter's urban policy. Young let it be known that he was "constantly on the phone to the White House" and that he spent several days a month in Washington. In 1977, Carter named him vice chairman of the Democratic National Committee, and Young became a major player on the national political stage, appearing on talk shows, pulling strings in the Democratic Party, active in the U.S. Conference of Mayors.

Young's ties to the president paid off big for Detroit, pulling in federal dollars by the millions. Starting with LBJ's Great Society, Republicans as well as Democrats in Washington had seen it as their role to bolster big cities in times of trouble. But Young, always thinking in racial terms, had taken the notion one step further. In keeping with his theory that the larger white society had caused Detroit's ills, he maintained that the federal government was responsible for the city's well-being, on a permanent basis. To those who argued that outside money would be of little help until the city's black community began to put its own house in order, he answered angrily that they were blaming the victim, and he pushed the city toward greater and greater dependence on outside aid.

By the late 1970s, that dependence had reached alarming proportions, even by the standards of strapped rust-belt cities. In Young's first four years in office, state aid to Detroit doubled, and federal aid increased by over half. In the course of a decade, direct cash grants multiplied by a factor of six. Some of the money was earmarked for community development, employment training or other specific needs. But most of it was fungible and loosely regulated, if at all. In 1978—the peak year—outside funding accounted for 41 percent of the Detroit budget. Add the aid that came to the city school board, to Wayne County, to the regional development group, SEMCOG, and to two smaller municipalities tucked inside the boundaries of Detroit proper—all money eventually funneled into the city—and the total grew by nearly a third, to over $400 million. None of the city's monumental development projects could have been accomplished without federal dollars or tax breaks. Without state aid, the zoo, the library and the art museum would have had to close their doors. Between a quarter and a third of all city employees were paid with federal money, and even the most basic city services—police, firemen and sanitation department—required outside help to continue functioning.

Still, through the seventies, city services declined markedly. By the end of the decade, there was 30 percent less bus service than at the beginning, 50 percent less trash collection and 20 percent fewer firemen on duty. The $900 million allotted by President Ford to build a subway sat unused in the bank while city and suburb squabbled over how it should be spent. Detroit scraped through several severe budget crises, but there was no large-scale structural change of the kind that might have enabled the city to get off the federal dole. Even the showy construction projects meant to bring jobs and businesses to downtown generated on average only seven hundred jobs a year—a hardly noticeable improvement in the endemic unemployment that plagued Detroit. Still, through the mid- and later 1970s, Young rallied black supporters with an irresistible racial message, at once blaming white people—the feds and suburban taxpayers—for Detroit's decline and boasting about the millions of dollars he had wrung out of them. Far from being a source of concern, his dependence on outside aid was a matter of pride; he had, he crowed, "brought home the bacon" for the city.

The 1977 mayoral election exposed the region's racial polarization in stark relief. Young's main opponent was black city council member Ernest C. Browne, Jr. A reserved, churchgoing man with nearly three decades of government experience, Browne built his campaign around crime and values, scolding Young for setting a bad example with his irresponsible lifestyle and "gutter" vocabulary. On matters of policy, he promised to spend more money in the neighborhoods and make them safer by ending police affirmative action programs and reviving declining standards in the uniformed services. Though stiff and a little pompous, in his way he called Young's bluff brilliantly, charging the mayor bluntly with neglecting his people's needs while distracting them with empty race baiting—emotionally satisfying in the short run, but ultimately self-defeating. Yet, apt as it was, the message was lost on black Detroit. Early polling showed Young coasting easily with the support of 72 percent of black voters, compared to a measly 3 percent who said they favored Browne.

Both the Detroit business elite and the national liberal establishment came out for Young in a big way. Henry Ford corralled friends and associates for a thousand-dollar-a-plate fund-raiser at the tony Detroit Club. Prominent blacks flew in from all over the country: Coretta Scott King, Jesse Jackson, representatives from the Tuskegee Airmen and a variety of civil rights groups. Even the union movement—heavily white working-class as it was—threw its clout behind Young's candidacy. By the time November came around, there was no suspense. The mayor won in a landslide. Ernest Browne and his telling criticism disappeared from view; Young went back to business as usual. "The Young administration couldn't clean or light the streets," said *Detroit News* columnist George Cantor. "It wasn't delivering jobs, arresting criminals or even explaining its budgets to the newspapers. Still, the people went on voting for Young—because he said what they wanted to hear about whites and white racism."

Meanwhile, Young grew ever more unpopular in the white suburbs. The big fights of the later seventies were over transportation: first the subway, then a proposed new road between the city and Oakland County. Virtually nothing—no policy initiative, grant or agreement—could have done more for race relations or to boost the flagging Detroit economy. Increasingly isolated, jobless and poor, Detroit stood so close to Oakland's thriving new towns that many city dwellers could see the gleaming office towers from their windows. With new businesses mushrooming across the city line, the region desperately needed better roads—both to take Detroiters out to the suburbs to work and to bring suburbanites into town to spend money. By 1978, even Young was beginning to recognize this, and he called publicly for "détente" with the suburbs. But once again, as so often in the past, he couldn't bring himself to make the necessary compromises. Instead of détente, negotiations led only to the usual name-calling; instead of integration, more angry isolation. "Some major roads were not built," one suburban politician said bluntly, "because of the influence of Detroit officials." Within a year, relations had grown so sour that a group of suburban mayors called for seceding from Detroit's Wayne County, and the state legislature considered a bill to create a new county called Suburbia. Young's by now familiar response: "This is racism. [They're trying] to take over Detroit."

In the late 1970s, as earlier, nothing did more to keep suburbanites out of the city than their fear of crime. Affirmative action had succeeded in transforming the police department. The new black chief, William L. Hart, was a well-liked detective with twenty years of experience, and he presided over an increasingly black force: two of his five deputies, ten of twenty-one commanders and 34 percent of all patrolmen. Yet, year by year, recruitment scandals only seemed to grow worse. Applicants who had difficulty with qualifying exams were allowed to take them repeatedly until they passed, or were given the answers by an instructor. Force veterans complained that many rookies were physically unfit for the job. One press report found that the average recruit was reading at a fourth-grade level. Another discovered a dozen female officers who were supplementing their salaries with welfare checks. Then, in mid-1978, came a rash of shootings by trigger-happy rookies. Four inadequately trained young officers accidentally shot and killed themselves with their service revolvers. Five others killed or wounded civilians—in several cases because they didn't like the way someone talked back to them. Determined, despite the scandals, to meet its racial quotas, for the most part the Young administration ignored the flaps.

As the color of the department changed, so did its values. Chief Hart boasted of the "sensitivity" of his new recruits. Black cops went out of their way to take account of community concerns and on occasion, when they thought the law was insensitive, to look the other way. "I wouldn't write tickets for black kids," recalled Freddie Williams. "I wouldn't pick up people for loitering. A lot of people who talk about law and order are just people trying to protect their property. I wouldn't do things that didn't make sense to me ethically." Even when the crime statistics began to rise again, with the economic downturn in 1979, the black department dismissed calls for a return to stiffer, conventional standards. "Racism and sour grapes," responded Chief Hart to complaints about what affirmative action was doing to the department. (In 1992, Hart himself would be convicted of embezzling $2.6 million from the police force.)

Still, for the region's whites—inside Eight Mile Road and beyond—crime remained the city's number one problem. Whites living in the northwest corner of the city reported being burglarized two, three and four times in as many months. Friends from the suburbs wouldn't come to visit because if they parked their cars on the street, they would be stolen. One young professional who moved east from Detroit was so frightened that he wouldn't go back to visit his parents' graves; things had gotten so bad, he heard from friends, that local bands were mugging and raping white visitors to the cemetery. Under pressure from Ford and Fisher, Mayor Young would occasionally talk tough about dealing with criminals. "The perception," said Oakland County prosecutor Brooks Patterson, "was that Young gave lip service to cracking down. But when proposals came up—for tougher laws in Lansing, for tougher judges on the bench—he was AWOL in the fight. By the time he got religion, or seemed to, it was too late. By then the schools were out of control. The streets were out of control. You couldn't put the genie back in the bottle."

The 1980 Republican National Convention, held just a few blocks from the RenCen, exposed the racial isolation of Detroit for all the nation to see. The idea of luring the gathering to Detroit was classic Young. Like his monumental downtown development, the convention would bolster the city's image and, he insisted hopefully, "catalyze" other business. Max Fisher helped woo the Republican Party. The nearly bankrupt city spent $2 million to spruce up downtown. Dozens of derelict buildings were demolished, abandoned cars removed from boulevards. Huge murals were painted to camouflage X-rated moviehouses. Policemen were put on twelve-hour shifts. The administration used community development funds to finish the Joe Louis Arena just in time for the convention, though it had to close the inner-city Detroit General Hospital for lack of funds. Some delegates arrived from the airport by helicopter. Others whizzed in on recessed, landscaped express-ways. Mayor Young addressed the opening session: "You [have] offered us the opportunity to show you and the world our revitalized city." But most visiting journalists saw through the sham, and many did stories on what one called "The Detroit the GOP Won't See."

Journalists noticed that virtually no delegates ventured beyond walking distance from the riverfront. Newsmen who did a little research discovered that for all the showy new construction downtown, fewer than ten building permits had been issued the year before for single-family houses anywhere in the city. Heading out of the central business district, reporters gasped when they came to the edge of the Potemkin Village created by the murals and the unlikely palm trees planted the week before. Touring the neighborhoods, they stumbled on all the things that had been hidden or removed from downtown: twenty thousand abandoned homes and vacant lots, piles of old machinery rusting in the streets, homeless people, drug dealers and able-bodied youths with nothing to do. With one in four city residents unemployed, there were plenty of people in the streets to interview, and most of them made clear that they felt hopelessly remote from what they saw as the white world. "Politics is a game, man," said one youth. "The convention being here—it don't make no difference." Many people asked had never heard of Ronald Reagan, being nominated for president just a few blocks away. One twenty-five year old, out of work, said he didn't care who lived in the White House. "Whoever is up there," he explained, "is not worried about us."

Even Detroiters who still hoped for one regional community knew that it was all over when the downtown Hudson's finally closed its doors eighteen months after the GOP convention. For more than ninety years, the great department store had been the Macy's of the Midwest, the nation's third largest retail outlet and a legendary presence in Detroit. The building took up an entire block: fifteen vast shopping floors, complete with crystal chandeliers, wood-paneled elevators and brass water fountains. The gleaming glass cases had once been stocked with top-quality merchandise, everything from pots and pans to silver fox furs. The store's reputation as treasure trove and arbiter of regional taste outshone even the opulent decor, and shoppers had come from as far away as Lansing and Toledo to register their weddings, furnish their homes, buy the latest fashions or treat their kids to a Christmas outing. But by the late seventies, most of the Hudson Company's business had moved to its nine new branches in suburban malls, and the once magical downtown store was unrecognizable.

Too quiet by half and more than a little musty, the big brick building stood almost empty. Guards manned the doors. The great display windows were dark. Several floors were closed, and bored salespeople chatted noisily among themselves, waiting for customers who did not come. Hoping against hope, the civic-minded store management kept the flagship open long after its profits ceased and most other major retailers had left town. But in 1982, Hudson's gave up and announced that it would close at the turn of the year. Even the last holiday shopping season was hardly worth the store's while, and in January 1983 there were chains on the doors of the old, grand Woodward Avenue entrance. Mayor Young and other city officials accused company executives of racism: "I guess," said city council president Erma Henderson, "the blacks, the poor and the elderly . . . don't fit into their plans." But most of the great department store's loyal clientele were more mournful than angry. "For me," said one customer of forty years, "Hudson's *was* Detroit. And when it's gone, there will be nothing left."

By the early 1980s, a bumper sticker had appeared in the city: "Will the last one who leaves please turn out the lights." The recessions of the seventies had made it more difficult for the working class to go as it became harder and harder to sell a house in Detroit. But whites continued to trickle out to the suburbs even in the worst of economic times, and as in the past, it took about five years for a neighborhood to go from all white to all black. In the course of the 1970s, the city had lost a fifth of its population—Young would call this the biggest demographic shift "in the history of man"—and, worse still, nearly a quarter of its jobs. In the late 1970s and early 1980s, downtown commercial activity declined by nearly half and, according to Young, homes and other buildings "were abandoned faster than we could tear them down." As even a casual visitor could tell, the city was dying.

By then, all of America had heard about the black underclass. No one yet talked much about its isolation or the role that isolation—from jobs, hope or mainstream values—played in causing pathological patterns of poverty. But anyone could see that Detroit was leading the nation in black destitution and joblessness. With white employment hovering around one in ten, black unemployment exceeded 27 percent—and the rate among black teenagers reached into the 60 percent range. By decade's end, one in three city blacks lacked any earned income. More than 90 percent lived in segregated neighborhoods. Nearly a quarter of the population had sunk below the poverty line, and according to some estimates, more than half received some kind of public assistance.

The city's physical isolation was mirrored in its mood: separatism, alienation, prejudice and conspiracy theories. A survey conducted by the *Detroit Free Press* compared 1980 with 1977 and found the city's blacks far more mistrustful of whites, far less interested in racial mingling. The number who thought whites couldn't care less about blacks had doubled, to 43 percent. So had the count of those who felt they could trust no white people—now a full one-third. Support for integration had declined markedly, to 23 percent. Only one in five people favored desegregated schools, and two-thirds now opted for better housing in a black neighborhood rather than a home in a mixed enclave. Consumed with issues of racial pride, self-sufficiency, block voting and what they still called "civil rights activism," city residents hardly seemed to notice the degree to which their isolation was breeding suspicion, making further isolation all the more likely—along with more mistrust and more prejudice. As for the city's dwindling whites, by 1980, 70 percent agreed with the sentence: "Ever since blacks became the majority in Detroit, white people are often discriminated against here."

As ever, Coleman Young led the way in this mistrust, preaching anger, blame and self-segregation. The mayor's personal style became ever more insular and embattled. By the late 1970s, a small circle of friends more or less ran the city. The press was given less and less access. The mayor grew more eccentric and more secretive. He consulted aides on the telephone after midnight, often disappeared from the office for days at a time and took to giving interviews in his bathrobe and slippers. With Detroit visibly falling apart,

Max Fisher noted—and he meant it as a compliment—that Young was holding the city together by the "sheer force of his will and personality."

If anything, the more besieged the city grew, the better the mayor seemed to like it. Young's list of enemies had not changed much since 1974—the press, the feds, the suburbs and the police—and, together with other outsiders, they were responsible for all that was wrong in the city. Unemployment was big business's fault—or the Arabs' or the Japanese'. Low school achievement scores could be blamed on the state's inequitable funding. The deterioration of Detroit's housing stock was the work of discriminatory mortgage policies. Crime was a product of white racism: prejudice caused unemployment caused black rage caused murder and mayhem. At the same time, Young insisted, crime was not really that bad in Detroit, just much exaggerated by a sensationalist media. Anyone who criticized the city was by definition bigoted. So were those who tried to hold black people accountable or suggest they were in any way responsible for the troubles that beset them. "We're not in control of our own destiny," the nation's most powerful black mayor told a reporter. "Anybody who tells you [that we are] is somebody you ought to take a second look at—because that's a racist." "Young fought the same battle over and over," commented columnist George Cantor. "Any sort of racism, persecution or outside threat: he'd point to it and rally black Detroiters behind him. He'd found a good song—and he kept on singing it."

By 1983, after nearly a decade in office, Young was still one of the most popular elected officials in the country. Older, grayer, a little heavier, but buoyant as ever and still mischievous, he knew—and Detroit knew—that the mayor's job would be his as long as he wanted it. The breaking of a major corruption scandal came as a nasty surprise, but it in no way knocked the mayor off his stride. The Vista deal was, by all appearances, a fairly conventional kickback scheme. It involved a sewage company; a $7.5 million city contract; a black entrepreneur, Darralyn Bowers—one of Young's closest friends and campaign contributors—and a top city aide, Charles Beckham, charged with taking bribes in connection with the letting of the contract to Bowers's Vista sludge-hauling concern. Investigations revealed no illegality on the mayor's part. Nevertheless, in trademark style, Young responded to the probe by siding with the accused, once again rallying Detroit blacks against what he claimed was the oppressive white system.

As so often in the past, the forces of law and order were cast as racist. Young accused the FBI of targeting him personally—because he was black and powerful. "I can just picture [them]," he charged, "salivating at the thought of nailing my black ass." The mayor insisted that the charges against Bowers and Beckham were unfounded, fabricated by the feds as part of their effort to undo him. Revelations that the FBI had bugged Young's town house and recorded hours of conversation between him and the accused entrepreneur played right into the mayor's hands, and instead of retreating, he escalated his assault on federal authority, claiming that the government had been out to get him for forty years. "To attack Coleman Young," he charged, "is to attack Detroit—and to attack Detroit is to attack black."

Eventually, six people—including Bowers and Beckham—either pleaded guilty or were convicted in court of conspiracy, bribery and fraud in connection with the Vista case. Still, Young maintained their innocence, and if anything his conspiracy theories grew wilder. Like Marion Barry a decade later—and he would defend Barry in precisely these terms—Young dismissed not just the case but the legal system as inherently biased. The city's black elite rallied behind the mayor, toasting Beckham at a gala fund-raiser the night before his sentencing. "Char-lee, Char-lee," the crowd chanted, as one prominent speaker after another took the stage to proclaim his innocence and call the system racist. TV cameras panning the room revealed a *Who's Who* of black Detroit: three hundred of the most influential black politicians and businessmen in America. The next day, Beckham was sentenced to three years in prison, and when the fund-raiser was broadcast on local TV, it fueled angry indignation across Detroit's neighborhoods: a new surge of alienation from what was described bitterly as "the white man's law."

It was hard to imagine the city's racial isolation growing worse, but in the wake of the Vista probe, according to pollsters, black Detroiters' distrust of the FBI doubled. Poor neighborhoods and middle-class enclaves alike reviled the federal government and the court system as they had long reviled local police. Years before the O. J. Simpson trial revealed what many blacks thought of the criminal justice system, black Detroiters had already given up on it, and most seemed to have no sense of how their mistrust was devastating the city.

Out in the suburbs, many whites had lost interest, but many also mourned the place they once called home. George Cantor, by now a leading voice of white disenchantment, remembers giving a speech in suburban Troy not long after Beckham was sentenced. "My fondest wish," he told his audience, "is that someday this city will once again be the thriving and vibrant place it was when I grew up here." Before he could go on, the columnist recalled, the room burst into spontaneous applause. But no one, Cantor included, knew how to reach out to the black city. Aggrieved, isolated—and encouraged by racemongering leadership—much of black Detroit wanted nothing to do with the white world. Severed from the regional economy, cut off from meaningful contact with whites, many city dwellers drifted beyond the pale of hope, their racial fantasies blossoming wildly, and even when race and poverty didn't bar them from the mainstream, their alienation sealed the door shut.

Part Three

ATLANTA

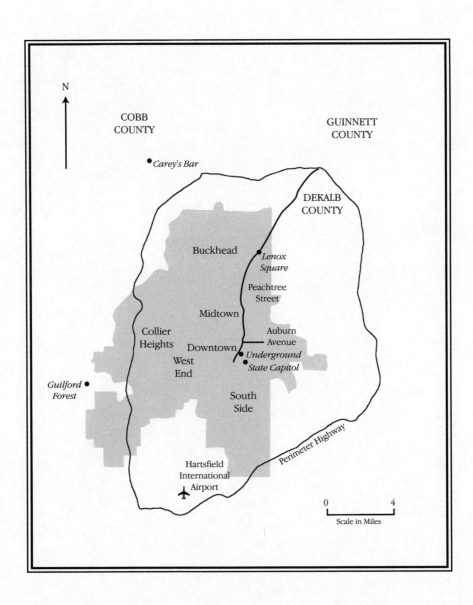

N

COBB
COUNTY

GUINNETT
COUNTY

• *Carey's Bar*

DEKALB
COUNTY

Buckhead

• *Lenox*
Square

Peachtree
Street

Midtown

Collier
Heights

Auburn
Avenue

Downtown

• *Underground*
State Capitol

West
End

Guilford •
Forest

South
Side

Perimeter Highway

Hartsfield
International
Airport

0   4

Scale in Miles

Chapter 12

TO LAY DOWN THE BURDEN

The photo of Andrew Young striding across the airstrip leaped off the front page of *The New York Times,* at once reassuring readers and bolstering their most hopeful assumptions. Whatever had been going on in Detroit through the past decade, it was a long time since many white Americans had thought much about race. Richard Nixon's turbulent presidency, the last years of the Vietnam War, the unfolding Watergate debacle: other seemingly more pressing matters had pushed blacks off the front pages, and many whites assumed that the problem had been solved—that now, with legal barriers removed, blacks were quietly making their way into the mainstream. Smiling, confident, handsome, Andrew Young seemed to confirm these unspoken hopes. A packed briefcase tucked under one arm, pretty wife and tousle-haired young son trudging at his side, Young was on his way to work—for the new president he had all but elected. The story beneath the photo explained what had happened: among Jimmy Carter's closest political allies, touted by the former governor as "one of the best personal friends I have in the world," Young was credited with legitimizing Carter in the eyes of blacks and helping swing the South—by now a lost cause for most Democratic presidential hopefuls—into the Georgian candidate's column.

The symbolism seemed almost fairy-tale perfect—at last a happy ending to the long, ugly history. Here was one of Martin Luther King's chief lieutenants, a man who only years before had been risking his life at protest

marches, journeying by private plane to the home of the president-elect—
not very far from the streets where he had braved police dogs and water
hoses—to claim his reward for the campaign effort: a cabinet-level position
as chief United States delegate to the United Nations. Not only that, but the
thoughtful young congressman was full of praise for the racial progress he
felt had been achieved in the past decade: "It isn't 'The Kingdom' yet," he
said, "but it's genuine. . . . The fundamental changes are there, and they're
not just for a few people. A broad base of opportunity has been established."

With his manner even more than his presence, Andrew Young told the
nation that blacks had arrived. Well-spoken, mild-mannered and yet
supremely self-confident, a consummate behind-the-scenes player who
never seemed to get angry, Young personified the kind of leadership many
whites had hoped to see emerging from black America. Walking across the
grass runway at Plains, his comely, middle-class family at his side, he seemed
in a flash to obliterate years of bad memories of Stokely Carmichael, of inner
cities burning through the night and fists raised angrily in the air. A dignified
black man, Young nevertheless wore his race lightly—as if it hardly mattered
to him. Asked by reporters about Carter's debt to black voters, he dismissed
the question and the divisions it implied: "It's the same debt that he owes all
American people. One of the things about black people is that they are people and they suffer the same problems and they are concerned about the
same things as a good many white people." The country's most powerful
black man, an emblem of racial triumph, Young presented himself—and it
seemed to be true—as a rising insider who just happened to be black.

By 1976, "integration" was a rarely used word, but it wasn't hard to see the
larger significance of the Carter victory. Outside of Carter's home state,
Georgia, Gerald Ford had polled a solid majority of southern whites. But
they were outnumbered by southern blacks who had turned out big and
voted overwhelmingly for Carter, ensuring his victory in ten of the eleven
Deep South states. (Pivotal black votes also gave Carter a winning margin in
three border and northern states.) With this, blacks more than fulfilled the
dream at the heart of the civil rights struggle: black registration had doubled
in the decade since the Voting Rights Act, and now as Martin Luther King
had predicted, black people were using this prize to win all others. Movement veteran and stalwart integrationist John Lewis called the day: "Hands
that once picked cotton now can pick a president." No one understood this
better than Lewis—a man who had had his skull cracked at Selma demonstrating peacefully for the right to vote. Though long overdue and hardly

enough for many understandably impatient blacks, this was, Lewis and Young knew, a huge triumph for their people—a critical step over the threshold of American society.

Basking in the Carter victory, Young launched a single-handed media campaign to talk about how far both black and white had come. He steered every interview in this direction and brought the subject up in every speech. "I'm ready to lay down the burden of race," he declared jubilantly, waving aside hundreds of years of history. "You don't have to demonstrate when you can pick up a phone and call someone," he said on another occasion. Pressed on whether there really was a New South—what about white voters' Republicanism, their continued resistance to busing?—he confidently dismissed the question. What about George Wallace and his supporters? Even they "weren't necessarily racists," Young argued. "People were alienated because they weren't being paid attention to." Forgiving, optimistic, determined to work within the system, Young was convinced that bigotry was abating north and south, and if he had one reason for backing Carter, it was because the governor grasped this. "Carter understands that people can change," Young explained. "He has seen people change. He knows what is necessary to help them change." Appealing to whites' goodwill, not their guilt, voicing blacks' hopeful faith instead of their anger, Young tantalizingly recalled the King legacy—and seemed for a moment to be opening a door that many thought had slammed forever shut.

Most startling of all, picking up where King had been brusquely silenced, Young dared to revive talk of color blindness. When introduced as a champion of the black man, he would interrupt: "And whites, and whites." Queried about who would be in the Carter cabinet, he assured reporters that there would be plenty of blacks, but because of their qualifications, not their color. "There are almost no specifically black problems," he insisted. "Black people get sick and have trouble paying the hospital bill, but so do white people . . . in larger numbers than blacks." Taking the concept of integration to its logical extreme, Young touted a radically new notion—what he called "deracialization." Blacks want what all Americans want, he argued, and they "are sophisticated enough to realize that their problems have got to be deracialized." As for himself: "I have never wanted to be, and have always insisted that I would not be, the black intermediary with the Carter administration. . . . No black leader should try to just deal with black issues."

Just how many blacks, north or south, Young represented was hard to tell. Outside of Detroit and a few other places like it, the mid- to late seventies were a time of relative quiet in the black movement—a lull between the angry battles of the late sixties and early seventies and the fights to come over affirmative action. There had been no big demonstrations in several years, no riots and few shoot-outs with white policemen. The blacks in the news were mostly "black firsts": the first black secretary of HUD, the first black president of the U.S. Conference of Mayors, the first black Secretary of the Army, the first black Episcopal bishop, the first black astronauts and the first black Wimbledon champion. The television show *Roots* aired in 1977, drawing 130 million viewers, but for its author and protagonist, Alex Haley, African pride still seemed to sit easily with a deeply felt American patriotism.

Opinion polls were more ambiguous: surveys done through the 1970s showed persistent black alienation from white society. There had been some improvement early in the decade—five- to ten-point increases in the number of blacks who felt race relations were better, who trusted whites, eschewed violence and welcomed white neighbors. Yet most polls continued to show deep skepticism about the future and high levels of racial mistrust, if not outright hostility. One sounding found that more than twice as many blacks (56 percent) felt close to people in Africa than felt close to white Americans (24 percent). More than half expected the next twenty years to bring less discrimination, but close to a third worried that "things will probably remain the same." As for Andrew Young's claim that he was willing to lay down the burden of race, even as they made their way into the mainstream, most other American blacks seemed uncertain. Asked, "Which would you say is more important to you—being black or being American?" 20 percent answered, "being black," 9 percent said, "being an American," and a full 71 percent fell into the cloudy, catch-all category labeled uninformatively "equally important."

Like Carter and his astonishing victory at the hands of blacks, Andrew Young's home city, Atlanta, was widely regarded as an emblem of improved race relations. The success story of the civil rights movement, the most enlightened and cosmopolitan city in the South, it was a place where both blacks and whites seemed to be prospering—and living more or less comfortably with each other. In the past decade, like Detroit, Atlanta had become a black Mecca and a national showcase of black political power. But unlike in Detroit, the white money had stayed, and instead of a "black city," Atlanta was seen as a biracial one. There was no wholesale emptying of downtown, not even—despite a national recession—a noticeable pause in growth. Blacks controlled City Hall; whites dominated the economy. But both black and white leaders saw the advantages of compromise and they seemed to be running the city together—to all appearances, harmoniously. By the time Young traveled to Plains to claim his reward in 1976, "the city too busy to hate" had emerged as the showpiece of the New South—an entire region, the congressman and others claimed, now ready to lay down the burden of race.

Founded in the 1840s as a railroad depot, Atlanta had always been quintessentially southern and yet different. The city was geographically blessed with a temperate climate and a natural raison d'être as a regional market center, and it became the seat of the South's then tiny middle class: a bustling traders' town where, it was said, a small boy's first words were "Sell, sell, sell." Even at the turn of the century, when most of the region was still rural, Atlanta's Peachtree Street was a place to get insurance, hire a lawyer, write a contract or issue stock. And unlike much of the rest of Dixie, which was dominated by landowners committed to the status quo, Atlantans devoted themselves to economic growth regardless of the racial consequences.

This difference emerged with a vengeance in the 1940s as the city's scrappy traders prepared to take advantage of the postwar economic boom. To northern eyes, Atlanta was still a distinctly southern small town, painfully class-conscious and stratified by rigid Jim Crow custom. A small business elite decided all municipal matters. Coca-Cola was the only big-time company in town, and together with the banks, utilities, important realtors and department storeowners who dominated Peachtree Street, it all but appointed the city government. Coca-Cola's longtime president, Robert Woodruff, had lunch every day for nearly a quarter of a century with longtime mayor William Hartsfield, who boasted unashamedly, "I have never taken an action as mayor but what I would consider the effect of national publicity about it on the Coca-Cola Company." Like all of his peers, Hartsfield was an unembarrassed segregationist. "Total segregation and subjugation of the Negro was a reality that was seldom questioned, even by the Negro himself," Hartsfield's successor Ivan Allen, Jr., said of their era. "They were there—as our maids, as our yard men, as our street sweepers—but we never actually saw them. . . . That was the system . . . and the thought of challenging it occurred to few southerners."

Nevertheless, in the mid-1940s, the city's business leaders realized they needed black voters, and unlike their rural neighbors, they were flexible enough to make common cause with them. Hartsfield and his Peachtree

Street backers were determined to refurbish the city, positioning it for big-time growth. But with the white middle class already fleeing and poorer whites too committed to the Jim Crow order to risk any change, only the black middle class shared the mayor's interest in development. The city's six traditionally black colleges had spawned a thriving black bourgeoisie: one of the country's first black millionaires, black banks, black fraternities, black Boy Scout troops and a luxurious black middle-class neighborhood. Comfortable, confident and increasingly restless, in 1946 this black aristocracy launched a massive voter registration drive, raising the black community's participation from 2 to 27 percent. Hartsfield knew a windfall when he saw one and immediately reached out, inviting the city's black elders into an unusual coalition. Whites and blacks were far from equal partners—that was unthinkable even in Atlanta. Still, a tacit deal was struck, an understanding based on mutual interest, that paved the way for improving race relations for decades to come.

The Hartsfield coalition was still intact when the civil rights revolution began to well up a decade later. By then, Morehouse College was revered across black America as "the black Harvard." The black business center on Auburn Avenue had taken on an almost mythic renown as "Sweet Auburn": a city-within-a-city with a complete array of merchants, doctors, lawyers, accountants, construction companies and bonding agents. Tradesmen and contractors who ventured to visit white colleagues across town still had to use the back door of any white business establishment. But in their own world, on the south side of the city, they lived in a style not unlike their richer white peers': a small, insular world, structured by old friendships and exclusive clubs, where a close-knit elite took all decisions for the community, usually behind closed doors and without public discussion. Martin Luther King, Jr., was born into this world. Andrew Young and other movement leaders joined it when they moved to Atlanta in the late fifties. One of King's closer friends was rising black contractor Herman Russell, and decades later, when Russell had become one of the richest black men in America, his office would be decorated with photos of his and King's young families at poolside.

White Atlantans knew virtually nothing of this world, but when it came time for the city to vote, the two elites worked in choreographed harmony. Though the black elders were only "silent partners," informed rather than consulted about policy changes, they knew the votes they controlled were crucial to the coalition, and they traded them carefully for improved public services. The city's black community became known for its moderation on racial matters. The white "power structure"—the term was coined in the fifties to describe the elite in Atlanta—got the social peace needed for the city to take off economically. Together, black and white leaders conspired to work around the city's poorer, more prejudiced whites. And the black middle class, with its gradually expanding power, began to share in the wealth generated by the city's growth.

The civil rights revolution when it came was less a revolution than a quiet molting, discreet and almost consensual. Hartsfield set the pattern in the late fifties when he decided it was time to get rid of the "White" and "Colored" signs on restrooms at the airport. Instead of taking them down all at once in a public show that might antagonize white voters, he gradually reduced them in size until they could hardly be seen and then removed them. Not long after, when the federal government declared segregated buses illegal, the mayor and his silent partners arranged for a group of prominent blacks to stage a symbolic challenge: a short ride on an all-white bus route to provide the basis for a local court case. Even so, instead of harassing the protesters, the bus driver gave them a friendly tour of the city, and the police chief, who had to be importuned to make arrests, refused to close the cell door. In 1961, the Peachtree elite all but orchestrated the desegregation of the city's schools with a sympathetic PR campaign, earning congratulations from both President Kennedy and the national media. The desegregation of the city's public accommodations was somewhat more contentious. Defying elders' pleas for a moderate, prearranged protest, black students organized sit-ins, and several hundred were arrested. But the national publicity, contemptuous and unrelenting, was exactly what business leaders had been dreading, and it wasn't long before they voted unanimously to capitulate.

From the beginning, the civic elite was out way ahead of its followers. Residential neighborhood change was as panicked in Atlanta as anywhere, and whites fled the public schools rather than integrate them. As late as 1965, the city had no black elected officials, and public hospital wards were strictly segregated. Most of the decade's enlightened decisions were taken by a few men, meeting quietly behind the scenes, whether at the all-white Commerce Club or over grits and fried chicken at the movement's unofficial headquarters, Paschal's Motor Lodge.

Still, as the years went by, it seemed that ordinary people too might be signing on for gradual, Atlanta-style racial change. After the sit-ins, there were hardly any confrontational demonstrations downtown. The city's one riot— if it could be called that—was a small disturbance provoked by outsider

Stokely Carmichael, and it was over by nine in the evening, leaving few serious injuries. The business leaders were notoriously wary of rank-and-file whites, and their doubts seemed confirmed in 1966 when Georgians elected Lester Maddox as governor. But businessmen who used this as an excuse to go on governing the city over lunch or at the club failed to notice other, contradictory signs: the defeat of Maddox twice for mayor of Atlanta and the election of the outspokenly liberal Ivan Allen to City Hall. Whatever white people really felt, one poll-taker recalled, already in the mid-sixties it was unfashionable to sound racist in Atlanta. A flattering national reputation as "the city too busy to hate" appealed to the pride of the common man as well as the magnate. "Eventually, it rubbed off on the general public," business insider Dan Sweat remembered. "The typical traveling salesman from Atlanta is as proud as anybody else. He goes around boasting of the good race relations we have here—even if he doesn't know anybody of the other race."

Envious visitors would ask what made Atlanta different, and some proud residents thought southern culture was key. "We blacks and whites had grown up together," one man explained, "eating the same food and learning the same southern manners. We know each other." Still others talked about what was at stake for both whites and blacks: their investment, big and small, in a city said to be "growing higher each month" and plainly, in the sixties, poised for yet more fantastic growth. Still others credited the local leadership—able, moderate blacks patient enough to let reform take its course and a white civic elite smart enough to see the racial future. Some of the explanations, even by insiders, were more cynical than others. "It's all boosterism," said some: a "myth," a "lie," a "veneer," "hypocrisy." The white old guard gave up just enough power, this view held, to keep the peace and maintain an image for investors, but it never really let go of the reins—and meanwhile most ordinary whites fled to the suburbs. ("The city too busy moving to hate" was a skeptical version of the boosters' slogan.)

But whatever their motives, the fact was that people modified their lives in the sixties, often dramatically, and many, particularly those who came of age in these years, talked of their sense of relief at finally walking out from under Jim Crow. "There's no question about it," political columnist Bill Shipp recalled. "There was a sense of relief—relief that you no longer had to maintain the old customs. You could stop worrying that you'd gotten too far to the back of the bus, that you'd drunk from the wrong fountain or wandered into the wrong restroom. The change was a freeing of both races." In Atlanta, as in other parts of the South—then later, the North—shame about the racial past proved to be a powerfully effective goad for change, and it set a standard that future generations would feel compelled to live up to. "The resistance melted surprisingly fast," commented Andrew Young. "The refusal to hate, the willingness to forgive and begin a new pattern of relationships. . . . We experienced one of the most radical shifts in law and tradition in human history."

By the early 1970s, Atlanta's racial moderation was paying off big. Growth came not in spurts but in a long, steady push, at levels that astounded even the Peachtree Street elite. One Fortune 500 headquarters sprang up after another, and in the period between 1960 and 1972, the city added a startling twenty-three thousand jobs a year. As pundits across the nation bemoaned "the crisis of the city," Atlanta seemed in a world apart, its skyline growing visibly taller with each lucrative quarter. Northern mayors like John Lindsay and Jerome Cavanagh watched with envy as young people flocked into town, looking to make their lives in a dynamic but livable city. "There was nowhere else in the South to go," remembered one young woman who came then, part of a newcomer population dubbed "the youngest, wealthiest, smartest and most ambitious in the country." The once rough market outpost became known for its cosmopolitanism and gracious charm, a combination, one newsman said, of "Yankee briskness" and "Southern manners."

By proving to the North that the racial past was really past, Atlanta broke the spell that had isolated the South since the Civil War. The old sense of defeat and humiliation—the habit of mind that had long defined the region—gave way overnight to an optimism based on the prospect of unlimited business growth. The great symbolic moment came in 1966, when Atlanta opened its new stadium, welcoming the Deep South's first major league baseball and football teams. "Atlanta had arrived," Ivan Allen recalled. That "single structure . . . signified [that we were] a national city." The most common comparison was with Birmingham, another southern city just 120 miles to the west. In 1950, Birmingham and Atlanta had been the same size, two small, dusty, old-fashioned towns, vying to become the region's capital. By 1970, there was no comparison—and everyone in Atlanta knew why. "We did the right thing," one business lawyer put it, "while Birmingham gave itself a black eye."

E ven so, in the early seventies, a half decade before Andrew Young traveled to Plains, Atlanta was beginning to look more and more like other American cities. In the South as in the North, the problem in big urban areas was a problem of race, and in Atlanta as in Detroit, there was no escaping it. Atlanta was less than half the size of Detroit, warm, civil and genteel—not gritty, grimy or violent. Its much younger economy was vastly healthier, and unlike the Motor City, whose soul was quintessentially industrial, Atlanta had always been a service-sector town. The heart of the place, once the train station, was now the air terminal: one wag joked that downtown was "a bunch of buildings and stuff next to the Atlanta airport." And the work the hub generated—retail, regional sales, professional services, tourism and the convention trade—only reinforced the city's white-collar ethos. Educated, gracious, leafy and spread out, Atlanta was as different as different could be from crumbling Detroit. But in Atlanta too, by the early seventies, a growing population of poor, unskilled migrant blacks was transforming the character of the city.

The black population welled up over the majority mark at just about the same time in both places. By the early seventies in Atlanta, gangs were a much-discussed problem, and the neighborhoods tipping one after the other from white to black learned to brace themselves for the inevitable shoplifting and muggers. The continuing influx of out-of-town white professionals made it hard to track the extent of middle-class white flight, but already by the start of the seventies, there was no mistaking the general population trend or its likely impact on the tax base. Then, in 1973, after a brief and plainly transitional, final white mayoralty, Atlanta elected the South's first big-city black mayor, Maynard Jackson, sworn in the same week as Detroit's Coleman Young.

Jackson came from a cultured, middle-class family so patrician, it was said, that "if he'd been born in Boston, he would have been a Cabot or a Lodge." He was an academic prodigy, a Morehouse graduate with a thriving business-law practice, witty, well-spoken, even grandiloquent in an old-fashioned southern way. But he also represented a new generation of younger, angrier blacks. Only thirty-five when he was elected mayor, he had come of age during the civil rights struggle and had defied Atlanta's black elders, who felt that he should "wait his turn" to run for office. Over six feet tall, weighing close to three hundred pounds, Jackson called himself the "youngest, fattest, blackest mayor in America," and he plainly enjoyed the way his quips and his alligator-skin boots unsettled the old guard, black as well as white.

The Peachtree elite were not sure how to read or handle him. Put off by the campaign rhetoric of outgoing mayor Sam Massell—his slogan, "Atlanta's Too Young to Die" was an explicit reference to the likely racial transition—many civic leaders had supported Jackson, or at least hedged their bets. As in Detroit, many in the elite felt a black mayor might be best equipped to govern the changing city, and, as one said, "we were running hard to keep up with our image" on racial matters. When election day came, Jackson pulled down more than 20 percent of the white vote, and most business leaders seemed reconciled to the changing of the guard. Some insiders even remember a brief honeymoon. But in Atlanta as in Detroit, the racial peace did not last long.

The civic elite did not give up on the city, and there was astonishingly little local business flight. Unlike Detroit, the regional economy was still relatively centralized, and an incredible building boom—seventeen new skyscrapers, $1 to $1.5 billion in new construction in progress—made pulling out unthinkable for leading investors. The institutional arm of the elite, a business association called Central Atlanta Progress (CAP), campaigned hard, sometimes with Jackson, to attract new, out-of-state business. In typical Atlanta fashion, the Peachtree crowd also tried to paper over its friction with the mayor—the last thing anybody wanted was a round of bad national press—and to a large degree, they succeeded.

But out of the public eye, Atlantan leaders hunkered down for what would later be called "the Eight Years' War"—an unrelenting, behind-the-scenes struggle between the black mayor and the power structure. The issues were the same in Atlanta as in Detroit: the cops, the schools, metropolitan consolidation, downtown crime, white flight and the newest black demand—for affirmative action. For all its middle-class élan, black Atlanta was also a desperately poor city—by one measure, the second poorest in the country (after Newark, New Jersey). The disadvantaged part of the population was far more alienated than the rest, and both it and the middle class were increasingly taken with black pride and Black Power. The election of a black mayor raised expectations to the boiling point, and—whatever his temperament—Jackson could ill afford the deferential patience of the older black elite. Like Coleman Young, he campaigned and governed on a racially charged promise to bring outsiders into government and high-level business circles. He made no secret of his own racial pride or his desire to make Atlanta an important black capital. "Atlanta is the best city in America for black people to live," he announced early on, and devoted himself, at the expense of much else, to the goal of black empowerment.

"Black and white communication is an old thing in this town, but this was a new game," remembered CAP chairman Dan Sweat. "It's one thing to sit down with a few college presidents or ministers, another thing to sit with a great big, impressive black mayor with real political power." Precisely because, unlike Detroiters, they could not leave, Atlanta's white businessmen were much more threatened by an ideologically hostile mayor they could not control. What bothered most of them was not so much Jackson's color as his grit and bristling racial agenda: his suspicion and resentment of the old white elite, his outsiders' determination to take power rather than share it. "We all knew that the city had to change from lily-white to salt-and-pepper, if not black," said another prominent businessman. "But Maynard Jackson did it poorly in a public relations way. He wanted to rub the change in the faces of the white community."

One of the biggest fights was over police reform. Like Coleman Young in Detroit, Jackson was determined to overhaul what he saw as a racist force, no matter what the consequences for the city. He began by firing the existing chief, but the man resisted in court, and Jackson trumped him by creating a position above his—a job he filled with a black man with no police experience, who happened to be an old college roommate. The new chief, Reginald Eaves, was then in and out of the news for several years in connection with one scandal after another: nepotism, influence peddling, misuse of police funds and cheating on the police promotion exam. Eventually Jackson was forced to get rid of Eaves, but not before the mayor had convinced the Peachtree crowd that he was more concerned with curbing the police than pursuing criminals. "No more 'police brutality' has come to mean no more pushing around of blacks," said downtown developer and longtime liberal John Portman. "The word is out that Atlanta is soft on crime." "You can call down to the police station and you can say two black fellows just robbed me," another white merchant complained, "and it'll be fifteen minutes before it gets on the radio—to give them time to get away." Within a few years, the growing lawlessness forced Jackson to crack down, significantly increasing the size of the police department. But by then it was too late; as in Detroit, the crime rate in Atlanta was out of sight—by the end of the decade, the worst in the country.

A second major controversy involved the city's schools, still largely segregated in 1973. Atlanta spent considerably more per child than the average suburban Georgia district, but students were failing in large numbers and dropping out, and, increasingly, white families were withdrawing their kids. Already by 1970, white enrollment had fallen to half what it was in 1963; by 1973, the white share was down to 23 percent. Though black opinion was less interested in desegregation than community control, an NAACP suit threatened a metropolitan busing scheme, and the region erupted in uncharacteristic racial conflict. But this time, instead of resisting, the business elite did the easy thing: it went along, capitulating to black demands for control, rather than risk a busing battle, sure to scare away new business and investment. The deal civic leaders struck traded jobs for black teachers and administrators in exchange for a busing cap: for better or worse, less than 3 percent of the city's children were ever bused. "It was the end of integration in Atlanta," one rueful liberal would later recall. "The school deal killed whatever chances it might have had." By the end of the seventies, the middle class—both white and black—had abandoned the public schools, leaving them over 90 percent black and among the nation's worst.

More and more, in their confrontations with Jackson, the businessmen gave in, at considerable cost to the city's traditional racial compact. As in Detroit, in the seventies the civic elite considered a variety of metropolitan solutions to the city's problems—everything from formal annexation of some neighboring towns to a regional scatter-site public housing plan. But like Coleman Young, Jackson saw regionalization as a hostile racial ploy to dilute black votes and curb black political power, and he opposed every overture, including a rapid transit system that would link the city and its wealthy suburbs. Outlying whites also resisted any metropolitan ties, particularly busing and the light rail MARTA system. In an earlier era, the business elite might have endeavored to bring them along, convincing or cajoling them to do the right thing. But by the seventies the Peachtree crowd saw little point in bucking the black leadership, risking racial turmoil by pressing for change that blacks no longer seemed to want. As in the rest of the country, declining black support for integration conveniently let whites off the hook, and both races retreated, often relieved, into separate spheres of influence.

Still, the mood of racial crisis persisted through the Jackson era. Despite the city's historic aversion to airing even the smallest family quarrel, the racial rhetoric escalated in an unseemly, un-Atlantan way. The old elite, used to unlimited access to the mayor, griped that Jackson would not take their phone calls, much less their advice. One survey of business attitudes found him widely regarded as "anti-white." The *Atlanta Constitution,* celebrated for its longtime liberalism on race, ran a seven-part, front-page series called "A City in Crisis" that roundly blamed Jackson and his policies. "In the white community, they think he is a mayor for the black community," developer John Portman told the press. "He is perceived as taking every issue and turning it into a race issue." Worse still, like Coleman Young, Jackson was said to be using race to elude accountability. "Any time the . . . City Hall crowd fails to perform up to snuff, and someone points it out," a local journalist noted, "the immediate response is 'racism.'"

As in Detroit, racial politics—and its policy consequences—drove whites from the city at an alarming rate. "Maynard was responsible for the building of the perimeter," one insider claimed about the several multi-million-dollar malls and countless apartment complexes that went up along the beltway in the 1970s. "Housing values fell through the floor in the city, and residential construction changed the face of outlying counties." Opinion surveys using the same tester cards that Reynolds Farley had developed in Detroit showed much the same racial attitudes in Atlanta: if anything, Atlanta whites were a little more tolerant than Detroiters, willing to live on an integrated block where as many as one-third of the families were black. But white Atlantans did not like Jackson's attitude or the feel of the streets when they ventured downtown, and seventy thousand of them—14 percent of the population, or four in ten whites—left the city in the 1970s, while the black share of the census rose from half to two-thirds. People spilled out into surrounding counties, with nearby Gwinnett quadrupling in a matter of years. Both Gwinnett and Cobb voted repeatedly against raising taxes to pay for MARTA lines. (Residents preferred to spend an hour stuck in traffic twice a day.) And for every local businessman who could not afford to abandon his investment in the downtown construction boom, there was a national corporation or business service that moved to a suburban office park.

The results in Atlanta were nothing like what happened in Detroit. Downtown construction continued at an astonishing clip: a huge new convention center, a modern sports complex, several large hotel developments and 10 million square feet of new office space in the late seventies alone. The city's economic engine, Hartsfield International Airport, had a $500-million overhaul; the billion-dollar MARTA system neared completion and began to spread the construction boom out through the city. Republican-leaning working whites moved to the suburbs, but better-off liberals stayed put, and gentrification gave new life to city neighborhoods that had been written off as dead. Economics, good intentions, guilt, shame and the city's unusually appealing quality of life: together, the combination proved stronger than the growing racial antagonism, and public Atlanta held together in a way Detroit never did.

As angry as they might be at Jackson, the civic leadership continued to champion the idea of a black mayor. Open race baiters in their midst were quickly denounced and silenced, and the businessmen remained ready to do whatever was needed to help the city. "If Maynard had been able to go to them," Dan Sweat maintained, "to say directly, 'I need your help,' eight out of ten would have done whatever he asked. I used to tell him that, but he couldn't bring himself to ask them." Determined to break with the old Atlanta mayoral tradition—what he called the "slavish, unquestioning adherence to downtown dicta"—Jackson found the businessmen meddlesome and threatening, always trying, in his view, to grab back their lost power. It was a classic racial misunderstanding, one that might have destroyed another city. Still, in Atlanta, the elite hung on, often pretending that nothing significant had changed.

The outcome of the 1970s was not segregation, as in Detroit, but it was not integration, either—more like uneasy coexistence. Racial separation seemed to have a logic all its own. Custom, geography, even architecture added to the inertia, with downtown's walled-off, air-conditioned new atriums quickly emerging as a white city-within-a-city. Even so, many whites used crime as an excuse to avoid downtown, and blacks and whites divided up the landscape like a battleground. Sometime in the seventies, localized shopping nodes eclipsed the old central hub, and by the end of the Jackson era, Atlanta had two downtowns: the deteriorating black downtown in the center city and the new white downtown, Buckhead, six miles to the north. With the city's upscale restaurants, its choicest hotels and newest office towers, Buckhead paid taxes to Atlanta and in an important way helped keep it alive, but its residents had less and less to do with the black people on the south side of town.

Not even the city's upscale middle classes—black and white—seemed to share much sense of community. "Already in the early seventies," one insider remembered, "it was the 'in' thing not to leave town." But in gracious Atlanta, wealthy whites could eat their cake and have it too, looking down their noses at those who were fleeing the city, while enjoying all the comforts—and racial isolation—of the suburbs. The lush, leafy neighborhoods in the northern tier of town near Buckhead were as nice as the nicest suburbs of most cities: quiet, crime-free and filled with glorious old houses. Residents sent their children to private school and spent their weekends at all-white golf and tennis clubs. Like their parents, part of a system they never thought to question or change, they went to white churches, white charity balls, white college football games. (Middle-class blacks, on the south side of town, were just as inclined to stick with their own kind.) Occasionally, a black family would move into a white neighborhood—Jackson and his family lived in one of the most exclusive enclaves—but by and large, as in most cities, residential segregation ruled. "It was as gracious—and segregated—a life as it had ever been," one out-of-town journalist commented. "In those north-side neighborhoods, it might as well still have been 1958." Visitors from Detroit looked on with envy: this was no chocolate city with vanilla suburbs. But nor exactly was it a case study in integration.

Then, in 1979, came the missing and murdered children. The first body, found in a field in poor, black southwest Atlanta, created little stir among either blacks or whites. The city was in the midst of an alarming crime wave, and for some time no one perceived a pattern of missing kids. The idea that this was a series, and that there might be a single killer, began to emerge only in July 1980. A group of black parents noticed that the apparently random crimes had something in common and brought them to the attention of the police, who organized a special task force. The rest of the nation didn't pick up on the story until October, when the parents' group signed up neighborhood volunteers for a weekend search of the nearby woods and found the heart-rending skeleton of seven-year-old Latonya Wilson. By then, there were nine children dead, five others missing, and the grisly pattern was all too clear. All the victims had been black, poor, often runaways or street kids, and all between the ages of seven and fifteen. Evidence suggested they had gone willingly with their captors and eventually been suffocated or strangled, then dumped in a field or wooded area. It was at this point that the national media took notice. *The New York Times* began to run a story a day, and what had been a local police matter became a nationwide racial cause célèbre.

From the beginning, the outpouring of concern was white as well as black, with whites contributing the lion's share of a $100,000 reward fund and coming out in force for continuing weekend patrols. But already in the first weeks, there was an accusatory edge to many blacks' charges. The community's initial reaction was to blame its old adversary, the police; the second impulse was to assume unquestioningly that the murderer was white—a bigot preying on black children. Talk swirled on the south side of Emmett Till, of the not so distant years of lynchings and white vigilante violence. The increasingly angry parents' group—it also included a number of activists—

accused Maynard Jackson of conspiring with the Peachtree businessmen to ignore if not suppress the murders. A boiler explosion in a south side housing project was immediately assumed to have been caused by a racist's bomb, and even assurances from the city's black police chief could not convince many Atlanta blacks otherwise. Fear and rumors spiraled wildly, and within a week of the first big news stories, the media were running pieces about a national black-killing wave.

The quote that opened *Newsweek*'s report captured the building frenzy. "When you pick up the newspaper and read about this black being killed here and another black being killed there, it does something to your psyche, something bad," the magazine cited one man saying. "It leads to the perception that it's suddenly hunting season on blacks again." The Atlanta killings were linked, in this story and others, to entirely unrelated murders in Buffalo, Oklahoma City, Indianapolis, Cincinnati and Salt Lake City. *Newsweek* noted a "palpable climate of fear" spreading among blacks as far away as Oakland, California. "The mood is extremely tense," the piece concluded, quoting another black man, in Atlanta: "If one more kid is snatched, this town could blow up." Recent racial rioting in Miami—the first in a decade or so—gave credibility to the threat in Atlanta, and the city prepared for the worst, amid spreading rumors that the Ku Klux Klan was organizing to provoke a race war. Several days later, the Justice Department held a closed-session meeting with Atlanta activists to address the notion that the murders were "racist attacks." No evidence whatsoever supported the by now universal assumption that the killer was white, but already the story had as much to do with racial myth as with the horrors being committed in Atlanta.

The murders continued grimly—like clockwork, one every three to four weeks. The weekend searches ballooned to one thousand and then three thousand volunteers. In an effort to protect children, Maynard Jackson canceled Halloween, then imposed a nightly curfew. The police task force grew to seventy and then three hundred officers—local, state and FBI. Homicide experts were brought in from five other cities. Scores of police went door-to-door across the south side asking for tips and information about potential witnesses. There were helicopter patrols, computer tracking stations, a raft of FBI behavioral scientists, even a New Jersey psychic flown in to give advice. By March 1981, the task force had spent over $1 million and still had virtually nothing to show for it. By then, twenty children were dead and two others unaccounted for.

Concern spread rapidly across the nation. Earnest interracial "conversations" were organized, and money poured into the ever-growing reward fund. Horrified as they were by the killings, many whites seemed to appreciate the chance to show their concern, to say in effect that the nation was suffering as one community. The Coca-Cola Company's public service ad campaign seemed to many to say it all: "Let's keep pulling together, Atlanta." Newly inaugurated vice president Bush traveled to Georgia with a promise of several million dollars in crisis aid. "This is a question of conscience," he told Mayor Jackson. "You have our support."

Still, in Atlanta and elsewhere, blacks continued to blame the murders on white racism. In addition to the murderer himself and the racist climate that made his actions possible, Atlanta activists denounced the whites they knew best—the cops and the local press. The fact that the mayor, the police chief and the commissioner of public safety were black was irrelevant; in the community's eyes, all three were tools of the white establishment. Like the police, the press was charged with abetting the murders by ignoring them during the first year. "We were accused of withholding information, then of printing too much," one journalist recalled. "No matter what we did, it was wrong." As for the national outpouring of concern, many blacks, including James Baldwin, in his word, "dismissed" it: the response was nothing, he complained, imputing a racist double standard, like the "American reaction to the fate of the hostages in Iran." It was at about this time that a number of journalists in Atlanta began to realize that the murderer probably was not white: white people simply did not go to the south side of Atlanta, and would have been noticed immediately if they did. But this was not a view that got much hearing in the spring of 1981, as the national racial passion play came to a climax.

The green ribbons first appeared in early March; within weeks, millions of people, black and white, were wearing them. The head of the Atlanta parents' group, Camille Bell, traveled to Harlem for a well-attended prayer vigil; there were several big marches in Atlanta, then a rally at the Lincoln Memorial. Jesse Jackson addressed the crowd. "It is open season on black people," he charged. "These murders can be understood only in the context of affirmative action and Ronald Reagan's conservative politics." By now, conspiracy theories had reached a fever pitch. Some blacks were convinced that the Klan was behind the disappearances. Others believed that it was the FBI, pursuing a genocidal plot to eliminate the race. Comedian and activist Dick Gregory had perhaps the most outlandish suggestion: that the Atlanta Centers for Disease Control were kidnapping and murdering black boys to harvest the anticancer drug found in the tips of their penises. As the spring wore on, Atlantan blacks began to organize armed vigilante patrols and on one occasion confronted the police in a tense standoff in a housing project.

By the time police zeroed in on black suspect Wayne Williams in June 1981, it had been the nation's biggest and most sophisticated homicide manhunt. The clues that led to Williams were anything but vague: he was stopped for questioning just moments after he threw the body of his last victim into the Chattahoochee River. But even Williams's trial—and his conviction by a largely black jury—had little effect on the deepest levels of black paranoia. Once it turned out that the suspect was not white, black interest in the case visibly plummeted. Journalists covering the trial filled their stories with praise for the city's racial calm, but wondered among themselves why so few blacks seemed interested in attending. The south side parents' group maintained throughout the trial that the "fat boy" mayor and his white supporters were using Williams as a scapegoat, covering up for the real, white killer. Instead of rejoicing at the cessation of the murders—and they did stop the day Williams was apprehended—many blacks across the country seemed angry or defeated. "They win," one Atlantan told James Baldwin, meaning whites. "They got us."

A reporter who visited south side housing projects on the day of the verdict could find almost no one who felt that justice had been done, not even on a block that had lost three children. "I don't believe he's guilty," said the sister of one victim. All but incontrovertible blood and fiber forensics linked Williams to the two deaths he was tried for—there were seven hundred pieces of fiber evidence alone—but many blacks in the projects dismissed this as merely circumstantial evidence and insisted even after the trial that the conviction had been driven by race. "Most people think the verdict was predetermined," one south sider commented, "the case was over before it began." Another journalist found the same reaction in better-off black parts of town. "Even educated, middle-class blacks dismissed the verdict," the *Atlanta Constitution* city editor, Joseph Dolman, remembers. "People were deeply, deeply skeptical—convinced that Williams had been framed." For Camille Bell, grieving mother and head of the parents' committee, it went beyond doubt. "With this conviction," she told the press, "Wayne Williams, at 23, became the 30th victim of the Atlanta slayings."

In typical boosterish Atlanta fashion, the city struggled in the months to come to put the best face on the episode. The city's black police commissioner, Lee P. Brown, became a national celebrity. The two Atlanta newspapers responded with increased coverage of the south side poor and patted themselves on the back for discovering "a face of the city" they had not known before. "There has been an accommodation of blacks and whites," Andrew Young commented, "that I don't think works like this any place else in the world." But in truth, the alarmists and conspiracy theorists were probably closer to the mark. White concern—shallow or deep—had been no match for black alienation. In Atlanta, as elsewhere in America, it seemed impossible to overcome the racial past. Whether elite Atlanta saw it or not, the missing and murdered children had revealed a chasm no one in the nation knew how to bridge.

Chapter 13

A PIECE OF THE PIE

W hen J. W. Robinson looks back over his career as an architect, he remembers two eras: life before affirmative action and the new life that came after it. Robinson came to Atlanta in 1949, a soft-spoken young man from South Carolina looking for a place to build a career. Few blacks graduating from professional school in the postwar years chose to settle in the South, still firmly in the grip of Jim Crow. But Robinson liked Atlanta—liked the hustle and bustle and hope on Auburn Avenue—and he found a job in a minority-owned office designing homes for the city's growing black middle class. The firm he joined prospered through the 1950s, a beneficiary, like other black businesses on Atlanta's south side, of segregation and the captive market it created. "I was a successful designer even before affirmative action," Robinson would later say proudly. Still, the Jim Crow ceiling was ever present and uncomfortably close. Not only could Robinson's firm never hope for a white client, but Catch-22 internship rules barred him and other blacks from the all-important status of "registered practitioner." (To become registered, you had to work under a registered mentor, but all registered architects in the city were white, and blacks were not allowed to work in white firms.) Robinson couldn't even walk through the front door on the odd occasion that he visited a white firm.

When segregation began to ease in the early sixties, Robinson proved both resourceful and lucky. A maverick white architect keen to get in on the black housing market shepherded him through the registration process, then asked him to head up a south side branch office. Black middle-class expansion kept them in business, though before long Robinson was complaining that it was not enough—that black housing alone could not sustain a firm of any size. Then, just in time, came his first opportunity to design a church. Several more churches followed—all for south side black congregations— then some school buildings for the city's black colleges. By 1970, Robinson had made the big break, opening his own firm, J. W. Robinson & Associates. An inflow of federal housing money—from Model Cities and other Great Society programs—meant a stream of new construction work. Unlike local building efforts, these jobs were open to blacks as well as whites, not yet affirmative action but strictly nondiscriminatory. Still, as Robinson saw things, he was living with a hedged-in future: "Blacks still had to fight for everything," he would remember bitterly.

Other south side entrepreneurs recall much the same kind of change in the sixties—limited. The civil rights era was soon reflected in Atlanta business, and by the time of Ivan Allen's mayoralty, a handful of black builders were taking part in mainstream construction jobs. Among the most successful was Herman Russell, Martin Luther King's friend and contemporary. A wiry, energetic man with drive of true Horatio Alger proportions, Russell had been working and saving since his first paper route at the age of ten. "I came from the other side of the railroad tracks," he reminisced in a thick country accent. "And I learned early on the art of working." Inheriting a small plastering business from his father, he made good money in the postwar growth of single-family black homes, not just plastering work but also buying land and developing it himself.

The surge of larger, downtown construction that began in the sixties meant more shuffling of the old Jim Crow categories, and Russell broke through a critical barrier, becoming the first black subcontractor to work on a downtown high-rise. A modest, likable man, he showed a knack for ingratiating himself with employers and partners. "I just like people," he said later, explaining his success, "all kinds of people. And besides, it was recognized that I was damned good." Before long, still with no help from affirmative action, he was doing a healthy share of north side subcontracting, and by the decade's end had built up a solid, small-time business—in one top employee's estimate, worth a couple of million dollars.

Still, Russell and his aides remember, there was always a feeling of second-best. In 1962, Russell was admitted to the Chamber of Commerce—by mistake. A form letter sent to all businesses of a certain size invited him to join, and he promptly sent it back, with dues. When the chamber brass discovered what had happened—their first black member—they were too embarrassed to back down, and together they and Russell tried to overlook the noisy resignations of resistant whites. But more than forty years later, Russell could still remember the slights at the first chamber dinner he attended, at a tony downtown hotel barred to black guests. In the workplace too, Russell employees often felt snubbed. "If you kissed enough behind," one subordinate recalled, "or would take jobs at a loss, you could get work. But things were far from perfect."

To many, Russell's and Robinson's advances suggested that blacks were rising quickly into the mainstream—that the old economic escalator was working as well as it ever had and that blacks would be able to take advantage of it as well as any group before them. But Atlanta's newly prosperous middle-class blacks still felt put upon and locked out of opportunity, and pressure began to grow in the early seventies for Mayor Maynard Jackson to do something about this. Whether you worked for yourself or were employed by a white firm, before affirmative action, it was said, you could never forget the ceiling. "There was only so far you could go," recalled Haywood Curry, another black contractor then working for J. A. Jones, a white-owned company. "I don't think," Curry added, making a common leap of logic, "that there was any way to break down the barriers without designating jobs for blacks."

Affirmative action was still only in the rough, early stages of implementation, but its seductive appeal and some of the problems it would create were apparent already in the early seventies. The first use of the term dated back to 1961, when President Kennedy's executive order 10925 required federal contractors to "take affirmative action" to ensure that employees were treated without regard to race, color, creed or national origin. The language of the order was vague and weak-sounding, but the reasoning behind it was blunt and hard for Americans of goodwill to reject, then or later.

Kennedy and his aides had been among the first to understand that the mere dropping of barriers would not be enough. Prejudice was still so keen and blacks so educationally and economically disadvantaged that merely banning discrimination was not going to produce enough progress to satisfy the pent-up demand. Equal opportunity, acculturation, entrepreneurship and hard work of the kind Robinson and Russell were doing in Atlanta would no doubt pay off in the long run. But most blacks were in too much of a hurry to wait that long, and for both moral and political reasons, Kennedy felt it was imperative to produce some visible change fast. Results—tangible, concrete, bankable results—were what seemed to matter, whatever it took to get there.

Already in the early sixties there were signs that this results-driven approach would come at a cost and would be unpopular with the larger white public. Goaded by the southern struggle, the majority was willing to ban discrimination, but not to guarantee a foreordained outcome, and much of the opposition to the 1964 Civil Rights Act grew out of fear that a press for rapid progress would lead to quotas. Concern about promising results carried enough weight among both liberals and conservatives that several amendments were added to the measure emphasizing that it covered only intentional acts of discrimination—not statistical discrepancies, which might or might not be evidence of exclusion and could be used as a rationale for quotas. Still, even before the bill passed, the federal government was requiring federal contractors to keep track of the statistical composition of their workforce. Already, the growing national determination to produce results for downtrodden blacks was leading inexorably in the direction of defining discrimination numerically and—the inevitable corollary—hiring by color.

By the time Lyndon Johnson took over the White House, the concern with tangible results had grown still more pressing and explicit. "It is not enough," Johnson insisted in his famous June 1965 Howard University speech, "just to open the gates of opportunity. All our citizens must have the ability to walk through those gates. . . . We seek . . . not just equality as a right and a theory, but equality as a fact and as a result." Many Americans, white and black, thrilled to the newly articulated ideal, and this time around, goaded by a new sense of urgency, fewer people thought to question what would be necessary to achieve it. Little attention was paid at the end of the summer when Johnson issued executive order 11246—the document generally credited with launching affirmative action, mainly by creating an alphabet soup of federal committees to implement the idea—and hardly anybody noticed a few weeks later when the newly empowered Equal Employment Opportunity Commission (EEOC) made what would turn out to be one of its most important decisions, announcing at a White House conference that it would define discrimination statistically. What about the Civil Rights Act and its provisions forbidding just that? A "big zero, a nothing, a nullity," was how one EEOC official characterized it, reflecting the new consensus in the movement and government circles.

In 1969, President Nixon's Labor Department took a concrete step to implement order 11246: the first presidentially approved preference program, requiring federal contractors in Philadelphia to set numerical targets for minority hiring. Within a few years, some version of the Philadelphia Plan had been adopted in fifty-five cities, in each case requiring contractors to count man-hours worked by blacks and whites, and to aim for a share of black workers equal to their share in the local population. In some places, including Philadelphia, the plans were a response to egregious discrimination. But in many cities, no past mistreatment was even charged; it didn't have to be, because justice had been arbitrarily redefined as proportional representation. The requirements were said to be "good-faith" goals, not quotas, though already this was a distinction without much difference, since contractors could be barred from federal work if they did not meet them. "We here at the EEOC believe in numbers," said a federal official. "The only accomplishment is when we look at all those numbers and see a vast improvement in the picture."

The media and much of the public were quick to accept the assumptions behind discrimination statistics. The numbers were so shocking: in the late 1960s, 96 percent of college professors were white and only 2 percent were black, 83 percent of auto workers compared to 15 percent, 87 to 13 percent of construction apprentices. In the face of discrepancies like these, it seemed churlish to ask about possible explanations other than discrimination—or about alternative, more gradual remedies to close the gaps in education and interest that might also be holding blacks back. The statistical shorthand was so useful, the remedial tool so powerful—"the only effective way to prove that discrimination has ended," *The New York Times* editorialized, is by "counting"—that within a few years it proved irresistible, and by the early 1970s, statistics were firmly ensconced in the driver's seat of civil rights law. In 1971, the Supreme Court endorsed the EEOC's decision to define discrimination numerically. Reasoning that it was just too difficult for plaintiffs to prove discriminatory intent—as the Civil Rights Act plainly required—the *Griggs* v. *Duke Power Company* decision held that the disproportionately low number of blacks in a North Carolina utility's workforce was enough, in itself, to prove that the company's hiring tests were biased.

Then, in 1972, the public's ambivalence surfaced again. Increasingly committed as they were to the goal of racial justice—and even to a results-oriented approach—people still didn't like the means the government was using to get there. The first constituencies to complain were blue-collar workers, who had begun to pay the price of the thumb on the scale, and Jewish groups, worried about the consequences for the nation of enshrining racial categories in law. Nixon, running for reelection, sniffed out these doubts and made a major campaign issue of his opposition to quotas. "The way to end discrimination against some," he thundered, "is not to begin discrimination against others." Democratic candidate George McGovern was no less emphatic. "I share the concerns you have expressed," he told Nixon, "and reject the quota system as detrimental to American society."

Still, inside the federal bureaucracy, regulations enforcing goals and quotas were proliferating. Rail as he might, Nixon did nothing to stop the spread of "good-faith" requirements for contractors, or the new effort by the federal bureaucracy to impose minority-hiring goals on government-funded universities. Many schools, led by the University of California at Berkeley, went looking for affirmative action coordinators, then began to rethink traditional color-blind hiring procedures. To spur the change, through 1972—even as the campaign rhetoric against quotas heated up—the government withheld $23 million from colleges that failed to institute color-coded goals. In midsummer, the media predicted that quotas could be the issue of the election. But as with busing, as November approached, neither candidate—nor their followers—appeared to want to press the sensitive racial question. Nobody seemed to like quotas, but nobody wanted to be the one to stop what seemed like progress, either. Entranced by their commitment to the program's noble integrationist end, both Democrats and Republicans averted their eyes from the dubious means, and the issue was quietly dropped from the campaign agenda. It was an early sign of just how difficult an issue affirmative action would become and how hard it would be to check the spread of preferences despite widespread doubts about them.

In Atlanta, as elsewhere in the nation, by the early seventies affirmative action was opening all kinds of doors—or beginning to, anyway. There were corporate goals and timetables, pioneered in the early sixties by the Lockheed Corporation. The city government, struggling to hire blacks, had committed itself to a 50 percent goal, then scoured the nation, in a widely publicized search effort, for black applicants for personnel chief and public works director. Several local colleges were in on the act, and all federal contractors in the area were under orders. But it was in the local construction business—not so much in hiring as the letting of contracts—that Atlanta was conducting its most innovative experiment with preferences.

Unlike many affirmative action programs, launched with a blast of ideological fanfare—talk of racial grievances and promises of justice—Atlanta's minority business program was born quietly, a child of old-fashioned backroom politics. The Peachtree elite, used to making decisions for the public, had expected widespread support for a proposed rapid transit system. But when a referendum was held in 1968, neither blacks nor suburban whites supported the proposed MARTA train lines, and civic leaders were forced to reach out to their old Sweet Auburn allies. Local black businessman Jesse Hill emerged as the natural negotiating partner. Scrappy and rough-edged, self-made president of the venerable Atlanta Life Insurance Company, Hill and contractor Herman Russell represented a new kind of behind-the-scenes black leadership. More aggressive than the old generation of ministers who had cooperated meekly with white authority, these two hardworking businessmen were still far from radical. They knew little of civil rights rhetoric or social engineering. They didn't see themselves as victims in need of redress, and the deal they worked out with the Peachtree elite was an old-fashioned horse trade—a promise of black votes in exchange for jobs and contracts. The black middle class got its share of the pie: 20 percent of all MARTA design, engineering and construction work set aside for minority-owned businesses. It was the first racial preference of its kind instituted by a local government. Yet neither side, black or white, seemed to grasp the significance of what they had established—the new racial regimen quietly replacing Jim Crow.

By the time Maynard Jackson was inaugurated as mayor in 1974, the MARTA program and other shifts were changing the face of black business in Atlanta. Scores of enterprises had popped up overnight to take advantage of the set-aside program. In some cases, laborers simply went out and bought a truck or printed up a business card. In other instances, white contractors recruited blacks—often people who had been working for them in the past—and set them up as 51 percent owners of the company. Even the big national construction firms hired blacks to represent them in Atlanta. Haywood Curry was among those who came to town in the early seventies on behalf of the white-owned North Carolina contractor J. A. Jones. "They saw the minority stuff taking off," he recalls, "and I became their minority—the minority who connected them to minorities." The city's already growing black middle class started to snowball—the quiet beginnings of the fastest middle-class growth in history.

How much was due to affirmative action, how much simply to the level-ing of barriers and the release of long-pent-up talent was already impossible to say. By 1974, Herman Russell's contracting business was doing $8 million in annual sales, and it ranked eighteenth on *Black Enterprise* magazine's list of national black companies. Some of this was MARTA work: Russell built stations alone and in partnership with white construction firms. But now as in the past, the bulk of his business was south side housing development—homes for black families benefiting from the end of Jim Crow, for the already-middle class moving in from elsewhere *and* for people getting a leg-up from the MARTA program.

Nor was the MARTA set-aside as much of a boon as it sometimes seemed for Atlanta's fledgling black business class. The numbers of firms grew steadily, and together they won a larger and larger percentage of govern-ment contracts. But these figures failed to reflect the many start-ups that went out of business almost as fast as they formed—or the large percentage that turned out to be "fronts." The preferred term in Atlanta was "rent-a-skin": a white-owned company nominally headed by a black man in order to snag a MARTA contract. "There were a zillion of 'em," recalled one tran-sit authority lawyer, "mom-and-pop cheat organizations." But in Atlanta in the early seventies, few people seemed to be counting. Certainly on the south side, where all kinds of businesses were starting to take off, no one really cared whether it was due to the set-aside or just a level playing field.

Maynard Jackson made clear from the start that he was going to take the preference program high profile and significantly expand it. Though a strong supporter of the MARTA set-aside, he was far from satisfied with the results. Like the other young men around him, movement veterans now rising into the middle class, he wanted more, and he wanted it faster. "There was a tremendous pressure to produce," former mayor Sam Massell remembered, "to overcome the shortcomings of a hundred years, and more. An all-out effort to promote minority business was the natural next step."

In office, Jackson moved immediately on several fronts to make affirma-tive action business as usual in Atlanta. His predecessor, Sam Massell, had created the position of city "affirmative action officer"; Jackson filled it for the first time and put the pressure on. Exactly half of his appointive positions went to blacks; hiring and promotion procedures were revamped to put less emphasis on standardized tests. As in Detroit, a new residency requirement made it easier to integrate the police force, and within three years, Jackson had raised the black percentage in the department to 33 percent. But by far the most important part of Jackson's push—the most original and relevant for his constituency—was his minority business program. "Minorities didn't just need jobs," Haywood Curry explained. "Minorities already know how to dig a ditch. They know how to go to work every day and pick up a paycheck. What you need is real entrepreneurial experience. That's what Maynard's program promised."

The idea from the beginning was to expand the MARTA program—to apply it to all city purchasing and contracting—and put some teeth in it. When Jackson arrived in City Hall, less than half of 1 percent of Atlanta contracts were going to blacks, already 54 percent of the population. There was plenty of city work in the offing. In addition to routine purchasing needs, Jackson had inherited plans for several big-league construction projects: a new water treatment system, a new jail, a new library, and—largest of all, at a projected $500 million—a new airport. The problem from the beginning was how to bring blacks in: how to force whites to make the change, but also—possibly even harder—how to use fledgling black companies effectively. In Atlanta, as elsewhere in the country, even the top black businesses were inexperienced and unprepared for multi-million-dollar jobs, in no position to compete with established white firms. The one thing Jackson knew was that change was going to take muscle, and as ever he relished the chance to put it to the Peachtree set.

He started close to home, with the people he knew best: his own law firm, Patterson & Parks. When Jackson was elected, and for decades before, the white-shoe firm of King & Spaulding had handled all of Atlanta's bond work. It was the only bond counsel of any size in the city. "You didn't go to Wall Street without their opinion," mayoral aide George Berry recalled. Jackson approached King & Spaulding in his first days in office and asked them to share the work with a black law firm—a firm that, in the circumstances, could have no knowledge or experience of municipal bond work. King & Spaulding, incredulous, refused. "And before you could say anything," Berry went on, "a new bond counsel was found for the city of Atlanta." The city's longtime law firm was replaced by three: a big-time Chicago office, a local white firm with some bond experience and Patterson & Parks—in the role of apprentice or protégé. "They didn't know a thing about the bond business," Berry recalled, "and everybody knew it. This was a way for them to learn." The partners were anything but equal or voluntary, but the Jackson team, determined to put the best face on things, called its new shotgun marriage a "joint venture."

The Atlanta establishment was still reeling from the bond deal when Jackson announced his next step: that the city's new international airport was going to be built entirely by joint ventures. "You had to start somewhere," recalled aide Dave Miller. "Why not take the largest government program available and make it your vehicle? The airport was a good opportunity to experiment." The Peachtree crowd was stunned. The airport was the city's biggest, most important asset—the engine of its economic growth and key to its future well-being. The expansion had been under discussion for more than a decade, every detail subject to intense scrutiny and endless backroom debate. As it was, construction would have involved more than a fair share of black laborers and subcontractors. But besides Herman Russell and one or two other firms, there were no black general contractors in town capable of building even a small part of the facility, designed to be the largest and most mechanized passenger terminal in America. "People thought it was crazy," said big-time contractor Lawrence Gellerstedt, Jr., "totally ridiculous. I'd been educated at Georgia Tech. I'd been in the construction business for thirty years. How are you going to tell me to take a black kid with no education, no experience, and put him into business with me?"

The negotiations with the white elite—if they could be called negotiations—were something that no one who took part in them would ever forget. As ever in Atlanta, they took place behind closed doors. But it didn't take long for the rest of the city to get word, and the meetings were soon the stuff of local legend—like the sit-ins and Dr. King's funeral, a critical milestone in Atlanta racial history. A tall, heavy man, Jackson was an imposing figure, and he used his size for all it was worth in hectoring the white business establishment. "Maynard stood there," Berry recalled. "He put his chin out. He looked them in the eye, and he said, 'This is the way it's going to be done.'" The businessmen who attended the meetings remember being thrown back in their chairs as if by gale-force winds. "Maynard didn't come in and sit down and negotiate. He dictated from on high, pompous and righteous," remembered Gellerstedt. "He could scare the britches off a white man, articulating the wrongs done over the years to blacks." "He crammed it down their throats," said a lawyer who worked with several of the big construction firms.

Jackson's leverage was as blunt as it was powerful: he simply refused to build the airport unless his "goals" were met. "Weeds will grow," went the legendary phrase. "That's what Maynard used to say," explained Berry. "Meaning that nothing would happen—that unless we got minority participation, nothing would be built." Berry, soon promoted to aviation commissioner, also made the case to the business elite. "I said to them, 'You can sue us, and you might win. But you cannot force us to do this airport project. It's a five-hundred-million-dollar project and Maynard wants to give 20 percent of it to minority firms. That means you all have a chance at four hundred million. Do you want that chance or not?'"

As it happened, weeds did grow for about a year while businessmen stewed and the administration fine-tuned its set-aside strategy. Jackson aides recall months of thinly veiled business hostility, grumbling editorials and angry questions at city council meetings. In a northern city like New York or Detroit, no one would have been surprised by the dug-in polarization. But this was not the way things worked in Atlanta, and it was all downtown could do to keep the racial standoff out of the national press. In the end, what finally turned things around was not so much Jackson's hectoring or even what he sneeringly called the businessmen's "profit motive," but primarily the sense among the elite that the city must have a new air terminal—that the economic future depended on it. "We knew the airport had to be built," said Gellerstedt. "So we were stuck."

By the time work began in 1975, Jackson and his aides had developed an ingenious enforcement mechanism—a precedent that would later form the basis of most minority business programs nationwide. In Jackson's Atlanta, there were no legal requirements. Berry and his colleagues were too clever for that. "We did it informally," he explained, "because we weren't sure. If we had done it with a law and the law was knocked down, we would have been in a poor position." Contracts were negotiated case by case—always with the same implied threat: "No minority, no deal." Instead of an explicit quota, Berry and colleagues came up with a stratagem they called "prequalification." Before they could even bid on airport work, companies had to submit detailed plans for ensuring that 20 to 25 percent of the job would be done by minority-owned companies. Then and only then, with the cost of using an inexperienced partner already built into the budget, the three or four firms that had "prequalified" would bid, and—as required by law—the lowest bidder would get the job. Finally, when the contract was drawn up, it would include the winner's plan for minority participation, as far as any outsider could tell, an entirely voluntary arrangement.

For the city's blacks—or a majority of them—Jackson became an instant hero. "Maynard's program," said contractor Haywood Curry, "was amazing to see. And the reason it was amazing, the reason it worked, was that Maynard required it. He said, 'If you want this job, you *have* to bring in minorities.' It was great, great—an eye-opening experience." Jackson had won his middle-class constituency many millions of dollars' worth of work and thrilled even those blacks who had no hope of benefiting from the set-aside by proving that the city's first black mayor was not a tool of the white establishment. "Maynard was forceful and convincing, and he made whites mad," said architect J. W. Robinson with a little grin. "But not so mad that it was counterproductive. Maynard was the spokesman. He got the whole country to look at Atlanta. Whites stopped and looked. And eventually what he did took over in the rest of the country, too."

Jackson made no apologies for his bullying tactics. "There is no way in hell," he told a reporter near the end of his tenure, "these age-old customs would have changed without someone making them change. I used political leverage and negotiating skills in order not to embarrass these people. What was said publicly that could be considered embarrassing is only one one-hundredth of what could have been said." If anything, the brash young mayor seemed to delight in the antagonism he had fostered. "I would have thought the heavens were falling down," he said later. "We were threatened with litigation six, seven times a day. A lot of litigation occurred." (In fact, there was only one suit in eight years.) And even in triumph, Jackson still seemed to feel an urge to needle his adversaries: "What the business community will never give me credit for is that all of this came with a great big plus for them. They now have a reputation for being progressive and open."

Once the airport contracts were settled, the battle over affirmative action moved into new realms: first the banks, then local business boards, the letting of cable-TV licenses and other construction projects. In each case, Jackson aide Dave Miller remembered, white businessmen "would get defensive. They would say, 'Not here, not in our business. Maybe it works in some other area—but we're unique.'" The banks were an obvious target, affirmative action the only way to get financing for inexperienced black contractors working at the airport and elsewhere. Noticing that loans were not forthcoming, Jackson demanded that bankers name more minorities to their boards and make it easier for blacks to rise to executive-level positions. When the bankers refused, the mayor threatened to move the city's cash accounts to Birmingham, and within a matter of months most Atlanta bank boards were integrated. "We used to tell the business crowd," said Miller, "'You'll soon get used to this.'" And gradually, like it or not, most of them did.

After a year or two of backroom deals, Jackson and his aides were emboldened to make affirmative action legal, and the city council passed a measure that made it easier still to muscle recalcitrant businessmen. Known as the Finley Ordinance, it dealt not with contracts but with hiring, requiring all firms doing business with the city to employ a certain percentage (in the 20 to 30 percent range) of minority workers. Most Atlanta firms did not come close to the required figure, but the mayor's office did not really expect them to. A local affirmative action official later explained how City Hall used its new weapon: "If a firm came in and wanted to do business with the city, Maynard's people would take them in a room and say, 'You don't meet our requirements. You don't have enough minorities in your workforce. You don't have *nearly* enough minorities. But,'" and here the official's voice softened, "'I'll tell you what you can do. You can form a joint venture with this minority firm we'll introduce you to, and together you all will meet our requirements—and then you'll have a shot at that contract you say you want.'"

Hardball tactics were nothing new in affirmative action law and not unique to Atlanta. A slight variation of the Finley Ordinance was already being used at the federal level. There, the weapon was the Supreme Court's 1971 *Griggs* decision, declaring a statistically imbalanced workforce proof of discrimination, and it was used to prod corporations toward preferential hiring. But Atlanta took the stratagem one step further, using the statistical definition to force companies into sharing responsibility and profits with inexperienced partners—and after a few months of backroom threats, even those conversations were unnecessary. Businessmen grasped that taking on a start-up minority partner was the price of doing business in Atlanta. Some contractors gave up bidding on city jobs, preferring to work in the private sector or the suburbs. But most settled more or less grudgingly into the new routine.

In typical Atlanta fashion, as the joint ventures proliferated, a hush fell over the business establishment. The controversy did not die, but the outrage went underground—so fast that it became hard to find Atlantans willing to speak out against affirmative action. Quiet grumbling continued behind the scenes: complaints that the set-aside increased costs for the city as well as business, that whites had to take on unqualified partners, that the program was an invitation to fronts and that in the end it would only sharpen racial antagonism. But as ever in Atlanta, the white elite dreaded nothing as much as what Dan Sweat called "the perception of racism," and the need to keep up a good racial image trumped all other concerns, even financial ones.

The last gasp of elite public criticism was heard in late 1975—the exception that proved the new rule of tacit acquiescence. An architect from the old, downtown office of Stevens & Wilkinson complained that the mayor's office had threatened to cancel his firm's airport contract if it did not bring in a black partner. This was the kind of thing that was happening every day in 1975, but only Stevens & Wilkinson senior partner Minton Braddy, Jr., dared to air it in the newspaper, accusing the administration of "blackmail." Jackson immediately denied the charge, and within twenty-four hours Braddy's colleagues had repudiated him, removing him from his job as head of their airport design team. The firm's president issued a statement praising Jackson "for giving black-owned firms experience in fields from which their previous experience had always excluded them," and within a few days, Braddy himself backed off, announcing that he had used the word "blackmail" hyperbolically.

By the time the first airport building appeared on the skyline, this hush had become a fact of life in Atlanta—a fact that would seriously distort public debate about affirmative action for decades to come. On the airport and later on a wide range of other jobs, whites bit their tongues and signed their contracts. Builders declined to talk to reporters; preference-minded politicians moved ahead assuming themselves to be unopposed. "Whites here are pragmatic," said Berry without irony. "This became the way we do business in Atlanta. And after the first few outbursts—really very, very few—it was not much discussed or grumbled over." Professionals competing for city work put a somewhat different spin on the silence. "Everybody's affirmative action story is off the record," said an architect. "You fear for your livelihood. You'd lose all your work. If I was retiring, I'd have a lot to tell you. But I'm not ready to retire yet. You don't alienate the power structure."

By the time Jackson left City Hall in 1981, the joint venture idea had spread to every area of city business. Affirmative action language was written into every municipal contract, and a third of the city's purchasing dollars was going to minority firms. Unlike in Detroit, the city's white business establishment had too much at stake to pull up and move their operations to the suburbs. The relationship was never a happy one; even when the fireworks subsided, it was neither trusting nor stable. But like it or not, the business leaders were married to the city and its black mayor, and after some hard swallowing, they managed to make their peace with him. Affirmative action, said George Berry, "became a given in Atlanta. If you did business with the city, you had to address this. And eventually, that made it second nature."

With downtown convinced or at least colluding in the mayor's program, the set-aside was put to the test on the ground: at construction sites and in offices where joint ventures brought black and white Atlantans together. J. W. Robinson was wary from the start of any job he did not earn himself or carry on his own shoulders. The first work he got because rather than in spite of his color were small city projects: a swimming pool and a fire station thrown his way in the early seventies by the city's first black officials. Robinson made a special effort to point out that however he got these jobs, when it came to the design, he did it by himself and won awards for his superior artistry. Like all Atlanta black builders of any size, he then did some MARTA work: his first joint venture, designing a south side station. It was not a bad experience—Robinson felt he did a good job and got the respect he was due—and he was game for more when the airport project came along. "Joint venturing is good," he said later, "if you can use it to pull yourself up—if you can take the experience and learn something from it, then build up your own company so it can stand on its own."

Supporters of the joint venture idea, white and black, agreed unanimously that this was the goal. It was understood that a joint venture would be something like an apprenticeship: the experienced whites would take the time to tutor and nudge, bringing their black partners along until they were able to make it on their own. Fledgling businesses with no experience would get a running start. Mid-sized firms like Robinson's would learn bigger-league business practices—bidding, bonding, accounting or management. Even relatively successful ventures like Herman Russell's construction company would have something to learn from association with a white firm: in his case, moving from $1- to $2-million partnerships up into the reaches of $3- to $5-million projects. It occurred to no one at the outset that it might be hard for beneficiaries to let go of the training wheels, or that there might be incentives, on all sides, to maintain the dependent partnerships.

The problem, as Robinson and others quickly found, was that the inequality of the joint venture bred contempt—contempt with an inevitably racial edge. Seasoned as he was, Robinson was in no position to do anything like 20 percent of the architectural work at the airport. Recognizing this, Jackson's people brought the city's four black architects into yet another backroom and told them, like it or not, that they were now one firm: Minority Airport Architects + Planners, or MAAP. Thrown together willy-nilly and effectively labeled "black," the architects' consortium was then paired up with two white "mentors"—the Atlanta firm, Stevens & Wilkinson, and another, more experienced, out-of-town concern. Even consolidated into one firm, the black architects were still what one city official called "weak and inexperienced," and the disparity skewed every aspect of the job. Decades later, Robinson was still smarting from his treatment by designers from the out-of-town partnership—men with what he called a "big-firm, country-club attitude."

At the time and afterward, Robinson tried to put the best face on the relationship. MAAP was responsible for one of four airport concourses, and the minority architects worked, he was keen to point out, on their own, out of "a separate office." Even so, years later, Robinson complained about partners "who've always got to be looking or guiding or whatever, who want to manage it all—and leave you out of the loop." Though he knew he was there to learn, he did not like the position this put him in, and he found that he was always struggling to maintain his dignity—to prove that he was equal to his partners, whether or not, in fact, this was the case. Not only were the training wheels humiliating, but in the end, Robinson found, they limited what he could learn about the business. "If someone else is managing you," he said, "and you don't have any input to speak of, you aren't going to get but a very little bit out of it." Finally, struggling to justify the arrangement, Robinson came up with a face-saving description. "Each brought something to the table," he said, screwing up his self-respect: the big companies provided the "expertise" and the minority firm brought "political connections." In fact, that was precisely the division of labor in most early Atlanta joint ventures. But it wasn't exactly an arrangement to make a man like Robinson proud, and his defensiveness was evident even two decades afterward. "The problem," he said, "is when you feel that the only way a minority can function is in a joint venture, with somebody telling you all the time what you should do. It's not good for you, it's not a way to build yourself up."

Managers who took part in early joint ventures amply confirm Robinson's—and other blacks'—suspicions about white attitudes. The contempt was rarely overt. "Ninety-nine percent of the time," Berry remembered caustically, "the discrimination was done in a very cordial, civilized way, by people being very nice to each other." Still, among blacks and whites alike, there was no mistaking how many whites felt, and things could get raw on the site and in the construction trailer. "Nobody likes being force-fed," said an estimator for a big firm that got a piece of the airport. "They felt the minorities didn't have the ability." "They thought it was a joke," echoed J. A. Jones man Haywood Curry, "and they didn't bother to hide their feelings. The comment—the comment you heard all the time—was, 'Is this really a joint venture? Or is it just a way to put some money in the minority partner's pocket?' " Like suburban families forced to submit to busing, white men in joint ventures were often thrown together with blacks they could not consider their equals, and more often than not, the encounter only reinforced their stereotypes.

This white contempt was hardly lost on already sensitive black junior partners. "The majority companies could dictate whatever they wanted," said building supplier Lincoln Watson, Jr., who like others complained that white contractors abused their superior position. In some instances, blacks charged, they weren't told about meetings where associates made decisions. In others, the top partner would conveniently forget promises he had made—about helping, say, to get insurance or meet bonding requirements. In still other cases, minorities who expected an apprenticeship found that once the deal was done—once the white company had "its black" and its share of airport work—there was little time for any kind of mentoring. Some blacks even suspected that their white associates, who as majority partners kept the books, were cheating them out of their fair share of profit. This kind of fraud was rarely if ever proved, but the mere suspicion poisoned many Atlanta joint ventures.

Some black contractors responded with indignation, and for them the affirmative action experience only fueled their own racial resentment. Lincoln Watson recalled the office he was given by his partners on the airport job: "It was the damnedest thing. They put a phone in there, and we could only receive calls—we couldn't dial out. I said to my dad, 'Looks like they don't even trust us with a phone.' " Other minority partners were more mortified than angered by the position the preference put them in, and they tended not to want to talk about their experience. "In most cases," said one black architect, still unwilling twenty years later to speak in his own name, "the entity you were joint venturing with didn't want you there to begin with. If I were them, I'd think the same way: 'Why do I have to do this?' A firm that's done this kind of job fifteen to twenty times before and one that's never done it, even once, being forced together. It puts a strain immediately—a very, very strong barrier. They don't want you there in the first place, and you never forget it."

The widespread fraud that plagued the set-aside program hardly enhanced white contractors' opinions of their partners. Some of the "rent-a-skin" schemes were more sophisticated than others. The simplest were old-fashioned fronts: situations in which there really was no black company, only a former employee now nominally president of a largely white enterprise—perhaps a division of the majority firm, spun off and then associated again through a joint venture or subcontract deal. In such situations, the minority and majority partners would often have the same address, the same receptionist, the same bookkeeper, the same lawyers—and when the job was done, the "minority company" would disappear as quickly as it had appeared. A slightly more elaborate kind of fraud involved a black venture that functioned as a "pass-through"—in effect, a kind of broker. As part of meeting its minority requirement, a majority company would buy building materials from a black supplier, though in fact the supplier had no warehouse, no trucks or even an office. An individual with a letterhead or an order book, this "entrepreneur" merely collected a check: what the materials would ordinarily have cost, plus a hefty add-on. In later years, when these scams were exposed, there would be much debate about who should be blamed—the whites ostensibly in charge or the blacks who had allowed themselves to be used. In fact, the corruption took two, but the driving force was the city's unrealistic set-aside and its attempt to short-cut the normal building up of a business class. And whatever harm it did whites—usually a small increase in operating costs—it would have been hard to invent a scheme that did more to mock the dignity of the blacks involved.

More advanced still and by far the most common kind of set-aside fraud was what came to be called "passive joint venturing." In these cases, unlike the others, there were bona fide minority partners, but they did no more of the job than a fictitious rent-a-skin would have. A white manager from one of the city's biggest construction firms described how it worked: "A minority contractor would come to you and say, 'I'll be your partner. You pay me X percent.' And in exchange for that money, instead of agreeing to do some part of the job, they would promise not to get in your hair. The minority turned the contract over to you. You did the work. They collected the check." Black builders remember that offers could also come from the other side of the table: "The majority firm would tell you, 'We'll give you your percentage, and you don't have to send anyone. Don't assign anyone. Don't show up.'" Mayor Jackson's former law partner, Bernard Parks, was offered a deal like this in the early seventies. When he seemed affronted, Parks recalled, the white pitchman "said I could come to all the meetings." Mechanical contractor Tom Cordy, a black entrepreneur who did well at the airport, received a similar overture—with a payoff of $50,000. By the time the airport neared completion, in the late seventies, there had been so many silent partnerships—and exposés of them—that many Atlantans assumed it was the norm for joint ventures: the way they all worked. "People get partners," said one businessman, "and ask them not to show up, not to screw up the business. That's affirmative action now."

As white managers explained the construction business, passive joint venturing was almost inevitable—a natural outcome of trying to marry two ill-matched and unequal partners. By the time the airport project arose, the big enterprises that expected to get contracts—firms like J. A. Jones and Lawrence Gellerstedt's Beers Inc.—had been in operation for many decades. Used to building big skyscrapers, operating in several states, a company of this size had amassed not only vast experience but also a large reserve of capital. This meant that it could bond at an unusually good rate, enabling it to stretch its big pile of capital much further than a smaller firm could stretch its small pile. The biggest contractors made far fewer mistakes than most firms. Their estimators were more accurate, so their overtime costs were lower. Because they could pay in cash, they bought supplies considerably cheaper than competitors who relied on credit. "It's always easier and cheaper," said Beers's estimator, Herbert Edwards, "to go with the biggest, oldest, most established company."

In contrast, a fledgling firm, black or white, is almost sure to be expensive. It pays a high rate for bonding, it makes mistakes and has to pay overtime, it bids lower than it can do the job for and ends up needing to be bailed out. In the eyes of the management at a place like Jones or Beers, a start-up partner can only get in the way. And in the intensely competitive contracting business, where even a few thousand dollars' difference can mean losing a bid or, later, blowing your profit, not even the biggest, most successful companies can afford a weak associate. No wonder, given the way joint ventures were conceived and implemented, many larger Atlanta firms were skeptical—and preferred taking on a passive partner.

Yet passive joint venturing played into exactly the same stereotypes as other set-aside fraud: the image of blacks as unqualified and not interested in hard work, scammers looking to make an easy buck. As committed a liberal as business insider Dan Sweat betrayed what many whites felt when he told the press: "These so-called minority businesses sit on the sidelines, collect their paychecks and don't do anything but grin and shuffle all the way to the bank." Black professionals and craftsmen couldn't help noticing that what they were wanted for was their skin. Bernard Parks, who eventually did get a piece of the $390,000 airport bond issue, began to sense that he was being ignored in meetings. "Even though I'd been doing this kind of work for six years, when they got ready to ask a question, they turned to my white partner." Blacks in every field complained that no matter how hard they worked, they were tagged by white colleagues as lazy freeloaders. "It was the dummy companies that gave us the black eyes," said Robinson. "That's what gave joint venturing a bad name." "What creates the racist backlash," said another entrepreneur, "is that they have seen the scams. If they had seen a black Sheetrocker or plasterer who was pricing well, doing his job and building up a business—then they would have felt very differently."

The Jackson administration mostly ignored the growing criticism, writing it off as so much racism. By the time the airport was under way, MARTA had seen just about every kind of scam under the sun, and the transit authority had a large office to detect them. But the city did not want to tie up manpower in administration, and when it finally set up a contract compliance office, it was less than a quarter the size of MARTA's. City Hall insiders insisted that the difference between a legitimate minority partner and a sham was too fine a distinction to prosecute in a court of law. Meanwhile, minority fronts caught and rejected by the MARTA compliance office regularly got work at the airport and in the federal set-asides springing up in the Atlanta area. Black Atlantans were not exactly pressing the mayor to crack down. Not only did they tend to blame the white contractors who they felt were initiating the frauds, but many also seemed hesitant to prosecute black start-ups. "A certain segment of the black population says, 'So what if it is a sham?'" one contractor explained. "'The guy is going to get thirty or forty thousand a year, and so what? What's wrong with that after all the money white people have made here?'" Years later, Jackson aides who ran the affirmative action program still shrugged off charges about passive joint venturing. "It was a learning process," said Richard Stogner. "We kept trying to tighten it up." "We policed it the best we could," said George Berry.

By the time the airport program was in full swing, the pattern was clear, and most minority beneficiaries fell into one of two categories. The first were what Herbert Edwards called "people who were looking for a way to make money quick, people who would never have succeeded under any circumstances." Many middle-class blacks were able to raise the money to start a business, and scores of small ventures got airport work. The difficulty, as insiders explained it, was turning that onetime opportunity to account—an almost impossible challenge given the natural hierarchies of the construction trade. "It's a very competitive business," explained Edwards, "very easy to get into. Any guy with a pickup truck can declare himself a building contractor. But it's very, very hard to make a go of it over time." Even in situations where the minority partner showed up for work and was given assignments, he often found them impossible to learn from. "The city took one-year-old firms," one architect said, "and tried to shove steak down their throats. The jobs were just too big. There was no way most of these guys could handle them." City officials tried to force managing partners to break the work down into smaller pieces, also to make more frequent payments than usual—a key boost for new firms with poor cash flow. Still, as one program official put it, "There was no way we could build expertise in a vacuum." "For most firms," said Edwards, "it takes a lifetime—maybe even two generations—to get started. The government plan for affirmative action budgeted five to ten years."

By the time the airport was up and running, the business failures were legion, once again feeding white stereotypes about blacks and black businesses. "How many minority contractors from the airport are still in business?" one young white builder asked scornfully. "Most of them are bankrupt. What good did that do anybody, black or white?" The other category—the firms that succeeded in joint venturing—were minority companies that had already been doing well: businesses like Robinson's or H. J. Russell's. And these, most Atlantans were convinced, would have succeeded with or without affirmative action.

The Atlanta preference programs gave J. W. Robinson's career a huge boost, promoting him to a kind of project he could never have aspired to and providing him with a stream of work over several decades. Mixed as his experience was, he remained a committed supporter of affirmative action, but he was eager to differentiate himself from the small-time failures and scammers. He remembered being embarrassed and ashamed to see preferences portrayed on television. "People watched *60 Minutes,*" he recalled, "and saw a guy—a guy who was supposed to be the president of the company—who didn't even know where the office was located." Robinson was sharply critical of start-up contractors who accepted jobs they were not qualified for. ("You wonder why the houses fall down," he said scathingly.) And he knew plenty of whites in the building trades who had been burned by their experience with set-asides: people who took on a black partner who couldn't handle his job, and after that declined to work with blacks under any circumstances. "It was a program," Robinson noted sadly, "with good intentions that did sometimes end up confirming people's worst, nasty ideas." In the seventies and beyond, Robinson struggled to come to terms with these mixed feelings—to reconcile his own pride and his confidence in his work with what he saw happening around him in Atlanta. In the end, his answer was one that preserved his pride, but it was no tribute to affirmative action. "I try to sell myself as an architect," said the man who had been benefiting from preferences for two decades, "but not necessarily as a minority architect. Because sometimes you carry something when you sell yourself as a minority architect. I'm an architect, and it just happens I'm a minority."

Even more than Robinson, Herman Russell was considered the model minority partner, the success story of the airport set-aside. As the city's top black builder—and Maynard Jackson's political godfather—he was inundated with offers for joint venture jobs. Known already around town as a prodigiously hard worker, frugal, disciplined, with a shrewd business sense, with or without his political connections he would have been a highly desirable partner, and his name in itself seemed a kind of guarantee that there would be no question of passive joint venturing. Still, even for Russell, the jobs were much bigger than anything he had done before, and he was paired with firms that dwarfed his own in both size and expertise. By the time the airport was done, he had been part of six joint ventures, including—the first and biggest—a three-way deal, with J. A. Jones and a local white contractor, to build the $21-million tunnel for the people-mover connecting the terminal's four passenger concourses. Russell's share of the job was 25 percent: he put up 25 percent of the capital, was expected to do 25 percent of the work and took home 25 percent of whatever profit it produced. "This set the table for H. J.," said Haywood Curry, who would later work in Russell's company. "It set the table for the rest of his life. From that job on, he would be involved not at the subcontractor level, but as a general contractor. Without it, he would be a basic plasterer, a drywall contractor—and he would have been great at that. But he wouldn't be what he is today if the city hadn't required that J. A. Jones get a minority partner."

Yet even Russell found that his experience of affirmative action could be humiliating. "Race relations," he said years later, "that was the toughest part. With executives and top management, you knew what you were getting

into. Where we ran into the most resentment was with the rank-and-file."
Curry, then working for Jones, recalled that many of his white co-workers
were scornful of the Russell firm, considering it "just another sub," hardly on
a par with their own company. As Russell remembered this and other early
joint ventures, the biggest problem had to do with job assignments. Again
and again, he found, middle-level supervisors—white men who worked for
the majority partner—would "pigeonhole" black staffers in dead-end, scut-
work positions: slots where little was expected of them and, chances were,
they would learn nothing. For Russell, looking back later, it was easy to see
this as bigotry. But according to Curry, who remembered little mistreatment,
that was not always the case. "It had nothing to do with racism," Curry said.
"A lot of these guys were very friendly with me. They just thought the joint
venture—the forced joint venture—was a stupid arrangement."

In the end, Russell profited very handsomely from his airport partnerships.
The six joint venture contracts he participated in were worth nearly $50 mil-
lion, and by all accounts Russell's overall share was about 30 percent—$15
million worth. This, in combination with his other development projects,
soon boosted him from eighteenth to fifth place on the list of the nation's
black businesses. In the first four years the airport was going up, his annual
profits quadrupled—to $32 million—and by the late seventies his was the
biggest black-owned construction company in America. Still, like Robinson,
while he strongly supported affirmative action, Russell was always uncomfortable with the idea that he had needed it, and he tried to put the memory
behind him. "I never had the benefit of any so-called set-aside programs," he
said twenty years later. "When I began my entrepreneurship, you didn't have
no program. There was nothing but cold, hard segregation. And by the time
the programs came along, I was too large to qualify. So in my case, I guess, it
boiled down to hard work, determination and not gonna let nobody turn me
around." True or not, this was the only way for Russell to maintain his dignity—to escape from the inevitable humiliation of joint venturing.

The airport opened in September 1980, just as Maynard Jackson was
nearing the end of his second and, by local law, final term. Named in
honor of the city's most famous previous mayor, the man who had first
cracked the door of segregation, Hartsfield International Airport was seen as
Jackson's towering achievement: the key to Atlanta's economic future and its
first major multiracial accomplishment—proof positive that blacks and

whites could work together to make the city great. The opening was an occasion for tremendous hoopla—the kind of party only Atlantans know how to throw. President Jimmy Carter was the first official passenger, flying in on Air Force One the day before the ribbon-cutting to give a speech in support of affirmative action. This was followed by several days of parties, with every institution in town, from City Hall to the art museum, hosting an event of its own. The final, crowning do—a catered, black-tie gala—brought twelve thousand people out to the airport. Pantsuits and dashikis mixed with the gown-and-tux set, and together the integrated crowd spilled over the terminal, riding the people-mover and testing the six-language information system, many of them, downing Jack Daniel's and caviar, getting hopelessly lost in the process.

The terminal was the biggest in the world and the most modern, thanks to the people-mover and mechanized baggage handling. Seventy-one of the two hundred firms that built it were said to be minority-owned, and according to Jackson, airport work had created twenty-one black millionaires. "We have established beyond question," he noted in one speech, "that hard-nosed, businesslike practices can be followed—that project schedules and budgets can be maintained—and at the same time desirable and necessary social goals can be met." It was a boast that would echo in Atlanta for decades to come: the terminal, it was said by everyone from Andrew Young to Lawrence Gellerstedt, had come in "on time and under budget." Conveniently, given the year that "weeds grew" at the site, no one was counting too precisely. "We used to joke," said former mayor Sam Massell, one of the few who dared to question the conventional wisdom. "On time and under budget—yeah. But the budget was already inflated and the schedule stretched out to who knows when."

More objective measures of the airport set-aside would dribble in slowly over the years. An early assessment by the usually supportive *Atlanta Journal* revealed widespread corruption at the site: not quite as bad, perhaps, as the worst white stereotypes predicted—not every black-owned business was a sham—but still shocking to most well-intentioned Atlantans. Minority subcontractors came out looking the worst—if not more fraudulent, at least more easily caught than joint venture partners. Of $70 million subcontracted to allegedly black-owned businesses, some $12 million, or 17 percent, went to out-and-out fronts—a white company headed by a black figurehead. Another 12 percent, or $8.5 million, went to "pass-through" conduits: black middlemen taking what Atlantans call a "rake-off." Still another 10 percent went to companies so ill-equipped to participate that they were already out of business before the terminal opened. And a final 15 percent went to white-controlled firms that didn't even bother to put up a front but were still mistakenly considered by the city to be minority-owned. Together, these frauds ate up 54 percent of "black" subcontract dollars. As for the rest, more than half of it—23 percent of the total thought to end up in minority hands—went to one firm, the Illinois-based paving company, F. O. Thacker, another already established, successful black venture, like Russell's or Robinson's, hardly in need of affirmative action. "A few black contractors were strengthened," said the *Journal* disappointedly, "but most were shuffled aside by the fast-buck artists."

What about bona fide black subs—the few fledgling companies that completed a piece of airport work? Seven years later, a shocking number of them were also out of business. Thacker was still going strong; so was the number two subcontract recipient—another already robust entrepreneur, an electrician, who had gotten about 10 percent of the $70-million total. But a full half of the others had proved unable to make it on their own. "The airport program offered them a false sense of security," said one city official, "and when it was no longer there . . . many of them just died on the vine." More and more, it seemed that what white construction workers had suspected was true: the set-aside had succeeded in putting money in a few black contractors' pockets. A tiny handful of men—Russell, Robinson, Thacker and Cordy—had amassed a slightly larger stake than they began with. But the dream of an apprentice program that would produce a black business class had come to virtually naught—and if anything had further soured race relations in Atlanta.

Jackson's effort to fill the airport shops and restaurants with black vendors was equally unsuccessful. Even more than the construction preference, the concession set-aside was sold as an opportunity for start-ups: a way for poor blacks to get a foothold in the system. Unlike contractors, these first-time entrepreneurs would not need much capital or experience; and, it was imagined, they would learn from doing—in shoeshine stands, newspaper shops and flower kiosks. But again the reality turned out differently. In fact, it was discovered in the mid-eighties, every one of the blacks who got space at Hartsfield, whether for an ice cream parlor, a lounge or a fast-food restaurant, was already wealthy or politically well connected. There were thirteen in all, and they included Herman Russell, Jesse Hill, Maynard Jackson's ex-wife, Bunny, and the head of the Atlanta Urban League.

Even so, many of the ablest blacks at the airport were only passive partners. Rents were high at Hartsfield, it was hard to make money, and before
long several of the original black concessionaires had gone bankrupt or
bailed out. (By 1988, only five of the original thirteen were still in business.)
Some sold to whites, but the whites still needed black partners—the city
required it—and political connections were a more important qualification
than retail expertise. So, for a decade, Atlanta's best connected black entrepreneurs passed shares of airport concessions around like footballs, and in
most cases, each new black owner was even less involved than the one before.
One investigating reporter found that the 30 percent owner of the ice cream
concession knew virtually nothing about day-to-day details. The 100 percent owner of the hot-dog operation knew even less: the international airport caterer, Dobbs House, simply managed the business for him. In the
kiosks and restaurants, even more than in the building of the airport, it was
a small group of experienced black businessmen who were making money;
indeed, the two groups overlapped, with Russell and the Thacker family at
the center of both. Meanwhile, no mom-and-pop black entrepreneurs had
succeeded in launching a business. There had been no apprenticeship, and
no new start-up companies had taken off.

None of these revelations seemed to matter much to black supporters of
the airport set-asides. Maynard Jackson continued to trumpet the minority
business program as the defining accomplishment of his mayoralty. "We
rewrote the book on affirmative action," he often said. By the time he left
office in 1981, the share of city contracting going to minority entrepreneurs
had risen from virtually nothing to nearly 34 percent. Some blacks inside the
construction business questioned the relevance of these numbers. "Those are
meaningless figures," said one top Russell manager. "You have to look at the
back side of the operation—are you really building up black businesses?"
Construction insiders, black and white, agreed unanimously that no more
than a handful of ventures, most of them already doing well, had really benefited from the program. But Jackson and his aides were undeterred. For
them, a few success stories were worth whatever it cost. Confronted by
reporters asking about airport rent-a-skins, the mayor pounded on the table
and gave questioners a taste of vintage Jackson treatment. "Imperfections in
the program?" he roared. "Yes. Missteps? Yes. Have we tried hard? Yes. Have
our hearts been in the right place? Yes. Who's copying us now? We're cited
across the nation. That's the bottom line."

For ordinary black Atlantans, too, the numbers seemed beside the point. Whatever the city's vast network of set-asides did for the entrepreneurial middle class, there was no appreciable trickle-down to the third of the black population below the poverty line. During Jackson's mayoralty, Atlanta unemployment grew from under thirteen thousand to roughly nineteen thousand. The welfare rolls shrank slightly but, local officials conceded, only because of tightened eligibility requirements. And even with the nation's largest public housing system, when Jackson left office, there were two thousand families on the waiting list. Still, polls showed, poor black Atlantans were as enthusiastic as the middle class about the city's minority contracting policy: 80 percent of those with incomes under $10,000 supported it, compared with 81 percent of better earners. Pollster John Hutcheson explained why he thought this was so: "because of the fact that many poor black people in this city see other black people who have made it." Whether it worked for them personally or not, blacks seemed to find something satisfying about affirmative action. Color-coded loyalties were already proving stronger than self-interest, and poorer black Atlantans made no move to demand more— to hold the black city government responsible for programs that might make a real difference in the ghetto. If anything, Maynard Jackson left office more popular than when he was elected, with south side favorability ratings in the 65 percent range. But the poison of affirmative action was already working its way among both black and white Atlantans.

Chapter 14

THE TUG OF SOLIDARITY

T he occasion was Herman Russell's twenty-fifth wedding anniversary, but the party, at Russell's roomy south side home, was also a celebration of Atlanta's mushrooming black middle class. There was a crackerjack four-piece dance band, a mountain of crab claws and everyone who mattered in black Atlanta: the old professional elite, the new airport millionaires, Maynard Jackson's brassy lieutenants and a swarm of white-collar newcomers to the city. With Jackson now in 1981 winding down his second term, leaving Atlanta the national capital of affirmative action–backed black business, Russell and his guests had plenty to be thankful for. But they were also thinking about the future and were pleased that Andrew Young could be among them—the most promising black candidate to replace Jackson as mayor.

Young worked the crowd quietly: no need for speeches here, at his home base. It was one of the few rooms in Atlanta where he could hope to raise a little money. By now—it was late August 1981, with the first round of voting scheduled for October—he had collected hundreds of thousands of dollars in New York and Los Angeles, where the national black establishment, from Harry Belafonte to Miles Davis, had been giving parties and getting the word out. But here in Atlanta, Young was way behind, mainly because of the Peachtree civic leaders. Not only had the businessmen rallied all but unanimously around white state legislator Sidney Marcus, but—for the first time in memory—they were not even hedging their bets by giving a little to the other major candidates. For all practical purposes, Young had been frozen out, and even as his poll numbers rose, the white men avoided him around town.

In ordinarily discreet and conflict-shy Atlanta, the businessmen's racial boycott was nothing short of shocking. Naturally mild-mannered and conciliatory, Young had always found it easy to get along with whites. As long ago as Birmingham and before, he had been the movement's moderate negotiator: playing "good cop" to the angry, marching men's "bad cop," he had gone to see local businessmen when the demonstrations were done and worked out a deal both sides could live with. Now a nationally known figure, former congressman and until recently UN ambassador with cabinet rank, he assumed he would have an easy time winning in Atlanta. Instead, the Young camp watched as downtown distanced itself. The first signals were veiled. "We're getting a new code word," said a Jackson aide. "People say, 'We need an administrator,' and the list is all white." Then one prominent developer who had backed Young in the past wrote him an explicit letter. "He told me," Young remembered, "'You know, you were a good congressman. You probably would be a good mayor, too. I really wish I could support you. I just wish you were white.'"

Many blacks Atlantans saw the Peachtree attitude as simple bigotry. But Young was sure it wasn't, sure that even the developer's letter "wasn't a hate statement"—and that the businessmen's reservations were less about him than about Maynard Jackson. Still reeling from eight years of confrontations with Jackson, the civic elite now felt free to complain about him—and though they rarely mentioned race, his racial politics were plainly part of what bothered them. Some griped about their lack of access to City Hall: "We kind of hate to stand around with our thumbs in our mouths," said one merchant. Others recalled the hectoring backroom meetings: "Maynard had a way of rolling his eyeballs," noted a developer. "People were up to their neck and right to the nose with Maynard," explained another business insider. "He ended up with no goodwill in the business community, and everyone feared that Andy would be more of the same." Like antibusing mothers who hated first the judge, then the buses, then the color of the kids who rode them, the Atlanta elite resented affirmative action—and, by extension, the color of the man who foisted it on them. Still, ever the conciliator, Young was convinced he could overcome these misgivings.

The 1981 mayoral race was a three-way contest: Young, Marcus and Reginald Eaves, Maynard Jackson's old college chum and controversial black police chief. Lawyer and businessman Sidney Marcus was a quintessential son of the Peachtree elite. A sense of civic duty had pulled him away from the family contracting business, and he had spent over a decade in state government, pursuing a liberal, integrationist agenda. "He's a consensus seeker," said one insider approvingly. At the other end of the spectrum—with a radically different tone and appeal—stocky, combative Reginald Eaves was an out-of-towner, originally from Boston, with a northern willingness to play on racial resentment in a way not even his mentor Jackson had dared to do. At the police department, he had pushed affirmative action and the need to defang the "occupying army" in blue. Forced to resign after a string of scandals, he had taken this militancy into politics and made a name for himself as an angry irritant. Together, Marcus and Eaves defined the boundaries of the campaign: a well-meaning white who didn't dare talk about race and a black man who did nothing but. This left Young to wander around in the middle: like just about everyone in Atlanta, preoccupied with color, but handling it gingerly.

Eaves played on the race issue day in, day out, harping on police brutality, the racist criminal justice system, the possibility of riots if the mayoralty were to revert to white hands. In his view, and he made it explicit, his main qualification was his color. "Symbolically," he said, "a black mayor here is important to young people. We cannot at this point create the image that blacks cannot succeed." Many Atlantans seemed put off by this outright race baiting, and polls consistently showed Eaves running a distant third. Still, it became clear, he was only saying what many others thought. Speaking from the pulpit of one of the city's biggest black churches, Maynard Jackson echoed the candidate's color-coded appeal: "We think we're free, but what little progress we've made can slip through our fingers. . . . There never has been a second black mayor elected in a major city." Former movement leader Julian Bond was even more explicit, talking to reporters of the "tragedy" in the offing. "If Andy loses and Sidney wins," he warned, "blacks around the country will wonder, 'Maybe we can't do it here either. Maybe our black candidate ought not to run.'"

On TV and with reporters, Young tried tirelessly to raise the level of the rhetoric. Not only did he downplay—and explicitly pardon—the businessmen's racial campaign against him, but again and again he went out of his way to appease whites' fears and speak to their concerns. Unlike Eaves and others who made careers out of complaining about whites, Young preferred whenever he could to talk about how race relations were improving. He constantly reminded voters that he had been elected to Congress by a majority-white district. With Marcus's campaign war chest running three times the size of his own, he still declined to bait or guilt-trip downtown. Before both black and white audiences, he talked thoughtfully about the legitimate white concerns that he felt were often mistaken for racism: concerns about the city's schools, its crime rate, its unskilled workforce. He promised to make suburbanites feel more welcome in the city and even broke with orthodox black opinion to come out in favor of more metropolitan government. Jimmy Carter underscored these appeals when he endorsed his old friend, praising Young for his "special ability to bring people together."

Still, integrationist as he was and determined to transcend the animosities of the past, as the campaign wore on, not even Young could entirely resist the tyranny of racial politics. The unbending rejection of the white businessmen didn't make things any easier. Among Peachtree regulars, only Charles Loudermilk, CEO of a large office furniture rental firm, came forward to support the former congressman. A conventional southerner, wealthy, Republican, Loudermilk was an unlikely trailblazer. But he grasped that for better or worse the next mayor would probably be black, and admiring the way Young handled himself, he tried to persuade other insiders to back him. "Over my dead body," responded leading banker Robert Strickland, shouting into the telephone. "This is our last chance of having a white mayor." Young never answered in kind or publicly blamed the elite, but their rebuff freed him to spend more time on the south side and to run, implicitly at least, on the qualification of his black skin.

Meanwhile, the pull on the black side—the pull of solidarity—was unrelenting. Eaves led the charge, followed by the Black Power advocates who dominated the campuses of the city's five black colleges. Their bitter taunts, implicit and explicit, rarely made the papers, but occasionally a reporter would catch the innuendo: that Young was "not black enough." He dismissed the accusations with characteristic aplomb. "Some people have attacked my—I don't know how to put it—my blackness, my militance. The irony is that these people are armchair militants who were never involved in the real struggle." Still, like it or not, Young had to appeal to voters where they lived—and for blacks, even in moderate Atlanta, that meant appealing to them as blacks first.

It all seemed innocent enough at the outset. Campaigning in south side churches, Young told and retold his movement war stories. With the Herman Russell set, he talked about his popularity in Africa and his dream of bringing African business to Atlanta. But as the campaign wore on, just like Eaves and Jackson and others, Young found himself reaping votes by encouraging stereotypes and alienation. Welcoming the endorsement of the nationalist Shrine of the Black Madonna, he grew more and more comfortable complaining about "racist" Republicans, stirring up resentment of ghetto police and blaming Atlanta's problems on bigoted northern bankers.

The racemongering escalated sharply after the first round of voting eliminated Eaves, pitting Young against Marcus in an openly color-coded runoff. "For twenty years," *Atlanta Journal* city editor Dick Williams said later, "without designation on the ballot, the White Party and the Black Party have vied for office in Atlanta. It was no different in 1981. There were no accidents. Young and his supporters played the race card, and both candidates focused on getting out the vote on their side of town." The campaign's culminating moment came just days before the vote: a speech by Maynard Jackson at the Butler Street YMCA, unofficial headquarters of the Auburn Avenue power structure. Taking aim at middle-class blacks who had broken ranks to support Marcus, Jackson laid down the law, stern and implacably color-coded. Blacks who support white candidates are "shuffling and grinning . . . slick-talking Negroes," he charged, "trying to justify their relationship with [white power] . . . jockeying for positions closer to the table so that when [the white man] is reminded to throw them a crumb, they will be in a position to grin and catch it."

Discreet, integrationist Atlanta had never heard anything like it—certainly not from a member of the downtown establishment. Then, even more astonishing, Young refused to repudiate the speech. By election day, his campaign was so sure that voters were choosing solely by color that it chartered buses to ferry south siders to polling places, and journalists remember seeing signs in largely black precincts: "North Side Voting Heavy. Go to the Polls." With the city by now some 67 percent black, Young carried the day by an easy margin.

Then, after the election, he immediately snapped back to his old conciliatory, integrationist self, forgiving and eager to transcend the color line. "I would hope that most of the polarization and the hostility was in the press," he said of the campaign, "and that it really does not exist in this city nearly to the extent we thought it does." He met with Peachtree insiders at an off-the-record lunch and reassured them that he had no intention of governing, as Jackson had, without their cooperation and support. He sounded the same theme again and again before blacks as well as whites: an urgent call for racial healing. "Those divisions between black and white are essentially artificial," he insisted. "We'll move forward together—or destroy ourselves." And remarkably enough, in a matter of days, both blacks and whites had rallied around him, welcoming the chance to paper over the unsightly gap revealed during the campaign.

The changes were small but everywhere, the key difference one of style. But style and tone seemed to be what it took to transform the city, and the adversarial tone of the Jackson era soon gave way to easy, open communication. Unlike Jackson, Young was always available, unfailingly polite, eager to cooperate, and before long white business was trumpeting the difference between the two men. "Andy Young's style is much easier for a white person to deal with," said Dan Sweat. "He doesn't come down so heavy-handed, and so much isn't made into a racial issue." "From his first day in office," said another man, a retailer, "you knew he represented everybody. You knew he had respect for the white people as well." It was a pleasant honeymoon, testament to both sides' yearning for integration. But even in boosterish Atlanta, most people knew it was a small, fragile achievement—no more than the tentative beginnings of community and still shadowed by deeply ingrained color consciousness.

The 1981 election was not the first or last time Young would find himself struggling to strike a balance between his racial loyalty and his integrationism. Like any black child growing up in America in the 1930s and 1940s, he could hardly escape an awareness of bigotry or an inevitably bittersweet race consciousness. But he was also bright and better-off, and the circumstances of his upbringing conspired to help him look beyond color. Third-generation middle-class, born and raised in the racially mixed city of New Orleans, he grew up with stories of a Jewish great-grandfather, a trader from Poland who had married into his mother's family. His father, Andrew Young, Sr., a dentist and leader of his church, was a classic "exaggerated American." Young's was the only black family in the Irish-Italian neighborhood where he grew up, and he and his brother were the only middle-class children in their all-black elementary school.

The lessons of childhood reinforced his basic integrationism. By Young's account, his father was intent on passing along two messages—that he should succeed in the white world and never get angry. It didn't take Young long to reject his father's dream that he become a dentist. But even as he charted his own activist path, he never lost sight of his family's emphasis on accomplishment and on the idea that blacks and whites should share the same standards. His father's second message had even more impact. "Daddy was a very calm man who saw emotion as a weakness," Young later wrote. "He never seemed to let anything touch him. . . . and he taught me never to lose my cool." Father and son spent hours shadow-boxing: lessons in self-control under pressure. "Don't get mad, get smart," was Young Senior's constant refrain and one that his son thoroughly internalized. It was a teaching that would serve him well in the civil rights movement and after, when he never let his anger at whites—however understandable or justified—get the better of his self-interest.

Young continued to search for his racial balance through college and beyond. He chose traditionally black institutions—first Dillard, in New Orleans, then Howard—where he was a carefree, good-times youth. The years after graduation brought a religious awakening, then ordination in the largely white Congregational church. In the mid-fifties, he went through what he called "my black consciousness." "I was on the verge of being absorbed by the white community," he later explained, "so I totally rebelled culturally." For some months, he listened to only black music, read all he could about Africa, applied (unsuccessfully) for permission to establish a church mission in Angola and eventually landed a pulpit in a small southern town where he could "be around plain, wise, black folk." It was there that he met his first wife, Jean, and apparently worked through his identity questions, reporting later, "That's when I decided I could be black in the midst of the white world. I've taken it for granted ever since." By the late fifties, the couple had made their way to New York, where Young was again working in a largely white universe—in the youth department of the National Council of Churches. There, in his home in middle-class Queens, he and Jean watched the early sit-ins on TV. "I have rarely been so moved by a television program," he said later. "We could literally feel God calling us back to the South."

In the movement as before, Young stood out as a man of easy self-assurance—confident enough, no matter what the circumstances, to move to his own beat. It was his church and the Field Foundation that first sent him to the South to oversee rural voter registration. This work brought him into contact with Dr. King, whom he joined officially in 1961, rising eventually to be the executive director of the SCLC. He spent some time training recruits and occasionally led a demonstration, but his relaxed confidence soon cast him in another role: as Julian Bond described it, "King was the spear-thrower and Andy came behind and put it all together." Forthright, intuitive, naturally man-to-man—even across the color line in the Old South—Young had the presence not only to confront powerful whites but also to weather the doubts of fellow activists who quickly, and not always jokingly, labeled him the movement Uncle Tom. "Where was Andy," another veteran would later ask bitterly, "when the rest of us were getting our heads bashed in?" "I didn't have any problem talking to white people," Young responded. "In fact I wanted to talk to white people. I always went into a negotiation figuring that if I could solve my opponents' problem, my problem would be solved. Once you dealt with their ungrounded fears, then you could go on and show them the positive side of what you wanted them to do."

His years with King crystallized Young's integrationism and gave him the confidence to shrug off questions about "how black" he was. His faith in an interracial future was reflected in his casual vocabulary: his preference even years later for phrases like "the human family," "human rights" and "human relations"—rather than "civil rights" or "black progress." "As we learn more about people," he insisted, "we have less and less to fear. There is much more that even the most divergent among us have in common than that which divides us." For him, integration meant freedom from hate—which he saw as a burden mainly for the hater—and from imprisoning race consciousness. Determined to see beyond bigotry— to "de-moralize" and understand it as mere "ethnocentrism"—he could sympathize with white southerners and even white South Africans, whom he saw as a group trapped by history. Looking back later, he was proud that Americans had "been successful enough in integration so that being black is not the total defining part of some people's lives." Never exactly color-blind—what American black could be?—Young nevertheless forged what seemed like a diamond-hard faith in the need to transcend color and put his racial resentment behind him.

The years after King's death were not so easy. Singled out among movement veterans to run for office largely because of his crossover appeal, Young was elected to Congress in 1972 by a majority-white district. He saw this as a point of pride: "If a white majority elects a black man to Congress," he argued, "it will say that the American dream is still possible." When he got to Washington, he found himself pigeonholed as a black leader, expected to speak for black voters on black issues, but even then he seemed to keep his racial balance. As Georgia's first black congressman since Reconstruction and a charter member of the Congressional Black Caucus, he pursued his lifelong fascination with Africa and usefully informed himself about the economics of poverty—all without letting go of his innate integrationism. Impressed colleagues noted his almost color-blind friendliness, his calm pragmatism, the habit of working man-to-man, behind the scenes, and before long he was even breaking occasionally with the racial orthodoxies of the Black Caucus. The year he spent helping Jimmy Carter win the presidency—proclaiming the New South and calling for a "deracialized" America—was the high point of Young's integrationism. Then President-elect Carter appointed him ambassador to the United Nations.

The UN job and his forced departure from it would sorely test Young's interracial commitment. His main qualification for the post was his black skin; his main task, as he described it, "sticking his head out [as] a black man [to] ask another black to trust a white man." Committed as he was to overcoming color, Young liked the role, and he soon grew comfortable doing something he had always eschewed as polarizing: sounding off about racism, both abroad and at home. He spent thirty-three months at Turtle Bay, America's highest-ranking black man. But it was when the news of his contacts with the Palestine Liberation Organization (PLO) broke that he truly became a black hero—now no longer an Uncle Tom, but what one admirer called "a living martyr." Forced to resign from the United Nations, he emerged overnight, one news account put it, "as the Number One leader for America's black community." "We've had no symbol like that," said a prominent pastor, "since movement days." "Thank God," echoed Washington mayor Marion Barry, "we've got another voice out there now." The more Jewish groups and other whites criticized him, the more Young was celebrated as a scapegoat—unjustly wronged and a permanent outsider. One overwrought black elected official even compared his resignation to the martyrdom of Martin Luther King. "I had the same sense of loss and a feeling of profound sadness," the man said, "and then I got angry."

In the wake of the PLO incident, Young could not resist a little race baiting. "They tried to put me in my place," he said angrily of the State Department. "The United States will not let a black man run foreign policy." He repaired to Africa, where he traveled as a business consultant, nursing his wounds. Then, in the months that followed, he discovered a new career: freelance speaker and op-ed columnist. A more sought-after lecturer than anyone from the administration except the president and Rosalynn, Young was especially popular with black organizations: not just political groups, but fraternities and color-coded clubs like One Hundred Black Men and the

Links. More recognized, more often cartooned, more frequently roasted and toasted than any other black spokesman in America—including the emerging Jesse Jackson—Young, the sometime integrationist, now sometime race man, looked around for what to do next. By now, he was using the word "we" interchangeably to mean both "we Americans" of all colors and "we blacks," that special, alienated interest group. And just as he often seemed to strike an admirable balance, so he occasionally seemed in the grip of confusion, torn between his universalist aspirations and the tug of his racial loyalties.

Young seemed to find his balance again in his first years as mayor of Atlanta. He was not known as a hands-on executive; in his first twelve months in office, he took three extended trips abroad in an effort to lure Third World trade to Atlanta. But when at home, he worked assiduously on maintaining good relations with the Peachtree crowd. There were regular gatherings with groups and intimate one-on-one talks over meals. The white men remember Young showing up early at meetings and staying late to shmooze, calling late at night for advice or to tell them in advance about something he was going to do the next day. Even the most skeptical insiders were impressed. Robert Strickland, the banker who had shouted in Charles Loudermilk's ear that Atlanta would elect another black mayor only "over my dead body," emerged as one of Young's biggest fans, one among many. Praising the mayor's "God-given gift" as a conciliator, Strickland owned that "the relationship between the business community and City Hall is better now than it has been in a long, long time." It was the old "Atlanta style" all over again: mayor and business leaders running the city together behind closed doors—only now the mayor was black and the alliance straddled the color line.

This cooperation did not sit particularly well with ordinary black Atlantans, and before long Young was under pressure to prove just where his racial loyalties lay. Two big fights in the first year of his mayoralty—one about taxation, the other over a proposed highway through a residential area—turned into racial litmus tests. In both cases, Young took what opponents saw as the "white side," business-friendly at the expense of the less fortunate: in favor of the new road, and of replacing property tax revenue with a sales tax. Advocates for the south side poor bitterly denounced the mayor as a "sellout": the "new black pharaoh in City Hall." "He has curtailed white fears and middle-class blacks are profiting," charged one critic, "but we have sacrificed the poor. That's a hell of a price to pay for a relationship with the white community." Self-assured as ever, confident of his support among the black rank-and-file, Young barreled ahead, confronting critical ministers in front of their own congregations and putting the proposed tax before the people in a referendum. As it turned out, he knew his constituency—particularly working-poor black Atlantans—and even among blacks the vote went his way. "Andy Young is the only elected official who could have gotten it passed," commented city councilman John Lewis. "[Black] people trust him. They feel he won't let them down. He gets support in both [black and white] camps because of his stature in both communities."

Still, the question of what his blackness meant hung heavily over the new mayor, as it hung over all elected black officials in those years. By the early eighties, there were nearly three hundred black mayors in America, including in four of the country's biggest cities. The Congressional Black Caucus was a highly visible, active body; black influence in the Democratic Party, particularly in presidential elections, was recognized as pivotal. Yet in the cities, where most blacks lived, it was far from clear what black politicians could do to help—to influence even unemployment, let alone the cycle of poverty, rising crime, drugs or the deteriorating family. Should the goal be helping blacks as blacks, or improving race relations, or simply priming the economy in the hope that a rising tide would lift all boats? "The biggest problem we face as black mayors," Young noted, "is living up to the expectations of black voters." As a lifelong integrationist, he also had to ask himself what integration meant now—just how relevant it was and how it could help in a city with the problems of Atlanta.

The national black leadership seemed to have little sense of direction. In August 1983, the movement and its followers convened in Washington for the twentieth anniversary of the 1963 march. Some 250,000 people gathered on the Mall, almost exactly the number that had come 20 years before, and those who attended both events agreed that the day was much better organized this time around. Still, no one who had been in Washington in 1963 seemed to feel that the spirit of that day had been rekindled. This was a sweltering, humid Saturday, 90-plus degrees, with storm clouds hovering. Failing acoustics did not help, and the crowd tended to drift as the afternoon wore on: swelling, dwindling, swelling again, yet never very intently focused. Jesse Jackson, Coretta Scott King, Reverend Joseph Lowery were featured speakers, but the oratory that seemed most to move the crowd—and the one text printed the next day in *The New York Times*—was Martin Luther King's twenty-year-old "I Have a Dream" speech, aired over the giant loudspeakers that lined the Mall.

The most thoughtful of the leadership, including Young, struggled to wrest some meaning out of the day. A Sunday morning news-show host put the question bluntly to the mayor: "Yesterday's demonstration was a march for 'Jobs, Peace and Freedom'—sort of like being for motherhood, isn't it? . . . You're the one who has turned to political action. Will there be some kind of political offshoot?" Young spent the next thirty minutes scrambling for an answer. He called for a rejection of "militarism and materialism," for political pressure on South Africa, for a lowering of interest rates ("With 14 to 16 percent interest," he said, "nobody can . . . bring themselves up by their own bootstraps"). If his comments had a theme, it was the same as that of the march: easy jabs at Ronald Reagan. Determined as he was to find a policy solution—something the government could do for blacks—Young seemed unable to articulate his own living integrationism. The closest he got to the idea of reconciliation or racial harmony was to talk in passing about the gentrification of city neighborhoods. Martin Luther King's refrain, "Where do we go from here?" had rarely seemed so apt. Plainly enough, the movement had run out of answers, and even those, like Young, who were working gradually toward a response were having difficulty making it heard over the din of ritualized protest.

At home in Atlanta, Young continued to champion integration, and as he struggled to find practical ways to realize the dream, Jackson's minority business program began to look more and more appealing—a way to spur black entry into the system that also happened to be popular with the rank-and-file who doubted Young's racial authenticity. By now, it was clear to all that the main barrier holding blacks back was economic, and as his supporter Charles Loudermilk recalled, "Andy wanted to give as many blacks as possible an opportunity to get a piece of the action—not just the political action but the money action, too." The black middle class would lead the way into the mainstream, and before long poor blacks would also profit, as black entrepreneurs and the businesses they created generated jobs for people in the ghetto. This sort of change was already happening in Atlanta, but for Young and his backers, it was too important to be left to time and spontaneous effort. Ever the activist, Young was convinced he could help by speeding up the clock, and if the integrationist in him thought twice about the racial categories—the stigmas and stereotypes—he would be perpetuating, he never let on to anyone.

Young moved ahead aggressively in his first year as mayor to strengthen the city set-aside. A new team of sharp, young professionals was brought on board: mostly twenty-something, middle-class, too young to have participated in the protests of the fifties and sixties, they were determined to make their mark now—helping to advance black business. Rodney Strong, typical of this group, had come to Atlanta to attend Morehouse College and was active even in his student days organizing demonstrations in support of Maynard Jackson. Close to two hundred pounds, sharp, shrewd and articulate, Strong could have been Jackson's son carrying on his legacy—only more sophisticated. Trained as a lawyer, invariably pinstriped but still talking the language of the movement, he oversaw a huge expansion of the city's affirmative action bureaucracy. "The period before Andy," he later recalled, "was the float-like-a-butterfly, sting-like-a-bee period in minority business. What we did was institutionalize and aggressively enforce the program."

An ordinance signed by the mayor in his first hundred days put an end to the old backroom meetings. From now on, minority participation would be a legal requirement written into every contract. An elaborate system was established to ferret out fronts and pass-throughs. Companies claiming to be minority firms had to submit tax returns and sworn financial statements, and when in doubt, the city zeroed in with formal audits and on-site inspections. Still more bureaucracy was added to maintain a running list—"the register"—of bona fide black businesses, making it harder for white firms to plead they could not find a minority partner. Money was even spent on PR agents and glossy brochures to remind incoming corporations—they were still streaming into Atlanta—just what the local rules and expectations were.

Meanwhile, the Peachtree set's attitude was changing too, as more and more of the businessmen grasped that affirmative action could be in their interest. Lawrence Gellerstedt, Jr., the owner and chairman of Beers Inc., had been one of the original skeptics. Among the city's leading contractors, a pillar of the downtown elite, he had not participated in the airport set-aside and had always assumed the worst: that white business had gone along because "there was no alternative." "Then," he recalled, "I did my first joint venture." His partner was Herman Russell; the job, building a library for one of the black colleges that make up Atlanta University.

It turned out to be a typical Atlanta joint venture—typically unequal. Negotiated as a 51–49 percent partnership, it required rough parity in capital and bonding. But when it came to staffing the job, far from doing his share, Russell sent only one man to join the managerial team in the trailer. A young, handsome Antiguan, educated at the Wharton Business School, Egbert Perry had just come to work for Russell, and though he knew more about big, commercial construction than anyone else at the black-owned firm, he was way out of his depth among the seasoned Beers men. As assistant to the project manager, it was Perry's job to follow the white man around and do his bidding—as Beers's Herbert Edwards put it, "whatever we told him." "There was no question," said Gellerstedt, "on that deal, Herman was not doing a thing but going to school."

After more than two decades in business for himself, Russell was by far the most successful black businessman in Atlanta: a local legend overseeing a broadly diversified corporation—everything from building single-family homes to a local beer distributorship and TV station—with revenues of nearly $40 million a year. Still, no one close to the operation, black or white, had any illusions about its capacity for large-scale construction—an entirely different line of work from building single-family houses. Egbert Perry remembered that when he joined the company in 1980—a year when Russell did some $10 to $20 million in high-rise construction work—there were only four technical professionals on that side of the business. Haywood Curry, still an employee at J. A. Jones, one of Russell's main joint venture partners, recalled him sending only one or two people to big skyscraper jobs, in wild disproportion to the number Jones sent. "We were getting attention as a sizable minority firm," said one Russell man, "but when you opened the door, there was nothing to substantiate the image. Herman did nothing on the big construction deals—nothing. How could he have?" Joint ventures had meant incredible opportunity, and in less than a decade, the Russell company had gone from $500,000 a year in work to fifty-fifty partnership in projects worth over $100 million. But the set-asides had allowed Russell to appear as a major player without doing what was necessary to build up his operation. "If you're in a joint venture," said Curry, "and the other guy is providing most of the personnel, you don't need to train anyone. You don't need to buy equipment. You don't even have to worry about what happens on the job." "All we had to do," said another insider, "was show up and get a check."

Still, in Gellerstedt's eyes, the Atlanta University joint venture was "a fabulous success." "If every joint venture worked that way," he said, "there would be no problem." For the big white builders, Russell's appeal transcended his experience and expertise. To do business in Atlanta, even business not strictly regulated by the government, builders needed a minority partner, and Russell was the one least likely to cause them trouble. Unlike his south side competitors, he could get the necessary bonding. Hardworking, disciplined, dependable, he was also undyingly good-natured. "He didn't wear the race issue on the outside," one Atlantan noted. "He didn't put whites off." Whether or not he or his people could do the job—whether they found the experience educational or merely humiliating—hardly mattered to the white men. "What Russell brought," said Gellerstedt, "was an atmosphere. It created a sense in the city that something was happening."

What the businessmen were discovering, exactly as Young had predicted, was that in a black-run Atlanta, they too benefited from the set-aside program. Part of the incentive was government work. "Whites looked at the dollars being passed through the city," said J. W. Robinson. "It was a big pot of money, and it was worth going after—worth doing a joint venture." Part of the lure was private money: as builders like Lawrence Gellerstedt and his friend and rival, Robert Holder, soon grasped, private clients like Delta and the Coca-Cola Company were keen to appease the buying public and didn't mind picking up the extra cost of a minority partner. But more than anything, the Peachtree set began to notice that they needed affirmative action to maintain their influence over city affairs—that they could trade minority participation for guaranteed access to the black government in City Hall. "It was an alliance of need," explained Charles Loudermilk. "We might be 90 percent of the wealth. But they have 98 to 100 percent of the political power."

When it came to political access, Herman Russell was the perfect joint venture partner. After more than thirty years of groundwork, his political connections reached wide and deep. He had started in the sixties, when the first blacks were elected in Atlanta, and had been among the first black businessmen to back both Maynard Jackson and Andrew Young. Other black entrepreneurs had followed in his footsteps, funding black candidates at every level of government. Even savvy newcomers had learned to play the game, and some of them were now even better plugged in than many old-time Atlantans. Altogether, these givers were a small group, but for better than a decade they dominated the joint ventures that pulled down the city's biggest contracts. "You have to spend a lot of time nurturing relationships in Atlanta," said one architect who did public-sector work. "The minority firms that have been successful have all worked hard at this kind of 'business development.'"

Not all the black businessmen were big givers—not even Russell gave large sums of money—and what they got in exchange was rarely illegal.

Contributors used their ins to get and hold concessions at the airport, to catch the ears of city council members with some say over procurement, to learn in advance of big construction jobs and other contracts in the offing. Most city purchasing and contracting jobs were bid, so a political connection was no guarantee of work; but judging by the outcome, it never hurt to have a link to someone in City Hall. "If you give, you may get the job," said one black architect. "If you don't give, you definitely will not get it."

For Atlanta's white establishment, the benefit of joint venturing with these black insiders was obvious. The first to profit were the white architects and engineers who won contracts to build the airport. But even in the early years, the white businessmen grasped that taking on a black partner could help with more than snagging city work. "The only way whites can reach the black political establishment," one black entrepreneur explained, "is through Herman Russell or the likes of Herman Russell." White builders and merchants used their joint venture partners to make their needs and wishes known to black officials, and usually they got what they asked for—not just from City Hall but also from Washington. Young called on his black friends in Congress and the Democratic Party to bolster the racial accommodation emerging in Atlanta, and over the decade the rewards rolled in: first supplementary funding for MARTA, then several federal grants to complete the expressway system, and in 1988 the lucrative Democratic National Convention took place in Atlanta. With each success, Young reminded downtown, "Whether you know it or not, this affirmative action stuff is paying off." "The money began to pour in," remembered Gellerstedt, "and in that circumstance, the logical businessperson says to himself, 'Well, there isn't much to be said about this. Even if I don't like it, the results are excellent.'"

Herman Russell was not the only black businessman to profit from the new civic order, but he was by far the most successful. The major builders jockeyed fiercely for the privilege of joint-venturing with him. Even in the early eighties, when he would still have had trouble with a $5-million building, his was among the half dozen firms invited to bid on all the big-league projects going up around town. J. A. Jones brought him in as a partner on the $150-million Georgia-Pacific Company's downtown headquarters, then the largest office building in the Southeast. In 1984, Jones and Robert Holder both courted him to bid with them on a major expansion of the Coca-Cola Company headquarters. Later that year, John Portman singled him out as the black he wanted included on his newest project—a glitzy downtown parking deck. From then on, for nearly a decade, Russell was the only black contractor getting work on big-time downtown construction jobs. The fact that he still struggled to carry his weight—and didn't exactly need the help—hardly seems to have troubled anyone.

By now, most of Atlanta understood that only a small group of blacks was benefiting from the set-aside. White developers looking for minority partners went back again and again to the few black contractors they knew to be reliable, and the importance of political connections narrowed the circle still further. Even as the decade wore on and other blacks had a chance to build up their businesses, the same names appeared again and again on the signs posted at the big construction sites: general contractors Herman Russell and Dave Moody, electrical contractor Tom Cordy, engineer Floyd Thacker, architects Oscar Harris and Pelham Williams. Administration officials saw nothing wrong with this; they were creating a new class of powerful black businessmen. But smaller minority contractors, devoted to the vision behind the set-aside, hardly knew what to make of the way it was panning out: a program that had promised to level the field, dispersing opportunity, seemed instead to be making the pyramid steeper—brutally competitive and with room for only a few at the top. "The purpose of the program was to take the lower middle class and move them into the middle class," complained one disappointed builder. "It was not to take a Herman Russell and pump him up higher." "A great deal of work," agreed city councilman John Lewis, "has gone to firms that were already at the top of the business community. Those who were driving a Mercedes are now driving a Rolls-Royce. But those who were walking are still walking."

By the mid-1980s, the Peachtree set was completely sold on affirmative action. With all city jobs now required by law to include 25 percent minority participation, anyone who wanted public-sector work had to find ways to meet the quota. Private-sector building was unregulated, and the vast bulk of it involved no preferences. But even in the private sector, many big, high-profile projects were racially sensitive, and most of the big-time builders and architects had had some occasion to use a minority partner. "Joint venturing is just a way of doing business here now," said one insider. "People trying to get something off the ground say, 'I've got the money. I've got the black.' Then all they have to worry about is the details." It was understood by people in business that teaming up with a less experienced minority would cost them a little more: estimates of the add-on ran between 10 and 15 percent—to search for the black firm, for the extra paperwork and to pick up the partner's end if he fell short. The extra burden discouraged many smaller white contractors. But for the power brokers, the benefits of joint venturing far outweighed the costs.

Only a few insiders, most of them black professionals, understood the possible dangers of the new civic compact, and none of them were in a position to make their doubts known. Herman Russell's top assistant Egbert Perry, J. A. Jones man Haywood Curry and developer Noel Khalil: twenty- and thirtysomething, highly educated, hardworking, astute and determined to make it in business, all three watched with alarm as the joint venture process became entrenched in the eighties. Fifteen years later, they still hesitated to make their complaints public. All were committed in principle to the idea of a minority business program. "Without affirmative action, I'd be a preacher or a teacher now," said Curry. "If you didn't require white companies to take on black partners, there would have been no progress." But even years afterward the former staffers were still outraged by what they had seen of Russell's partnerships with the likes of Jones, Beers and the Holder construction company.

The young black professionals hated the label "minority" and the stigma that came with it. "I refused to play the minority business game," said Perry. "I would never market the company as a minority company." He and the other critics heaped scorn on the way a few prominent whites and blacks had conspired to use their joint ventures for political advantage. "It was all about a few [black] firms that developed a good pimping game," said another staffer. "The only question was which group, black or white, could use the other the most." And all three insiders were convinced that the partnerships had been a boon for whites without doing much of anything to boost black firms. "It was a program for the majority firms," said still another man. "It cost them nothing. It put them in a preferred position, and they worked the economics so that the minority contractor had nothing in the end."

But the thing that troubled the insiders most was what they saw as both blacks' and whites' utter disregard for the original aim of joint venturing: the idea of building up black businesses. "The white businessmen could have taken the spirit of the law," one said indignantly. "They could have actually mentored blacks, trained them, created businesses. But for most white firms, doing a joint venture was just a way to get their hands on some city money. They used the black to get the job, they did the work, they took most of the money—and they gave a couple dollars to a token black guy." "Minority contractors," said Curry, "should have been insisting, 'Here is 25 percent of the money. Now take 25 percent of my people—to fill 25 percent of the jobs at every level, including the superintendent and the engineers.'" The young men didn't blame Russell. "I call him my superstar," said Curry. "He has lived the ultimate dream for a black man in this town." But they felt he too had lost sight of the goal: "I didn't see him building up a business," Curry said sadly.

From the time Egbert Perry arrived at the Russell company in 1980, he devoted himself to just that. Russell, flinty and skeptical, resisted every step, but Perry pressed him tirelessly to try a few changes. The younger man started with hiring: the best in the business, or the best he could lure away from the big white companies Russell had been working with. Jack Byrd and Julius McEver came from J. A. Jones, where both had been top-level managers. Older, experienced white men who knew the building trades inside out, they brainstormed with Perry about how get the Russell company off the ground. "Perry said, 'I want to really get in the construction business,'" Byrd remembered. "That's when things got going over there. That's when they caught fire." Perry convinced Russell to begin investing in the company. He told Byrd and McEver to get busy recruiting. "They didn't have the people," said Byrd. "Or the people they had weren't capable of doing what we wanted them to do." Then Perry pressed Russell to scale back a little on the size of the jobs they were going for. "We could bid on $20-million projects," Perry told a reporter. "But the smaller projects are [more] consistent with our growth plan." "We want $5-million to $10-million projects," Byrd explained. "We can train more people that way."

Most important in his eyes, Perry persuaded his boss to start bidding on stand-alone projects. In more than thirty years of construction work, Russell had built hundreds of single-family homes—rudimentary two-by-four and plywood construction. He had worked as a plastering subcontractor on scores of downtown skyscrapers and joint-ventured as a general contractor on a dozen more—the biggest of them in the $150-million range. But until 1983, he had never undertaken to put up a major steel-and-glass building by himself. He was still so uncomfortable with the idea that Perry had to threaten to resign to get him to take on the project. It was a medium-sized office block— a service center for the Atlanta Gas Light Company—in the $4- to $5-million range, and Russell had to borrow some Jones supervisors to get the job done. But for Perry and the company, it was a critical milestone.

After that, there were three or four more small independent jobs and finally, in 1985, a stand-alone project that broke the $10-million ceiling. A headline on the business page of the *Atlanta Constitution* announced that Russell was now "Building Toward the Big Time"—positioning the company, the text said, "to move up to big national projects." In the story, just as Perry had been urging, Russell eschewed the label "minority," and for a moment it looked as if he might actually escape—might graduate from the joint venture business and all the dependence that went with it.

It was not to be. There was too much at stake in Atlanta, and Russell was too much at the center of it. He was still the only sizable black general contractor in town, the only one with access to significant capital or bonding. He was the only black the big white builders knew and felt they could trust—the only one who had been to their clubs and visited them in their vacation homes. They needed him as their black partner—their ticket to public-sector projects and corporate construction work. And they needed him as their connection to the city's black political establishment. It was a financial but also psychological need—with joint venturing by now a critical part of the white men's self-image. If there had been other blacks to step in and fill his shoes, Russell might have escaped. But there weren't, or they weren't good enough to replace him, and his very success—his affability, dependability and connections—trapped him in the joint venture business. Besides, joint venturing had significant advantages for him, too. It required far less capital on each job than solo contracting, less overhead investment in the company, less time and effort spent training and drumming up business. Whatever a man like Perry saw as the humiliations and the ultimate glass ceiling, in Russell's eyes joint ventures were simply good business. Like the low-interest loans, tax breaks and other special subsidies he got because he was willing to build in the ghetto, affirmative action was just too good for Russell to pass up.

Before the eighties were over, Russell would help meet the minority quota on ten out of fifteen of the major construction projects undertaken by the city and county: several water treatment plants, the new Fulton County Jail, a new skyscraper addition to City Hall, several projects at the airport and the renovation of the city's vast Grady Memorial Hospital. High-profile public companies and utilities—Coca-Cola and Delta were the most persistent— would continue to request that whatever white builders they hired pair up with Russell. Gellerstedt could not remember joint-venturing with anyone else in these years. But it was his competitor, Robert Holder, who managed to win the largest number of coveted spots on the busy Russell dance card. Over the course of a decade, the two men did more than a billion dollars' worth of construction work together, including the Georgia Dome stadium and one of the biggest new downtown skyscrapers, the 191 Peachtree Tower. The big signs outside the construction sites announced the partnership in block letters: HOLDER-RUSSELL—invaluable goodwill advertising for both the white builder and the company that had hired the black-white pair. Egged on by the young Turks who worked for him, Russell continued to build some buildings on his own, developing a prosperous, competitive construction firm. But even in the later eighties, when his operation took in close to $150 million a year and ranked among the top three or four black companies in America, Russell could not let go of the role of subordinate minority partner.

Nor, even when he tried to stand on his own, could he escape the helping hand of City Hall. One of the biggest projects the Young administration undertook in the mid-eighties was a new set of parking decks at Hartsfield International Airport. There was $24 million at stake: $14 million for a first garage and another $10 million for a matching deck at the other end of the airport, both jobs guaranteed to go to the same builder. The bids were due on August 10, 1985, at 2:00 P.M., and as usual in competitive bid situations, it was expected that the top contenders would wait until the last minute to submit.

By law in Atlanta, bid deadlines were counted out by the city clock—a time-punch in the purchasing office. Builders' representatives routinely showed up there an hour or so before the deadline to synchronize their watches, while estimators back at the office took calls from subcontractors who, fearing that other builders would undercut them, had waited as long as they could to make their prices known. The general contractors would fiddle and adjust their bids up until the very last moment, then rush them over to the purchasing office just in time to submit them. "Literally a few seconds make all the difference in the world," Perry explained. On this Wednesday, all the city's big builders were bidding, including Russell, on his own, and J. A. Jones, teamed up with another minority firm, the E. R. Mitchell Construction Company.

Haywood Curry brought over the J. A. Jones bid just moments before the deadline: the clock stamped one copy 1:59, a second exactly 2:00 P.M. Curry watched for a few minutes as a municipal employee loaded all the bids on a cart to take them across the street to City Hall, where they would be read and a winner announced. Then, just as Curry was walking out of the purchasing office, Russell's representative ran through the door and handed in a bid. A city official took the packet and stamped it 2:03, but warned the Russell man that the bid was late and could not be accepted. Another courier from a Savannah-based construction company showed up with a bid and was sent away. Russell's man and the official argued for several minutes, then headed across the street for the announcement. There, to Curry's surprise, Russell's bid was read among the others. Not only that, but it was lower than any of the rest, $10,000 lower than Jones's, which would otherwise have won the bidding.

Everything in the city process—the rules, the individuals, custom—argued against Russell. The clock was unequivocal. The official who took the Russell bid not only pronounced it late but eventually testified in court that it should have been out of contention. Two other top-level city officials agreed: administrative services commissioner Clara Axam and Dave Miller, then director of purchasing, advised the mayor that the estimate was out of bounds and should be rejected. At the very least, when the Jones company objected to the reading of the contested bid, the out-of-town contractor should have been granted a hearing. Instead, contrary to city law, Jones's protests were ignored. On April 29, three weeks after the bidding, the city announced that Russell had won the contract. A month or so later, returning home from a trip out of town, Curry noticed the familiar Russell sign hanging at the airport construction site. Together, the two Hartsfield decks would add up to one of the biggest jobs Russell's firm ever did on its own. "They, more than anything, put us on the map," said a top officer of the company.

Eventually Jones sued the city, and the mayor testified in court. Prickly and defensive, he seemed to many observers to have only a dim grasp of what had happened, but he saw nothing wrong with the outcome: it seemed, he said, to save the city money. His careless testimony only confirmed what many thought: as Curry put it, "Andy Young made the decision, and he said, 'Herman Russell is going to get this contract.'" "Young would not have done what he did for anyone else," said another builder, "not for someone who had never contributed." Even City Hall insiders appeared to concede the point, one telling a reporter that any other contractor turning in a late bid "wouldn't have gotten the time of day." Pressed to explain his action, Young was vague, but he seemed to see it as only fair that a black builder should get the job. "I just see," he said with a shrug, "J. A. Jones building all over town. I mean, we got all kinds of city work going on and I don't know what all this fight is about."

In January 1988, J. A. Jones won its suit, and a jury awarded it nearly a million dollars. The city appealed and the case floated slowly up through the judicial system. Then, at the end of the decade, long after both parking decks had been completed, a panel of state supreme court judges overturned the jury award. Six out of seven justices agreed that Jones had been wronged and deserved some compensation; one went so far as to accuse Young of an "illegal act." But with the city strapped for cash and without any means of raising an extra million dollars, a majority of the panel agreed that all Jones had forfeited was the cost of preparing a bid, and the contractor's compensation was severely reduced, to a mere $22,000.

By now, the Atlanta public was all too used to affirmative action scandals, and the verdict was greeted with silence by blacks and whites alike. With both the Peachtree set and the black city government profitably wedded to racial preferences, neither questioned the improprieties that seemed inevitably to come with them. Just as Herman Russell could not escape joint venture work, so for Andrew Young, black solidarity had proved stronger than any scruples or standards, and once he started bending the rules, it had been hard to know where to stop. For him, the end justified the means, and what began as a small adjustment in the name of color had come to mean just about anything goes—for blacks or simply for a friend. "I thought the city would want to do the right thing," Haywood Curry said years later, "especially with all the racial issues involved. Whether [Russell] saved the city some money or not, whether he was a black man building up the business—that's not the point. Russell was late. The bid was late. They broke the rules, and it doesn't help anyone in the city to push blacks ahead that way."

The issue of color consciousness would dog Andrew Young through the decade and beyond, surfacing again with a vengeance in the spring of 1983 with the idea of a black run for the presidency. Blacks had tried for the office before: marginal protest candidates like Shirley Chisholm and Dick Gregory. But the notion emerged anew, with a new seriousness, in the aftermath of black candidate Harold Washington's bid for the Chicago mayoralty. A variety of black leaders, stung by the Democratic Party's lackluster support for Washington, spoke up for the anger surging in black circles. "It's time," Jesse Jackson asserted, "[for blacks] to renegotiate our relationship with the . . . party." Several movement figures began to talk about a symbolic presidential run—whatever was necessary, said Mayor Richard Hatcher of Gary, Indiana, to keep the Democrats from "taking us for granted." Young, though sympathetic to the festering resentment, was immediately dubious about a color-coded candidacy, and by the time the group that called itself the "black leadership family" met to discuss the idea in Atlanta in early March, he outspokenly opposed it.

The idea of fielding a candidate gathered steam as the spring wore on, and with it Young's opposition. There were more meetings, official and unofficial, in Atlanta, Gary, Washington and Chicago. Jesse Jackson emerged as the person most likely to make a run, and Young, working the media, produced a stream of speeches and interviews questioning his judgment. A black candidacy could be racially divisive, Young warned in *The New York Times*, alienating black voters from the eventual white nominee. Blacks shouldn't be asking the party, he told the *Atlanta Constitution*, to "mortgage" itself to any "special interest." "I come out of the side of the civil rights movement that rejected symbolic politics," he argued. "A black presidential candidacy is a symbolic political effort that will reap some symbolic benefits. My concern is to find ways to reap real benefits in this election."

Young's opposition was based in principle—deep-seated, integrationist principle. "My feeling," he insisted emphatically to one interviewer, "is that there is no need for a [black] candidate." But he was also thinking pragmatically and was convinced that Jackson's effort would backfire. "If people had talked about John Kennedy's candidacy as a Catholic candidacy," Young complained, "it would have put the kiss of death on it." In the real world, Young argued, where he and other southern black elected officials had to operate, they depended on white voters and white coalition partners—and the last thing they needed was another round of fiery racial politics. "Jesse was concerned about power within the black community," Young said years later, "I was concerned about power within the nation. And I thought the quest for power within the black community was limiting blacks' potential power within the nation."

A variety of black leaders joined Young in the coming months in opposing Jackson's candidacy. Birmingham mayor Richard Arrington, Philadelphia mayor Wilson Goode, Los Angeles mayor Tom Bradley, Coleman Young, Julian Bond, Coretta Scott King and Martin Luther King, Sr., among others, would all endorse Vice President Walter Mondale before the primary season was over. But Jackson, getting ever more attention in the media, showed no sign that he heard their arguments. Voters galvanized by a black candidacy began to register in large numbers. And as the most vocal, eloquently integrationist of the doubters, Young started to feel caught out on a limb.

With the campaign picking up momentum, younger blacks put pressure on the skeptics. The old question about "how black" Young was began to make the rounds in black circles, and back home in Atlanta, where he would soon be facing reelection, some of the angrier ministers denounced him. Ever politic, Young lauded Jackson's registration effort and the "enthusiasm" he was generating; he admired his old friend's eloquence and the "psychological impact" of his campaign. Still, Young insisted, what the Democrats needed was a "consensus candidate." Blacks could not come into the convention as a divisive racial phalanx. Poor blacks should not be encouraged to hope for something that could never come to pass. If Reagan were to win in November, Young warned, "folks are going to blame Jesse." In one speech, to Atlanta blacks, he even called Jackson's campaign "dangerous." "All of us," he told a reporter of himself and his friends in the movement, "have spent years of our lives urging people not to vote on account of race, and we can't just suddenly reverse that."

It was a courageous stand, a vote against all odds for integrationism, but by spring 1984, with Jackson's poll numbers still spiking upward, even the confident Young was reduced to evasion and wishful thinking. The week before the Super Tuesday primaries, he appeared on *Meet the Press,* asserting—despite all signs to the contrary—that there was still some hope of a color-neutral outcome. "One of the things we've known about black voters in the South," he maintained hopefully, "is that they really are independent and they basically will not vote primarily racially." But Young also saw how Jackson's popularity was snowballing, and he now hesitated to criticize the candidate, refusing to comment even on his "Hymietown" jab at New York Jews. "I don't want to be the one," Young hedged awkwardly, "that pours cold water on the possibility of [a Jackson] candidacy." When the Super Tuesday ballots were counted later in the week, Jackson carried an overwhelming majority of black voters in Georgia and across the South.

By the time of the convention, in July 1984, millions of other black voters had made the same choice, endorsing Jackson's color-coded protest over Young's coalition politics. A face-to-face encounter, on the floor in San Francisco, brought Young's defeat home in brutal clarity. The occasion was a discussion of one of Jackson's four proposed platform planks, his call to end the old southern custom of runoff primaries. The hall was packed with Jackson delegates; millions of Americans, black and white, were watching on television. Young stood up to oppose the Jackson measure: the runoff system wasn't necessarily racist, he said; he and many other black candidates had profited from it. But he had gotten only a few sentences into his speech when the Jackson delegation erupted in a chorus of boos. Young struggled to get through his remarks, accompanied to the end by angry jeers, hissing and shouts of "Shame on you!" By the time he left the stage, he was visibly shaken; his wife Jean, standing near, was in tears. The next day, when Coretta Scott King addressed a meeting of Jackson delegates and told them they owed Young an apology, she too was booed and heckled to the point of tears. To her pleas for tolerance and free expression, one loud voice in the crowd shouted, "It don't justify prostitution."

Witnesses commenting in the days and weeks to come could not help comparing Young's humiliation to Jackson's triumph. "One was treated as a modern-day savior of his people, the other reviled as a Judas," said a man on the floor. Though the most eloquent living spokesman for Martin Luther King's dream, Young had proved unable to carry his political base. Whatever most blacks felt about integration, many were still caught on the horns of their "two-ness," and they could not resist the call of an angry black protest candidate. As for Young, he would never fully recover from the defeat in the eyes of the black political establishment or among black voters. "Around the country, it hurt him," said John Lewis. It hurt his ability "to sell a political candidate or an issue to the black community."

Back home in Atlanta, Young scrambled to cover his back. Among the Georgia contests looming in November was a race for the fifth congressional district—Young's old seat. The man who had replaced him there, white liberal Wyche Fowler, was widely popular among both blacks and whites and had been repeatedly returned to Washington. But the district had recently been reapportioned—it was now over 65 percent black—and local activists were intent on trying to recapture it. The most likely black candidate was Hosea Williams, flamboyant movement veteran and good-natured troublemaker, much beloved in black Atlanta but not really anyone's idea of congressional material.

It was not an easy test for Young. No one who knew the mayor or the candidates thought he believed Hosea Williams would be a better congressman than Wyche Fowler. But it was also said by aides that Young "still flinched" when reminded that his old seat, once a historic black first, had never been recaptured by a black candidate. Whatever the reason—his own gut feelings or a political need to make up for opposing Jackson—sometime that summer Young put his signature to a piece of campaign literature sent out to black homes, reminding voters of the redistricting and urging them to support Williams. "His election," the letter said, "would give us the only black Congressman from the Deep South." When the document was discovered by the press, it produced an uproar among white Atlantans, right and left. Fowler called the letter "sad and disappointing"; an *Atlanta Journal* editorial and several columnists denounced it. The letter was "a blatant appeal to black voters to vote strictly on a racial basis," the editorial said. "It is appalling, and reflects a racist way of thinking." As for the city's blacks, ambivalent as they seemed about integration, the fifth district reelected Fowler by a substantial margin.

Young had occasion to comment on Jackson's candidacy one more time that summer at the annual meeting of the National Association of Black Journalists. Once again, he outlined his integrationist objections. Noting that in the end Jackson had actually accomplished rather little—he took 85 percent of the black vote but lost big on all four platform planks—Young added, "I know Jesse, I like Jesse. . . . But Jesse scares the hell out of white folks. Now, it makes us feel good to scare the hell out of white folks. But ultimately it's counterproductive. . . . We're only 11 percent, and to get anything in America we've got to get 50 percent plus one." Self-assured as ever, relaxed and persuasive, Young urged the assembled journalists to support Walter Mondale for president. Yet even as he pressed for coalition politics and putting aside color, the mayor also got in a little racial innuendo. "I don't think we can afford not to work for this election," he said, "just because nobody on the Mondale staff will listen to me. They don't listen because they're a bunch of smart-ass white boys."

It seemed an inconsequential aside, too oblique and equivocal to have much impact on the campaign, but blacks and whites in Atlanta and elsewhere reacted as if to a major statement. The Association of Black Journalists greeted the speech with a standing ovation. The racially sensitive national press was sternly disapproving, the Mondale campaign defensive and indignant. A spokeswoman for the vice president said she found Young's language personally objectionable, adding that Mondale's staff, in keeping with his beliefs on affirmative action, was fully "representative of this country." For black and white alike, it was an occasion for racial politics as usual. Only in Atlanta did the reaction break the bounds of convention. "The national press went nuts," columnist Dick Williams said later. "But here in Atlanta, everybody loved what Young had done. It was fun. It was how we differentiated our race relations from the rest of the country. He was saying it was okay to joke about this."

The Peachtree leaders were the first to rally around their wounded hero, and when they came together, it was typical Atlanta style—part southern charm, part unrelenting business. Former mayor Sam Massell set the ball rolling when he decided, on a whim, to have twenty-five campaign-style buttons made up to distribute among the Peachtree regulars. Massell's buddy Albert Maslia, owner of a greeting card and knickknack chain, did the design: SMART ASS WHITE BOY, in block letters, on a plain white background. Charles Loudermilk, who attended the meeting, liked the buttons so much that he ordered another two hundred to hand out to friends—an emblem of how far the black and white establishments had come that they now could laugh easily about this sort of thing. A few of the buttons trickled down to journalists; a picture of one appeared in the newspaper, and within days orders were pouring in from blacks and whites all over the Atlanta area. Soon Maslia was making coffee mugs, T-shirts and ballpoint pens—some printed with the full phrase, some with simply SAWB—and by the time the craze was over, he had made more than $30,000 on fourteen thousand buttons and who knew what else. In its small, odd way, the episode was a hopeful sign, suggesting that in the right circumstances even the bitterest race consciousness could be neutralized. Still, for all the racial change apparent in Atlanta, there could be no ignoring what it papered over—in the city's business or its politics. If anything, color seemed more firmly entrenched than ever, integration more elusive and far-fetched.

Chapter 15

THE PROGRAM THAT
WOULD NOT DIE

J. Ben Shapiro had never expected to find himself in a standoff with Andrew Young. Raised in Atlanta, in college and law school at Emory in the early sixties, Shapiro was part of the generation that came of age with the New South. Born into a middle-class Jewish family, he grew up in a segregated city, but already as a teen, in the early fifties, he had begun to find the race code odd. He remembered one supposedly citywide high school track meet without a single black: "It was ludicrous," he recalled. Like most of the people in his world in Atlanta, he believed implicitly in integration, and by the time he got out of law school, he hardly recognized the town he had known as a child. "I'm proud of Atlanta," he said earnestly. "I'm proud of the race relations we have here." Liberal-minded, sober, responsible, more workmanlike than crusading, the young attorney specializing in construction law was the last person anyone who knew him expected to take on the city's establishment and its conventional wisdom about race. But in the early eighties, when a group of Atlanta builders decided to fight the city set-aside, Shapiro emerged as their unlikely spokesman.

By the time he got involved with the issue, the public-sector preference was well entrenched in Atlanta. Every year since 1976, at least 20 to 30 percent of city contracting dollars had gone to minority businesses, and in 1978, the black share had risen as high as 38 percent. Much of this minority portion was concentrated in a few trades—the ones the city needed most and in which it was easiest to start a business—with the result that certain

432

kinds of nonminority contractors were all but frozen out of city work. Like the black firms that replaced them, these white-owned businesses were almost always small and family-run: a guy with a small office and a pickup truck who provided one kind of simple, labor-intensive contracting service. After eight years of Maynard Jackson, many of these small-time entrepreneurs were pressed to the breaking point, and they were stunned in 1981 when the city council proposed the law to make the set-aside permanent.

Several Atlanta area contractors who Shapiro's firm had represented in other matters came to his office to air their concerns about what the law would mean for them. "A client," he remembered, "would come to me and say, 'I'm qualified to do this job. I want to do this job for the city. But I can't get the job because my skin is white.'" Shapiro was troubled by the men's stories and decided to take their case. But both he and the builders hoped to avoid a showdown. The letters he wrote to city authorities that summer on behalf of the local chapter of the American Subcontractors Association were disgruntled yet, in typical Atlanta style, consensus-seeking. "We want to stress," Shapiro wrote, "that we are not opposed to affirmative action." Instead of a color-coded quota, he proposed convening an interracial task force—"blacks and whites, men and women, general contractors and sub-contractors"—to devise color-neutral measures to bring blacks into the construction trades. "We don't have all the answers," the lawyer conceded, "[but] with input from all of the sectors which are affected, an ordinance could be drafted which is fair [to all] . . . and at the same time achieves affirmative action."

Shapiro's letters pricked the conscience of a few uneasy city council members, and before the bill could come up for a vote, it was pulled from consideration. Still, Shapiro had meant what he said about alternative means to bring black businesses into the building trades, and even in victory he got to work to organize a task force. There was another round of letters and several meetings with council members. Most encouraging to the young lawyer was the influence he seemed to be having on black council president Marvin Arrington, a law school classmate and personal friend. The two men corresponded daily over a period of weeks, hand-delivered notes about what would be the best and least divisive way for the city to boost minority entrepreneurs, not just with a onetime leg-up but with substantive help in forming and growing their own businesses. Finally, after much discussion, the two friends met for lunch and talked about possible language for an alternate bill. Shapiro was encouraged. "I was convinced," he said later, "that we could find another way for Atlanta to help small businesses, black and white—a way to help them get off the ground without penalizing anyone else."

Then, in April 1982, the city council passed another minority business bill—to Shapiro's surprise, virtually identical to the first proposed ordinance. Nothing had been done to the legislation to ease its rigid color coding. No measures of the kind Shapiro and his clients had recommended were added to teach start-up entrepreneurs new skills or help them find capital or bonding. The new law spoke for itself: what mattered to the council and its constituency was that the people who got city work be black, and all other concerns were shrugged off as trivial or bigoted.

Shapiro was stunned and bitterly disappointed. "I came to realize," he recalled, "that there was not going to be a compromise. The politicians in the city government didn't want a compromise. They wanted a program that would be financially rewarding to their constituents." He had always considered himself a liberal, but now the label seemed irrelevant. "I was proud of Dr. King," he explained. "I supported the civil rights movement. I believed in equality—for all individuals. But I don't think the people who were supporting the set-aside understood the implications. I don't think they realized that a racial preference would inevitably discriminate against someone else. My clients were being discriminated against—real discrimination." Finally, convinced there was no other course, the lawyer decided he would have to sue.

In May 1982, he filed suit—actually two suits, on behalf of two different local contractors' groups. Choosing to try his chances in state court, he took a scattershot approach, marshaling every argument he could think of—everything from reverse discrimination to the added cost the preference posed for Atlanta taxpayers. He appealed to every possible legal standard: the U.S. Constitution, the city charter and a number of state laws. Named as defendants were the city, the city council and the mayor. Shapiro knew he might be in for a long haul—a difficult process of trial and error—but he was convinced he could find a way to beat the set-aside. He had no idea how resilient the program would prove or how difficult it would turn out to be to persuade anyone else in Atlanta to think seriously about better stratagems to bring blacks into the economic mainstream.

By the mid-1980s, affirmative action had taken root in just about every realm of American life. More than 60 percent of private companies, including virtually all large corporations, had instituted some kind of volun-

tary hiring and promotion goals. Federal authorities required careful personnel counting from every university that took federal money and every enterprise that did business with the government: all told, some fifteen thousand
companies, with more than 23 million workers. Many local governments,
particularly in big cities, had instituted formal and informal hiring plans like
those in Detroit and Atlanta: plans that covered City Hall employees, but
even more significantly, the uniformed services—cops and firefighters.

Business set-asides like Atlanta's were springing up across the country, as
often as not modeled directly on the pioneering Georgia program. George
Berry's ingenious "prequalification" stratagem, Rodney Strong's tough certi-
fication process, the language of the 1982 act: all were soon in use in cities
from Washington to Los Angeles. Even the personalities in the Atlanta
drama were showing up in other places. When he left City Hall, Maynard
Jackson took a job with a Chicago law firm trying to develop business with
cities run by black mayors, and before long he had put together a multi-bil-
lion-dollar list of clients: black politicians around the country presiding over
set-asides similar to Atlanta's. In the course of advising these clients, Jackson
made sure to introduce them to the aides who had developed the Atlanta
preference, and within a few years, there were members of "the Atlanta
mafia" in the government of every big city with a black mayor or heavily
black city council: Chicago, Los Angeles, Houston, Detroit, Newark and
Gary, Indiana, among others. Then, as often as not, when it came time to
hire a black entrepreneur, these officials reached out to the businessmen they
knew best—the same handful of well-connected black businessmen who
were benefiting from the set-aside in Atlanta.

The federal government's business preferences, also in some cases modeled on Atlanta's, were growing even faster than local programs. Every agency
and department in Washington had its own purchasing quota, known as a
"procurement objective." Other, overlapping set-asides administered by the
Small Business Administration (SBA) channeled dollars from every government agency to "disadvantaged business enterprises," more than 95 percent
of them minority-owned. The largest program, run by the Department of
Transportation, reserved 10 percent of all federal highway construction, or
about a billion dollars' worth of work each year, for minority- and female-
owned pavers, landscapers, dirt and gravel haulers, sign and guardrail
installers. Still other quotas earmarked contracts for minority firms building
schools, subways, hospitals, parks, sewer systems, water purification plants
and other public works across the country. All told, by the mid-1980s, fed-

eral set-asides were channeling $3.5 billion a year to minority companies, just under 4 percent of all government expenditure, while the SBA dispensed another $2.7 billion.

Just what impact all this color-coded hiring and spending had was harder to say. Civil rights groups and affirmative action bureaucrats—a growing profession—traded optimistic statistics. According to the NAACP, hiring programs put in place in the seventies had brought the ranks of black policemen up from 23,000 to 43,000, the number of black electricians from 15,000 to 37,000. Though not quite so dramatic, the U.S. Census Bureau's count of minority-owned businesses shot up impressively in the mid-1980s, from 308,000 to 424,000. But other observers in government and elsewhere were increasingly dubious about the effects of racial preferences—unsure about where the dollars were going or how many people were actually being helped.

One important academic study by James P. Smith and Finis Welch looked at the effects of hiring preferences and found that the largest increase in black employment had occurred before affirmative action—in the years between 1966 and 1970, after discrimination had been declared illegal, but before the federal government began enforcing job preferences. Hiring by color had made some difference, the scholars found, but it was very small and affected mainly black managers moving laterally from one company to another. "Education and migration," Smith and Welch concluded, "were the primary determinant of the long-term black economic improvement. Affirmative action has marginally altered black wage gains." A second study a year or so later came to much the same conclusion about minority business programs. "Set-asides do not appear to have encouraged the formation of minority-owned firms," noted the U.S. Civil Rights Commission. Blacks accounted for no larger share of self-employed workers in 1982 than they had in 1972; they comprised a smaller percentage of self-employed building contractors; and minority business programs had triggered virtually no "economic ripple effect [in] minority employment." "I think it is debatable," new EEOC chairman Clarence Thomas summed up the emerging doubts, "whether affirmative action has resulted in any changes that wouldn't have occurred naturally."

In Atlanta, the public-sector set-aside was making some dent in the old order, but less than many of its advocates liked to imagine. The mayor and his aides boasted of the six hundred black-owned firms that had gotten city work since the program was initiated. The official register of certified minority businesses now contained over four hundred names in a wide range of trades, and in the first three years of Young's mayoralty, more than $100 million in city money went to these entrepreneurs. Still, construction insiders warned, the numbers told only part of the story.

Of the four hundred concerns listed in the register, reporters discovered that many could not be found or had gone out of business. As for the number of contracts the city claimed had been let to blacks, these were contracts awarded, not contracts completed—and as the set-aside became entrenched, this was a distinction that made more and more of a difference. Frequently, according to insiders, general contractors would hire an inexperienced black subcontractor who turned out to be unable to do the job, then replace him with another and possibly another, finally ending up with a seasoned white concern. Nor did the numbers say anything about the size of the contracts being won by black entrepreneurs. Of the 152 minority operations that actually got work the year Shapiro sued, few bigger firms made a good living out of it. But most of the contracts issued to minorities were too small to keep even a mom-and-pop operation in business: their median value was $33,000, one-one-hundredth the size of the median contract won by white companies. In most cases, these were the only jobs the black concerns could handle, but the money was rarely enough to help them take off. Even the larger black firms getting city work had a hard time making a go of it. Of the several dozen that had joint-ventured at the airport, 75 percent were no longer in operation less than a decade later; of the twenty-five that landed the biggest contracts in the mid-1980s, eleven had either gone out of business or been revealed as frauds within three years.

More than a decade of preferences had had virtually no effect on the city's socioeconomic profile. A full 95 percent of the businesses within city limits were still owned by whites, and the few black firms there were took in less than 1 percent of all business revenue. A 1982 Census Bureau report on black business growth nationwide showed Atlanta lagging well behind other cities that had no set-aside programs or much smaller ones: far from coming in first, as the city's black politicians had assumed it would, Atlanta ranked fifteenth, hardly on the chart. Nor did the city's preferences seem to be having much trickle-down effect. Compared to the suburbs, Atlanta was hemorrhaging jobs, average family income was plummeting, and 27 percent of residents were living below the poverty line—a larger percentage than in any city in America except Newark. Black unemployment, hovering around 20 percent, was more than twice the national figure and many times the rate in suburban Atlanta.

In Atlanta as elsewhere, the black middle class was coming into its own. Blacks accounted for half the police force, 65 percent of City Hall employees, twelve out of nineteen council members and a majority of public school teachers. The percentage of black doctors and lawyers was twice the national average. More than 15 percent of employed blacks held professional or managerial jobs, and it was hard to find middle-class Atlantans, black or white, who did not at least occasionally work with someone of the other race. Still, it was unclear how much of this progress was due to affirmative action, and after working hours the city remained largely segregated, with neighborhoods, churches, private clubs and schools almost as starkly color-coded as they had ever been.

Andrew Young, among others, black and white, seemed to be revising his definition of integration to suit the more limited prospects of the day. He no longer talked as he had ten years before about a "deracialized" America in which color would count for less and less: how could he in a city driven by color-coded preferences? Instead, he now envisioned integration as "learning to accept and not be threatened by cultural differences." "The illustration I use most," he explained, "is the stew rather than the soup. In a stew, the potatoes, the carrots, the peas maintain their identity—whereas in a soup everything becomes blended and homogenized." And even by Young's hedged definition, the city was far from the goal. "People do and can live anywhere they want in Atlanta," the mayor noted. "It's not a segregated town. It's just not an integrated town. There's a difference."

Still, even in the face of this mounting evidence, in Atlanta and elsewhere the public remained surprisingly ambivalent about affirmative action. When asked specifically about quotas, large majorities were strongly against them. One Gallup survey found only 11 percent of all respondents (and 30 percent of nonwhites) supporting "preferential treatment in getting jobs and places in college." A second poll, conducted in 1983 by the Anti-Defamation League, reported 73 percent opposing quotas and maintaining that work should be gotten "solely on merit." Yet, despite this apparently overwhelming consensus, most people remained committed to the idea of helping blacks into the mainstream, and no one seemed to want to look too closely at any means likely to advance that end.

In Atlanta, black opinion ran strongly in favor of the city set-aside. Black politicians were unanimous in their support. By the mid-1980s, most put it top and center of their agendas—"I feel that this is my obligation as a black elected official," said Fulton County commissioner Michael Lomax—and those, like Young and Marvin Arrington, who took the strongest stands were invariably reelected by huge margins. White concern about frauds and favoritism was shrugged off as so much bigotry; so were reports that only a tiny handful of politically savvy black entrepreneurs were benefiting from the preference. "Just as this is the American dream," said Lomax, "so it's the African-American dream. The black community understands that it has to create a wealth class."

White Atlantans were a little more hesitant, caught between their doubts and their hopes for the program. In the South as in the North, polls showed between 70 and 80 percent opposed to special treatment on the basis of skin color, and by the mid-eighties most Atlanta whites knew all about what was wrong with the set-aside—the corruption and the persistent elitism. Still, most brushed aside their misgivings or kept quiet about them. Some seemed to do so out of genuine concern for the people the preference was meant to help. Others worried that challenging the black city government would leave them sounding like bigots. Still others, largely unaffected by the program and grateful for the racial peace it had brought Atlanta, simply didn't want to rock the boat. The real costs of the quota—the demeaning dependence it encouraged, the racial stereotypes, the premium it put on scamming rather than skill and hard work—these were all costs paid by blacks, of little consequence to most white people.

Even white Atlantans with the gravest doubts hesitated to call for an end to affirmative action, and when pressed to think about the problem preferences were meant to solve could be surprisingly supportive. The wealthy, well-connected owner of a large convenience-store chain, Dillard Munford was a quintessential member of the Atlanta establishment: he belonged to all the right clubs, sat on all the right boards and owned one of the finest quail-hunting plantations in South Georgia. What made him different from other business leaders were his outspoken right-wing views, which he aired in a newspaper column published in nearly thirty suburban weeklies and eventually in the *Constitution*. On affirmative action, Munford was sharply opposed—to the color-coded patronage, the reverse discrimination, the failure to reduce unemployment or bring poor blacks into the system. Then, in the mid-eighties, he decided it was time to move beyond criticism and do something practical to ease the city's race problems. Hoping to set an example for other businessmen, he organized an outreach hiring program and asked the city's black churches to find him one hundred employable, at-risk youth he could put to work in his convenience stores. It wasn't exactly a quota, but anyone else would have called it affirmative action. "It's good for the company," Munford declared proudly to a reporter, "and it's good for the city of Atlanta."

Munford's fellow columnist Dick Williams was another conservative white male with surprising views about affirmative action. Some thirty years younger than Munford, a former political reporter, Williams emerged as a columnist in the early eighties, and before long he had earned a reputation as the voice of Atlanta's white suburbs—not the old traditionalists Munford wrote for, but the new, make-money, Republican South. Unlike most of his colleagues on the *Journal-Constitution,* Williams did not hesitate to criticize affirmative action: the unending abuses, the waste of taxpayers' money, the all too short list of beneficiaries. Still, acerbic as he could be, he worried about what else the city could or would do to help "ordinary black men and women looking for a chance to work," and he thought the goals of the set-aside were too important to let go of it entirely. Stretching to justify the program, or at least excuse its flaws, he told himself and his readers that it was no worse than ordinary, old-fashioned patronage. "It's a modern-day spoils system," he explained with a shrug. Besides, Atlanta voters had repeatedly endorsed it: "If voters know the costs of the program," he maintained, "and those black voters continue to approve the politicians who back it—well, that's their choice. As long as it's defended in that way, and not on constitutional grounds, then I don't mind."

Even the set-aside's most determined critics—the men who fought it in court—seemed when pressed to be of two minds. McNeil Stokes was Ben Shapiro's partner, an older man and veteran construction lawyer who had been listening to contractors' complaints for nearly two decades. Yet, when he reflected on his experience, Stokes wasn't sure what he thought about affirmative action. "I draw the line on quotas," he mused, "but no right-thinking person could disagree with equal opportunity—with outreach and training and a little extra effort to find people beyond the usual daisy chain." Looking back over the seventies and eighties, Stokes wondered if he had been on the right side of the issue. "I didn't like it philosophically," he said, "but I'm not sure it hasn't done a decent job. In the long run, I'm not so sure history hasn't proven the other guys right." Even Ben Shapiro, though still in the midst of battle, sometimes showed a bit of a soft spot. "Without these programs," he conceded, "some qualified people would not have had opportunities. Because of the program, they got a chance and they've succeeded and I'm proud of them." The lawyer squirmed uncomfortably, grappling with his mixed feelings. "Bottom line, am I saying two different things? Yes and no. When you ask if the law should be color-blind, I'm a purist. But I will admit these programs have opened the door for people."

In Atlanta as elsewhere by the mid-eighties, much of the white public quietly resented affirmative action. Many, black and white, had misgivings about the color-coded stereotypes it encouraged, and a small group of conservatives was beginning to raise questions about its long-term effectiveness. But by and large the only people willing to stand up and oppose counting by color were those directly hurt by it—mostly contractors' groups—and none of them spoke for large numbers of Americans or galvanized much support when they began to file suit in the early eighties. For better or worse, it was becoming clear, uprooting preferences would be a political challenge of the highest order—despite the public's overwhelming and consistent opposition to quotas.

The ruling in Ben Shapiro's set-aside case was announced without much fanfare in October 1984. The unanimous decision by the Georgia Supreme Court was short and to the point: overturning the city ordinance. Tailored as narrowly as possible, the terse three-page ruling hardly mentioned race, and it set no important affirmative action precedent. Still, in its limited way, the decision was a verdict for fairness and color-blind standards—specifically the city charter's requirement that contracts be awarded "to the lowest and/or best bidder." "The legislative purpose in the Atlanta city charter," the court declared, "was to [ensure] that contracts be awarded without favoritism." Shapiro seized on the phrase as an endorsement of his principles and announced triumphantly to his clients that the Atlanta set-aside was dead. "I encourage minority and female business enterprises to bid on city work," he told the press, "but let the job go to the lowest responsible bidder."

City officials took a different view, and within hours they announced that they intended to find a way around the decision. Director of contract compliance Eugene Duffy called it "a setback, but a very small setback." "The technical problems within our charter can be corrected," he told a reporter. City councilman Robb Pitts, a sponsor of the now void 1982 ordinance, said he was "disappointed," but ready "to do whatever's necessary" to reinstate the law. "We remain firmly committed," he declared, "to minority and female businesses." Shapiro and his clients were dumbstruck: apparently city officials were going to override the decision, trumping the court's power with their own, smashing judge-made law with their electoral mandate.

Andrew Young took the first step, a dramatic, high-stakes move, declaring a moratorium on all city purchasing that effectively shut down the Atlanta government, putting a halt to the letting of contracts and even to routine supply buying. Not only was the bureaucracy determined to reinstate the set-aside law but black entrepreneurs were not going to forfeit a dollar of business in the meantime. Council president Marvin Arrington delivered the follow-up punch, promising quick legislative action. "The city council has the ability to amend the city charter," he said, "so that we will preserve the intent, spirit and fulfillment of the city's clear commitment to participation by minority enterprises."

This time around, there was no talk of compromise, no discussion— between Shapiro and Arrington or anyone else—of reshaping disputed means to achieve a common end. Whatever their ambivalence about affirmative action, no one who was anyone in Atlanta wanted to side with the white contractors against the city government. Virtually all public comment on the court ruling defended the set-aside, and no one came forward to question the city's counterpunch. If anything, in the name of popular opinion, most of the media encouraged the city to act unilaterally to overrule the court. "There is no question," a *Constitution* editorial declared, "that set-asides are proper or that enhanced black economic power is in the best interest of the total community." Editorial page editor Tom Teepen went further still in a signed column. "Yes," he wrote, "this is sort of the old spoils system—but with a difference. It has clear rules, negotiated publicly through the political process and written into . . . law." In other words, because the majority of voters were behind it, racial preferences were desirable, whatever their shortcomings.

It took the city less than two months to restore its preference program. An amendment to the city charter inserted a single word—"responsible"—into existing language about acceptable bidders. Three days later, Mayor Young lifted the moratorium and issued an administrative order reinstating the set-aside in words virtually identical to the ordinance that had been overturned in court. "There is no question," Shapiro noted later, "that [both] the charter amendment and administrative order . . . were designed to continue the same minority and female business participation program which had been declared unlawful by the Georgia supreme court." Then, in January 1985, not content with reestablishing the preference, Young increased the percentage of city business to be reserved for minority entrepreneurs from 25 to 35 percent. Even years later, Shapiro could hardly believe the city's audacity.

"These people don't care what you do," he said. "They don't care what any judge says. Even if the current system were declared unconstitutional, they would probably devise another one. As long as they control the government, they are going to keep coming back with another ordinance."

The Reagan administration, fighting affirmative action on the national front, was also finding it all but impossible in the early eighties to uproot color-coded favoritism. The president took up the issue at his very first news conference. "I'm old enough to remember," he said, "when quotas existed in the U.S. for the purpose of discrimination, and I don't want to see that happen again." The Justice Department fleshed out his argument in a more formal declaration of war. The government, it announced, "will no longer insist upon or in any respect support the use of quotas or any other numerical or statistical formulae designed to provide to non-victims of discrimination preferential treatment based on race, sex, national origin or religion." In substance, the statement contained nothing to offend the majority consensus, firmly opposed to quotas. Yet from the start the Justice Department's tone was offputting: not just cold but, with that little, unnecessary jab, "non-victims," likely to grate even on many potential allies—people who wanted to get rid of preferences but remained nevertheless sympathetic to black suffering. It was the kind of mistake Justice would make again and again, characteristic of its civil rights division chief, William Bradford Reynolds.

Reynolds was a lawyers' lawyer: razor-sharp, combative, driven by principle and closer to the law than to the facts on the ground. He was never particularly popular or convincing, and as the architect of the Reagan civil rights policy, he set a tone that would polarize the nation. The administration's early initiatives were a series of public relations disasters, and by the time Reynolds got around to tackling the vast federal system of goals, timetables and quotas, he had virtually no credibility left on race issues. But even if Reynolds and his team had been more deft, few Americans were ready to repudiate preferences in the early eighties. No matter what the Justice Department proved in court, no matter how much corruption reporters unearthed, counting by race had become a way of life, institutionalized and bolstered with expectations, black and white. Corporate executives were the staunchest defenders, but government officials also balked at change. "I don't get the kind of resistance to affirmative action I did ten to 15 years ago," said one lawyer and business consultant. "In the midst of this success, Reynolds is just a speck on the ceiling shooting his mouth off."

Still convinced he could prevail even in this climate, Reynolds launched a major campaign against preferences. He thought he had a court victory in 1984. The case had originated years before in Memphis, where a black firefighter, Carl Stotts, had sued the city for discriminatory hiring. He won the case, the court ordered an affirmative action hiring plan, and eighteen blacks were recruited for the department. But then, a year later, when the city fell short of money and had to lay off firefighters, the new blacks were the first to go. Stotts sued again and won, but this time the largely white firefighters' union sued back, complaining that members' seniority privileges should not have to be sacrificed to affirmative action. The Supreme Court agreed with them, 6–3, and the majority opinion, strongly sympathetic to "the innocent employee" whose seniority rights had been trampled, suggested that it might be desirable to limit court-ordered civil rights remedies to actual victims of discrimination rather than oppressed groups—just the line of reasoning Reynolds had been pushing in other cases.

Reynolds seized the opportunity to declare victory. "There's a great deal of satisfaction," he told reporters, "that we now have a Supreme Court decision that confirms [our] position. The era of the racial quota has run its course." Calling the ruling "exhilarating" and "unequivocal," he interpreted it in the broadest possible manner—as applying not just to situations where whites were being fired because of affirmative action, but actually barring all use of quotas in hiring and promotions. "*Stotts* may well represent the most significant victory for civil rights in this nation in a great many years," Reynolds exulted, "not a victory for whites or males or union members or any discrete group in our pluralistic society, but a victory for all Americans."

He and his staffers spent the next nine months scouring Justice Department records for other cases of court-ordered affirmative action. Out of seventy orders in place across the country, Reynolds decided that fifty-one had been invalidated by the Memphis ruling, and he wrote to all fifty-one cities and states urging them to modify their plans. It was the largest government initiative yet undertaken against preferences. Letters went out to the Los Angeles Police Department, to a half dozen fire departments in New Jersey, to the Arkansas state police, Boston, Chicago, Miami, Milwaukee, Philadelphia, St. Louis and New York State—all places where the Justice Department had originally supported affirmative action as a means to open up a uniformed service.

The initiative triggered a storm of criticism from press and public. Civil rights groups prepared to go to court in the fifty-one jurisdictions that had received letters. Other advocates stepped up their denunciations of Reynolds. When a member of the U.S. Civil Rights Commission suggested that *Stotts* might be a civil rights victory—might advance Martin Luther King's dream of color-blind justice—King's former lieutenant Joseph Lowery charged that it was "an act of blasphemous proportions" for a rights official even to question affirmative action. A handful of nationally syndicated columnists, including Robert Samuelson and Richard Cohen of *The Washington Post,* tried to speak to the public's ambivalence about preferences, welcoming the death of color-coded quotas, but urging the Justice Department to replace them with other, more effective programs to enhance job or business opportunities for black people. Mostly, though, the ensuing debate was starkly partisan—unquestioningly for preferences or against them—and sterile. With both sides citing King's moral authority and neither listening to the other's arguments, the bitter back-and-forth droned on like a broken record, quashing all hope of the kind of discussion that might have given rise to a better answer than preferences.

At the local level, officials dug in their heels and refused to consider Reynolds's suggestions. Of the fifty-one cities and states, twenty-five threatened to go to court to oppose the federal government. Others simply ignored Reynolds's letter. Despite the public's well-documented dislike of quotas, almost none moved to dismantle or modify their programs, and not one even considered the possibility of a less divisive alternative remedy. "The Justice Department is trying to reopen this wound and nobody here is excited about the prospect," grumbled a lawyer for the city of Norfolk, Virginia. "No community that has been through this and achieved the success we have is anxious to go back and revisit it." "It's usually more expensive to upset the apple cart than to keep it rolling," explained another attorney. Whether or not it was actually working to bring blacks into the mainstream, affirmative action helped to ease white consciences. Whether or not it encouraged stereotyping or resentment, it was keeping the racial peace—and no one wanted to derail that.

Reynolds made little effort to persuade the other side of his views and instead returned combatively to the court system. Holding to his argument that the *Stotts* decision had invalidated quotas, he filed controversial briefs in several cases elsewhere in the country. In response, civil rights groups stepped up their ad hominem attacks, calling him a racist and an enemy of justice. Court battles proliferated and worked their way up through the system: angry, adversarial standoffs that allowed for no reflection or compromise on either side. Within a year, three appeals courts had disappointed Reynolds, finding that the Memphis case applied only when layoffs were at issue. In 1986, three more appellate panels concurred. By 1987, four new affirmative action cases had reached the Supreme Court, and in every one of them the justices repudiated Reynolds, sanctioning quota-based hiring and promotion as the law of the land.

Even Reynolds's own administration resisted his efforts to scale back affirmative action. Breaking abruptly with fifteen years' precedent, he declined to enforce the Justice Department's internal hiring and promotion goals and urged the rest of the federal government to follow suit. But only two other government departments complied, the rest determinedly persisting with their employee quotas. Reynolds's new boss, Attorney General Edwin Meese III, was even more staunch in his opposition to affirmative action than his predecessor, William French Smith, had been. But according to department spokesman Terry Eastland, neither Meese nor Reynolds was successful in convincing other Republican insiders to overcome their "soft spot" for business set-asides. Then, in 1985, Reynolds was personally rebuffed when liberal members of the Senate Judiciary Committee managed to block his nomination as Associate Attorney General.

Meese and Reynolds met their most spectacular defeat in 1986, when they tried to rescind the original 1965 presidential decree requiring affirmative action hiring by all contractors in business with the federal government. Issued by Lyndon Johnson, executive order 11246 had given rise to the Philadelphia Plan and all the similar goals and timetables that followed; by the mid-1980s, it affected 27 million employees working on jobs worth over $100 billion. As with many other preferences, the results were far from spectacular: only one in ten companies actually met the targets fully, and overall the program was said to have increased demand—and salaries and promotions—only for highly educated minorities, with little effect on employment of unskilled workers. Still, for both advocates and opponents, the order was a major symbol: proof positive that the country was trying to help, or Exhibit A of all it was doing wrong. Reynolds and Meese derided the decree and urged that it be radically revised. Voluntary affirmative action might continue, the two men allowed, but no contractor should be penalized for failing to meet a statistical goal, and there should be no "legal basis" for granting any preference on the basis of race.

This initiative too met with overwhelming opposition not just in the predictably hostile media but also inside the Reagan administration and among

Republicans in Congress. Labor Secretary William Brock led the resistance in the name of business interests. "It works. Why change it?" a spokesman for the National Association of Manufacturers asked a reporter. A survey of heads of major corporations found 122 out of 128 would continue preferential hiring even if the law did not require it. "We don't need the government involved in this," said one executive, from Merck. "Affirmative action is a way of life here."

The national Republican establishment rallied around Brock and the status quo: Senator Bob Dole and his wife, Transportation Secretary Elizabeth Hanford Dole; Secretary of State George Shultz; Treasury Secretary James Baker III; the National Association of Manufacturers; the Business Roundtable; and some two hundred congressmen, Republicans as well as Democrats. "Our board of directors came out unanimously in favor of goals and timetables," said a spokesman for the manufacturers' group. "A lot of [people] couldn't believe it. . . . But there has been a change in the country. . . . We've all benefited from affirmative action." From the business point of view, preferences had turned out to be a relatively cheap, easy way to help— cheaper certainly than massive programs to rebuild the ghetto, wholesale job training or revamping the public schools—and management knew that hiring and promoting by number would spare them costly discrimination suits. Republicans in Congress were driven by an additional fear—of another political firestorm like those that had erupted over Reagan's earlier flat-footed civil rights initiatives. No elected official or businessman wanted to be cast as a racist. No one wanted to go to the trouble of finding new ways to satisfy black demands, or to face what one corporate spokesman described as "a situation where 50 states pass 50 different laws and we'd be subject to compliance reviews in 50 different areas." Once again, it was simply easier just to keep the applecart rolling, and before long both Meese and Reynolds had retreated into silence.

The evidence against set-asides continued to pile up through the mid-1980s, but even the worst revelations did little to change public opinion in Atlanta or elsewhere. Spring 1986 brought the release of two major scholarly studies, one by the staff of the U.S. Civil Rights Commission, the other by a Georgia institute called Research Atlanta. The Civil Rights Commission report documented in painstaking detail the corruption that by now everyone knew plagued set-aside contracting. Twenty percent of SBA clients, one-third of the firms enrolled in the Department of Transportation's preference, 60 percent of the disadvantaged businesses certified by the state of Illinois, as many as 80 percent and an average of 20 to 25 percent in other state and local programs—all were shams of one kind or another. The Research Atlanta study, though nominally supportive of set-asides, was no less damaging in its findings. The report praised Atlanta area preferences for increasing the share of public work that went to minority firms: up from virtually nothing to over 30 percent. But even the study's enthusiastic authors had to admit that most of these jobs were relatively small and that they benefited only a handful of entrepreneurs. The city program involved no more than 150 firms a year, and even five and ten years later 75 percent of the beneficiaries remained dependent on government set-aside work. Bottom line, the report noted in its most startling and often quoted sentence, in more than a decade, all four Atlanta area preferences combined had produced no more than "a dozen clear-cut cases of [minority business] success."

Devastating as they were, neither report had much impact. When the federal study came up for approval by the full Civil Rights Commission, ideological division prevented the panel from accepting it, and the report was sent back to the staff for "revision," never again to see the light of day. A handful of editorial writers in Atlanta and elsewhere repeated the study's findings for their readers, but mostly it was reviled by civil rights activists, who dismissed it and its authors as racist. Atlanta city council president Marvin Arrington told a local group that someone "should take a baseball bat after" commission chairman Clarence Pendleton, Jr., and not even the Reagan administration gave serious thought to the report's recommendation that the federal government suspend its set-asides. The mountain of troubling evidence in the Research Atlanta report also went largely ignored by the public. Most editorials emphasized the study's positive conclusions. "'Only a dozen' [successful beneficiaries] isn't too shabby," reasoned the *Constitution*. "Standard Oil wasn't built in a day." "Metro Atlanta's programs to encourage minority businesses are working," the newspaper concluded optimistically in the face of massive evidence to the contrary. Predictably enough, within a few months, most Atlantans had all but forgotten the upsetting document.

By the mid-eighties, a handful of Atlantans, black and white, were coming to a quiet consensus about the set-aside's central shortcoming. Even more than corruption and color-coded stigmas, the problem was that the program did not work. "If the concept is to economically benefit minorities, then it's failing," said former mayor Sam Massell. "White firms are taking in minority partners without giving them any responsibility or learning experience." Ben Shapiro spelled out the difficulty: "You can't go from being a tradesman one day," he said, "to being a businessman the next. There's a lot you need to know before you can open your door as ABC Contracting. All start-up businesses need this kind of education and training. But the program is not providing it." Even Young's friend and supporter, Charles Loudermilk, agreed. "The question," he said, "is not what black person is going to be president of what company. It starts way below that. We should work more toward teaching the black community how to succeed in business. How to act in the business world: the clothes, the manners, what's expected. Under the city's program, this is not being done."

What was needed was obvious: better education and training, on the job, but also before. Every now and then, someone like Massell or Shapiro would say this to the press or the mayor and his aides. But mostly, for their own reasons, even the whites who grasped the point did not voice it. Whether out of deference or patronizing indifference, they hesitated to advise the black city government how to help its own people. The kinds of education and training that were needed would have been much more expensive than affirmative action. The mayor and city council were more than happy with the black "wealth class" the program was creating. And even less advantaged blacks who might benefit from a different kind of training initiative seemed gratified by the set-aside and annoyed by whites who criticized it, constructively or not. For better or worse, most whites remained silent, and the city's black politicians assumed they had a unanimous mandate. "It never got to be an issue," Young mused a decade later. "This was the way we did business in Atlanta, and we never really heard much dissent about it."

Still, even in this adverse climate, Ben Shapiro had no intention of giving up. Within a few weeks of the city's action amending the charter, the lawyer and his clients were meeting again. The mayor got word of their deliberations and tried to discourage them by questioning their motives. Another suit, Young said, would introduce "an element of racial discord . . . jeopardizing the prosperity of the entire region." Shapiro ignored the barb and pressed ahead. His second suit was filed in April 1985. "It was the same lawyers," he said, "the same court, the exact same minority business program at issue."

The second case took even longer than the first to make its way up through the state court system. In 1987, the local trial court in Fulton

County once again found in favor of the city, and the following year Shapiro again appealed to the state Supreme Court. By late 1988, the second suit had been pending for over three years, and it was nearly seven since Shapiro had first declared the city set-aside dead. Still, the Georgia court hung back, hesitant to rule on Shapiro's suit until the U.S. Supreme Court decided a similar case from Richmond, Virginia.

Activists on both sides of the issue waited tensely through the autumn as the Court deliberated in the Richmond case. In substance, the suit involved a set-aside much like Atlanta's: a contracting preference under challenge by a white-owned plumbing firm, the J. A. Croson Company. Neither supporters nor foes knew how the three new justices appointed by the Reagan administration would rule on affirmative action, but most people expected they would be critical and open to the new legal arguments about preferences crystallizing in conservative legal circles. The most significant and pointed of these new ideas concerned the rationale for affirmative action. In the past, judges, bureaucrats and businessmen instituting preferences had appealed to a wide variety of justifications—the need to compensate victims of past discrimination, to make up for current effects of past exclusion, to fight continuing discrimination, provide role models, foster a black middle class, promote "diversity" and meet current "operational needs" for, say, black policemen in black neighborhoods. But by the mid-eighties a group of federal judges was trying to clarify this murky tangle, radically narrowing the legally acceptable rationale: to past discrimination and, more strictly yet, past discrimination by the government. As both Shapiro and the Atlanta black political establishment knew, the city's preference programs might have trouble meeting this new standard, and both sides watched the *Croson* case carefully to see if the Court adopted it. "This is the first time," Rodney Strong told a reporter, "the Supreme Court has ever looked squarely at a municipal minority business program, and it could have serious national implications. It could be real trouble."

Shapiro was in his car when he heard the *Croson* verdict reported on the radio. "I was elated," he remembered, "just elated. I knew right away this could be the deciding factor in our case." The *Atlanta Constitution* splashed the news across the front page: "a serious blow" to affirmative action. Sandra Day O'Connor, writing for a plurality of justices, had declared the Richmond set-aside unconstitutional.

Her reasoning picked up the new argument about past discrimination and took it a step further. A city like Richmond could not justify a set-aside by claiming that the South in general had been a racist place. Nor would it be enough to show that city authorities had a history of bigotry, or even that contractors in Virginia had in the past been shut out of public work. "An amorphous claim," she wrote, "that there has been past discrimination in a particular industry cannot justify the use of an unyielding racial quota." Counting by race, Justice O'Connor reasoned, was such an unpleasant remedy that it should be used only "in extreme cases." In order to take the "suspect" step of categorizing, say, bricklayers on the basis of their color, authorities had to prove—with facts and figures—that the city of Richmond had in the past discriminated against black bricklayers. Otherwise, given the country's odious racial history, there would be no end to color coding. Plainly troubled by the small number of successful black businessmen, eager to remedy any past wrongdoing, O'Connor did not want to jettison affirmative action entirely. Still, she hoped she could severely limit the use of racial categories—to the instances in which it seemed truly justified and necessary.

The decision set off alarms in Atlanta, where Shapiro's suit was still awaiting a decision. Shapiro and his clients were jubilant. *Croson,* he announced, had "sounded the death knell" for the city set-aside—and many on the other side, including Rodney Strong, feared he was right. "I would imagine," Strong said grimly, "there will be some effect on all minority business programs, including ours." Officials huddled in the corridors of City Hall, anxious phone calls crisscrossed the city. Both sets of lawyers prepared supplemental briefs and waited nervously for some sign from the state's seven justices.

As expected, the state court followed the Supreme Court's lead to the letter, striking down the Atlanta set-aside for precisely the same reasons O'Connor had ruled against Richmond. The decision was unanimous and beyond appeal. The premise, stated explicitly, was that counting by color was playing with fire—a remedy to be used only in extreme circumstances. "Classifications based on race," the ruling said, "carry a danger of stigmatic harm. Unless they are strictly reserved for remedial settings, they may in fact promote notions of racial inferiority and lead to a politics of racial hostility." Atlanta, the court found further, had played with this fire in a particularly reckless way: the evidence it offered of past discrimination was "woefully inadequate," its remedy was too broadly drawn—not limited to victims but often benefiting those who needed no help—and officials had made no effort to try racially neutral alternatives. Shapiro once again declared victory: "That program is illegal as of right now," he said. "We are extremely pleased," he told another journalist. "This decision reaffirms the principle that race and sex have no bearing on an individual's ability to do a good job."

Still, even in the face of these rulings—a Supreme Court verdict and a unanimous state court decision—Atlanta officials refused to concede defeat. City attorney Marva Brooks maintained that Atlanta would find a way around the ruling; Rodney Strong talked about the possibility of another moratorium. Then Mayor Young held a press conference. Though relaxed and genial as ever, he made clear that he read the decision as simple bigotry and was determined to fight it with all the power at his disposal. O'Connor's distinctions held little interest for him: "Slavery did exist," he noted indignantly. "There were a hundred years of segregation based on race"—and for him this more than justified affirmative action. The Georgia decision, he declared, would have no effect in the short term; like Maynard Jackson in the 1970s, he would negotiate minority participation deal by deal. "There is no choice," Young concluded, "but for us to go back to the drawing board." "We're going to be doing something," Marva Brooks echoed later the same day, "that we feel will be positive, upbeat, legal and hopefully lead to the survival of the program."

The weeks following the decision brought a burst of apparently dramatic change in local affirmative action programs all over the country. Pursuing Atlanta's lead, eleven other federal and state courts moved to strike down set-asides. Within six weeks, twenty preferences had been voluntarily suspended, and thirty-five others were being contested in court. For the first time in more than two decades of affirmative action, it looked as if a major class of preferences—the most corrupt, the most patently punitive to white competitors and the one involving the most money—was about to be rolled back. And local contractors felt the effects almost immediately. In Atlanta, Young's promises notwithstanding, it proved impossible to negotiate every municipal contracting deal, and minority participation in city business dropped precipitously, from more than a third to only 15 percent.

Shapiro, earnest as ever and keen to find an alternative way to help, thought this might be the moment for the compromise he had been dreaming of since 1981. He and his clients resurrected their old plan for a race-neutral city program to promote any and all small businesses. He wrote letters to other local governments inquiring about what they had done to boost start-up entrepreneurs; he contacted banks and bonding agencies to discuss just what kinds of stratagems were likely to work best. There were approaches to other Atlanta builders and meetings with city officials. Finally, after months of preparation, Shapiro drafted a proposal for a new city ordinance and sent it to members of the city council. His recommendations were specific and technical: more frequent payments to ease small builders' cash flow, stronger legislation to prevent discrimination by bonding agencies, simplified bidding procedures, reduced paperwork requirements and an official city-sponsored mentoring program. At Shapiro's prodding, a group of local subcontractors endorsed the plan and asked city officials to meet with them to discuss it. They sat down over coffee at Paschal's, the old movement hangout on the south side of Atlanta, and the white builders explained their proposals. Contractor Greg Sweetin later recalled a cordial meeting, but he suspected even then that little would come of it. "I felt they weren't interested," he said, still disappointed years later. "My sense was that they wanted to have programs that were in favor of African Americans."

Frustrated and angered by the court's decision, the mayor's team was determined to fight back, and in the weeks after the ruling, Young hosted several "emergency meetings" to discuss strategy. One of the more emotional gatherings drew three hundred minority contractors to City Hall. Brooks, Strong, Young and Arrington addressed the crowd, each speaker more dramatic and righteous than the one before. "This program is morally right and good for business," Young declared. "This is a reminder that the struggle continues." Rodney Strong asked anyone in the audience who had experienced discrimination to raise his hand; a forest of arms shot up—by one account, virtually every hand in the hall. Arrington went a step further, asking contractors to begin keeping records of discrimination, making detailed notes and tape-recording conversations if necessary. The largely black audience responded with a chorus of cheers. "I am prepared to die for affirmative action, so help me God," Arrington announced to another round of roaring amens. Among the stratagems discussed at the meeting and elsewhere in those early weeks: further litigation, mass protest and a black boycott of insurance companies that provided bonding for white contractors who did not voluntarily joint-venture with blacks.

The defense the city finally settled on was to try to meet Justice O'Connor's challenge head-on: to provide enough evidence of discrimination, past and present, to justify a set-aside. A team was hired to do the job: fittingly enough, a joint venture formed between former Federal Reserve Board member Andrew Brimmer, who was black, and Carter administration labor secretary Ray Marshall, who was white. The study was to take three months and cost the city just over half a million dollars. The two economists and their staff would look at statistical and anecdotal evidence to determine whether discrimination had occurred or still existed. But there was little doubt in the minds of the Atlanta establishment about what the outcome of the investigation would be. As city officials announced unembarrassedly, they were hiring "a team of experts to help Atlanta bolster its legal case for reinstating the affirmative action effort." "We know that a certain past discrimination existed," councilwoman Myrtle Davis explained. "Now it's time to document it." "We will pursue the study," Brimmer confirmed to a reporter, "on the assumption that the record will show disparity."

The Brimmer-Marshall study was delivered in July 1990 and received with great hoopla in City Hall. The eight thick volumes, some 1100 pages in all, had taken a year of work by more than a dozen experts: lawyers, economists, business consultants, local historians and others. These professionals had scoured the morgue of the *Journal-Constitution,* interviewed scores of minority business people and pored over reams of economic data: U.S. Census tables, Bureau of Labor statistics, City Hall affirmative action files. They had thought about every conceivable defense of preferences— legal, historical, emotional—drawing on sources from the ancient Code of Hammurabi to contemporary anecdotes about racial exclusion. Since no one in the city bureaucracy had any doubt about what the study's findings would be, people were only encouraged by the breadth of the research that had gone into it. "To have to hire experts to prove that discrimination has existed in Atlanta is ludicrous," said Maynard Jackson on accepting the report. "But we have hired the very best experts this nation has to offer . . . and the evidence they present is incontrovertible."

In fact, very few people in Atlanta ever read the Brimmer-Marshall study. A handful of Peachtree regulars saw the short executive summary, and the local newspapers reprinted a few of the more dramatic anecdotes. But at over $300 a copy, the eight volumes were not widely distributed, available only at City Hall and in local law libraries. Still, the report's findings soon became conventional wisdom around town. "Discrimination in Atlanta's business sector," one often-cited line maintained, "is deeply rooted in the city's history, has become institutionalized, but also continues to be overt."

Most Atlantans, white and black, saw little reason to question the report's claims. A sharecropper's son who had risen to serve on the Federal Reserve Board, Andrew Brimmer was a "black first" of superstar proportions, and both he and his co-author were distinguished public servants with unassailable academic credentials. Besides, Atlantans figured, you didn't have to be an economics professor to know about the South's ugly racial past or its continuing legacy. A *Constitution* editorial welcoming the study reminded readers how little things had changed: "In Atlanta, 66 percent black, only 41 percent of the income goes to the black community. And only one-quarter of 1 percent of the business receipts." If affirmative action could be justified anywhere, well-meaning citizens reasoned, surely it was here in Atlanta. The Brimmer-Marshall study had been necessary to satisfy the courts, but almost no one doubted its legal or moral arguments: what the *Constitution* called a "compelling case for new set-asides."

This left it to out-of-town lawyers, most of them published only in obscure law journals, to ask whether the Brimmer-Marshall team had actually done what the city paid it for: prove that Atlantans were guilty of the kind of discrimination that the Supreme Court said they had to have committed in order to justify an affirmative action program. That legal standard, developed in the *Croson* decision, was not, it turned out, an easy concept for the general public to understand, mainly because it flew in the face of most people's notion of affirmative action. Still, as law, it was explicit and clear, and beyond dispute by 1990. Appalled as the bench was by the injustices that had been perpetrated over the decades in the Old South and elsewhere, the Court had ruled specifically that generalized, "societal discrimination" could not be used to warrant a racial preference. If it were, *Croson* and a consistent string of earlier cases had held, the state's remedial job would never be done, and affirmative action—with all its potentially poisonous side effects—would become a permanent way of life in America. Residents of Atlanta, like many others, north and south, were understandably ashamed of their ugly racial past. But this did not, the Supreme Court had repeatedly ruled, justify a new set of government programs classifying people and granting or denying them benefits on the basis of their skin color.

Trying to limit the use of this dangerous medicine to the cases where it seemed truly called for, the justices had laid out a strict set of criteria. Affirmative action could not be used simply as a way to carve up the pie more fairly. Nor was it a tool to fight current discrimination; there were other laws to take care of that. Preferences like Atlanta's were warranted, the Court said, only as a remedy for past discrimination by a government body, acting in a direct or at least "passive" way, as an accomplice. Not only that, Sandra Day O'Connor had argued, but past prejudice on the part of another government—the feds, say, or the state of Georgia—could not justify an Atlanta set-aside. A long history of Atlanta slights against black architects was not enough reason to reserve work for black contractors. The remedy had to match the past injustice, place by place and trade by trade, with only an identified class of victims qualifying as beneficiaries. This was the *Croson* mandate, as clear as it was precise. Justice O'Connor even went so far as to tell local governments what kind of numbers they would have to find to exonerate their programs: "a significant disparity between the number of qualified minority contractors willing and able to perform a particular service and the number of such contractors actually engaged by the locality." In that case, but only in that case, would a set-aside be permissible.

Thorough as it was and filled with evidence of past wrongdoing, the Brimmer-Marshall study did not meet this standard. In all its thousand-plus pages, the study found no smoking gun: not a scrap of hard evidence that the Atlanta city government had discriminated against black contractors. Construction insiders were not surprised. That was the point of the low-bid system: to prevent discrimination and other patronage. "There is not a single reported instance in the study," one attorney said, "where a minority or woman firm in Atlanta is the lowest bidder and didn't get the contract." But this failure to meet its mandate did not stop the Brimmer-Marshall team, which found plenty of evidence of other, more amorphous kinds of discrimination for the city to use as ammunition in making its case.

Much of the economists' report, particularly the historical and anecdotal volumes, simply ignored O'Connor's new standard of proof. Rationalizing perhaps that the long history of societal discrimination in the South would have an emotional impact if not a legal one, the study's authors laid on chapter after chapter of unsavory description of the Old South: stories about the Civil War, anecdotes from the 1920s, personal testimony about all manner of slights by whites against blacks. Still another volume relied on contemporary stories from minority contractors in the Atlanta area: anecdotes about late payments, inadequate notice of job opportunities, deals made on the golf course, jobs handed out to children of friends and through other networks inaccessible to black people. The stories were gripping and often horrific; together, they made for a powerful indictment of Jim Crow and its legacy. But by the Supreme Court's standards, all of these tales were irrelevant. Virtually none, historical or contemporary, dealt with government discrimination. Many of the newer anecdotes were unattributed and could not be verified. And even if the report proved that there had been extensive private discrimination among Atlanta contractors, by the Supreme Court's new standard, this would not justify a government set-aside.

The Brimmer-Marshall team's second stratagem was to take explicit issue with the *Croson* mandate. The authors criticized O'Connor's criteria as both too narrow and ill-conceived, likely to underestimate the true extent of past discrimination. Ignoring the justice's strict standards, they developed a test of their own—what lawyers would later call the "but for" thesis—that they held up as an alternative to O'Connor's logic. But for discrimination in the past, this argument held, black businesses in the South and elsewhere would be as large and prosperous and well-connected as white firms—and any discrepancy between the two kinds of companies was incontrovertible proof of discrimination.

At first blush, the economists' reasoning made sense: the "but for" logic sounded accurate enough and only fair—and, for most of the public, it remains the central justification for affirmative action. The problem was that this was exactly the kind of thinking and evidence that O'Connor had ruled inadmissible. Not only was it wildly speculative and impossible to prove: after all, not all disparity was the result of discrimination. But more important, O'Connor argued, if implemented on a wide scale, the "but for" argument would open the way to an unending web of preferences—a system in which government-adjusted, color-coded proportionality took precedence over any kind of individual initiative, achievement or accident. The Brimmer-Marshall team devoted most of its resources to careful comparisons of white- and black-owned firms in the Atlanta region—and to no one's surprise found black-owned firms falling short in all areas. Still, whatever the emotional power of these comparisons, like the long historical section of the report, they were strictly beside the point.

The Brimmer-Marshall study came closest to meeting the Supreme Court's standard in the chapters that were the hardest for the public to understand—the statistical portion of the study. Justice O'Connor had specifically required that a city maintaining a set-aside prove that the percentage of local minority-owned companies willing and able to do the work in question was greater than the share of city jobs that actually went to such firms. It was a finicky, technical standard, but not one removed from common sense: if there were only five black architects in town, after all, out of two thousand total, it would hardly be fair for them to get 30 percent of all city design work—no matter what percentage of the overall population was black.

The Brimmer-Marshall team made an exhaustive effort to compile this kind of comparison, generally known as a "disparity ratio." The problem, according to the skeptical lawyers who would later take this and other similar studies to court, was that the statistics used in the Atlanta report left much to be desired. Most of the census data was badly out of date. The economists' vocational categories were not specific enough to meet O'Connor's criteria, and the authors took no account of the size or capacity of the minority firms they counted. This last omission was a particularly significant mistake, one that went to the heart of what had gone wrong with the Atlanta set-aside over the years. Minority contractors might well make up a third of all contracting firms in the city, but if only one or two black-owned companies were actually capable of doing the work that had to be done—as was the case on many of the jobs that went to Herman Russell and the few others like him—then it hardly made sense for the city to reserve one-third of all its building work for them.

Among the lawyers—and they were not many—who could understand the arcane complexities of Brimmer-Marshall, the verdict was clear. "It was a pseudo-discussion," said one Atlanta attorney. "There is just no proof of discrimination in the [city's] construction industry." "The team knew what it was looking for," said another lawyer, "and they found it. But to a large degree, the contents of the study did not support its conclusions." "There's an awful lot of general information and opinion in there," said a third man, a recently retired U.S. Attorney. "It seems to be the justification for . . . a preconceived solution."

Still, in the public's eye, the social scientists' report was a triumph. The lawyers' refutations, like Justice O'Connor's strict standard, struck many Atlantans as cold and elaborately nitpicking, and it was easy to cast the naysayers as mean-spirited or hostile to minorities. Certainly, the attorneys' fine-toothed arguments were no match in the public's eye for the wrenching stories and stirring rhetoric in the hired team's long report. To Atlantans, blacks and concerned whites, the moral case for set-asides—amorphous and uncertain as it was—trumped any reasoned legal argument against the programs, and the Brimmer-Marshall study was heralded as a landmark document in the history of affirmative action.

Rodney Strong and others in the city government proclaimed triumphantly that they had complied with the Supreme Court's requirements and met its challenge. "I believe we're in a position that's unassailable," Strong declared, "on the basis of current constitutional law." The city held five days of public hearings to dramatize and publicize the Brimmer-Marshall findings, and within a year the city had a new minority business ordinance that incorporated all 1,100 pages of the much-celebrated study.

Those who thought the *Croson* case had put an end to local set-asides could not have been more surprised. Not only did the new Atlanta law reinstate the city preference virtually intact; it even extended the scope and power of the program. Among other changes, the measure required a significantly expanded affirmative action bureaucracy. As mandated by the new law, the new quota was much less vulnerable than the old one to legal challenges by small white contractors who felt shut out of city work. Most radically, in the wake of the Brimmer-Marshall study, the city council expanded the Atlanta set-aside so that it regulated not just the public sector but also private contracting. Once again, Atlanta was leading the nation in the use of ever larger, more ingenious and legally sophisticated preferences—in this case, using public muscle to restrict what private companies did in private business. It was an unprecedented extension of the reach of municipal affirmative action programs, and lawyers familiar with the city ordinance strongly doubted that it would withstand a legal challenge. This did not stop the city council from passing it unanimously, without hesitation or debate.

As so often when it came to affirmative action, the rest of the nation soon followed Atlanta's lead. The years since *Croson* had been nearly fatal for local set-asides. Contractors all over the country had gone to court with reverse discrimination suits, and a number of local programs had been struck down. More than thirty other jurisdictions dismantled their preferences voluntarily rather than face costly legal battles. Still others scrambled to scale back their requirements to comply with Justice O'Connor's standards. But the apparent turning of the tide did not last long. As Atlanta's program had been the "granddaddy" of preferences, so Brimmer-Marshall was the progenitor of what came to be known as "disparity studies"—and the new generation of bulletproof preferences they spawned.

A raft of professional imitators picked up where Brimmer and Marshall left off: academics, lawyers and big accounting firm executives who traveled from city to city preparing similar reports. Jurisdictions from coast to coast seized on the two economists' logic to shore up their threatened set-asides: New York City, Chicago, Washington, D.C., Seattle, Phoenix, the states of Texas and Florida, the Port Authority of New York & New Jersey, among other places and agencies. Six months after the Atlanta study was finished, twenty-nine others had been done elsewhere in the country, thirty-seven more were already in the pipeline, and cities that had not yet commissioned their own could write to a central clearinghouse in Washington for a list of consultants for hire. Not all the documents were as long or as expensive as Atlanta's; they ranged in length from fifty to a thousand pages and in price from $50,000 to Atlanta's half million. But by the time the *Croson* case was five years old, there were more than ninety disparity studies floating around the country—some thirty thousand pages of documentation that had cost local taxpayers more than $45 million.

Most of the studies were much like Brimmer-Marshall's: a lot of anecdotal evidence and general history hung on the framework of a "but for" thesis. According to lawyers who tracked the new cottage industry, for all the proliferating reports, no jurisdiction anywhere in the country was ever found guilty of outright discrimination in its allotment of public-sector construction work. As often as not, as in Atlanta, the documents were padded with irrelevant information. Like the original Brimmer-Marshall text, most paid lip service to the *Croson* mandate, but then proceeded to ignore it. As for Justice O'Connor's central question—about the ratio of qualified contractors to those getting city work—many studies, like Atlanta's, actually demonstrated the opposite of what they were intended to prove: they found that the local set-aside goal far exceeded the percentage of available and qualified minority contractors. Still, virtually every disparity study claimed to find what it had set out to find: a justifying need for a set-aside program.

Attorneys like Ben Shapiro with experience fighting set-asides initially assumed that disparity studies would be easily defeated in court, but the lawyers were quickly disillusioned. Not only was it now more expensive and time-consuming to sue: challengers had to refute the elaborate quantitative analysis in the disparity studies with extensive quantitative research of their own. But the seeming moral mandate at the heart of the studies had also significantly swayed public opinion in many jurisdictions, bolstering support for set-asides among well-meaning liberals. The handful of small contractors in every town who were most put out by the preferences now felt even more isolated than before. Local governments, feeling protected by their expensive research efforts, fended off challenges before they emerged, gently and not so gently dissuading would-be litigants. Ben Shapiro, for one, finally decided not to sue again; it was just too much trouble, too frustrating and thankless. Recognizing the increased difficulty of mounting a case, the national contractors' associations tried to coordinate and streamline challenges. But in the end that effort too foundered on expense and public opinion.

In the long run, it was as if *Croson* had never happened. Judges were not on the whole impressed by disparity studies. In one much-watched case, in Philadelphia, the court found the city's report, also by Andrew Brimmer, to be so full of "serious methodological and scientific flaws" that it could not be relied upon. Some studies, particularly those based largely on testimony by interested minority contractors, were dismissed out of hand. But other judges, often those who approved of set-asides to begin with, sensed that this was once again a wide open issue—and a number ruled boldly to uphold local programs. Lawyers began to talk about the *Croson* case, once seen as an all but definitive ban on local preferences, as "inconclusive" and "open to interpretation." "Strict scrutiny," said one attorney, using the legal term for O'Connor's mandate, "expresses a mood. It doesn't decide a case."

Six or seven years after the Supreme Court's decision, it had given rise to over a hundred lower court cases, and the outcome was a toss-up: about as many victories as defeats for local set-asides. More flexible programs fared better than others, as did those that seemed to be voluntary, temporary or to include at least some race-neutral measures. In some jurisdictions, preferences were scaled back to take account of the Supreme Court's concerns. But in other places, like Atlanta, programs were strengthened and expanded. In 1988, the year before the *Croson* ruling, organizations that monitor local government counted 225 set-asides nationwide; in 1992, a new tally found 234 jurisdictions with minority business preferences. "We won in state court," Ben Shapiro commented. "We won in the U.S. Supreme Court. But in cities like Atlanta, where there is a majority controlling city government, even if you get a program struck down, they just say, 'Well, we'll pass another ordinance.' The astonishing thing is that they have gotten away with it."

As for the color coding that Sandra Day O'Connor had tried so hard to restrict, not much of the public, in Atlanta anyway, seemed to notice or care. If anything, the disparity study business had added new racial rancor to the atmosphere in cities like Atlanta: inflating evidence of discrimination, reopening the old wounds inflicted by history, sharpening the mistrust and polarization that already divided black from white. Assuming, largely erroneously, that local set-asides were helping to create a new class of black businessmen, most of the public seemed to feel that they were worth it—that the benefits exceeded the costs of a little more racial awareness. Thanks to the disparity industry and the public that rallied around it, the programs now had a new lease on life. For better or worse, the Atlanta city government would remain a major force for race consciousness, relentlessly reminding people just how much their color mattered and hardening resentments among both blacks and whites.

After nearly a decade of fighting racial quotas in court, J. Ben Shapiro had nothing to show for his effort: an early warning to those in years to come who would try to dismantle affirmative action, not just in contracting but also on the job and in universities. Once again, as with busing, the racial issue was just too charged, and meaningful public discussion had proved all but impossible. Most Americans seemed to believe in integration, but for whatever reasons could not bring themselves to focus thoughtfully on the best means to achieve it. Instead, heartened by any talk that held out the possibility of racial justice, they tended to look politely away from the uncertain methods being used to get there. "The majority of the American people," Shapiro said later, "don't accept racial preferences. There have been lots of studies now to show this. On the other hand, they are not as vocal as civil rights advocates. Besides, Americans feel they have a moral obligation to repair the damage done by three hundred years of racial discrimination. They want to do the right thing. They want to help people—and they have no idea how much damage they are doing."

Chapter 16

BETTING ON
TRICKLE-DOWN

ell into the 1980s, even as Atlanta prospered as never before, at the center of the city where a town square or public park should have been, there was nothing but a rubbish-strewn wasteland. Just a block or two from the skyscrapers of downtown, the dilapidated streets had the lost, rusty look of an old industrial corridor, the kind of place you find on the outskirts of some cities, long abandoned but too remote for anyone to want to rebuild there. In Atlanta, this strip was what divided the white sections of town—downtown and the residential neighborhoods to the north of it—from most of the historically black parts of the city. A permanent, subliminal reminder of the racial past, it stood forlorn and crumbling, an unhealed breach.

The missing hub had a long history. Back as far as the Civil War, the Western & Atlantic Railroad had cut a wide, uninhabited swath between the bustling white-owned shops at the Five Points corner and the always shabbier frame buildings on the other side of the tracks. For more than half a century, custom and then Jim Crow law reinforced the physical barrier, confining black homes and businesses to strictly zoned enclaves, most of them south and west of downtown. In the 1920s, the emerging Peachtree elite decided to cover over the railroad, too dirty and noisy for a modern city. An elaborate system of viaducts was built, burying not just the train line but also the nineteenth-century streets that ran alongside it. Merchants abandoned their shops and rebuilt on the new street level, a floor or so above their old real estate. The ghost town underneath was left to rot, its cast-iron store-fronts and cobblestoned streets a fading memory. In the decades that followed, blacks and whites gravitated to different hubs: Atlanta's two Main Streets, white Peachtree Street and black Auburn Avenue. And the area where the two worlds might have met, the streets above the tracks, remained a transitional neighborhood: warehouses, freight-loading docks, industrial supply stores, small, seedy shops about to go out of business. It was, as Andrew Young would often say, "a hole in the middle of downtown": a crusty scar where the heart of the city should have been.

In the late sixties, architect Paul Muldawer convinced two real estate developers to try refurbishing the subterranean hollow. Their $10-million restoration produced a small entertainment complex, Underground Atlanta. Mostly kitschy theme-park stuff—player pianos, gaslight, a lot of period stained glass—for five years it was a successful tourist attraction. Still, it was not a town center, nobody's idea of the civic heart of the growing city, and within a decade it was heading for dereliction again. In the early eighties the last nightclub closed its doors, leaving the padlocked cavern to vandals and winos.

By the time Andrew Young took over City Hall, the old knot of tunnels was a sight to behold: a now twice-abandoned ghost town, littered with condoms and liquor bottles, the wrought-iron fence that had ringed the nightclub complex already rusting, its turnstiles twisted grotesquely askew. Just ten blocks north, John Portman was building a showy cluster of new skyscrapers: atrium hotels, office towers, state-of-the-art convention facilities. Just two blocks south, the state capitol stood imperturbable, its great gold-leafed dome rising sedately above a handsome neoclassical facade. But in between the two, at the city's geographical middle, there was still nothing but that old, burnt-out hole, an unending nightmare for the city police force. Worse still, the decay was spreading, and the streets around the hollow were in a tailspin: rapidly emptying, wracked by crime, increasingly black and desolate after office hours.

By the early 1980s, the Peachtree set knew that something had to be done with the empty cavern. The businessmen had two concerns. Most immediately, they wanted to shore up the convention trade. For some years now, Atlanta had been pouring money into its hospitality industry. Much of the new construction of the past decade was in high-rise hotels. Together, they, the restaurants, entertainment spots and other visitor services were the city's largest employer, and Atlanta was already the third most popular convention destination in the country. The one problem—the only obstacle to further growth—was that there was almost nothing for off-duty visitors to do in downtown Atlanta. As a result, conventioneers rarely brought along their spouses, and they generally left as soon as their meetings were over, severely cutting into Atlanta's potential profit. To the city's businessmen, an entertainment district was the obvious answer, and though not exactly the perfect spot, the old Underground was the easiest place to build one.

The businessmen's larger concern, more civic and socioeconomic, was the problem plaguing all American cities—the problem that had all but killed Detroit a decade earlier. Whites and, in Atlanta, middle-class blacks were moving to the suburbs. The city's tax base was shrinking even as its need for social services soared. The larger metro area was thriving, but even it, businessmen feared, could be dragged down by a dying center city. Some kind of development was needed to shore up the region's core—to prevent the blight that had already sprouted in Underground from taking over a larger and larger area. In Atlanta, as in Detroit, many big businessmen were shifting their own investments beyond the city line, but they saw that it would be worth their while to contribute a little something to create the impression— all-important to other investors—of a safe and vibrant downtown.

The idea of developing Underground had gripped Andrew Young even before he was elected mayor. In the period between the vote and his inauguration, he traveled to Maryland to confer with James Rouse, developer of Boston's Faneuil Hall and Baltimore's Harbor Place, about what the Rouse Company might do in Atlanta. Then, once he was sworn in, the first piece of legislation Young pushed through the city council was an official expression of interest in refurbishing the Underground cavern. The businessmen's vision—a restoration of the old nightclub complex—did not promise much for poor black Atlantans. Like Detroit's Renaissance Center, it would be a showy investment with few civic side effects, hardly even a Band-Aid on the cancer eating at the heart of downtown. "We'd all been to Detroit," said Rodney Strong. "We all knew what had happened in Detroit." But Young was convinced that Atlanta could do better, meeting the white business establishment's needs while also doing something for the city's poor blacks.

The newly restored Underground he hoped to create would be a "bridge" across the divided city or, as he put it, a North African "casbah"—finally, after all these years, a common hub for centerless Atlanta. "Andy's idea," columnist Dick Williams remembered, "was to create the town hall of a disconnected city. Everybody would come together. It would be Atlanta's public square." Many Atlantans, white and black, saw this as the height of folly. "We needed an entertainment complex," said business leader Lawrence Gellerstedt, Jr. "But why would you build it in the black-controlled heart of the city, where all the crime was?" Others could not imagine what magnet, cultural or otherwise, could possibly draw both whites and blacks—both suburban families and city street kids—to any one spot on the urban landscape. "But Andy insisted he could make it work," said Williams, "if only he could control the music. It was brilliant—typical Andy. You'd have reggae at one place, country and western next door, soul down the block. You'd attract everyone, and they'd all get along." It was only a symbol, and a modest one at that, but Young and his allies insisted that Underground Atlanta would "reestablish downtown as the biracial heart of metro Atlanta."

Even more ambitious and more significant, Young saw Underground as an engine of trickle-down racial justice. Like Detroit and other cities, Atlanta faced a grim financial future: less and less federal aid and a rapidly shrinking tax base. Young's response to these straits—not that different from Detroit's response—was what he called "public-purpose capitalism": using private financing to pay for development the city alone could never pull off. "We would use city money," he explained, "for the feasibility studies and to package the project, then leverage private investment at about a ten-to-one ratio." But unlike Coleman Young in Detroit, Andrew Young was determined that some of this infusion be spent in black neighborhoods. Unlike the RenCen, built as far as possible from the poor enclaves of black Motown, the Underground site sat just inside black Atlanta, and redeveloping the tunnels could not help but bring some jobs and money into the black community. Both contractors and the tourism industry could be pressed to hire from the neighborhood. Money pumped into black districts would have a multiplier effect. "I saw it as an economic engine," Young said later.

The idea at the core of the trickle-down strategy—its key component— was affirmative action: joint venture contracting, joint venture retail, affirmative action hiring at every stage of the project. "Young made clear to me early on," said the city's top affirmative action bureaucrat, Rodney Strong, "that he wanted me to make Underground Atlanta my biggest priority. It was the most important project of our entire administration, our biggest opportunity for African-American business development. It was the whole heart and soul of what we were trying to do [in promoting preferences] and it had implications across the board." The largest construction project in Atlanta since Maynard Jackson's rebuilding of Hartsfield International Airport, Underground became Young's chance to match his predecessor and better him by using affirmative action on a much broader scale to open up opportunities for all blacks.

This was not as easy as it sounded. Elsewhere, at the airport and downtown's construction sites, the city's joint venture efforts, public and private, had helped enrich only a handful of already wealthy men. But Young and Strong and others on the city council were convinced that counting by race could boost the many, making economic integration a reality for even the poorest of Atlantans. "Spending with minority contractors," said Young, "means that minority contractors [are] hiring and training minority young people. It means that these young people begin to think of themselves as entrepreneurs." Well-meaning white Atlantans welcomed the prospect. "I don't like the program," said Dick Williams. "I never did. But if it's about a black man or woman rolling up their sleeves and working—that's a different thing." "Of course, costs are inflated by the preferences," echoed Charles Loudermilk. "But I can live with that if it's an educational process."

Spurred by Young's determination and idealism, Underground became the ultimate test of the black political establishment's long-deferred promise that affirmative action would have "ripple effects": that it generated jobs, created new wealth, made new entrepreneurs and provided role models for the less fortunate still at the bottom of the ladder. Young made the project his personal priority and pursued it unrelentingly through his eight years in City Hall. Betting all he had that he could use a city set-aside to reach even the poorest south siders, he staked his future and downtown Atlanta's on his trickle-down theory of affirmative action.

The mayor's first challenge—before even the first joint venture issues could be addressed—was to put together the money. This alone would consume nearly five years and involve negotiations with everyone who was anyone in Atlanta public life. The first stages went smoothly enough. The Rouse Company expressed interest in the project and did a feasibility study. The city kicked in just enough money to turn that exploration into a preliminary plan, then applied for and received a $10-million Urban Development Action Grant (UDAG) from the federal government. Not two full years into Young's first term, the mayor predicted confidently that whatever obstacles arose, the Underground project was "a foregone conclusion." Then he started to look for the other $130 million that was needed to turn the dream into reality.

None of the obvious people were interested. The Rouse Company, which usually underwrote and developed its festival marketplaces, declined in this case to follow its feasibility study with a serious investment: the Maryland firm would be happy to manage the Atlanta complex, but the company had no intention of putting up more than $1 million—in this context, next to nothing. The Peachtree civic leaders formally and informally endorsed the development and pressed everyone they could think of—mainly the city council and Fulton County—to get involved in the deal. But even when offered a hefty tax deduction for any money they invested, the businessmen were notably slow to reach for their wallets. As for public money, both Young and the Peachtree set knew that a referendum on a bond issue would go down to almost certain defeat.

The risks associated with the investment were plain to all. Would the entertainment mix succeed in luring both blacks and whites—and holding them together in one place? Would white Atlantans and suburbanites travel downtown in the evenings and on weekends? How would the city control the crime that had killed the first Underground complex? And even if the answers to all these questions were yes—even if the project were successful—it was not likely to be a high-return investment. Investors weren't just paying for an entertainment complex; they were also subsidizing a dicey urban renewal project—building in a devastated area, largely without infrastructure and plagued by crime—and the high cost of this cleanup effort would make it very difficult to recoup the original stake. Then there was the extra cost of joint-venturing at every level. Add it all up, and the total bill was staggering. As Rodney Strong admitted years later, "We always projected that Underground would lose money during the first ten years. We tried to make the estimates as thin as possible to make it as politically palatable as possible. But we always knew that the city was going to be subsidizing the project."

Still, in the end the business community had little choice but to do its share. Hotel and real estate developers were the first to sign on. The businessmen with the most obvious stake in the development, they put up nearly $5 million and convinced seventy-five other local companies to come in with them—enough to match the pending UDAG money and then some. All the Peachtree regulars ponied up: in addition to the hotel and real estate people, the major banks, the Coca-Cola Company, the Georgia Power Company, Bell South, Southern Bell, Equitable Life and many smaller investors—with contributions ranging from $100 to over $1 million. Some of the businessmen were reluctant. "The Chamber of Commerce coerced us," said shopowner Albert Maslia. "It was not really an investment. It was forced." But skeptical or not, most held their tongues. Whether out of guilt or good intentions or patronizing deference, they acceded despite their better judgment in the black mayor's hopeful strategy for racial uplift. Altogether, their share came to nearly $20 million, leaving still another $110 million unaccounted for.

With Rouse still refusing to have anything to do with developing the complex, in 1985 the Peachtree set put together its own corporation to do the job. To head up the project, they chose Joe Martin, a classic Atlanta mix of businessman and idealist. A city native, white, with a Harvard MBA, he had worked for Maynard Jackson and dabbled in private real estate development before signing on with the Underground project. Preppy in style, earnest in manner, he talked with a deep southern twang but as fast as any Yankee banker. As coordinator of the development, he oversaw an incredibly complex series of financial and legal transactions. But Martin also emerged early on as a spokesman for the vision behind the undertaking. "I believe very deeply in an integrated society," he told reporters. "I believe in this project because I believe in a pluralistic society. Downtown is a central meeting place. It is the one place in our community where everyone comes together. It's the crossroads. So if one believes in a pluralistic society, one of the means to that end is to make sure that downtown is really healthy—that there is a central marketplace."

So it was, as the eighties wore on, that the fuzzy hopes behind the project gradually crystallized into a civic credo. Like Martin, the Peachtree leaders wanted to feel good about their social investment. Whatever doubts they had about affirmative action were put aside. First Martin and then his backers embraced the trickle-down component of Young's strategy, encouraging the city in its joint venture requirements and boasting of the number of new jobs the project would create for minority workers. Before long, this well-intentioned hope had hardened into a definite promise: the figure bandied about town was precisely three thousand jobs. The city even convinced the federal government that it was true; in order to get permission to use $8.5 million in Community Development Block Grant (CDBG) money—funds earmarked for the poor—to build the entertainment complex, Young successfully persuaded the feds that Underground's clubs and shops would provide work for that many low-income south siders.

The hardest sell of all, perhaps because they were footing most of the bill, was to the people of Atlanta. As the project shaped up through the mid-eighties, Young remained technically true to his promise to limit the public's involvement in financing it: City Hall contributed only $14 million out of a total $140 million. Still, it turned out, one way or another, that taxpayers were ultimately responsible for all $120 million not covered by Peachtree investors. Both the UDAG and CDBG funds had to be repaid eventually, if not with profits from the complex, then out of city coffers. The bulk of the financing—the remaining $85 million—was met with a municipal bond issue. The voters had no direct say in approving this outlay; Young made sure that was left to the city council. But if the project flopped, this money too would have to be repaid by Atlanta taxpayers. All in all, critics projected, the public would be liable until the year 2016 for $8 to $9 million annually— over $100 extra in property taxes every year from the average middle-class homeowner. It was a hefty bill under any circumstances, but especially if, contrary to Young's promises, the project turned out to benefit only a handful of already wealthy black businessmen.

Young and the Peachtree set worked tirelessly through the early eighties to bring the public and the city council on board. There were newspaper editorials, backroom lobbying efforts, quiet uptown lunches and earnest public appeals. "All the citizens of Atlanta," said one *Constitution* editorial, "which need we say again is 66 percent black, stand to gain from a completion of a refurbished Underground Atlanta. Those who stand to benefit most directly include a host of marginally employed and unemployed menial laborers who live in the shadow of downtown. Many of those laborers are black." Still, much of the public, black and white, remained skeptical about the project.

Among the most doubtful from the start were local grassroots activists and councilmen from the south side. City council president Marvin Arrington gave a passionate speech at his 1986 inauguration warning that the city's poor would not benefit from the project. Several months later, Arrington stood up again in the council to suggest that the money being spent on the new complex should go instead to refurbishing the historic black shopping area, Sweet Auburn. Even in the project's early stages, there was plenty of evidence to confirm Arrington's doubts: well before the builders started to work, the often repeated promise of three thousand jobs had shrunk dramatically, to eighteen hundred. In 1987, two thousand union laborers marched on City Hall to complain that they were being left out of Underground construction work. Not long after, fifty inner-city residents mounted another protest. "What Does Underground Have to Do with Poor Mothers?" asked one of their placards. Civil rights activist Hosea Williams summed up critics' misgivings: "Underground is just an entertainment center for rich folks," he said. "We need to deal with our real problems."

Young's answer was to remind the council of his affirmative action promises. It was an irrefutable, surefire argument in 1980s Atlanta, and for all the public's skepticism, Young's reassurances worked. If anything, city council members took up the cause with greater zeal and vehemence than the mayor, embracing as their own his assumption that color-coding meant trickle-down. As the public's proxies, they kept an eagle-eyed watch over the Underground project, second-guessing every aspect of building, leasing and staffing the complex. And no matter what was at issue—from the early eighties until the end of the decade, well after Underground's opening day— the council's concerns turned on affirmative action: demands for additional preferences on more favorable terms, more earmarked jobs, more special loans, more reserved retail space and other dispensations.

The first battle over color coding occurred well before construction began, as Young and his team struggled to negotiate a financial agreement with the Rouse Company. The discussions were handled quietly, in a straightforward businesslike manner—until the city council was asked to approve a small sum of money for a preliminary design study. Council members had no reason to doubt Rouse's goodwill on race matters. Yet several decided to turn the negotiations into a racial standoff. "I'm prepared to make sure the project dies if we do not have some blacks involved," councilman James Howard told the Atlanta press in late 1983.

In fact, the Maryland firm had an impeccable record on race issues. "The Rouse Company was integrated at the managerial level before affirmative action was the law of the land," Young assured the council. Atlantan journalists visiting Rouse's Harbor Place complex in Baltimore found that nearly 15 percent of the tenants were minority entrepreneurs. The company was open to similar black participation in the Atlanta project and willingly accepted the city's requirement that 25 percent of all work on the project go to minority entrepreneurs. As the Underground negotiations were coming to a head, a delegation of black businessmen from Atlanta spent at week at Rouse headquarters. The leader of the group, Joseph Hudson, came home fully reassured. Rouse executives "have the sensitivity to make this project go," he told the city council.

But council members remained unconvinced, and their public ultimatums grew more and more shrill. By May 1984, the money for the design study still had not been approved, and the council then refused to pass legislation allowing the city to underwrite a bond issue, although the delay threatened to kill the pending $10-million federal UDAG grant. There were a series of feverish meetings between Young aides and council members. Still, the legislative body dragged its feet. Finally, with only days to go before the UDAG money expired, the council conditionally voted the necessary permissions—with the caveat that it could immediately cut off support if Rouse did not meet the 25 percent minority business goal and a still higher 50 percent requirement for local participation in Underground construction jobs.

At the time of its negotiations with Atlanta, the Rouse Company was riding high on a wave of national attention. *Time* magazine had just done a cover story on its trademark festival marketplaces, touted there and elsewhere in the press as the latest cure for urban blight. Both more and less than a conventional shopping mall, a marketplace was not for serious purchases; it was a public gathering place, where you met a friend for a drink or brought your kids on Saturday for entertainment. More than a collection of stores, it was a deliberate evocation of the urban street, and in other cities, it had miraculously revitalized the downtown neighborhoods around it. Rouse was not the only concern in the country that could conceivably develop Atlanta's entertainment complex. But it was the only entrepreneur that had used shopping centers to revive the inner city—and it had already walked away from a deal in Chicago when the black city government pressed too hard for a say in running the project.

No one close to the Atlanta negotiations had any illusions: the city needed Rouse more than Rouse needed the city. What's more, to the degree Atlantans had any leverage, they should, insiders said, have been using it to secure more Rouse investment in Underground. Instead, the city council pinned its approval almost exclusively on affirmative action commitments: color-coded shibboleths taking precedence over the city's interest in redeveloping its rotting core. "It often seemed," Joe Martin mused later, "that there was more interest in getting the joint ventures than there was in all the life-and-death issues of how the project was going to be run."

The city's second round of negotiations with the company was even more cantankerous than the first. At issue this time around was who was going to manage the complex, a job that in other cities Rouse always reserved for itself. By now, the festival marketplace was more or less a formula. Rouse had no need for local advice, took no partners in other cities and had no incentive to divvy up projected revenues. Whatever the company's commitment to affirmative action on other aspects of the project—on the design team, at the construction site, in tenant selection or retail hiring—there was little reason for it to want to share its own job. "Rouse just didn't want to do it," Rodney Strong later complained. "They said, 'If we do it like that here, then we're going to have to do joint ventures everywhere else.'" Still, the city of Atlanta insisted, without a management joint venture there would be no contract.

It didn't take long for the likely joint venture partners to emerge: there were only a few black Atlantans who were up to the job. Mack Wilbourn's retail expertise put him near the top of everyone's list. He had been one of the first Atlanta blacks to get a McDonald's franchise, and his political connections, with Maynard Jackson and others, had helped him win and keep a joint venture share of a major airport concession. The other obvious candidate was Herman Russell, one of the small handful of blacks in town with the necessary capital and business acumen. Neither man was remotely disadvantaged; Russell alone was taking in nearly $120 million a year by the mid-eighties. Nor could they justify their part of the management contract by claiming that any significant share of their profit would trickle down to poorer blacks; the running of the complex involved only a tiny staff—so no minority hiring to speak of. It wasn't difficult to understand why either man would want in on the unusually sweet deal: they would have to make only a token investment ($167,000 each), were guaranteed an annual management fee and a hefty percentage of any annual sales revenue, but—like their white partner—were liable for no losses whatsoever. What was harder to grasp was why the council should go to the barricades for these two men, two of the city's richest and best-connected black entrepreneurs.

Once again, the entire development was put on hold while city officials and grandstanding council members wrangled with Rouse executives. Rodney Strong remembered countless trips back and forth to Maryland, late-night harangues and threats to go to another developer. The Rouseketeers, as they came to be called in City Hall, proved to be iron-willed negotiators, threatening repeatedly to walk away from the deal. Still, the city council refused to vote any money until the management joint venture was worked out. "It is time to tell Rouse," said council member Bill Campbell, "that if they are unwilling or unable to consummate the joint venture agreement, then we don't need Rouse to do the project." Meanwhile, time ticked by and nothing was done to get the development off the ground. By May 1985, another year had passed, and the UDAG money, still unspent, threatened to expire again.

The cliff-hanger negotiations lasted through spring and summer 1985. Eventually, the press and public began to complain about the city's foot-dragging. "What about the 80,000 Atlantans who work in the convention and tourist business?" asked Dick Williams. "After all," echoed a *Constitution* editorial, "there is far more at stake here than the further enrichment of two very successful black businessmen." Finally, according to Rodney Strong, when he and other officials could make no headway with Rouse, Young called a meeting of Peachtree stalwarts and asked them to intervene on behalf of Russell and Wilbourn. Bank president Robert Strickland, the man who had once said he would vote for Young only over his dead body, volunteered to go to Maryland and do what he could. Whatever he told the Rouse executives, it persuaded them of what the Peachtree leaders had known for a long time: if you wanted to do business in Atlanta, you needed a joint venture partner with political connections.

When the deal was finally done and the contract signed, it was celebrated across Atlanta as a triumph of racial justice over bigotry. Several Rouse executives traveled to town for a last negotiating session at the airport, and the agreement was written up in the press as a major victory for the dignity of black businessmen everywhere. The contract signing took place in October 1986, at the old railroad freight depot overlooking the entrance to the deserted Underground site: a suitably festive occasion, with all the appropriate black officials and Peachtree executives in attendance. Still, for the city council, this was far from the end of the battle. Councilman Bill Campbell vowed to stay vigilant until the last nickel had been spent on the complex. "From the top to the bottom," he declared, "from the architects to the people who clean up at night, I am going to insist on joint venturing in the Underground project."

Once the management contract was signed, the other salt-and-pepper deals fell into place fairly smoothly. The preliminary design team had to include a black architect, again in a 25 percent joint venture. Though a junior role, this was one of the project's most important positions, and no start-up professional could be considered. To no one's surprise, the job went to Oscar Harris, the most established and best-known black architect in town. When it came time to pick a builder, Herman Russell's name came up, but he was asked not to bid for the job—only because of the potential conflict of interest with his management position. Instead, the contract went to Thomas Cordy, another regular beneficiary of the local set-asides. Engineering joint venture contracts went to similarly well-known and well-connected black men. By the time all the pieces were in place, the Underground lineup read like a *Who's Who* of black business in Atlanta.

Still, even as the Underground deals shaped up to include more and more big-name builders, the city's black leaders continued to talk about trickledown, and the political pressure to help poor, working blacks began to weigh more heavily. One obvious answer was subcontractors, and as in the building of the airport, everyone involved in the deal was encouraged to use black subs. The problem was how to avoid the pitfalls discovered at the airport: the shams and start-up firms with no experience—firms that went out of business as soon as the job was finished, if not sooner. Scores of would-be subcontractors flocked to a meeting at Paschal's restaurant where city officials explained the kind of work available at Underground, and insiders could not help noticing that many of them had been incorporated only weeks before. "It's not the sort of thing anyone can come into without being prepared," Joe Martin warned worriedly.

Another possible answer to the trickle-down problem was construction workers. Young, Strong and others assumed that using black builders would inevitably mean more jobs for black laborers, and just to make sure, the city council passed a resolution insisting that 50 percent of all jobs at the site go to minorities. The problem here, as any construction insider could have pointed out, was that black builders wanted to hire the same workers whites did—the most skilled. As it happened in Atlanta, this meant both blacks and whites: blacks in some trades—brickmasons, cement finishers, plasterers— that they historically dominated, and whites in others. "We would have hired white carpenters and black masons, no matter what," said one builder. "The hiring was mixed," another agreed, "roughly 40 percent black, 60 percent white, maybe fifty-fifty. It followed the trades, and no affirmative action program was going to change that." Once the Underground contracting team was chosen, the builders—both black and white—put pressure on the council to rescind its 50 percent minority resolution. All the contracting firms promised to make a good-faith effort to hire as many blacks as they could. But even if they met the halfway mark, with only a thousand or so slots to be filled, this was not going to mean a big ripple effect in the black community.

Still another conceivable trickle-down solution was tenants. The numbers involved here were not huge, either; the complex would have no more than a hundred retail outlets, with no more than a few jobs in each shop. Still, the city determined as early as 1984 that this was a good way to create some opportunity, and it was formally decreed that at least 25 percent of Underground retailers would be minority. Of course, like subcontractors, they too would face a high risk of failure. Because of the large sums that went into developing the project, the rents were going to be unusually steep, and given the city's stake in the complex, there was little room for amateurism or start-up sloppiness.

But city insiders thought of all this, and even before a brick had been laid, they began to prepare for it. An additional $3 million was inserted in the budget for business training and low-interest loans for the anticipated twenty-five minority tenants. Rodney Strong commissioned an expensive study of minority merchants at other Rouse malls and what could be done to improve the chances of those at Underground. "They reached the 25 percent goal in Philly," he explained, "but it took a very strong effort on the part of the local government working with tenants." No one in Atlanta questioned the additional spending or the extra effort Strong promised. On the contrary, the political establishment let out a sigh of relief. Finally, it had found a strategy to make its trickle-down promise a reality.

As Underground's black architect, Oscar Harris soon found himself something of a celebrity around Atlanta: a symbol of black involvement at the highest and showiest level of the project. One local newspaper profile nailed down his significance with a statistic: of the nation's one hundred thousand architects, only 2.4 percent were black. Virtually none had had a chance to design a central city square, and Harris's opportunity to do so was seen as a triumph for his people. Whether or not the south side poor were going to benefit from the Underground complex, as its designer he carried a standard for all black Atlantans, and he was duly celebrated as a local hero in the press and elsewhere. It was a role he understood and accepted with dignity. "As I saw it," he said later, "I represented something in a symbolic way to the minority community of Atlanta. On behalf of other minority Atlantans, I showed people that I could perform—that I could fight the fight, and be successful."

Harris's road to success had paralleled that of many black Atlantans of his generation—the generation after Herman Russell and, in architecture, J. W. Robinson. A tall, soft-spoken man with an elegant goatee and polished manners, Harris had been born in Pittsburgh to a relatively well-off family that assumed he would have a professional career. He came to Atlanta in 1972, working for a white-owned company hoping to do business with the city's black political establishment. He helped the firm snag a MARTA contract, then went on to participate in the airport set-aside and several that came after it. By 1977, he had bought out his white partners and was running his own design firm, Turner Associates. His carefully cultivated political connections were top-notch, and he was the obvious choice for any white firm bidding on the Underground project. In fact, all three finalists for the job listed him as the black man they would work with if they won the contract.

Still, from the first days of the project, Harris found the experience frustrating. As one of the architects who helped put together the preliminary planning study, he expected to play a prominent part in designing the complex. Though the city council's requirement for minority involvement was 25 percent, Harris thought he might do better: a 50 percent share, if not bigger. He had never built anything on the scale of Underground and had yet to head the design team on any big job. Still, he reasoned, he knew the city and the site. Instead, when Rouse put together the deal, Harris found himself very much the junior partner, teamed up with a flashy New England firm with extensive design experience. Once again, as in the case of Russell and Wilbourn, the city intervened in the negotiation, leaning on Rouse management to give Harris more favorable terms. In this instance too, the pressure worked, and the contract was rewritten as a fifty-fifty partnership. Then, before the team began to work, the New England firm was dropped from the deal. Again, Harris hoped he would be made the majority partner. Instead, he was paired with a local firm, also with more design experience, in another fifty-fifty arrangement. For Harris, insiders recalled, it was a galling affront. Whether or not he was capable of carrying the high-profile $140-million assignment, he felt he was entitled to it and resented what he saw as another humiliating partnership with a white firm.

Harris worked on the Underground project for nearly three years, and the job turned out to be a major stepping-stone in his career. Atlantans were generally happy with the look and feel of the complex: a crisply modern updating of the buried nineteenth-century streets, complete with charming detail—original signs, bits of carved stone, cast-iron ornaments and the like. Harris got at least as much credit for it as his white partners; in fact, as the high-profile "black first," he probably got more acclaim. The burst of attention led to other big jobs: the City Hall extension, the new Atlanta Zoo, the $10-million Coca-Cola Pavilion just outside Underground, and then a variety of other civic projects, including the new Fulton County Jail and government center. Thanks to his work at Underground, Turner

Associates' thirty-five designers grew to fifty-five, and Harris's reputation was made.

By then, it was common knowledge in Atlanta that most joint venture work—public- and private-sector—went to a few already well-to-do and well-connected black firms. But for some reason in the later eighties, the press began to document the problem, forcing Atlantans to recognize publicly what many had long known but hesitated to admit. One reporter scanned back over the $14.2 million of city money that had gone to minority businesses the year before and found that it was divided among two distinct groups: the top ten companies, including Turner Associates, which received 82 percent of the total, or on average more than a million dollars apiece—and seventeen small fry, who went away with an average $22,000 each. Another effort to assess the disparity went back over five years and found more or less the same two-tier skew: the top ten companies got away with more than half the total awarded. In 1989, there was yet another investigation, again with the same results. This report, by the *Atlanta Business Chronicle*, focused on Atlanta's four biggest minority entrepreneurs: Russell, Oscar Harris, contractor Thomas Cordy and architectural engineer Pelham Williams (the only one not working on Underground). Over the course of the eighties, the *Chronicle* found, there were no public-sector construction projects in Atlanta worth more than $5 million that did not include one or more of these four men.

Still, the more successful he got, the more Harris complained about racial inequality in his profession. As he looked back over his Underground experience and the rest of his career, what loomed large were not the opportunities but the endless obstacles. The man once featured in proud, upbeat profiles about minority business success became the source reporters went to when they wanted to hear how tough things were for blacks in Atlanta. Harris complained about discrimination by whites, about being shut out of professional networks. His early days in business on his own—that frightening moment every start-up firm knows, when the phone never seems to ring— became an almost legendary emblem of Atlanta racism, rehearsed in every article. Even when he landed his first big solo assignment, designing the new, $75-million international concourse at the airport, the news stories about Harris sounded a plaintive, angry note. "When [a corporation] selects a designer," he told a reporter, "a person like myself is not typically considered." In fact, by then, Harris had probably done more private work than any black entrepreneur in Atlanta except Herman Russell.

Toward the end of the decade, as set-asides came under increasing challenge, Harris became a leading proponent of the need to continue the program. By then, his firm was doing more than $6 million a year in work. He was a fixture in black political circles, an extensive contributor, close to anyone who was anyone in power. Having been involved over the Young era in seven out of fifteen of the metro area's largest public-sector construction projects, it was hard to see how he could credibly complain about discrimination in government work. Still, as in the past, he maintained that preferences were needed to make up for prejudice, and he was convinced that he still needed a leg-up. It was almost as if, in order to justify affirmative action, he had to dwell on the discrimination he felt made it necessary. "I need the same support now that I did then," he said at the pinnacle of his career. "Without the opportunity created by the program, I would only gravitate back to where I came from."

By the time the Underground construction neared completion, Rodney Strong had long been at work choosing the minority tenants who would fulfill the complex's all-important trickle-down mission. The concept behind his outreach effort tugged at the hearts of just about all Atlantans, and not only because it seemed an answer to the elitist bias of the city's other preferences. It was the same concept that had originally driven the airport concession set-aside: to give poorer entrepreneurial blacks—the kind of people who might open up a shoeshine stand or flower shop—a chance to help themselves into the economic mainstream. The city of Atlanta would make an extra effort to find them, reaching out to them in a way it might not reach out to prospective white tenants. But after that, they'd be on their own, their color no longer relevant to anyone.

As everyone in the city knew by now, the program had not worked out well at the airport. Not only were most of the tenants who won concessions already rich and well-connected—Maynard Jackson's friends and former associates—but high rents and the entrepreneurs' lack of management expertise meant that few had been able to make much of the opportunity. "It had not really done much to help economic development in the black community," Rodney Strong conceded. Still, Underground looked like a more promising spot to try the outreach strategy. A festival marketplace was supposed to remind shoppers of an urban melting pot: a place to find pushcart vendors as well as big, name-brand stores, with a busy carnival atmosphere and plenty of quirky local flavor in the shops and food outlets. It was easy to imagine a tenant mix that included both the Gap, paying a hefty rent, and a pushcart selling kente-cloth notions. If the first-time entrepreneur with the pushcart did well, he or she might later move up to a sandwich stand or gift shop. It seemed like affirmative action as originally conceived: just a little help onto an ordinary business ladder. In addition, Andrew Young made clear from the start, unlike at the airport there were to be no politics involved in the choice of tenants. "Andy said, 'I want you to maximize the number of minority business people,'" Strong recalled. "'But I want this to be an open process. Anybody's who's got a business concept, anybody who's got an idea, I want us to try to put them in business.'"

Strong had been working on it since 1984, sparing no effort. There had been an extensive review of the airport set-aside and its mistakes. Strong and his aides had traveled around the country meeting minority retailers at other Rouse marketplaces, then slogged through another round of negotiations with the Maryland company. "Andy said, 'I want you to do whatever you can—whatever it takes,'" Strong remembered, "and that's what we did." The minority "goal," as at all levels of the Underground deal, was 25 percent: not just 25 percent overall, but 25 percent in every area—retail, restaurants, entertainment, fast-food outlets. And given the Underground leasing structure, the target was even more ambitious than it looked. A certain amount of space in the complex had to go to large national stores: Gap, Ann Taylor, The Limited. "But if you took them out of the mix," Joe Martin noted, "then the 25 percent goal is more like 50 percent of all the small tenants."

Technically, the job of choosing the minority tenants belonged to Rouse and its joint venture partners, but the issue was too important to Strong to leave it to the Maryland company. A special outside consultant was hired by the city to seek out tenants and put together deals. An older black man who had been dabbling in business since the sixties—a gas station franchise, a steak house, a nightclub—L. C. Crowe was a lifelong affirmative action beneficiary who had had extensive dealings with the Small Business Administration. He and Strong organized what they called an "opportunity fair" for prospective Underground tenants. There was much more interest than expected: a crowd that filled and spilled out of one of City Hall's largest meeting rooms. One journalist working the room talked to a jewelry salesman who hoped to go into business for himself, a body-shop owner thinking about switching to a different kind of retail, a young fast-food handler who wasn't sure what it might mean for him. None of the gathered hopefuls knew exactly what they were getting into, and more than a few of them gulped when a Rouse executive started talking investment figures: at least $50,000 would be necessary, he said, and for some spaces as much as $1 million. "Underground is fixed against the grassroots minorities," complained one man in the crowd, but no one seemed to pay much heed to his warning.

It was Crowe's job to find the most promising aspiring tenants and help them overcome the financial start-up barrier. The opportunity fair and other public announcements produced more than eight hundred letters from prospective retailers. Crowe met with most of them in what Strong called "a kind of triage": a search for the candidates most likely to make it in the unforgiving Underground environment. Once Crowe had settled on the best-looking few, he tried to match them with the business opportunities outlined in Rouse's plan for the shops and restaurants it wanted in the complex. One woman who hoped to run a health-food stand was told that someone else had beaten her to that idea, but since she looked like a good business prospect, she was given her choice of other possibilities: T-shirts, kitchen utensils, dolls or hats. She went for hats, but since she had had no experience with clothing retail, she was asked to go into business with another promising applicant who had. "There were some stretches," said one Rouse official. "Everybody knew they were stretches. But we did all we could. You wouldn't need the programs if there were people out there with experience." Several minority entrepreneurs with successful nightspots were asked to move them to Underground. In other instances, would-be start-ups were introduced to national franchisers. Strong and Crowe were involved in every negotiation, and by the time it was done, they were deeply proud of their search effort. "It was the crowning achievement of our administration," Strong said.

Despite Young's instructions, according to insiders, the process was far from open. Sometimes the problem was old-fashioned patronage. According to one City Hall official, at least a few of the tenants were recommended by city council members, and others were friends of Strong's or Crowe's. "There was always a little fuzziness," Martin remembered. "Was this being done in the name of affirmative action or was it being done because so-and-so knew somebody?" Given the choice between a well-prepared white and a weaker black candidate, Crowe inevitably went with the minority. To white Atlantan retailers trying to get in on the action, this often looked like old-fashioned prejudice. Young supporter Albert Maslia was wooed by Rouse to bring his greeting card shop to Underground. But he had at least one friend or relative who wasn't so lucky. "A quarter of the tenants had to be minority," Maslia complained later, "and that could not mean a Jewish woman." "We didn't always make the right decisions," Martin conceded, "and sometimes we might have done something that wasn't in the best interest of the project in a strict financial sense because we wanted to keep faith with the [minority business] goal."

Strong's minority tenants got a huge financial boost from the city. Tenant allowances are common practice at shopping malls, but they are usually reserved for high-profit national chains—stores the management badly wants to include in the complex—and are almost never given to fast-food restaurants. At Underground, Strong insisted that his minority retailers, fast-food operators included, needed this kind of aid, and after a bitter fight with Rouse and Martin, he finally convinced them to allot the money. It came out of the city's Community Block Grant reserve, federal funds meant for helping poor people: the first lump sum of $3 million, then another $750,000 as opening day approached. Still, black city council members were convinced this was not enough, and a quasi-public arm of the city's affirmative action bureaucracy was authorized to make additional low-interest loans. This Atlanta Economic Development Corporation (AEDC) was told it could lend up to $100,000 each to the minority start-ups, and $1.9 million of city money was earmarked for them. The AEDC was also charged with coordinating bank loans to the tenants: up to $150,000 each, again at below-market rates, 90 percent of it to be guaranteed by the Small Business Administration.

By the time construction was completed, all the minority retailers had been lined up. There were twenty-seven in all, over half of them in fast-food outlets—more than 50 percent of the complex's smaller tenants. They were not the city's usual wealthy, well-connected affirmative action beneficiaries, but not exactly impoverished either, and several were already successful retailers—entrepreneurs transplanted from elsewhere in the city. Altogether, they had received more than $7 million in government money: CDBG funds, city-financed AEDC loans and SBA-backed bank loans. It was an unprecedented public experiment: city of Atlanta plays Pygmalion. It would be, most Atlantans understood, a high-risk gamble. "It's not over yet," said one Rouse official who described himself as "guardedly optimistic." "These are 8-year, 10-year leases. The important part is still to come." As for the trickle-down, by any objective standard, it seemed fairly limited; there were, after all, only twenty-seven of these people—subsidized to the tune of nearly $300,000 each—and none of them would hire more than a few employees. Still, most Atlantans seemed to see the effort as a major accomplishment, proof positive that affirmative action could mean social justice after all.

By spring 1989, the complex beneath the streets was almost finished. Construction had transformed the twelve-acre cavern. New features included a nightclub row called Kenny's Alley, Humbug Square (named for the salesmen and hustlers who had flourished there a hundred years before), a specialty food-shop area and the fast-food court. There was an outdoor plaza, complete with cascading fountains, and a variety of historical statuettes to enhance the quaint atmosphere. A nineteenth-century-style trolley on the street above completed the scene. With opening day just weeks away, Atlantans worked themselves into a frenzy of anticipation. "There's too much at stake for Atlanta to let Underground fail," said one city employee. "If it does fail, Atlanta will be an also-ran city."

The approaching launch spurred a flurry of new talk about the city's integrationist hopes for the project. Joe Martin was quoted every few days in the press comparing the complex to the Athenian agora and a traditional southern courthouse square. Oscar Harris talked hopefully about "a melting-pot atmosphere." But only builder Lawrence Gellerstedt dared to pose the question on everyone's mind: "Will people come downtown to an integrated space," he asked, "where they're going to see the facts of life of a city?" According to Rouse's projections, the bulk of Underground's customers would be tourists and convention goers, known in the trade as "tag people." But in order for the complex to succeed, a lot of Atlantans would have to come, too. Specifically, by Rouse estimates, 31 percent of long-term patrons would have to be local. "Underground must have a critical mass of middle class," wrote Dick Williams. "And though it violates Atlanta's sensible rules of polite public discourse, let's say it. The critical mass must be largely white."

When opening day came on June 15, it was a great success. There was a little ceremony, complete with the predictable speeches. "What we've done is put a new heart in the center of the city," Mayor Young declared jubilantly. His words were followed by an official pulling of ribbons. Then the crowds began to pour in, and by the end of the day many merchants were close to selling out. The rush continued over the weekend and beyond: a million visitors in the first four days, of every color and class, one of the best turnouts Rouse had seen at any mall opening anywhere. Those who went remember elbowing their way through a sea of smiles: "everything from bums to presidents of corporations," said one man. "It's a dream come true," beamed a minority tenant. It was Andrew Young's crowning moment, vindication of seven long years of hope, wheeling and dealing, arm-twisting and integrationist rhetoric. "There's no way we could have spent the same amount of money and done as much to alleviate poverty," he said. "Underground is going to be the rebirth of downtown, and it's going to bring along poor people too." Most Atlantans were inclined to give him the benefit of the doubt. "For some time," said one columnist on Monday morning, "Atlanta has been terribly wary of itself, edgy in its biraciality. . . . Underground is betting that we are moving beyond that. . . . And so far, about a million of us have said, just by showing up, 'About time.'"

The good times continued through the summer of 1989 and beyond. All kinds of people, black and white, came, mingled and bought. Sales in the first several months were 20 to 25 percent above predictions, and the summer ended without a single major incident on the police blotter. By June of the following year, there had been 13 million visitors, 60 percent of them from the metro area, and $75 million in sales—15 percent above projections. "The first year was incredible," said Albert Maslia, "just unbelievable." The problem from the start was that the success wasn't uniform, and before long a number of the minority tenants were complaining that they had been discriminated against.

Boston Lights was one of the first outlets to fail. A seafood restaurant run by a former air traffic controller, it was one of the largest minority-owned concerns in the complex. The owner's family had been in the restaurant business and he came in with some capital of his own, but he had also borrowed the maximum from the SBA and taken his share of city tenant allowance money. According to Dick Williams, among other customers, the place was in trouble from the start. "I went there the first day for lunch," Williams said. "It was terrible. You could just tell it wasn't going to make it." Within a year, the restaurant was in Chapter 11 and way behind on its rent. By the time the press got wind of its troubles, the owner owed nearly $60,000 in back rent plus $75,000 in back taxes and insurance premiums, not to mention the $250,000 he had borrowed from the bank and the city of Atlanta. It could have happened to anyone, white or black, and one or two white-owned nightclubs at Underground also had difficulty the first year. The difference was that small white-owned places had not been subsidized with city money and federal poverty funds.

As Underground's novelty wore off, customer traffic gradually subsided, and the complex's high rents began to take their toll on other businesses. Problems were particularly acute in the food court, with its concentration of minority tenants. Before long, five of them were heading for bankruptcy and the city's affirmative action bureaucracy stepped in to help them. There were additional how-to seminars and one-on-one consulting sessions. The city reached into its minority business contingency fund—another $250,000 allotted to the Underground trickle-down effort—to help tide over several of the struggling franchisees. Rouse's top Atlanta executive, William Coleman, allowed to a reporter that he thought tenant mismanagement was at the root of most of the failures. The minority retailers took a different view: the problem was that Rouse's rents were too high. Coleman was more than understanding. "There were frustrations," he said later. "Underground was not as successful as they had originally hoped." He wasn't sure what to make of the tenants' next round of complaints: that the expensive business consultant he had flown in from Virginia, a man with a national reputation, was of no use to the failing minority tenants. "We were being criticized because he was white," Coleman said.

The complaints got worse as time went on. Small black retailers griped about the locations they had been given: big white stores like The Limited had been rented better selling spots, they said. Others charged that they had not been allotted as much money as white tenants to design and decorate their shops. Rodney Strong accused Rouse and its partners of not being quick enough to restructure their arrangements with tenants who were going under. The most contentious specific issue was rent. Tenants complained that stores like The Limited were paying too little and they were paying too much, on less favorable terms. "Some rents didn't have to be paid for months," said Pam Alexander, the black woman who owned the Underground barbecue joint. "Some didn't have to be paid for a year. But minority rents had to be paid up front." Other retailers demanded that when business slowed, their rent bills should be lowered. Then, as more and more of them began to fall behind in their payments, they criticized Rouse for trying to collect the money it was owed. But the worst reproaches of all were the general, unanswerable ones. Tenants just felt they weren't getting enough "cooperation" from Rouse management. "Black tenants are treated differently from white tenants down here," said one.

Other Underground insiders, black and white, adamantly denied that there was any discrimination by Rouse and its partners. Shop locations and decoration allowances are generally business decisions, made at most shopping malls on the basis of supply and demand: the management makes its best offers to the tenants it thinks will make the most money and that it most wants to lure to its complex. If anything, at Underground Rouse had broken this business rule, leaning over backwards to help fledgling minority entrepreneurs as much or more than it helped cash cows like The Limited. On the question of rent, there was little the management team could do in the way of adjustments. Rents were steep because the investment required to develop the marketplace had been steep. If rents had been lowered when business grew slack, the burden would have fallen on the city—and eventually on the taxpayers liable for the investment. As for cooperating with struggling tenants and restructuring their deals when they failed, it was hard to imagine what else Rouse could have done to help. "All said and done, Underground has worked harder to keep minority-owned tenants in business than [it has] majority tenants," insisted Martin. Rouse manager Coleman, who bore the brunt of the racism charges, was still tormented by them half a decade later. "It was the furthest thing from what was in my heart," he said. "If I had had it in my heart, I never would have taken the job. I knew what I was going into at Underground."

The reality was that there were plenty of business reasons for the minority tenants' troubles. After the first year or so, business was not particularly good at Underground. The recession of the early nineties hit clubs and restaurants especially hard, then growing crime began to frighten off suburban customers. According to successful tenant Albert Maslia, after the first year, the complex also let down its end. "Everybody was so worried about affirmative action," he said, "nobody was taking charge of marketing the shopping center." "There's not a discriminatory problem down there," said Herman Russell's son, Jerome, who represented his father in the management partnership. "This is not just a black problem, it's a center problem." If minority tenants seemed to have a harder time handling the ups and downs, there were explanations other than color. At least two-thirds of them were first-time owners, and eight or ten had no prior retail experience. Besides, there were several notable black successes that gave the lie to the claim that minorities could not make it at Underground. Still, the complaints drummed on. "The minority tenants just did not feel they were making as much money as they wanted to make," said Strong. Despite or perhaps because of all the special help they had already been given on account of their color, the retailers felt they were entitled to more. By now they had come to believe they were entitled to success, and when their affirmative action patrons could not provide it, they read this as racism.

The disputes over rent grew more and more acute as the shopping seasons ticked by. It was only a few years before all the tenants together were more than $1 million in arrears. Blacks accounted for only 34 percent of the leases but owed 63 percent of the money due. "Because the city was behind Underground," said Martin, "and because the city supported minority participation, some people had the sense that they didn't have to pay their rent." Rouse and its partners were as understanding as they could be. "A lot of loans were forgiven," said Coleman "We often did not go after the past due rents. What would the point have been? We knew how badly these people were doing." In the cases where Rouse did try to collect, the company all but apologized for it. "We've tried to meet with every single tenant with rental arrearages to work something out," one manager told the press plaintively. Still, the retailers cried racism. "They tended to see the world through a racial prism," said one company executive. "Rouse was white. It was a white-black game. They didn't trust our motives. We were the enemy."

Many in the city affirmative action bureaucracy sided with the beleaguered tenants. According to Joe Martin, L. C. Crowe went so far as to advise black retailers not to pay the rent they owed. Crowe denied it: "The only thing I've done is—if someone is behind in rent—to [tell them to] go and compromise with the landlord to pay it back. I've told them to pay what you could." When Martin would not drop the matter, Crowe declared he was being punished for speaking the truth about bigotry. He fired off a memo to the Rouse Company, charging the firm with "eradicating the small minority businesses, replacing them with large white chains [and] franchises." "Crowe is a martyr," said one of the tenants who rallied to his defense, "and a martyr is always hurt because he is trying to help."

The rest of Atlanta's black political establishment stayed out of the conflict as long as it could—until former tenant Pam Alexander ran for a seat on the city council. Alexander's Underground barbecue place had fared poorly from the start. The city tried several times to save her, but she finally went out of business and then, looking around for something to do, took it on herself to become the voice of the aggrieved Underground retailers. Elected to the council, she came into office with one agenda—to get back at those she held responsible for her failure—and in a matter of months she had convinced her colleagues to order an audit of Rouse's management of the complex. It was completed in August 1994 and proved what had seemed obvious to many all along: that the company was indeed operating on a racial double standard—one that favored minority tenants.

By the time the complex was five years old, in 1994, twenty-one out of twenty-seven of the original minority tenants had gone out of business. Eager to justify Underground's landmark affirmative action program, just about everyone connected with the complex defended its record. "I don't look at the project as having been a failure," said Strong. "The survival rates were better than normal SBA rates," agreed Coleman. "Underground was a great success in terms of minority business participation," said Martin. "Everybody hasn't succeeded, but Underground made a tremendous commitment and delivered on it." Outsiders were more skeptical, even about the six merchants who had apparently made it: a florist, a pizza vendor, the man with the Gorin's ice cream franchise and three others. According to Albert Maslia, at least one of them was still not paying rent, but she was well connected enough that "the city can't close in on her. It would be called foul by the city council." "Some of them are hanging on," said Dick Williams, "but not one single entrepreneur really made it at Underground." Gellerstedt, still a strong supporter of the complex, summed up Peachtree's attitude to the minority retailers with a shrug: "I don't know any real success story." Successes or not, the city was still struggling with the bill. Counting only the $7 million in government funds spent before the complex opened (and no one knew how much more had been spent in intangibles since then), the six merchants still in business had cost Atlanta taxpayers $1.2 million each—money originally raised in the name of trickle-down social justice.

The consequences for race relations were harder to calculate. Within five years, William Coleman had left his job with Rouse—driven out, according to insiders, by the charges of bigotry. White merchants in the complex mostly averted their eyes from the conflict, but those who didn't, Albert Maslia among them, came away much disillusioned. "Race had nothing to do with it," Maslia said, "but the black tenants kept claiming it did. They didn't know what they were doing, and they kept crying foul. There is no question, it contributed to the racism around the city." As for the minority tenants, successful and not, most seemed if anything embittered by the affirmative action effort on their behalf. Once again, as in Oscar Harris's case, the program only exacerbated their mistrust and their color-coded sense of grievance. "The irony," said Martin, "is that Underground did more than anyone else for minority business participation. And yet Underground was picked on—vilified by the city council and others. I suppose that's because when the city sponsors something, people always expect more. People have unrealistic expectations. Certainly, I feel we got a bad rap." As a devoted supporter of affirmative action, it didn't occur to him to wonder how much racial preferences were fueling those expectations and the disappointment left in their wake.

For a few years, it seemed as if Underground might fulfill Andrew Young's dream of an integrated town square. Shops included Ann Taylor and African Pride; the atmosphere blended street funk with suburban family fun. The music mix worked out just as Young had hoped, and the diverse clubs lured a diverse public: middle-aged white couples, tourists and yuppies as well as black teens. Not only did local shoppers make up more than half the complex's customers—well over Rouse's one-third minimum—but they tended to return again and again. "In that sense," said Gellerstedt, "it worked out. It is a symbol for the city." For a while at least, it was a place where Atlantans could see themselves as they liked to think they were: diverse but comfortable together, blacks and whites naturally sharing the same streets. The trouble was that like all mirrors, Underground sometimes revealed a less than ideal picture. "Underground is the best place," Gellerstedt went on, "to put the thermometer for race relations. It's a tribute to the progress we've made here. But it also documents the point: we ain't solved the problem yet. And it may still belly up on account of race relations."

The problem began with crime—at first just minor incidents. Underground itself was heavily policed and fairly safe, but the intense security displaced vagrants and junkies, sending them a few blocks north into downtown proper. In the six months after the complex opened, the number of purse snatchings, holdups and late-night break-ins in the neighborhood jumped noticeably. Homeless people wandered up Peachtree Street at night; aggressive teens roamed where they had never gone before, breaking department-store windows and removing merchandise. Then, as with any crime in an interracial setting, the incidents began to poison attitudes. The more white Atlantans feared to come to the complex, the blacker its clientele grew—and the more this frightened those whites who did come. Word got out that Underground was, as Martin put it, "too black"—and this perception began to take a toll on leasing.

Meanwhile, the crime grew worse. Nuisance harassment blurred into the genuinely frightening, not just in the neighborhood but down beneath ground in the complex itself. According to insiders, management began to cover up unpleasant incidents. "The worse it got," said one journalist, "the less it was reported. They didn't want to frighten white suburbanites, though of course people were frightened anyway." If anything, the gap between what they heard from friends and what they read in the newspaper only inflamed whites' imaginations. Then, in August 1990, when the complex was just over a year old, there was an incident that even Rouse could not keep quiet.

It happened late one weekend night; there were about a hundred people on the plaza in front of Underground's main entrance. Two small nodes of black teens got into some kind of standoff. Everyone else ran for cover, but one twenty-one-year-old man, a bystander, tried to stop the fight. Before it was over, he was dead and two other people were wounded. The next day, it came out that the teens were Crips and Bloods. The following year there was another sensational crime in the neighborhood, this one a block away, at the Five Points MARTA station. Three out-of-town businessmen were shot in broad daylight, two of them fatally, by a lone gunman who later told the cops he hated white people.

From then on, Underground slid steadily downhill—ever more black and ever less appealing to white Atlantans. Martin was probably right: "The fear of downtown is heavily racial," he maintained. "It's predicated on some reality. But the reality is greatly exaggerated by the racial dimension." Still, in Atlanta, as in most places, this was a distinction people could not face or untangle. Within two years, it was clear that Underground was not going to anchor downtown as so many had hoped. Rich's legendary department store could not hold on and eventually closed its flagship outlet just a few blocks south of the complex. Two of the city's major banks moved their headquarters from Five Points to Midtown, three or four miles north, and they were followed by a host of law firms, accounting offices and other support services. Rouse Company surveys of Underground customers showed rapidly dwindling interest on the part of suburbanites. "It was soon mostly tourists," said Dick Williams. "If there's a convention in town, Underground does fine. But Atlantans don't come enough to keep it going."

The financial picture was even worse. Sales receipts plummeted. Rent revenues failed to cover the debt service, and just as skeptics had predicted, before long the city was picking up the tab: some $4 million in 1991 alone. By the time the complex was five years old, a number of the big national chains had left and more than fifty other merchants had gone out of business. Rouse scrambled to replace them. Still, nearly 10 percent of the retail space sat vacant—double what the Maryland company had projected. By then, operating losses totaled $28 million and backers had given up hope that the project would ever make money. "We've written off our investment there," Gellerstedt said with a shrug. Others doubted that the marketplace would remain open another five years. As for the dream of integration and trickle-down racial justice, it was not much talked about any more among Atlantans. "Just about all the positions in the shops and fast-food outlets were filled by African Americans," William Coleman said later, "though this had nothing to do with affirmative action. It was a function of who was close by—who lived in the neighborhood." The problem was that compared to many other kinds of investment, Underground had created relatively few jobs and, as Coleman noted, "none of them were high-paying positions."

Atlantans hoping for affirmative action ripple effects were equally disappointed by what happened in the building trades. In the years that the Underground project was in the works, Herman Russell had had some visible success in finding and hiring young blacks, particularly at the top levels of his company. Egbert Perry, Noel Khalil and Haywood Curry all put in time as his lieutenants, and each used his job with Russell to rise to a new level in the construction or real estate business. Boosted by their association with the legendary builder, each made a name for himself around town, with Perry in particular earning something like the reputation for acumen and integrity that Russell himself enjoyed among Atlantans, and eventually all three left to start their own businesses. "HJ's company was an incubator," said Curry with admiration and gratitude. "It's the only place that a young black with some business talent could get in on the inside of running something."

Still, even a man like Russell could go only so far in reaching out to young blacks. Part of the problem had to do with the size of his business. Even the biggest construction companies rarely keep a large staff on line: a handful of supervisors, estimators and other office types is enough to handle even a multi-million-dollar building job. The people who actually do the work—the artisans and laborers—are hired by the hour only, and since in Atlanta each trade comes color-coded, this leaves only a few full-time slots for an employer like Russell to fill with minority outreach. Russell's construction company was by far the biggest black-owned concern in Atlanta, but at any given moment in the late eighties, it employed no more than a few hundred people, most of them hourly laborers. Russell's closest competitors, Tom Cordy and Floyd Thacker, were paying far fewer: no more than sixty each and at times as few as fifteen. As for entrepreneurs outside the charmed top circle of set-aside beneficiaries, they had even less hope of helping to lift other blacks. Of the twenty-five minority companies that got the most city business in 1982 to 1987, fewer than half employed more than ten staffers. Whatever the intentions of the black entrepreneurs benefiting from public-sector preferences, they just did not have the weight to make much of a hiring ripple effect.

Besides, much as they wanted to help, black entrepreneurs were also pulled in other directions. Like any businessman, Russell wanted to hire people who knew the trade—and as often as not, they were white men. Especially in construction, insiders explained, where competitive bidding and small profit margins made every nickel important, no one could afford not to hire strictly on the basis of merit. Russell made some effort to get around these constraints, but in practice his managers remembered an uneven outcome: never quite as many blacks at any level as they had aimed for, and even those often disappointingly ill-prepared for the job. By Russell's own estimate, considering all his employees in all the businesses all over the country, his staff was half white, half minority. His longtime vice president, Jack Byrd, a white man, saw even less evidence of affirmative action. "In Russell's construction company," Byrd said, "most of the supervisors are white. It's the telephone-answering people and the secretaries who are black. It's the same at both white- and black-owned companies."

Even Russell's most vaunted successes seemed in the end to fall short of the goals of the set-aside program. Five years after they left his company, his most brilliant protégés were still feeding at the government trough. Noel Khalil was running a real estate development business that, according to insiders, relied heavily on city tax breaks, low-interest loans and other government money set aside to help black entrepreneurs and spur inner-city revitalization. Haywood Curry had set up his own engineering firm: the engineers were Iranian, but it was his color that enabled them to apply for much of the work they got around the city. Even the superstar Perry, once so committed to the goal of creating a stand-alone black business, was still leaning on the old crutch: like Khalil, he had specialized in developing affordable housing—a niche that entitled him to extensive government subsidies, many of them earned through political connections and, implicitly or explicitly, the color of his skin. "I'm disappointed," said Perry's one-time employee, Jack Byrd. "He's not investing, he's not building anything. He's not running the construction business he once talked and seemed to dream of."

In Atlanta, through the eighties and beyond, affirmative action changed the lives of many young blacks, particularly those who already had skills that recommended them to employers. "I live on a mixed block in a yuppie section of town," said former city official George Berry, "and on any given day I see an amazing number of successful black men and women. They wear the normal business uniform, complete with the briefcases and the late-model foreign cars. Mostly they've come from somewhere else, bought homes, worked their way up the ladder and entered the mainstream. Their success is not written in the headlines, but you can't say it's all been a bust." The question that no one could answer: would these people have been hired and promoted in any case, with or without corporate preference programs? As ever, proponents of the preferences were convinced not—convinced that white bigotry still held blacks back. Opponents were less certain—more inclined to give white employers the benefit of the doubt and to credit black workers with the kinds of skills that would enable them to make it on their own. The one thing that was clear was that the programs—corporate and municipal—weren't reaching people who did not start with one foot on the ladder: the poor, uneducated, unacculturated blacks who grew up in the worst sections of the city or were still streaming into Atlanta from the surrounding countryside.

In Atlanta as elsewhere, the black population fell increasingly into two groups: what demographers called "the two-humped camel." Two decades of the most aggressive public- and private-sector affirmative action in the nation had done nothing to alleviate the pattern: the rich got richer and the poor fell off the chart. Through the Young era and beyond, job growth in the Atlanta metropolitan area far outstripped national growth rates. The black middle class benefited as much as anyone, moving not just up the ladder but also out of town to the suburbs. By the late eighties, a majority of black children in the metro area were growing up in leafy enclaves beyond the city limits, and if their neighborhoods weren't always as nice as white suburbs, sometimes they were more plush.

But the black Atlantans who were left behind sank deeper and deeper into poverty. Most new economic activity was taking place beyond the town line: the five blackest neighborhoods in the metro area grew less than 5 percent in the first half of the eighties, while many parts of the suburbs, black and white, grew more than 500 percent. Some working-poor Atlantans rode the MARTA system out to the new suburban jobs, but many others, unable or unwilling to commute, were cut off from the growth and its benefits. Isolated in deteriorating schools, without role models or opportunities, they fell further and further behind. According to one study by the think tank Research Atlanta, even as affirmative action took off in the city, there was an 80 percent increase in the category of blacks who made the least money, a 25 percent increase in the class that was doing the best—and an 18 percent *decrease* in the middle group, the working poor.

By the time the first bills came due on the Underground complex in the early 1990s, the city's ten-year struggle with the project had soured many Atlantans' attitudes toward affirmative action. Some of the gripes were predictable—from men who resented their lost privilege and new competitors. But these weren't the only complaints emerging by the end of the Young era. Longtime liberal Sam Massell, a fixture of the Peachtree set and now known as the unofficial mayor of the white enclave in Buckhead, said for the record what many others seemed to feel. "My own philosophy from the very beginning," he explained, "was that it was not only okay but appropriate to give preference to minorities—if everything else was equal. I felt the same way about giving preference to veterans, or to Atlantans. But by the time of Underground, the pendulum had swung too far. The feeling had been building, but by then the pendulum had swung too far."

Disappointed first by the airport set-aside and then a second time by Underground, many onetime supporters were no longer sure that minority business programs could deliver. Most Atlantans, black and white, held Herman Russell in the highest esteem, and most believed he would have made it with or without the leg-up. "The program helped him go a little further," said Gellerstedt's top lieutenant, Herbert Edwards. "But he didn't need it— and that's true of most who succeeded." By the same token, most insiders had come to doubt that preferences could do much to help minority entrepreneurs who weren't destined to make it on their own. "If the purpose was to make black contractors or bring them up from nowhere," said Jack Byrd, "I don't know a single one who was brought up, not a single one that made it." "It hasn't worked very well in my opinion," Edwards concurred. "Only the able are going to make it in this business, and there isn't much any government program can do about that."

Worse still, twenty years of set-asides had only fed the stereotypes left over from an earlier era when whites and blacks had too little contact to know better. Whether it was the tenants at Underground or the fly-by-night subcontractors, affirmative action beneficiaries encouraged the impression that blacks were less able than whites. "City jobs are now all filled by blacks," said one man. "That's fine, but some are not all that capable." "By now we've seen so many black architects and builders that are not qualified," said another, a lifelong liberal. "It can't help but poison your outlook." Even many well-meaning whites, as they made their way around town, could not help noticing the occasional black person whom affirmative action had boosted beyond his or her competence. If the whites were thoughtful, they faulted the preference program. If they weren't, the experience made them think less of blacks. "I believe that in my city," Massell said, "whites feel very comfortable with blacks who are qualified to do whatever they are doing. But people are fed up with the poor service, the slow service, the inept service. The problem is affirmative action, but eventually people equate all that with racial change."

Still other whites, disapproving of the behavior of Underground's minority tenants, began to generalize about what they saw as the black retailers' bad attitudes. "There are two kinds of black people," said one man, "those who want to bust their butts and those who are waiting—waiting for a handout." People involved in the Underground project and many who weren't accused the tenants of "crying racism" and exaggerating stories of abuse by the project's white management. "The general feeling here in Atlanta now is that blacks have a chip on their shoulder," one Underground merchant complained. "Even the smart ones have a chip on their shoulder. Just the other day, a black woman who works in one of my shops came to me and said, 'When so-and-so is sick, you pay her. When I get sick, you tell me I have to come in anyway.' A lot of the blacks in my stores are so busy with that, they don't have time to work." "I don't begrudge them their wealth," said another man, a lawyer, about Herman Russell and Oscar Harris, "but whatever they say, it isn't a right."

By the time Young left office in 1990, no matter how much Atlantans tried to put the best face on things, the cynicism engendered by the set-aside hung heavily over the city. "I hate to sound callous," said Sam Massell. "But the bottom line is, how much does it cost. Is it fair to the rest of the public? Is it fair to pay that extra cost? Up to a point it is fair, especially if you are helping some part of the population. But at a certain point, that balance changes." Even the Peachtree leaders who still defended the program did so for the most grudging of reasons. "We would have been in bad trouble if we hadn't done it," shrugged Lawrence Gellerstedt. "It was the price of racial peace." Worse still, though no Atlantan white liked to admit it in public or private, many had grown deeply pessimistic about ever understanding or getting along with their black neighbors. "Whatever the set-aside has done," said one man wearily, "it has not increased the trust between blacks and whites. I don't think most whites will ever see civil rights the same way again."

Joe Martin was at a meeting in a suburban town just north of the city when he heard the news on April 30, 1992. Like most Americans, he was vaguely aware of the trial going on near Los Angeles: the trial of the four white policemen accused of beating black motorist Rodney King. Martin hadn't thought much about the impact for Atlanta; no one had. This was the city too busy to hate, after all: a city with a black mayor, a black police chief, dozens of black judges and a large black middle class—people with too much of a stake in the system to want to see it destroyed. Years later, Martin could still remember the exact words of the anxious staffer who interrupted his meeting: "Have you heard?" she asked. "They're tearing up Underground."

The Atlanta demonstration had started peacefully enough. A few hundred students from the largely black Atlanta University Center gathered at midday to protest the California verdict and decided to march to the Georgia capitol. As they did, the crowd grew larger—a mix of college students and street kids from the south side. By the time they reached the government district, a phalanx of youths had broken away from the rest. They began to run and jostle each other and overturned a car. Then someone got the idea of smashing windows: they started with cars—the windshields were easy game—but couldn't resist the mostly plate glass facade of the Fulton County government center. Then they moved down into Underground, just next door. The rampaging youths tore through the shopping center, smashing windows, upsetting displays, turning over planters and pilfering merchandise. The mostly minority-owned pushcarts were the easiest prey and they suffered the most—both damage and theft. It took only half an hour for the first roiling wave to make its way through Underground, but it left several thousand dollars' worth of damage in its wake.

If anything, the violence got worse when the crowd emerged on the north side of the complex—downtown. One band burst into Macy's and ransacked the first floor, knocking over tables and sweeping merchandise from counters. By the time the last youth ran out, the store's ground level was in a shambles. Only then did the police get serious. A large contingent of officers showed up—in cars, on horseback and on motorcycles, some of them in riot gear—and began blocking off streets. Thousands of white and black Atlantans at work in downtown office buildings rushed to their windows to watch the mayhem on the streets below. Joe Martin tried to drive through on his way to the Underground complex and was taunted by a cluster of kids, banging their fists on his car and trying to break his windshield.

The unrest lasted through the afternoon, most of it confined to the ten-block area around Underground. There were the usual clashes between police and demonstrators, the usual flying rocks, cans and bottles. A large rubbish fire filled the street with smoke. One store clerk was struck on the head with a cash register. Several youths took turns beating a woman who got in their way, then kicked her down the steps of an office building. A young white man in shorts and a fraternity T-shirt was beaten unconscious and left bleeding on the sidewalk. A black youth stood over him with a sign: "Justice 4 Rodney." A teenage girl nearby explained to a reporter, "What those cops did to Rodney King started this." Most downtown offices and shops closed up immediately, and their workers fled the area. By the time it was all over, at the end of the day, some 50 stores had suffered damage or looting, there had been 325 arrests and 41 people injured.

By Los Angeles standards, Atlanta's disturbance was a decidedly minor event: under $100,000 damage in all, no deaths, no more than half a day's lost business for even those stores that had been the worst hit. Still, insiders worried about what Atlantans would make of the riot—what it would do to people's perceptions of each other and of the city. The usual boosters moved in fast to downplay the trouble. Black city officials, white businessmen, clerics of every color and creed held meetings to discuss race relations. Rouse and the Underground tenants organized promotional events to lure suburbanites back to the complex. Editorials emphasized how well policed and safe the marketplace was. "There have been naysayers from the beginning of the project," said William Coleman. "We've been proving them wrong for years."

But it was already clear that many Atlantans were deeply frightened by the disturbance. Looking back, what Joe Martin remembered most vividly was the alarm he heard in the voices of people being interviewed on the radio. "If you ask anybody who was watching Atlanta TV or listening to the radio or reading the newspapers," he recalled, "you would have thought it was an armed insurrection." The department stores and other shops on Peachtree Street, just blocks north of Underground, recovered in a matter of days. But the festival marketplace, heavily dependent on weekend and after-hours customers, was another matter. Traffic plummeted; the upbeat promotional events went largely unattended. In the month after the disturbance, sales were down 40 percent; two months later—peak season—they were still off by 20 percent. Within weeks, three nightclubs had closed for good. At another bar, struggling to stay open, the manager told a reporter, "We've had virtually no business down here at night since [the trouble]." Several clubs tried offering free buffets, giving away cassette tapes, CDs and other prizes—all to no avail. Merchants fielded daily calls from customers asking if it was safe to come in. One suburbanite later recalled a conversation with friends about a proposed trip to the Coca-Cola Pavilion just outside the complex: "I don't think we're going now," was the friend's response. "I don't want to put our lives in jeopardy."

As many Atlantans understood immediately, the event was a turning point for the complex and the center city. "The psychological toll was devastating," said Martin. "We have never recovered." "It confirmed people's sense about Underground and about downtown," said Williams. It was as if the city had been waiting for the episode: the kind of disaster you know is going to happen and that forever after trumps all other evidence. "People aren't going to forget it quickly," said a realtor. The disturbance and all that came with it played too deeply into their racial fears—the deep-seated, often only half-conscious racial fears that Andrew Young had been trying so hard to overcome, now fatefully reasserting themselves.

Underground Atlanta had flourished briefly—a symbol of hope for race relations. But the skin-deep integration of Atlanta's interracial town square turned out to be no match for the failure of integration at a more profound level. Try as it might, the Young administration had been unable to give poor Atlantans a sense that they too were part of the city—that they too were citizens with enough stake in the system that they would hesitate before trashing it. No one who knew the south side's poorest, most cut-off blacks imagined that overcoming their alienation would be easy. Some doubted if that were possible in this generation or the next. But plainly enough, Young's optimistic trickle-down had not succeeded—and the little mingling Atlantans saw at Underground had changed few attitudes on either side of town.

Business at Underground never fully recovered. Traffic crept slowly back up toward the levels of the first three years, and the shopping center stayed in business. But the complex never made money. Petty crime remained a constant problem in the marketplace and in the surrounding area. The annual spring festival, Freaknik, that brought tens of thousands of black college students to Atlanta invariably took its worst toll at Underground. Participants flocked to the night spots in Kenny's Alley, followed by south side teens hoping to join the party, and together they left a wake of devastation: violent brawls, break-ins, looting and sexual assaults. The unending lawlessness only confirmed white Atlantans' fears, and many wrote off the marketplace entirely. "It's over," said Williams. "The night business has never come back," echoed Coleman. "Soon enough," Martin recalled, "you couldn't even get guests from the hotel district to walk to Underground. They wouldn't walk the three blocks out of fear of being accosted on the streets."

Not long after the Rodney King disturbance, a reporter wandering in Underground encountered a group of street kids and struck up a conversation with them. All were under twenty-two years old, without jobs, local youths with scant education and no prospects. They were exactly the kind of kids Young and others had hoped would one day work at the marketplace—or catch the attention of a black contractor or benefit from the spending the complex brought to the south side of Atlanta. In fact, the shopping center had meant nothing for their lives. It was just another place, indistinguishable from others, for them to hang out, whiling away their empty afternoons.

None of the young men knew anything about politics or about the civil rights movement. They had no agenda for change—for themselves or for society at large. Still, all seven had taken part in the rampage of a few days before, and they were still burning with the anger it had brought to the surface. "This is where it's going on," said one with a teenage swagger. "We gonna shake this mother up," he warned the reporter. "Black folks took this stuff in the 60s," said another, "but we ain't gonna take it. . . . We ain't gonna take it—even if we gonna die." Just what they were angry at was too tangled to name; what they hoped to achieve was even less clear. The concept of integration never crossed their minds, and if asked, they would surely have repudiated it. The integrated city that Young and others dreamed of would never be realized unless these youths were included. But if anything, the Young years had proved how hard that would be—and how little idea anybody had of how to get there.

Chapter 17

AS GOOD AS IT GETS

In the 1990s, as elsewhere in America, even boosterish and ever hopeful Atlantans began to feel a sense of the limits of racial change. By now, the momentum of the civil rights era was fully spent. The dramatic shifts of the past thirty years had long been taken for granted, and the high expectations that originally came with them—the euphoria associated with the New South—had given way to a more resigned mood. The symptoms showed up everywhere: in attitudes toward politics, friends, neighbors, investments. But few of the signs were more conspicuous or telling than the city's racial geography—a geography not so much of hate and fear as of incurious disengagement.

The color-coded map of the Atlanta metropolitan region was nowhere near as stark as Detroit's. The line between city and suburb did not divide rich from poor. Business flight and other disinvestment, though serious, was nothing like the virtual abandonment of the Motor City. Early in the Andrew Young era, City Hall had recognized the possibility that Atlanta would tip racially, and from then on, the mayor devoted himself to heading off the danger. His ammunition included hefty tax abatements, building subsidies, special land deals and low-interest loans, though as much as anything it was Young's insistent integrationism that convinced the Peachtree set to keep its money in town. The old Victorian neighborhoods that ringed the central city had flourished through the 1980s, gentrified by young white-collar workers, black and white and often gay. Even more unusual, the exclusive enclaves in the city's northern tier were holding, and if anything the suburban-style mansions there seemed to grow larger year by year. One way or another, into the nineties, the city maintained a stable population ratio just below the dreaded 70–30 tipping point, and virtually every white who lived inside the city line could boast of the prosperous black families on their block.

The relationship between city and suburb was also more relaxed in Atlanta. The Georgia metro area, unlike Detroit's, was far from lily-white. Blacks had been venturing over into south Fulton County for more than a decade now, and in the early nineties, they achieved a critical mass. Some of their sprawling subdivisions were modest enough, but some were as lavish as anything in the city's traditionally white northern suburbs. The developer of Guilford Forest—a young black hired by a local bank in the seventies under affirmative action pressure from Maynard Jackson—showed other builders what could be done. Dave Waller started out with one small pocket of houses, ranging in price from $200,000 to $300,000. But even before they were finished, Waller found himself swamped with high-end demand. The next pocket of homes he built was more expensive, yet the same thing happened there and with a still more expensive enclave after that, and before long the developer noticed he was selling out even in the subdivision's "estates area": several streets of miniature chateaux and Tudor mansions on immaculately manicured grounds, many with garages that could hold up to three and four cars.

Atlanta had its remote suburbs, and some outlying whites never came to town, but most blacks and whites beyond the perimeter remained connected to the city in a way that would have been unimaginable for Detroiters. In the early nineties and beyond, one of Atlanta's biggest problems was traffic congestion: rush-hour volume of black and white suburbanites traveling to and from their jobs in the city. While Detroit was changing the name of its airport, hoping with the new title, "Metro," to ease conventioneers' fears and lure new business to the outer region, suburbanites from Georgia's Cobb and Gwinnett counties still boasted to strangers that they came from Atlanta. No black elected official from the Georgia capital would have dreamed of thumbing his nose at the suburbs, let alone making political hay out of regional tensions. In Atlanta, civility mattered, and there was always business to consider: the city tax rolls were still heavily dependent on retail and services that catered to the far reaches of the metro area.

Also unlike Detroit, Atlantans maintained a semblance of social integration, particularly among the political and corporate elite. All businesses of any size counted on a racially mixed workforce, and just about everyone who participated in the mainstream economy occasionally worked with someone of the other race. As elsewhere in America, few extended these friendships after hours, and Atlanta homes—like homes everywhere—remained the last frontier of racial change. Still, a visit to Atlanta was nothing like a visit to Detroit.

Black as many of its most prominent residents were, it was not a black city. The surge of angry African-American awareness that swept through in the nineties was confined largely to the neighborhood known as the West End. The legendary Lenox Square mall in Buckhead—one of the largest and most opulent retail destinations in the Southeast—drew black suburbanites as well as whites. Out on the town—in theaters, museums and restaurants— it was plain that the Old South was gone forever and that middle-class blacks, more and more comfortable in the mainstream, were keen to share in the city's leisure-time pleasures, as often as not in the company of whites.

Still, for all this progress and relaxed interaction, in its way Atlanta's racial geography was as discouraging as Detroit's—graphic, unmistakable evidence of the limits of integration. The patterns on the ground mirrored the patterns in attitudes: carefully choreographed peaceful coexistence between two basically mistrustful communities. Wealthy as black suburbanites were, and much as their enclaves resembled white tracts, still the two did not overlap, and what residential integration there was remained largely token. Blacks came to Lenox Square to shop and eat, but they did not go across the street to Phipps Plaza, the newer and still tonier mall, preferred by some whites because there was no MARTA stop there—and as a result, no rowdy black youths at the movies. Whites who came to Underground came only at certain hours. Black families that opted into the voluntary school desegregation program could not make their teenagers want to eat with white kids, and in Atlanta as elsewhere most students hung out in strictly color-coded cliques. Nightclubs, bars and strip joints remained largely segregated. Even plugged-in journalist Dick Williams could count on the fingers of one hand the times he had been to a private home on the black south side of the city—and those had been mostly big parties given by Young or Fulton County commissioner Michael Lomax.

The education of the mayor's youngest child, Bo, showed just how clear the geographical lines were and what kind of careful navigating they required. Hoping to teach his son something about getting along with others, Young sent him first to an integrated elementary school in a wealthy white neighborhood on the north side of the city. Then, in fourth grade, the child transferred back to a south side school—expressly to get a taste of a black environment. Middle school brought him up north again, but high school was back on the south side, close to home and among his own. Not everybody in Atlanta took advantage of the options in this way—in fact, hardly anybody else did. But for everyone, with the exception of the very poor, the city's racial patterns were self-conscious and largely voluntary. "Nothing says to blacks that they cannot live in a neighborhood or go to a certain church or fellowship with whites," explained Michael Lomax. "All you need is the interest and the money, and you can do it. But the disposition in Atlanta remains to be segregated."

In the nineties even more than before, what made the choreography work was Buckhead, the largely white and rapidly growing second downtown some six or seven miles north of Underground—the region's new city-within-a-city. It wasn't a large enclave, more like an overgrown village—still leafy, automobile-friendly, but distinctly cosmopolitan, a kind of in-town "edge city" ringed by lavish private homes. By the early nineties, there were sixty thousand people living in Buckhead: just about a fifth of the city's residents and all in upper-income tax brackets. Another two hundred thousand came every day to work or shop. Still others who worked just a few miles away in Midtown or the office towers on the perimeter highway came to Buckhead after hours to eat or listen to music. The city's nicest hotels, restaurants and night spots were all there. It was a place with sidewalks and storefronts, where you could stroll after dinner and taste the fast-paced excitement of an urban street. For most white suburbanites, by the nineties, Buckhead *was* Atlanta, the glittering linchpin that held the region together by making them feel they were still part of a proud, dynamic city.

Still, vibrant as it was and critical for the health of the region, there was no mistaking the racial implications of Atlanta's new in-town anchor. Middle-class blacks used the amenities of Buckhead; there was no discrimination, overt or covert. But everyone understood that this was the new white city-within-the-city, and few black were truly at home there. As for the poorest of Atlantans, the black underclass, they never saw the streets of Buckhead—and its residents never saw them. As a metro area, Atlanta held together in a way few other American city-suburb combinations did. But if this was urban integration, it didn't amount to very much.

Like the residents of the old, divided Berlin, Atlantans lived in self-contained zones, not exactly antagonistic, but cut off and indifferent to each other. The CEOs who lived in the opulent homes of Buckhead were, by nature or status, a little more socially responsible than their neighbors in the white suburbs of Cobb and Gwinnett counties: most grasped that they had a stake in the city, and most supported efforts to keep downtown alive. Still, the lifestyle of the in-town middle class, black and white, was not that different from life in the northern suburbs. People lived in large family houses on tree-lined streets; they spent their weekends in the backyard or at private clubs. They drove to and from shopping malls where they rarely encountered anyone from outside their social class, and not many—not even many of the blacks in this milieu—had much time for community service. Just as Cobb and Gwinnett had once vetoed MARTA, so now the middle-class blacks of Cascade Heights tried to block a highway extension that would provide easier access from the center city. Into the nineties and beyond, racial progressivism meant support for affirmative action, but few people, white or black, went out of their way to do much more than that.

By the nineties, in Atlanta as elsewhere, the main obstacle to race relations was no longer active hostility. There was still plenty of mistrust and resentment over past and present slights and the frictions of racial politics. But the real poison now was more lack of concern and curiosity: a sense that the other group was different and wanted to be, that they weren't part of the community that mattered to you or yours. "Race relations?" asked one man, a longtime integrationist. "We don't have race relations in Atlanta any more." Call it color consciousness, clannishness or sheer indifference, it set the limits of racial progress in 1990s Atlanta.

On the black side of the divide, by the early nineties, more and more people seemed to be deliberately cultivating a certain separation from the mainstream. Local official Michael Lomax's journey was, he felt, fairly typical of the changes taking place in middle-class black Atlanta. A slender, courtly man from California, Lomax had come to Georgia in the 1960s and stayed on to make a dual career as a politician with a day job in academia. At the historically black Spelman College, his expertise was Renaissance literature; at City Hall, he began as an aide to Maynard Jackson, then worked his way up to chief executive of Fulton County and in 1989 lost to Jackson in a sharply contested race for mayor. Erudite, elegant, an avid arts patron tagged in the press as the "consummate buppie," Lomax had for many years come down firmly on the integrationist side of black debates about goals and strategy. In 1989, his mayoral campaign portrayed him as part of a new, more accommodationist generation. Unlike the confrontational Jackson, he was keen to make alliances with whites and understand their concerns, including their fears of black crime. Still, his campaign foundered badly and he withdrew from the race, dropping out of public life and surfacing a few years later in a small entrepreneurial business. It was at this point, astounding the Atlantans who had known him over the decades, that Lomax started telling people he had given up on integration.

The story, as Lomax told it, centered on his family, beginning with a now grown-up daughter from his first marriage. "I tried integration," he remembered. "I tried it for a long, long time." Though both he and his wife were black, they lived, he said, "as if we were white and acted as if there were no color line, and I did everything I could think of to ensure that my daughter had experiences that were racially and culturally integrated." For whatever reason, the experiment did not work. The child didn't make friends at her largely white private school; she didn't get invited to sleepovers; as an adolescent she adamantly rejected her integrated experience and insisted on going to a black college. By the time she joined the workaday world, according to her father, she had no white friends and "her life was totally in the black community." "She said, 'Hey, I'm not interested,'" Lomax explained, "and I learned from her."

The second time he started a family, Lomax did it all very differently. He and his new wife chose to live on the south side in an all-black subdivision, and their two daughters were sent to an all-black private school. "In my neighborhood, we have all the amenities we could have," he said, "and none of the hostility." His goal this time around was to give his children what he called a stronger sense of themselves. "I'm not going to have anybody telling my kids they're not attractive," he said sharply. And everyone in the family, parents and children, seemed to like things better this way. "The whole integration movement was one where you were always worried," Lomax said. "'What do white people think of me, what impression am I making?' I think it's very healthy that that's no longer the case. These days, black folks are less interested in impressing white people than in satisfying ourselves."

If anything, according to Lomax, he was behind the curve traveled by many black Atlantans. Asked if they as a group believed in integration, Lomax's answer was a flat no. In his view, the city's long tradition of educated and successful blacks had made isolation all the easier and more appealing. He described the growing south side subdivisions as a kind of idyllic refuge: a world of all-black churches, black private schools, top-rank black colleges, black fraternities, sororities, sports leagues and all-consuming social organizations like One Hundred Black Men or, for women, the Links, that more than compensated for the rejection he and others felt among whites. "That's what I do after work and on the weekends," he said. "I stay in my neighborhood. I stay with my friends. We have everything that you could need there." As for blacks who tried moving out of the community, according to Lomax, most eventually came back, disappointed and chastened. "The idea that we've got to be wherever whites are is just not the attitude any more," he said. "There is if not a rejection of integration, certainly a sense of its limitations."

The wave of African-American consciousness that washed over the city in the early nineties fed on and fueled this deliberate insularity. Beginning in 1988, Lomax organized a series of annual black arts festivals, drawing up to half a million out-of-towners to Atlanta every year to listen to jazz and watch African-inspired theater and dancing. In 1990, the Rouse Company transformed a mall in the black suburbs into an "Afrocentric retail center," complete with special, targeted marketing and color-coded merchandise: everything from Malcolm X T-shirts to expensive African art. Also at about this time, educators reported a surge of interest in the city's historically black colleges. Bill Cosby's $20-million gift to Spelman in 1988 gave the trend a big boost, and by the early nineties Atlanta neighborhoods were abuzz with gossip about the talented young people given scholarships to Yale and Harvard who chose to go to Morehouse and Spelman instead. Not all Atlanta blacks were happy with this new color consciousness. "I don't do my major shopping there," said one man of the Afrocentric mall, explaining that he didn't like the "ethnic" clothes he found there. "When the stores see an area that's all black," he complained, "they assume we're all the same. They assume we're all rappers. We're not." Still, dissenters seemed to be a distinct minority, and young Atlantans in particular seemed taken with the new racialism.

The growing insularity spread most rapidly in the West End, near the city's five traditionally black colleges, where the upbeat, self-help side of Afrocentrism tended to come tinged with angrier, more conspiratorial impulses. The Shrine of the Black Madonna, founded by onetime Detroit militant Reverend Albert Cleage, now known as Jaramogi Abebe Agyeman, was part church, part bookstore, part youth center and part political ward hangout. Strongly influenced by the teachings of Malcolm X, the Shrine encouraged blacks to cultivate their social and economic independence from whites: among other things, to grow their own food and vote only for other blacks. Members committed themselves, Muslim-like, to a strictly austere personal code and intensive secrecy, particularly from white people. Through the 1970s and 1980s, the organization published an influential "Black Slate" of preferred political candidates—usually black candidates and the most radical running. But it wasn't until the early 1990s that the group's cultural message began to catch on more widely, galvanizing the nearby campuses. Recruitment could be a little intense. "It's similar to Jehovah's Witnesses," said one young woman. "It comes to the point where they're actually badgering." But many students were excited by the heady talk of self-respect and autonomy from white society, and the Shrine's West End meetings overflowed with young people.

Well before most Americans had heard the word "Afrocentrism," the Shrine and like-minded campus forums were introducing students to the group of racially preoccupied academics coalescing under that banner: men like Molefi Asante, John Henrik Clarke, Haki Madhubuti and Atlanta's own Asa Hilliard III. Atlanta college students flocked to their lectures and came away high on the exhortations to reclaim their African roots and rediscover the truths left out of Eurocentric history books. Tapes of the Afrocentrists' talks circulated like samizdat on the Atlanta University campuses. The Shrine bookstore could hardly stock enough copies of the African-American Baseline Essays series, one of the movement's seminal texts, detailing the African foundations of civilization allegedly suppressed by white historians. Once again, as in the civil rights era, Atlanta seemed to be at the cutting edge of the black movement, and the excitement spread through the West End campuses. "I'd rather meet a scholar than a Michael Jackson," one enthusiastic student told a reporter.

It took only a few months of national exposure to reveal how wild and inaccurate many of the Afrocentrists' fundamental claims were. Mainstream scholars summarily refuted the notion that Cleopatra had been black, that the culture of ancient Egypt was derived from Central Africa, that the Ten Commandments and modern mathematics had originated there. Still, much of Atlanta's black establishment and its liberal allies seemed entranced by the new color-coded scholarship. Thrilled college administrators reported a leap in undergraduate interest in academic careers. The *Atlanta Constitution* published an admiring trend piece, then an editorial lauding the visiting Afrocentric scholars and their ideas. City fathers began to talk about revising the public school curriculum to make everyday lessons more color-conscious.

There may have been people in the community with private reservations. Andrew Young, for one, could speak scathingly in a different context about "the West End intellectuals uncomfortable with nonviolence and any multiracial partnership." But virtually no one in black Atlanta or the city's white liberal circles raised their voices to question the historical inaccuracies being encouraged by the Afrocentrists.

Asa Hilliard, a professor at Georgia State University, made some of the most extravagant claims of anyone in the new Afrocentric pantheon. He, along with Leonard Jeffries, had been one of the original "melanists." Confusing the pigment, melanin, which makes black skin black, with the very different chemical, neuromelanin, found in the brains of all human beings—in similar amounts regardless of race—Hilliard and like-minded activists argued that blacks were more feeling than whites, more talented, smarter, more psychically sensitive and generally superior. As a scientific claim, the idea was universally ridiculed. As racial doctrine posing as science, it was poisonous.

Still, or perhaps precisely because of its implications, Hilliard and his melanin theory caught on big in Atlanta. After ten years of celebrating Black History Month, the city school board decided in the late eighties that four weeks a year of hit-and-miss race-conscious instruction were not enough. Plans were made, at Hilliard's urging, to implement a comprehensive "African Infusion Curriculum" that would weave Afrocentric teachings into every subject and every class period all year long. Hilliard, who had played a role in developing the African-American Baseline Essays and had helped the Portland, Oregon, schools implement a pioneering infusion program, was the natural figure to oversee the curriculum change. Widely lauded around town as a distinguished scholar and role model for young blacks, he cast a long shadow over the incubation of the new lesson plans, and by the time the infusion program was ready to go, his melanin theory was one of its central principles—what one local educator called "the thread [and] the core of the project."

The new curriculum was ushered in virtually unopposed by Atlantans. Several conferences were held in the West End to boost the idea; a million dollars was allocated for implementation. Teachers were paid to attend "infusion workshops," and detailed lesson plans were provided for instructors at all grade levels. "Every discipline—science, mathematics, English, social sciences, art and music—will be revised to include factual materials about our African-American heritage," said one school board official. In mathematics, this meant using Swahili numbers: the figure 9,147, for example, represented not by numerals but by nine lotus flowers, one coiled rope, four oxen yokes and seven vertical strokes. In science, it meant learning that ancient Egyptians traveled in airborne gliders; in art class, that the pyramids were built by black emperors, endowed, thanks to their melanin, with ESP. After the curriculum was introduced, educators claimed that both attendance and test scores improved notably. And, even as the new teaching spread through the schools, no one in Atlanta came forward to question it. "No one took it on," said a reporter who covered Atlanta education in these years. "The only fight," recalled Joe Martin, "was over who would get the political credit."

By the 1990s, it was clear in Atlanta as elsewhere that color consciousness had become a driving force in the lives of many black Americans. Most whites were inclined to regard this as a good thing—something like patriotism or family loyalty—and they saw no reason not to encourage it. Even when it emerged that many young blacks didn't want to do well in school on the grounds that this was "acting white," well-intentioned educators embraced Afrocentrism and its message that studying could be a "black thing." In their eyes, "positive" race consciousness seemed the natural antidote to the young people's negative preoccupation with color, and few whites tried to come to grips with the emotions that lay behind the popularity of the new revisionist history.

Liberal white Atlantans were not unaware of the anger swirling in the black community. "There's more anti-white feeling among blacks than there is anti-black feeling among whites," said one worried pollster. "That negative attitude toward society, government, the white community, we're seeing it even among more affluent blacks," noted Charles Loudermilk. "Here at my company, in the elevators, I look at young blacks and I see hatred in their eyes." Some whites, Loudermilk among them, grasped that this was something young blacks were being taught. "They've been told," he said with concern, "programmed from the cradle, that I am a bad guy because I am white." "The problem is not the rank-and-file," Dan Sweat said later. "The problem is the Afrocentrism movement."

Still, even these Atlantans, troubled as they were by the alienation coming to the surface, hesitated to suggest publicly that the infusion curriculum might be doing more harm than good. No one asked if the uplift was worth the price. No one wondered if the two strands of black race consciousness—the pride and the anger—could be separated. The racial resentment welling up in black Atlanta was nothing new, and men like Albert Cleage and Asa Hilliard had been stirring up the community for decades. Just why their teachings should have such currency now, at a time when more blacks than ever were getting a foothold in the mainstream, was hard to say. But even if they did not share Hilliard's implicit hatred of white people, few middle-class blacks or their white allies were ready to repudiate his teachings. Neither blacks nor whites seemed to want to draw a line between Michael Lomax's comforting insularity and the isolating anger of the infusion curriculum. And virtually no one, black or white, asked what if anything could be done to ease the racial bitterness eating at the city's young people instead of encouraging it.

It was the old pattern all over again. Just as McGeorge Bundy in New York and Max Fisher in Detroit had acceded in their day to the demands of the angriest and most radical black leaders in the field, so now the Atlanta public acquiesced in Asa Hilliard's separatist curriculum. Some whites, like those on the approving *Constitution* editorial board, seemed driven mainly by guilt. The unsigned editorial welcoming the new lesson plans talked of "embarrassment" that there had been nothing like them before—nothing but conventional Georgia history books paying unseemly attention to "early white settlers [with] European backgrounds." Still other Atlanta whites were simply indifferent to what happened in the overwhelmingly black schools. "It was part of the old deal," the newspaper's education reporter explained, "the 1973 Atlanta Compromise. It was then that we gave up on desegregation—nobody wanted that. And in exchange, the city's whites told the black leadership, 'You can have the schools, and we won't say anything.'" By the early nineties, when the infusion curriculum was introduced, it was hard to say which was more damaging: the liberals' well-intentioned but unthinking assent, or the rest of the public's sheer indifference.

By the mid-nineties, the new mood in the black community was giving rise to a pronounced backlash among these less concerned white Atlantans— particularly those who had come of age since the 1960s. Greg Sweetin, born in 1961, had no memories of the Old South and little sense of guilt by association. All of two years old when Martin Luther King spoke at the March on Washington, not yet eight when King was assassinated, Sweetin knew of the black struggle only from history classes, and the latter-day black spokesmen he had listened to growing up in the seventies had not elicited much sympathy from him. He was in his late twenties when he took over his father's small contracting business, and though he had never been directly affected by affirmative action—he kept away from public-sector work expressly to avoid it—he was no supporter. He had absorbed enough of the New South to be worried about how he sounded when he talked about race. "I hope you won't take me for some kind of a southern bigot," he said twice in the course of one conversation. Still, there was no mistaking the edge in his voice, an edge that wasn't there with older businessmen like Gellerstedt and Loudermilk and probably not with Sweetin's father.

Disillusioned and sometimes resentful as he was, the younger Sweetin did not seem to dislike black people just because they were black. What he objected to were the policies used to engineer racial progress and what he saw as many blacks' increasingly angry, demanding attitudes. His high school had been part of a voluntary desegregation effort, with, he thought, detrimental consequences: lowered academic standards, discipline problems, tensions among students. As an adult, his small family-owned company had been hit with a discrimination suit. In the end, the EEOC found no wrongdoing, but the charges still stung years later. "It's very frustrating," Sweetin said, "you're constantly being accused of something, but you can't vindicate yourself." More than anything, what the young man complained about was what he called blacks' "give-me attitude." "We're paying homage to something our forefathers did or supposedly did hundreds of years ago," he said, "Okay, maybe there is a debt to be paid. But you're in charge of your own destiny. It's yours to make it and yours to lose it."

Sweetin was hardly alone, and far from the worst of his generation. "Yes," sighed another Atlantan, old enough to be the contractor's father, "there was originally a pleasure and pride in walking out from under the shadow of the southern past. But it didn't last long." By the 1990s, this man and others who had been expecting continued racial progress were surprised and saddened to see how little interaction there was between whites and blacks in the younger generation. Because they didn't know each other, it was evident to the older men, the twenty- and thirtysomethings tended to jump more easily to conclusions and to racial stereotyping of a kind that would have embarrassed their parents. As for the ideals of the sixties, they were clearly a thing of the past. "We used to talk about a cosmopolitan world, where we would enjoy our differences but look beyond them in getting along with everyone," said another man, a professor. "That is entirely lacking in my students. No one is dreaming of integration anymore."

After years of relative racial peace in the Atlanta area, the late 1980s and early 1990s brought a resurgence of ugly incidents: racial threats, vandalism, violence in high schools, even several cross burnings in one northern county. The Malcolm X T-shirts and baseball caps that appeared in the city prompted a like response among young whites: shirts stamped with Confederate flags and the slogan, "You wear your X, I'll wear mine." Even more raw were the bumper stickers: "Don't Blame Us, We Voted for Jefferson Davis" and "If I'd known it would be this much trouble, I'd have picked my own damn cotton." The emergence of former Klansman David Duke—elected first to the Louisiana state legislature and then close to victorious in his 1990 run for senator—struck many Atlantans as appalling but understandable. "The old patterns of race relations have broken down," said one man about Duke's age, older than Sweetin, but younger than Gellerstedt or Loudermilk. "And we haven't really replaced them. It's led to a lot of alienation—alienation that came with the effort to make it 'equal.' People think you can change things, just like that. But you can't. You can't legislate equality." "The thirty-year-olds are different," commented journalist Dick Williams uneasily. "They say, 'I didn't discriminate. I went to school with these people. I worked hard. I did as well as they did. Why are they getting ahead of me?' Affirmative action and the new color consciousness and the anger that comes with it are breeding a generation of racism far more virulent than anything that came before it."

It took Andrew Young more than a year to decide to run for governor, and by the time his campaign kicked off in earnest in 1990, everyone in Atlanta had their own racial assumptions about the contest. The outgoing mayor enjoyed the warm support of a wide variety of Atlantans. When he left City Hall, the Peachtree set expressed its appreciation with a lavish gift: a matched set of luxury cars for Young and his wife. Working whites in the metro region seemed ready to back their local star's new quest. "By the time he ran for governor, the suburbs had gotten past his race," said Dick Williams. "He'd won them over, as he won over everyone else—because he was such a decent man with such interesting ideas." Black misgivings about Young's priorities as mayor were no secret to anyone: grassroots leaders and many of their followers had long considered him too business-oriented. Still, most political observers, professional and not, assumed his candidacy would have the support of most black Atlantans. Whatever quibbles they had about what he did in City Hall, they were expected to vote for him as governor—if only because of his color. With city whites, suburbanites and blacks in his column, this left only rural whites—and they were seen as a loaded racial question mark.

The assumption, local and national, was that the election would be a test of the New South. Young seemed more than qualified to be governor of Georgia. A former UN ambassador, one of the nation's most able black politicians, he had brought racial peace to transitional Atlanta and presided over an economic boom that was the envy of every city in the country. He would, it was assumed, have plenty of money and had all the connections he needed to the media, local and national. There was virtually no way, handicappers figured, he could lose the race—unless rural whites declined to vote for a black man. He wouldn't even need a very large percentage of the white vote; assuming he brought along just about all of the black electorate—27 percent of the total—he could get by with as little as one-third of the state's white ballots. There were almost enough white votes to fill this quota in the Atlanta area alone. Still, the press and pundits worried: what might yet be lurking in the hamlets of rural Georgia? "It's going to be tough in the small towns," a resident of little Jesup was quoted by a reporter in one of the dozens of speculative pieces published that spring. "They still got segregation, and a lot of people there haven't accepted change."

Young himself, ever upbeat, did not seem worried. The local elections of 1989 had introduced a new phrase into the nation's political vocabulary: "racial crossover." Douglas Wilder's election as governor of Virginia and Mayor David Dinkins's success in New York were only the two most impressive on a list of victories by moderate, integrationist blacks running in heavily white jurisdictions. To Young, it looked as if this was his moment in history—the moment he'd spent all his life preparing for—and he was convinced that not just he but his state's rural voters were up to the challenge. Kicking off the campaign, he went so far as to tell reporters that he thought his color would be an advantage. "Georgians are tired of being called racist," he said. "I think the level of racial harmony around Georgia is greater than the level in almost any other state in the union." As for the possibility that his opponents or anyone else would try to make an issue of his color, he was indignant at the idea. "The good people of Georgia won't stand for that," he said.

In the spring of 1990, Young went to work to prove the point. The campaign focused from the start on rural Georgia. It was not unusual for the candidate to drive five hundred miles a day, patiently stumping and shaking hands in the kind of remote little towns he had once been afraid to drive through. He met with factory workers and farmers, frail old ladies and brawny young men with pickup trucks. Young was received politely wherever he went, but journalists on the campaign trail were not sure this counted for much. They were quick to note the uncomfortable body language of many whites, and every news story quoted at least one old-timer with a mind shut tight against racial change: people like Alamedia Crosby, who told a reporter, "I would rather elect a white. I'm more comfortable with that. I understand some colored people are just as nice as they can be. But I think the coloreds are trying to overpower. . . . the whites."

Still, Young soldiered on, unfazed, going anywhere and doing anything he could think of to prove his bona fides to his target group. There were photos taken at a firing range, trying out new pistols for the Atlanta Police Department, and at evening after evening of hometown events like the annual Pig Jig in Vienna, Georgia. Young softened his stance on the death penalty, long an issue of principle for him and many other blacks. He hired a good old boy from South Georgia to be his campaign manager and even spoke warmly of rival candidate Lester Maddox. Wherever he went, Young presented himself as a friend of business, a friend—in the local racial code—of the white power structure. But more than anything, in rural Georgia and at home, he talked about his faith in racial progress: his belief in whites' and blacks' goodwill and in the possibility of real harmony. "I didn't come to the civil rights movement out of any sense of anger or frustration," he declared on the stump. "My parents taught me that whites just didn't know any better. My daddy used to say a doctor doesn't get mad with a patient who's sick. You have to heal them."

It was classic Young, integrationist, forgiving, the man who had solidified racial understanding in Atlanta by urging both whites and blacks to forget the past and move on to something better. Now, as before, he refused to pose as a victim or to play on white people's sense of guilt. If anything, he went one step further in 1990, all but absolving whites of bigotry. Asked about the recent controversial death of a young black man in the Howard Beach neighborhood of New York, Young argued that the incident had had more to do with "hooliganism" than racial hatred. When his opponent Zell Miller claimed that "racism and its dangers are increasing," Young disagreed: "Racism in this country was once like a cancer," he said. "It is now like acne." It was a clever campaign tactic: Young knew he stood the best chance with white voters who could put aside their race consciousness and all that came with it. But he also seemed genuinely to believe what he said—and to feel that by claiming it, he could make it happen. Whatever he had done in Atlanta to encourage racial thinking, now once again he seemed to find a rare balance that allowed him to combine his blackness with faith in the possibility of transcending color.

He ran a different kind of campaign in black neighborhoods. Both he and his aides understood that they couldn't treat black voters the same way they treated whites. It wasn't just that blacks didn't watch as much TV, that they wanted to meet candidates in person and hesitated to back anyone who hadn't been endorsed by a local minister or a group like the Shrine of the Black Madonna. More important, as the Young team knew, the south side liked politicians who had paid their racial dues—who had been part of the civil rights movement, like Young and John Lewis, or grown up poor, like Marvin Arrington, or made a point of defying white people, as Maynard Jackson had. Even this wasn't always a guarantee, and black candidates who tried too hard for crossover appeal often found themselves repudiated in the black community. It had happened to Lewis in 1986, when he ran for Congress against Julian Bond. Despite his impeccable movement credentials, Lewis did poorly among black voters, managing to win the seat thanks only to a swing vote by the district's white yuppie minority. Michael Lomax fared even worse: drummed out of the 1989 mayoral race as a result of campaign ads that looked at crime from what was seen to be too white a point of view.

Young budgeted some time and money to meet these black concerns. He went out of his way to make up publicly with Jesse Jackson and pay court to Atlanta's influential ministers, who boasted they could reel in 90 percent of their congregations. The Young team knew that when it came time to vote, turnout would be key: most blacks who came to the polls would vote for Young, but if not enough came out, he would be in trouble. And in order to guarantee turnout, he was willing to pay some walking-around money—described as printing costs or consultant fees—to groups like the Shrine of the Black Madonna that could get out the vote in the projects. Still, given the competing demands of the campaign, Young and his aides assumed they could go easy in the black community. Despite black criticism of his pro-business outlook, he was convinced he had a permanent place in the hearts of the rank-and-file. "They love me," he said years later, with characteristic assurance. "I never lost touch with them. I never had a problem with them." Whatever his appeal to whites in the metro area or further afield, he was counting on a solid base of black votes.

By late spring 1990, it was clear that Young's campaign was in trouble. For all his early promise, he ran a disorganized, unfocused race, no match for Zell Miller's effort, orchestrated by the then unknown James Carville. Young brought no new ideas to the contest, only vague promises of economic development, while Miller rallied both blacks and whites by pledging to introduce a state-run lottery. In contrast to Miller, who had been lieutenant governor for sixteen years, Young had little hands-on administrative experience: in Atlanta, he had left day-to-day affairs to his staff, and the outcome was widely seen as disastrous. Neither the state Democratic Party nor the Peachtree set supported him, and his fund-raising efforts were a disappointment. Even Herman Russell, who gave $30,000 to Young, hedged his bets with a contribution to Miller. But as much as any of these other problems, it became clear as the campaign wore on, Young's major stumbling block was going to be race—though not necessarily white racism.

The problem was that he was trying to have it both ways: to bring black voters out in the name of solidarity, even as he urged white Georgians to let go of color. He tried for a while to hedge the issue. "We're trying to find a way to [appeal to] both," he told reporters. But in the end, whether driven by pragmatism or his integrationist beliefs, Young and his team opted for the high road: a largely nonracial campaign.

If anything, he leaned over backwards not to look too black. He wouldn't let himself be photographed with Jesse Jackson or Douglas Wilder, wouldn't invite Jackson to Georgia to campaign with him. When grassroots activists complained that he had done little or nothing to help the city's poor, he brushed them off. "I was elected mayor, not Messiah," he said. His team even hesitated to mount rallies in black communities, in Atlanta or around the state. "It's a touchy thing," said Young. "If we work to get out a big black rally, we scare away the white people. So we're trying to pull together community leaders [in smaller, private groups]." Young's aides were candid about their strategy. "I don't know of a black candidate for any office beyond a predominantly black district, with the exception of Jesse Jackson, who has run and accentuated his blackness," said longtime staffer Stoney Cooks. "You stress qualifications and experience and, as in Wilder's case, you make the race issue difficult to raise."

The black community was not pleased, and reactions ranged from mild offense to smoldering outrage. There were complaints about Young's "racist" stand on the death penalty. Others grumbled about his campaign tactics. "His TV ads were designed not to offend white voters," said one local official. "But they are not arousing black people." Still others, talking in a kind of racial code, bemoaned what they called Young's campaign "style": too low-key, no "fire in the belly," not "emotional" enough, not like Jesse Jackson—no black anger, and no victim's guiltmongering. At the heart of the matter for many activists was the old question that wouldn't go away—whether Young was "black enough." "I support Andrew Young," SCLC chief Joseph Lowery said grudgingly, "[but] not because he's colored. For one thing, he ain't all that colored."

As the campaign wore on, black attacks escalated, and questions about Young's racial authenticity grew sharper. Local activists urged followers not to vote for him; several influential clergymen questioned his fitness for office. "I've seen nothing he's done for us," said the minister of one of the city's largest black churches. "The black political leaders have basically become house niggers who run errands for the white man," charged a second pastor. Others who could not bring themselves to criticize Young greeted his campaign with silence. Maynard Jackson, now mayor again, refused to endorse him before the election. Most black city council members sat on their hands. The city's leading black newspaper, the *Atlanta Voice,* took no stand in the governor's race. "What we're looking for is delivery," said the editor. "He's got to start at the grassroots." In a contest where turnout was everything, this lack of enthusiasm was as bad as criticism. As the months ticked by, the expected surge in black registration failed to materialize, and south side Atlanta hardly seemed to notice or care.

The last straw for many Atlanta blacks was Young's visit to Carey's. A popular sports bar in heavily Republican Cobb County, not far from Dobbins Air Force Base, Carey's was a dark, casual place, decorated mostly with illuminated beer signs, that served a mixed suburban and blue-collar clientele—people who liked to think of themselves as southern and "country." The owner, Carey Dunn, a longtime Young supporter, had another, more yuppified bar in Buckhead, a club that specialized in reggae music. But Young deliberately chose to come to Carey's to make the point that he was comfortable in Cobb County, the lily-white home turf of the region's most southern southerners. The candidate didn't mind Carey or his joking boast, "Our necks aren't fire-engine red, just a little pink." He didn't mind the bar's down-home patrons. He didn't even mind Carey's jukebox or its two infamous records with the word "nigger" in their titles.

Just as Young planned, the visit turned into a major media event. In fact, there were no voters there: only some two dozen journalists, local and national. Young sat at the head of a long row of tables: a noisy, integrated crowd eating hamburgers and drinking beer. Young and Carey acted out a little ritual, the bar owner temporarily removing the two offending records from the jukebox, Young offering him two others to replace them, Carey declining—with all the goodwill in the world. Aficionados insisted that the two unfortunately titled songs weren't actually racist—that both were in fact send-ups of the kind of person who would use the "N-word."

Cameras rolled and flashbulbs snapped, and the next day all Atlanta knew about the party. As campaign choreography went, it may have been a little silly and over the top. But it was also hallmark Young: an effort to reach out to white voters where they lived—to convince them, as Dick Williams put it, that "he was not the enemy." Once again, as so often before, Young was asking voters to forget the past and ignore their color. "If I want to be governor," he told a reporter of Carey's patrons, "I have to be governor for them, too. I'll go anywhere to talk to anybody about the future of Georgia."

Black Atlanta was incensed by the visit. "Is that any place for a black leader to be?" asked an anguished *Constitution* editorial by a black writer. Joseph Lowery denounced the candidate and his gambit. Indignant community leaders lambasted it as the last step in the "Wilderization" of Young—as if there were nothing worse in the political universe than an effort to appeal to voters across racial lines. Young and his aides seemed mostly indifferent to the criticism: one joked to Dick Williams that the candidate was getting as much flak for this hamburger as he got at the United Nations when he met with representatives of the PLO. But most black Atlantans weren't laughing, and they made no secret of their indignation. A month before the election, even *Time* magazine was speculating on Young's racial authenticity: a national news outlet, in effect, endorsing and adopting black Atlanta's color-coded litmus test. Meanwhile, in Georgia, polls showed only about 65 percent of the black electorate planning to vote for its onetime hero. "The jury is still out on the turnout," one political insider warned on the eve of the balloting.

The first round of the election was a rout for Young. He came in second out of five candidates, but a very poor second, pulling down only 29 percent of the vote to Zell Miller's 42 percent. The white turnout was high, particularly in rural areas, and most of it went to Miller. The black turnout was disappointing and badly split, with as much as 20 percent in some precincts going to the white front-runner. Among blacks, Young did better in rural parts of the state than in the Atlanta metro area. Local pundits speculated that this was because he looked better to blacks who did not know him and saw only his color. Some commentators took comfort from the complicated crossover returns; after all, quite a few blacks and a good number of whites had voted for a candidate of the other race. Still, in the end, it was hard not to see the outcome as a triumph for racial clannishness. The prospect of a black-white runoff, necessary because no candidate had gotten more than 50 percent of the vote, seemed to promise more of the same—with the ironic twist that color coding might mean black voters coming out against a not-black-enough black candidate.

White prejudice seemed to have played some part in Young's poor showing, though less than many had expected. According to one exit poll, he got about one-third of the white vote in Atlanta, but only one-fifth in the suburbs and one-tenth in small country towns. The large turnout in rural areas could have been a sign of white resistance: a push to vote for anybody but the black man. One much-discussed statewide survey around the time of the balloting found two-thirds of all whites in favor of integration. While low by national standards—overall, the figure ran in the 90 percent range—this was considered fairly enlightened for the rural South. Still, it suggested to others that one-third of the white electorate would not vote for a black man. Young himself never blamed white voters for his loss, though his supporters sometimes did. "I never thought Andy could win," said his longtime backer Charles Loudermilk. "The prejudice was too strong. And in the end, his effort only caused further racial splits."

But the black voters' message—Atlantans called it "payback"—was at least as damaging and was widely seen as a key factor in Young's defeat. His longtime alliance with white businessmen, his apparent neglect of Atlanta's black poor, the unforgivable treachery on Jesse Jackson: together, it was just too much for many people. And whatever most Georgia blacks felt about inclusion—whatever ambivalent "two-ness"—Young's crusading integrationism was not something that inspired them to come out to vote, either in South Atlanta or on the black side of the tracks in rural Georgia. "Race is the most significant factor in who votes for whom here," said pollster Claibourne Darden. "There is no second place." It was an old saw, still true, but now it seemed that race didn't mean just skin color. Thanks to ever-growing race consciousness, a candidate who looked right could still lose an election if he didn't fit the stereotypes.

In the three weeks between the first round of voting and the runoff, Young abruptly switched tactics. All but ignoring white voters, he mounted a frantic effort in the black community. He did not exactly abandon the integrationist rhetoric that had long defined him. He still made much of his role in the movement and still measured racial progress by participation in the mainstream. But the thrust of the new campaign, totally unlike the previous months' push, was to appeal to blacks' color consciousness and racial solidarity.

The last-minute effort left no stone unturned. There were ad campaigns on black radio stations; the Shrine of the Black Madonna issued hundreds of leaflets. On Sundays, Young raced from church to church on the south side, taking the pulpit to make his case. During the week, he addressed "buppie" breakfast groups, asking them if they had forgotten their debt to the movement. Now that the election had become a black-on-white contest, black support was intense and emotional. Joseph Lowery abruptly changed his tone. Grassroots south side activists lined up behind the mayor they had been vilifying for eight years, and a variety of national movement figures came to Atlanta to stump on Young's behalf. All the surrogates pressed the same message: that this was now a racial campaign and black voters must rally around their own. "The next governor of this state is going to be a black man," one minister declared fervently from the pulpit. "What is this large, monolithic black vote worth if we don't use it for leverage?" asked another activist.

It was too late. Three weeks could not undo eight years, and the outcome of the runoff mirrored the first vote. This time, Miller won by 62 percent to Young's meager 38. There was no surge in black turnout. Miller collected most of the votes that had gone to other white candidates in the primary, and once again he walked away with 20 to 25 percent of the ballots in black areas of Atlanta. Afterward, Young's aides told reporters that they thought the problem had been mainly in-house: a disorganized and ineffective campaign. Young was philosophical and still would not fault white voters. "I haven't had anybody call me any name," he said. "I haven't had anybody shoot me a bird. And that represents a new day in Georgia." But few black Atlantans seemed to hear him or share his view, and most continued to blame the white electorate. "The racism is not manifest in the crude old ways, it is manifest more subtly," said one, an elected official and political scientist. "If he had been a white ambassador, if he had been a white congressman, if he had been the white mayor of a successful city," said another, "he'd have been a favorite son. It's because of his race. That's the factor." Try as he had, as candidate and mayor, Young just could not get his message of forgiveness and inclusion across. The old assumptions about prejudice ran too deep and had left too much residue of counterprejudice.

When the Olympics came to town in 1996, Atlanta was still riding high on its reputation as one of the most racially harmonious cities in the country. Among the reasons it was chosen as an Olympic site was its promise to put on an integrated spectacle: an image, for all the world to see, of diversity that worked. Spectators and journalists alike marveled at the black middle-class haven Atlanta had become. Even skeptical visitors came away inspired by what one reporter called the "pageant of interracial unity." The image conveyed by the TV coverage only slightly exaggerated what most Atlantans believed. "The whole world looks to us as an example when it comes to race," said business insider Dan Sweat. "Race relations in Atlanta are as good as they get," agreed an out-of-town journalist.

Out of the glare of the Olympic lights and the boosterism that went with it, Atlantans, like Americans everywhere, were trying in the mid-nineties to take stock of where they were on race. In the South, even more than in other regions, there was no denying that astonishing progress had been made. Andrew Young, always reminding people of the momentous shifts, made the point to a group of black doctors from Alabama. The physicians were grumbling among themselves about the continued frustrations they faced. "One of them," Young recalled, "said, 'Things are no better now than they were thirty years ago.' And I had to remind them, 'Thirty years ago, you all would have been shining shoes in Alabama.'" Still, for all the dramatic change, many people in Atlanta as elsewhere wondered if race relations weren't in some ways worse than they had been in the past. Black economic and social advances seemed to have done surprisingly little to ease mistrust on either side. The means used to create change were producing new, unexpected resentments. And after all the hope generated by the sixties, the sheer difficulty of the task—the long, slow, zigzagging route toward social transformation—had given rise to a pitch of disappointment that often seemed to overshadow any progress. "Expectations were too high, then reality set in," said one white Atlantan. "We still don't really know each other—and we don't accept the fact that we need to understand and accept each other."

Atlanta was a step ahead of many other American cities, but even there people weren't sure: was the glass half empty or half full? "The conventional wisdom is more true than anything else," said former city official George Berry, "that the negatives are overwhelming whatever progress we've made. But don't dwell on that to the point of ignoring the good." Dick Williams's assessment was equally mixed and uncertain. "It's a richly harmonious city," he said. "Okay, maybe it's only peaceful coexistence. But it's good peaceful coexistence—coexistence with respect." Lawrence Gellerstedt sounded more upbeat. "Look at what's happened to black-white relations since 1973," he said. "There's been such a shift, it's hard to even think about it." Still, ten minutes later, Gellerstedt was not so sure. "The veneer is thin—very, very thin," he said. "One bad incident could set the whole thing way back. That's why every time some little thing happens at Underground, the press says Atlanta is exploding."

Except for the ever optimistic Young, virtually all Atlantans, when they talked about race, seemed to feel some undercurrent of disappointment. Some tried to put the best face on their feelings, others didn't bother. But there was no mistaking the diminished expectations. The train had been slowing down for so long, it was hard for anyone to imagine a new spurt of forward motion. And if this was it—if this really was as good as it got—what did that mean? Was this good enough, for blacks or whites? Was this all there was to look forward to in race relations?

Everybody in Atlanta had their own idea of what was blocking further progress—mostly the perennial culprits. Many people, white and black, blamed white bigotry. "Anybody who tells you they are not prejudiced is either not telling you the truth, or hasn't thought about it," said one white man starkly. Other people pointed to class and the way it exacerbated mistrust between, say, black city and white suburb. Still others, even those who understood and sympathized with black alienation, felt that the future depended as much on black change as on anything white people could do. "The black community really needs to reassess its position," said Charles Loudermilk. "When are they going to see the need to be part of this country rather than being a fringe group? Thirty and forty years ago, white people— enlightened white people—started telling their children it was not right to hate anybody because of their color. If we could say it then, they should be saying it now. It's time we found black leaders willing to say this to their people." White racism, black anger, mutual indifference: there was plenty of blame to go around. But beyond blame, few people were sure where to go or what to do next. For whatever reason, the old visions hadn't panned out, and no one seemed to know what to replace them with.

By now, most Atlantans' definitions of integration were pretty limited— narrow, mechanical, emotionally hedged. "Call it integration if you like," said one white man, a journalist. "But what we have here is really power sharing more than integration." Instead of talking about community or understanding, blacks and whites watched each other warily and kept a running scorecard of who controlled what—the conventional wisdom being that whites had ceded political power, but maintained their economic dominance of the city. Hopeful and skeptical alike clung to a largely adversarial view of race relations. "There is, I can't say exactly a battle of equals," Michael Lomax noted. "But the black community is not powerless." Even the idealistic Young now defined racial harmony pragmatically. "What we're really talking about is integrating the money," he said, adopting a view long prevalent among more mistrustful blacks. "Integration is not about sitting next to white people or going to the same school. It's about having equal access to the resources."

At best, by the 1990s, good race relations seemed to mean workaday communication, tolerance and the absence of disruptive antagonism. Virtually no one was still holding out for the old Martin Luther King dream: one "beloved community," more or less color-blind. Andrew Young put a positive spin on the idea that had replaced it: peaceful coexistence by irrevocably different and separate color-coded groups. "It's like the ecumenical movement," he said. "You know you aren't going to see Baptists become Catholics. You aren't going to get meditative Quakers to become born-again Pentecostals—and you wouldn't want to." Others, like George Berry, saw the same landscape but bathed in a bleaker light. "There are two subcultures," Berry said, "and the twain will never fully meet. Integration has never meant that everybody would come out coffee-colored—and as long as they're not, I'm not sure blacks will ever be fully accepted." Berry's longtime friend and political ally Richard Stogner was equally grim. "Are we at the content-of-our-character stage?" he asked. "I don't think we'll ever see it."

Mixed in with the general disappointment, it wasn't hard to find pockets of hope. Despite what they saw all around them, people didn't want to give up on race relations: didn't want to accept the half a loaf that passed for progress in Atlanta. "Deep down," said one man, a black journalist, "the black middle class in Atlanta is still integrationist." "It's all of our problem," agreed Charles Loudermilk. "We're living together. And we all need to work on the problems—problems shared by black and white communities." "The idealism still moves a lot of us," said another, younger man, a white journalist. "That spiritual, theological strain in the civil rights movement—in our way, we hold on to that. That's why we set so much store by leaders like Andrew Young and John Lewis." Still, by the mid-nineties, most people, black and white, had no idea how to move forward. Comforting as their idealism was, it no longer seemed particularly useful either as a beacon or a goad for change.

Yet, even in this largely hopeless climate, Andrew Young had an idea—a vision of what he liked to call "a way out." Hopeful as ever, forgiving and conciliatory, Young was still confident that his city and the rest of the nation were marching toward a better future. "The movement has come in off the streets," he maintained, "and people are carrying on the battle in the political and economic arena"—struggling in their everyday lives for some kind of inclusion. In Young's view, the black political leadership was now integrationist. "In the political corridors you have to be," he said. "In order to get a vote passed, you have to put together a majority." Ordinary rank-and-file blacks were trying in one way or another to get ahead, and as Young saw things, this too was integrationist. "I quantify revolution in dollar terms," he said. "Martin Luther King, when he was running the movement, never had more than half a million dollars a year to work with. Now I see black people driving around Atlanta in cars that are worth one hundred thirty thousand dollars. That's integration. I keep running into young people who are starting their own businesses. That's integration. I used to know everyone in black Atlanta who could afford to take an airplane. Now I see black folks I don't even know flying first class. These people are carrying on the struggle."

It was easy to see Young's new vision as prosaic and mechanical, a long way from the inspiring King dream he once championed. It came with little rhetoric, moral or otherwise. It said nothing about relations between blacks and whites or about how to heal the wounds of the past. In his new mood, Young didn't even seem to care much what people felt or claimed they were doing. "Watch what they do, not what they say," he urged, when asked about the spread of separatist rhetoric. At the same time, there was something encouraging about his down-to-earth view and the minimal expectations that came with it. His new idea of how to get to the future offered no false promises: no quick fixes, no automatic understanding, no instant equality. It didn't hinge on shared idealism or altruism. And it didn't count on people, black or white, to act like heroes—just ordinary folks pursuing their self-interest. Young was still a strong proponent of affirmative action, but as he laid out this vision in the mid-nineties, it didn't seem to require much social engineering. More than anything, it was a view of change driven by personal striving: getting onto the old immigrants' escalator of schooling, a job and a stake in the system. Though less exciting than the vision Young and others had held out in the past, it also seemed potentially more practical.

What about the emotional side of race relations? Young's new blueprint had nothing to say about white bigotry or black anger or the other complicated cross-currents that swirled between the two groups. "It's not that there isn't racism still," he said, "but in business, money is green." Once blacks got onto the escalator, once they had the tools to make their own way in the mainstream, white people's feelings would no longer matter as much as they once had. As for black feelings, the more success people had in school or business or politics, the less resentment and alienation they would harbor. In the long run, Young seemed to be saying, the feelings would take care of themselves. In the mid-nineties, it sounded like an outlandish notion. But here and there in Atlanta and elsewhere, some ordinary blacks and whites were starting to bear him out.

For Haywood Curry, the mid-nineties brought a major personal change—a seismic shift in relations among his family members that also seemed a kind of parable for the rest of the nation. Curry had grown up in a small North Carolina town, where even into the sixties blacks and whites had little to do with each other. He knew virtually no whites, mistrusted the few he knew, and as a young man, like most of his generation, he embraced the Black Power movement. "I was out in front with the banners and the marches," he recalled. "I had the biggest Afro around. I wanted blacks to be blacks and didn't want to have much to do with white people." In later years, the demands of starting a career cut back on his activism but did little to change his feelings about race relations. By the seventies, thanks to affirmative action, he was working for the large construction firm of J. A. Jones, and was thrilled to be transferred to Atlanta, where he hoped to help the company get business in the black community.

New in town, largely without friends, Curry struck up an acquaintance with another newcomer: a white law student who lived in the same apartment complex. One night, the acquaintance asked Curry to come out to dinner with him and a group of fellow students. Among them was a young white woman from Virginia, Linda Bryant. Despite his initial mistrust, she and Curry hit if off. There were a few more group dinners, then some on their own, and it wasn't long before Curry and Bryant were dating. Curry was deeply ambivalent. "I said, 'This can't be happening. This shouldn't be happening. This is not going to work.' I tried dating other people. I tried to break it off." Both he and Bryant were worried about what their families would think. "But it wasn't just my family," said Curry. "It was a problem for me. I had never gone out with a white woman before."

Still, the relationship had its own momentum. Bryant urged Curry to keep trying, and he did. Eventually, both realized that their attraction was more than a passing thing. Neither imagined that their romance was a solution to the race problem and both would have felt uncomfortable with anyone who did. But after a while, neither felt that race was as important as what they felt for each other. "The more we saw each other, the more we came to the realization," Curry recalled, "that we were people who were in love and the color of our skin didn't make that much difference." It was a long, uncertain courtship, even so; but finally in 1979 Curry and Bryant were married. It was then, more or less without warning, that her parents made clear they wanted to have nothing to do with the couple or any children they might have.

Curry's family, though not exactly enthusiastic, gradually made its peace with the marriage. His mother, who worked in other people's homes, cleaning and taking care of children, soon warmed to Linda. His sister, who like him came of age in the sixties, was a little more suspicious, but she was never antagonistic. On Linda's side, the younger generation and then two aunts accepted the match, and Curry began to go to regular family gatherings at the home of Linda's sister in a Washington suburb. Still, the Bryant parents held out. A middle-class couple from Newport News, Virginia—both of them were engineers—the Bryants were part of the New South, or should have been. But the Currys' interracial marriage was just too much for them. Part of the problem was upbringing: both the Bryants had been raised in the Deep South, with all the assumptions that came with it. Part of what held them back now was social; Mrs. Bryant in particular could not face introducing Curry to her country-club friends in Virginia. In the years after the wedding, there was no communication between the Bryants and their daughter, no sign from them when the young couple's first child, Sarah, was born in 1985, or when the second, Ross, appeared three years later.

By the early 1990s, life looked pretty good for the Curry family. Both Haywood and Linda were doing well in their careers: each had recently started a business, and both concerns were taking off. The family lived in an integrated suburb in DeKalb County, just west of the city. The children went to a mixed school; both parents had black and white friends whom they saw separately and together. Husband and wife were pleasantly surprised by how little prejudice they encountered. Curry could still remember the stares the couple had gotten when they started dating, particularly traveling around the South. "You could feel their eyes," he said with a laugh. But neither he nor his wife seemed to put much store by people's looks: "We were sometimes seen as a curiosity," Linda recalled. "But we were never mistreated."

If anything, according to Linda, the couple felt that their friends and colleagues had encouraged them in their choice. "It might have been different," she said, "if we had started dating and horrible things had happened, like my father warned me. 'You'll never have friends,' he said. 'You'll never get a job. Your life will be ruined.' In fact, none of that happened—and mostly what we had were experiences that reinforced what we had done." In Linda's eyes, her parents were the exception that proved the rule: just how much America had changed and how little race now mattered. "My kids have never experienced prejudice head-on," she said. "They don't even know what it is really, and can't understand when I try to tell them why we don't see my parents. I've explained it again and again to my son, but he doesn't get it. 'Why is it, again?' he asks. 'Are you sure they're not dead?' Maybe we've been lucky. We don't really know. But the only real problem we've had is my parents. Our lives in Atlanta have made things easier for us."

After more than twenty years together, neither Curry nor his wife thought much about each other's color; it just didn't cross their minds very often. Asked whether he saw his children as black or white, Curry answered, "We think of them as kids." His own racial identity was still important to him. "I'm proud of being black," he said. "I still have things that matter to me from the black tradition—the church, things I learned from family. And it's become part of the kids." The children didn't live in a totally color-blind universe—how could they? But when color came up, they were told that they were both black and white. Confronted with questions about race on census queries or other forms, Linda checked both "white" and "black" or "other." "I want my children to be able to choose for themselves," she explained. "We tell them people are people," said her husband. By now, even among strangers, Curry seemed largely indifferent to people's color. "It's like when you first meet somebody who is Chinese," he said. "At first you recognize that they are Chinese or Japanese or whatever. But after that, it goes away." Linda believed that if anything, she was now more aware of race than her husband was, more sensitive to what might be slights or racial resentments. "What counts," said Curry, "is when you get to know people. In a relationship, it will come out whether someone likes you or dislikes you, whether you can trust them or not. I don't think I trust people because they are black, and I don't think I distrust people because they're white—because I know plenty of black people I don't like and plenty of whites I do."

What happened in 1994 surprised everyone, younger and older generation alike. By then, Linda's parents were getting on and her father's health was failing. That summer, as always, the Bryants rented a house at the shore, where they were visited by their other children and their families. One day, Linda's sister Janet and her father were alone on the beach and Bryant asked his daughter if she ever saw Linda and Haywood. "Yes," she told him, "as a matter of fact we all get together—all the siblings—every year, in Alexandria." Bryant said nothing and nearly six months passed without another sign from him. Linda tried writing to her parents, reaching out to them as she had every few years, but as usual there was no reply. Then, in early spring of 1995, Mrs. Bryant called Janet at home and asked her where and when the next siblings' gathering was going to be—the parents wanted to come.

Originally, it was to be a short visit, a quick stopover en route from one place to another, but when the time came, the Bryants spent all day with their gathered children, the Currys and their children among them. It wasn't a particularly eventful meeting. "We met them. We all talked— about nothing really," Curry reported. "We acted like we had seen each other two weeks before." There were a few awkward moments. "I don't think they had ever been around anybody black before," Curry said, "except maybe the lady who cleans their house. They didn't really know what to say or ask, though I think by then they had been asking Linda's sisters and brothers a lot of questions and I think they had a lot of information about us." Still, Linda was convinced, the meeting had gone well. A few months later, eleven-year-old Sarah Curry got a birthday card from her grandparents. It was a small thing, but in the Curry family it meant a lot.

As astonishing as the Bryants' change of heart had been, Curry's reaction was in its way even more surprising. His mother, worried about her grandchildren, wanted to know how the family was taking the new situation. Were the kids upset, was Linda, did Curry think he could ever forgive the Bryants and come to look on them as family? Curry didn't have to think twice. "I don't know these people," he said. "I never met them before, or met them only once, when Linda and I were dating, at a party. I'm upset that they've treated Linda the way they treated her. But I don't know these people, so how can I be mad at them? How can I not like them when I don't even know them?" What mattered to him, Curry said, was that the Bryants were coming around now. They seemed like nice people to him, and the way he figured it, they had been trapped in something they didn't understand. "I think they got stuck," he said. "They said some things about me and about Linda at the beginning, and they didn't know how to go back—how to retract those things or say they were sorry. Now they are trying to figure that out, making amends, or trying to, in their own way." Curry wasn't sure there was much he could do to help his white in-laws, but for his part, he was open to whatever was going to happen next.

When it came to race relations outside the family, Curry was no more sanguine than the next person. His experience as a contractor had left him deeply skeptical about white Atlantans and their exclusive old-boy networks. Whether or not they were actually prejudiced, Curry found, few white builders reached out to him except when they had to—when they thought his minority participation would help them get a city contract. Nor was he particularly hopeful about what had happened in the black movement. His brother had gone to the Million Man March called by Louis Farrakhan in October 1995, but Curry couldn't bring himself to go along. "When you talk about something like that, putting so much emphasis on being black," he said, "you're isolating yourself. A lot of the problems with the family nowadays—the problems of husbands and fathers—you find them in white neighborhoods, too. I can't accept the things Farrakhan talks about. I can't follow that belief." In Atlanta, Curry was dismayed by what he saw in his church, a predominantly white church he and his family attended mostly because it was convenient to where they lived. Most Sunday mornings, Curry's was the only black face there, and he had a hard time reconciling that with what he read in the scriptures about the universal brotherhood of man. He didn't blame his fellow parishioners. "It's not that they don't invite blacks to the church," he said. "They do. But the blacks don't come. It's the same in black churches—they'll reach out to white people. But the whites don't go."

Still, for all his misgivings, Curry was clear about one thing. "I keep saying," he maintained, "we gotta forget. What so-and-so's dad did to my dad—we got to forget it. It's over with. If we keep bringing it up, it will always be there. That's the real problem I have with things like the Million Man March—it just pointed to these issues and made it harder for people to get over them, made it harder and harder for people to come together." Curry had no idea how to get other black people to come to his church, or how to help his white friends get to know other blacks. All he knew was that this was what had to happen. "As long as we keep apart from each other the way we do, uncomfortable talking with or being with or living with each other, it's always going to be there—this black and white thing. I don't think it's ever going to go away," he said, "but we could learn to live with it much better than we do."

Epilogue

WHERE DO WE GO
FROM HERE?

The late 1990s have brought a spate of race anniversaries and, with them, the old question: just what can we learn from history? It's been nearly thirty-five years since the March on Washington, thirty years since the Detroit riots—and five years since the latest riot, in Los Angeles, far worse than any that came before it. For all the progress we've made, we remain trapped in the old patterns—and many of us are beginning to give up hope that there's a way out. Still, weary as we are, few of us can shrug off the race issue.

In New York, Detroit and Atlanta, the more things change, the more familiar they seem. The problems that dogged each city through the sixties, seventies and eighties still dog them today—so much so that at times the sense of déjà vu seems almost painful. Still, all three cities have made some progress in recent years in coming to grips with their particular race syndromes, and if the change isn't enough exactly to justify hope, it can help point the way for the future.

In New York City, John Lindsay's well-intentioned failures left a bitter legacy of division. Middle-class whites excluded from his racial compact managed to elect the next mayor, Abe Beame, and the one after that, Ed Koch. But most borough-based whites would never feel the same about the city, and as soon as they could, they left—at a rate of about one hundred thousand a year, reducing the percentage of whites in the population from nearly two-thirds to under 40 percent. Once it was clear how hard it would be to solve the race problem, even the most liberal Manhattanites grew tired of it, and though they continued to defer to the rhetoric of whatever angry spokesmen emerged from the ghetto, the gap between poor blacks and well-off whites only grew wider year by year. The election of black mayor David Dinkins did little to ease black alienation or improve overburdened services in poor neighborhoods. Finally, when it seemed that things could get no worse, a series of racial incidents in the late eighties and early nineties turned New York into a national symbol of all that was still wrong between black and white.

It was the polarization and demagoguery of the Lindsay era, only worse. The Tawana Brawley rape hoax, the roving bands that attacked black youths in Howard Beach and Bensonhurst, the deadly riots in Crown Heights, the fatal fire at Freddy's clothing store in Harlem: the episodes rarely involved many people, but they left both blacks and whites despairing that they could ever get along. As in the sixties, blacks blamed white racism, whites faulted black leadership—and each used the other as an excuse to stop trying. The black political agenda changed little over the years: police brutality, educational genocide, angry demands for respect and ghetto autonomy. Even the leaders were familiar, with both Sonny Carson and Al Sharpton setting the tone among black New Yorkers into the late nineties.

Still, divided as New York grew, there were occasional glimmers of hope: hints that blacks were making progress, and that blacks and whites alike might find ways to rise above their bitterness. Already by 1990, the census showed that middle-class black families in Queens had met and surpassed the average annual income of the borough's middle-class whites. A burgeoning entrepreneurial spirit was transforming Harlem even before it was designated as a federal empowerment zone, promising tax breaks and other incentives to spur the creation of still more start-up businesses. Republican mayor Rudolph Giuliani bore down hard on crime and refused to play cat-and-mouse with race men, dramatically reducing their power to set both blacks and whites on edge. "One city, one standard," the mayor declared, declining to grant special favors or negotiate with activists. Resolute to the point of gruffness, he refused to make symbolic racial gestures and abolished the special City Hall office devoted to black issues. Then, in 1996, with his approval, the state legislature finally freed the city from the tyranny of community control, drastically reducing the powers of the thirty-two local boards, many of them scandal-ridden and corrupt, that had been mismanaging the public schools since the Ocean Hill–Brownsville episode.

Not all black New Yorkers were happy with Giuliani's mayoralty. His new, proactive police strategies made life safer in the ghetto, but they also brought an upsurge in complaints about brutality and pressure to strengthen the civilian review board, which had been reinstated in the early nineties. Many blacks were still so alienated from what they saw as white authority that their representatives voted to retain community control despite its proven failure in the city's schools. Angry activists kept up a drumbeat of criticism: denunciations of the "racist" mayor and his "war on black New York." But unlike Lindsay, Giuliani ignored the demagogues, and though he had some trouble speaking convincingly to the city's minorities, he seemed to know what would do most to help them in the long run. "People in this city don't need special things," he told one reporter. "They need more of certain general things—safety, education, jobs." Confounding all expectations, many in the black silent majority agreed. In 1997, according to a *New York Times* poll, one in three black New Yorkers believed that Giuliani's first term had been a success, while more than two-thirds approved of the way his administration was handling crime. This was hardly model race relations, and conditions in poor neighborhoods were far from satisfactory. But already, stern and unsympathetic as he sometimes seemed, Giuliani had shown what might be done to reverse the damage wrought by decades of New York–style racial politics.

The challenge of leadership was even more evident in the black community, and no one personified the difficulties better than Al Sharpton. Embracing his early lessons in confrontation tactics, Sharpton emerged in the eighties as the quintessential black protest leader: a master of flamboyant, symbolic politics, color-coded and inflamed by grievance, that rallied the city's blacks and alienated whites while doing little or nothing to improve life in the ghetto. A tireless opportunist, willing to exploit any tragedy, Sharpton played a leading role in all the ugly episodes of the era, inviting young blacks to blame the system for their problems—in the case of upstate teenager Tawana Brawley, he encouraged her false claim that she had been raped—and fostering a sense, among both whites and blacks, of an unbridgeable racial divide.

In the early nineties, much to New Yorkers' surprise, Sharpton decided to try mainstream politics. Modeling himself on Jesse Jackson, he lost weight, trimmed his hair, declared himself a moderate in the Martin Luther King mold and ran for office, twice for the Senate and then, in 1997, for mayor. A man of considerable political talent, Sharpton was a lively, thought-provoking candidate, his transformation an ironic tribute to the enduring power of the integrationist vision. Still, even at his best, he remained more a gadfly than an effective leader. Like his heroes Adam Clayton Powell and Jesse Jackson, he saw it as his job to express blacks' complaints, not work the system to their advantage. He never ran for an office he could win, and like many black politicians formed in the protest era, never moved beyond symbolic issues—sweeping, unaddressable claims about white racism and injustice—that if anything diverted attention from the real, pressing problems plaguing black New Yorkers.

It looked as if black politics might be mired forever in rage and resentment—until, in the late nineties, the black silent majority began to grow restless, and a group of alternative leaders began to emerge in New York. Most were ministers and businessmen as down-to-earth as Sharpton was flamboyant. Among the most impressive was Floyd Flake, a six-term congressman and the charismatic pastor of a 9,000-member church. In Queens and in Washington, Flake was a consummate problem solver, always thinking of new ways to deliver for his constituents. By the late nineties, his church-based empire was a national model for what could be done to heal the ghetto: with nearly five hundred new housing units, a street of shops and an elaborate network of cradle-to-grave social services, it provided jobs for thousands of people and pumped millions of dollars a year into the local economy. An earnest, plain-spoken man, Flake rarely charged anyone with racism; he made a habit of working with both Republicans and Democrats and did not hesitate to pooh-pooh the symbolic issues that preoccupied many fellow black leaders. Like Giuliani, he believed that government could help—mostly through programs, like school vouchers and home ownership incentives, that encouraged poor people to help themselves. But above all, what he proved was the difference leadership can make, encouraging even the poorest blacks to believe they can succeed in the mainstream.

By the time an alternative leadership emerged in Detroit, in the early nineties, the city was on the verge of collapse. Increasingly derelict, dangerous and empty, Motown had lost another third of its population and 40 percent of its jobs, with General Motors alone reducing its in-town workforce from over 30,000 to a mere 9,200. One in three city residents now lived below the poverty line, and in some neighborhoods more than half were unemployed. Crime, drugs, welfare dependency and teenage pregnancy were endemic, to the point where over 70 percent of male high school students had had some involvement with the criminal justice system, often for major offenses. Coleman Young remained popular—even beloved—among black Detroiters, but city government had all but ceased to function: obtaining routine permits and licenses often required bribes, and outside of downtown there was virtually no police protection or even trash collection. The one public service that continued to operate was the demolition crews, speeding the spread of the ubiquitous meadow taking over where working families had once lived.

The gap between city and suburbs grew worse with every passing year. Thanks to the crime rate and an unrelentingly hostile political climate, almost no new businesses were being created in town. In many neighborhoods, there was no retail to speak of, not even mom-and-pop groceries. One in five downtown commercial buildings stood empty or close to it; and in 1996, GM bought the long-bankrupt RenCen for less than one-fifth of what it had cost to build two decades before. Meanwhile, the surrounding suburbs continued to grow, the booming engine of a state economy that ranked first in the nation in business creation. But unlike in other metro areas, including New York, Atlanta, and Washington, D.C., virtually no Detroit blacks made the move across the city line. Coleman Young had achieved his dream—Black Power in one city—but cut off from the larger world, it had turned to dross around him.

The city's new mayor, Dennis Archer, promised a 180-degree shift: first a crackdown on crime, then an all-out effort to create new businesses and attract jobs. Archer's friendly overtures were warmly welcomed in the suburbs, and small groups of outlying whites began to venture into town to participate in cleanup crews and other symbolic gestures of concern. After twenty years in Pontiac, the Detroit Lions agreed to move back to the city, and a new football stadium was planned for them, along with a new baseball park and three gambling casinos. Commercial developers put up a stand of new middle-class housing—the first in the city in years. The Big Three and large local banks began to talk about reinvesting, and General Motors announced that it would not move its headquarters out of town after all. The problem in Detroit was that after decades of devastation, there were limits to what even the most enlightened leadership could do. Even the announcement that the Motor City had qualified as a federal empowerment zone—a designation that, over a decade, would bring in $100 million in grants and $250 million in tax breaks—was greeted with caution bordering on skepticism. "We have to be realistic about our expectations," warned HUD secretary Andrew Cuomo. "One hundred million dollars is in one sense a drop in the bucket," echoed city council member Sheila Cockrel. "The migration of capital out of the city was so huge."

The challenge that Archer and his allies face is the same one that has dogged Detroiters for over three decades: just what can business or government do to heal the ghetto and accelerate black inclusion? But both the empowerment zone concept and the way it is being implemented in Detroit point to some promising new thinking about what might work. Unlike in the seventies, Detroit's concerned white businessmen are no longer inviting angry blacks to "vent" their feelings, and there is far less talk on either side of top-down social engineering. Both business and government seem to grasp that the best path into the mainstream is the old-fashioned one: schooling, jobs and a stake in the system. Local officials, state and city, are trying to remove impediments—the worst is crime—and improve the school system. Big industry hopes to help not so much with handouts as by spurring small-business creation. The logic in both cases is the same: relatively small but strategic interventions that will help people find ways to help themselves.

Detroiters have responded with a burst of entrepreneurial enthusiasm; roughly thirty business initiatives, many of them start-ups, are to be launched in the empowerment zone in the next decade, bringing over $2 billion into the center city. Local banks will lend money at below-market rates; the Big Three have promised to do business with fledgling inner-city companies. The challenges are daunting: to create real, viable businesses, to wean them of dependence, to avoid patronizing color-coded favors and spin an enduring web of trade and business contacts that connects the ghetto and its residents with the outside world. The signs are not all good. The Detroit City Council is still reflexively antibusiness, and its foot-dragging could kill any revitalization. The new stadiums and casinos could be a troubling repeat of RenCen: more showy bricks-and-mortar development with little trickle-down into poor neighborhoods. Though the empowerment zone concept shifts the emphasis from color to location, outsiders' criteria for aiding small firms still often involve race—and no one pretends to know how to fight the hopelessness that still grips much of black Detroit. Change is sure to be slow; there will be no sudden "Renaissance" in the Motor City. Still, over time, if it stays Archer's course, the city may gradually edge its way back from its disastrous isolation.

The racial picture in Atlanta is still much better than in either New York or Detroit—or most of America, for that matter. Atlanta's black middle class is still growing and gaining in confidence. No massive flow of whites is streaming out of town, and the sense of metro cohesion is holding, linking city and suburbs, many of them black, with an ever-strengthening net of business and personal ties. Occasionally, there are even signs that the old, ingrained race consciousness may be ebbing. The Supreme Court decision overturning Georgia's racially gerrymandered congressional districts brought howls of outrage from the local black establishment. But on election day 1996, more white Atlantans than blacks turned out to vote for black incumbent Cynthia McKinney: proof positive, as many commentators noticed, of how much attitudes have changed even in the heart of the South.

More than anything, Atlanta proves that the old immigrants' escalator is still the best way for any impoverished group to make it into the system. Like Queens' middle-class black families and Detroit's new start-up entrepreneurs, black Atlantans are advancing toward integration one step at a time, mostly through hard work, self-help, determination and faith in the system. Even prosperous middle-class Atlantans aren't quite there yet. The road from outside to inside still takes a generation at least. There are far fewer shortcuts than we hoped in the sixties, and real social integration—the last frontier— remains a distant dream. But imperfect as it is, Atlanta stands out as an example of what can be done to make economic and political inclusion a reality—even without a full sense of belonging in a single, shared community.

The problem in Atlanta, as elsewhere, is that old habits die hard, particularly the habit of seeing and counting by color. The 1996 Olympics were originally conceived as a showcase of how far Atlanta had come; the city traded on its civil rights history to secure the games, promising a pageant of interracial harmony in keeping with American ideals and Olympic tradition. Even the economic rationale for hosting the event had an integrationist edge to it. The metaphor was a rising tide that would lift all boats, pumping money into the local economy, irrespective of color. "The Olympics are an expanding pie," one local columnist wrote. "There is enough for everyone." Still, when it came time to determine who would get which piece, Atlantans could not help deciding largely on the basis of race.

Affirmative action considerations shaped every aspect of the competition. The Atlanta Committee for the Olympic Games was not initially inclined to mete out contracts by color, but Maynard Jackson, then in his second stint as mayor, once again harangued civic leaders behind closed doors, and the committee eventually agreed to hew to the city's 36 percent set-aside goal. Minority-owned companies helped build every Olympic venue and participated in almost every vending contract—a total of nearly $390 million worth of business. "There has never been that much money coming into the black community," crowed Andrew Young. The problem was that, as in the past, the biggest beneficiaries were a few well-known insiders. Herman Russell, by then the nation's largest black contractor, participated in all three of the biggest, most lucrative jobs: building the main stadium, the Centennial Olympic Park and the Coca-Coca Company's Olympic City theme park. Some lesser-known, inexperienced builders got breaks, but as in the past there was also plenty of "passive joint venturing" and incompetence that only soured white attitudes and further stigmatized blacks.

The biggest disaster was the city program to recruit and license street vendors. The idea, as at the Atlanta airport and at Underground, was to reach out to first-time minority entrepreneurs, giving them a critical boost over the start-up threshold. The difference was that this time they had to pay the city for the opportunity—up to $20,000 for what were said to be choice vending spots near Olympic venues. Would-be entrepreneurs came from all over the country, in some cases staking their life savings on a barbecue stand or shaved-ice cart. But it turned out that city authorities could not control foot traffic or limit competition, and they provided none of the fundamental support services they had promised—electricity, water or security. In the end, not a single minority vendor made money, and most of them lost tens of thousands of dollars, though the city and the freelance consultant in charge of the program netted $4.8 million between them. It was a new low—affirmative action profits not for minority entrepreneurs but for the city government running the program—that could only add to white Atlantans' growing cynicism about black business and how to encourage it.

Still, for all their doubts, neither Atlantans nor the rest of the nation seemed able to get rid of preferences. The late nineties brought a swell of opposition nationwide: once unthinkable attacks by mainstream politicians and pundits, followed by a welter of precedent-upsetting court cases and legislative proposals. California governor Pete Wilson made a promise to end affirmative action the central plank of his 1996 run for the presidency, and state universities in California and Texas began to phase out programs. The groundswell culminated in November 1996 with passage of California's Proposition 209, an unequivocal, democratically backed call for banning preferences in state employment, education and contracting. Still, as in Atlanta after the *Croson* decision, affirmative action would not die. President Bill Clinton appeased some people's doubts by promising to "mend" offending programs, but after much foot-dragging his administration eliminated only one of the federal government's scores of quotas: an obscure Pentagon procurement regimen.

It was easy to accuse the White House of straddling, but the obstacles to change were bigger than that. Across the country, as in Atlanta, even whites who disliked preferences hesitated to do away with them. People didn't want to look racist, or didn't want to seem to slam the door shut in blacks' faces. Not even preferences' staunchest opponents liked the idea that eliminating them might mean there would be few blacks at the nation's top colleges. On the other side, too, many people were quietly ambivalent: eager to help but uneasy with the idea of granting special favors on the basis of color. If it were any other issue—anything but race— the two sides would have gotten together and hammered out a compromise: a package of alternative remedies, including recruitment programs, remedial classes, color-neutral scholarships and the like, that would work better than race-based preferences to help larger numbers of truly needy blacks into the mainstream. But the debate about affirmative action was already far too polarized for that.

Instead of a constructive discussion about the best means to a shared end, both sides erupted in angry name-calling. Those in favor of affirmative action dismissed anyone with questions as hard-hearted racists; opponents responded with defensive counterattacks, demonizing the programs and their backers. The issue of what might actually work to solve the problem got lost in a sea of shouting. Once again as so often in the past—on questions of busing, ghetto policing, education and affirmative action—the aura of moral righteousness that surrounds race issues made it all but impossible to talk about them or move ahead toward a better remedy.

Nationally, when it comes to race, it's often hard not to feel that we're trapped in the past—and will remain so forever, no matter what we do. Almost every episode in this book had an eerie echo in the later nineties. The black paranoia about the criminal justice system that gripped Detroit under Coleman Young and Atlanta at the time of the missing and murdered children surfaced again with a vengeance during the O. J. Simpson trial. The misguided white impulse to win blacks' favor by dwelling on their alienation is more common than ever now. The old black "two-ness" is as agonized as in the past, and the nation as a whole has even less idea today than in the sixties if it wants the future to be color-blind or not. No wonder we aren't sure if we still believe in integration as an achievable goal.

As we look back over the decades and then stumble again into the same pitfalls, it's easy to wonder if it is possible to move forward. Are there other choices? Or are the mistakes we keep making all but inevitable—the tragic playing out of history we can't hope to undo? Many of the errors of the past thirty-five years probably were unavoidable. It was almost inconceivable, given what came before, that blacks would not be angry, at once alienated and convinced that they deserved special help. Once whites of goodwill saw this, it is hard to imagine them reacting with anything but compassion and some indulgence even for flailing activists. Then, when liberals reached out, they often had little choice but to make alliances with race men: constructive, gradualist leaders were in short supply, and they had little credibility with the impatient black public. The recurring patterns that wind through this book only reinforce the sense of inevitable tragedy: black mistrust of the police, the appeal of racial solidarity, a tendency on all sides to feel that the stakes are too high to permit compromise—how could it have been otherwise? And even if both blacks and whites had somehow managed to transcend the past, the play of larger economic forces was always making the climb steeper, hemming in a city like Detroit, eroding jobs, discouraging even limited government efforts to spark personal change.

Still, choices were made, all too many of them poor ones, and along with the tragedy, the past is also a moral tale. The better choices being made now in New York, Detroit and Atlanta point to some of the avoidable errors made in previous decades. Besides, a number of the givens that once seemed hopelessly intractable have changed with time as the past loses its grip. The black political spectrum is broader now; some chastened whites have learned to think more carefully about the consequences of their goodwill. Many blacks' economic advance has eased their insularity, and increased interracial contact is softening white prejudice. Even the worst failures of the past few decades can point the way to better strategies, and though this is not the place for a detailed inventory of solutions, a few basic principles can be distilled from history.

The first and perhaps the toughest to swallow is that integration will not work without acculturation. Many blacks don't like the ring of this—the idea of values imposed from outside—and relativist as we are, wary of racial condescension, most of the rest of us empathize with this distaste. That's part of why we couldn't win the War on Poverty: when it turned out that it required extensive acculturation—programs to change people's habits, their attitudes toward school, work and the law—many otherwise well-meaning whites lost the will to fight the battle. For more than thirty years, we tried to ignore the development gap, and those who dared to mention it were written off as bigots. But the difficult truth remains that people who cannot speak standard English or have never seen anyone hold down a regular job have little hope of fitting into the system or sharing its fruits. If anything, the past few decades have taught us that the preparation gap is wider than we thought, and more needs to be done than we ever imagined: everything from getting poor mothers into prenatal care to teaching job applicants about deferring to a boss's authority. What makes this hard is that acculturation is a long, slow process—one that will require a kind of patience till now largely lacking on race matters.

A second basic question has to do with top-down assistance: can outsiders help, and with what kinds of intervention? Even if we start from the assumption, borne out in New York, Detroit and Atlanta, that the best way into the system is the immigrants' route—school, job and entrepreneurship—that doesn't mean that there is nothing government or business can do to accelerate the process. The free market alone cannot make the inner city safe for children or business. The economy no longer provides adequate job opportunities in urban neighborhoods, and it cannot heal the alienation that prevents many blacks from taking advantage of what chances they do get. Popular as the idea of self-help may be among both black activists and white conservatives, mainstream America cannot wash its hands of these problems, assuming that they will take care of themselves.

The temptation in the past was to step in and "fix" things, but what we've learned is that government works best at the margins—and so, by extension, do any outsiders. Incentives are better than heavy-handed engineering. Small, locally run social services generally outperform large, federal ones. The state can play a role: with funding and, even better, tax breaks. Well-meaning whites can find ways to sponsor achievement-oriented students and expand corporate outreach efforts. Even the old idea of government-mandated mingling can work, if updated for the nineties. In the right circumstances, racial interaction is its own reward—the only real way to overcome prejudice. But here as in other realms, far more effective than forced efforts like busing are situations that rely on color-neutral inducements: magnet schools, school choice, the volunteer career-track army. Both business and government can help to create more of these circumstances where blacks and whites get to know each other—but both must learn to approach race matters with a lighter touch.

The third big question is color coding, and I believe the past makes more than clear: it is playing with fire. No one who understands what makes America great can quarrel with ethnic pride. At home, on the weekend, in the family and the neighborhood, Jews will be Jews, Italians Italian—and there is no reason blacks should be any different. Religion and ethnicity are essential parts of all our lives, and government should not curtail how we express them in the private sphere. But when it comes to public life, even the benevolent color coding of recent decades has proved a recipe for alienation and resentment. Under the law and as people make their way up the ladders of school and career, they must operate as individuals, not members of a group. Society need not be color-blind or color-less, but the law cannot work unless it is color-neutral, and the government should not be in the business of abetting or paying for the cultivation of group identity. Nothing in the history of the past three decades suggests that America should stop requiring people to find a way of reconciling their ethnicity and their citizenship.

There are many reasons why color-coded remedies caught on the way they did, but one of the most important was that they seemed relatively easy. Busing seemed easier—and cheaper and quicker—than the wholesale desegregation of city neighborhoods; affirmative action seemed easier than the slow acculturation that would naturally prepare blacks to compete at school and on the job. But after two to three decades of grappling with the hidden costs of these "easy" answers, it should be growing clear that there are no shortcuts.

Affirmative action is a Band-Aid on the cancer of black underdevelopment. Vastly improved public schooling, some form of school choice or vouchers, more money for community colleges, need-based scholarships and remedial tutoring, job-training programs, apprenticeships, outreach and mentoring networks: this is only the beginning of the long, hard assault that is necessary to develop black capacities in a way that will truly level the playing field. This need not—could not—be a single, coordinated government push. Quite the contrary, it will take a welter of small, piecemeal efforts, less top-down than bottom-up, many of them local and privately run. This kind of developmental approach will look for a while like a step backward from the apparent progress achieved with affirmative action. But in the long run, there can be no other choice if we mean what we say about integration.

The fourth and perhaps most important lesson of history is the need for better leadership, both black and white, to foster the common values of a shared society. So many of the mistakes of the past can be traced to feckless leadership: racemongering demagogues, patronizing civic elites, would-be racial healers who confused compromise with appeasement and ended up creating standoffs instead of helping people listen and reach out. We will spend at least the next decade undoing the harm these men and women did, and even then, we will have lost a generation to separatism and indifference. What would better leadership look like? The first principle is to do no harm: stop sending the message that because of racism there is no point in trying, that blacks are fundamentally different from whites and right to ground their lives on a bed of old grudges. Public policy could start by deemphasizing the difference race makes, whether in the voting booth or on an application for a government contract. Corporations could rethink in-house diversity training that fosters color consciousness and rubs salt in old wounds. Popular culture could let go of the idea that skin color is what makes a role model. Politicians, entertainers, sports heroes and others could use their bully pulpits not to air old gripes but to remind people that we're making progress—that there's plenty of reason for hope and individual effort.

But even this is only the beginning of what's needed. Whatever else government can do, it cannot, in Martin Luther King's phrase, teach men to "treat other men as thou." It cannot help people, black or white, let go of the past. It cannot force an indifferent public to face up to the costs of the poverty and exclusion in our midst. Only leadership can do these things—leadership that creates a sense of community.

Part of the challenge is articulating a set of common values and allegiances: first and foremost, our national ideals—freedom, democracy, equal opportunity. These are the foundations of our common culture, the necessary condition of the pluralism that means so much to us. But in the short run, it may take something more than this traditional creed to convince most people to look beyond their differences. Intoxicated with their roots and ethnic identities, many find it hard to focus on these big, abstract concepts. Others are too angry to think about common values. Still others, probably the majority, take the old ideals for granted if they think about them at all—not exactly rallying points for a new civic culture.

Perhaps a better place to start is closer to the ground: in fragmented cities, resegregated schools and other places where blacks and whites rub shoulders—but without a sense of shared belonging or common purposes. Why couldn't teachers bring students together without counting or mentioning color and get them excited about common projects—cleaning up the neighborhood, say, or a shared political interest? Politicians may never restore the bond between center city and suburb, but no one has more in common than property holders worried about safe streets and real estate values. Metro cohesion could start with local alliances—between adjacent black and white enclaves and even pockets on either side of the city line. The key in each case is bringing people together around common goals—goals that in most cases have nothing to do with color. The army does it; so do mixed-race work crews, sports teams, corporate management units and even, occasionally, juries. It's a small step, but it's a start, and far more likely to be effective than awkward interracial dialogues. Then, when we begin to remember what we have in common, perhaps we'll be able to celebrate the big national ideals together.

Where we do we go from here? Martin Luther King's answer is as apt today as when he posed the question in 1967. The choice is "chaos or community"—and the challenge for all of us is to foster a greater sense of shared allegiance. This will not be easy in today's fragmented climate. To the degree it happens, it will build slowly and will suffer many zigzagging reversals. Still, if we do not eventually change course, it's hard to see how the nation will hold together in the long run.

The first step is the hardest: deciding that integration is what we want. But that may not be as much of a leap as it sometimes seems. After all, many of us made the commitment once already several decades ago, and despite our failures, few of us seem to have changed our minds. Most whites are still ashamed by the nation's grim racial history, and most still feel that the country must somehow come to grips with it. The public rallied enthusiastically to President Clinton's call for a national debate about race; polls consistently show that voters would be willing to spend more for social programs—including acculturation programs—if they were persuaded that the government knew what worked. The hope that still surrounds integration shows itself in all kinds of ways, including the reaction, in the mid-nineties, to Colin Powell's emergence as a national leader. Whatever his strengths and weaknesses as a presidential candidate, Powell made clear that he was ready to lay down the burden of race—and huge numbers of whites, including conservative southern Republicans, responded with admiration and support. Blacks sometimes seem less enthusiastic about the old dream, particularly when it's labeled "integration." One recent poll by *The Wall Street Journal* found that only 8 percent of black respondents considered this a primary concern. Still, even where the sense of two-ness seems strongest, very few blacks have given up all hope of inclusion.

It would be hard to find a more skeptical group than the men who gathered in October 1995 at Louis Farrakhan's Million Man March. It was a brazenly exclusive event, black men only, led by an avowed and bitter separatist. The obvious parallels to the 1963 March on Washington only highlighted the differences and the way the black mood seemed to have soured in the decades between the two gatherings. I wandered among the men on the Mall, talking to anyone who would catch my eye—asking if they thought integration was still possible and if it was something they hoped to see. The surprise in store for me could not have been greater. Every man I spoke to— with no exceptions—expressed some sympathy for the integrationist vision.

From James Burrell, a middle-aged Virginia businessman: "I'd like to see the day when we are all one people." From James Stewart, sixty-seven, a retired personnel manager from North Carolina: "You can't live separate in society. It's like a family. Man and wife can't live in the same house and carry on as if they were living separately." From postal worker Mark Sheffield, forty, of Atlanta: "King's message is more relevant today than it was thirty-two years ago. We [blacks and whites] have got to be patient with each other and let go of the past." For most of the two dozen men I spoke with, this inclusive hope was mixed with very different feelings: disappointment, alienation, sadness, sheer provocativeness or racial pride, often with a strong separatist tinge. Almost all defended Farrakhan, some more angrily than others, and though the themes of the day were self-help and "atonement," most of the men were clear: this was also a protest march. "We're not happy," said one older man. "We're trying to tell you that. If we were happy, we wouldn't be out here."

Still, even the gruffest of the marchers were of two minds about integration. James Bilal, thirty-seven, a supervisor for a Washington air-conditioning company, was plainly irritated to see a white woman in the crowd. He refused to make eye contact, didn't want to talk and answered my questions with curt monosyllables. What is the biggest problem black people face today? "White supremacy," he said. What kind of change is necessary? "Whites have to change," he answered. "The only other option is to kill each other." I was about to give up on the conversation when, virtually without prompting, he offered: "Of course, whites and blacks will have to learn to live together in one country. People are people. We all breathe air and drink water. Underneath, we're all the same." What does integration mean for this man? What does he think it would be like "to live together"? He wasn't ready to talk about that yet, but he was sure of one thing—there was no alternative.

A NOTE ON SOURCES

The stories told in this book are drawn primarily from interviews and press coverage found in the newspaper morgues at *Newsweek,* the *Detroit News,* and the *Atlanta Journal-Constitution.*

Among the periodicals consulted and cited in the Notes:

ABA Journal	*Journal of the American Bar Association*
Am News	*Amsterdam News*
Am Op	*American Opinion*
AP	*Associated Press*
AJC	*Atlanta Journal-Constitution**
Atl Biz Chr	*Atlanta Business Chronicle*
Balt Sun	*Baltimore Sun*
Biz Atl	*Business Atlanta*
Chi Trib	*Chicago Tribune*
Cleve Pln Dlr	*Cleveland Plain Dealer*
Chr Sci Mon	*Christian Science Monitor*
CQ	*Congressional Quarterly*
Current Bio	*Current Biography*
Det News	*Detroit News†*
Det FP	*Detroit Free Press†*
Ga Trend	*Georgia Trend*
Look	*Look* magazine
LA Times	*Los Angeles Times*
Mich Chr	*Michigan Chronicle*
Mil Jrnl	*Milwaukee Journal*
Nat Observer	*National Observer*
NY Mag	*New York* magazine
NYPost	*New York Post*
NYT	*New York Times*
Nwk	*Newsweek*

Observer	Observer Newspaper group†
Phil Inq	*Philadelphia Inquirer*
Sat Eve Post	*Saturday Evening Post*
Sat Rev	*Saturday Review*
TNR	*The New Republic*
US News	*U.S. News & World Report*
VV	*Village Voice*
WP	*Washington Post*
WSJ	*Wall Street Journal*

Also useful were the John V. Lindsay papers at Yale University's Sterling Memorial Library, the Ford Foundation's internal archives, and the Shirley Wohlfield papers at the University of Michigan. In the Notes, they are abbreviated as follows:

JVL papers	John V. Lindsay papers
FF archives	Ford Foundation archives
SW archive	Shirley Wohlfield archive

---

*The *Atlanta Journal* and the *Atlanta Constitution* are jointly owned and jointly published, one in the morning, one in the evening, but they maintain separate editorial pages.

†Though linked since the late 1980s by a joint operating agreement that consolidated advertising, delivery and printing costs, the *Detroit News* and the *Detroit Free Press* are two entirely separate newspapers with different editorial outlooks.

Several editions of the *Observer* newspaper are published each week in suburban Detroit. All editions carry local reportage and advertising, though they share a common editorial page. Together, they make up roughly half of the Observer & Eccentric Newspaper group.

NOTES

NEW YORK

1. Stall-in

The account of the stall-in and its historical context draws on interviews with Sonny Carson, James Farmer, Roy Innis, Kenneth Clark, Robert Curvin and Jervis Anderson, as well as the contemporary press.

Useful books include Sonny Carson's memoir, *The Education of Sonny Carson;* James Farmer's memoir, *Lay Bare the Heart;* James Farmer, *Freedom—When;* August Meier and Elliott Rudwick, *CORE;* Theodore H. White, *The Making of the President 1964;* Benjamin Muse, *The American Negro Revolution;* Anthony Lewis, *Portrait of a Decade;* Robert Penn Warren, *Who Speaks for the Negro?;* Diane Ravitch, *The Great School Wars;* and *Public Papers of the Presidents: Lyndon B. Johnson 1963–64,* Vol. I.

page

16   "I didn't know any": Carson interview.
16   "The NAACP is the Justice Department": Time 6/28/63.
17   "Is he white": Farmer, *Freedom—When?*
17   "When I look": Ibid.
18   "often, for those": Farmer interview.
18   "I think some": NYT 4/21/64.
19   "There was another brother": Carson, *The Education of Sonny Carson.*
20   "on sympathy": Farmer interview.
20   "Don't tell us": Farmer, *Lay Bare the Heart.*
20   "I knew what": Farmer interview.
21   "Harmony is not": Carson interview.
21   "It tore me": Farmer interview.
21   "channelize them": Ibid.
22   "White folks": Carson interview.
22   "would bring New York": Muse, *The American Negro Revolution.*
22   "a Deep South": NYT 2/3/64.
23   "destroyed" and "maybe": Ravitch, *The Great School Wars.*
23   "The battle for": Lewis, *Portrait of a Decade.*

24   "More dramatic": NYT 3/8/64.

24   "a disservice": Muse, *The American Negro Revolution.*

24   "nihilism": Muse, Ibid.

25   "drastically inconveniences": Look 11/21/64.

25   "We are for": NYT 3/4/64.

25   "If I got": NYT 3/16/64.

26   "turn New York City": Ibid.

26   "Civil wrongs": NYT 4/15/64.

27   "We do not see": NYT 4/12/64.

27   "I think" and "We wanted": Carson interview.

27   "relevant confrontation": NYT 4/12/64 and Meier and Rudwick, *CORE.*

27   "hare-brained": Farmer, *Lay Bare the Heart.*

28   "growing frustration": NYT 4/12/64.

29   "positive" and "focused": Ibid.

29   "civil rights president": Farmer interview and writings.

30   "Farmer is our"; Muse, *The American Negro Revolution.* For more on the stall-in itself, see Time 5/1/64, Nwk 5/27/64 and 5/4/67, NYT 4/23/64, Meier and Rudwick, *CORE,* Carson, *The Education of Sonny Carson,* Farmer, *Lay Bare the Heart,* and White, *The Making of the President, 1964.*

31   "We do not try" and "a world": NYT 4/23/64 and *Public Papers of the Presidents: LBJ.*

31   "We were on": Farmer interview.

2. *Out of Sync*

For perspective on the history of the integration idea, I spoke with Kenneth Clark, August Meier, C. Vann Woodward, Jack Greenberg, Glenn Loury, Juan Williams, Robert Curvin, James Farmer, Nathan Glazer, David Garrow, Peter Goldman, Arthur M. Schlesinger, Jr. and Theodore Sorensen, among others.

Useful books on the black protest movement and the history of the integration idea include: Frederick Douglass, *Narrative of the Life;* W. E. B. Du Bois, *The Souls of Black Folk;* David Levering Lewis, *W. E. B. Du Bois;* August Meier, Elliott Rudwick and Francis L. Broderick, eds., *Black Protest Thought in the Twentieth Century;* John Hope Franklin and August Meier, eds., *Black Leaders of the Twentieth Century;* August Meier, *Negro Thought in America;* August Meier and Elliott Rudwick, *From Plantation to Ghetto;* Joanne Grant, ed., *Black Protest;* Harvard Sitkoff, *The Struggle for Black Equality;* Henry Hampton and Steve Fayer, *Voices of Freedom;* Fred Powledge, *Free At Last?;* Juan Williams, ed., *Eyes on the Prize;* E. Franklin Frazier, *The Negro Church in America;* Robert Penn Warren, *Who Speaks for the Negro?;* Charles E. Silberman, *Crisis in Black and White;* Richard Kluger, *Simple Justice;* Bayard Rustin, *Down the Line;* Bayard Rustin, *Strategies for Freedom;* David J. Garrow, *Bearing the Cross;* Taylor Branch, *Parting the Waters;* James M. Washington, *A Testament of Hope;* Martin Luther King, Jr., *Why We Can't Wait;* Martin Luther King, Jr., *Where Do We Go from Here?;* James H. Cone, *Martin and Malcolm and America;* Andrew Young, *An Easy Burden;* James Farmer, *Lay Bare the Heart;* James Farmer, *Freedom—When?;* James Baldwin, *The Fire Next Time;* Kenneth Clark, *Dark Ghetto;* Derrick Bell, *And We Are Not Saved;* Derrick Bell, ed., *Shades of Brown;* and William Brink and Louis Harris, *The Negro Revolution in America.*

Among the books cited on black nationalism and Harlem in the early 1960s: John Henrik Clarke and Amy Jaques Garvey, eds., *Marcus Garvey and the Vision of Africa;* Jervis Anderson, *This Was Harlem;* Samuel M. Johnson, *Often Back;* Essien Essien-Udom, *Black Nationalism;* Theodore Draper, *The Rediscovery of Black Nationalism;* Raymond L. Hall, *Black Separatism;* Neil Hickey and Ed Edwin, *Adam Clayton Powell;* Charles A. Hamilton, *Adam Clayton Powell, Jr.*; Adam Clayton Powell, Jr., *Adam on Adam;* Malcolm X with Alex Haley, *The Autobiography of Malcolm X;* Joe Wood, ed., *Malcolm X;* Peter Goldman, *The Death and Life of Malcolm X;* Bruce Perry, *Malcolm;* George Breitman, ed., *Malcolm X Speaks;* and Harold Cruse, *Plural But Equal.*

Helpful books on white attitudes toward race and integration: Gunnar Myrdal, *An American Dilemma;* Nathan Glazer and Daniel Patrick Moynihan, *Beyond the Melting Pot;* Theodore H. White, *The Making of the President 1964;* Harris Wofford, *Of Kennedys and Kings;* Henry Fairlie, *The Kennedy Promise;* Arthur M. Schlesinger, Jr., *Robert Kennedy and His Times;* Theodore C. Sorensen, ed., *Let the Word Go Forth;* Theodore C. Sorensen, *Kennedy;* and Charles and Barbara Whalen, *The Longest Debate.*

page

33   **"Any black opponent"**: Meier et al., *Black Protest Thought.*
34   **"I tell you"**: Ibid.
34   **"The masses," "hand-picked,"** etc.: Ibid.
34   **"redeem"**: Washington, *Testament of Hope.*
35   **"vengeance" "hatred"** and **"burning house?"**: Baldwin, *The Fire Next Time.*
35   **"The people"**: Meier et al., *Black Protest Thought.*
35   **"'beat' generation"**: Washington, *Testament of Hope.*
35   **"Two–four"**: Powledge, *Free at Last?*
36   **"One feels his"**: Du Bois, *The Souls of Black Folk.*
37   **"Deep in the"**: Farmer, *Lay Bare the Heart* and interview.
37   **"The goal seemed"**: Woodward interview.
38   **"exaggerated Americans"**: Myrdal, *An American Dilemma.*
38   **"The Negro must"**: Meier et al., *Black Protest Thought.*
39   **"Integration became the official agenda"**: Farmer interview.
39   **"Invented by a Northern liberal"**: Malcolm X, *Autobiography.*
40   **"that there was no future"**: Anderson, *This Was Harlem.*
40   **"torrential"**: Hall, *Black Separatism.*
40   **"Up you mighty race"** and **"I am the equal"**: Ibid.
41   **"It was one of the greatest thrills"**: Powell, *Adam by Adam.*
41   **"the fight against racism"**: Clark interview.
41   **"Negro artists"**: Hall, *Black Separatism.*
41   **"voluntary"** and **"diversity"**: *Journal of Negro Education,* Summer 1935.
41   **"wider contacts"**: Ibid.
42   **"hated"**: Ibid.
42   **"What [else]"**: Meier et al; *Black Protest Thought.*
42   **"only a fluid"**: Myrdal, *An American Dilemma.*
43   **"chauvinism"** and **"all-out"**: Ibid.
44   **"desegregated"** and **"the same"**: Bell, *Shades of Brown.*
44   **"the antithesis of racism"**: Clark interview.

44 "of one mind": Woodward interview.

44 "My generation": Bundy interview.

45 "the American Creed" and "the ideals": Myrdal, *An American Dilemma.*

45 "long ago": Ibid.

45 "early definition": Farmer, *Freedom—When?*

45 "doing the same?": Glazer and Moynihan, *Beyond the Melting Pot.*

46 "Separate educational": Kluger, *Simple Justice.*

46 "uncommon word": Cruse, *Plural But Equal.*

47 "eliminated from the nation": Powledge, *Free at Last?*

47 "the Ph.D's": Cone, *Martin and Malcolm.*

47 "tired": Ibid.

48 "end to segregation": Ibid.

48 "Coca-Cola": Farmer, interview.

48 "hotheads" and "freedom high": Young, *An Easy Burden.*

48 "to get in": Warren, *Who Speaks for the Negro?*

49 "negative," "creative" and "dignity": Washington, *Testament of Hope.*

49 "beloved community" and "not enough": Ibid.

49 "proximity," "elbows," "thou," "obligation," etc.: Ibid.

50 "lavish dish": Cruse, *Plural But Equal.*

50 "Boot-Strap": Warren, *Who Speaks for the Negro?*

50 "God's instrument": Cone, *Martin and Malcolm.*

50 "freedom": Washington, *Testament of Hope.*

50 "The moral dimension": Cone, *Martin and Malcolm.*

50 "beacons": Bell, *And We Are Not Saved.*

51 "No one has thought": Glazer and Moynihan, *Beyond the Melting Pot.*

52 "The Man": NYT 7/14/63.

52 "lemme," "too hot" and "hollering": NYT 8/12/63. See also NYT 4/13/63, 5/12/63, and 8/13/63.

53 "Damn" and "Crumbs": NYT 4/13/63.

53 "I deplore their methods": NYT 3/2/61.

53 "the spirit of militance": Johnson, *Often Back.*

54 "the first bad": Hamilton, *Adam Clayton Powell, Jr.,* and Hickey and Edwin, *Adam Clayton Powell.*

54 "Loser," "old ladies" and "Prince": Warren, *Who Speaks for the Negro?,* and Hickey and Edwin, *Adam Clayton Powell.*

55 "The white man": Malcolm X, *Autobiography.*

55 "Separation": Goldman, *The Death and Life.*

55 "General Motors": Meier et al., *Black Protest Thought.*

55 "He didn't take": Wood, *Malcolm X.*

55 "cringe" and "beg": Malcolm X, *Autobiography.*

56 "an American nightmare": Cone, *Martin and Malcolm.*

56 "biscuits": Farmer, *Lay Bare the Heart.*

56 "Malcolm says things": Silberman, *Crisis in Black and White.*

57 "depend," "fight" and "nationalism": NYT 3/24/63. See also Am News 3/30/63, and Hickey and Edwin, *Adam Clayton Powell.*

57 "set back": Am News 3/30/63.

57 "given up": NYT 4/17/63.

57 "stupid," "enemy" and "charity": Am News 3/30/63.

58 "seceded": NYT 4/23/63.

58 "swept along": NYT 8/12/63.

58 "every segment": NYT 4/23/63.

59   "What precisely": Brink and Harris, *The Negro Revolution.*
59   "seemed peripheral": White, *The Making of the President 1964.*
60   "an intellectual grasp": Schlesinger interview.
60   "Negroes laugh," etc.: Brink and Harris, *The Negro Revolution.*
60   "mingle": Sat Eve Post 9/7/63.
60   "there wasn't any interest": Schlesinger, *Robert Kennedy.*
60   "If tokenism": Fairlie, *The Kennedy Promise.*
61   "a moral issue": Sorensen, *Let the Word Go Forth.*
61   "use the word": Sorensen interview.
61   "treated": Sorensen, *Let the Word Go Forth.*
61   "This issue could cost": Whalen, *The Longest Debate.*
62   "Real men": Goldman, *The Death and Life.*
62   "I must catch": Sitkoff, *The Struggle for Black Equality.*
62   "the healthy discontent" and "hate": Warren, *Who Speaks for the Negro?*
63   "Blood may soon": NYT 8/13/63.
64   "two Negro communities" and "kind of culture": White, *The Making of the President 1964.*
64   "principal intellectual leader": Nwk 8/3/64.
64   "cruel": Warren, *Who Speaks for the Negro?*
64   "how psychologically naive": Nwk 5/11/65.
65   "racial damage," "core of doubt" and "inner anxieties": Clark, *Dark Ghetto.*
65   "president," "despondent," "mop" and "flag": Ibid.
65   "dignity": Am News 4/20/63.
66   "emotional horde": NYT 8/29/63.
66   "consensus": Hampton and Fayer, *Voices of Freedom.*
66   "marveled": Sorensen, *Kennedy.*
66   "People were moved": Schlesinger interview.
66   "the finest hour": Am News 8/31/63.
67   "Farce": Goldman, *The Death and Life.*
67   "scorched earth": NYT 6/25/67.
67   "what it meant" and "had no idea": Farmer interview.
68   "golf course": Warren, *Who Speaks for the Negro?*
68   "without bloodshed": NYT 4/23/63.
68   "no mixing": Brink and Harris, *The Negro Revolution.*
69   "go to parties," "like an animal" and "eat with": Ibid.
69   "moral force": NYT 6/20/64.
69   "flower": NYT 6/21/64.
70   "shrug," "paper" and "overdue": NYT 6/20/64.
70   "The Negro mood": Brink and Harris, *The Negro Revolution.*

3. *Looking for "the Solution"*

The story of Lindsay's effort to solve New York's race problem draws on the Lindsay papers in Yale University's Sterling Memorial Library and on interviews with John Lindsay, Barry Gottehrer, Jay Kriegel, Kenneth Clark, Roy Innis, Sonny Carson, James Farmer, McGeorge Bundy, David Garth and Roger Starr, among others.

Useful books include John Lindsay, *The City;* William F. Buckley, Jr., *The Unmaking of a Mayor;* Nat Hentoff, *A Political Life;* Daniel E. Button, *Lindsay;* Woody Klein, *Lindsay's Promise;* Kenneth Clark, *Dark Ghetto;* August Meier and

Elliott Rudwick, *CORE;* Jewel Bellush and Stephen David, eds., *Race and Politics in New York City;* Anthony Lewis, *Portrait of a Decade;* Benjamin Muse, *The American Negro Revolution;* Harvard Sitkoff, *The Struggle for Black Equality;* Theodore White, *The Making of the President 1964;* Lee Rainwater and William L. Yancey, *The Moynihan Report and the Politics of Controversy;* Arthur M. Schlesinger, Jr., *Robert Kennedy and His Times;* Joanne Grant, ed., *Black Protest;* Stokely Carmichael and Charles V. Hamilton, *Black Power;* Samuel Johnson, *Often Back;* and John Henrik Clarke, ed., *Harlem.*

This account draws heavily on the local press, including the *Amsterdam News.* A particularly helpful magazine piece is Roger Starr, "John V. Lindsay: A Political Portrait," *Commentary,* February 1970.

page

72　"Police brutality": NYT 7/12/64.

72　"C'mon": NYT 7/17/64.

72　"It is time to let the Man": Meier and Rudwick, *CORE.*

72　"That's right": Ibid.

73　"a necessary phase": Johnson, *Often Back.*

73　"they find out we mean business": Langston Hughes, "The Harlem Riot," Clarke, *Harlem.*

74　"controls life": Hughes, "The Harlem Riot," Clarke, *Harlem.*

74　"It was a very live issue": Farmer interview.

74　"is the hottest": Nwk 5/31/65.

75　"the foremost issue": notes for a speech, JVL papers.

75　"discrimination": press interview, JVL papers.

75　"to fulfill": Howard University speech, Rainwater and Yancey, *The Moynihan Report.*

76　"longer evade": Rainwater and Yancey, *The Moynihan Report.*

76　"leap-frog": Ibid.

76　"hobbled" and "liberate": Howard University speech, Rainwater and Yancey, *The Moynihan Report.*

77　"gut instinct": Lindsay interview.

77　"first-class": Buckley, *The Unmaking of a Mayor.*

78　"Lochinvar": Nwk 5/31/65.

78　"the solution": Button, *Lindsay.*

78　"to solve the crisis": *Meet the Press* 6/12/66.

78　"There is no shortage": JVL campaign "Policy Statement on Civil Rights," 10/23/65.

79　"All I ask": Nwk 5/31/65.

79　"time for a change": Ibid.

79　"scoundrel" and "a special pleading": Buckley, *The Unmaking of a Mayor.*

79　"junior savages" and "relocate": Ibid.

79　"synthetic," and "members": Ibid.

81　"integrated dust": Ibid.

81　"scared the liberals": Ibid.

83　"governable": Nwk 5/31/65.

83　"Fun City": Pilat, *Lindsay's Campaign.*

84　"Just listen to mine": Klein, *Lindsay's Promise.*

85　"city cared": Lindsay, *The City.*

85　"somebody is interested": NYT 7/19/66.

85   "the ugly silences": Lindsay interview.

85   "how deep poverty": Ibid.

85   "social problems": Ibid.

85   "same old trite phrases": campaign "Policy Statement," 10/23/65.

88   "partners of their city government": notes for speech, JVL papers.

89   "mistakes and there was conflict": Lindsay, *The City.*

89   "very modest expenditure": Klein, *Lindsay's Promise.*

90   "feudal hierarchies": Hentoff, *A Political Life.*

90   "Sometimes I feel": Ibid.

91   "Labor hates": Klein, *Lindsay's Promise.*

91   "puzzling tendency": Ibid.

91   "before he took office": Time 12/16/66.

93   "White blood," "Seize" and "Overrun!": Sitkoff, *The Struggle.*

93   "BLACK POWER": Ibid.

93   "despicable," "inferior," "Race" and "supremacy": Carmichael and Hamilton, *Black Power,* and Grant, *Black Protest.*

93   "I was thrilled": Carson interview.

94   "a feeling of emptiness": Muse, *The American Negro Revolution.*

95   "riot waiting": NYT 9/5/65.

95   "You going to treat us right": NYT 7/9/66.

95   "Is this cat": NYT 7/19/66.

96   "year's most spectacular": NYT 1/7/67.

96   "We don't want": Gottehrer, *The Mayor's Man.*

97   "turf": NYT 6/25/66.

97   "I do not think": Lindsay, *The City.*

97   "It will take more": Klein, *Lindsay's Promise.*

98   "no strategy": Lindsay, *The City.*

98   "bleeding hearts": Klein, *Lindsay's Promise.*

98   "It was a symbolic": Kriegel interview.

99   "raise the morale": flyer, JVL papers.

100   "improper": NYT 5/3/66.

100   "that Negro crime": Buckley, *The Unmaking of a Mayor.*

100   "Who's going": Klein, *Lindsay's Promise.*

101   "terrible": notes of press conference, JVL papers. See also NYT 10/11/66.

101   "injecting a thinly veiled racism": Rogowsky et al., Bellush and David, *Race and Politics.*

101   "inflammatory": Klein, *Lindsay's Promise.*

101   "The suggestion that": Starr, "A Political Portrait," Commentary, February 1970.

101   "I told them": Klein, *Lindsay's Promise.*

102   "Why do you always kowtow": NYT 10/5/66.

102   "doing so much": Klein, *Lindsay's Promise.*

102   "If you're black, get back": NYT 10/20/66.

102   "I can tell": Klein, *Lindsay's Promise.*

103   "They just hadn't registered": Garth interview.

103   "I would regard that as irrelevant": Klein, *Lindsay's Promise.*

103   "on balance," "Negroes" and "racist": Rogowsky et al., Bellush and David, *Race and Politics.*

104   "pushing" and "generally violent": Ibid.

104   "special procedural guarantees": Ibid.

105   "If you're black, get back": NYT 10/20/66.

4. The Fire Next Time

On the Lindsay administration's ghetto outreach and its relationship with Sonny Carson, I spoke with John Lindsay, Sonny Carson, Barry Gottehrer, Roy Innis, Kenneth Clark and Jay Kriegel. I also relied heavily on the local press.

Useful books include: Barry Gottehrer, *The Mayor's Man;* John Lindsay, *The City;* Sonny Carson, *The Education of Sonny Carson;* Woody Klein, *Lindsay's Promise;* August Meier and Elliott Rudwick, *CORE;* William Brink and Louis Harris, *Black and White;* Nat Hentoff, *A Political Life;* Godfrey Hodgson, *America in Our Time; The Report of the National Advisory Commission on Civil Disorders* (Kerner Report); Tom Hayden, *Rebellion in Newark;* Jack Newfield, *Robert Kennedy;* Jervis Anderson, *Bayard Rustin;* Robert Weisbrot, *Freedom Bound;* Benjamin Muse, *The American Negro Revolution;* and Henry Hampton and Steve Fayer, *Voices of Freedom.*

Page

106	"complaints" and "liaison": Gottehrer interview.
107	"potential leaders": Ibid.
107	"would hurt the poor": Gottehrer, *The Mayor's Man.*
108	"power brokers" and "poverty pimps": Ibid.
108	"expression of racial unity": Ibid.
108	"the Al Sharpton": Lindsay interview.
109	"There were lots of kids": Gottehrer interview.
109	"They would stand on a soap box": Ibid.
109	"A black man today": Time 8/11/67.
109	"What the Negro wants": Meier and Rudwick, *CORE.*
110	"the father": NYT 7/8/66.
110	"What we need is a few more riots": Time 7/15/66.
110	"make integration irrelevant": NYT 7/2/66 and Meier and Rudwick, *CORE.*
110	"I don't want to be a white man": NYT 7/8/66.
110	"sell-outs": NYT 7/2/66.
110	"self-determination": Meier and Rudwick, *CORE.*
111	"We are not anti-white" and "I would be against myself": NYT 7/4/66.
111	"What Black Power is all about": NYT 7/24/66.
111	"ultimate solution": Ibid.
111	"dying philosophy": NYT 7/3/66 and Meier and Rudwick, *CORE.*
111	"are no longer": Meier and Rudwick, *CORE.*
111	"but being black is not a program": Anderson, *Bayard Rustin.*
113	"Students don't see": NYT 10/25/65.
113	"the long, cold winter": Brink and Harris, *Black and White.*
114	"[We thought] integration": NYT 6/18/67.
114	"open invitation": Weisbrot, *Freedom Bound.*
114	"It is time": Muse, *The American Negro Revolution.*
115	"opening up a few more play streets": Hentoff, *A Political Life.*
115	"No, I don't believe so": *Meet the Press* 6/12/66.
116	"Last summer": NYT 4/29/67.
116	"to get to": Kriegel interview.
117	"lollipop programs": Muse, *The American Negro Revolution.*
117	"I ain't got no quarrel": Hampton and Fayer, *Voices of Freedom.*
117	"[These kids] now believe": NYT 8/6/67.
118	"We want jobs!": NYT 7/8/67.

119   "symbol of the oppression": Muse, *The American Negro Revolution.*
120   "two separate nations": NYT 7/24/67.
120   "I love violence": Time 7/28/67.
120   "Everyone knows Whitey's a devil": NYT 7/24/67.
121   "stomped [him]": Time 7/28/67.
121   "Get your guns" and "to explode": Muse, *The American Negro Revolution.*
121   "not a riot": NYT 7/24/67.
121   "Manhattan was ravaged": NYT 7/28/67.
122   "close to the top": Gottehrer, *The Mayor's Man.*
122   "good way": Carson interview.
122   "ball game is being played": Newfield, *Robert Kennedy.*
123   "committed to change": Gottehrer interview.
123   "represented something": Lindsay interview.
123   "somebody we had to deal with": Gottehrer interview.
123   "call on Friday": Ibid.
123   "If there were an incident": Ibid.
124   "I doubt he ever stopped anything": Ibid.
124   "small insurrection": NYT 7/30/67.
124   "We have a long way": Ibid.
124   "We're tired" and "Yeah!": Ibid.
124   "was only a skirmish": Ibid.
125   "Kids are sore": Ibid.
125   "That was power": Carson interview.
125   "white cop": Gottehrer, *The Mayor's Man.*
125   "uglier mood": Lindsay, *The City.*
125   "[The mayor's] presence": Gottehrer, *The Mayor's Man.*
126   "pure fury" and "Look": Lindsay, *The City.*
126   "was listening": Ibid.
126   "tall, blond John": Carson, *The Education of Sonny Carson.*
127   "a lot of gunfire": Gottehrer, *The Mayor's Man.*
128   "mad dogs": Time 8/4/67.
128   "a bunch of savages": Ibid.
128   "go kill": Hayden, *Rebellion in Newark.*
128   "anti-rat," etc.: Muse, *The American Negro Revolution.*
128   "Their people are as mad as hell": Time 8/11/67.
128   "It's like laughing": Harris and Brink, *Black and White.*
129   "Those monkeys": Time 8/4/67.
131   "The meeting": Gottehrer, *The Mayor's Man.*
131   "when you are in control": Carson interview.
131   "immediately": Gottehrer interview.
131   "Sonny was mainly interested": Gottehrer, *The Mayor's Man.*

5. The Last Gasp of Liberalism

The story of Lindsay and the Kerner Commission draws heavily on the Lindsay papers at Yale University's Sterling Memorial Library and on interviews with John Lindsay, Jay Kriegel, Barry Gottehrer, Kenneth Clark, James Farmer, Sonny Carson and David Garth.

Useful books include: *Report of the National Advisory Commission on Civil Disorders* (Kerner Report); Peter Goldman, *Report from Black America;* Fred Harris and

Roger Wilkins, eds., *Quiet Riots;* William H. Grier and Price M. Cobbs, *Black Rage;* August Meier and Elliott Rudwick, *CORE;* John Lindsay, *The City;* Barry Gottehrer, *The Mayor's Man;* Christopher Lasch, *The Agony of the American Left;* Nathan Glazer and Daniel Patrick Moynihan, *Beyond the Melting Pot;* Kenneth Clark, *Dark Ghetto;* Harvard Sitkoff, *The Struggle for Black Equality;* and Benjamin Muse, *The American Negro Revolution.*

page

133   "abrasive": NYT 1/11/68.
133   "He was engrossed": Kriegel interview.
133   "I began feeling": Nwk 11/20/67.
134   "expert": Kriegel interview.
134   "The situation facing the Negro": Nwk 12/4/67.
136   "dress rehearsals": NYT 8/7/67.
136   "rebellions against oppression": NYT 8/1/67.
136   "a necessary phrase" Time 8/4/67.
136   "We condemn": Muse, *The American Negro Revolution.*
136   "killing" and "Negro": NYT 7/27/67.
137   "young men": NYT 8/6/67.
137   "coherent" "riots," and "looting": NYT 8/13/67.
137   "the difficulty," "unbalanced," "self-destructive" and "suicidal": NYT 8/6/67.
138   "I find myself": Ibid.
138   "fever pitch" and "Stop expressing": NYT 8/20/67.
138   Poll figures on black reaction are from Goldman, *Report.*
139   "the white man's errand boys": Time 8/11/67.
139   "moderate" and "gradualist": Ibid.
140   "American as cherry pie": Sitkoff, *The Struggle for Black Equality.*
140   "it would be controversial": Lindsay interview.
140   "then best-sellers in history": NYT 3/14/68.
140   "overstate the importance": John Herbers, Harris and Wilkins, *Quiet Riots.*
141   "tough and fiery": Kriegel interview.
141   "and it was a stunner": Ibid.
141   "the Negro can never forget": Kerner report.
142   "white society" and "white morality": memo, JVL papers.
142   "white racism": Kerner report.
142   "to tell it like it is": Nwk 3/11/68.
142   "It was a report about choices": Kriegel interview.
142   "These programs will require unprecedented": Kerner report.
142   "We're on our way to the moment of truth": Nwk 3/11/68.
143   "would voluntarily": Ibid.
143   "a single nation": Ibid.
143   "divide people": NYT 3/7/68.
143   "group guilt": NYT 3/25/68.
145   "greatest mayor": NYT 4/20/68.
145   "exactly the right phrase": Nwk 3/18/68.
145   "America uncomfortable": ABC *Issues and Answers* 2/28/68.
146   "excuses": NYT 3/10/68.
146   "Spend more": Congressman Durward Halls, NYT 3/2/68.
146   "and everybody else": Time 3/15/68.
146   "message," "with vacuous" and "slogans": NYT 4/22/68.

147   Figures on public reaction are from a Harris poll released by the LA Times syndicate 4/16/68.
147   "**although higher taxes**": Ibid.
147   "**the etiquette**": Glazer and Moynihan, *Beyond the Melting Pot.*
148   "**right to live**" and "**maintain**": NYT 1/17/68.
148   "**bigotry**": Ibid.
148   "**We do not seek**": Goldman, *Report.*
148   "**It didn't come about**": NYT 10/1/67.
148   "**peaceful coexistence**": NYT 12/17/67.
148   "**The assimilationist argument**": Lasch, *The Agony of the American Left.*
148   *The Partisan Review* symposium was in the Spring 1968 issue.
149   "**Separatism has become**": NYT 12/17/68.
149   "**gathering momentum**": Ibid.
149   Figures on black attitudes toward integration come from Goldman, *Report.*
150   "**bitch**," "**Reich**," "**killed**" and "**on fire**": NYT 2/25/68. For more on the I.S. 201 meeting and New Yorkers' reactions, see also NYT 2/22/68, 2/26/68, 2/27/68, and 3/1/68.
150   "**hunting season**": NYT 2/25/68.
150   "**racism**": NYT 2/26/68.
150   "**that such pilot efforts**": press release, JVL papers.
151   "**People like Ferguson**": NYT 2/25/68.
151   "**condemning that kind of talk**": Ibid.
151   "**very difficult**," "**showdowns**" and "**fanned the flames**": Ibid.
151   "**my life is over**": NY Mag 4/19/93.
152   "**I'm sorry**": Lindsay interview.
152   "**Brothers—**": Nwk 4/15/68.
152   "**was holding**": Lindsay interview.
152   "**Cohen's**": Nwk 4/15/68.
153   "**My King**": Ibid.
153   "**Go home**," "**I don't want**," and "**war**": Ibid.
153   "**This is the only answer**" and "**die fighting**": Ibid.
153   "**cool it**": Kenyatta, NYT 4/6/68.
154   "**older established persons**": notes for remarks, JVL papers.
154   "**temptation to strike back**": NYT 4/6/68.
154   "**Hello**" and "**for five bucks**": Gottehrer, *The Mayor's Man.*
155   "**tribute**" and "**remembrance**": NYT Mag 4/19/93.
155   "**kept the faith**" and "**[skeptics] are wrong**": NYT 4/8/68 and speech notes in JVL papers.
155   "**this tragedy**": NBC 4/7/68, transcript, JVL papers.
155   "**you will**," "**under you**," "**you, the young**" and "**not abandon you**": broadcast text, JVL papers.
156   "**too late**": NYT 4/11/68.
156   "**to create a single society**": notes of press conference, JVL papers.
157   "**Band-Aids**": NYT 4/20/68.
157   "**riot-stopping**": Ibid.

6. "It's Not an Either/Or"

My account of the New York school situation relies heavily on the contemporary press and the Ford Foundation's internal archives, as well as on interviews with McGeorge Bundy, John Lindsay, Kenneth Clark, Frederick Nauman, Sonny Carson, Al Sharpton, Barry Gottehrer, Jay Kriegel, James Comer and David Shipler.

In the Ford Foundation archives, McGeorge Bundy's speeches, memos, and draft writings were particularly helpful, along with Mario Fantini's memos of 11/21/66 and 11/28/66.

Useful books include David Rogers, *110 Livingston Street;* Diane Ravitch, *The Great School Wars;* Jewel Bellush and Stephen David, eds., *Race and Politics in New York City;* Maurice R. Berube and Marilyn Gittell, eds., *Confrontation at Ocean Hill–Brownsville;* Sonny Carson, *The Education of Sonny Carson;* Stokely Carmichael and Charles V. Hamilton, *Black Power;* Woody Klein, *Lindsay's Promise;* Barry Gottehrer, *The Mayor's Man;* William F. Buckley, Jr., *The Unmaking of a Mayor;* and Henry Hampton and Steve Fayer, *Voices of Freedom.*

Particularly helpful articles include Martin Mayer, "Washington's Grant to the Ford Foundation," NYT 11/13/66; Maurice J. Goldbloom, "The New York School Crisis," *Commentary*, January 1969; and Fred Ferretti, "Who's to Blame in the School Strike," *New York* magazine, 11/18/68.

page

158   "community control": Carmichael and Hamilton, *Black Power.*
159   "We had to do something": Lindsay interview.
160   "My idea of the solution": Bundy interview.
161   "It implies": internal memo in FF archive, November 1966.
161   "have their own control": Ibid.
161   "be presented": Ibid.
162   "society is going to want": NYT 11/13/66.
162   "obvious issue": Bundy interview.
162   "The road from right": speech in FF archive, 8/2/66.
162   "improvements in skills": Ibid.
163   "Picketing is better than": press interview text in FF archive.
163   "the New York City syndrome": Rogers, *110 Livingston Street.*
163   "immediately" and "Anyone who talks": Ravitch, *The Great School Wars.*
165   "destroyed" and "instant": Ibid.
165   "unrealistic": speech, November 1963, text in author's possession.
166   "Have child" and "sick child": Rogers, *110 Livingston Street.*
167   "here as in the South": Bundy interview.
168   "they were hateful of blacks": background interview.
169   "interests," "accountable" and "conflict": Rogers, *110 Livingston Street*, and Ravitch, *The Great School Wars.*
169   "Integration or": NYT 8/13/66.
169   "We feel that the involvement": Ravitch, *The Great School Wars.*
170   "responsible for any action": Ibid.
170   "Ginzburg and Rosenberg": Ibid.
171   "the hell with it": Klein, *Lindsay's Promise.*
172   "poor return": Lindsay interview.
173   "radical": Roy Innis, NYT 3/2/67.
173   "community," "evaluate" and "fired": Carson interview.
173   "we are kidding": Ravitch, *The Great School Wars.*
173   "I hope you die." Carson, *Education.*
173   "this great big": Ibid.
174   "The Germans": NYT 9/13/67.
174   "race hatred": report in FF archive.

174 "effort-free": Bundy interview.
175 "find someone": Ibid.
176 "They were punching": Shipler interview.
176 "I had been a strong supporter": Nauman interview.
177 "defensive" and "excited": Hampton and Fayer, *Voices of Freedom.*
178 "Any suggestions": Ibid.
178 "The ending of oppression": Ravitch, *The Great School Wars.*
179 "keep teachers in line": Ibid.
179 "Don't come back": Kemble, Berube and Gittell, *Confrontation.*
180 "It was not skills": Hampton and Fayer, *Voices of Freedom.*
180 "[We were] taking on": Ibid.
180 "were representative": Nauman interview.
180 Poll numbers are in Berube and Gittell, *Confrontation,* and Hampton and Fayer, *Voices of Freedom.*
181 "community didn't exist": Shipler interview.
181 "advising the board": Carson interview.
181 "family-like" and "I'm locked": Ferretti, "Who's to Blame in the School Strike," NY Mag 11/18/68.
181 "to destroy": VV 6/6/89.
181 "was an ideologue.": Nauman interview.
182 "[We] put our trust": draft report in FF archive.
183 "racial feelings": Bundy interview.
183 "There is only one bar": preface to FF 1967 annual report.
183 "It's not an either/or": Bundy interview.
183 "the plainest of facts": preface to FF 1967 annual report.
183 "the preachers of hate": Ibid.
183 "spume on the wave": Ibid.
183 "legitimate": Ibid.
184 "Integration must be deferred": report in FF archive.
184 "shows an incredible lack": Goldbloom, "The New York School Crisis," Commentary, January 1969.
184 "Negro teachers": Ibid.
184 "a potential breeder of apartheid": Ravitch, *The Great School Wars.*
184 "interference": Ibid.
185 "terror" and "Threats and intimidation": NYT 2/6/68.
186 "We would oppose any": Ravitch, *The Great School Wars.*
188 "begging" and "we'll either be independent": NYT 7/14/68.
188 "Wake up": Goldbloom, "The New York School Crisis," Commentary, January 1969.
188 "could not share": Nauman interview.
188 "steal from" and "graveyard": Goldbloom, "The New York School Crisis," Commentary, January 1969.
188 "frightened" and "to see things differently": Nauman interview.
189 "a confrontation": NYT 11/13/66.
189 "hunting season": Ravitch, *The Great School Wars.*
189 "to contain guerrilla warfare": Ibid.

7. *"Confrontation Works"*

This account of the Ocean Hill–Brownsville experiment and the 1968 strikes relies heavily on the contemporary press and the Ford Foundation's internal archives, as well as on interviews with Frederick Nauman, Sonny Carson, Al

Sharpton, McGeorge Bundy, John Lindsay, Kenneth Clark, David Garth, Barry Gottehrer, Jay Kriegel and David Shipler.

Useful books include Diane Ravitch, *The Great School Wars;* Naomi Levine with Richard Cohen, *Ocean Hill–Brownsville;* Maurice R. Berube and Marilyn Gittell, eds., *Confrontation at Ocean Hill–Brownsville;* Jonathan Kaufman, *Broken Alliance;* Sonny Carson, *The Education of Sonny Carson;* Barry Gottehrer, *The Mayor's Man;* Allon Schoener, ed., *Harlem on My Mind;* August Meier and Elliott Rudwick, eds., *Black Protest in the Sixties;* Harold Cruse, *The Crisis of the Negro Intellectual;* Eldridge Cleaver, *Soul on Ice;* and Henry Hampton and Steve Fayer, *Voices of Freedom.*

Among many contemporary articles about the strikes, Maurice J. Goldbloom's "The New York School Crisis," *Commentary,* January 1969, was particularly useful.

Two other helpful documents were the ADL report, "Anti-Semitism in the New York City School Controversy," January 1969, and the report of Mayor Lindsay's Special Committee on Racial and Religious Prejudice, January 1969.

page

190   **"own rules"**: Ravitch, *The Great School Wars.*
191   **"community"**: Berube and Gittell, *Confrontation.*
191   **"At no time"**: Hampton and Fayer, *Voices of Freedom.*
191   **"Not one"**: Ravitch, *The Great School Wars.*
191   **"disloyalty"** and **"baby-sitting"**: Berube and Gittell, *Confrontation.*
191   **"mind control"**: VV 6/6/89.
191   **"means we decide"**: Ravitch, *The Great School Wars.*
191   **"The kids"**: NYT 5/14/68.
193   **"One strike"**: Time 5/29/72.
193   **"The [smaller]"**: Current Bio 1969.
194   **"We in the UFT"**: NYT 5/11/68.
195   **"sabotage,"** **"inappropriate,"** and **"failing"**: Rivers Report, Berube and Gittell, *Confrontation.*
195   **"hearsay"**: Ibid.
196   **"oppose"** and **"constructive"**: Ibid.
196   **"[We] never formally"**: Goldbloom, "The New York School Crisis," Commentary, January 1969.
196   **"transfers"**: contemporary press and Lindsay interview.
196   **"great guy"**: NYT 7/16/68.
197   **"I am a dictator"**: NYT 9/4/68.
198   **"open up a field day"**: NYT 9/1/68.
198   **"washed their hands"**: Hampton and Fayer, *Voices of Freedom.*
198   **"The union really had no choice"**: Ibid.
199   **"no longer act as a buffer"**: Ravitch, *The Great School Wars.*
199   **"the lights out"**: Goldbloom, "The New York School Crisis," Commentary, January 1969. For more on what happened that day at I.S. 55, see also NYT 2/2/69, Naomi Levine, *Ocean Hill–Brownsville,* Sandra Feldman exchange with Maurice Berube in Berube and Gittell, *Confrontation,* and the ADL's January 1969 report, "Anti-Semitism in the New York City School Controversy."
199   **"faggots"**: Levine, *Ocean Hill–Brownsville.*
200   **"pine boxes"**: Feldman-Berube exchange, Berube and Gittell, *Confrontation.*
200   **"little lady"**: Levine, *Ocean Hill–Brownsville.*

200   "**He told us**": Nauman interview.
200   "**pigs**": ADL report "Anti-Semitism," January 1969.
200   "**Why don't**": Levine, *Ocean Hill–Brownsville*.
201   "**99 percent**" and "**affectionate**": VV 10/21/68.
201   "**more or less**": NYT 2/2/69.
201   "**All of the abuse**": NYT 11/24/68.
201   "**drop dead!**": Ibid.
201   "**The students**" and "**belched**": Ibid.
202   "**There were a lot of volatile moments**": Hampton and Fayer, *Voices of Freedom*.
203   "**No one was immune**": Sharpton interview.
203   "**You couldn't avoid it**": Sharpton interview.
203   "**teachers who give a damn**": Nwk 10/28/68.
204   "**I don't want**": Kaufman, *Broken Alliance*.
204   "**You can't just have biology**": Karima Jordan, Hampton and Fayer, *Voices of Freedom*.
204   "**atmosphere of warmth**": Sol Stern, *Ramparts* 12/17/68.
204   "**The holy flame**": NYT 11/6/68.
204   "**I can see**": NYT 9/20/68.
205   "**The real**": Ibid.
205   "**some abstract something**": Karima Jordan, Hampton and Fayer, *Voices of Freedom*.
205   "**I saw them as role models**": Sharpton interview.
206   "**Whitey doesn't want to give us anything**" and "**Molotov**": Goldbloom, "The New York School Crisis," Commentary, January 1969, and Berube and Gittell, *Confrontation*.
206   "**I'm not sure**": Nauman interview.
206   "**transformed**": Carson interview.
207   "**frequent demonstrators**": NYT 19/15/68.
207   "**White people**": Gottehrer, *The Mayor's Man*.
207   "**repudiation of Carson**": Nauman interview.
208   "**Middle-East murderers**": Kaufman, *Broken Alliance*.
208   "**If African American history and culture is important**": Ibid.
209   "**We're gonna piss**": Ibid.
000   "**The Weinsteins**": ADL report, "Anti–Semitism," January 1969.
209   "**The Jew**": NY Mag 19/10/83.
209   "**whitey textbooks**": Kaufman, *Broken Alliance*.
209   "**You have to**": Ibid.
210   "**Joseph McCarthy**": NYT 11/11/68.
210   "**The countless incidents**": report of Mayor Lindsay's Special Committee on Racial and Religious Prejudice, January 1969.
211   "**We had become sort of heroes**": Hampton and Fayer, *Voices of Freedom*.
211   "**Lindsay leans**": NYPost 3/12/69.
211   "**He's a blankety-blank**": Ibid.
211   "**say 'Jew'**": NYT 4/9/67. See also Baldwin, "The Harlem Ghetto," Commentary, February 1948.
211   "**anti-white**": NYT 10/20/89.
211   "**was incidental**": Hampton and Fayer, *Voices of Freedom*.
212   "**Jew pig!**": Levine, *Ocean Hill–Brownsville*.
212   "**Nigger lover!**": Time 10/25/68.
212   "**Middle-East murderer!**": ADL report, "Anti-Semitism," January 1969.
213   "**We will die for Rhody**": Nwk 10/28/68.
213   "**specifics**": John Doar, CBS *Face the Nation* 11/10/68.
213   "**extremists**": NYT 10/16/68.

214   "We want": Ibid.
214   "Jewish faith": Ibid.
214   "Lindsay Must Go!": Ibid.
215   "what Shanker had done": Gottehrer interview.
215   "was not all that distressing": Bundy interview.
215   "I still believe in that track": Ibid.
217   "Operation Liberation": NYT 12/6/68.
217   "You better": Ibid.
218   "little Sonny Carsons": Carson interview.
218   "excitement": Sharpton interview.
218   "Everyone was involved": Ibid.
218   "It was like a rampage": Ibid.
219   "Hey, Jew boy": Kaufman, *Broken Alliance.*
219   "People should": Ibid.
219   "beautiful" and "true": Nwk 2/10/69 and ADL, "Anti-Semitism," January 1969.
219   "no anti-Semitic overtones": NYT 1/20/69.
219   "more power to Hitler": NYT 1/25/69.
219   "I'm particularly disturbed": NYT 1/19/69.
219   "Behind every": NYT 1/22/69.
220   "Our contempt": Ibid.
220   "I assumed": Allon Schoener, Schoener, *Harlem on My Mind.*
220   "confrontation works": Sharpton interview.
221   Poll is reported by Rowland Evans and Robert Novak in the NYPost 3/12/69.
221   "The days": Ibid.
221   "The forces of reaction": Nwk 6/30/69.
222   "What's a": NYT 8/10/69.
222   "Moses" and "My heart": Ibid.
223   "He's the guy": Time 10/17/69.
223   "chiselers": NYT 8/10/69.
223   "limousine": Time 10/3/69.
223   "one standard": NYT 10/17/69.
223   "coddling criminals" and "blow": NYT 8/10/69.
223   "rape was": Cleaver, *Soul on Ice.*
224   "I'm a bigot": Nwk 11/17/69.
224   "I'm not the man you want": WP 9/29/69.
224   "anti-black": anonymous Jewish leader, NYT 10/10/69.
225   "ball game": NYT 9/15/69.
225   "I made a mistake": Garth interview.
225   "The Jewish voter": NYT 9/15/69.
225   "liberal faith": Nwk 11/17/69.
226   "the Athens": Nwk 10/6/69.

DETROIT

8. *Bending the Rules*

The story of Max Fisher and the New Detroit Committee draws on the local press, including the suburban Observer Newspaper chain, and interviews with Fisher, Joseph Hudson, Irving Bluestone and Douglas Fraser. For Detroit's racial past, I spoke with Coleman Young, Philip Power, Damon Keith, Max Fisher, Joseph Hudson, Douglas Fraser, Irving Bluestone, Pete Waldmeir, Richard Austin, Brooks Patterson, Irene McCabe, Freddie Williams, Reynolds Farley, Thomas Bray, George Cantor, Ze'ev Chafets, Tom Sugrue, Tom Delisle and Bob Berg, among others.

Useful books include Sidney Fine, *Violence in the Model City;* Robert Conot, *American Odyssey;* Melvin Holli, ed., *Detroit;* Joe T. Darden et al., *Detroit, Race and Uneven Development;* B.J. Widick, *Detroit;* Joel D. Aberbach and Jack L. Walker, *Race in the City;* Scott McGehee and Susan Watson, eds., *Blacks in Detroit;* The New Detroit Committee's 1968 *Progress Report;* Jon C. Teaford, *The Rough Road to Renaissance;* Eleanor P. Wolf, *Trial and Error;* Peter Golden, *Quiet Diplomat.*

Three helpful academic articles: Reynolds Farley et al., "Chocolate City, Vanilla Suburbs," Farley et al., "Barriers to the Racial Integration of Neighborhoods," and Tom J. Sugrue, "Crabgrassroots Politics." I have also quoted from the transcripts of the Detroit Strategic Planning Project's July 1987 *Conference on Race Relations.*

page

229   "It was quite a shock": Fisher interview.
230   "I'd lived here": Ibid.
231   "old pair of socks": from Teaford, *Rough Road.*
231   "They thought": Hudson interview.
232   "We got involved": Ibid.
232   "putting out fires": Golden, *Quiet Diplomat.*
232   "change attitudes": Fisher interview.
232   "We thought": Ibid.
232   "It was a new thing": Ibid.
232   "invite blacks to parties": Ibid.
232   "No matter": NDC *Progress Report.*
233   "dealt in harsh realities": Young interview.
233   "the niceties of life": Ibid.
235   "Negro invasion": Sugrue, "Crabgrassroots."
237   "White people cannot abide a situation": Ibid.
238   "American Dream": Power interview.
238   "revolt": Aberbach and Walker, *Race in the City.*
238   "What you had in 1967": Detroit Strategic Planning Project 1987 *Conference on Rice Relations.*
239   "the birth pangs": Ebony, April 1978.
239   "a surprise pregnancy": Ebony, Ibid.
239   "Black Metropolis": Widick, *Detroit.*
239   "chocolate city": Farley et al., "Chocolate City."
239   rebellion: Widick, *Detroit.*
239   "Negroes in Detroit" and "only militant and more militant": Fine, *Violence in the Model City.*
240   "It is our duty": Widick, *Detroit.*
240   "as much our problem": Observer 7/26/67.
240   "bring blacks into the process": Fisher interview.
241   "We knew": Hudson interview.
241   "the Hudson committee": Fine, *Violence in the Model City.*
241   "Street kids and CEOs": Hudson interview.
241   "the natural Americanization machine" and "part of American society": Golden, *Quiet Diplomat.*
241   "within a fairly short space": NDC *Progress Report.*

241　"ventilation": Fisher interview

241　"haranguing": Hudson interview.

241　"It was a place for airing": Fisher interview.

242　"We crusty CEOs": Hudson interview.

242　"stone faces": Conot, *American Odyssey.*

243　"White customers were upset": Hudson interview.

243　"fat cats": Fine, *Violence in the Model City* and Bluestone interview.

243　"some crumbs": Ibid.

244　"bloody": Ibid.

244　"Burn whitey": Widick, *Detroit.*

244　"There was a great, great need": Hudson interview.

244　"It eased the antagonism": Bluestone interview.

245　"guys with rifles": Nwk 4/14/69. Other accounts of the New Bethel incident include NYT 3/31/69, NYT 4/1/69, NYT 4/4/69, WP 4/1/69, Time 4/11/69, Det News 4/6/69.

246　"sacrifice them": Fine, *Violence in the Model City.*

247　"that he doesn't belong on the court": anonymous judge, NYT 2/19/74.

247　"con man": Ibid.

248　"in the only appropriate way": Fine, *Violence in the Model City.*

249　"hero of these trying times": NYT 4/4/69.

249　"If Crockett goes": Fine, *Violence in the Model City.*

249　"The people who elected me": Esquire, December 1970.

249　"If the white judge's law in Alabama": Am Op June 1969.

249　"to pore through the law": Det News 4/6/69.

249　"If you don't get me an appointment": Fisher interview.

250　"You don't know", "Let us," and "In my honest judgment": Golden, *Quiet Diplomat.*

250　"It was a hard call": Fisher interview.

250　"justifiable basis": NDC statement, text in author's possession.

250　"regret": Fine, *Violence in the Model City.*

251　"as a losing battle": Tom Delisle interview.

252　"almost every white": Time 4/6/70.

252　"Walk in twos after dark": Time 4/6/70.

252　"They didn't seem that interested": Fisher interview.

252　"volunteer fatigue": Widick, *Detroit.*

252　"largely unfulfilled": NDC *Progress Report.*

253　"unrealistic" and "irrelevant": Ibid.

253　"employers unwittingly supported the myth": Ibid.

253　"screen them in": Fine, *Violence in the Model City.*

256　"We became aware of ourselves": Chr Sci Mon 7/23/86.

257　"debating society": Hudson interview.

257　"get down to programs": Conot, *American Odyssey.*

257　"force the market": Golden, *Quiet Diplomat.*

258　"You won't get": Hudson interview.

258　"give something back": Golden, *Quiet Diplomat.*

9. Blocking the Buses

The story of Irene McCabe and the Detroit-area busing wars relies on interviews with her, Brooks Patterson, Philip Power, Coleman Young, Richard Austin, Douglas Fraser and Gary Orfield, among others. On the national busing story, I also spoke with Kenneth Clark, Nathan Glazer and Diane Ravitch.

Along with other local and national press sources, I drew on reporting and editorial comment in the suburban Observer & Eccentric Newspaper chain, including Philip Power's regular column through this period. Also extremely helpful was the Shirley Wohlfield archive at the University of Michigan in Ann Arbor.

Useful books include Eleanor P. Wolf, *Trial and Error;* J. Harvie Wilkinson, III, *From Brown to Bakke;* Paul R. Dimond, *Beyond Busing;* Gary Orfield, *Must We Bus?;* Sidney Fine, *Violence in the Model City;* Robert Conot, *American Odyssey;* Scott McGehee and Susan Watson, eds., *Blacks in Detroit;* Joe T. Darden et al., *Detroit, Race and Uneven Development;* Joel D. Aberbach and Jack L. Walker, *Race in the City;* Douglas S. Massey and Nancy A. Denton, *American Apartheid.*

Helpful articles: William R. Grant, "Community Control vs. School Integration—The Case of Detroit," Reynolds Farley et al., "Chocolate City, Vanilla Suburbs," Farley et al., "Barriers to the Racial Integration of Neighborhoods," and Tom J. Sugrue, "Crabgrassroots Politics."

The U.S Supreme Court decision is *Milliken, Gov. of Michigan, et al.* v. *Bradley et al.*

page

260   "blue-collar working-class": Det News 10/10/71.
260   "I never used to even stop to think": Ibid.
260   "Publicity, attention—every day": Nat Observer 4/10/72.
260   "You can't run over the American flag": NYT 9/9/91.
261   "We've shown what the people of Pontiac think": NYT 9/15/71.
262   "undesirable elements" and "hordes": Sugrue, "Crabgrassroots Politics."
262   "this is a free country": Darden et al., *Detroit.*
263   "I don't know why you'd want to buy": Dimond, *Beyond Busing.*
263   "mental maps": Wolf, *Trial and Error.*
263   "belong": Reynolds Farley interview.
265   "I was so naive": Nwk Feature Service 3/16/72.
266   "We're dumb": Det News 10/10/71.
266   "one of my closest girl friends": Ibid.
267   "A mother is a mother": NAG leaflet, SW archive.
267   "guinea pigs," "losing control" and "giant social experiment": NAG documents and Wohlfield speeches in SW archive.
267   "I think the black parents instilled hatred": Det News 10/10/72.
267   "crime-blackboard jungle": and "no discipline": speech notes, SW archive.
267   "It's in an area of town": Det News 10/10/72.
267   "There was an incident": Nwk Feature Service 3/16/72.
268   "In some schools": Carl Gregory, NYT 4/15/68.
268   "If you think about it": Power interview.
270   "They did not want their children bused": Wolf, *Trial and Error.*
270   "None of us": Dimond, *Beyond Busing.*
271   "most people": Malcolm Dade, Wolf, *Trial and Error.*
271   "If you don't know anything": McGehee and Watson, *Blacks in Detroit.*
271   "The issue had been drawn": Dimond, *Beyond Busing.*
272   "We were groping": NAACP general counsel Nathaniel Jones, Dimond, *Beyond Busing.*
274   "by the numbers," "forced feeding" and "integration's sake": Dimond, *Beyond Busing,* and Wolf, *Trial and Error.*
274   "a conscious, deliberate, progressive and contnuous attempt": Dimond, *Beyond Busing.*
274   "pockets": Ibid.

274   "The quandary of a man": Ibid.
275   "forces of evil" and "unfortunate": Wolf, *Trial and Error.*
275   "conversion": Dimond, *Beyond Busing.*
276   "There is enough blame": Ibid.
277   "The court has made its determination": Ibid.
279   "Rumor and mythology": Wolf, *Trial and Error.*
279   "detest the idea": Observer 8/5/72.
279   "Pith" and "molester": Dimond, *Beyond Busing.*
280   "I hope": Ibid.
280   "ducking the issue": Observer 4/26/72.
280   "Parents who may": Observer 2/25/70.
280   "We were losing control": McCabe interview.
280   "The ordinary guy": Observer 8/9/72.
281   "class excursions": Wilkinson, *From Brown to Bakke.*
281   "Busing legitimated a white backlash": Power interview.
281   "The Agony of Busing": Time 11/15/71.
282   "If the federal government is going to reach": Ibid.
282   "merely slowed": Aberbach and Walker, *Race in the City.*
282   "Two valid aspirations": NYT 9/26/71.
283   "Marie Antoinette liberalism": Stewart Alsop, Nwk 10/18/71.
283   "I feel like I'm inferior": Time 3/13/72.
283   "This busing is callous and asinine": Time 3/11/72.
284   "to do whatever is necessary": CQ 12/7/71.
285   "It's not the distance": Wilkinson, *From Brown to Bakke.*
285   "The North": Ibid.
285   "Taken together": Orfield, *Must We Bus?*
285   "At a certain point": McCabe interview.
286   "bankrupt and suicidal method": Time 3/27/72.
286   "People are always inviting us": Nat Observer 4/10/72.
287   "the other girls": Ibid.
289   "a giant step backward": Marshall dissent to *Milliken.*
289   "*Milliken* ended a dream": Wilkinson, *From Brown to Bakke.*
289   "second post-reconstruction": NAACP's Herbert Hill, Wilkinson, *From Brown to Bakke.*
290   "root and branch": *Milliken.*
290   "Disparate treatment": Ibid.
290   "is a task": Ibid.
291   Wicker column: NYT 7/28/74.
291   Wechsler column: NYPost 7/30/74.
291   "We never felt we were guilty": Nwk 8/5/74.
291   "in the name of saving it": Michael Novak, WSJ 7/25/75.
292   "I'll never forget the faces filled with hatred": Clark interview.
292   "the futile shuffling": NYT 6/22/75.
293   "total black and white segregation": US News 5/8/78.
293   "That was the end of it": Power interview.

10. *"The People's Mayor"*

The story of the Young mayoralty and his relationship with the suburbs draws on interviews with Coleman Young, Damon Keith, Philip Power, Max Fisher, Joseph Hudson, Irene McCabe, Brooks Patterson, Thomas Bray, George Cantor, Pete

Waldmeir, Ze'ev Chafets, Douglas Fraser, Richard Austin, Ron Gault and Bob Berg, among others.

Along with other local and national press sources, Richard Willing's January 1994 series on Coleman Young in the *Detroit News* was particularly useful.

Helpful books include Coleman Young and Lonnie Wheeler, *Hard Stuff;* Studs Terkel, *American Dreams;* James H. Buckley, *Bringing Home the News;* Wilbur C. Rich, *Coleman Young and Detroit Politics;* Joe T. Darden et al., *Detroit, Race and Uneven Development;* Ze'ev Chafets, *Devil's Night;* Thomas J. Anton, *Federal Aid to Detroit;* Jon C. Teaford, *The Rough Road to Renaissance;* Peter Brown, *Minority Party;* Joel Garreau, *Edge City;* Robert Weisbrot, *Freedom Bound;* J. Harvie Wilkinson, III, *From Brown to Bakke;* Howard Schuman, Charlotte Steeh and Lawrence Bobo, *Racial Attitudes in America;* Gary Orfield, *Must We Bus?;* Peter Carroll, *It Seemed Like Nothing Happened;* and *The Quotations of Mayor Coleman A. Young.*

page

295   **"Detroit is coming together"**: Nwk 1/14/74, Time 1/14/74.
295   **"from Superfly to super straight"**: NYT 1/6/64.
295   **"Let it be said"**: Mich Chr 1/5/74.
296   **"first believe in ourselves"**: Det News 11/7/73.
297   **"The biggest chore"**: Ibid.
297   **"We can no longer afford"**: Mich Chr 1/8/74.
298   **"Hit the road"**: Ibid.
298   **"innocent enough"**: Young interview.
298   **"If you've seen one city slum"**: Weisbrot, *Freedom Bound.*
299   **"The question"**: Wilkinson, *From Brown to Bakke.*
299   Statistics on white attitudes in the early seventies are from Schuman, Steeh and Bobo, *Racial Attitudes in America*, and Orfield, *Must We Bus?*
300   **"a stillness"**: Carroll, *It Seemed Like Nothing Happened.*
301   Poll on 1973 Detroit attitudes is Det News 10/4/73.
302   **"sigh of relief"**: Mark Lilla interview.
302   **"never quite the same person"**: Young and Wheeler, *Hard Stuff.*
303   **"I got screwed"**: Terkel, *American Dreams.*
303   **"an adversary role toward society"**: Young and Wheeler, *Hard Stuff.*
303   **"proud"** and **"ornery"**: Terkel, *American Dreams.*
303   **"tweaking the system," "scams"** and **"hustles"**: Ibid.
303   **"an extra antenna"**: interview with *Prime Time Live* reporter Judd Rose 9/6/90.
303   **"cheated them out of dues"**: Willing series, Det News 1/23–26/94.
303   **"It was a climate"**: Young and Wheeler, *Hard Stuff.*
304   **"only fools"** and **"deliberately screwed up"**: Ibid.
304   **"hate liberals"**: Young interview.
304   **"I reveled"**: Young and Wheeler, *Hard Stuff.*
304   **"Negro," "speak"** and **"slurring"**: Young and Wheeler, *Hard Stuff,* Terkel, *American Dreams,* Det News 1/25/94.
305   **"un-American"** and **"stool pigeon"**: Ibid.
305   **"I felt like Joe Louis"**: Young and Wheeler, *Hard Stuff.*
305   **"come in out of the cold"**: Willing series, Det News 1/23–26/94.
306   **"it's *Senator* Motherfucker"**: Young and Wheeler, *Hard Stuff.*
306   **"We need to have a black mayor"**: Darden et al., *Detroit.*
307   **"completely off-target and unacceptable"**: Young and Wheeler, *Hard Stuff.*

307   "I do not believe that integration is an end": Young interview.

307   "take power in the city": Young and Wheeler, *Hard Stuff.*

308   "criminals on the streets" and "I carried on a crusade": Ibid.

308   "an official vehicle": Ibid.

308   "a victory by Nichols": Ibid.

308   "The pattern was developing": Terkel, *American Dreams.*

309   "a classic confrontation": Ibid.

309   "I'm a mayor": Det News 11/9/73.

309   "Many of us had great hopes": Power interview.

311   "There is no way in hell": Observer 3/25/76.

312   "I'm a victim of it": Det News 11/7/73.

312   "He was an arrogant son": Young and Wheeler, *Hard Stuff.*

313   "at suburban cocktail parties": Ibid.

313   "part of a white conspiracy": Cantor interview.

313   "If they work for me": *Prime Time Live* interview 9/6/90.

313   "pandering to his support group": Power interview.

314   "Some deep combative influence": Hudson interview.

314   "Suburban isolation" and "We're all in this": Power columns in Observer, 1970–71.

315   "edge cities": Garreau, *Edge City.*

315   "We need the city": Power interview.

315   "forty-five percent view": Ibid.

316   "My modus operandi": Young and Wheeler, *Hard Stuff.*

316   "He wasn't acting rationally": Ron Gault interview.

316   "Those people who fled": Darden et al., *Detroit.*

317   "Detroit's fiscal problems": Ibid.

317   "In Young's eyes": Power interview.

317   "I might feel differently": Darden et al., *Detroit.*

317   "ripping off the suburbs": Observer 5/1/75.

317   "take over a city utility": Young interview.

318   "Detroit's ours now": NYT 7/26/76.

318   "the black working-man's capital": Ibid.

318   "He'll tell white people": NYT 9/17/89.

319   "need for control": Young interview.

319   "Get the hell": Observer 3/25/76.

319   "raiding parties": Ibid.

319   "stealing" and "sabotaging": Young interview.

319   "throwing all those rocks": *The Quotations of Mayor Coleman A. Young.*

319   "suburban cooperation": Observer 10/9/75.

319   "I think he uses racism as an alibi": Det News 9/25/85.

319   "at war": Observer 10/2/75.

319   "our assailants": Young and Wheeler, *Hard Stuff.*

320   "economically pillaging the city": Ibid.

320   "have dissociated themselves": Ibid.

320   "can't stand": speech to Booker T. Washington Business Association, 8/22/84.

320   "I'm honestly not dumb enough": Young and Wheeler, *Hard Stuff.*

320   "say 'ouch' ": unpublished interview with Detroit Free Press editorial board, 1/15/87.

320   "Coleman Young as much as told people": McCabe interview.

320   "He was trying to drive whites": Waldmeir interview.

320   "staunched the flow": Young interview.

320   "We need": Young and Wheeler, *Hard Stuff.*

11. A Mandate for Anarchy

The story of Coleman Young's relationship with the Detroit police force draws on interviews with Freddie Williams, Gil Hill, Douglas Fraser, Coleman Young, Joseph Hudson, Max Fisher, Damon Keith, Brooks Patterson, Irene McCabe, Philip Power, George Cantor, Irving Bluestone, Pete Waldmeir, Bob Berg, Thomas Bray and Ze'ev Chafets. On the RenCen and Detroit politics of the late 1970s, I spoke with Max Fisher, Joseph Hudson, Coleman Young, George Cantor, Pete Waldmeir, Damon Keith, Philip Power, Douglas Fraser, Irving Bluestone, Thomas Bray, Bob Berg, Brooks Patterson, Irene McCabe and Ze'ev Chafets, among others.

In addition to the contemporary press, local and national, I drew on transcripts of several of Young's speeches and press interviews made available by his office.

Helpful books include Coleman A. Young and Lonnie Wheeler, *Hard Stuff;* Joe T. Darden et al., *Detroit, Race and Uneven Development;* Scott McGehee and Susan Watson, eds., *Blacks in Detroit;* Studs Terkel, *American Dreams;* Wilbur C. Rich, *Coleman Young and Detroit Politics;* Sidney Fine, *Violence in the Model City;* Jon C. Teaford, *The Rough Road to Renaissance;* Peter Golden, *Quiet Diplomat;* Elijah Anderson, *Streetwise;* and *The Quotations of Mayor Coleman A. Young.* Also useful was Thomas Bray, "Jimmy Carter's Favorite Mayor," *Policy Review,* Spring 1984.

page

322   "**Blacks were confined**": Williams interview.
322   "**You walked the beat**": Ibid.
322   "**NAACP Blood Bank**": Hill interview.
322   "**The guys weren't all bad**": Williams interview.
323   "**There were reformist efforts**": Fraser interview.
323   "**it was the only issue**": Young interview.
325   "**they could go for things**": Hill interview.
325   "**The department had to change**": Fraser interview.
325   "**a bunch of out-and-out racists**": WP 6/25/78.
325   "**at the top**": Cleve Pln Dlr 3/17/74.
326   "**The same problem exists throughout**": Ibid.
326   "**law and order**": speech to the Association of Black Psychiatrists of America, May 1974.
326   "**but not *the* problem**": Det News 5/22/77.
326   "**I have to decide**": Cleve Pln Dlr 3/17/74.
326   "**I'd planned on building**": Det News 9/7/75.
326   "**With a shooting**": WSJ 1/16/75.
327   "**traitors**": Hill interview.
327   "**You join up**": NYT 8/11/74.
327   "**to bring the force**": Det News 4/11/74.
327   "**The typical [black] resident**": Young and Wheeler, *Hard Stuff.*
328   "**the way the public accepts**" and "**ho-hum**": WSJ 1/16/75.
328   "**It's wild, just wild**": NYT 4/3/75.
329   Photos of police rally are NYT and WP 5/10/75.
330   "**beer-can throwing**": Daily World 5/14/75.
330   "**I'd leave in a minute**": WP 1/29/75.

330   "maybe he can keep the lid on": LA Times 5/7/75.

331   "Not a single shot": Terkel, *American Dreams.*

331   "I'm just as disappointed": NYT 7/31/75.

332   "this was the turning point": Terkel, *American Dreams.*

332   "the mores of the society": WP 1/4/76.

333   "a racist perception of the city": *The Quotations of Mayor Coleman A. Young.*

334   "Black Killers!": Nwk 8/30/76.

335   "I don't care who you are": Ibid.

335   "It's time to clamp down": NYT 8/19/76 and Nwk 8/30/76.

336   "I want the pimps, prostitutes": NYT 8/17/76.

336   "How come you're hassling us": Nwk 10/11/76.

336   "I've been writing": Observer 8/19/76.

336   "By attacking the police": McCabe interview.

337   "Coleman Young had a chance": Patterson interview.

337   "respect for any kind of police": Hudson interview.

337   "oppositional culture": Elijah Anderson, *Streetwise.*

337   "Eight Mile will really be a wall": Observer 8/19/76.

337   "an Emerald City of Oz": Nwk 3/28/77.

340   "Would it spark a meaningful revival": Nwk 8/28/77.

340   "Detroit is a young woman with acne": Ebony, April 1978.

340   "For a city that was declared dead": Ibid.

342   "We were never in it for the money": Young and Wheeler, *Hard Stuff.*

342   "they figured things must really be bad": Cantor interview.

342   "a Noah's ark" and "a fortress": Darden et al., *Detroit.*

343   "doing for themselves;" NYT 7/26/76.

343   "self-determination": Ibid.

343   Ebony profile is April 1978.

343   "blacks exercised more power": *Prime Time Live* interview 9/6/90.

343   "sentimentalists": Ebony, April 1978.

343   "I've never been concerned": Young interview.

343   "We refuse in Detroit" and "to kiss": *Prime Time Live* interview 9/6/90.

343   "He's fighting back": WP 6/25/78.

344   "as American as apple pie": Det News 5/22/77 and Young and Wheeler, *Hard Stuff.*

344   "constantly on the phone": NYT 12/16/79.

345   "brought home the bacon": AP Biographical Service, July 1980.

346   "The Young administration": Cantor interview.

346   "détente": Det News 1/18/78.

346   "Some major roads": Oakland County executive Daniel Murphy, Det News 1/18/78.

346   "This is racism": Det News 11/25/79.

347   "sensitivity": NYT 4/23/80.

347   "I wouldn't write tickets": Williams interview.

347   "Racism and sour grapes": Det News 8/7/77.

347   "he was AWOL in the fight": Patterson interview.

348   "our revitalized city": Mil Jrnl 7/15/80.

348   "The Detroit the GOP Won't See": WP 5/21/80.

348   "Politics is a game": anonymous, Phil Inq 7/17/80.

348   "is not worried about us": Leonard Greenwood, NYT 7/17/80.

349   "I guess" : Darden et al., *Detroit.*

349   "Hudson's *was* Detroit": Marguerite Hague, Nwk 12/27/82.

349   "please turn out the lights": bumper sticker, SW archive at the University of Michigan.

349   **"in the history of man"**: Young interview.
350   **"were abandoned faster"**: Ibid.
350   The attitude survey is from McGehee and Watson, *Blacks in Detroit.*
350   **"to keep blacks down," "civil rights activism"** and **"Ever since"**: Ibid.
351   **"sheer force of his will"**: Rich, *Coleman Young and Detroit Politics.*
351   **"We're not in control"**: transcript of interview with Remer Tyson 5/13/87.
351   **"Young fought the same battle"**: Cantor interview.
352   **"my black ass"**: Young and Wheeler, *Hard Stuff* and Det News 1/27/85.
352   **"To attack"**: *Prime Time Live* interview 9/6/90.
352   **"Char-lee"**: Det News 1/27/85.
352   **"My fondest wish"**: Cantor interview and Det News 11/15/86.

ATLANTA

12. To Lay Down the Burden

For perspective on Atlanta's racial history, I spoke with Sam Massell, Dan Sweat, Lawrence Gellerstedt, Jr., Charles Loudermilk, Bill Shipp, Paul and Carol Muldawer, Andrew Young, Michael Lomax, J. W. Robinson, Lee May, Jeff Dickerson, J. Ben Shapiro, Wendell Rawls, Joseph Dolman, Michael Hinkelman, Ellen Wolf and Mark Silk. Among those interviewed on Maynard Jackson's Atlanta: Dan Sweat, Michael Lomax, Bill Shipp, Sam Massell, George Berry, Richard Stogner, Dave Miller, Charles Loudermilk and Paul Muldawer. My account of the missing and murdered children episode draws on extensive local and national press coverage and interviews with, among others, Joseph Dolman, Lawrence Gellerstedt, Jr. and Wendell Rawls.

Useful books include Earl Black and Merle Black, *Politics and Society in the South;* Clarence N. Stone, *Regime Politics;* Peter K. Eisinger, *The Politics of Displacement;* Ivan Allen with Paul Hemphill, *Mayor;* Gary Orfield and Carole Ashkinaze, *The Closing Door;* Andrew Young's memoir, *A Way Out of No Way;* Pat Watters, *Coca-Cola;* John D. Hutcheson, Jr., *Racial Attitudes in Atlanta;* Chris Geller, Keith Ihlanfelt and David Sjoquist, *Atlanta in Black and White;* Gerald David Jaynes and Robin M. Williams, Jr., eds., *A Common Destiny;* Glenn Loury, *One by One from the Inside Out;* and James Baldwin, *The Evidence of Things Not Seen.*

Two helpful academic studies were Mack H. Jones, "Black Political Empowerment in Atlanta," and Adolphe Reed, "A Critique of Neo-Progressivism in Theorizing About Local Development Policy: A Case from Atlanta."

page

357   **"best personal friends"**: NYT 12/17/76.
358   **"It isn't 'The Kingdom' "**: NYPost 7/24/76.
358   **"It's the same debt"**: *Issues and Answers* 11/14/76.
358   **"Hands that once picked cotton"**: NYT 11/14/76.
359   **"I'm ready to lay down"**: NYPost 7/24/76.
359   **"when you can pick up a phone"**: WP 7/25/76.

359   "weren't necessarily racists": NYPost 7/24/76.

359   "understands that people can change": *Meet the Press* 7/18/76.

359   "And whites and whites": WP 7/25/76.

359   "There are almost no specifically black problems": *Meet the Press* 7/18/76.

359   "that their problems have got to be deracialized": *Issues and Answers* 11/14/76.

359   "No black leader should try": *CBS Morning News* 12/17/76.

360   Poll findings on black alienation: Jaynes and Williams, eds., *Common Destiny.*

361   "I have never taken an action": Watters, *Coca-Cola.*

361   "That was the system": Allen, *Mayor.*

363   "power structure": phrase coined by Floyd Hunter in his pathbreaking 1953 study, *Community Power Structure.*

364   "Eventually, it rubbed off": Sweat interview.

364   "We know each other": May interview.

364   "growing higher each month": Hutcheson, *Racial Attitudes.*

364   "It's all boosterism": Calvin Trillin, Time 7/25/88.

364   a "myth": Hinkelman interview.

364   a "lie": Dolman interview.

364   a "veneer" and "hypocrisy": Rawls interview.

364   "The city too busy moving": Hutcheson, *Racial Attitudes.*

364   "There was a sense of relief": Shipp interview.

365   "melted surprisingly fast": Young, *A Way Out of No Way.*

365   "There was nowhere else": Wolf interview.

365   "the youngest, wealthiest": National Geographic, July 1988.

365   "Yankee briskness": NYT 2/26/75.

365   "single structure": Allen, *Mayor.*

365   "gave itself a black eye": Shapiro interview.

366   "a bunch of buildings and stuff": Calvin Trillin, Time 7/25/88.

366   "a Cabot or a Lodge": WP 10/3/77.

366   "youngest, fattest, blackest mayor in America": NYT 10/3/77.

367   "we were running hard": Massell interview.

367   "the Eight Years' War": AJC, numerous stories.

367   "Atlanta is the best city": Current Bio, September 1976.

367   "an old thing in this town": Sweat interview.

368   "He wanted to rub the change": Loudermilk interview.

368   "Atlanta is soft on crime": Business Week 12/28/81.

368   "to give them time to get away": J.K. Ramey, NYT 12/7/79.

369   "It was the end of integration": Berry interview.

369   "anti-white": from document known as the "Brockey Letter" mailed from CAP to Jackson on 9/16/74, copy in author's possession.

369   "mayor for the black community": Time 4/21/75.

370   "response is 'racism' ": NYT 12/2/79, echoed in Peter Eisinger's 1975 and 1978 attitude surveys.

370   "building of the perimeter": Muldawer interview.

371   "eight out of ten": Sweat interview.

371   "slavish, unquestioning": Stone, *Regime Politics.*

371   "it was the 'in' thing": Shipp interview.

372   "been 1958": Dolman interview.

373   "being killed," "perception," "climate of fear" and "The mood": Nwk 10/27/8.

374   "This is a question of conscience": NYT 1/30/81.

374   "We were accused": Dolman interview.

374   "dismissed": Baldwin, *The Evidence of Things Not Seen.*

374 "open season on black people": Loury, *One by One.*
375 "They win": Baldwin, *The Evidence of Things Not Seen.*
375 "I don't believe" and "the verdict was predetermined": NYT 3/1/82.
375 "convinced that Williams had been framed": Dolman interview.
375 "the 30th victim": NYT 3/1/82.
376 "a face of the city": AJC "Black and Poor in Atlanta" series, autumn 1981.
376 "There has been an accommodation": NYT 1/3/82.

13. A Piece of the Pie

The picture of early black entrepreneurship in Atlanta is drawn from interviews with Herman Russell, J. W. Robinson, Lawrence Gellerstedt, Jr., and various Russell employees including Egbert Perry, Jack Byrd, Noel Khalil and Haywood Curry. On the MARTA deal and Maynard Jackson's affirmative action initiative, I spoke with Jackson aides George Berry, Richard Stogner, Michael Lomax and Dave Miller, as well as Sam Massell, Dan Sweat, Rodney Strong, Charles Loudermilk, Lawrence Gellerstedt, Jr., Oscar Harris, Paul Muldawer, Andrew Young, J. Ben Shapiro and Terrence Lee Croft. For what happened on the ground in the early set-asides, I have relied on interviews with J. W. Robinson, Herman Russell, Oscar Harris, George Berry, Richard Stogner, Lawrence Gellerstedt, Jr., Dave Miller, Paul Muldawer, Egbert Perry, Haywood Curry, Herbert Edwards, Jack Byrd, Albert Maslia, Noel Khalil and Greg Sweetin, among others. The story of the airport concession set-aside draws on conversations with Michael Hinkelman and Richard Stogner, among others.

The early history of affirmative action has been covered in innumerable books and articles. Among the books I drew on directly: Charles and Barbara Whalen, *The Longest Debate;* Herman Belz, *Equality Transformed;* and Nathan Glazer, *Affirmative Discrimination.* Lyndon B. Johnson's Howard University speech is printed in full in Lee Rainwater and William L. Yancy, *The Moynihan Report and the Politics of Controversy.* The story of Maynard Jackson's first initiatives has not been well reported, though there was some discussion in the contemporary press, in Clarence N. Stone, *Regime Politics;* Peter K. Eisinger, *The Politics of Displacement;* Henry Hampton and Steve Fayer, *Voices of Freedom;* and in two academic studies, Adolphe Reed, "A Critique of Neo-Progressivism in Theorizing about Local Development Policy: A Case from Atlanta," and Mack Jones, "Black Political Empowerment in Atlanta."

page
377 "I was a successful designer": Robinson interview.
378 "Blacks still had to fight for everything": Ibid.
378 "And I learned early on the art of working": Russell interview.
378 "I just like people": Ibid.
379 "If you kissed enough behind": background interview.
379 "so far you could go" and "without designating jobs": Curry interview.
379 "take affirmative action": Belz, *Equality Transformed.*
380 "It is not enough": Rainwater and Yancy, *The Moynihan Report.*

380   "big zero": Arch Puddington, "What to Do About Affirmative Action," Commentary, June 1995.
381   "improvement in the picture": EEOC chair Clifford Alexander, Belz, *Equality Transformed.*
381   "the only effective way": NYT 9/10/72.
382   "The way to end discrimination": Nwk 9/18/72.
382   "I share the concerns": Ibid.
383   "and I became their minority": Curry interview.
384   "There were a zillion": Croft interview.
384   "There was a tremendous pressure": Massell interview.
385   "Minorities already know how to dig a ditch": Curry interview.
385   "You didn't go to Wall Street," "a new bond counsel" and "and everybody knew it": Berry interview.
386   "You had to start somewhere": Miller interview.
386   "People thought it was crazy": Gellerstedt interview.
386   "He put his chin out": Ga Trend, August 1987.
386   "He dictated from on high": Gellerstedt interview.
386   "he crammed it down": Shapiro interview.
386   "Weeds will grow": Berry interview.
387   "Do you want that chance or not": Ibid.
387   "profit motive": Jackson, AJC 3/30/80.
387   "So we were stuck": Gellerstedt interview.
387   "We did it informally": Berry interview.
387   "was amazing to see": Curry interview.
388   "Maynard was forceful": Robinson interview.
388   "There is no way in hell": AJC 11/30/80.
388   "We were threatened": Hampton and Fayer, *Voices of Freedom.*
388   "a great big plus": AJC 11/30/80.
388   "would get defensive": Miller interview.
388   "You'll soon get used to this": Ibid.
389   "Maynard's people would take them": Strong interview.
389   "the perception of racism": Sweat interview.
390   "blackmail" and "experience had always excluded": Business Week 11/17/75.
390   "Whites here are pragmatic": Berry interview.
390   "You fear for your livelihood": background interview.
391   "became a given": Berry interview.
391   "if you can use it to pull yourself up": Robinson interview.
392   "weak and inexperienced": Miller interview.
392   "big-firm country-club": Robinson interview.
392   "a separate office," "who want to manage," "and you don't have any input," "Each brought" and "The problem": Robinson interview.
392   "cordial, civilized way": Berry interview.
392   "Nobody likes being force-fed": Byrd interview.
393   "They thought it was a joke": Curry interview.
393   "dictate whatever they wanted": Biz Atl, November 1985.
393   "It was the damnedest thing": Ibid.
393   "didn't want you there to begin with": background interview.
394   "not to get in your hair": Edwards interview.
394   "Don't assign anyone": background interview.
395   "said I could come to all the meetings": AJC 3/31/80.
395   "People get partners": Maslia interview.

395   "it's always easier": Edwards interview.

395   "These so-called minority businesses": Biz Atl, November 1985.

396   "they turned to my white partner": AJC 3/31/80.

396   "It was the dummy companies": Robinson interview.

396   "What creates the racist backlash": Khalil interview.

396   "A certain segment": Will Fortson, AJC 3/31/80.

396   "It was a learning process": Stogner interview.

396   "We policed it the best we could": Berry interview.

396   "to make money quick" and "very competitive business": Edwards interview.

397   "and tried to shove steak": background interview.

397   "it takes a lifetime": Edwards interview.

397   "How many minority contractors": Sweetin interview.

397   "*60 Minutes*" and "the houses fall down": Robinson interview.

398   "with good intentions" and "I try to sell myself:" Ibid.

398   "This set the table": Curry interview.

398   "Race relations": Russell interview.

399   "Just another sub": Curry interview.

399   "pigeonhole": Russell interview.

399   "It had nothing to do with racism": Curry interview.

399   "When I began my entrepreneurship": Russell interview.

400   "We have established beyond question": AJC 9/16/80.

400   "We used to joke": Massell interview.

400   The *Journal* series on the airport set-aside, by Dale Russakoff and Fred Hiatt, ran from 3/30/80 through 4/1/80.

401   "A few black contractors": AJC 1/8/80.

401   "a false sense of security": Charles Brazzeal, Atl Biz Chr 12/21/87.

401   For the story of the airport concessions, see Atl Biz Chr 6/6/88, AJC 11/23/84, 3/29/92 and 3/31/92.

402   "rewrote the book": Hampton and Fayer, *Voices of Freedom*.

402   "You have to look at the back side": background interview.

402   "Imperfections in the program?": AJC 4/3/80.

403   Black public opinion numbers come from the AJC "Black and Poor in Atlanta" series, autumn 1981.

403   "have made it": AJC "Black and Poor in Atlanta" series, autumn 1981.

14. The Tug of Solidarity

The account of the 1981 campaign is drawn from the contemporary press and numerous interviews, including Andrew Young, Charles Loudermilk, Dick Williams, Sam Massell and Dan Sweat. The overview of Young's life and his integrationism relies heavily on an interview with him, as well as his writings and numerous press profiles. The story of joint venturing in Atlanta in the early 1980s is based on many interviews: Andrew Young, Lawrence Gellerstedt, Jr., Herman Russell, Herbert Edwards, Egbert Perry, Haywood Curry, Jack Byrd, Dan Sweat, Rodney Strong, Michael Lomax, Dave Miller, Albert Maslia, Carl Trimble, Oscar Harris, J. W. Robinson, John Busby, Jr., Stanley Daniels and Claiborne Darden, among others. On the inside workings of the Russell company and his joint ventures, I spoke with Russell himself, Egbert Perry, Haywood Curry, Lawrence Gellerstedt, Jr., Noel Khalil, Jack Byrd and Herbert Edwards. The account of the 1984 primary season and what came after in Atlanta draws on interviews with Andrew Young, Dick Williams, Albert Maslia and the contemporary press.

Useful books include Young's memoir, *A Way Out of No Way,* and the first volume of his autobiography, *An Easy Burden.*

page

405   "a new code word": David Franklin, AJC 9/20/80.
405   "He told me": Young interview.
405   "wasn't a hate statement": Chi Trib 8/23/81.
405   "we kind of hate": Dillard Munford, WSJ 10/6/81.
405   "rolling his eyeballs": Dan Sweat interview.
405   "to their neck": Charles Loudermilk interview.
406   "a consensus seeker": TNR 9/23/81.
406   "Symbolically": Miami Herald 9/13/81.
406   "We think we're free": NYT 10/5/81.
406   "tragedy": Ibid.
407   "special ability": AJC 8/18/81.
407   "Over my dead body": quoted by Loudermilk in interview.
407   "not black enough": Balt Sun 10/5/81.
402   "my blackness": Ibid.
408   "For twenty years": Williams interview.
408   "shuffling": NYT 10/18/81 and WP 10/25/81.
408   "North Side Voting": Williams interview.
408   "I would hope that": WP 10/29/81.
409   "Those divisions": NYT 10/29/81.
409   "Andy Young's style": LA Times 12/25/82.
409   "represented everybody": Maslia interview.
410   "Daddy was": Young, *A Way Out of No Way.*
410   "Don't get mad": Young, *A Way Out of No Way* and countless profiles.
410   "on the verge": Playboy, July 1977.
410   "black folk": Current Bio 1977.
410   "That's when I decided": Playboy, July 1977.
410   "I have rarely": Young, *A Way Out of No Way.*
411   "spear-thrower": NYT 12/17/76.
411   "Where was Andy": anonymous activist, WP 8/8/79.
411   "I didn't have": Young interview.
411   "the human family," "human rights," and "human relations": Young, *A Way Out of No Way.*
411   "As we learn": Ibid.
411   "to de-moralize" and "ethnocentrism": Playboy, July 1977.
411   "been successful enough": unpublished interview with editors and reporters at LA Times Washington, D.C., bureau 12/29/94.
411   "If a white majority": Current Bio 1977.
412   "sticking his head": WP 8/8/79.
412   "a living martyr": WP 8/26/79.
412   "the Number One": Nation 8/15/79.
412   "We've had no symbol": Robert Pruit, WP 8/17/79.
412   "Thank God": WP 8/17/79.
412   "I had the same": Mayor Richard Hatcher of Gary, Nwk 8/27/79.
412   "They tried": Chi Trib 11/4/79.
413   "God-given gift": AJC 1/2/83.

413   "new black pharaoh": Young interview.
414   "sacrificed the poor": Charles King, WP 1/3/83.
414   "Andy Young is the only": WP 1/3/83.
414   "The biggest problem": Chi Trib 6/5/83.
415   "Yesterday's demonstration": George Herman, CBS *Face the Nation* 8/28/83.
415   "militarism" and "bootstraps": CBS *Face the Nation* 8/28/83.
415   "Where do we go": *Where Do We Go from Here: Chaos or Community?* is the title of Martin Luther King's 1967 book-length essay on Black Power and integration.
415   "Andy wanted to give": Loudermilk interview.
416   "The period before": Strong interview.
416   "There was no alternative": Gellerstedt interview.
417   "whatever": Edwards interview.
417   "There was no": Gellerstedt interview.
417   "We were getting": background interview.
417   "If you're in": Curry interview.
417   "a fabulous": Gellerstedt interview.
418   "He didn't wear": Ira Jackson, AJC 7/1/90.
418   "What Russell brought": Gellerstedt interview.
418   "Whites looked": Robinson interview.
418   "an alliance": Loudermilk interview.
418   "You have to spend": Daniels interview.
419   "If you give": Trimble interview.
419   "The only way": Ibid.
419   "paying off": Young interview.
419   "The money began": Gellerstedt interview.
420   "The purpose of the program": anonymous, Biz Atl, November 1985.
420   "A great deal of work": Ga Trend, August 1987.
420   "Joint venturing": Maslia interview.
421   "Without affirmative action": Curry interview.
421   "the minority business game": Perry interview.
421   "It was all about": background interview.
421   "It was a program": background interview.
421   "The white businessmen": background interview.
421   "Minority contractors": Curry interview.
422   "I call him": Ibid.
422   "Perry said": Byrd interview.
422   "We could bid": AJC 3/22/85.
422   "We want $5-million": Ibid.
423   "Building Toward": Ibid.
424   "Literally a few": AJC 7/27/88.
425   "They, more than anything": background interview.
425   "Andy Young made": Curry interview.
425   "Young would not have": Trimble interview.
425   "the time of day": Atl Biz Chr 9/28/87.
425   "I just see": Ibid.
426   "illegal act": Justice P. J. Smith, AJC 12/6/90.
426   "I thought the city": Curry interview.
426   "to renegotiate": NYT 3/30/83.
427   "mortgage": AJC 5/29/83.
427   "I come out": AJC 1/1/84.
427   "My feeling": CBS *Face the Nation* 8/28/83.
427   "kiss of death": WP 8/29/83.

427   "Jesse was concerned": Young interview.
428   "enthusiasm," "psychological impact" and "consensus": CBS *Face the Nation* 8/28/83.
428   "folks": Nwk 5/7/84.
428   "dangerous": AJC 10/13/83.
428   "All of us": NYT 2/2/84.
428   "One of the things": *Meet the Press* 3/11/84.
428   "pours cold water": Ibid.
429   "Shame": Boston Globe 7/20/84.
429   "It don't": WP 7/19/84.
429   "One was": Boston Globe 7/20/84.
429   "Around the country": Ibid.
429   "still flinched": AJC 7/7/84.
430   "This election": Ibid.
430   "sad and disappointing": NYT 7/16/84.
430   "blatant appeal": AJC 7/9/84.
430   "I know Jesse": WP 8/18/84.
430   "I don't think": Ibid.
430   "representative of this country": AJC 8/18/84.
430   "The national press": Williams interview.

15. *The Program That Would Not Die*

The story of J. Ben Shapiro and his suits draws on several interviews with him, court documents, contemporary press reports and correspondence from the files of his firm, Shapiro, Fussell, Wedge, Smotherman & Martin. Also useful were interviews with McNeil Stokes, William O. Miller, Rodney Strong, Greg Sweetin and Andrew Young, among others. The story of the Brimmer-Marshall study draws on local and national press accounts, as well as on interviews with Rodney Strong, Terrence Lee Croft, J. Ben Shapiro, William O. Miller and Charles Shanor.

My assessment of the Brimmer-Marshall study relies on the work of George R. LaNoue and John Sullivan. Among the most helpful of LaNoue's articles are those in *The Public Interest*, Winter 1993, and the *Annals of the American Academy of Political and Social Science*, September 1992. He and Sullivan collaborated on an informative piece in the *Columbia Human Rights Review*, Winter 1992–93. Also extremely helpful were the Atlanta chapters from Sullivan's unpublished dissertation. Other useful articles and reports include John P. Smith and Finis Welch's *Closing the Gap*, Nathan Glazer's "The Affirmative Action Stalemate," the U.S. Civil Rights Commission's unpublished 1986 report on set-asides and Research Atlanta's 1986 study, *The Impact of Local Government Programs to Encourage Minority Business Development*.

The U.S. Supreme Court decision is *City of Richmond* v. *J. A. Croson Company*.

page

432   "It was ludicrous": Shapiro interview.
432   "I'm proud": Ibid.
433   "A client": Ibid.
433   "We want to stress": Shapiro letter to councilwoman Barbara Asher 2/2/82.
433   "I was convinced": Shapiro interview.

434   "a compromise": Ibid.
434   "I was proud": Ibid.
436   The Smith and Welch study, *Closing the Gap,* was published in 1986 by the Rand Corporation.
436   **"Education and migration"**: Glazer, "The Affirmative Action Stalemate."
436   **"Set-asides do not"**: U.S. Civil Rights Commission unpublished 1986 report.
436   **"I think it is"**: Time 2/25/85.
438   **"learning to accept"**: NYT 5/6/85.
438   **"The illustration"**: Young interview.
438   **"People can and do"**: AJC 7/1/84.
438   Poll numbers taken from Commentary, April 1982, and NYT 9/25/83.
438   **"this is my obligation"**: Lomax interview.
439   **"create a wealth class"**: Ibid.
440   **"It's good"**: UPI 3/2/82.
440   **"ordinary black"**: Williams interview.
440   **"It's a modern-day"**: Ibid.
440   **"I draw"**: Stokes interview.
440   **"I didn't like"**: Ibid.
440   **"Without these programs"**: Shapiro interview.
441   **"Bottom line"**: Ibid.
441   **"to the lowest"**: *Georgia Branch, Associated General Contractors of America Inc., et al.* v. *City of Atlanta, et al.*
441   **"The legislature purpose"**: Ibid.
441   **"I encourage"**: AJC 10/12/84.
441   **"a setback"**: Ibid.
441   **"disappointed"**: Sullivan dissertation.
442   **"The city council"**: AJC 10/15/84.
442   **"There is no"**: AJC 10/13/84.
442   **"the old spoils system"**: AJC 10/20/84.
442   **"There is no question"**: motion for summary judgment filed with the Fulton County Superior Court.
443   **"These people"**: Shapiro interview.
443   **"I'm old enough"**: Time 2/25/85.
443   **"will no longer"**: CQ Researcher 5/17/91.
443   **"speck on the ceiling"**: unnamed lawyer, Time 2/25/85.
444   **"There's a great deal"**: Nwk 6/25/84.
444   **"exhilarating"**: Fortune 4/23/84.
444   **"unequivocal"**: Current Bio 1988.
444   **"*Stotts* may well"**: speech, 11/14/84.
445   **"blasphemous"**: AJC 2/1/85.
445   **"go back and revisit it"**: Philip R. Trapani, NYT 5/4/85.
445   **"It's usually more"**: Stephen Bokat, Fortune 7/23/84.
446   **"soft spot"**: Commentary, January 1989.
446   **"legal basis"**: WP 10/25/85.
447   **"It works"**: Jim Conway, Nwk 12/20/85.
447   **"We don't need"**: Lawrence Branch, NYT 3/3/86.
447   **"came out unanimously"**: William McEwen, WP 3/29/87.
447   **"a situation where"**: William McEwen, WP 1/23/86.
448   **"a dozen clear-cut"**: Research Atlanta, *Impact.*
448   **"take a baseball bat"**: AJC 4/10/86.
448   **"Only a dozen"**: AJC 5/29/86.
448   **"Metro Atlanta's"**: AJC 5/28/86.

448   "If the concept": Biz Atl, November 1985.
449   "You can't go": Shapiro interview.
449   "The question": Loudermilk interview.
449   "It never got": Young interview.
449   "an element": AJC 12/12/84.
449   "It was the same": Ibid.
450   "This is the first": AJC 10/16/88.
450   "I was elated": Shapiro interview.
450   "a serious blow": AJC 1/23/89.
451   "An amorphous": *City of Richmond* v. *Croson.*
451   "in extreme cases": Ibid.
451   "sounded": AJC 2/25/89.
451   "I would imagine": AJC 1/24/89.
451   "Classifications": *American Subcontractors Association, Georgia Chapter Inc.* v. *City of Atlanta, et al.*
451   "woefully": Ibid.
451   "That program": AP 3/3/89.
451   "We are extremely": crib sheet in Shapiro's files.
452   "Slavery": WSJ 3/6/89.
452   "There is no choice": AJC 3/3/89.
452   "We're going": Ibid.
453   "I felt": Sweetin interview.
453   "This program": notes of the meeting in Shapiro's files.
453   "This is a reminder": AJC 3/9/89.
453   "I am prepared": Ibid.
454   "a team of experts": AJC 3/4/89.
454   "We know": AJC 7/13/89.
454   "We will pursue": AJC 6/19/89.
454   "To have to hire experts": Jackson statement to the press 7/16/90.
454   "is deeply rooted": Atl Biz Chr 8/20/90.
455   "In Atlanta, 66 percent black": AJC 7/22/90.
455   "compelling case": Ibid.
456   "a significant disparity": *City of Richmond* v. *Croson.*
456   "There is not": background interview.
458   "a pseudo-discussion": Terrence Lee Croft interview.
458   "The team knew": Charles Shanor interview.
458   "There's an awful lot": Robert Barr, AJC 10/8/90.
458   "I believe": AJC 9/17/91.
461   "serious methodological": Philadelphia judge, ABA Journal, September 1995.
461   "inconclusive" and "open": Ibid.
461   "Strict scrutiny": Ibid.
461   "We won": Shapiro interview.
462   "The majority": Ibid.

16. *Betting on Trickle-Down*

This account of the background, financing, building, leasing and opening of Underground Atlanta comes from interviews with Andrew Young, Rodney Strong, Joseph Martin, Richard Stogner, George Berry, Herman Russell, Oscar Harris, William Coleman, Paul Muldawer, Albert Maslia, Lawrence Gellerstedt, Jr., Dick Williams, Sam Massell, Wendell Rawls and others, in addition to contemporary press accounts.

Background on Harris and Russell draws on interviews with both of them, as well as with Paul Muldawer, Stanley Daniels, John Busby, J. W. Robinson, Haywood Curry, Jack Byrd, Herbert Edwards, Egbert Perry and Carl Trimble, among others.

There is a short discussion of the building of Underground in Clarence N. Stone's *Regime Politics*. Also useful for this chapter were the U.S. Civil Rights Commission's unpublished 1986 report on set-asides and David Sjoquist's 1989 Research Atlanta study, *The Economic Status of Black Atlantans*.

page

464   "a hole": Young interview.
465   "We'd all been": Strong interview.
465   "bridge": AJC 6/11/89.
465   "Casbah": AJC 6/28/87.
465   "Andy's idea": Williams interview.
466   "We needed": Gellerstedt interview.
466   "But Andy insisted": Williams interview.
466   "reestablish downtown": AJC 6/28/87.
466   "public-purpose" and "feasibility": Young interview.
466   "I saw it": Ibid.
466   "Young made clear": Strong interview.
467   "Spending with": unpublished interview with reporters and editors at LA Times Washington, D.C., bureau 12/29/94.
467   "I don't like": Williams interview.
467   "Of course, costs are inflated": Atl Biz Chr 2/20/89.
467   "ripple effects": U.S. Civil Rights Commission's unpublished 1986 report.
467   "a foregone": AJC 9/23/84.
468   "We always projected": Strong interview.
468   "The Chamber": Maslia interview.
469   "I believe": AJC 8/29/85.
470   "All the citizens": AJC 5/20/85.
470   "What Does": AJC 6/28/87.
471   "Underground is just": AJC 6/4/89.
471   "I'm prepared": AJC 11/11/83.
471   "The Rouse Company": AJC 6/30/85.
471   "have the sensitivity": AJC 6/6/84.
472   "It often seemed": Martin interview.
473   "Rouse just didn't": Strong interview.
473   "It is time": AJC 5/16/85.
474   "What about": AJC 5/19/85.
474   "After all": AJC 5/20/85.
474   "From the top": AJC 7/2/85.
475   "It's not": AJC 11/20/85.
475   "We would have": Edwards interview.
475   "The hiring was": Byrd interview.
476   "They reached": AJC 6/28/85.
476   "As I saw it": Harris interview.
478   The Atlanta Business Chronicle story is dated 2/20/89.
478   "When [a corporation] selects": MBE magazine, January–February 1992.
479   "I need": Harris interview.
479   "It had not": Strong interview.

480   "maximize the number": Ibid.
480   "whatever it takes": Ibid.
480   "But if you took": Martin interview.
481   "Underground is": Herman Pitts, AJC 6/28/87.
481   "a kind of triage": Strong interview.
481   "some stretches": Coleman interview.
481   "It was the crowning": Strong interview.
481   "There was always": Martin interview.
481   "could not mean a Jewish woman": Maslia interview.
482   "the right decisions": Martin interview.
482   "It's not over": Dana Nottingham, AJC 5/3/89.
483   "too much at stake": Ted Sprague, head of the Convention and Visitors Bureau, AJC 6/11/89.
483   "a melting-pot": AJC 6/12/89.
483   "Will people": AJC 6/11/89.
483   "Underground must have": AJC 3/25/89.
483   "new heart": AJC 6/16/89.
483   "everything from bums": Dante Stephensen, AJC 6/16/89.
483   "It's a dream": Pam Alexander, AJC 6/15/89.
484   "to alleviate poverty": AJC 6/14/89.
484   "For some time": Tom Teepen, AJC 6/20/89.
484   "The first year": Maslia interview.
484   "I went there": Williams interview.
485   "There were frustrations": Coleman interview.
485   "Some rents": Pam Alexander, AJC 4/2/94.
485   "Black tenants": Tena Sutton, AJC 4/28/94.
486   "All said and done": AJC 6/12/94.
486   "It was the": Coleman interview.
486   "Everybody was": Maslia interview.
486   "There's not a discriminatory problem": AJC 4/28/94.
486   "The minority tenants": Strong interview.
487   "Because the city": Martin interview.
487   "A lot of loans": Coleman interview.
487   "We've tried to": Bob Grahamslaw, AJC 4/29/94.
487   "They tended": background interview.
487   "The only thing": AJC 5/4/94.
487   "eradicating": AJC 5/4/94.
487   "Crowe is a martyr": Jackie Johnson, AJC 5/4/94.
488   "I don't look": Strong interview.
488   "The survival rates": Coleman interview.
488   "Underground was": Martin interview.
488   "the city can't": Maslia interview.
488   "Some of them": Williams interview.
488   "I don't know": Gellerstedt interview.
488   "Race had nothing": Maslia interview.
488   "The irony": Martin interview.
489   "In that sense": Gellerstedt interview.
489   "Underground is the best place": Ibid.
489   "too black": Martin interview.
489   "The worse": Rawls interview.
490   "The fear of": Martin interview.

490   "It was soon": Williams interview.
490   "We've written off": Gellerstedt interview.
490   "Just about all the positions": Coleman interview.
491   "high-paying positions": Ibid.
491   "HJ's company": Curry interview.
492   "In Russell's": Byrd interview.
492   "I'm disappointed": Ibid.
492   "I live": Berry interview.
493   Demographic figures from David Sjoquist, *The Economic Status of Black Atlantans.*
494   "My own philosophy": Massell interview.
494   "The program": Edwards interview.
494   "If the purpose": Byrd interview.
494   "It hasn't worked": Edwards interview.
494   "City jobs": background interview.
494   "By now": background interview.
495   "I believe": Massell interview.
495   "There are two kinds": background interview.
495   "crying racism": background interview.
495   "a chip on their shoulder": Maslia interview.
495   "I don't begrudge": background interview.
495   "I hate": Massell interview.
495   "We would have": Gellerstedt interview.
495   "Whatever the set-aside": background interview.
496   "Have you heard?": Martin interview.
497   "Justice": AJC 5/1/92.
497   "What those cops": Ibid.
497   "There have been": NYT 5/12/92.
497   "If you ask": Martin interview.
497   "We've had": Anna Butler, AJC 5/16/92.
498   "I don't think": Melba Johnson, NYT 5/12/92.
498   "The psychological toll": Martin interview.
498   "It confirmed": Williams interview.
498   "People aren't": Christopher Curth, NYT 5/12/92.
498   "It's over": Williams interview.
498   "The night": Coleman interview.
498   "Soon enough": Martin interview.
499   "shake this mother up": AJC 5/2/92.
499   "Black folks": Ibid.

17. As Good As It Gets

The description of Atlanta's racial geography and disengagement draws on contemporary press accounts and many interviews. Among the most helpful: Andrew Young, Michael Lomax, Herman Russell, Oscar Harris, Lee May, Egbert Perry, Haywood Curry, Jeff Dickerson, Lawrence Gellerstedt, Jr., Charles Loudermilk, Dan Sweat, Sam Massell, George Berry, Richard Stogner, Dick Williams, Joseph Martin, Claibourne Darden, Albert Maslia, Paul and Carol Muldawer, Manual Maloof, Douglas Cumming, Mark Silk, John Hutcheson, Joseph Dolman, J. Ben Shapiro and Greg Sweetin.

page

503   "Nothing says": NYT 5/6/85.

504   "We don't have": Berry interview.

504   "consummate buppie": US News 7/25/88.

505   "I tried": Lomax interview.

505   "her life was": Ibid.

505   "all the amenities": Ibid.

505   "not attractive": Ibid.

505   "always worried": Ibid.

506   "That's what": Ibid.

506   "The idea that": Ibid.

506   "We're not": Emerson Bryan, WSJ 2/26/92.

507   "It's similar": Deborah Collins, AJC 3/31/91.

507   "I'd rather meet": Riche Richardson, AJC 11/28/92.

508   "West End intellectuals": Young interview.

508   "the thread": Gladys Twyman, Time 4/4/94.

508   "Every discipline"; Myrtice Taylor, AJC 1/19/89.

509   "No one": Douglas Cumming interview.

509   "The only fight": Martin interview.

509   "There's more anti-white": Claibourne Darden interview.

509   "That negative": Loudermilk interview.

509   "They've been told": Ibid.

509   "The problem": Sweat interview.

510   "It was part": Douglas Cumming interview.

511   "I hope you": Sweetin interview.

511   "very frustrating" and "give-me": Ibid.

511   "We're paying": Ibid.

511   "there was originally": Manuel Maloof interview.

511   "We used to talk": Dan Carter interview.

512   "You wear" and "Don't Blame": NYT 8/3/94.

512   "If I'd known": bumper sticker.

512   "The old patterns": Claibourne Darden interview.

512   "The thirty year olds": Williams interview.

512   "By the time": Ibid.

513   "It's going to be": Willie Mae Yarbrough, WP Weekly 4/9–15/90.

513   "Georgians are tired": US News 7/23/90.

513   "I think the level": LA Times 7/19/88.

513   "The good people": 7/13/88.

514   "I would rather": WP 4/1/90.

514   "I didn't come to the civil rights movement": Chi Trib 5/13/90.

514   "hooliganism": Phil Inq 1/20/90.

514   "dangers are increasing" and "Racism in": unpublished chapter by John Hutcheson, Jr., and Carol Perannunzi.

515   "They love me": Young interview.

516   "We're trying to": AJC 7/29/90.

516   "I was elected": NYT 1/7/90.

516   "It's a touchy": WP 4/1/90.

516   "I don't know": NYT 11/26/89.

516   "His TV ads": anonymous quote, WP 8/6/90.

516   "fire in the belly": anonymous, AJC 7/16/90.

516   "emotional": op-ed article by John Head, AJC 7/16/90.

517   "I support": Time 7/16/90.

517   "I've seen": Rev. Jasper Williams, AJC 7/16/90.

517   "The black political": Rev. A. Cottrel, US News 7/25/88.

517   "What we're looking": Lowell Ware, WSJ 7/27/90.

517   "Our necks": NYT 11/26/89.

518   "he was not": AJC 12/2/89.

518   "If I want": NYT 11/26/89.

518   "Is that any place": AJC 11/23/89.

518   "The jury": anonymous, AJC 7/16/90.

519   "I never": Loudermilk interview.

519   "payback": AJC 7/16/90.

519   "Race is the": Darden interview.

520   "The next governor": Rev. William Smith, AJC 7/16/90.

520   "What is this": David Scott, AJC 7/27/90.

520   "I haven't had": AJC 8/5/90.

520   "The racism": Bob Holmes, AJC 8/5/90.

520   "If he had been": Michael Jones, AJC 7/26/90.

521   "pageant of interracial": NYT 8/5/96.

521   "The whole world": NYT 5/6/85.

521   "Race relations": Joseph Dolman interview.

521   "One of them": NYT 5/11/94.

521   "Expectations": Manual Maloof interview.

521   "The conventional": Berry interview.

521   "It's a richly": Williams interview.

522   "Look at": Gellerstedt interview.

522   "The veneer": Ibid.

522   "Anybody who": Claibourne Darden interview.

522   "The black community": Loudermilk interview.

522   "Call it": Joseph Dolman interview.

523   "There is": Lomax interview.

523   "What we're really": Young interview.

523   "It's like": Ibid.

523   "There are two": Berry interview.

523   "Are we at": Stogner interview.

523   "Deep down": Lee May interview.

523   "It's all of": Loudermilk interview.

523   "The idealism": Douglas Cumming interview.

524   "a way out": the title of Young's memoir, also used frequently in his speeches, is *A Way Out of No Way.*

524   "The movement": Young interview.

524   "In the political": Ibid.

524   "I quantify": Ibid.

524   "Watch what": Ibid.

525   "It's not that": Ibid.

525   "I was out," etc.: All the quotes used in the story of Haywood Curry and the Curry family reconciliation are drawn from interviews with Haywood and Linda Curry.

EPILOGUE

page

531   "One city": WSJ 9/19/97.

532   "war on black": WP 2/16/97.

532   "People in": Ibid.

534   "We have to be": NYT 4/11/97.
534   "One hundred million": Ibid.
536   "The Olympics": Jeff Dickerson, AJC 6/25/96.
537   "There has never": Andrew Young interview.

SELECTED
BIBLIOGRAPHY

GENERAL

Allport, Gordon W. *The Nature of Prejudice.* Doubleday, 1954.

Anderson, Elijah. *Streetwise: Race, Class and Change in an Urban Community.* University of Chicago Press, 1990.

Anderson, Jervis. *Bayard Rustin: Troubles I've Seen.* HarperCollins, 1996.

Anson, Robert Sam. *Best Intentions: The Education and Killing of Edmund Perry.* Vintage, 1988.

Armor, David J. *Forced Justice: School Desegregation and the Law.* Oxford University Press, 1995.

Auletta, Ken. *The Underclass.* Vintage, 1982.

Baldwin, James. *Notes of a Native Son.* Beacon Press, 1955.

———. *Nobody Knows My Name.* Delta, 1962.

———. *The Fire Next Time.* Laurel, 1962.

Bates, Timothy. *Banking on Black Enterprise: The Potential of Emerging Firms for Revitalizing Urban Economies.* Joint Center for Political and Economic Studies, 1993.

Bell, Derrick. *And We Are Not Saved: The Elusive Quest for Racial Justice.* Basic Books, 1987.

Bell, Derrick, ed. *Shades of Brown: New Perspectives on School Desegregation.* Columbia University Teachers College, 1980.

Belz, Herman. *Equality Transformed: A Quarter Century of Affirmative Action.* Transaction, 1991.

Berman, Paul, ed. *Blacks and Jews: Alliances and Arguments.* Delacorte, 1994.

Blauner, Bob. *Black Lives, White Lives: Three Decades of Race Relations in America.* University of California Press, 1989.

Bolick, Clint. *Unfinished Business: A Civil Rights Strategy for America's Third Century.* Pacific Research Institute, 1990.

———. *The Affirmative Action Fraud: Can We Restore the American Civil Rights Vision?* Cato, 1996.

Branch, Taylor. *Parting the Waters: America in the King Years 1954–63.* Simon & Schuster, 1988.

Breitman, George, ed. *Malcolm X Speaks: Selected Speeches and Statements.* Grove, 1965.

Brink, William, and Louis Harris. *Black and White: A Study of Racial Attitudes Today.* Simon & Schuster, 1967.

————. *The Negro Revolution in America.* Simon & Schuster, 1964.

Carmichael, Stokely, and Charles V. Hamilton. *Black Power: The Politics of Liberation in America.* Vintage, 1967.

Carroll, Peter. *It Seemed Like Nothing Happened: The Tragedy and Promise of America in the 1970s.* Holt Rinehart Winston, 1982.

Carter, Stephen L. *Reflections of an Affirmative Action Baby.* Basic Books, 1991.

Clark, Kenneth B. *Dark Ghetto: Dilemmas of Social Power.* Wesleyan University Press, 1965.

Clarke, John Henrik, and Amy Jaques Garvey, eds. *Marcus Garvey and the Vision of Africa.* Random House, 1974.

Cleaver, Eldridge. *Soul on Ice.* McGraw-Hill, 1968.

Cone, James H. *Martin and Malcolm and America: A Dream or a Nightmare.* Orbis, 1991.

Cose, Ellis. *The Rage of a Privileged Class.* Basic Books, 1993.

————. *Color-Blind: Seeing Beyond Race in a Race-Obsessed World.* HarperCollins, 1996.

Crouch, Stanley. *Notes of a Hanging Judge: Essays and Reviews 1979–1989.* Oxford University Press, 1990.

Cruse, Harold. *The Crisis of the Negro Intellectual: A Historical Analysis of the Failure of Black Leadership.* Quill, 1984.

————. *Plural but Equal: Blacks and Minorities in America's Plural Society.* William Morrow, 1987.

Curry, George E., ed. *The Affirmative Action Debate.* Addison-Wesley, 1996.

DeMott, Benjamin. *The Trouble with Friendship: Why Americans Can't Think Straight About Race.* Atlantic Monthly, 1995.

Douglass, Frederick. *Narrative of the Life of Frederick Douglass.* Doubleday, 1963.

Draper, Theodore. *The Rediscovery of Black Nationalism.* Viking, 1970.

D'Souza, Dinesh. *Illiberal Education: The Politics of Race and Sex on Campus.* Free Press, 1991.

————. *The End of Racism: Principles for a Multiracial Society.* Free Press, 1995.

Du Bois, W. E. B. *The Souls of Black Folk.* New American Library, 1969.

Dunbar, Leslie, ed. *Minority Report.* Pantheon, 1984.

Duneier, Mitchell. *Slim's Table: Race, Respectability and Masculinity.* University of Chicago Press, 1992.

Early, Gerald, ed. *Lure and Loathing: Essays on Race, Identity and the Ambivalence of Assimilation.* Penguin, 1993.

Eastland, Terry. *Ending Affirmative Action: A Case for Colorblind Justice.* Basic Books, 1996.

Eastland, Terry, and William J. Bennett. *Counting by Race: Equality from the Founding Fathers to Bakke and Weber.* Basic Books, 1979.

Edsall, Thomas Byrne with Mary D. Edsall. *Chain Reaction: The Impact of Race, Rights and Taxes on American Politics.* Norton, 1991.

Essien-Udom, Essien. *Black Nationalism: A Search for an Identity in America.* University of Chicago, 1962.

Fairlie, Henry. *The Kennedy Promise: The Politics of Expectation.* Doubleday, 1973.

Farmer, James. *Freedom—When?* Random House, 1965.

Frady, Marshall. *Jesse: The Life and Pilgrimage of Jesse Jackson.* Random House, 1996.

Franklin, John Hope, and August Meier, eds. *Black Leaders of the Twentieth Century.* University of Illinois Press, 1982.

Frazier, E. Franklin. *Black Bourgeoisie: The Rise of a New Middle Class in the United States.* Collier, 1957.

————. *The Negro Church in America.* Schocken, 1974.

Garreau, Joel. *Edge City: Life on the New Frontier.* Doubleday, 1991.

Garrow, David J. *Bearing the Cross: Martin Luther King, Jr. and the Southern Christian Leadership Conference.* Random House, 1986.

Gates, Henry Louis, Jr. *Colored People: A Memoir.* Knopf, 1994.

Gitlin, Todd. *The Twilight of Common Dreams: Why America Is Wracked by Culture Wars.* Metropolitan Books, 1995.

Glazer, Nathan. *Affirmative Discrimination: Ethnic Inequality and Public Policy.* Basic Books, 1978.

———. *Ethnic Dilemmas, 1964–1982.* Harvard University Press, 1983.

———. *We Are All Multiculturalists Now.* Harvard University Press, 1997.

Glazer, Nathan, and Daniel Patrick Moynihan. *Beyond the Melting Pot.* MIT Press, 1970.

Goldman, Peter. *Report from Black America.* Simon & Schuster, 1969.

———. *The Death and Life of Malcolm X.* University of Illinois Press, 1979.

Goodwin, Richard N. *Remembering America: A Voice from the Sixties.* Little Brown, 1988.

Graham, Hugh. *The Civil Rights Era: Origins and Development of National Policy.* Oxford University Press, 1990.

Grant, Joanne, ed. *Black Protest: History Documents and Analysis, 1619 to the Present.* Fawcett, 1968.

Grier, William H., and Price M. Cobbs. *Black Rage.* Basic Books, 1968.

Hacker, Andrew. *Two Nations: Black and White, Separate, Hostile, Unequal.* Scribner's, 1992.

Hall, Raymond. *Black Separatism and Social Reality.* Pergamon Press, 1977.

Hampton, Henry, and Steve Fayer. *Voices of Freedom: An Oral History of the Civil Rights Movement from the 1950s through the 1980s.* Bantam Books, 1990.

Harris, Fred R., and Roger W. Wilkins. *Quiet Riots: Race and Poverty in the United States.* Pantheon, 1988.

Herrnstein, Richard J., and Charles Murray. *The Bell Curve: Intelligence and Class Structure in American Life.* Free Press, 1994.

Hodgson, Godfrey. *America in Our Time.* Random House, 1976.

Hughes, Robert. *Culture of Complaint: The Fraying of America.* Oxford University Press, 1993.

Jackson, Kenneth T. *Crabgrass Frontier: The Suburbanization of the United States.* Oxford University Press, 1985.

Jaynes, Gerald David, and Robin M. Williams, Jr., eds. *A Common Destiny: Blacks and American Society.* National Academy Press, 1989.

Jencks, Christopher. *Rethinking Social Policy: Race, Poverty and the Underclass.* Harvard University Press, 1992.

Katz, Michael B., ed. *The Underclass Debate: Views from History.* Princeton University Press, 1993.

Kearns, Doris. *Lyndon Johnson and the American Dream.* Harper & Row, 1976.

King, Martin Luther, Jr. *Why We Can't Wait.* NAL, 1963.

———. *Where Do We Go from Here: Chaos or Community.* Beacon Press, 1967.

Kluger, Richard. *Simple Justice: The History of Brown v. Board of Education and Black America's Struggle for Equality.* Random House, 1975.

Lamar, Jake. *Bourgeois Blues: An American Memoir.* Plume, 1991.

Landry, Bart. *The New Black Middle Class.* University of California Press, 1987.

Lasch, Christopher. *The Agony of the American Left.* Knopf, 1969.

Lemann, Nicholas. *The Promised Land: The Great Black Migration and How It Changed America.* Knopf, 1991.

Lewis, Anthony, and The New York Times. *Portrait of a Decade: The Second American Revolution.* Random House, 1965.

Lewis, David Levering. *W. E. B. Du Bois: Biography of a Race 1868–1919.* Henry Holt, 1993.

Liebow, Elliot. *Tally's Corner: A Study of Negro Streetcorner Men.* Little, Brown, 1967.

Lipset, Seymour Martin, and Earl Raab. *The Politics of Unreason: Right-Wing Extremism in America, 1790–1970.* Harper & Row, 1970.

Loury, Glenn. *One by One from the Inside Out: Essays and Reviews on Race and Responsibility in America.* Free Press, 1995.

Lukas, J. Anthony. *Common Ground: A Turbulent Decade in the Lives of Three American Families.* Vintage, 1986.

MacInnes, Gordon A. *Wrong for All the Right Reasons: How White Liberals Have Been Undone by Race.* New York University Press, 1966.

Magida, Arthur J. *Prophet of Rage: A Life of Louis Farrakhan and his Nation.* Basic Books, 1996.

Malcolm X, with Alex Haley. *The Autobiography of Malcolm X.* Ballantine Books, 1965.

Massey, Douglas S., and Nancy A. Denton. *American Apartheid: Segregation and the Making of the Underclass.* Harvard University Press, 1993.

McCall, Nathan. *Makes Me Wanna Holler: A Young Black Man in America.* Random House, 1994.

Meier, August. *Negro Thought in America 1880–1915.* University of Michigan Press, 1963.

Meier, August, and Elliott Rudwick, eds. *Black Protest in the Sixties.* Quadrangle, 1970.

———. *From Plantation to Ghetto.* Hill and Wang, 1976.

Meier, August, Elliott Rudwick, and Francis L. Broderick, eds. *Black Protest Thought in the Twentieth Century.* Macmillan, 1971.

Mfume, Kweisi, with Ron Stodghill II. *No Free Ride: From the Mean Streets to the Mainstream.* Ballantine Books, 1996.

Mills, Nicolaus, ed. *Debating Affirmative Action: Race, Gender, Ethnicity and the Politics of Inclusion.* Delta, 1994.

Moskos, Charles C., and John Sibley Butler. *All That We Can Be: Black Leadership and Racial Integration the Army Way.* Basic Books, 1996.

Murray, Charles. *Losing Ground: American Social Policy, 1950–1980.* Basic Books, 1984.

Muse, Benjamin. *The American Negro Revolution.* Indiana University Press, 1968.

Myrdal, Gunnar. *An American Dilemma.* Harper & Brothers, 1944.

Novak, Michael. *The Rise of the Unmeltable Ethnics: Politics and Culture in the Seventies.* Macmillan, 1972.

Ogbu, John U.. *Minority Education and Caste: The American System in Cross-Cultural Perspective.* Academic Press, 1978.

Parsons, Talcott, and Kenneth B. Clark, eds. *The Negro American.* Beacon, 1966.

Perry, Bruce. *Malcolm: The Life of a Man Who Changed Black America.* Station Hill, 1991.

Powell, Colin L. *My American Journey.* Random House, 1995.

Powledge, Fred. *Free At Last? The Civil Rights Movement and the People Who Made It.* Little Brown, 1991.

Preston, Michael B., Lenneal J. Henderson, Jr., and Paul L. Puyear, eds. *The New Black Politics: A Search for Political Power.* Longman, 1987.

Rainwater, Lee, and William L. Yancey. *The Moynihan Report and the Politics of Controversy.* MIT Press, 1967.

Roberts, Paul Craig, and Lawrence M. Stratton. *The New Color Line: How Quotas and Privilege Destroy Democracy.* Regnery, 1995.

Rodriguez, Richard. *Hunger of Memory: The Education of Richard Rodriguez.* Bantam Books, 1982.

Rossell, Christine H., and Willis D. Hawley. *The Consequences of School Desegregation.* Temple University Press, 1983.

Rusk, David. *Cities Without Suburbs.* Johns Hopkins University Press, 1993.

Rustin, Bayard. *Down the Line.* Quadrangle, 1971.

———. *Strategies for Freedom: The Changing Patterns of Black Protest.* Columbia University Press, 1976.

Schlesinger, Arthur M., Jr. *A Thousand Days: John F. Kennedy in the White House.* Fawcett, 1965.

———. *The Disuniting of America.* Whittle, 1991.

Schuman, Howard, Charlotte Steeh, and Lawrence Bobo. *Racial Attitudes in America: Trends and Interpretations.* Harvard University Press, 1985.

Siegel, Fred. *The Future Once Happened Here: New York, D.C., L.A. and the Fate of America's Big Cities.* Free Press, 1997.

Silberman, Charles E. *Crisis in Black and White.* Random House, 1964.

Simms, Margaret C., ed. *Economic Perspectives on Affirmative Action.* Joint Center for Political and Economic Studies, 1995.

Sitkoff, Harvard. *The Struggle for Black Equality 1954–1980.* Hill and Wang, 1981.

Sleeper, Jim. *The Closest of Strangers: Liberalism and the Politics of Race in New York.* Norton, 1990.

———. *Liberal Racism.* Viking, 1997.

Smith, Robert C. *We Have No Leaders: African Americans in the Post-Civil Rights Era.* State University of New York Press, 1996.

Sniderman, Paul M., and Thomas Piazza. *The Scar of Race.* Harvard University Press, 1993.

Sorensen, Theodore C. *Kennedy.* Harper & Row, 1965.

———, ed. *Let the Word Go Forth: The Speeches, Statements and Writings of John F. Kennedy.* Delacorte, 1988.

Sowell, Thomas. *Civil Rights: Rhetoric or Reality.* Quill, 1984.

Staples, Brent. *Parallel Time: Growing Up in Black and White.* Pantheon, 1994.

Steele, Shelby. *The Content of Our Character: A New Vision of Race in America.* St. Martin's Press, 1990.

Sykes, Charles J. *A Nation of Victims: The Decay of the American Charter.* St. Martin's Press, 1992.

Tatum, Beverly Daniel. *Assimilation Blues: Black Families in a White Community.* Greenwood Press, 1987.

Taulbert, Clifton L. *Once Upon a Time When We Were Colored.* Council Oak Books, 1989.

Taylor, Jared. *Paved with Good Intentions: The Failure of Race Relations in Contemporary America.* Carroll & Graf, 1992.

Terkel, Studs. *Race: How Blacks and Whites Think and Feel About the American Obsession.* The New Press, 1992.

Thernstrom, Abigail. *Whose Votes Count? Affirmative Action and Minority Voting Rights.* Harvard University Press, 1987.

Thernstrom, Stephan, and Abigail Thernstrom. *America in Black and White: One Nation Indivisible.* Simon & Schuster, 1997.

Warren, Robert Penn. *Who Speaks for the Negro?* Random House, 1965.

Washington, James M. *A Testament of Hope: The Essential Writings of Martin Luther King, Jr.* Harper & Row, 1986.

Weisbrot, Robert. *Freedom Bound: A History of America's Civil Rights Movement.* Norton, 1990.

West, Cornell. *Race Matters.* Beacon Press, 1993.

Whalen, Charles, and Barbara Whalen. *The Longest Debate: The Legislative History of the 1964 Civil Rights Act.* NAL, 1985.

White, Theodore H. *The Making of the President 1964.* Atheneum, 1965.

Wideman, John Edgar. *Brothers and Keepers.* Penguin, 1984.

Williams, Juan, ed. *Eyes on the Prize: America's Civil Rights Years, 1954–1965.* Viking, 1987.

Williams, Robert F. *Negroes With Guns.* Marzani and Munsell, 1962.

Williams, Walter E. *The State Against Blacks.* McGraw-Hill, 1982.

Wilson, William Julius. *The Declining Significance of Race: Blacks and Changing American Institutions.* University of Chicago Press, 1980.

———. *The Truly Disadvantaged: The Inner City, the Underclass and Public Policy.* University of Chicago Press, 1987.

———. *When Work Disappears: The World of the New Urban Poor.* Knopf, 1996.

Wofford, Harris. *Of Kennedys and Kings: Making Sense of the Sixties.* Farrar, Straus & Giroux, 1980.

Wolfe, Tom. *Radical Chic and Mau-Mauing the Flak Catchers.* Farrar, Straus & Giroux, 1970.

Wood, Joe, ed. *Malcolm X: In Our Own Image.* St. Martin's Press, 1992.

Woodson, Carter G. *The Mis-Education of the Negro.* Africa World Press, 1990.

Young, Andrew Young. *An Easy Burden: The Civil Rights Movement and the Transformation of America.* HarperCollins, 1996.

NEW YORK

Altshuler, Alan A. *Community Control: The Black Demand for Participation in Large American Cities.* Bobbs-Merrill, 1970.

Anderson, Jervis. *This Was Harlem: A Cultural Portrait, 1900–1950.* Farrar, Straus & Giroux, 1982.

Bellush, Jewel, and Stephen David, eds. *Race and Politics in New York City.* Praeger 1971.

Berube, Maurice R., and Marilyn Gittell, eds. *Confrontation at Ocean Hill–Brownsville: The New York School Strikes of 1968.* Praeger, 1969.

Buckley, William F., Jr. *The Unmaking of a Mayor.* Viking, 1966.

Button, Daniel E. *Lindsay: A Man for Tomorrow.* Random House, 1965.

Carson, Sonny. *The Education of Sonny Carson.* Norton, 1972.

Clarke, John Henrik. *Harlem: A Community in Transition.* Citadel Press, 1964.

Farmer, James. *Lay Bare the Heart: An Autobiography of the Civil Rights Movement.* Arbor House, 1985.

Gottehrer, Barry. *The Mayor's Man.* Doubleday, 1975.

Green, Charles St. Clair, and Basil Wilson. *Struggle for Black Empowerment in New York City: Beyond the Politics of Pigmentation.* Praeger, 1989.

Hamilton, Charles A. *Adam Clayton Powell, Jr.: The Political Biography of an American Dilemma.* Atheneum, 1991.

Hayden, Tom. *Rebellion in Newark: Official Violence and Ghetto Response.* Random House, 1967.

Haygood, Wil. *King of the Cats: The Life and Times of Adam Clayton Powell, Jr.* Houghton Mifflin, 1993.

Hentoff, Nat. *A Political Life: The Education of John V. Lindsay.* Knopf, 1969.

Hickey, Neil, and Ed Edwin. *Adam Clayton Powell.* Fleet, 1965.

Johnson, Samuel M. *Often Back: The Tales of Harlem.* Vantage, 1971.

Kaufman, Jonathan. *Broken Alliance: The Turbulent Times Between Blacks and Jews in America.* Scribner's, 1988.

Klein, Woody. *Lindsay's Promise: The Dream That Failed.* Macmillan, 1970.

Levine, Naomi, with Richard Cohen. *Ocean Hill–Brownsville: A Case History of Schools in Crisis.* Popular Library, 1969.

Lindsay, John V. *The City.* Norton, 1969.

Meier, August, and Elliott Rudwick. *CORE: A Study in the Civil Rights Movement, 1942–1968.* Oxford University Press, 1973.

Moynihan, Daniel Patrick. *Maximum Feasible Misunderstanding: Community Action in the War on Poverty.* Free Press, 1969.

Newfield, Jack. *Robert Kennedy: A Memoir.* Dutton, 1969.

Osofsky, Gilbert. *Harlem: The Making of a Ghetto.* Harper & Row, 1966.

Pilat, Oliver. *Lindsay's Campaign: A Behind-the-Scenes Diary.* Beacon Press, 1968.

Powell, Adam Clayton, Jr. *Adam by Adam.* Dial, 1971.

Public Papers of the Presidents: Lyndon B. Johnson 1963–64, Vol. I. Government Printing Office, 1965.

Ravitch, Diane. *The Great School Wars: A History of the New York City Public Schools.* Basic Books, 1974.

Report of the National Advisory Commission on Civil Disorders. Bantam Books, 1968.

Rieder, Jonathan. *Canarsie: The Jews and Italians of Brooklyn against Liberalism.* Harvard University Press, 1985.

Rogers, David. *110 Livingston Street.* Random House, 1968.

Schlesinger, Arthur M., Jr. *Robert Kennedy and His Times.* Houghton Mifflin, 1978.

Schoener, Allon, ed. *Harlem on My Mind.* The New Press, 1995.

Sharpton, Al, with Anthony Walton. *Go and Tell Pharoah: The Autobiography of the Reverend Al Sharpton.* Doubleday, 1996.

Walter, John C. *The Harlem Fox: J. Raymond Jones and Tammany, 1920–1970.* State University of New York Press, 1989.

DETROIT

Aberbach, Joel D., and Jack L. Walker. *Race in the City: Political Trust and Public Policy in the New Urban System.* Little Brown, 1973.

Anton, Thomas J. *Federal Aid to Detroit.* Brookings Institution, 1983.

Bray, Thomas. "Jimmy Carter's Favorite Mayor." *Policy Review.* Spring 1984.

Brown, Peter. *Minority Party: Why Democrats Face Defeat in 1992 and Beyond.* Regnery Gateway, 1991.

Buckley, James H. *Bringing Home the News: A Case Study of the Community Press.* Suburban Communications Corporation, 1991.

Chafets, Ze'ev. *Devil's Night and Other True Tales of Detroit.* Random House, 1990.

Conference on Race Relations: Text of Presentations made on July 25, 1987. Detroit Strategic Planning Project.

Conot, Robert. *American Odyssey: A History of a Great City.* Wayne State University Press, 1986.

Darden, Joe T., Richard C. Hill, June Thomas, and Richard Thomas. *Detroit, Race and Uneven Development.* Temple University Press, 1987.

Dimond, Paul R. *Beyond Busing: Inside the Challenge to Urban Segregation.* University of Michigan Press, 1985.

Farley, Reynolds, et al. "Chocolate City, Vanilla Suburbs: Will the Trend Toward Racially Separate Communities Continue?" *Social Science Research 7* (1978).

Farley, Reynolds, Suzanne Bianchi, and Diane L. Colasanto. "Barriers to the Racial Integration of Neighborhoods: The Detroit Case," *Annals of the American Academy of Political and Social Science* 441 (1979).

Fine, Sidney. *Violence in the Model City: The Cavanagh Administration, Race Relations and the Detroit Riot of 1967.* University of Michigan Press, 1989.

Golden, Peter. *Quiet Diplomat: A Biography of Max M. Fisher.* Herzl Press, 1992.

Grant, William R. "Community Control vs. School Integration—The Case of Detroit," *Public Interest* (Summer 1971).

Holli, Melvin G., ed. *Detroit.* Franklin Watts, 1976.

McGehee, Scott, and Susan Watson, eds. *Blacks in Detroit.* Detroit Free Press, 1980.

Orfield, Gary. *Must We Bus? Segregated Schools and National Policy.* Brookings Institution, 1978.

Progress Report of the New Detroit Committee, April 1968.

The Quotations of Mayor Coleman A. Young. Droog Press, 1991.

Rich, Wilbur C. *Coleman Young and Detroit Politics: From Social Activist to Power Broker.* Wayne State University Press, 1989.

Salins, Peter D. "Cities, Suburbs and the Urban Crisis," *Public Interest* (Fall 1993).

Sugrue, Tom J. "Crabgrassroots Politics: Race, Homeownership, and the Fragmentation of the New Deal Coalition in the Urban North, 1940–1960," *Journal of American History* (September 1995).

Teaford, Jon C. *The Rough Road to Renaissance: Urban Revitalization in America.* Johns Hopkins University Press, 1990.

Terkel, Studs. *American Dreams: Lost and Found.* Pantheon, 1980.

Widick, B. J. *Detroit: City of Race and Class Violence.* Quadrangle Books, 1972.

Wilkinson, J. Harvie, III. *From Brown to Bakke: The Supreme Court and School Integration 1954–1978.* Oxford University Press, 1979.

Wolf, Eleanor P. *Trial and Error: The Detroit School Segregation Case.* Wayne State University Press, 1981.

Young, Coleman, and Lonnie Wheeler. *Hard Stuff: The Autobiography of Coleman Young.* Viking, 1994.

ATLANTA

Allen, Ivan, with Paul Hemphill. *Mayor: Notes on the Sixties.* Simon & Schuster, 1971.

Baldwin, James. *The Evidence of Things Not Seen.* Henry Holt, 1985.

Black, Earl, and Merle Black. *Politics and Society in the South.* Harvard University Press, 1987.

Eisinger, Peter K. *The Politics of Displacement: Racial and Ethnic Transition in Three American Cities.* Academic Press, 1980.

Geller, Chris, Keith Ihlanfelt, and David Sjoquist. *Atlanta in Black and White: Racial Attitudes and Perspectives.* Research Atlanta, 1995.

Glazer, Nathan, "The Affirmative Action Stalemate," *Public Interest* (Winter 1988).

Horton, Nehl. *The Young Years: Report on the Administration of the Honorable Andrew Young, Mayor of Atlanta 1982–1989.* Office of Mayor Andrew Young, 1989.

Hunter, Floyd. *Community Power Structure: A Study of Decision Makers.* University of North Carolina Press, 1953.

Hutcheson, John D., Jr. *Racial Attitudes in Atlanta.* Emory University Center for Research in Social Change, 1973.

The Impact of Local Government Programs to Encourage Minority Business Development. Research Atlanta, 1986.

Jones, Mack H. "Black Political Empowerment in Atlanta: Myth and Reality," *Annals of the American Academy of Political and Social Science* (September 1978).

LaNoue, George R. "Split Visions: Minority Business Set-Asides," *Annals of the American Academy of Political and Social Science* (September 1992).

———. "Social Science and Minority 'Set-Asides.' *Public Interest* (Winter 1993).

———. "Selective Perception: The Role of History in the Disparity Study Industry," *Public Historian* (Spring 1995).

LaNoue, George R., and John Sullivan, "'But For' Discrimination: How Many Minority Businesses Would There Be?" *Columbia Human Rights Law Review* (Winter 1992–93).

Naipaul, V. S. *A Turn in the South.* Knopf, 1989.

Orfield, Gary, and Carole Ashkinaze, *The Closing Door: Conservative Policy and Black Opportunity.* University of Chicago Press, 1991.

Reed, Adolphe, "A Critique of Neo-Progressivism in Theorizing about Local Development Policy: A Case from Atlanta," in Clarence N. Stone and Heywood T. Sanders, eds., *The Politics of Urban Development.* University Press of Kansas, 1987.

Sjoquist, David. *The Economic Status of Black Atlantans.* Research Atlanta, 1989.

Smith, James P., and Finis Welch. *Closing the Gap: Forty Years of Economic Progress for Blacks.* Rand Corp., 1986.

Stone, Clarence N. *Regime Politics: Governing Atlanta, 1946–1988.* University Press of Kansas, 1989.

Unpublished and untitled 1986 draft report on set-asides by the staff of the U.S. Civil Rights Commission.

Watters, Pat. *Coca-Cola: An Illustrated History.* Doubleday, 1978.

Young, Andrew. *A Way Out of No Way.* Thomas Nelson Publishers, 1994.

ACKNOWLEDGMENTS

Many people helped me write this book, and it is impossible to thank them adequately. For generous financial support, I am grateful to the National Endowment for the Humanities, the Alicia Patterson Foundation, the John M. Olin Foundation, the Joyce Foundation, the Smith Richardson Foundation, the Frederick P. and Sandra P. Rose Foundation, the Daniel and Joanna S. Rose Fund, the Klingenstein Third Generation Foundation, the Neil A. McConnell Foundation, Virginia Gilder, Stanley Goldstein and the Hauser Foundation. James Piereson, William Hammett, Lawrence Mone, Leslie Lenkowsky and Margaret Engel combined help in securing funding with much appreciated encouragement and insight. The Manhattan Institute provided administrative support as well as inspiration.

Librarians at the periodical morgues at *Newsweek,* the *Detroit News* and the *Atlanta Journal-Constitution* could not have been more patient or helpful. Archivists at Yale University, the University of Michigan and the Ford Foundation were tolerant of a journalist in their midst. Ze'ev Chafets knows Detroit as no one else does, and he generously took the time to share his knowledge with me. Jeffrey Goldberg gave me an important nudge when I needed it. Sheldon Birenhack tracked down loose ends in the library. Thomas Bray, Douglas Lavin, Mark Silk and Paul and Carol Muldawer provided much-appreciated hospitality and leads in Detroit and Atlanta. In the course of researching and writing this book, I talked with more people than I can count about the subject, and almost all were helpful in one way or another. Although they are too many to name here, I am deeply grateful to everyone I interviewed in New York, Detroit and Atlanta. Among friends and colleagues, I am indebted to Shelby Steele, Glenn Loury, David Garrow, Jim Sleeper, Fred Siegel, Michael Meyers and Mitchell Duneier.

Shelby Steele, David Garrow, Anthony Lewis, Martin Peretz, Midge Decter, Thomas Bray, Gary Baumgarten, Mark Silk, Jonathan Rosen, Mitchell Duneier, Cynthia Farrar, Rosanna Warren, Maud Lavin, Tom Klingenstein, Ruth Kozodoy, Susan Rabiner and Jack Schwartz read all or part of the manuscript and offered invaluable insights. Sherwood Harris showed me how to cut it by more than I care to say—and all but painlessly. My agent Amanda Urban stood by me from start to finish. Bob Asahina believed in me enough to buy the book and wait patiently for early drafts. Adam Bellow pushed me to make the final product all it could be, deftly helping to frame and polish the story. Elizabeth Maguire shepherded the text through the last stages of the editorial process. A long list of other people at The Free Press helped the book to see the light of day, but Chad Conway, Edith Lewis and copy editor Ann Adelman deserve special thanks. William Shinker, Jonathan Rosen and Sandee Brawarsky offered indispensable advice on how to be happily published. Ronald Steel made me want to be a writer and encouraged me all along the way. David Kohn heard the stories in the book as I discovered them, supported me when my energy flagged and put up with my partial presence for much longer than he should have had to.

INDEX